Anthi Chrysanthou
Defining Orphism

Trends in Classics – Supplementary Volumes

Edited by
Franco Montanari and Antonios Rengakos

Associate Editors
Stavros Frangoulidis · Fausto Montana · Lara Pagani
Serena Perrone · Evina Sistakou · Christos Tsagalis

Scientific Committee
Alberto Bernabé · Margarethe Billerbeck
Claude Calame · Jonas Grethlein · Philip R. Hardie
Stephen J. Harrison · Stephen Hinds · Richard Hunter
Christina Kraus · Giuseppe Mastromarco
Gregory Nagy · Theodore D. Papanghelis
Giusto Picone · Tim Whitmarsh
Bernhard Zimmermann

Volume 94

Anthi Chrysanthou
Defining Orphism

The Beliefs, the *teletae* and the Writings

DE GRUYTER

ISBN 978-3-11-077809-0
e-ISBN (PDF) 978-3-11-067845-1
e-ISBN (EPUB) 978-3-11-067853-6
ISSN 1868-4785

Library of Congress Control Number: 2020932271

Bibliographic information published by the Deutsche Nationalbibliothek
The Deutsche Nationalbibliothek lists this publication in the Deutsche Nationalbibliografie;
detailed bibliographic data are available on the Internet at http://dnb.dnb.de.

© 2021 Walter de Gruyter GmbH, Berlin/Boston
This volume is text- and page-identical with the hardback published in 2020.
Editorial Office: Alessia Ferreccio and Katerina Zianna
Logo: Christopher Schneider, Laufen
Printing and binding: CPI books GmbH, Leck

www.degruyter.com

To my Family

Contents

List of Tables —— IX
Abbreviations —— XI

1 Introduction —— 1

2 Non-Orphic material referring to Orphic practices, beliefs and writings —— 9
2.1 'Those affiliated to Orpheus...' —— 9
2.2 Itinerant Priests, Sacred Books and *Hieroi Logoi* —— 20
2.3 References to specific Orphic Rites, Mysteries and Practices —— 43
2.4 Orphic writings and their authors —— 70
2.5 Conclusion —— 82

3 The Myth of Dionysos' Dismemberment —— 85
Conclusion —— 112

4 The Gold Tablets – Practical and Eschatological Aspects —— 113
4.1 Introduction —— 113
4.2 Archaeological and Geographical Information —— 113
4.3 New Discoveries: New Theories —— 121
4.4 Textual Analysis —— 124
4.5 Ritualistic Analysis —— 151
4.6 Mnemosyne – Memory —— 191
4.7 The Olbian Bone Tablets —— 198
4.8 Conclusion —— 203

5 Papyrological Evidence: The Derveni Papyrus and the Gurôb Papyrus —— 205
5.1 The Derveni Papyrus —— 205
5.2 The Gurôb Papyrus —— 264
5.3 Conclusion —— 272

6 *Hieroi Logoi in 24 Rhapsodies* —— 274
6.1 Introduction —— 274
6.2 West's Reconstruction of the Orphic theogonies —— 280
6.3 Methodology of the Reconstruction of the *Orphic Rhapsodies* —— 282

6.4	Reconstruction of the *Orphic Rhapsodies*	**286**
6.5	Analysis of the *Orphic Rhapsodies*	**299**
6.6	Conclusion	**349**

7 Conclusion — 351

Appendix — 358

Bibliography — 371
Index of the *Orphic Rhapsodies* — 385
General Index — 389
Index of Primary Sources — 399

List of Tables

Tab. 1: List of Orphic works with a specific title along with sigla of Bernabé's edition —— 75
Tab. 2: Sources of Dionysos' Dismemberment myth —— 85
Tab. 3: List of gold tablets with sigla of most recent editions —— 115
Tab. 4: Textual divergences between tablets from group B —— 129
Tab. 5: Sources of the *Orphic Rhapsodies* —— 284

Abbreviations

ARV	Beazley, J.D. (1963). *Attic Red-Figure Vase-Painters*, Oxford: Clarendon Press.
BT	Olbian Bone Tablets
CMS	Corpus of Minoan and Mycenaean Seals
DFHG	Digital Fragmenta Historicorum Graecorum [Online] Available at: http://www.dfhg-project.org/
DK	Diels, H. and Kranz, W. (1952), *Fragmente der Vorsokratiker* (6th edn.), Weidmannsche Buchhandlung.
DP	Derveni Papyrus
EOAG	Wilson, N. (2013). *Encyclopedia of ancient Greece*. London: Routledge.
FGrHist	Jacoby, F. (1923–). *Fragmente der griechischen Historiker*. Weidmann: Berlin.
GT	Gold Tablets
IC	Inscriptiones Creticae [IC] III [Online] Available at: https://epigraphy.packhum.org/book/292?location=1362
IG	Inscriptiones Grecae [Online] Available at: https://epigraphy.packhum.org/biblio#b20
KPT	Kouremenos, Parássoglou, Tsantsanoglou edition and translation of the Derveni Papyrus. Kouremenos, T., Parássoglou G.M., Tsantsanoglou, K. (2006). *The Derveni Papyrus*. Firenze: Leo S. Olschki Editore.
KRS	Kirk, G.S., Raven, J.E., Schofield, M. (1983). *The Presocratic Philosophers: A critical history with a selection of text*. Cambridge: Cambridge University Press.
OF(number) (Kern)	Orphic Fragments from Kern's *Orphicorum Fragmenta* (1922).
OF(number)F	Orphic Fragments from Bernabé's *Orphicorum et Orphicis similium testimonia et fragmenta*. Pars II, Fasc. 1 and 2 (2004–2005)
OF(number)T	Orphic Testimonia from Bernabé's aforementioned edition of the Orphic fragments.
OR	The text and translation of the *Orphic Rhapsodies* by the author as found in section 6.4.
PEG	Bernabé, A. (ed.) (1987). *Poetae epici Graeci, testimonia et fragmenta*. Pars I. Leipzig: B.G. Teubner.
Pf	Pfeiffer, R. (1949). *Callimachus*, vol. i: *Fragmenta*. Oxford: Clarendon Press.
TrGF	Snell, B., Kannicht, R., Radt, S. (eds.) (1971–2004). *Tragicorum Graecorum Fragmenta*. Göttingen: Vandenhoeck & Ruprecht.

1 Introduction

When I began my research on Orphism I quickly realised that there was not a specific and widely accepted definition of this phenomenon and that the vast amount of sources referring to Orphism is not directly proportionate to how important its place in ancient Greek history is considered by scholarship. By the time I reached the end of my research I was more convinced than ever that there needs to be a major shift in the way that the disputed matter of Orphism is perceived by scholars. Despite the long and significant history of Orphic scholarship I believe that as time went by the study of Orphism has been somewhat inhibited by academic blind-spotting rooted deeply into doctrines of what is and is not acceptable or expected in ancient Greek religion. In this book, I aim to approach the material with a fresh look, without any presuppositions and limitations in order to reach a clear understanding of this phenomenon. This is not of course to say that previous theories on the matter will not be taken into consideration or to take away of the significance of previous scholarship but that the attitude of this book will be more exploratory rather than deterministic. More specifically, this book aims to bring together in one discussion all the basic constituents of Orphism and the majority of non-Orphic ancient sources which refer to Orphism in order to propose a redefinition of what exactly Orphism was and to evaluate its place in ancient Greek religion. The basic constituents I will be analysing are: the Derveni Papyrus, the Gold and Bone Tablets and the *Orphic Rhapsodies*, which are broadly considered by scholarship to be important sources relating to Orphism.[1] Other ancient sources range from Platonic passages to archaeological remains and coins, ranging chronologically from the archaic period to Late Antiquity. I hope that this book can offer new insights into the matter and a new definition of the Orphic phenomenon while at the same time serve as a concise introductory guide for Orphic researchers.

The general tendency of scholarship on Orphism has been constantly changing. Perhaps one of the first scholarly opinions on Orphism can be considered the

---

I would like to thank the University of Leeds for giving me the opportunity to undertake the research which led to the publication of this book. I would also like to express my sincere gratitude to Dr. Emma Stafford and Prof. Malcolm Heath for their support and constructive feedback. This book would not have been possible without the constant encouragement of my family: Anna, Chrysanthos, Tania, Antonia and Michalakis. Finally, I would like to thank my husband Dovydas for always being there for me.

1 I will be referring to them as DP, GT, BT and OR respectively throughout the book. If a translator is not specified, the translation is by the author (throughout the book).

one of Proclus who in the 5th century A.D. claimed that the totality of Greek theology springs from the Orphic mythical doctrine.[2] In the 1900s the belief that such a thing as Orphism existed in antiquity was the prevailing one. Diels would write in 1897 'people calling themselves Orphics did indeed exist in Archaic Greece, they were roughly contemporaries of Pherekydes, and they maintained cosmogonic doctrines quite comparable to his in several respects'.[3] In 1903, Harrison, in her *Prolegomena to the Study of Greek Religion* analysed Orphism, asserting as its 'cardinal doctrine' the apotheosis element, the ὁσιότης, and also identifying the gold tablets as Orphic and discussing them as a source of Orphic eschatology.[4] Kern's edition of the *Orphicorum Fragmenta* in 1922 was undoubtedly the first and most important work that would allow scholarship on Orphism to go even further.[5] In 1935 (revised in 1952) Guthrie published *Orpheus and Greek Religion: A Study of the Orphic Movement*, where he tends to acknowledge Orphism as a religion with certain beliefs 'founded on a collection of sacred writings', but not in the strict sense of a sect.[6] When he refers to it as a religion he does not use the term in its modern meaning but points to the difficulties in defining the boundaries of Orphism. He claims, thus, that Orphism was a particular modification of religion with Orphic rites but that the Orphics did not 'worship a different god' and their means of worshipping were not 'always obviously different'.[7] Orphics, as Guthrie claimed, moulded the primitive mythology to 'suit their own conceptions'.[8]

Linforth shifted scholarly opinion on Orphism in the opposite direction. In *The Arts of Orpheus* in 1941 he collected a large number of ancient sources related to Orphism, divided them to *ante* and *post* 300 B.C. and analysed them to conclude that there is no such thing as a systematic set of Orphic beliefs. Dodds, in his discussion of Orphism in *The Greeks and the Irrational* (1951), mentions that his view on Orphism was influenced by Linforth's work, which led him to suggest that Orphism as a concept stands on fragile ground, patched up with material from 'the fantastic theogonies' of Proclus and Damascius'.[9] In 1962, the discovery

---

[2] Procl. *Theol. Pl.* 1.6.
[3] Diels, 1897.
[4] Harrison, 1903, p.474–78; p.572ff; p.659: '…the last word in ancient Greek religion was said by the Orphics…'
[5] Kern, 1922.
[6] Guthrie, 1952, p.10.
[7] Guthrie, 1952, p.9.
[8] Guthrie, 1952, p.130.
[9] Dodds, 1951, p.148.

of the Derveni Papyrus containing an allegorical interpretation of an Orphic Theogony would stir the waters again due to its early date, since the papyrus is dated to the 4th century B.C. and the theogony itself even earlier.

The prevalent tendency amongst more recent scholars has been to identify Orphism through its literature, and define as Orphic the works associated with Orpheus and the religious 'spirit' that pervades these works. Gruppe maintained that there is a doctrine prevalent in the Orphic theogonies, which he summarised in a single phrase attributed to Musaeus: 'Everything comes to be out of One and is resolved into One'.[10] Focusing on the literary aspect of Orphism was also Alderink's and West's approach, as becomes apparent from the latter's work *The Orphic Poems* dealing solely with the Orphic Theogonies. He suggested that 'the only definite meaning that can be given to the term is the fashion for claiming Orpheus as an authority'.[11] Alderink suggested the term 'Orphic theology' and considered Orphism to be 'a mood or spirit which animates the selected literary texts' and a 'soteriological thrust which was expressed in literary form'.[12] He also claimed that if there were Orphic mysteries then they had to be literary, emphasizing the importance of knowledge.[13]

Scholarship up to now has approached Orphism as something problematic, as a part of Greek religion that should not exist. This is due to its apparent strong differentiation from anything that we know about ancient Greek religion. Certain aspects attributed to Orphism such as vegetarianism or emphasis on texts, for example, do not conform to the various 'norms' of ancient Greek society. Edmonds is the most recent scholar representing one of the extreme sides of the debate and he has published an abundance of articles and books which offer new insights and alternative interpretations of Orphic material. His contribution, thus, has also been invaluable, especially in terms of stirring the debate. In his book *Redefining Ancient Orphism* (2013) he discusses the history of Orphism and its literary and religious aspects. He addresses the non-conformity of Orphism mentioned above, claiming that:

> Orphism, however, must not be understood as the exception to the rule, the doctrinal current within Greek religion or the forerunner of the doctrinal tradition of Christianity that followed. Rather, Orphism, to use a modern '-ism' term to designate a modern scholarly

---

10 Diog. Laert. *Prooem*. 3. Gruppe, as referenced by Guthrie, 1952, p.74–75.
11 West, 1983, p.2–3.
12 Alderink, 1981, p.17; p.19/41/95.
13 Alderink, 1981, p.89.

concept, can be understood as the category that includes those things that the ancient Greeks associated with the name of Orpheus, the Orphica –whether text or ritual.[14]

Edmonds, thus, whom Bernabé has characterised as a 'crusader' against Orphism, does not accept that Orphism as a religion with specific beliefs and mysteries ever existed.[15] I believe that the fact, that –ism is a modern scholarly concept, most probably used for the sake of convenience, should not be taken as a reason to reject the possibility of a coherence in beliefs that is consistent with some fluidity through time and space. The –ism designating a modern scholarly concept is also applied for example to Pythagoreanism, which no scholar will deny included cosmological philosophy and religious beliefs and also influenced later school of thoughts despite its fluidity through time. The 'label' Orphism, then, might not be so much like the case of 'Buddhism' but more like the case of 'Pythagoreanism' with a similarly complex nature.

Edmonds also argues extensively against the existence of an Orphic belief in an original sin based on the Zagreus myth, since he claims that the anthropogony of the Titans is an interpolation by the Neoplatonist Olympiodorus.[16] Edmonds, moreover, argues for a polythetic definition of the term Orphic: 'if something – person, text, or ritual – boasted of extraordinary purity or sanctity, made a claim to special divine connection or extreme antiquity, or was marked by extra-ordinary strangeness, perversity, or alien nature, then that thing might be labelled Orphic, classified with other Orphic things, and perhaps even sealed with the name of Orpheus'.[17] This approach seems useful *prima facie*, but in my opinion it turns out to be too broad, for according to this definition, Empedokles or the *Sibylline Oracles* for example, should – or 'might' – be classified as Orphic. Edmonds' book also demonstrates another problem for the study of Orphism since there is not a systematic analysis of all the Orphic and non-Orphic evidence, and the absence of a systematic analysis makes a complete and coherent picture impossible. For example the text of the *Orphic Rhapsodies* is not discussed by Edmonds in *Redefining Ancient Orphism* (2013) but only its nature. A definition of the totality cannot be complete if all the components are not examined. Edmonds, of course, discusses all the components in separate works such as his most recent edition of the gold tablets. But it is essential that if a single study is to define Orphism, it should take adequately into consideration all the components.

---

14 Edmonds, 2013, p.396. Even though this work is taken into consideration, this book in no case constitutes a reply to Edmonds' work. The titles are similar incidentally.
15 Bernabé, 2006, p.5.
16 Edmonds, 2013, p.393. Edmonds, 2008a.
17 Edmonds, 2013, p.7.

The other extreme of the most recent scholarship is represented by Bernabé. His edition of the Orphic fragments in two volumes in 2004–2005 (*Orphicorum et Orphicis similium testimonia et fragmenta. Poetae Epici Graeci. Pars II. Fasc. 1 and 2. Bibliotheca Teubneriana*) is a significant addition to Orphic studies and should be used by every researcher working in this area. It includes new fragments that were not included in Kern's edition, with a literature apparatus and it is the edition used in this book.[18] It is indicative of the importance of this new edition of the Orphic fragments that a collection of short essays on selected fragments has been published in honour of Bernabé (*Tracing Orpheus: Studies of Orphic Fragments in Honour of Alberto Bernabé*, 2011). Bernabé has written numerous insightful works on every aspect of Orphism. He argues that Orphism had a core of specific Orphic doctrines: the duality of humans as body and soul, the belief in an 'original sin' for which the soul is being punished, the possibility of escaping this punishment through a cycle of reincarnations, and the purpose of the soul to be united with the divine. Bernabé has also edited, with Casadesús, the two volume *Orfeo y la tradición órfica. Un reencuentro*, which deals comprehensively with all aspects of Orphism and includes articles by a variety of scholars, including Bernabé and Casadesús themselves, Graf, Brisson, West and Burkert.[19] These two volumes consist of no fewer than 1600 pages. Though this book is an essential resource for researchers on Orphism it once again demonstrates the need for a concise and coherent representation of the Orphic and non-Orphic material, since its length and the variety of perspectives represented mean that it cannot achieve a unified account of Orphism, which this book aims to provide.

The fact, then, that there is not a book available which discusses in a concise and all-encompassing way all the main components of Orphism has led me to the production of this work. I aim to define the nature of Orphism from the Archaic to Hellenestic times, through literary analysis and examination of the main components of Orphism (DP, GT, BT, OR) and of other literary ancient sources which can offer insight into the notion of Orphism. In addition, I will be looking at other types of evidence such as inscriptions and coins. I will initially examine non-Orphic material which refers or relates to Orphism and thus will help us identify ancient attitudes towards Orphism. I will next discuss the myth of Dionysos' dismemberment by the Titans, since it is a central point of the scholarly debate. I will then discuss the gold tablets, Derveni Papyrus and the *Orphic Rhapsodies* and juxtapose them to the picture created by the earlier chapters. I will not deal with the *Orphic Hymns* and the Orphic *Argonautika*, which are relatively late

---

18 Bernabé, 2004a, 2005a, 2007.
19 Bernabé *et al.*, 2010.

sources and are not so relevant to the earlier form of Orphism but rather to its evolution in later times, which is not part of the present project. These particular works differ from the Neoplatonic commentaries which I will be examining, since even though in both cases we have works composed in late antiquity, the former ones are poetic Orphic works while the latter preserve and comment on passages from the *Orphic Rhapsodies* thus retaining material from earlier periods.

A systematic juxtaposition of the Derveni Papyrus, the gold and bone Tablets and the *Orphic Rhapsodies* in a single work will facilitate the analysis of possible parallels or divergences. Even though the gold and bone Tablets and the Derveni Papyrus have been studied separately and extensively by scholarship, this is not the case with the *Orphic Rhapsodies*. Until now the latter has been approached via the hundreds of fragments through which it survives and mostly through West's reconstruction of its basic narrative. To facilitate a detailed analysis of the *Orphic Rhapsodies*, and its comparison with other Orphic and non-Orphic material, I have attempted a more elaborate reconstruction, with the incorporation and arrangement of all the quoted verses we have available. In this way there is the possibility that the text of the *Orphic Rhapsodies* may become visible as an entity in its own right, instead as a fragmented chaos. Through the analysis of ancient textual and archaeological evidence, in combination with the discussion of the main components of Orphism (the OR, DP, GT and BT), we will be able to discern possible Orphic religious beliefs and mysteries through time and space and decipher their nature and relationship to one another. We will also be able to examine whether Orphic ideas and texts/myths had any role in the formation of otherwise well-known rites and mysteries, such as the Eleusinian ones. Most importantly, this book will bring together all of Orphism's main components in a single study, highlighting both parallels and divergences between a wide range of sources. Juxtaposing and comparing the totality of the Orphic components and sources is the only way to examine whether Orphism was a religious phenomenon with specific beliefs and mysteries that were transmitted through time and space, a mere 'label' denoting a theological literary spirit, a specific type of mysteries or a mythological tradition, or all or none of the above. Focusing on one source at a time, as has been the tendency up to now, is a restricted methodology that leads to an incomplete analysis and definition of Orphism.

I also hope to fill in a gap in the scholarship on the *Orphic Rhapsodies* since the absence of a basic reconstruction makes its examination extremely difficult. The mere reconstruction of the storyline by West is not adequate, since we need to have the ancient text as well in order to draw parallels with other Orphic and non-Orphic literary sources. The preliminary reconstruction and translation of the *Orphic Rhapsodies* in this book can form the starting point for its clearer understanding as a whole and offer new insights as far as the chronology of its content is concerned. Through having the *Orphic Rhapsodies* in front of us as a single entity it will be possible to outline a chronological frame for its mythological background, exploring new possibilities of its ideas and their relation to ancient Greek literature.

A complete definition of Orphism is necessary because many ancient texts have been examined without considering the possibility of a relationship to Orphism. This is due to confusion around the notion of Orphism and the lack of literature addressing the matter in its totality. I do not suggest that we should force the concept of Orphism into the literary analysis of, for example, Sophoclean plays or Platonic dialogues, but the absence of a definition of Orphism prevents us from recognising possible parallels where they might be present. The possibility of re-examining ancient sources in the light of a potential Orphic context will create new ways of understanding and perhaps solving existing problems. Having a clear idea of what Orphism was, might lead to a new sociological and anthropological analysis and understanding of ancient Greek society and mentality. If Orphism turns out to be distinctively different from mainstream socio-religious currents, this will be a matter which will have to be taken into consideration for the understanding of ancient Greek culture. Orphism will never be part of our understanding of the socio-religious reality of antiquity if we do not first of all define and understand what exactly Orphism is.

After this Introduction, Chapter 2 will discuss non-Orphic material referring to Orphic practices, beliefs and writings. The majority of the sources are Classical and Hellenistic and I will also refer to a few possible indirect references to Orphism through the figure of Orpheus. This will give us the opportunity to form an initial idea about the ancient approaches to Orphism before proceeding to the discussion of the Orphic material. This will be important, since we will be able to identify if the term Orphic as a distinguishable category existed in antiquity. I will also deal with the apparent importance of texts in Orphism and examine their possible use in the sphere of Orphism. I will finally discuss specific references to Orphic practices in a variety of areas and refer to the texts attributed to Orpheus. Following the discussion of non-Orphic material and before proceeding to the material which is, or has been, associated with Orphism, I will analyse the myth of Dionysos' dismemberment. This is essential, since it is a central point of Orphic studies especially in relation to the idea of a primal sin. Chapter 3 will be concerned with matters such as the narrative of the myth, its date and interpretation, as well as with the various sources through which it survives.

In Chapter 4 I will examine whether the gold tablets should be considered Orphic. There will be a four-layered analysis: discussion of archaeological and geographical information in order to examine possible parallels; a textual analysis and the examination of whether the tablets derive from an archetype; a discussion from a ritual perspective attempting to detect any performative and ritual elements; and a discussion of the eschatological and religious beliefs of the owners of the tablets. This chapter is prior to the discussion of the Derveni Papyrus and the *Orphic Rhapsodies* since it is easier to determine specific religious practical activity first and then detect a possible relation to theogonical/cosmogonical material. The Olbian Bone Tablets will also be discussed since they constitute the earliest evidence of the use of the term Orphic, and they have similarities to the gold tablets in that both are inscribed tablets used for religious purposes.

In Chapter 5 I will discuss the Derveni Papyrus, which contains an allegorical interpretation of a theogonical Orphic poem and it is one of the most important finds that shifted the academic debate about Orphism and led to new considerations about who the Orphics were. I will firstly discuss the contents of the Orphic poem quoted by the author and following his interpretation. In addition, I will deal with questions such as the author's identity and purpose, whether he can be considered to be an Orphic, the text's purpose and use, and its connection to Pre-Socratic philosophy. The Gurôb Papyrus will also be discussed in order to establish its possible relation to Orphic practices. The analysis of the Derveni Theogony will allow us to proceed to the discussion of another Orphic text of theogonical nature, namely the *Orphic Rhapsodies* in Chapter 6, and will enable us to make a comparison of their contents. Chapter 6 will also include the reconstruction of the text of the *Orphic Rhapsodies* and its analysis. Apart from the reconstruction of the text, a commentary justifying the arrangement of the fragments will also be included in the Appendix. The reconstruction will help us move away from the *Orphic Rhapsodies'* fragmented state, while having a continuous outline will allow for a better literary analysis of key elements and ideas to take place. Examining the *Orphic Rhapsodies* as a continuous whole will also help us better understand its nature and whether it was just a Theogony, as it has been mostly treated, or a more complex text.

2 Non-Orphic material referring to Orphic practices, beliefs and writings

The non-Orphic material which provides evidence about Orphism comes from a variety of periods and is, thus, of diverse nature. This needs to be taken into consideration when examining non-Orphic sources. However, the large majority of the sources examined in this chapter are Classical or Hellenistic. Any non-Orphic material which relates particularly to the Orphic sources to be discussed in the following chapters, will be discussed when we become familiar with the aforesaid sources. Some of the references to Orphism are made in an indirect way through the figure of Orpheus. In discussing such references to the mythical character of Orpheus, I do not of course suggest that Orpheus truly existed and wrote Orphic works or instituted Orphic mysteries; this would not be possible as he was only a legendary figure. We must, however, take these references into consideration since there is a difference between acknowledging Orpheus as a singer enchanting the cosmos with his music and acknowledging him as someone who instituted mysteries. The first case belongs entirely to the imaginary sphere while the second case has some referential connection to reality, in the sense that mysteries might have been instituted based on mythology or works attributed to the legendary figure of Orpheus. Most of the sources discussed in this section are dated to the 5th–4th centuries B.C. and are of a philosophical nature.

2.1 'Those affiliated to Orpheus...'

When trying to establish whether Orphics existed in ancient times, it would be very convenient to have direct references to them as a group of people. It would be very difficult to make a case for the existence of Orphics if they were not identified in any non-Orphic sources. This is why two passages from Plato are particularly important. The first comes from *Cratylus*:

> καὶ γὰρ σῆμά τινές φασιν αὐτὸ εἶναι τῆς ψυχῆς, ὡς τεθαμμένης ἐν τῷ νῦν παρόντι· καὶ διότι αὖ τούτῳ σημαίνει ἃ ἂν σημαίνῃ ἡ ψυχή, καὶ ταύτῃ σῆμα ὀρθῶς καλεῖσθαι. δοκοῦσι μέντοι μοι μάλιστα θέσθαι οἱ ἀμφὶ Ὀρφέα τοῦτο τὸ ὄνομα, ὡς δίκην διδούσης τῆς ψυχῆς ὧν δὴ ἕνεκα δίδωσιν· τοῦτον δὲ περίβολον ἔχειν, ἵνα σῴζηται, δεσμωτηρίου εἰκόνα· εἶναι οὖν τῆς ψυχῆς τοῦτο, ὥσπερ αὐτὸ ὀνομάζεται, ἕως ἂν ἐκτείσῃ τὰ ὀφειλόμενα, τὸ σῶμα, καὶ οὐδὲν δεῖν παράγειν οὐδὲ γράμμα.

> ...for some say it is the tomb (σῆμά) of the soul, their notion being that the soul is buried in the present life; and again, because by its means the soul gives any signs (σημαίνει) which

it gives, it is for this reason also properly called "sign" (σῆμα). But I think it most likely that [those affiliated to Orpheus] (οἱ ἀμφὶ Ὀρφέα) gave this name, with the idea that the soul is undergoing punishment for something; they think it has the body as an enclosure to keep it safe, like a prison, and this is, as the name itself denotes, the safe (σῶμα) for the soul, until the penalty is paid, and not even a letter needs to be changed.[20]

Fowler translates οἱ ἀμφὶ Ὀρφέα as 'the Orphic poets'.[21] However, if Socrates is referring simply to the Orphic poets we need to find an explanation of why he attributes this particular interpretation of the word 'body' to them. If we simply have to do with works of a poetic nature, then how can Socrates be confident that this is the interpretation of the creators of these works (plural because *oi* ἀμφὶ Ὀρφέα so unless he is referring to a single co-created work, which is unlikely, then he must be referring to a multitude of works)? We have to accept either that these Orphic poets offer an explanation next to the poem or that their work was not of a poetic nature, but of a philosophical and explanatory religious nature. There is a third possibility: that he is not referring to the creators of the Orphic works but to people who interpreted works attributed to Orpheus in this way. In this case, the Orphic texts would be of an allegorical nature and the word σῆμα would be referenced by Plato from a work of explanatory nature. The third case is more probable, and I have therefore amended the translation to 'those affiliated to Orpheus'. We can safely assume that Socrates is not referring here to those actually being around Orpheus, who was in any case a mythical person of the past, but to a group contemporary to him (Socrates), as the present tense of the verb δίδωσιν suggests. The same phrase is found in *Protagoras*, this time in reference to Orphic mysteries:

ἐγὼ δὲ τὴν σοφιστικὴν τέχνην φημὶ μὲν εἶναι παλαιάν, τοὺς δὲ μεταχειριζομένους αὐτὴν τῶν παλαιῶν ἀνδρῶν, φοβουμένους τὸ ἐπαχθὲς αὐτῆς, πρόσχημα ποιεῖσθαι καὶ προκαλύπτεσθαι, τοὺς μὲν ποίησιν, οἷον Ὅμηρόν τε καὶ Ἡσίοδον καὶ Σιμωνίδην, τοὺς δὲ αὖ τελετάς τε καὶ χρησμῳδίας, τοὺς ἀμφί τε Ὀρφέα καὶ Μουσαῖον·

Now I tell you that sophistry is an ancient art, and those men of ancient times who practised it, fearing the odium it involved, disguised it in a decent dress, sometimes of poetry, as in the case of Homer, Hesiod, and Simonides sometimes of mystic rites and soothsayings

---

20 Pl. *Cra.* 400c (Tr. Fowler).
21 This passage is also discussed in p.181. This phrase was often used periphrastically for persons grouped about one. However, saying 'Orpheus' group' instead of 'those surrounding Orpheus' does not alter the meaning significantly and the periphrastic use becomes more common in Hellenistic and later Greek.

(τελετάς τε καὶ χρησμῳδίας), as did Orpheus, Musaeus and their sects (τοὺς ἀμφί τε Ὀρφέα)[22]

Protagoras suggests that some men would practise sophistry disguised as something else, more decent, due to fear of being abominated. Some of his examples are Orpheus and Musaeus and their sects, who would disguise it as mystic rites and soothsaying. Perhaps Protagoras is trying to give his profession a respectable past through these references and not suggest that Orphics were sophists. In any case, the important information we get from this reference is the association of 'those affiliated to Orpheus' to mystic rites (τελετάς). The consistency with which Plato refers to this group of people also shows that they were identified by their contemporaries in reference to Orpheus. The passage from *Protagoras* supports the argument that Plato is not referring to Orphic poets in the *Cratylus*, but to a different group of people who were somehow related to Orpheus – as we saw possibly through the way they interpreted the works attributed to him. The association of these people in *Protagoras* with religious initiatory practices invalidates their poetic capacity and supports their religious capacity. It is also possible that they had both capacities, if we have to do with works of a religious explanatory nature.

In the passage from the *Cratylus*, Socrates notes that these people believe that the body (σῶμα) is the tomb (σῆμα) of the soul. The soul is materialised in order to pay the penalty for a punishment it is undergoing. The body is the safe receptacle which will protect the soul until the penalty is repaid. Socrates does not reveal what is the reason that the soul is being punished but makes clear that the body serves as the 'tomb' of the soul until what is being owed is repaid in full: ἕως ἂν ἐκτείσῃ τὰ ὀφειλόμενα. The soul, then, is 'trapped' in a bodily, earthly existence and can only be released when the penalty is paid. This idea draws a clear dichotomy between body and soul and also imposes the question of what happens to the soul after it is released from its containment. It appears, then, that those affiliated to Orpheus believed in the duality of body and soul and in an afterlife existence which is presumably better than the present one, judging by the negative overtones of the notions of punishment, imprisonment and entombment which Socrates uses to explain their interpretation.[23] The confidence of Socrates in attributing this interpretation to those affiliated to Orpheus suggests that it was an interpretation used by the majority of such people. At the least, it allows us to assume the existence of a specific group of people interpreting Orphic works in this specific way. What is more, their interpretation was 'circulated enough' to

---

22   Pl. *Prt.* 316d (Tr. Lamb).
23   In Socrates' capacity as a character voicing words attributed to him by Plato.

be referenced by Plato. If we combine the two Platonic passages linked by the same phrase, we can argue that there existed in Plato's time a group of people associated with Orphic writings; these people interpreted the Orphic works in a specific way, they believed in the duality of body and soul, to an afterlife existence which was better than the present bodily life which they conceived as a punishment, and they also performed mystic rites.

This suggestion is supported by a passage in *Rhesus*, a 5th–4th century B.C. play written around the time of Plato. It is attributed to Euripides but its authorship is disputed.[24] The following words are spoken after Rhesus' death by his mother – an un-identified Muse – who refers to him:

ΜΟΥΣΑ: οὐκ εἶσι γαίας ἐς μελάγχιμον πέδον·
τοσόνδε νύμφην τὴν ἔνερθ' αἰτήσομαι,
τῆς καρποποιοῦ παῖδα Δήμητρος θεᾶς,
ψυχὴν ἀνεῖναι τοῦδ'· ὀφειλέτις δέ μοι
τοὺς Ὀρφέως τιμῶσα φαίνεσθαι φίλους.
κἀμοὶ μὲν ὡς θανών τε κοὐ λεύσσων φάος
ἔσται τὸ λοιπόν· οὐ γὰρ ἐς ταὐτόν ποτε
ἔτ' εἶσιν οὐδὲ μητρὸς ὄψεται δέμας·
κρυπτὸς δ' ἐν ἄντροις τῆς ὑπαργύρου χθονὸς
ἀνθρωποδαίμων κείσεται βλέπων φάος,
Βάκχου προφήτης, ὅς γε Παγγαίου πέτραν
ᾤκησε, σεμνὸς τοῖσιν εἰδόσιν θεός.

---

24 Some scholars date the play to around 460 B.C. (Kennedy and Davis, 1998, p.7). A work by the name *Rhesus* is included in the *Records of Dramatic Performances (Didascaliae)*, originating from Aristotle, in the Euripidean plays (Arist. fr.626 Rose. Ritchie, 1964, p.14–18 on the *Didascaliae* in relation to *Rhesus*. Kennedy and Davis, 1998, p.5.). Crates of Mallos (2nd B.C.) suggests that an astronomical error in *Rhesus* 527–36 was due to Euripides being young when he wrote the play (Fr.89 Broggiato). The opposition, ancient and modern, rests on internal evidence, such as style and quality (Kennedy and Davis, 1998, p.4; Diggle, 1994, p.430). Liapis, whose discussion deals with language, metre and style thinks that the play is of low quality (Liapis, 2012, p.liii ff.). Ritchie defends an Euripidean authorship based on external evidence (Ritchie, 1964, p.260–73. Also, Braun, 1992, p.4; Kennedy and Davis, 1998, p.5). Euripidean authorship supported by: Kennedy and Davis, 1998, p.3–10; Murray, 1913, v–xi; Lattimore, 1958, p.5; Braun, 1992, p.3–4. It is not possible to elaborate on the lengthy debate over the authorship of *Rhesus*, but the usefulness of the passage does not depend on Euripidean authorship. If Euripides is not the author, we have evidence for someone else writing in the 5th–4th B.C., who was aware of Orphic mysteries related to the afterlife. Liapis argues that the play was composed in the mid 4th century for a Macedonian audience (Liapis, 2009, p.71–82). As we will see, Macedonia is the finding place of the Derveni Papyrus as well as of several gold tablets, both constituting Orphic material to be discussed in the following chapters. If Liapis is correct, this would enhance the presence of Orphic activity at the area.

MUSE: He will not go down into the black earth: I will make this request of the maid below, the daughter of fruitful Demeter, that she send up his soul. She is under obligation to me to show that she honors the [friends] of Orpheus. For me, he will be hereafter as one who has died and looks no more on the light: we shall never meet and he will never see his mother. But he shall lie hidden in the caves of the silver-rich land as a man-god, looking on the light, a spokesman of Bacchos, who came to dwell in the cliff of Pangaeon as a god revered by those who have understanding.[25]

The author of this work, through the mouth of the Muse, notes that Persephone is indebted to set Rhesus' soul free. This is an act that Persephone is obliged to do because the Muse or Rhesus has been a friend of Orpheus. Not only is this the same concept found in the *Cratylus* passage mentioned above, but the phrase τοὺς Ὀρφέως... φίλους could correspond to 'those affiliated to Orpheus' mentioned by Plato. On the other hand, this could be a mythological reference which applies exclusively to this occasion. Orpheus' place of origin was Thrace and according to most ancient sources he was the son of Oeagrus and muse Kalliope.[26] Even though we do not know who is the specific Muse in the *Rhesus* we know that Rhesus is a Thracian king and a cousin of Orpheus, since he is described in *Rhesus* as Ὀρφεύς, αὐτανέψιος νεκροῦ ('Orpheus, full cousin to the dead man').[27] However, if this is the case, it is not clear why Persephone would be impelled to turn Rhesus into a god and set his soul free just because she has an obligation to Orpheus. The reason behind this obligation is not stated. There might be a hint a few lines earlier where Orpheus is referred to as the one who revealed some secretive mysteries: μυστηρίων τε τῶν ἀπορρήτων φανὰς ἔδειξεν Ὀρφεύς ('...and it was Orpheus who revealed your ineffable mysteries with their torch processions...').[28] This reference might connote that these mysteries are related to the debt of Persephone to set the souls of Orpheus' beloved ones free. In fact, it is not a simple act of setting the soul free, but Rhesus will actually become a 'man-god' (ἀνθρωποδαίμων) who will be 'revered by those who have understanding'. This is a notable idea in itself, considering the time at which this play was composed – either 5th or 4th century B.C. – since the prevalent view about the soul did not

---

25 Eur. *Rhes.* 962–73 (Tr. Kovacs). My amendment. The word 'kinsmen' which Kovacs has does not correspond to the Greek word φίλους which means 'friends'.
26 Some other places, most of them areas of Thrace, such as Haemus, Rhodope, Bistonia, Odrysae, Sithone, Mount Pangaeus, Olympus and Leibethra are mentioned by a variety of writers. See OF923T-OF937T. OF890T: Pind. Fr.128c: υἰὸν Οἰαγροθ <δὲ> Ὀρφέα χρυσάορα. OF891T: schol. Eur. *Rhes.* 346.
27 Eur. *Rhes.* 944 (Tr.Kovacs).
28 Eur. *Rhes.* 943–44.

involve the possibility of it being deified and the most known mysteries, the Eleusinian ones, did not make such a promise. According to the passage from *Rhesus* the mysteries which Orpheus has revealed were also secret or not to be spoken and included torch processions. This must mean that the mysteries were so sacred that it was not allowed to utter them out loud or speak about them. As Bremmer argues, referring to the Eleusinian mysteries: '…it is the very holiness of the rites that forbids them to be performed or related outside their proper ritual context'.[29] These mysteries shown by Orpheus, then, either had concealed knowledge or were of the utmost sacredness. We will need more evidence to decide which of the two it was.

So far, the references to Orpheus are associated with eschatological and religious matters, namely the soul and the afterlife. Apart from Plato, his pupil Aristotle (384–322 B.C.) also refers to a belief about the soul found in the Orphic writings in his work *De Anima* written c.350 B.C.:

> τοῦτο δὲ πέπονθε καὶ <u>ὁ ἐν τοῖς Ὀρφικοῖς ἔπεσι καλουμένοις λόγος</u>· φησὶ γὰρ τὴν ψυχὴν ἐκ τοῦ ὅλου εἰσιέναι ἀναπνεόντων, φερομένην ὑπὸ τῶν ἀνέμων. οὐχ οἷόν τε δὴ τοῖς φυτοῖς τοῦτο συμβαίνειν οὐδὲ τῶν ζῴων ἐνίοις, εἴπερ μὴ πάντα ἀναπνέουσιν. τοῦτο δὲ λέληθε <u>τοὺς οὕτως ὑπειληφότας</u>.

> The theory in the so-called poems of Orpheus presents the same difficulty; for this theory alleges that the soul, borne by the winds, enters from the universe into animals when they breathe. Now this cannot happen to plants, nor to some animals, since they do not all breathe: a point which has escaped those who support this theory.[30]

The theory argued in the Orphic poems according to Aristotle is that the nature of the soul is airy and that it enters all living beings through breath. We do not necessarily need to interpret the word ἔπεσι as poems since it was often used for denoting a written work, a story, or an oracle. We need to also consider that Aristotle is not referring to one Orphic work or poem but to several. However, he does refer to only one theory (λόγος). This again imposes the question of whether this was a theory in the form of allegorical poetry or in the form of a more explanatory religious and philosophical prose/poetry. Considering the way it is expressed by Aristotle, there must have been a collection of Orphic works and we cannot exclude the possibility that it included poems as well as prose concerned with the interpretation of texts or with religious/philosophical matters. The existence of

---

[29] Bremmer, 2014, p.16–17. Strabo (1st B.C), 10.3.9: '…the secrecy with which the sacred rites are concealed induces reverence for the divine, since it imitates the nature of the divine, which is to avoid being perceived by our human senses' (Tr. Jones).
[30] Arist. *De an.* A5 410b29–411a3 (Tr. Hett).

such a collection would suggest that it was deliberately compiled by specific people and its interpretations followed by others. These would be the τοὺς οὕτως ὑπειληφότας mentioned by Aristotle; the ones that upheld this theory. It becomes clear that whatever the nature of the Orphic works, they also had scientific overtones. We notice that Aristotle, like Plato, refers to a theory which has to do with the soul. This theory again presupposes the duality of body and soul and that the soul pre-exists the body. There is, thus, a consistency in our sources which enhances their reliability. According to Aristotle, the soul enters the body ἐκ τοῦ ὅλου meaning that during the time that it is not inside a body, it is part of the whole, of the universe. This is a theory that comes closer to philosophical/scientifical interpretations of the human condition. In the case that Aristotle's τοὺς οὕτως ὑπειληφότας are the same as Plato's τοὺς ἀμφί...Ὀρφέα in *Protagoras*, then we have to do with a religious philosophy which dealt with eschatological questions and was practised through mysteries.[31] It is too early to draw such conclusions but it is essential to decipher any information from non-Orphic sources so we will be able to juxtapose them with Orphic sources and examine if they have any corresponding ideas and overarching patterns.

The 'scientific nature' of the Orphic writings is supported by another passage, namely a fragment of Heraclides of Pontus (4th B.C) who also was a contemporary of Plato and Aristotle and a student at the Platonic Academy in Athens. This source, then, belongs to the same category of philosophical texts as Aristotle and Plato. The fragment in question is the following one:

> Ἡρακλείδης καὶ οἱ Πυθαγόρειοι ἕκαστον τῶν ἀστέρων κόσμον ὑπάρχειν γῆν περιέχοντα ἀέρα τε ἐν τῶι ἀπείρωι αἰθέρι. ταῦτα δὲ τὰ δόγματα ἐν τοῖς Ὀρφικοῖς φέρεται. κοσμοποιοῦσι γὰρ ἕκαστον τῶν ἀστέρων.
>
> Heraclides and the Pythagoreans (say) that each of the stars is a world, containing land and air in the infinite aether. These doctrines are circulated in the Orphic writings. For they make a world out of each of the stars.[32]

It is not clear whether this passage suggests that it is the Pythagorean doctrines that were circulated in the Orphic writings or doctrines similar to the Pythagorean ones. Both cases can be explained by the possibility of ideas being interchanged between these traditions, and we cannot exclude the possibility that Pythagoreans were behind the Orphic writings. As we will see later on in this chapter, some

---

[31] Pl. *Prt.* 316d (Tr. Lamb).
[32] Heraclid. Pont. fr.75 Schütrumpf (Tr. Schütrumpf = ps.-Plut. 2.13 888 F = Euseb. 15.30.8 = ps.-Gal. 52. Gottschalk. 1998.

Orphic works are attributed to specific Pythagoreans. However, this could also go the other way around if our ancient sources attributed Orphic works to Pythagoreans because of their potential similarities to Pythagorean ideas. In any case, once again, the reference is not just to one but to many writings in which this theory (along with other doctrines as Heraclides says) about the stars is found.

As was earlier argued, it appears that from the mid 5th- late 4th century B.C., the period which all the sources discussed so far come from, there was a collection of Orphic works on which specific religious, eschatological and perhaps cosmogonical/scientific ideas were based. The fact that all our sources always refer to the plural instead of the singular supports the argument that we are dealing with a collection and not a single poem/work. If the theories mentioned in our respective sources were taken from a single work each time, then there would be no reason for the authors to refer to them in the plural. Also, the totality of the non-Orphic sources discussed so far are of a philosophical nature – apart from *Rhesus* – this supports that the Orphic writings included texts of an explanatory nature which instigated this philosophical intertextual 'dialogue'. This does not mean that our sources were not interested in non-philosophical matters but since Plato, Aristotle and Heraclides Ponticus were all interested in matters of the soul, it becomes more probable that they were interested in these theories found in the Orphic writings because they were stated explicitly and thus could be addressed directly. If we had to do with simple religious poems such as a theogony, Aristotle could not have been so assertive in rejecting the airy nature of the soul, since he could have been mistaken in his interpretation of the poem. Also, it was not common to find theories about the substance of the soul expressed explicitly in religious poems such as a theogony. The same goes for Plato who built his argument around a specific word (σῆμα) giving its semasiological explanation according to the Orphic writings. This would perhaps not have been possible if he was referring to a religious poem.

But what about other kind of sources, such as Herodotus? He was a contemporary of Socrates who was often used by Plato in his later dialogues and the one referring to the ἀμφὶ Ὀρφέα in the *Cratylus* passage discussed at the beginning of the chapter. In the following passage we find an intermingling of traditions similar to that in Heraclides Ponticus:

ὁμολογέουσι δὲ ταῦτα τοῖσι Ὀρφικοῖσι καλεομένοισι καὶ Βακχικοῖσι, ἐοῦσι δὲ Αἰγυπτίοισι καὶ Πυθαγορείοισι· οὐδὲ γὰρ τούτων τῶν ὀργίων μετέχοντα ὅσιον ἐστὶ ἐν εἰρινέοισι εἵμασι θαφθῆναι. ἔστι δὲ περὶ αὐτῶν ἰρὸς λόγος λεγόμενος.

In this they agree with practices called Orphic and Bacchic, but in fact Egyptian and Pythagorean: for it is not pious either, for someone participating in these secret rites to be buried in woollen garments. There is a sacred story about this.³³

Herodotus is making a clear statement about rites identified as Orphic (τοῖσι Ὀρφικοῖσι καλεομένοισι) and he closely links them to Bacchic rites. The specific rite he is referring to is the forbidding of being buried in woollen garments. Herodotus refers to those participating in these rites as τούτων τῶν ὀργίων μετέχοντα. This in itself does not allow us to identify them as Orphic as we do not know yet the nature of the Orphic cult, or even if it was a cult at all or something closer to a religious philosophy. The people mentioned by Herodotus as participating in these rites could have participated in other cults too and may not have identified themselves as exclusively Orphic. We can however get more information on Orphic rites from this passage. Herodotus refers to *orgia*, which are usually interpreted as 'secret rites'. The secrecy of the meaning of this rite is furthermore signified by the fact that Herodotus says there is an ἱρὸς λόγος (sacred story) about this but does not give any more information about the contents of the story. A few paragraphs earlier, Herodotus mentions some Egyptian rites of Osiris 'of which it is not right for <him> to speak' (οὔ μοι ὅσιον ἐστὶ λέγειν).³⁴ Edmonds argues that, since according to the available evidence the rites of Osiris were not secret, Herodotus must be referring to some Greek rites resembling the Egyptian ones and which were indeed forbidden to talk about.³⁵ He also claims that these mysteries were possibly related to the myth of Dionysos' dismemberment and thus the parallelism with Osiris who was also dismembered.³⁶ Even if Edmonds is not right in his suggestions, we can be sure that Herodotus considered the Orphic rites to be secret.

Let us dwell some more on the matter of secrecy. In the second book of Plutarch's *Table-Talk* written somewhere between 99–116 A.D. the question of 'Which came first: the chicken or the egg?' is discussed.³⁷ One of the speakers, Firmus, refers to an Orphic *hieros logos* and even mentions some details from the story. He goes on, however, to say that he cannot reveal the parts related to the mysteries and even mentions Herodotus as his 'role model' for keeping these matters secret:

---

33 Hdt. 2.81.
34 Hdt. 2.61.
35 Edmonds, 2008a.
36 This myth will be discussed in extent in the following chapter.
37 Plut. *Quaest. conv.* 2.3: πότερον ἡ ὄρνις πρότερον ἢ τὸ ᾠὸν ἐγένετο; Date: Pelling, 2011, p.207.

ἡ γὰρ ὕλη λόγον ἔχει πρὸς τὰ γιγνόμενα μητρὸς ὥς φησι Πλάτων καὶ τιθήνης· ὕλη δὲ πᾶν ἐξ οὗ σύστασιν ἔχει τὸ γεννώμενον. "Τὸ δ' ἐπὶ τούτοις," ἔφη γελάσας, "'<u>ἀείσω ξυνετοῖσι</u>' τὸν <u>Ὀρφικὸν καὶ ἱερὸν λόγον</u>, ὃς οὐκ ὄρνιθος μόνον τὸ ᾠὸν ἀποφαίνει πρεσβύτερον, ἀλλὰ καὶ συλλαβὼν ἅπασαν αὐτῷ τὴν ἁπάντων ὁμοῦ πρεσβυγένειαν ἀνατίθησιν. καὶ τἄλλα μὲν 'εὔστομα κείσθω' καθ' Ἡρόδοτον, ἔστι γὰρ μυστικώτερα·…"

For matter has the relation of mother or nurse to things which exist, as Plato says; and matter is all from which whatever is created has its substance. "What is more", he added with a laugh, ['I will sing for those who are wise' the sacred discourse of Orpheus], which not only declares the egg older than the hen, but also attributes to it the absolute primordiality over all things together without exception. [As for the other parts, as Herodotus says 'I shall keep a reverent silence', since they are connected with the mysteries][38]

Through Firmus' lips, Plutarch most probably refers to the birth of Phanes from the cosmic egg as found in the *Orphic Rhapsodies* to be discussed in Chapter 6.[39] Phanes was the first god who created the totality of the cosmos and thus Plutarch's attestation is in accordance with the *Orphic Rhapsodies*. He quotes Herodotus from a passage where he refers to Egyptian rites forbidden to be revealed and where he describes the Thesmophoria.[40] We can see that a theogony such as the *Rhapsodic* one could be an *hieros logos* related to mysteries whose sacredness made them unatterable. We once more, establish a connection of Orphic texts with religious rites and it seems that it was not the text in itself which was secret but its application/interpretation into mysteries.

A similar verse to the one quoted by Plutarch is quoted in the Derveni Papyrus (mid 4th B.C.) from the Orphic poem which the Derveni author commented on and possibly dating as early as the 6th century B.C.[41] In the passage in question, the Derveni author notes that Orpheus is saying holy things [ἱερ[ολογ]εῖται], from the beginning to the end:

[κ]αὶ ἀνθρώ[ποις] αἰνι[γμ]ατώδης, [κε]ὶ [Ὀρφεὺ]ς αὐτ[ὸ]ς
[ἐ]ρίστ' αἰν[ίγμα]τα οὐκ ἤθελε λέγειν, [ἐν αἰν]ίγμασ[ι]ν δὲ
[μεγά]λα. ἱερ[ολογ]εῖται μὲν οὖν καὶ ἀ[πὸ το]ῦ πρώτου
[ἀεὶ] μέχρι οὗ [τελε]υταίου ῥήματος. ὡ[ς δηλοῖ] καὶ ἐν τῶι

---

38 Plut. *Quaest. conv.* 2.3.2, 636d–636e (Tr. Clement). Translation in brackets [ ] is by the author.
39 See p.301.
40 Hdt. 2.171.1–2: 'On this lake they enact by night the story of the god's sufferings, a rite which the Egyptians call the Mysteries. I could say more about this, for I know the truth, but let me preserve a discreet silence. Let me preserve a discreet silence, too, concerning that rite of Demeter which the Greeks call Thesmophoria, except as much of it as I am not forbidden to mention'.
41 Sider, 2014, Tzifopoulos, 2014, p.137, Burkert, 1997: Date the poem at 6th B.C. Janko (2002, p.1) and Tsantsanoglou (KPT, 2006, p.10) date the Derveni author's treatise at the late 5th century B.C.

[εὐκ]ρινήτῳ[ι ἔπει· "θ]ύρας" γὰρ "ἐπιθέ[σθαι" κελ]εύσας τοῖ[ς]
["ὠσὶ]ν" αὐτ[οὺς οὔτι νομο]θετεῖν φη[σιν τοῖς] πολλοῖς
τὴ]ν ἀκοὴν [ἀγνεύο]ντας κατ[ὰ]

> This poem is strange and riddling to people, though [Orpheus] himself did not intend to say contentious riddles but rather great things in riddles. In fact he is speaking mystically, and from the very first word all the way to the last. As he also makes clear in the well recognizable verse: for, having ordered them to 'put doors to their ears', he says that he is not legislating for the many [but addressing himself to those] who are pure in hearing[42]

The particular *hieros logos* from the Derveni Papyrus, which is also a cosmogony, is addressed only to those who are prudent, just as is the case with Plutarch's cosmogony. I will not at present elaborate more on the Derveni Papyrus which constitutes one of our major Orphic sources since it will be discussed in depth in Chapter 5. In any case, the information which we get from Plutarch is that secretive mysteries were related to an Orphic *hieros logos* which was also apparently recited to a restricted, pure audience; under which circumstances we still do not know.

Finally, there is one more parallel between Plutarch and Herodotean references to Orphic ideas since Plutarch intermingles Orphic and Pythagorean beliefs: 'But my companions at one of Sossius Senecio's dinners suspected me of being committed to beliefs of the Orphics or the Pythagoreans and holding the egg taboo, as some hold the heart and brain, because I thought it to be the first principle of creation.'[43] According to Plutarch, Orphics and/or Pythagoreans did not eat eggs because they considered the egg to be the 'principle of generation'. This might be a rule stemming from the Orphic myth of the creation of the world by Phanes who was born from an egg and it is found in the *Rhapsodies* as mentioned earlier.[44] Also, Plutarch claims through Firmus' voice that this is the reason that an egg is offered to Dionysos during his secret rites: 'It is therefore not inappropriate that in the rites of Dionysus the egg is consecrated as a symbol of that which produces everything and contains everything within itself.'[45] If this is true, then this constitutes another evidence of mystic rites being based on Orphic mythology and texts. It also relates Dionysos to Phanes who was the deity that

---

42 DP, Col.VII.5–11 (Tr. Tsantsanoglou-Parássoglou).
43 Plut. *Quaest. conv.* 2.3.1, 635e: ὑπόνοιαν μέντοι παρέσχον, ἑστιῶντος ἡμᾶς Σοσσίου Σενεκίωνος, ἐνέχεσθαι δόγμασιν Ὀρφικοῖς ἢ Πυθαγορικοῖς καὶ τὸ ᾠόν, ὥσπερ ἔνιοι καρδίαν καὶ ἐγκέφαλον, ἀρχὴν ἡγούμενος γενέσεως ἀφοσιοῦσθαι· (Tr. Clement).
44 See OR7–12.
45 Plut. *Quaest. conv.* 2.3.2, 636e: ὅθεν οὐκ ἀπὸ τρόπου τοῖς περὶ τὸν Διόνυσον ὀργιασμοῖς ὡς μίμημα τοῦ τὰ πάντα γεννῶντος καὶ περιέχοντος ἐν ἑαυτῷ συγκαθωσίωται. (Tr. Clement).

came out of the egg. I will, however, cross-examine the egg-related information in Chapter 6 where the *Rhapsodies* will be discussed in depth.

The passages from Herodotus and Plutarch, even though they are six centuries apart, both entail four major points which have also become evident in the passages of Plato and Aristotle discussed earlier: 1) the Orphic religious practices and beliefs are associated with sacred written or unwritten stories, 2) a level of secrecy surrounds Orphic religious practices possibly due to their sacredness, 3) Orphic ideas seem to be intermingled with Pythagorean ideas and 4) Orphic ideas are concerned with eschatological beliefs about the soul and the afterlife and with cosmogonical/scientific matters. These points will come up throughout the book and they will be discussed in more depth in the context of the sociological and religious background of the Archaic and Classical period to which most of our sources belong. For the present I will deal with the first point. In the next section, I will examine non-Orphic sources which refer to the use of 'sacred stories' as an aetiological device for mysteries in relation to Orphism. I will also discuss how widespread the use of 'books' was in rituals and by whom was this practised. In this way, we will be able to establish how closely Orphism was related to literature and what this means for the place of Orphism in Archaic and Classical times.

2.2 Itinerant Priests, Sacred Books and *Hieroi Logoi*

Sources from Plato onwards attest Orphic *bibloi*, conventionally translated 'books', but 'books' in the modern sense of the term did not exist in ancient times. What would be roughly equivalent to modern books is papyrus rolls inscribed with 'an organised written text, or a collection of texts, identified by a title'.[46] These rolls 'served as repositories for written texts whose survival depended on the durability of the inscribed surfaces that transmitted them'.[47] Texts were, however, also transmitted orally or survived through memorisation and recitation. The question I will be dealing with is whether such 'books' (or texts) were used during rituals or if they had any religious purpose in general. I will firstly discuss any non-Orphic sources referring to such practices in relation to Orphism and then I will deal with the use of 'books' or *hieroi logoi* in general in Classical Greece in order to provide context or possible parallels for the use of the Orphic texts.

---

46 Henrichs, 2003, 210.
47 Henrichs, 2003, 210.

Let us, then, discuss the non-Orphic sources which attest that Orphic 'books'were used during rites.[48] The first one comes, once again, from Plato's *Republic* (370s B.C.) through the lips of Adeimantus:

> βίβλων δὲ ὅμαδον παρέχονται Μουσαίου καὶ Ὀρφέως, Σελήνης τε καὶ Μουσῶν ἐκγόνων, ὥς φασι, καθ' ἃς θυηπολοῦσιν, πείθοντες | οὐ μόνον ἰδιώτας ἀλλὰ καὶ πόλεις, ὡς ἄρα λύσεις τε καὶ καθαρμοὶ ἀδικημάτων διὰ θυσιῶν καὶ παιδιᾶς ἡδονῶν εἰσι μὲν ἔτι ζῶσιν, εἰσὶ δὲ καὶ τελευτήσασιν, ἃς δὴ τελετὰς καλοῦσιν, αἳ τῶν ἐκεῖ κακῶν ἀπολύουσιν ἡμᾶς, μὴ θύσαντας δὲ δεινὰ περιμένει.

> And they produce a babble of books by Musaeus and Orpheus, descendants, as they claim, of Selene and the Muses, and using these they make sacrifices, and persuade not only individuals but cities that they really can have atonement and purification for their wrongdoing through sacrifices and playful delights while they are still alive and equally after death. These they actually call initiations, which free us from evils in the next world, while terrible things await those who neglect their sacrifices.[49]

In this passage Plato clearly refers to the use of 'books' during or in association with certain *teletas* of a purificatory nature which assured the avoidance of 'evils' in the afterlife. The phrase βίβλων δὲ ὅμαδον indicates that these 'initiators' perhaps made use of texts by more than one author. This is also suggested by the fact that Adeimantus refers to Musaeus *and* Orpheus as the authors of the texts. It is noted that the books were used while performing sacrifices, an act mentioned two lines later as a means of averting evils in the afterlife. Adeimantus also refers to childish playful acts of pleasure (παιδιᾶς ἡδονῶν) being part of these apotropaic practices. These 'books', then, possibly included information or allegorical texts justifying specific views about the afterlife and on how to be purified from wrongdoings in order to avoid the 'terrible things' awaiting the uninitiated. There is a hint of contempt in the Platonic passage against these people and their 'clients', the reason for which is not immediately evident.

The context of the passage can provide more information as it deals with justice and injustice and whether it is better to be just or unjust. The discussion prior to the above passage deals with how rich citizens might get a better lot in life despite being unjust:

> ΓΛΑΥΚΩΝ:
> ...καὶ θεοῖς θυσίας καὶ ἀναθήματα ἱκανῶς καὶ μεγαλοπρεπῶς θύειν τε καὶ ἀνατιθέναι, καὶ θεραπεύειν τοῦ δικαίου πολὺ ἄμεινον τοὺς θεοὺς καὶ τῶν ἀνθρώπων οὓς ἂν βούληται, ὥστε καὶ θεοφιλέστερον αὐτὸν εἶναι μᾶλλον προσήκειν ἐκ τῶν εἰκότων ἢ τὸν δίκαιον

---

48 I will refer to them as 'books' for convenience.
49 Pl. *Resp.* 2.364e–365a (Tr. and date Emlyn-Jones).

GLAUCON:
... He will make sacrifices and dedicate votive offerings to the gods on an appropriately magnificent scale, and do service to the gods and any humans he wishes far more effectively than the just person, so that it is reasonable to suppose that he is also more loved by the gods than the just person. Thus they say, Socrates, that a better life has been provided by gods and men for the unjust than for the just person.[50]

After a quotation from Homer about the rewards to a just person by the gods, Adeimantus says:

Μουσαῖος δὲ τούτων νεανικώτερα τἀγαθὰ καὶ ὁ ὑὸς αὐτοῦ παρὰ θεῶν διδόασιν τοῖς δικαίοις· εἰς Ἅιδου γὰρ ἀγαγόντες τῷ λόγῳ καὶ | κατακλίναντες καὶ συμπόσιον τῶν ὁσίων κατασκευάσαντες ἐστεφανωμένους ποιοῦσιν τὸν ἅπαντα χρόνον ἤδη διάγειν μεθύοντας, ἡγησάμενοι κάλλιστον ἀρετῆς μισθὸν μέθην αἰώνιον. οἱ δ' ἔτι τούτων μακροτέρους ἀποτείνουσιν μισθοὺς παρὰ θεῶν· παῖδας γὰρ παίδων φασὶ καὶ γένος κατόπισθεν λείπεσθαι τοῦ <u>ὁσίου καὶ εὐόρκου</u>. | ταῦτα δὴ καὶ ἄλλα τοιαῦτα ἐγκωμιάζουσιν δικαιοσύνην· τοὺς δὲ <u>ἀνοσίους αὖ καὶ ἀδίκους</u> εἰς πηλόν τινα κατορύττουσιν ἐν Ἅιδου καὶ κοσκίνῳ ὕδωρ ἀναγκάζουσι φέρειν, ἔτι τε ζῶντας εἰς κακὰς δόξας ἄγοντες, ἅπερ Γλαύκων περὶ τῶν δικαίων δοξαζομένων δὲ ἀδίκων διῆλθε τιμωρήματα, ταῦτα περὶ τῶν ἀδίκων λέγουσιν, ἄλλα δὲ οὐκ ἔχουσιν. ὁ μὲν οὖν ἔπαινος καὶ ὁ ψόγος οὗτος ἑκατέρων.

But Musaeus and his son sing of still more splendid rewards that the just can expect from the gods. For the story goes that when they have conducted them down to Hades they sit them down to a wine party for the pious that they have laid on, and have them pass the whole time drinking with garlands on their heads in the belief that the finest reward of virtue is to be drunk for all eternity. But others extend the rewards from the gods even farther; they say the children's children and the family of a man who is pious, and keeps to his word are preserved thereafter. So with these and similar commendations they extol justice. But the impious and unjust, on the other hand, they bury in some sort of mud in Hades and force them to carry water in a sieve. In fact while they are still alive even they bring them into evil repute, and all the punishments which Glaucon described as falling on the just who are supposed to be wicked, they talk of as belonging to the unjust: they don't have any others. Such is the praise and censure of the just and unjust.[51]

Adeimantus essentially argues that some men choose to be just not for the sake of it but because of the rewards or punishments which await them; in this particular passage, in the afterlife. It could be said, thus, that Plato portrays a negative attitude towards these beliefs. However, earlier in the dialogue Socrates places justice in the finest class: that 'which any person aiming at future happiness must

---

50 Pl. *Resp.* 2.362c (Tr. Emlyn-Jones).
51 Pl. *Resp.* 2.363c–e (Tr. Emlyn-Jones).

value both for its own sake and for its consequences'.[52] We can see, thus, that Socrates does not directly condemn the beliefs in rewards or punishments for the just or unjust since this can be good in itself and has good consequences. Glaucon's point was that one could get the rewards without actually being just while Adeimantus says that people are led to believe that justice is good because of its rewards and not for its own sake. It is not entirely clear from Adeimantus' words if, according to the beliefs he discusses, the rewards are given to men performing sacrifices and rites despite being unjust or if someone has to be truly just to receive these rewards and avoid the punishments. I would suggest that this passage refers to people actually being just, as can be extracted by phrases such as: '... of the pious and oath-keeping man' or 'the impious and unjust they bury in mud in the house of Hades' and 'while they still live, they bring them into evil repute'. The first phrases show that to receive the rewards or avoid the punishments you actually have to be pious, while the second shows that unjust men suffer while still alive. This view does not correspond to how rich men paying their way to blissfulness have been portrayed earlier and it could be said that Adeimantus' criticism is against those who act justly being driven solely by the rewards and punishments. Adeimantus even says that all the sufferings that Glaucon has said befall just men who are thought to be unjust are enumerated by these writers as befalling the unjust.[53] There seems to be a contrasting attitude, then, towards what is said in the works of Musaeus and Orpheus and how what is said is being used for the wrong purposes by those convincing individuals and whole cities that they can get atonement from their wrongdoings from sacrifices and rituals alone. The condemnation expressed in the *Republic*, thus, might not turn against Orphic beliefs, texts and practices but against the way these were used by specific individuals.

It is not possible or relevant to my purpose to analyse the *Republic* here but we can still get an idea of attitudes towards such beliefs and practices, and valuable information. We can say that there were specific works attributed to Musaeus (and his son) which dealt with justice and piousness, and the consequences in the afterlife for someone just or unjust. Musaeus is a figure closely associated with Orpheus. He was said to be the father of Eumolpus and he is frequently mentioned alongside Orpheus, while some ancient authors identify him as Orpheus'

---

[52] Pl. *Resp.* 2.358a: ὃ καὶ δι' αὐτὸ καὶ διὰ τὰ γιγνόμενα ἀπ' αὐτοῦ ἀγαπητέον τῷ μέλλοντι μακαρίῳ ἔσεσθαι (Tr.Emlyn-Jones).
[53] Let us not forget that the *Republic* ends with the Myth of Er, which has been related with Orphic ideas amongst others, and it will be discussed in Chapter 4: see p.193 ff.

son, teacher or student.⁵⁴ A passage from the *Parian Marble*, a *stele* of 264 B.C. referring to the years from the 16th century B.C. to the 3rd century B.C, mentions that Eumolpus instituted the Eleusinian mysteries sometime between 1397 B.C. and 1373 B.C. and made known the works of his father Musaeus.⁵⁵ The entry right before this one refers to Orpheus' poem about Kore's rape and Demeter's quest.⁵⁶ As Rotstein suggests mentioning Musaeus after Orpheus might indicate 'a father and son genealogical link'.⁵⁷ The works, thus, often attributed to Musaeus could be related to Orphic practices and/or beliefs. It is more probable, however, that the idea of rewards or punishments being directly linked to leading a just or unjust life was related to Orphic beliefs and practices rather than with the Eleusinian Mysteries which we know promised a better lot in the afterlife to their initiates without linking it to the present lifestyle. This matter will be discussed further in the following chapter. For the moment, it can be argued that there were in Plato's time, in Athens, a group of people who either wrote works under the name of Musaeus or interpreted them in a way which suggested that someone's lot in the afterlife was directly determined by how justly he acted during his lifetime. The attribution of these works to Musaeus who is in turn closely linked to Orpheus suggests that these ideas were considered Orphic. This argument is supported by all the other non-Orphic sources discussed so far, which indicate a clear association of Orphic beliefs and practices with written (or unwritten) works and which suggest that the nature of Orphic beliefs was eschatological.

Do we have evidence by whom were these works used? The following passage from the *Republic* which comes right before the first passage discussed at the beginning of this sub-chapter gives an answer:

ἀγύρται δὲ καὶ μάντεις ἐπὶ πλουσίων θύρας ἰόντες πείθουσιν ὡς ἔστι παρὰ σφίσι δύναμις ἐκ θεῶν ποριζομένη θυσίαις τε καὶ ἐπῳδαῖς, εἴτε τι ἀδίκημά του γέγονεν αὐτοῦ ἢ προγόνων,

---

54 Clem. Al. *Strom.* 1.21.107.4; Euseb. *Chron.* II 46 Schone. An Attic red-figure pelike dated to the late 5th century B.C. and attributed to the Meidias painter shows Mousaios, in Thracian garments, standing next to a young Eumolpos, which shows that the genealogy of Mousaios-Eumolpos was known at least as early as the late 5th century B.C. New York, Metropolitan Museum of Art 37.11.23. Beazley, ARV2 1313.7.
55 *Marm. Par.* saec. III a.C.n. (*IG* 12 (5), 444,15) = OF1096T: [ἀφ' οὗ Εὔμολπος ...] [...]ΝΟΥ τὰ μυστήρια ἀνέφηνεν ἐν Ἐλευσῖνι καὶ τὰς τοῦ [πατρὸς Μ]ουσαίου ποιήσ[ει]ς ἐξέθηκ[εν ἔτη ΧΗΔ, βασιλεύοντος Ἀθηνῶν] [Ἐριχθέ]ως τοῦ Πανδίονος.
56 *Marm. Par.* saec. III a.C.n. (*IG* 12 (5), 444,14): [ἀφ' οὗ Ὀρφεὺς ὁ Οἰάγρου καὶ Καλλιόπης] υἱὸ[ς τὴ]ν [ἑ]αυτοῦ πο<ί>ησιν ἐξ[έ]θηκε Κόρης τε ἁρπαγὴν καὶ Δήμητρος ζήτησιν καὶ τὸν αὐτου[ργηθέντα ὑπ'αὐτῆς σπόρον καὶ τὸ] [ἐκεῖθεν ἔ]θος τῶν ὑποδεξαμένων τὸν καρπόν, ἔτη ΧΗΔΔΔΓ, βασιλεύοντος Ἀθηνῶν Ἐριχθέως.
57 Rotstein, 2016, Ch.6.

ἀκεῖσθαι μεθ' ἡδονῶν τε καὶ ἑορτῶν, ἐάν τέ τινα ἐχθρὸν πημῆναι ἐθέλῃ, μετὰ σμικρῶν δαπανῶν ὁμοίως δίκαιον ἀδίκῳ βλάψει ἐπαγωγαῖς τισιν καὶ καταδέσμοις, τοὺς θεούς, ὥς φασιν, πείθοντές σφισιν ὑπηρετεῖν. | τούτοις δὲ πᾶσιν τοῖς λόγοις μάρτυρας ποιητὰς ἐπάγονται οἱ μὲν κακίας πέρι, εὐπετείας διδόντες, ὡς 'τὴν μὲν κακότητα καὶ ἰλαδὸν ἔστιν ἑλέσθαι | ῥηϊδίως· λείη μὲν ὁδός, μάλα δ' ἐγγύθι ναίει· | τῆς δ' ἀρετῆς ἱδρῶτα θεοὶ προπάροιθεν ἔθηκαν' καί τινα ὁδὸν μακράν τε καὶ τραχεῖαν καὶ ἀνάντη· οἱ δὲ τῆς τῶν θεῶν ὑπ' ἀνθρώπων παραγωγῆς τὸν Ὅμηρον μαρτύρονται, | ὅτι καὶ ἐκεῖνος εἶπεν 'λιστοὶ δέ τε καὶ θεοὶ αὐτοί, | καὶ τοὺς μὲν θυσίαισι καὶ εὐχωλαῖς ἀγαναῖσιν | λοιβῇ τε κνίσῃ τε παρατρωπῶσ' ἄνθρωποι | λισσόμενοι, ὅτε κέν τις ὑπερβήῃ καὶ ἁμάρτῃ.' βίβλων δὲ ὅμαδον παρέχονται Μουσαίου καὶ Ὀρφέως...

Wandering priests and prophets <u>approach the doors of the wealthy and persuade them</u> that they have a power from the gods conveyed through sacrifices and incantations, and any wrong committed against someone either by an individual or his ancestors can be expiated with pleasure and feasting. Or if he wishes to injure any enemy of his, for a small outlay he will be able to harm just and unjust alike with certain spells and incantations through which they can persuade the gods, they say, to serve their ends. For all these stories they call on the poets as support. Some, granting indulgences for vice, quote as follows: 'Indeed evil can be obtained easily in abundance, smooth is the way, and it lives very close by. But the gods have placed sweat in the path of virtue' [Hes. *Op*. 287–89], and a long hard uphill road. Others bring in Homer as a witness for the beguiling of gods by men, since he too said: 'The gods themselves can be moved by supplication; And humans, with sacrifices and soothing prayers with libations and sacrifices, turn their wills by prayer, when anyone has overstepped the mark and offended' [Hom. *Il*. 9.497,499–501]. And they produce a babble of books by Musaeus and Orpheus...[58]

We can see that the 'wandering priests and prophets' use a variety of works to convince their clients. Plato quotes Homer and Hesiod as being part of their elaborate case in favour of being acquitted of their evil-doings through sacrifice, libations and religious practices. If these itinerant priests did not use exclusively Orphic works to justify their expertise in religious matters, this allows us to identify them as a phenomenon which is 'external' to Orphism: itinerant soothsayers traditionally made use of a variety of religious practices, taking elements from several cults and beliefs and created a bricolage of numerous sources in order to project a persona of religious expertise. Orphic works such as the ones described by Plato and which referred to punishments and rewards in the afterlife would be very fitting and useful to the itinerant priests in validating the necessity of religious rites and sacrifices to secure a happy afterlife. The fact that such itinerant priests used Orphic material does not constitute enough evidence to conclude that Orphic beliefs and practices were scorned by ancient authors. The itinerant priests in this passage are identified by many scholars as *Orpheotelestae* even

---

[58] Pl. *Resp*. 2.364b–e (Tr. Emlyn-Jones).

though they are not identified by Plato as such. Plato refers to them as 'ἀγύρται δὲ καὶ μάντεις', meaning beggar prophets.[59] Edwards – who also considers the itinerant priests to be *Orpheotelestae* – agrees with the suggestion that they would not 'have been confused by Plato' with the Orphics who according to him could be either 'celebrants of mysteries attributed to Orpheus', 'writers of poems under the name of Orpheus', 'interpreters of such poems and mysteries', or a combination of the above.[60] Whether or not the itinerant priests mentioned by Plato identified themselves as *Orpheotelestae* is uncertain, but I believe that they constitute only one strand of Orphism and not its totality. As Edwards also suggests: 'The Orphics and the *Orpheotelestae* were alike in that they both believed in future reward and punishment, but the core of Orphic doctrine is that the gods reward us not for our disbursements but for the purity of our souls'.[61] This emphasis on purity in Orphic and non-Orphic sources will become evident in the following paragraphs and chapters.

Do we have any sources at all who use the specific term *Orpheotelestēs*? The only classical source in which this term is found is a passage from Theophrastus' *Characters* (late 4th B.C.) where he describes the character of a δεισιδαίμων. Could Theophrastus be referring to these itinerant priests criticised by Plato?[62] The term δεισιδαίμων is literally translated as the one who fears the gods but from the end of the 4th century and onwards the term is often used, especially in philosophical works, in a negative way which comes closer to the term 'superstitious'.[63] Theophrastus was a pupil of Aristotle and a contemporary of Heraclides of Pontus. He falls, thus, in the same timeframe as the majority of sources discussed so far. It is also generally agreed that his *Characters* refer to Athenians and were written in the last quarter of the 4th century.[64] This work, then, also falls in the same socio-political context as our other Athenian sources – apart from Plato who is early 4th century. It is, however, of a different nature than Platonic philosophical works for example, since its nature is descriptive rather than theoretical. Theophrastus begins by identifying the δεισιδαίμων as someone who feels δειλία

---

[59] Parker, 2007, p.121: 'Orphic purifications may sound like one thing, magical attacks like quite another, and one might suspect Plato of conflating two different threats to public morals purveyed by two different types of religious specialist. But perhaps we should recognise late survivors of the kind of charismatic all-purpose man of god best illustrated for us by Empedocles, in his actions a wonder-worker and in his writings a prophet of metempsychosis'.
[60] Edwards, 2000, p.215.
[61] Edwards, 2000, p.215.
[62] Theophr. *Char.* 16.
[63] Bowden, 2008, p.57.
[64] For a discussion of the *Characters*' date see Diggle, 2004, p.27–37.

(fear/cowardice) towards the gods. One might think that this was a good feeling to have as it shows respect to the gods. However, Theophrastus mocks or criticises the person whose *excessive* fear towards the gods leads him to perform excessive devout acts mostly of an apotropaic nature. The δεισιδαίμων will not start his day unless he first: 'washes his hands, sprinkles himself with water from a shrine, puts a sprig of laurel in his mouth'.[65] The list of acts is quite long and Bowden has rightly paralleled Theophrastus' *deisidaimōn* to a person suffering from OCD, a pathological condition that leads someone to excessively perform specific actions in a daily or regular basis.[66] Anyone who has been unnecessarily sour towards an unsuspecting black cat will sympathise with Theophrastus'*deisidaimōn*.

One of the acts mentioned by Theophrastus is a monthly visit to the Orphic priests to participate in a rite:

> καὶ τελεσθησόμενος πρὸς τοὺς Ὀρφεοτελεστὰς κατὰ μῆνα πορεύεσθαι μετὰ τῆς γυναικός, ἐὰν δὲ μὴ σχολάζῃ ἡ γυνή, μετὰ τῆς τίτθης καὶ τῶν παιδίων.
>
> He goes to the Initiators of Orpheus every month to be inducted, with his wife – if she has no time, he takes his children and their wet-nurse.[67]

This passage first and foremost constitutes evidence for the existence of Orphic priests who performed *teletae*. I suggest that these rituals are not being ridiculed by Theophrastus because each act listed by him taken individually was considered normal; for example the avoidance of a dead body or a woman in childbirth in fear of pollution (16.9) or a visit to a seer (16.11) would not be considered as something out of the ordinary. As Bowden argues: 'It is clear that what these writers condemned was much closer to the normal ritual activities of their contemporaries than they imply'; a point also made by Diggle: 'His actions and his attitudes, taken one by one, would probably not have seemed abnormal to the ordinary Athenian'.[68] In general, many seers were no doubt wholly respectable, as Parker notes and 'the city did not merely tolerate seers, but actually needed and employed them'.[69] It is the combination of *all* the acts listed and their excessive practice driven by extreme fear which is being mocked by Theophrastus.

---

65 Theophr. *Char.* 16.2: ἀπονιψάμενος τὰς χεῖρας καὶ περιρρανάμενος ἀπὸ ἱεροῦ δάφνην εἰς τὸ στόμα λαβὼν (Tr. Rusten).
66 Obsessive Compulsive Disorder. Bowden, 2008, p.68–69.
67 Theophr. *Char.* 16.11 (Tr. Rusten).
68 Bowden, 2008, p.56. 'These writers' because Bowden also discusses Plutarch's *Peri Deisidaimonias*. Diggle, 2004, p.350.
69 Parker, 2007, p.134.

Also, we cannot be sure that the information that people visited the Orphic priests monthly is correct, since Theophrastus might be exaggerating in order to create the persona of the *deisidaimōn*. Theophrastus portrays the visit to the Orphic priests as a 'family thing', since the *deisidaimōn* is accompanied by his children and wife. This suggests that men, women and children could participate in these particular rites and that the presence of a woman might have been required. In general, we can argue that as early as the late 4th century B.C., Orphic priests in Athens performed rituals for members of the public; children and women also participated in these rituals which must have been private. Considering that the other practices mentioned by Theophrastus were not out of the ordinary, it can be argued that a visit to the Orphic priests was also a standard procedure. What is being mocked in this case is the monthly repetition of the visit. Finally, whether or not Theophrastus' *Orpheotelestae* are the same as Plato's itinerant priests we cannot be sure. It might be of importance that in Theophrastus' passage the person visits the *Orpheotelestēs* while in Plato's passage the begging priests are wandering from door to door. Another reference related to *Orpheotelestae* is from Plutarch in a work written around the end/turn of 1st century A.D. He refers by name to a specific *Orpheotelestēs* called Philip, who was extremely poor and proclaimed a happy afterlife for those who would become his initiates.[70] To him Leotychidas said: 'You idiot! Why then don't you die as speedily as possible so that you may with that cease from bewailing your unhappiness and poverty?'.[71] Leotychidas' mockery indicates that Philip must have suggested that the afterlife was better than this life. This emphasis on the afterlife must not have been appealing to the rich clients of the itinerant priests that Plato mentions and who also offered non-eschatologial services such as harming their clients enemies. Philip, thus, must be distinguished by Plato's itinerant priests who should not be definitively identified as *Orpheotelestae*.

The fact that the itinerant priests in Plato's *Republic* performed *sacrifices* using the books of Musaeus and Orpheus contrasts with another Platonic passage referring to the so-called 'Orphic life':

ΑΘΗΝΑΙΟΣ: Τὸ δὲ μὴν θύειν ἀνθρώπους ἀλλήλους ἔτι καὶ νῦν παραμένον ὁρῶμεν πολλοῖς· καὶ τοὐναντίον ἀκούομεν ἐν ἄλλοις, ὅτε οὐδὲ βοὸς ἐτόλμων μὲν γεύεσθαι θύματά τε οὐκ ἦν τοῖς θεοῖσι ζῷα, πέλανοι δὲ καὶ μέλιτι καρποὶ δεδευμένοι καὶ τοιαῦτα ἄλλα ἁγνὰ θύματα, σαρκῶν δ' ἀπείχοντο ὡς οὐχ ὅσιον ὂν ἐσθίειν οὐδὲ τοὺς τῶν θεῶν βωμοὺς αἵματι μιαίνειν,

---

70 Plut. *Apopht.* 224e. See also Philodem. *De poem. P. Hercul.* 1074 fr. 30.
71 Plut. *Apopht.* 224e: "τί οὖν, ὦ ἀνόητε," εἶπεν, "οὐ τὴν ταχίστην ἀποθνήσκεις, ἵν' ἅμα παύσῃ κακοδαιμονίαν καὶ πενίαν κλαίων" (Tr. Cole Babbit).

ἀλλὰ Ὀρφικοί τινες λεγόμενοι βίοι ἐγίγνοντο ἡμῶν τοῖς τότε, ἀψύχων μὲν ἐχόμενοι πάντων, ἐμψύχων δὲ τοὐναντίον πάντων ἀπεχόμενοι.
ΚΛΕΙΝΙΑΣ: Καὶ σφόδρα λεγόμενα ἅ γ᾽εἴρηκας, καὶ πιστεύεσθαι πιθανά.

ATHENIAN: The custom of men sacrificing one another is, in fact, one that survives even now among many peoples; whereas amongst others we hear of how the opposite custom existed, when they were forbidden so much as to eat an ox, and their offerings to the gods consisted, not of animals, but of cakes of meal and grain steeped in honey, and other such bloodless sacrifices, and from flesh they abstained as though it were unholy to eat it or to stain with blood the altars of the gods; instead of that, those of us men who then existed lived what is called an Orphic life, keeping wholly to inanimate food and, contrariwise, abstaining wholly from things animate.
CLINIAS: Certainly what you say is widely reported and easy to credit.[72]

In this case, the Athenian refers to the so-called 'Orphic life' where bloodshed and sacrificing and eating animals were prohibited. The people living the *Orphikos bios*, then, must have been different from the clients of the priests mentioned in the *Republic* and which performed sacrifices. Moreover, we do not have the same negative attitude to those living the *Orphikos bios* as we have seen in the previous Platonic passage about the itinerant priests. The different attitude and the act of sacrificing might be indicative of two different strands of Orphism – at least in Athens – or possibly even more. The Athenian refers to the vegetarian lifestyle as something which was more common in the past while this kind of life is now called 'Orphic' and thus practiced by specific people. The clients of the *Orpheotelestae*, thus, could not be the same people following the *Orphikos bios*, which supports my suggestion about different strands of Orphism.

Other sources referring to the Orphic life might be useful in determining its presence in Classical times. In a passage from Euripides' *Hippolytos*, first produced in 428 B.C. in Athens, Theseus relates vegetarianism and the use of books in rites to the figure of Orpheus. Theseus has just discovered that his wife, Phaedra, has hanged herself. He has found a letter on her in which she falsely accuses Hippolytos of raping her. Theseus addresses the following words to Hippolytos and later on curses him to death despite Hippolytos pleading his innocence:

σὺ δὴ θεοῖσιν ὡς περισσὸς ὢν ἀνὴρ
ξύνει; σὺ σώφρων καὶ κακῶν ἀκήρατος;
οὐκ ἂν πιθοίμην τοῖσι σοῖς κόμποις ἐγὼ
θεοῖσι προσθεὶς ἀμαθίαν φρονεῖν κακῶς.
ἤδη νυν αὔχει καὶ δι᾽ ἀψύχου βορᾶς
σίτοις καπήλευ᾽ Ὀρφέα τ᾽ ἄνακτ᾽ ἔχων

---

[72] Pl. *Leg.* 6.782c–d (Tr. Bury).

βάκχευε πολλῶν γραμμάτων τιμῶν καπνούς·
ἐπεί γ' ἐλήφθης. τοὺς δὲ τοιούτους ἐγὼ
φεύγειν προφωνῶ πᾶσι· θηρεύουσι γὰρ
σεμνοῖς λόγοισιν, αἰσχρὰ μηχανώμενοι.
τέθνηκεν ἥδε· τοῦτό σ' ἐκσώσειν δοκεῖς;
ἐν τῷδ' ἁλίσκῃ πλεῖστον, ὦ κάκιστε σύ·
ποῖοι γὰρ ὅρκοι κρείσσονες, τίνες λόγοι
τῆσδ' ἂν γένοιντ' ἄν, ὥστε σ' αἰτίαν φυγεῖν

Are you, then, the companion of the gods, as a man beyond the common? Are you the chaste one, untouched by evil? I will never be persuaded by your vauntings, never be so unintelligent as to impute folly to the gods. Continue then your confident boasting, take up a diet of greens and play the showman with your food, make Orpheus your lord and engage in mystic rites [honouring the smoke of many writings]. For you have been found out. To all I give the warning: avoid men like this. For they make you their prey with their high-holy-sounding words while they contrive deeds of shame. She is dead. Do you think this will save you? This is the fact that most serves to convict you, villainous man. For what oaths, what arguments, could be more powerful than she is, to win you acquittal on the charge?[73]

In this passage, Theseus essentially identifies Hippolytos as an Orphic. Some of Hippolytos' characteristics are that: he considers himself to be worthy to dwell in the company of the gods, to be a man out of the ordinary, to be extremely pure and having committed no evil, to be a vegetarian, to have Orpheus as his lord, to perform bacchic mysteries (βάκχευε) using many writings and to expect that oaths and arguments will acquit him from wrongdoing. As Henrichs notes: 'For the first time in the Greek record, religious writings are explicitly recognised as a constitutive element of a person's religious identity' and even though the term 'γράμματα is ambiguous, the term clearly signifies the written word'.[74] The epithet πολλῶν signifies that we have a variety of texts. The use of the term βάκχευε implies, as did the Herodotus passage discussed above, that Orphic mysteries were closely related to the Bacchic ones and rejects Hippolytus' identification as a Pythagorean rather than an Orphic follower – at least in this context. Hippolytus' participation in Bacchic rites is linked by Theseus to the honouring of many writings, which again suggests a connection between Orphic rites and written texts. Texts which could either be used during the mystery or constitute the base

---

73 Eur. *Hipp.* 949–961 (Tr. Kovacs). I have replaced Kovacs translation [in brackets] who previously had 'holding the vaporings of many books in honor' because vaporings does not seem the most suitable word to translate καπνούς and γραμμάτων translation as 'books' is not entirely accurate.

74 Henrichs, 2003, p.212–13.

for the formation of the mystery. This could be a reference to contemporary practices in Athens like so many other elements in tragic treatments of myth. Especially considering that many of the components of Theseus' description of Hippolytus as an Orphic – such as the use of 'books', vegetarianism, promises of acquittal from wrongdoing, the link to Bacchic rites – are found in the Classical sources referring to Orphism previously discussed. I suggest, thus, that the *Orphikos bios* was still being practised at the time of Euripides.

If Theseus' words are read in isolation, his accusations against Orphics, or followers of Orpheus, of being mere imposters who perform rites and pretend to be pure while they in fact perform shameful deeds could appear as corresponding to reality. Theseus warns everyone to stay away from such people – a warning which might be addressed to Euripides' audience. This attitude comes closer to the Platonic passage from the *Republic* where the itinerant priests using books of Orpheus and Musaeus are presented with contempt and as people who deceive their 'clients' and even whole cities with fake promises for a blissful afterlife. However, the larger context reveals that the accusation is in fact false. By the end of the play Theseus finds out that he has wrongly accused Hippolytos, who is in fact truly chaste and has not committed the evil deeds or bloodshed of which he is being accused. Hippolytos, then, has been true in pleading innocence and his purity is emphasised repeatedly by Artemis (1339–1340) ('…the gods do not rejoice at the death of the godly [εὐσεβοῖς]…'), Hippolytos (1364–65) ('…holy [σεμνὸς] and god-revering one [θεοσέπτωρ]') and Theseus (1454) ('Oh, what a noble, godly heart [εὐσεβοῦς τε κἀγαθῆς] is lost!'). Moreover, we know that Hippolytos is a virgin having renounced sexual intercourse. This is why he is so dear to Artemis and so hated by Aphrodite who is the one behind the events which lead to his death. Extreme purity and chastity, then, could have been part of the 'Orphic life'. It is perhaps important that Artemis herself reassures Hippolytos that his chastity will be rewarded in the afterlife:

ΑΡΤΕΜΙΣ:
ἔασον· οὐ γὰρ οὐδὲ γῆς ὑπὸ ζόφον
θεᾶς ἄτιμοι Κύπριδος ἐκ προθυμίας
ὀργαὶ κατασκήψουσιν ἐς τὸ σὸν δέμας,
σῆς εὐσεβείας κἀγαθῆς φρενὸς χάριν·

ARTEMIS:
Let it be! For even though you will be in the darkness under the earth your body beaten by the dishonourable desires of goddess Aphrodite's eagerness, your heart's piety and virtue will be rewarded.[75]

Apart from this, we have already seen Theseus accusing Hippolytos of claiming to be worthy to dwell with the gods. This could be interpreted as a blissful afterlife existence next to the gods. The negative attitude of Theseus is, then, negated by the positive representation of Hippolytos by the end of the play. We cannot, thus, treat this non-Orphic reference to Orphics in the same way as the negative Platonic passage from the *Republic*. We need to examine why Euripides portrayed Hippolytus in this way through Theseus' words and what was the reason for Hippolytus' final justification. Firstly, there was no need for Euripides to associate Hippolytus with Orphism if, on the one hand the extreme purity and virtuousness of Hippolytos which must have been known to the audience, did not correspond to the contemporary Orphic persona, and on the other hand if the audience was not aware of this Orphic persona.[76] Also, the initial hostile representation of Hippolytus, only to be justified at the end, might be an indication of a negative attitude towards contemporary Orphics which comes in contrast with the positive representation of an Orphic in this play. The fact that Hippolytos is portrayed as an Orphic must be rooted in Euripides' contemporary sociological background since it is certainly not attested anywhere in the mythological tradition. It furthermore contributes to the dynamics of the plot since it helps to make Theseus' hostility to his son seem plausible: he is displaying a kind of prejudice which would be recognisable to the audience and which some might share. Moreover, as we will see, there are several Euripidean passages which seem to refer to Orphism and this might indicate his interest in Orphic beliefs and practices.

As mentioned in Chapter 1 Edmonds argues that it is this extra-ordinary level of concern with purity and appeasement of the powers of the underworld that characterises the evidence labeled Orphic in the ancient sources and not any central nucleus of dogmas or beliefs.[77] This, however, contrasts with the abundance of classical sources we have examined so far and which clearly refer to specific beliefs of those affiliated to Orpheus, such as the airy nature of the soul, the transmigration of the soul, the entering of the soul into the body through breath and

---

75 Eur. *Hipp.* 1416–19.
76 Gantz, 1993, p.287: 'Whether he was so presented <as totally chaste> in the other plays, or in the earlier tradition, we cannot say, although aspects of his cult at Troizen (maidens dedicating locks of hair to him) would seem to indicate that this was the case'.
77 See p.4.

the existence of punishments and rewards in the afterlife, one of which could possibly be to dwell with the gods. Commenting on the Platonic sources, the passage by Theophrastus and Euripides' *Hippolytus*, Edmonds notes that: '...this mix of positive and negative evaluations of the same extra-ordinary concerns with purity and special relations with the gods is characteristic of the evidence for the ancient idea of Orphism'.[78] Instead of interpreting, however, these mixed references as positive and negative evaluations of 'extra-ordinary' religious concerns, there might be a different explanation. As already argued, we should consider the possible existence of two or more different strands of Orphism, at least in Athens of the 5th–4th century B.C. where all the above sources come from. The itinerant priests to whom Plato refers to could be people who used the Orphic works for their own purposes. Such people could be the itinerant practitioners who performed incantations, purifications and rites on demand using a bricolage of religious material available to them. The constant refrain of our ancient sources referring in detail to the secret Orphic mysteries and their meaning is perhaps evidence that they were highly revered, so sacred that they should not be uttered. Itinerant priestly practitioners made use of the most sacred and respected cults and religious material, in order to project greater authority. What is more, the constant juxtaposition in several sources of Orphic ideas to Pythagorean ones is another argument for their relation to eschatological and cosmogonical philosophical ideas, something which will be more explored in the following chapters. Considering the non-Orphic sources discussed so far, thus, I am more inclined to accept the existence of specific Orphic beliefs and mysteries which were closely related to Orphic texts, rather than deny such a possibility. Moreover, the negative attitude and criticism present in some sources might be directed to a specific type of people who used Orphic texts for their own gain and not to the totality of 'those who were affiliated with Orpheus'.

2.2.1 The use of 'books' and texts in religious practices

According to the non-Orphic Classical Athenian sources I have examined so far, then, Orphic beliefs and practices were closely linked to Orphic texts, whether written or orally transmitted. Orpheus' name had been linked to *hieroi logoi* already in the 5th century B.C.[79] The continuing association of Orpheus with sacred *logoi* through time is evident in the work attributed to him titled Ἱεροὶ Λόγοι ἐν

---

78 Edmonds, 2008a.
79 Henrichs, 2003, p.214.

ῥαψωιδίαις κδ' (*Sacred Discourses in Twenty Four Rhapsodies*) which scholars date from the 1st B.C. to the 2nd A.D. and which will be discussed in Chapter 6.[80] Going back, then, to the question at the beginning of this sub-chapter: how often were written or non-written texts (*bibloi* or *hieroi logoi*) associated with rites and religious eschatological or philosophical beliefs in Classical Greece? Did the use of 'books' relate to 'marginal' religious practices and were the *hieroi logoi* any different? Did the 'books' include *hieroi logoi* and did the latter term's meaning change over time?

Several religious documents survive in Greece such as: 'sacred calendars, oracles, cult regulations, ritual precepts, dedications to divinities, sales of priesthoods, statutes of religious clubs and associations, records of divine epiphanies' and magical papyri which range 'from individual texts and collections of spells to entire papyrus books composed of magical incantations and instructions'.[81] My interest lies in the category of *hieroi logoi* which were often associated with the name of Orpheus and secretive as already established from our sources.[82] An *hieros logos* possibly had an aetiological nature. For example, as we saw, Herodotus notes that there is an *hieros logos* about the prohibition against being buried in woollen garments in Orphic and Pythagorean practices and Plutarch refers to an Orphic *hieros logos* where an egg was the first being of the world in relation to religious dietary rules.[83] Confirming the secrecy surrounding *hieroi logoi*, they both refrain from revealing the contents of the sacred story and how it relates to the mysteries. The particular sacred story in Plutarch, must have been of a cosmogonical nature and indeed, as we will see, the egg is the first being of the world in the Orphic Ἱεροὶ Λόγοι ἐν ῥαψωιδίαις κδ' mentioned above. This suggests that an *hieros logos* was exactly that, a sacred 'reasoning' in the form of a story; possibly justifying an initiation rite or things uttered during a ritual, the so-called *legomena*.[84] The attitude towards an *hieros logos* which is treated with respect and

---

80 *Suda* s.v. Ὀρφεύς = OF91T = Sacred stories in 24 rhapsodies/books.
81 Henrichs, 2003, p.208–209.
82 Henrichs, 2003, p.209–210; p.235: 'From its first attestation in Herodotos to its final appearance in dozens of pagan and Christian writers of late antiquity, the very concept of the *hieros logos* is surrounded by an aura of deep mystery, extreme secrecy, and high religious authority'.
83 Hdt. 2.81; Plut. *Quaest. conv.* 2.3.2, 636d–636e.
84 Henrichs, 2003, p.237: '"There is a sacred λόγος being said (λεγόμενος) about this". Each time Herodotos uses this expression, he seems to imply that a *hieros logos* was a "sacred story" or "sacred account" exclusively or at least primarily in oral form, and that its function was to explain an existing sacred custom by means of narrative. This suggests at least for the time of Herodotos that strictly speaking *hieroi logoi* were aetiological myths having to do with gods or rituals'.

even perhaps 'fear' as to the consequences of revealing its contents, differs from the attitude towards the use of *bibloi* in rituals which seems to be treated as something to be scorned by those who did not use them. I have discussed passages from Plato and Euripides where their characters treated with contempt people using such books in rituals specifically in reference to Orpheus. We have other sources too which do not refer specifically to Orphism but are characterised by the same reprehensible attitude.

A passage from Demosthenes' speech *On the Crown* against Aeschines is possibly the earliest explicit reference to the use of a 'book' during a ritual. In this particular passage he attacks Aeschines through accusing him of helping his mother perform private initiation rites:

> ἀνὴρ δὲ γενόμενος τῇ μητρὶ τελούσῃ <u>τὰς βίβλους ἀνεγίγνωσκες</u> καὶ τἆλλα συνεσκευωροῦ, τὴν μὲν νύκτα νεβρίζων καὶ κρατηρίζων καὶ καθαίρων τοὺς τελουμένους κἀπομάττων τῷ πηλῷ καὶ τοῖς πιτύροις, καὶ ἀνιστὰς ἀπὸ τοῦ καθαρμοῦ κελεύων λέγειν "ἔφυγον κακόν, εὗρον ἄμεινον," ἐπὶ τῷ μηδένα πώποτε τηλικοῦτ' ὀλολύξαι σεμνυνόμενος καὶ ἔγωγε νομίζω·

> On arriving at manhood you assisted your mother in her initiations, reading the service-book while she performed the ritual, and helping generally with the paraphernalia. At night it was your duty to mix the libations, to clothe the initiates in fawn-skins, to wash their bodies, to scour them with the clay and the bran, and, when their lustration was duly performed, to set them on their legs, and order them to say: 'I have escaped from evil, I have found something better'; and it was your pride that no one ever emitted that holy ululation so powerfully as yourself. I can well believe it![85]

Demosthenes has no reserve in revealing many details of the rites Aeschines was participating in and even phrases from the book(s) used in the mysteries: this is a significant difference from Herodotus and Plutarch. Even though this might be due to Demosthenes' describing rites for which he has no respect and thus had no reason to maintain their secrecy, it might also be due to that there was no punishment for revealing these particular rites. However, this might also be due to the derogatory tone of Demosthenes and Martin argues that 'we should not take the accuracy of the account for granted' since Demosthenes is 'probably blurring elements of various cults and exposing his opponent to the audience's laughter'.[86] This, though, does not mean that Demosthenes is not drawing from a specific cult.[87] It is

---

[85] Dem. 18.259 (Tr. Vince). See also Parker, 2007, p.120–121.
[86] Martin, 2009, p.105. Many scholars, however, as Martin admits, identify a specific cult in this passage (p.106).
[87] Demosthenes' passage has been related by some scholars to a Ferrara krater made c.440–430 B.C. and showing some similarities to Demosthenes' description (*ARV*² 1052. 25=Ferrara 2897), but the interpretation of the image is debated (Martin, 2009, p.106–107).

generally argued that Aeschines' mother, Glaucothea, was a priestess performing rituals of the cult of Sabazios, 'a deity related to the Greek god Dionysos, but with roots in Phrygia and Thrace' and whose exotic nature was perhaps the reason she was presented in this negative way by Demosthenes.[88] Demosthenes informs us in another speech that her predecessor was condemned to death: '... whose mother, Glaucothea, heads a wild cult for which her predecessor was put to death'.[89] Her predecessor was Nino, the 'leader of a *thiasos* for the god Sabazios' and who according to the scholia was accused by Menecles for casting love charms on young boys.[90] However, Demosthenes himself in two other speeches referring to the conviction of Nino by Menecles, portrays him as a sycophant who did not give the reason for charging Nino or any other explanations.[91] Nino, then, seems to have been tried for 'witchcraft' and we cannot be sure that Aeschines' mother had the same capacity as Nino, who could have performed incantations and enchantments, or if this is just a 'rhetorical slander (διαβολή), typical of Athenian oratory' by Demosthenes.[92] Martin argues that: 'The ceremony of Aeschines' mother is a hotchpotch of various rites and the audience must have recognised at least some of them from their own participation in the celebration of mysteries'.[93] If the audience could not place these kind of practices under one category, then the effect of the slander loses its power. This suggests, that Demosthenes perhaps aims to bring into the audience's mind the itinerant priests who combine various religious elements and we have seen them being portrayed as charlatans. Perhaps, once more, as in the case of Theophrastus, it is not the individual religious practices described here which are being ridiculed but their combination. What we can take from this passage is that some of these religious practices or their combination constituted reasons for suspicion towards them. It has also been argued that the particular religious practices are related to the Orphic Dionysos' dismemberment myth. If Demosthenes is indeed evoking practices such as the ones offered by itinerant priests, this would be in accordance with their employment of Orphic elements as found in other sources discussed earlier. Since we are not yet familiar with this myth, however, this matter will be discussed in the following chapter.

---

[88] Yunis, 2005, p.95. Connelly, 2007, p.216. Martin, 2009, p.106.
[89] Dem. 19.281: καὶ Γλαυκοθέας τῆς τοὺς θιάσους συναγούσης, ἐφ' οἷς ἑτέρα τέθνηκεν ἱέρεια. Yunis, 2005, p.95/198.
[90] Connelly, 2007, p.216. Filonik, 2013, p.68. See also Parker, 2007, p.133.
[91] Dem. 39.2 and 40. Filonik, 2013, p.67.
[92] Filonik, 2013, p.68.
[93] Martin, 2009, p.111.

In any case, it appears that private initiation rites performed in closed groups, and perhaps the use of books, were treated with suspicion, possibly because they were performed in secret and were not part of the official religious practices of the polis.[94] As Dodds notes: '...the Greeks had neither a Bible nor a Church'.[95] Any religious practices, thus, involving books would be out of the ordinary and the unknown nature of the contents of such books makes things more complicated.[96] Demosthenes explicitly mentions that one of these religious practices was someone reading out loud from the book(s). The phrase: 'I have escaped from evil, I have found something better', could certainly correspond to the averting of evils which priests using such books promised to their clients, as mentioned in our previous sources and especially Plato. A name often given to women who led revel-bands like Aeschines' mother, was 'priestess' and as Parker notes: '...though functionally very distinct from the priestess of the public cults, shares their respectable title. But to her as not to them less pleasant names are also applied'.[97] However, as mentioned in the previous paragraph, the negativity might be due to the assimilation to itinerant priests performing a bricolage of rites outside of the established public cults. It is not easy to distinguish between the blurry lines of what was acceptable and what was not, concerning private religious practices, since we can see that even though Nino was sentenced to death, Glaukothea was not. As Parker argues: 'The study of magic is a study of the religious practices disapproved of in a given society, or a particular set of them; for 'bad religion' has different forms, some activities being laughed at as merely silly ('superstition'), others condemned as wicked and dangerous'.[98]

During the 5th century B.C. new cults characterised by ecstatic rites were introduced and enjoyed increased popularity in Athens.[99] Connelly notes that: 'Inscriptions preserve rules that governed the behavior of cult agents and that, in turn, ensured protection of their rights and privileges. Legal cases were brought when these rights were violated or when priestly personnel behaved in ways contrary to law'.[100] The introduction of new cults or foreign gods 'was subject to limitation by law, and thus implied official agreement or at least toleration on the

---

[94] Yunis, 2005, p.95, fn.196.
[95] Dodds, 1973, p.142.
[96] Bremmer, 2010, p.331: Referring to Orphism, Bremmer says that books 'were important in this movement and that singles them out from mainstream Greek religion'.
[97] Parker, 2007, p.120–121.
[98] Parker, 2007, p.122. [See also p.123: 'The concept of 'strong social disapproval' is also a slippery one'.
[99] Rubel and Vickers, 2014.
[100] Connelly, 2007, p.213.

part of the polis'.[101] As Parker argues: 'Elective religion is more directly responsive to the wishes of the individual than are the cults of the city, but it too is not and could not be a wholly spontaneous growth. What priests, magistrates, exegetes, assembly and the rest are to the cults of the city, that the religious professionals are to informal or elective religion'.[102] In general, we can see that unofficial religious practices were treated differently by each citizen and this might be one of the reasons for the mixed references to Orphic practices in our sources – in the cases that the references are to private Orphic practices such as the ones performed by an *Orpheotelestēs* or itinerant priests. However, this does not mean that public or official religious practices cannot be identified as Orphic and as already argued private initiations by *Orpheotelestes* must have been but one of the aspects of Orphism. The author of the speech *Against Aristogeiton I* refers to Orpheus as 'the prophet of our most sacred mysteries' [ὁ τὰς ἁγιωτάτας ἡμῖν τελετὰς καταδείξας Ὀρφεὺς] in a reference to the importance of Justice overseeing men.[103] This speech is supposed to be by Demosthenes but this is debated and even though Longinus quotes the first speech as genuine other authors doubt its authenticity.[104] If Demosthenes is the actual author then this indicates that these *teletas* instituted by Orpheus are not the same as the private initiations performed by an *Orpheotelestēs* and which are of the same nature as the ones scorned in the speech against Aeschines. If he is not the author, then the actual author thought that this was something that Demosthenes could say. Along the same lines are two other passages by the author of *Rhesus*, as we saw earlier, and from Aristophanes' *agōn* in the *Frogs*: 'Just consider how beneficial the noble poets have been from the earliest times. Orpheus revealed mystic rites to us, and taught us to abstain from killings'.[105] Private initiations, then, which included books with works by 'Orpheus' must belong to a different category than the ἁγιωτάτας τελετὰς revealed by Orpheus. In both cases, however, there seems to be a relation with a sacred story, whether written or unwritten. We have already seen that there are two contrasting attitudes towards Orphic practices and it was argued, that there

---

101 Rubel and Vickers, 2014. For the state's involvement in religion in Athens see Rhodes, 2009.
102 Parker, 2007, p.134.
103 [Dem]. *Against Arist.* I, 25.11.
104 Vince, 1935, p.515.
105 Ar. *Ran.* 1032: σκέψαι γὰρ ἀπ' ἀρχῆς | ὡς ὠφέλιμοι τῶν ποιητῶν οἱ γενναῖοι γεγένηνται. | Ὀρφεὺς μὲν γὰρ τελετάς θ' ἡμῖν κατέδειξε φόνων τ'ἀπέχεσθαι (Tr. Henderson). Linforth in reference to the passage from *Rhesus:* '...these specific mysteries are mentioned here 'as a benefaction to the Athenians' and that there would be no point to the reference if they were not highly important and valued by them' (1941, p.63).

were two different strands of Orphism at least in Classical Athens. I would furthermore suggest that the use of *bibloi* was linked to the more 'marginal' strand of Orphic practices, while the *hieroi logoi* were linked to those Orphic practices which were revered and considered highly sacred.

There might be an explanation for this distinction. An *hieros logos* in Greece 'remained by definition unwritten'.[106] However, Bremmer notes that perhaps this was the case in the fifth century B.C. but suggests that 'we cannot be sure that the texts from which Aeschines read … were not also called *hieroi logoi*'.[107] As Henrichs argues: 'Recording sacred tales in writing would have jeopardised their secrecy and even invited pious fraud; not surprisingly, *hieroi logoi* ascribed to individual authors are with one exception pseudepigrapha'.[108] If Orphic ideas or sacred mysteries were based on oral *hieroi logoi* or in other words had an aetiological *hieros logos*, and if subsequently itinerant priests and seers wrote down or claimed they had written down and possessed such *hieroi logoi*, this might explain the differing attitudes in our sources. Itinerant priests using 'books' might have been scorned because, since writing an *hieros logos* down was prohibited or not advised, violations of such prohibitions would cause condemnation. A later passage by Athenagoras (2nd A.D.) corroborates to the secrecy of the Orphic *hieros logos* through attesting that Diagoras of Melos, a renowned 'atheist' of the 5th century B.C. was accused of impiety for revealing to the public the Ὀρφικὸν λόγον:

> Διαγόραι μὲν γὰρ εἰκότως ἀθεότητα ἐπεκάλουν Ἀθηναῖοι, μὴ μόνον τὸν Ὀρφικὸν εἰς μέσον κατατιθέντι λόγον καὶ τὰ ἐν Ἐλευσῖνι καὶ τὰ τῶν Καβίρων δημεύοντι μυστήρια καὶ τὸ τοῦ Ἡρακλέους ἵνα τὰς γογγύλας ἕψοι κατακόπτοντι ξόανον, ἄντικρυς δὲ ἀποφαινομένωι μηδὲ ὅλως εἶναι θεόν.

> …with reason did the Athenians adjudge Diagoras guilty of atheism, in that he not only divulged the Orphic doctrine, and published the mysteries of Eleusis and of the Cabiri, and chopped up the wooden statue of Herakles to boil his turnips, but openly declared that there was no God at all.[109]

We cannot be sure that Athenagoras is correct about retribution in case of revealing the Orphic *hieros logos* since we are not aware of his source about Diagoras, but even if he is not correct, the fact that he brings the violation of Orphic secrecy

---

106 Henrichs, 2003, p.240.
107 Bremmer, 2010, p.332.
108 Henrichs, 2003, p.240.
109 Athenagoras, *Leg. pro Christ.* 4.1 = OF557T. Bremmer, 2010, p.333. On Diagoras of Melos being an 'atheist' see: Ar. *Av.* 1072; Ar. *Ran.* 316; Diod. Sic. 13.6; Lys. *Against Andocides*, 6.17.

as additional evidence of Diagoras' impiety suggests that it was at least considered impious to reveal the Orphic *hieros logos*.[110] In this case, Athenagoras juxtaposes the Orphic *logos* to the Eleusinian and Cabirean mysteries which were highly respected by the Athenians and the Greeks in general. This suggests that this *logos* was different than the stories being told by the scorned itinerant priests. If revealing the *Orphikos logos* led to accusations of impiety, then this particular sacred story must have been treated with respect and reverence by the city, as is also obvious by how cautiously it is treated by authors such as Plato and Herodotus. Bremmer argues that: '...the central oral text of the Orphic (-Bacchic) rituals must have been so prominent that in the course of time books with Orphic poems adopted the title *Hieros Logos* or *Hieroi Logoi*'.[111] This is a plausible argument and it would explain the different attitudes in the usage of the term depending on the circumstances. At any rate, the passages which we have argued to be referring to itinerant priests and seers do not in fact explicitly have the term *hieros logos*. We cannot be sure, though, that in the course of time, the *hieroi logoi* of the revered sacred mysteries mentioned by Plato, Herodotus and others were not written down, either for reasons of preservation or for other religious uses.[112] It is possible, thus, that multiple sacred 'books' containing *hieroi logoi* under the name of Orpheus were circulating but that not all of them were the initial oral ones or that a large proportion of them were forgeries. If this was the case, this would have made it very difficult for the itinerant priests/*Orpheotelestes'* clientele to be sure of whom was using the 'right' sacred text. This would also lead the itinerant priests to adopt competitive tactics to attract clients. Perhaps the people who visited such itinerant priests without giving it much thought, and easily paid them to be initiated, are the ones being scorned by Plato.

This does not exclude that Orphic mysteries had *legomena* – meaning texts uttered during a mystery – but whether or not these *legomena* were written down is a different story. It must be clarified that when referring to Orphic mysteries I mean mysteries that were exclusively Orphic in contrast to the ones performed by itinerant priests which as argued combined various religious elements and not

---

110 Janko argued that the author of the Derveni Papyrus which comments on an Orphic Theogony is Diagoras and thus the accusations of revealing an Orphic *hieros logos*. His arguments, however, are not plausible and this theory has been rejected by the majority of scholars. For this matter see Winiarczyk, 2016, p.118–126.
111 Bremmer, 2010, p.333.
112 Henrichs, 2003, p.250: Two conflicting tendencies in protecting the *hieroi logoi*: keeping it a secret through its ineffability outside of mysteries and the tendency to preserve it by writing it down.

just Orphic ones. The circumstances under which the *hieroi logoi* were communicated to the initiates is also difficult to pin down. They could have been spoken or read from written texts, either during or before a ritual. Again, Plato might be enlightening in relation to this problem. In the *Laws* the Athenian says:

Τούτων δὴ πάντων πέρι προοίμια μὲν εἰρημένα ταῦτ' ἔστω, καὶ πρὸς τούτοις, ὃν καὶ πολλοὶ λόγον <u>τῶν ἐν ταῖς τελεταῖς περὶ τὰ τοιαῦτα ἐσπουδακότων ἀκούοντες</u> σφόδρα πείθονται, τὸ τῶν τοιούτων τίσιν ἐν Ἅιδου γίγνεσθαι καὶ πάλιν ἀφικομένοις δεῦρο ἀναγκαῖον εἶναι τὴν κατὰ φύσιν δίκην ἐκτῖσαι, τὴν τοῦ παθόντος ἅπερ αὐτὸς ἔδρασεν, ὑπ' ἄλλου τοιαύτῃ μοίρᾳ τελευτῆσαι τὸν τότε βίον.

Concerning all these matters, the preludes mentioned shall be pronounced, and, in addition to them, that story which is believed by many when they hear it from the lips of those who seriously relate such things at their mystic rites, – that vengeance for such acts is exacted in Hades, and that those who return again to this earth are bound to pay the natural penalty, – each culprit the same, that is, which he inflicted on his victim, – and that their life on earth must end in their meeting a like fate at the hands of another.[113]

If a story is told to the initiates during the *teletae* about punishments in Hades, this confirms the exegetical and aetiological nature of the story. The word ἐσπουδακότων, which means that those who told the story were taking these matters seriously, suggests that Plato is not referring to the itinerant priests he has mentioned elsewhere. It is very hard to define whether the story was being read from a 'book' or if it was an oral *hieros logos*. We can be sure, however, that this story 'proves' that the actions of the present life have consequences in the afterlife. So to whom is Plato referring? The context of this passage refers to the punishment of murderous acts in the afterlife and how one should lead a just life and not chase wealth which is usually the cause of evils. They could not be the itinerant priests who Plato says knock on rich people's doors and offer atonement from the afterlife punishments through performing sacrifices using books, since he criticises their clients for performing the rites while remaining unjust. Even more, Plato says that these itinerant priests could harm their clients' enemies and such actions are strongly condemned in the context of this reference and in this sacred story. In this case, a lifelong commitment of being just is required and Plato also relates the punishments with reincarnation. Considering our discussion so far, the only plausible remaining religious 'candidate' is Orphism – Pythagoreanism is excluded due to the reference to mystic rites. We have examined evidence that repeatedly links Orphic eschatological beliefs with Orphic sacred stories; we have also seen that these eschatological beliefs have to do with the soul, reincarnation,

---

113 Pl. *Leg.* 9.870d–e (Tr. Bury) = OF433F.

the afterlife and post-mortem rewards or punishments. Finally, we have seen that there is a secrecy surrounding the references to Orphic beliefs, stories and practices. In this case, too, Plato does not reveal many details and is quite secretive about the contents of the story. All of these elements, thus, are found in this Platonic passage, making it very plausible that 'those who seriously relate such things at their mystic rites' were 'those affiliated to Orpheus'. And they were 'many', as Plato says.

There is further evidence which supports the Orphic identity of this *logos*. Plato refers to this sacred story again a few paragraphs later, this time, giving a slight inkling about what this story was about:

> ὁ γὰρ δὴ μῦθος ἢ λόγος, ἤ ὅ τι χρὴ προσαγορεύειν αὐτόν, ἐκ παλαιῶν ἱερέων εἴρηται σαφῶς, ὡς ἡ τῶν ξυγγενῶν αἱμάτων τιμωρὸς δίκη ἐπίσκοπος νόμῳ χρῆται τῷ νῦν δὴ λεχθέντι καὶ ἔταξεν ἄρα δράσαντί τι τοιοῦτον παθεῖν ταὐτὰ ἀναγκαίως ἅπερ ἔδρασεν·

> The myth or story (or whatever one should call it) has been clearly stated, as derived from ancient priests, to the effect that Justice, the avenger of kindred blood, acting as overseer, employs the law just mentioned, and has ordained that the doer of such a deed must of necessity suffer the same as he has done...[114]

This, then, was a story of kin-killing which leads to the same punishment. We notice that even Plato is unsure what to call this story. Is it a simple myth or a *logos*? This is due to his prior reference to the story where he has linked it with mysteries and which would make it an *hieros logos*. It seems unlikely that Plato is referring to a myth found in Hesiod, otherwise he would have mentioned it with no reserve. It is also unlikely that this myth relates to the Eleusinian mysteries which had an eschatological context, because the Eleusinian myth was the one of Persephone's abduction by Hades and does not refer to kin-killing or a punishment of the wrong-doer who in this case is Hades. The most plausible myth is the Orphic myth of Dionysos' dismemberment by the Titans and their subsequent punishment and banishment down to Hades by Zeus – where banishment to Hades essentially equals death. I will not dwell on this myth here because I will analyse it in detail in the following chapter. Moreover, in this passage Plato refers to the act of killing as temple-robbery because the body/temple is being robbed of its soul: '...he will be liable to most heavy penalties, and likewise for impiety and temple-robbing, since he has robbed his parent of life...'.[115] Plato's phraseology points to Orphism and relates to

---

114 Pl. *Leg.* 9.872e (Tr. Bury).
115 Pl. *Leg.* 9.869b: καὶ γὰρ αἰκίας δίκαις ταῖς ἐσχάταις ἔνοχος ἂν γίγνοιτο καὶ ἀσεβείας ὡσαύτως καὶ ἱεροσυλίας, τὴν τοῦ γεννήτου ψυχὴν συλήσας (Tr. Bury).

another Platonic passage where he refers to the Orphic belief that the body is the tomb/prison of the soul, namely the very first passage we discussed in this chapter.[116] Considering the above discussion and the association of Orphic beliefs/texts to punishments in the afterlife, we can identify other possible Platonic references to an Orphic *hieros logos*. In another passage from his *Epistles* Plato says that we should always truly believe those παλαιοῖς τε καὶ ἱεροῖς λόγοις which 'declare to us that the soul is immortal and that it has judges and pays the greatest penalties, whensoever a man is released from his body; wherefore also one should account it a lesser evil to suffer than to perform the great iniquities and injustices'.[117] In this case, too the avoidance of punishment is through leading a just life and thus comes closer to the *Orphikos Bios* rather than the itinerant priests' practices or the Eleusinian mysteries. We also notice that an emphasis on the role of Justice seems to be related to Orphic texts and beliefs.

2.3 References to specific Orphic Rites, Mysteries and Practices

We have an abundance of non-Orphic sources referring to specific Orphic rites, mysteries and practices, or which link them to Orpheus' name and they constitute direct evidence for the existence of Orphic rites.[118] I have already discussed passages from Demosthenes, Aristophanes and *Rhesus* identifying Orpheus as the one that revealed the most sacred mysteries. Diodorus (1st B.C.) also says that Orpheus was 'the first to introduce initiatory rites and mysteries to the Greeks' after becoming a student of the Idaean Dactyls and that he 'became the greatest man among the Greeks both for his knowledge of the gods and for their rites, as well as for his poems and songs'.[119] Similarly, Pausanias (2nd A.D.) claims that Orpheus 'excelled his predecessors in the beauty of his verse, and reached a high degree of power because he was believed to have discovered mysteries, purification from sins, cures

---

116 Pl. *Cra.* 400c. For text see p.9.
117 Pl. *Epist.* 7.335a: πείθεσθαι δὲ ὄντως ἀεὶ χρὴ τοῖς παλαιοῖς τε καὶ ἱεροῖς λόγοις, οἳ δὴ μηνύουσιν ἡμῖν ἀθάνατον ψυχὴν εἶναι δικαστάς τε ἴσχειν καὶ τίνειν τὰς μεγίστας τιμωρίας, ὅταν τις ἀπαλλαχθῇ τοῦ σώματος. διὸ καὶ τὰ μεγάλα ἁμαρτήματα καὶ ἀδικήματα σμικρότερον εἶναι χρὴ νομίζειν κακὸν πάσχειν ἢ δρᾶσαι. (Tr. Bury) = OF433F.
118 These are listed by Bernabé in mostly OF510T-OF535F and Linforth, 1941, pp.263–263.
119 Diod. Sic. V.64.4: καὶ πρῶτον εἰς τοὺς Ἕλληνας ἐξενεγκεῖν τελετὰς καὶ μυστήρια; IV.25.2: μέγιστος ἐγένετο τῶν Ἑλλήνων ἔν τε ταῖς θεολογίαις καὶ ταῖς τελεταῖς καὶ ποιήμασι καὶ μελῳδίαις.

of diseases and means of averting divine wrath'.[120] I will, now, move away from such generic references to mysteries and discuss those passages which refer to specific rituals or specific locations. Pausanias and Diodorus are the two authors who link Orpheus with particular mysteries the most and, as in other sources we have seen, they both connect the Orphic mysteries to Orphic texts in several instances. Additionally, many sources relate Orpheus and Orphic ideas/mythology to Dionysiac/Bacchic mysteries, while some authors draw a link to the Eleusinian Mysteries. However, I will discuss Bacchic and Eleusinian mysteries in a following chapter since we need to be familiar with the Orphic sources as well as the non-Orphic ones in order to be able to acknowledge the relation. We have references to rites taking place in areas around Mainland Greece, in Asia Minor and Magna Graecia, which indicates the vast spread of Orphic ideas and practices. I will also discuss any similarities or common elements between these rites and what could this mean. As already made clear, the attribution to 'Orpheus' of the establishment of a particular rite should not be taken literally, but the association with his name must indicate a relation to Orphic ideas, works or practices found elsewhere.

2.3.1 Mainland Greece

Pausanias whose travels took place in the 2nd century A.D. is the most prolific source for information on local cults and he often links Orpheus to specific cults in Mainland Greece. However, his attestations come in contrast to the absence of direct epigraphic evidence. Herrero de Jáuregui attributes this 'in part to chance, which has not furnished us with inscriptions confirming his references to Orphic cults, and in part to the fact that ... the Orphic presence in the region consisted primarily in *legomena* that accompanied or explained *dromena* in sanctuaries of esoteric coloration that prided themselves on the divine origin of their rites, open only to the faithful'.[121] Secrecy, might indeed be one of the reasons, especially considering our earlier discussion of secret *hieroi logoi* being linked to Orphism by various authors and of the possible private esoteric nature of Orphism.

---

120 Paus. IX.30.4: ὁ δὲ Ὀρφεὺς ἐμοὶ δοκεῖν ὑπερεβάλετο ἐπῶν κόσμῳ τοὺς πρὸ αὑτοῦ καὶ ἐπὶ μέγα ἦλθεν ἰσχύος οἷα πιστευόμενος εὑρηκέναι τελετὰς θεῶν καὶ ἔργων ἀνοσίων καθαρμοὺς νόσων τε ἰάματα καὶ τροπὰς μηνιμάτων θείων (Tr. Jones).
121 Herrero de Jáuregui, 2010, p.42.

References to specific Orphic Rites, Mysteries and Practices — 45

2.3.1.1 Phlya

Some sources refer to Orphic rites taking place at the Attic deme Phlya (modern Chalandri). I will firstly refer to a passage by Hippolytus of Rome (2nd–3rd A.D) who was one of the Church Fathers. In this passage, Hippolytus aims to accuse the Sethians of deriving their beliefs from the Ancient Greeks and we should, thus, be cautious of the validity of his sayings:

> ἔστι δὲ αὐτοῖς ἡ πᾶσα διδασκαλία τοῦ <u>λόγου</u> ἀπὸ τῶν παλαιῶν θεολόγων, Μουσαίου καὶ Λίνου καὶ τοῦ τὰς τελετὰς μάλιστα καὶ τὰ μυστήρια καταδείξαντος Ὀρφέως. ὁ γὰρ περὶ τῆς μήτρας αὐτῶν καὶ τοῦ ὄφεως λόγος καὶ <ὁ> ὀμφαλός, ὅπερ ἐστὶν ἁρμονία, διαρρήδην οὕτως ἐστὶν ἐν τοῖς Βακχικοῖς τοῦ Ὀρφέως. τετέλεσται δὲ ταῦτα καὶ παραδέδοται ἀνθρώποις πρὸ τῆς Κελεοῦ καὶ Τριπτολέμου καὶ Δήμητρος καὶ Κόρης καὶ Διονύσου ἐν Ἐλευσῖνι τελετῆς, ἐν Φλειοῦντι τῆς Ἀττικῆς· πρὸ γὰρ τῶν Ἐλευσινίων μυστηρίων ἔστιν ἐν τῆι Φλειοῦντι <τῆς> λεγομένης Μεγάλης ὄργια. ἔστι δὲ παστὰς ἐν αὐτῆι, ἐπὶ δὲ τῆς παστάδος ἐγγέγραπται μέχρι σήμερον ἡ τούτων πάντων τῶν εἰρημένων λόγων ἰδέα. πολλὰ μὲν οὖν ἐστι τὰ ἐπὶ τῆς παστάδος ἐγγεγραμμένα, περὶ ὧν Πλούταρχος ποιεῖται λόγους ἐν ταῖς πρὸς Ἐμπεδοκλέα δέκα βίβλοις, ἔστι δὲ τοῖς πλείοσι καὶ πρεσβύτης τις ἐγγεγραμμένος πολιὸς πτερωτὸς ἐντεταμένην ἔχων τὴν αἰσχύνην, γυναῖκα ἀποφεύγουσαν διώκων κυνοειδῆ. ἐπιγέγραπται δὲ ἐπὶ τοῦ πρεσβύτου 'Φάος ῥυέντης', ἐπὶ δὲ τῆς γυναικὸς 'περεη Φικόλα'...

> The entire system of their doctrine, however, is (derived) from the ancient theologians Musaeus, and Linus, and Orpheus, who elucidates especially the ceremonies of initiation, as well as the mysteries themselves. For their doctrine concerning the womb is also the tenet of Orpheus; and the (idea of the) navel, which is harmony, is (to be found) with the same symbolism attached to it in the Bacchanalian orgies of Orpheus. But prior to the observance of the mystic rite of Celeus, and Triptolemus, and Ceres, and Proserpine, and Bacchus in Eleusis, these orgies have been celebrated and handed down to men in Phlium of Attica. For antecedent to the Eleusinian mysteries, there are (enacted) in Phlium the orgies of her denominated the Great (Mother). There is, however, a portico in this (city), and on the portico is inscribed a representation, (visible) up to the present day, of all the words which are spoken (on such occasions). Many, then, of the words inscribed upon that portico are those about which Plutarch institutes discussions in his ten books against Empedokles. And in the greater number of these books is also drawn the representation of a certain aged man, grey-haired, winged, having his *pudendum erectum*, pursuing a retreating woman of azure colour. And over the aged man is the inscription *phaos ruetēs* and over the woman *pereē phikola* ...[122]

Firstly, we see the same association we have found elsewhere of Orpheus with Musaeus and their representation as theologians who instituted mysteries. The reference to Orpheus' Bacchanalian orgies suggests a Dionysiac nature of the Orphic rites. Hippolytus says that these rites were earlier than the Eleusinian and

---

[122] Hippol. *Haer.* V.15 (Tr. MacMahon).

had their beginning at Phlya. Hippolytus' reference to a specific inscribed portico which could still be seen in his day gives credibility to his attestation: if the portico was not real his claim could be instantly discredited. If Hippolytos is right, though, the portico suggests that the *legomena* of the mysteries were not secret, at least at Hippolytos' time (2nd–3rd A.D.). Finally, once again we see an association of the mysteries with a text and also a link to Empedokles which might indicate the 'scientifical' nature of Orphic writings attested elsewhere.

Hippolytus' testimony becomes more credible when cross-referenced with the following passages from Pausanias:[123]

> 1. Ὠλῆνος δὲ ὕστερον Πάμφως τε ἔπη καὶ Ὀρφεὺς ἐποίησαν· καί σφισιν ἀμφοτέροις πεποιημένα ἐστὶν ἐς Ἔρωτα, ἵνα ἐπὶ τοῖς δρωμένοις Λυκομίδαι καὶ ταῦτα ᾄδωσιν· ἐγὼ δὲ ἐπελεξάμην ἀνδρὶ ἐς λόγους ἐλθὼν δᾳδουχοῦντι. καὶ τῶν μὲν οὐ πρόσω ποιήσομαι μνήμην (IX.27.2).
> 2. ὅστις δὲ περὶ ποιήσεως ἐπολυπραγμόνησεν ἤδη, τοὺς Ὀρφέως ὕμνους οἶδεν ὄντας ἕκαστόν τε αὐτῶν ἐπὶ βραχύτατον καὶ τὸ σύμπαν οὐκ ἐς ἀριθμὸν πολὺν πεποιημένους· Λυκομίδαι δὲ ἴσασί τε καὶ ἐπᾴδουσι τοῖς δρωμένοις. κόσμῳ μὲν δὴ τῶν ἐπῶν δευτερεῖα φέροιντο ἂν μετά γε Ὁμήρου τοὺς ὕμνους, τιμῆς δὲ ἐκ τοῦ θείου καὶ ἐς πλέον ἐκείνων ἥκουσι (IX.30.12).
> 3. ἐγὼ δὲ ἔπη μὲν ἐπελεξάμην, ἐν οἷς ἐστι πέτεσθαι Μουσαῖον ὑπὸ Βορέου δῶρον, δοκεῖν δέ μοι πεποίηκεν αὐτὰ Ὀνομάκριτος καὶ ἔστιν οὐδὲν Μουσαίου βεβαίως ὅτι μὴ μόνον ἐς Δήμητρα ὕμνος Λυκομίδαις (I.22.7).
> 4. πρῶτοι δ'οὖν βασιλεύουσιν ἐν τῇ χώρᾳ ταύτῃ Πολυκάων τε ὁ Λέλεγος καὶ Μεσσήνη γυνὴ τοῦ Πολυκάονος. παρὰ ταύτην τὴν Μεσσήνην τὰ ὄργια κομίζων τῶν Μεγάλων θεῶν Καύκων ἦλθεν ἐξ Ἐλευσῖνος ὁ Κελαίνου τοῦ Φλύου. Φλῦον δὲ αὐτὸν Ἀθηναῖοι λέγουσι παῖδα εἶναι Γῆς· ὁμολογεῖ δέ σφισι καὶ ὕμνος Μουσαίου Λυκομίδαις ποιηθεὶς ἐς Δήμητρα (IV.1.5).

> 1. Later than Olen, both Pamphos and Orpheus wrote hexameter verse, and composed poems on Love, in order that they might be among those sung by the Lykomidae to accompany the ritual. I read them after conversation with a Torchbearer. Of these things I will make no further mention.
> 2. Whoever has devoted himself to the study of poetry knows that the hymns of Orpheus are all very short, and that the total number of them is not great. The Lykomidae know them and chant them over the ritual of the mysteries. For poetic beauty they may be said to come next to the hymns of Homer, while they have been even more honored by the gods.
> 3. I have read verse in which Musaeus receives from the North Wind the gift of flight, but, in my opinion, Onomacritus wrote them, and there are no certainly genuine works of Musaeus except a hymn to Demeter written for the Lykomidae.
> 4. The first rulers then in this country were Polycaon, the son of Lelex, and Messene his wife. It was to her that Caucon, the son of Celaenus, son of Phlyus, brought the rites of the

---

[123] All translations of Pausanias are by Jones/Ormerod.

Great Goddesses from Eleusis. Phlyus himself is said by the Athenians to have been the son of Earth, and the hymn of Musaeus to Demeter made for the Lykomidae agrees.

The Lykomidae were a priestly family active at Phlya and responsible for the mysteries there from Classical times.[124] Pausanias argues that they are said to sing an hexametric Orphic poem on Love while performing a rite and that they are said to know and chant the Orphic hymns in general during the conduct of their rituals. These Orphic hymns excelled in poetic beauty. Similarly to Pausanias, Plato referring to some Orphic hymns says that 'nor yet shall anyone venture to sing an unauthorised song not even should it be sweeter than the hymns of Orpheus or of Thamyras'.[125] Pausanias also mentions that Musaeus wrote a hymn to Demeter for them and gives some information about the content of the hymn, since he mentions that according to it Phlyus was the son of Earth. Combining these passages by Pausanias and Hippolytus, it seems that Eleusinian and Orphic rites had similar elements. The use of texts during Orphic rites, discussed in the previous section, is again attested by non-Orphic sources. Faithful to the pattern established so far, Pausanias is reserved in revealing the contents of the texts. We are, however, informed that the texts used were Hymns, some of which were in honour of Demeter and Eros. Pausanias says that he has read(?) the Hymns after coming in contact with a Torchbearer. A Torchbearer was an important member of the 'personnel' of the Eleusinian Mysteries, topped in hierarchy only by the *hierophantes* (the ones who showed the mysteries).[126] This might indicate that rites performed by the Lykomidae were similar to the formation of the Eleusinian mysteries and since a *dadouchos* was an official appointed by the city in the Eleusinian Mysteries, then, the same could have been done for the Orphic rites performed by the Lykomidae at Phlya. Herrero de Jáuregui argues that their cult: '...kept up a certain rivalry with the Eleusinian cult. They held that only the hymns that they sang were the authentic works of Orpheus and Musaeus'.[127] Pausanias agrees with their claim (see passage 3 above). In any case, it seems that Orphic texts were being read/recited to the initiates during the Orphic rites led by the Lykomidae, which comes in accordance with other sources we have discussed attesting the use of texts during Orphic rites.[128]

---

124 Herrero de Jáuregui, 2010, p.43.
125 Pl. *Leg.* 8.829d–e: μηδέ τινα τολμᾶν ᾄδειν ἀδόκιμον Μοῦσαν [μὴ κρινάντων τῶν νομοφυλάκων], μηδ' ἂν ἡδίων ᾖ τῶν Θαμύρου τε καὶ Ὀρφείων ὕμνων (Tr. Bury).
126 Larson, 2007, p.74.
127 Herrero de Jáuregui, 2010, p.43.
128 See also Herrero de Jáuregui, 2010, p.42.

Plutarch confirms that the Lykomidae owned a sanctuary at Phlya and argues that Themistocles must have been clearly connected to them because he restored their sanctuary after it was burned by the barbarians at his own costs (he gives Simonides as his source).[129] This sanctuary might have been dedicated to Kore Protogone since according to Pausanias there were shrines dedicated to them at Phlya and a deity called Protogonos is part of the *Rhapsodies* and the Orphic theogony found in the Derveni Papyrus.[130] He also quotes an inscription from a statue dedicated to a shrine of the Lykomidae by Methapos – the founder of the mysteries of the Cabiri – which refers to Demeter and Kore Protogone (Firstborn) in a passage where he discusses the mysteries of the Great Goddess.[131] The importance of Kore in Orphic rites is also attested in other sources, as we will see, while several authors relate Orpheus or Orphic works and ideas to the Samothracean and Eleusinian mysteries. Considering the reference to the *dadouchos* and specific sanctuaries it seems that the Orphic rites performed by the Lykomidae were not private, but simply secret in the revered sense of not being uttered or made known to the uninitiated. They certainly were not of the same kind as those performed by the itinerant priests.

2.3.1.2 Lacedaemonia

The pair of Demeter and Kore are associated to the figure of Orpheus in relation to Lacedaemonia by Pausanias. He refers specifically to Κόρη Σωτείρα (Saviour Maid) and Demeter Chthonia:

> 1. Λακεδαιμονίοις δὲ ἀπαντικρὺ τῆς Ὀλυμπίας Ἀφροδίτης ἐστὶ ναὸς Κόρης Σωτείρας· ποιῆσαι δὲ τὸν Θρᾶκα Ὀρφέα λέγουσιν, οἱ δὲ Ἄβαριν ἀφικόμενον ἐξ Ὑπερβορέων (III.13.2).
> 2. Δήμητρα δὲ Χθονίαν Λακεδαιμόνιοι μὲν σέβειν φασὶ παραδόντος σφίσιν Ὀρφέως, δόξῃ δὲ ἐμῇ διὰ τὸ ἱερὸν τὸ ἐν Ἑρμιόνῃ κατέστη καὶ τούτοις Χθονίαν νομίζειν Δήμητρα (III.14.5).
>
> 1. Opposite the Olympian Aphrodite the Lacedaemonians have a temple of the Saviour Maid (*Korē Sōteira*). Some say that it was made by Orpheus the Thracian, others by Abaris when he had come from the Hyperboreans.

---

129 Plut. *Them.* 1.3: 'However, it is clear that he was connected with the family of the Lycomidae, for he caused the chapel shrine at Phlya, which belonged to the Lycomidae, and had been burned by the barbarians, to be restored at his own costs and adorned with frescoes, as Simonides has stated' (Tr. Perrin).
130 Paus. I.31.4.
131 Paus. IV.1.7–8.

2. The cult of Demeter Chthonia (of the Lower World) the Lacedaemonians say was handed on to them by Orpheus, but in my opinion it was because of the sanctuary in Hermione that the Lacedaemonians also began to worship Demeter Chthonia.

Demeter Chthonia and Kore Soteira are eschatological deities and in this respect are relevant to the Orphic eschatological beliefs discussed earlier. Kore Soteira is none other than Persephone, and her role as a saviour needs to be interpreted in relation to the afterlife, since she was the queen of the underworld. The epithet Soteira points to eschatological ideas of a blissful afterlife awarded by Persephone; an idea evident in the gold tablets to be discussed in Chapter 4. The attribution of the building of a temple to Orpheus can hardly be taken literally, but the association between Orpheus and Kore Soteira might have a reason since as established from non-Orphic sources so far, Orphic practices related to a blissful afterlife which was mediated by Persephone.

Pausanias also claims (passage 2 above) that the Lacaedemonians themselves say that Orpheus instituted the cult of Demeter Chthonia. His personal opinion, though, is that they worship her because of her nearby cult in Hermione. There was indeed a famous cult of Demeter Chthonia in Hermione (modern Argolis).[132] As Larson notes, the cult in Hermione 'is unusual in its emphasis on the role of Hades' who is called *Klymenos* (the Renowned One).[133] It is confirmed by the 6th century B.C. poet Lasos of Hermione who refers to Kore as the 'wedded wife of Klymenos' that the triad Demeter, Klymenos and Kore was worshipped already in the late Archaic period.[134] Herodotus mentions that Lasos was the one who caught Onomakritos (mid 6th – early 5th B.C.) forging the writings of Musaeus:

ἔχοντες Ὀνομάκριτον ἄνδρα Ἀθηναῖον, χρησμολόγον τε καὶ διαθέτην χρησμῶν τῶν Μουσαίου, ἀναβεβήκεσαν, τὴν ἔχθρην προκαταλυσάμενοι. ἐξηλάσθη γὰρ ὑπὸ Ἱππάρχου τοῦ Πεισιστράτου ὁ Ὀνομάκριτος ἐξ Ἀθηνέων, ἐπ' αὐτοφώρῳ ἁλοὺς ὑπὸ Λάσου τοῦ Ἑρμιονέος ἐμποιέων ἐς τὰ Μουσαίου χρησμόν, ὡς αἱ ἐπὶ Λήμνῳ ἐπικείμεναι νῆσοι ἀφανιζοίατο κατὰ τῆς θαλάσσης. διὸ ἐξήλασέ μιν ὁ Ἵππαρχος, πρότερον χρεώμενος τὰ μάλιστα. τότε δὲ συναναβὰς ὅκως ἀπίκοιτο ἐς ὄψιν τὴν βασιλέος, λεγόντων τῶν Πεισιστρατιδέων περὶ αὐτοῦ σεμνοὺς λόγους, κατέλεγε τῶν χρησμῶν·

---

132 See Larson, 2007, p.78–79. Pausanias described the Chthonia festival at Hermione in 2.35.4–11: 'A procession of the whole town dressed in white and wreathed with Hyacinthus flowers performed a procession to the sanctuary while leading a heifer which they allowed to wander around until it entered the temple where it was sacrificed in secret by four old women waiting inside. Four cows in total were sacrificed.'
133 *PMG* 702 = Ath. 14, 624e. Larson, 2007, p.78.
134 Ath. 10.455c-d, 14.624e–f. Larson, 2007, p.79.

> With these came Onomacritus, an Athenian oracle-monger, one that had set in order the oracles of Musaeus; with him they had come, being now reconciled to him after their quarrel: for Onomacritus had been banished from Athens by Pisistratus' son Hipparchus, having been caught by Lasus of Hermione in the act of interpolating in the writings of Musaeus an oracle showing that the islands off Lemnos should disappear into the sea. For this cause Hipparchus banished him, though before that they had been close friends. Now he came to Susa with Pisistratus' kin; and whensoever he came into the king's presence they would use high language concerning him and he would recite from his oracles...[135]

As we saw, Musaeus was closely linked to Orphic writings and perhaps this shows a familiarity of Lasos with Orphic works and thus a presence of Orphic texts at Hermione. In a passage from Euripides' *Herakles*, after returning from his descend into the underworld where he has met the daughter of Hades (Ἅιδου Κόρης), Herakles says that he has brought the three-headed monster Kerberus in daylight and adds that the monster is now located at the groves of Demeter at Hermione.[136] Pausanias attests that near the temple of Klymenos which is opposite Chthonia's temple there is a chasm in the earth through which 'according to the legend of the Hermionians, Herakles brought up the Hound of Hell'.[137] He furthermore says that he conquered the monster in fight because he was lucky enough to witness the rites of the initiated.[138] This suggests a re-enactment of a *katabasis* ritual during initiation where the initiate would confront obstacles. The euphemistic name of Hades and the worship of the particular triad might signify influence by Orphic ideas since as we have seen, Orphism placed an emphasis on the afterlife in a positive way. The identification by Euripides through Herakles' mouth of Chthonia's grove at Hermione, and the reference of Herakles to initiation rites associated with the underworld, points to the presence of eschatological rites at Hermione. The fact that the legend of Herakles' locating the entrance (or the exit?) of the underworld at Hermione is attested both by Euripides and Pausanias – who also refers to initiates – corroborates the performance of *katabasis* rituals. Callimachus might indicate the justification of the special treatment of the Hermionians by Demeter and the story behind the *katabasis*:

---

[135] Hdt. 7.6.3 (Tr. Godley). See also Pausanias, in the passage quoted above (p.46, passage 3), who says that some verses he read which are supposed to be by Musaeus must have been by Onomakritos.
[136] Eur. *HF*, 607–615.
[137] Paus. 2.35.10.
[138] Eur. *HF*, 613.

'τοὔνεκα καὶ νέκυες πορθμήιον οὔτι φέρονται' (Hecale fr.278 Pfeiffer). ἐν Αἰγιαλῷ γὰρ καταβάσιόν ἐστιν εἰς ᾅδου, εἰς ὃ ἀπελθοῦσα ἡ Δημήτηρ ἔμαθε παρὰ τῶν περιοίκων περὶ τῆς Κόρης καὶ ἐδωρήσατο αὐτοῖς, ὥς λέγει, ἄφεσιν τοῦ πορθμηίου

> Therefore, even as dead they do not need to carry a ferry-fee. Since at Aigialos there is a descend into Hades, to which Demeter came and learned from the locals about Kore and she bestowed them, as he says, with an exemption of the ferry-fee.[139]

Callimachus' fragment indicates that what the initiates got in return was of an eschatological nature. At any rate, it appears that Pausanias is truthful when he says that the Spartans *themselves* say that Chthonia's cult was handed to them by Orpheus, since he still mentions this even though he has a different opinion. Based on the above, an influence of Orphic eschatological ideas in Sparta and perhaps Hermione is very probable.

2.3.1.3 Aigina

We have seen so far that in most cases the rites being associated to Orpheus involve the goddesses Demeter and Kore and have an eschatological nature. In the case of Aigina, Orpheus is linked to the cult of Hecate, another chthonic deity, who was prominent in Miletos and present in Athens by the 6th century B.C.[140] Pausanias attests the following:

θεῶν δὲ Αἰγινῆται τιμῶσιν Ἑκάτην μάλιστα καὶ τελετὴν ἄγουσιν ἀνὰ πᾶν ἔτος Ἑκάτης, Ὀρφέα σφίσι τὸν Θρᾷκα καταστήσασθαι τὴν τελετὴν λέγοντες. τοῦ περιβόλου δὲ ἐντὸς ναός ἐστι, ξόανον δὲ ἔργον Μύρωνος, ὁμοίως ἓν πρόσωπόν τε καὶ τὸ λοιπὸν σῶμα. Ἀλκαμένης δὲ ἐμοὶ δοκεῖν πρῶτος ἀγάλματα Ἑκάτης τρία ἐποίησε προσεχόμενα ἀλλήλοις, ἣν Ἀθηναῖοι καλοῦσιν Ἐπιπυργιδίαν· ἔστηκε δὲ παρὰ τῆς Ἀπτέρου Νίκης τὸν ναόν.

> Of the gods, the Aeginetans worship most Hecate, in whose honor every year they celebrate mystic rites which, they say, Orpheus the Thracian established among them. Within the enclosure is a temple; its wooden image is the work of Myron, and it has one face and one body. It was Alcamenes, in my opinion, who first made three images of Hecate attached to one another, a figure called by the Athenians Epipurgidia (on the Tower); it stands beside the temple of the Wingless Victory.[141]

---

139 *Suda* s.v. Πορθμήϊον, π' 2072.
140 Larson, 2007, p.165.
141 Paus. II 30.2.

Hekate has a special role in the Homeric *Hymn to Demeter,* where she witnesses along with Helios the rape of Persephone and she also visits Helios with Demeter.[142] She finally becomes Persephone's companion in her route from the underworld to the upper world and vice versa.[143] As Larson argues, this points to her subsequent role as a protective deity during transitions of various kinds.[144] She furthermore adds that this was due to her capacity of being intimate with and control over the dead.

She was also associated with magic. Her name is mentioned as early as the mid-fourth century B.C. in a curse tablet from Attica.[145] Her control over the dead would make it easier for the curse to reach them and be accomplished. Considering her eschatological nature and her role as a guide of Persephone in the underworld it would not be surprising if she was indeed linked to Orphic ideas by the Aiginetans as Pausanias says. As already mentioned, Persephone has an important role as Dionysos' mother in Orphic mythology and features prominently in the gold tablets, and in non-Orphic sources referring to Orphism. As Larson notes, the Aeginetan cult of Hekate is unusual because 'the goddess rarely achieved such full integration into any civic pantheon'.[146] Her special relation to Persephone and the fact that she knew her way around the underworld might be the reasons that she was associated with Orphic ideas by the Aiginetans.[147]

2.3.1.4 Macedonia

Macedonia is the place where one of our major Orphic sources was found, namely the Derveni Papyrus, which will be discussed in Chapter 5. In addition, ten out of the forty gold tablets we have available were found in Macedonia dating as early as the 4th century B.C. so it is very likely that Orphic works and ideas were present there already from the 5th–4th century B.C. Here I will refer to the non-Orphic sources linking Macedonia to Orpheus.

---

142 *Hom. Hymn Dem.* 20–75. A scholiast on Ap. Rhod. *Argon.* III.467 says that in the *Orphika* she was Demeter's offspring: ἐν δὲ τοῖς Ὀρφικοῖς Δήμητρος γενεαλογεῖται (schol. *In Ap. Argon.* III.467).
143 *Hom. Hymn Dem.* 438–440. Larson, 2007, p.166.
144 Larson, 2007, p.166.
145 Gager, 1992, no. 40.
146 Larson, 2007, p.167.
147 There is also a possible Orphic link with Aigina's major goddess Aphaia, a matter which will be pursued in future research.

In a passage from the *Alexander*, Plutarch mentions that the majority of the Macedonian women were involved in Orphic and Dionysiac rites from very ancient times and that these women were called Klodones and Mimallones, which are the Macedonian names for Bacchantes:

λέγεται δὲ Φίλιππος ἐν Σαμοθρᾴκῃ τῇ Ὀλυμπιάδι συμμυηθεὶς αὐτός τε μειράκιον ὢν ἔτι κἀκείνης παιδὸς ὀρφανῆς γονέων ἐρασθῆναι καὶ τὸν γάμον οὕτως ἁρμόσαι, πείσας τὸν ἀδελφὸν αὐτῆς Ἀρύμβαν. ἡ μὲν οὖν νύμφη, πρὸ τῆς νυκτὸς ᾗ συνείρχθησαν εἰς τὸν θάλαμον, ἔδοξε βροντῆς γενομένης ἐμπεσεῖν αὐτῆς τῇ γαστρὶ κεραυνόν, ἐκ δὲ τῆς πληγῆς πολὺ πῦρ ἀναφθέν, εἶτα ῥηγνύμενον εἰς φλόγας πάντῃ φερομένας διαλυθῆναι. ... ὤφθη δέ ποτε καὶ δράκων κοιμωμένης τῆς Ὀλυμπιάδος παρεκτεταμένος τῷ σώματι· καὶ τοῦτο μάλιστα τοῦ Φιλίππου τὸν ἔρωτα καὶ τὰς φιλοφροσύνας ἀμαυρῶσαι λέγουσιν, ὡς μηδὲ φοιτᾶν ἔτι πολλάκις παρ᾽ αὐτὴν ἀναπαυσόμενον, εἴτε δείσαντά τινας μαγείας ἐπ᾽ αὐτῷ καὶ φάρμακα τῆς γυναικός, εἴτε τὴν ὁμιλίαν ὡς κρείττονι συνούσης ἀφοσιούμενον. Ἕτερος δὲ περὶ τούτων ἐστὶ λόγος, ὡς πᾶσαι μὲν αἱ τῇδε γυναῖκες ἔνοχοι τοῖς Ὀρφικοῖς οὖσαι καὶ τοῖς περὶ τὸν Διόνυσον ὀργιασμοῖς ἐκ τοῦ πάνυ παλαιοῦ, Κλώδωνές τε καὶ Μιμαλλόνες ἐπωνυμίαν ἔχουσαι, πολλὰ ταῖς Ἠδωνίσι καὶ ταῖς περὶ τὸν Αἷμον Θρῄσσαις ὅμοια δρῶσιν, ἀφ᾽ ὧν δοκεῖ καὶ τὸ θρησκεύειν ὄνομα ταῖς κατακόροις γενέσθαι καὶ περιέργοις ἱερουργίαις, ἡ δὲ Ὀλυμπιὰς μᾶλλον ἑτέρων ζηλώσασα τὰς κατοχὰς καὶ τοὺς ἐνθουσιασμοὺς ἐξάγουσα βαρβαρικώτερον ὄφεις μεγάλους χειροήθεις ἐφείλκετο τοῖς θιάσοις, οἳ πολλάκις ἐκ τοῦ κιττοῦ καὶ τῶν μυστικῶν λίκνων παραναδυόμενοι καὶ περιελιττόμενοι τοῖς θύρσοις τῶν γυναικῶν καὶ τοῖς στεφάνοις ἐξέπληττον τοὺς ἄνδρας.

And we are told that Philip, after being initiated into the mysteries of Samothrace at the same time with Olympias, he himself being still a youth and she an orphan child, fell in love with her and betrothed himself to her at once with the consent of her brother, Arymbas. Well, then, the night before that on which the marriage was consummated, the bride dreamed that there was a peal of thunder and that a thunder-bolt fell upon her womb, and that thereby much fire was kindled, which broke into flames that travelled all about, and then was extinguished. ... Moreover, a serpent was once seen lying stretched out by the side of Olympias as she slept, and we are told that this, more than anything else, dulled the ardour of Philip's attentions to his wife, so that he no longer came often to sleep by her side, either because he feared that some spells and enchantments might be practised upon him by her, or because he shrank from her embraces in the conviction that she was the partner of a superior being. But concerning these matters there is another story to this effect: all the women of these parts were addicted to the Orphic rites and the orgies of Dionysus from very ancient times (being called Klodones and Mimallones), and imitated in many ways the practices of the Edonian women and the Thracian women about Mount Haemus, from whom, as it would seem, the word 'threskeuein' came to be applied to the celebration of extravagant and superstitious ceremonies. Now Olympias, who affected these divine possessions more zealously than other women, and carried out these divine inspirations in wilder fashion, used to provide the revelling companies with great tame serpents, which would often lift their heads from out the ivy and the mystic winnowing baskets, or coil themselves about the wands and garlands of the women, thus terrifying the men.[148]

The context of this passage refers to Alexander's lineage. Olympias was a kind of prominent figure of the *thiasos* which she would provide with snakes to be used during the mysteries and there is also the detail of the serpent stretching next to Olympias while sleeping. The serpent, as will be discussed in more detail in the following chapters, is directly linked to Dionysos, and once again we see Orphic rites being equated with the Dionysiac orgies. The carrying of secret winnowing baskets (τῶν μυστικῶν λίκνων) in conjunction with the snakes might be a reference to the Orphic myth of Dionysos' dismemberment where infant Dionysos is carried by Hipta in a basket encircled by a snake when he is born for the second time.[149] To the importance of the Dionysiac cult in Macedonia also point several tombs with paintings depicting scenes of a symposium whose main figure was Dionysos as well as the fact that Euripides wrote the *Bacchae* whose central theme is the cult of Dionysos, while in Pella, Macedonia.[150]

Plutarch also notes that these rites resembled those of the Thracian and Edonian women indicating that Orphic rites in various areas might had similar characteristics.[151] Since Edonis was an area in Thrace next to Macedonia, it is not hard to imagine these rites being transmitted from one place to the next. Ovid (1st B.C.) in his *Metamorphoses* has the Edonian women murder Orpheus on a hilltop by tearing him apart after one of them proclaims: 'See! Here is the poet who has scorned us'.[152] Perhaps the hilltop where Orpheus was said to be murdered was Mount Pangaion, located in Edonis, since it is also the site of Orpheus' death in Euripides' *Hypsipyle*.[153] According to Ovid, Dionysos is not pleased with Orpheus' murder and punishes the maenads:

> *Non inpune tamen scelus hoc sinit esse Lyaeus*
> *amissoque dolens sacrorum vate suorum*
> *protinus in silvis matres Edonidas omnes,*
> *quae videre nefas, torta radice ligavit...*

---

[148] Plut. *Alex.* 2 (Tr. Perrin).
[149] See Table 2 in p.85.
[150] Piano, 2016, p.53–58.
[151] See next section.
[152] Ov. *Met.* 11.1–84.
[153] Eur. *Hyps.* fr. 759a.

However, Lyaeus did not suffer such crime as this to go unavenged. Grieved at the loss of the bard of his sacred rites, he straightway bound fast all those Thracian women, who looked upon the outrage, with twisted roots.[154]

Dionysos grieves for Orpheus' death because he was the bard of his sacred rites. The way in which Orpheus is murdered is the same with Dionysos' way of death according to the Orphic myth of his dismemberment. This might be a subtle reference to the close connection of the Orphic rites and their development to Orphic works and in particular the dismemberment myth. Orpheus is identified as the 'bard' of the rites which suggests that they were based on his songs: Orphic works/mythology. Ovid's work is not of a historiographical nature but this does not mean that he was not inspired by real traditions, especially since Pausanias also relates the Edonian rites to Orphic ones. Ovid also says that Orpheus' soul escaped his body from his lips and 'breathed out, went faring forth in air'.[155] This notion about the airy nature of the soul is attested to be Orphic, as we saw, in sources such as Aristotle: the specification by Ovid suggest he might have been aware of such an Orphic idea.

This particular version of Orpheus' death is also found in Eratosthenes' *Catasterismoi*, a work which survives in an epitome dated to the 1st century A.D. but attributed to Eratosthenes of Cyrene who lived in the 3rd century B.C. The following passage discusses the constellation of Lyra:

> διὰ δὲ τὴν γυναῖκα εἰς Ἅιδου καταβὰς καὶ ἰδὼν τὰ ἐκεῖ οἷα ἦν τὸν μὲν Διόνυσον οὐκέτι ἐτίμα, ὑφ' οὗ ἦν δεδοξασμένος, τὸν δὲ Ἥλιον μέγιστον τῶν θεῶν ἐνόμισεν, ὃν καὶ Ἀπόλλωνα προσηγόρευσεν· ἐπεγειρόμενός τε τὴν νύκτα ἕωθεν κατὰ τὸ ὄρος τὸ καλούμενον Πάγγαιον προσέμενε τὰς ἀνατολάς, ἵνα ἴδῃ τὸν Ἥλιον πρῶτος· ὅθεν ὁ Διόνυσος ὀργισθεὶς αὐτῷ ἔπεμψε τὰς Βασσάρας, ὥς φησιν Αἰσχύλος ὁ τῶν τραγῳδιῶν ποιητής· αἳ διέσπασαν αὐτὸν καὶ τὰ μέλη ἔρριψαν χωρὶς ἕκαστον· αἱ δὲ Μοῦσαι συναγαγοῦσαι ἔθαψαν ἐπὶ τοῖς καλουμένοις Λειβήθροις.

> ...having descended to Hades because of his wife and seen how things were there, he did not any longer honour Dionysos, by whom he had been made famous, but considered Helios (the sun) to be greatest of the gods, whom he addressed also as Apollo. Rousing himself at night before dawn he awaited the rising of the sun at the mountain Pangaion, in order to be the first to see the sun. And so Dionysos was angry with him and – as Aeschylus the

---

154 Ov. *Met.* 11.67–70 (Tr. Miller).
155 Ov. *Mer* 11.41–43: *perque os, pro Iuppiter! Illud | auditum saxis intellectumque ferarum | sensibus in ventos anima exhalata recessit.*

tragic poet says – sent against him the Bassarai, who tore him apart and dispersed his limbs. The Muses gathered the limbs and buried them at the place called Libethroi.[156]

Pausanias offers a different explanation since, as he says, the Thracian women – flushed with wine – killed him because he convinced their husbands to follow him in his wanderings.[157] He does however agree with Eratosthenes in locating his tomb close to Leibethra, a town in Macedonia.[158] Plutarch refers to it in a story where he links Alexander himself to Orpheus. As he says, at the time when Alexander had begun his expedition to Persia, a statue of Orpheus at Leibethra was sweating abundantly.[159] This sign was feared by most of the people but Aristander told Alexander that he should receive it as a good omen, meaning that his deeds would be worthy of song and praise. The version of Orpheus being killed by women is also attested in Plato where Socrates tells Glaukon the story of Er who died and came back to life and described what he saw in the afterlife.[160] He records that Orpheus chose to be reborn as a swan because he did not want to be born by a woman due to his hatred of them.[161] On the other hand, in an epigram by Damagetus (2nd B.C.), Orpheus' tomb is located on the Thracian slopes of Mount Olympus. He also mentions that Orpheus established the mystical rites of Bacchos and managed to charm even Hades with his lyre.[162] In any case, the localization of Orpheus' tomb at Macedonia by various authors must be an indication of Orphic activity in the area, which is supported by the sources attesting the presence of Orphic rites in Macedonia.

---

156 *TrGF* vol.3, p.138, Aeschylos fr.23a Radt. = Eratosth. [*Cat.*] 24. See also Hygin. *Astr.* 2.7. Translation by Seaford – apart from the last sentence – of an edition of the text by West. Seaford, 2005, p.602.
157 Paus. IX.30.5.
158 Paus. IX. 30.9.
159 Plut. *Alex.* 14.5. See also Arr. *Anab.* 1.11.2. and Ps-Callisth. *Hist. Alex. Magn.* rec. β 1.42.
160 Pl. *Resp.* 10.613ff to the end.
161 Pl. *Resp.* 10.620a. For a third version of Orpheus being torn apart from women because of Aphrodite's wrath see P. Berol. 13426, saec. II, 1469ss (OF1036T) and Hyg. *Poet. astr.* 2.7. Another passage – although somewhat late (3rd A.D.) – indicating a connection with Bacchism is the one of ps.-Plutarch who references Clitonymus' report that there is an herb called *kithara* on Mount Pangaion, which grew out of Orpheus' blood. This herb, during the sacrifices to Bacchos, makes a sound like a *kithara* being played, while the natives covered with deer skins and carrying the thyrsus in their hands sing a hymn, including the following lines: 'If you are going to be wise in vain, then do not be wise at all' (Ps-Plutarch, *De fluvi.* 3.4).
162 Dam. *Anth. Pal.* 7.9.

Dio Chrysostom (1st A.D.) also draws a link between Macedonia and Orphism. In the following passage he refers to a story he heard from 'a Phrygian, a kinsman of Aesop':

ζῶντος μὲν οὖν Ὀρφέως συνέπεσθαι αὐτῷ πανταχόθεν ἀκούοντα ὁμοῦ καὶ νεμόμενα· καὶ γὰρ ἐκεῖνον ἔν τε τοῖς ὄρεσι καὶ περὶ τὰς νάπας τὰ πολλὰ διατρίβειν· ἀποθανόντος δὲ ἐρημωθέντα ὀδύρεσθαι καὶ χαλεπῶς φέρειν· ὥστε τὴν μητέρα αὐτοῦ Καλλιόπην διὰ τὴν πρὸς τὸν υἱὸν εὔνοιαν καὶ φιλίαν αἰτησαμένην παρὰ Διὸς τὰ σώματα αὐτῶν μεταβαλεῖν εἰς ἀνθρώπων τύπον, τὰς μέντοι ψυχὰς διαμένειν, οἷαι πρότερον ἦσαν.
Χαλεπὸν οὖν ἤδη ἐστὶ τὸ λειπόμενον τοῦ λόγου, καὶ δέδοικα πρὸς ὑμᾶς σαφῶς αὐτὸ εἰπεῖν. ἔλεγε γὰρ ἐξ ἐκείνων γένος τι φῦναι Μακεδόνων, καὶ τοῦτο αὖθις ὕστερον μετὰ Ἀλεξάνδρου διαβὰν ἐνθάδε οἰκῆσαι. καὶ διὰ τοῦτο δὴ τὸν τῶν Ἀλεξανδρέων δῆμον ἄγεσθαι μὲν ὑπὸ ᾠδῆς, ὡς οὐδένας ἄλλους, κἂν ἀκούσωσι κιθάρας ὁποιασοῦν, ἐξεστάναι καὶ φρίττειν κατὰ μνήμην τὴν Ὀρφέως. εἶναι δὲ τῷ τρόπῳ κοῦφον καὶ ἀνόητον, ὡς ἐκ τοιούτου σπέρματος· ἐπεὶ τούς γε ἄλλους Μακεδόνας ἀνδρείους καὶ πολεμικοὺς γενέσθαι καὶ τὸ ἦθος βεβαίους.

So then, as long as Orpheus was alive they <animals: mostly birds and sheep> followed him from every quarter, listening as they fed — for indeed he spent his time for the most part on the mountains and about the glens; but when he died, in their desolation they wailed and were distressed; and so it came about that the mother of Orpheus, Kalliope, because of her goodwill and affection toward her son, begged Zeus to change their bodies into human form; yet their souls remained as they had been before. Well, the remainder of the tale from this point on is painful and I am reluctant to tell it to you in plain language. For the Phrygian went on to say that from those wild creatures whom Zeus transformed a tribe of Macedonians was born, and that it was this tribe which at a later time crossed over with Alexander and settled here. He added that this is the reason why the people of Alexandria are carried away by song as no other people are, and that if they hear music of the lyre, however bad, they lose their senses and are all aquiver in memory of Orpheus. And he said that they are giddy and foolish in behaviour, coming as they do from such a stock, since the other Macedonians certainly have shown themselves to be manly and martial and steadfast of character.[163]

Even though, this passage refers to a legendary story, it is nonetheless indicative of the role of the ancient Greeks' aetiological stories about their rites and ancestry. This story is interesting not only because it seems to refer to ecstatic rites linked to Orphism – 'this is the reason why...they lose their sense they are all aquiver in memory of Orpheus' – but also there are subtle allusions to a soul doctrine and the origin of a Macedonian tribe which later on 'crossed over with Alexander' and settled in Alexandria in Egypt. This speech was given to the people of Alexandria, whom Dio Chrysostom criticised, defining life in Alexandria as a

---

[163] Dio Chrys. *Or.* 32.64–65 (Tr. Crosby).

'wild, ruinous revel of dancers, whistlers and murderers'.[164] According to this story, it seems that Dio is trying to attribute these traits to a Macedonian ancestry and more specifically, to a tribe which came into existence after a request to Zeus by Orpheus' mother Kalliope in order to honour their love for Orpheus. Dio Chrysostom most probably uses this parallelism to emphasise the wild lifestyle of the Alexandrians. The story, nonetheless, in conjunction with other sources linking Macedonia to Orpheus, adds to the argument for the existence of Orphic rites at the area. Finally, the reference to the soul by Dio Chrysostom might be an allusion to Macedonian beliefs about the incarnation of the soul. The Macedonian tribe members believed they were created by Zeus and their souls used to exist before they came into being, in animals. This presupposes the transmigration of souls and the reference to animals might be of importance if related to the *Orphikos Bios* entailing vegetarianism and abstinence from killing.

The non-Orphic sources which refer to Orphic rites in Macedonia and also locate Orpheus' death and tomb in the area, indicate that Macedonia was one of the most important Orphic centres, or an area where Orphic activity was more prominent than elsewhere.

2.3.2 Thrace and Phrygia

Thrace and Phrygia are geographically next to each other and the reason they are discussed together is that they are often mentioned together in our sources. Thrace has a special mythological connection to Orpheus since it was his place of origin. Sources from Pindar in the early 5th century to the Parian Marble (264 BC) and later make Orpheus son of muse Kalliope and Oeagrus, the king of Thrace.[165] Even though Orpheus comes from Thrace, an area which was considered barbarian by Greeks, we have seen him being identified as the establisher of the most sacred Greek rites, something which is perhaps an indicator of the strange nature of the Orphic rites, works and beliefs. Another example of this would be Dionysos who was identified by some ancient sources as a 'foreign god'

---

164 Dio Chrys. *Or.* 32.69. Swain, 2002, p.83.
165 OF513T: *Marm. Par.* saec. III a.Ch. *IG* XIII 5,444 ed. Hiller de Gaertringen. For text see fn.56. Some other places, most of them areas of Thrace, such as Haemus, Rhodope, Bistonia, Odrysae, Sithone, Mount Pangaeus, Olympus and Leibethra are mentioned by a variety of writers. See OF923T–OF937T. Pind. Fr.128c = OF890T: υἱὸν Οἰαγροθ <δὲ> Ὀρφέα χρυσάορα. OF891T: Schol. Eur. *Rhes.* 346. King of Thrace: OF874T. Kalliope, who is named by Timotheus and Parmenion as Orpheus' mother, was one of the nine Muses: OF902T: Timoth. *Pers.* Fr.791, 221–224. OF904T = *Anth. Pal.* 16.217.

coming from Asia Minor, though he was a purely Greek god whose name was found on Linear B tablets from Pylos which date from LM II to LH III B (1425 to 1190 B.C).[166] Identifying something as foreign might have been the Greek 'defence mechanism' for justifying 'barbaric' or 'ecstatic' elements of a Greek cult or myth; without, of course, excluding the interchange of cultural elements between civilisations. In any case, the colonisation of all Thracian coasts by Greeks began before and around the middle of the seventh century almost simultaneously, and slightly earlier in the Aegean and the Propontis.[167]

The connection of Orphic practices with Thracian and Phrygian rites might be due to their orgiastic nature and also because of the relation of Dionysos to the goddess Kybele, whose rites were considered to originate from these areas. Matar Kubileya was closely related to the Bronze Age goddess depicted in Minoan gems, as a mistress of wild nature. She is the equivalent of Titaness Rhea – mother of the Olympians – and Mountain Mother and closely associated to Dionysos as we will see, while the popular appeal and rapid spread of her cult already in the sixth century is attested by archaeological evidence depicting the goddess, such as figurines and votive reliefs, found in sanctuaries, domestic contexts and tombs.[168] Kybele herself is rarely mentioned in Orphic sources but her equivalent Rhea is found on several occasions, which might indicate her importance in Orphism.[169] In most of these occasions she is equated to Demeter.

Apollonius Rhodius refers to Orpheus' involvement in Phrygian religious rites, and more specifically to the use of the wheel and the drum for worshipping Rhea, who as already mentioned was identified with the Phrygian Kybele:

ἄμυδις δὲ νέοι Ὀρφῆος ἀνωγῇ
σκαίροντες βηταρμὸν ἐνόπλιον ὠρχήσαντο,
καὶ σάκεα ξιφέεσσιν ἐπέκτυπον, ὥς κεν ἰωὴ

---

166 Chadwick, 1967, p.13. Burkert, 1985 p.43–46. Tablets with Dionysos' name: Xa 06 and Xa 1419; Caskey, 1986, p.40. Edmonds, 2013, p.62, fn.181: 'Tablet KH Gq5 from Khania records the offering of honey to Dionysos, while a tablet from Pylos (PY Ea 102) refers to a fire altar for Dionysos'.
167 Damyanov, 2015, p.296. On the Greek colonisation of Thrace see Damyanov, 2015, pp.295–308.
168 Larson, 2007, p.170–71. Rhea: Hes. *Theog.* 463–91. Gantz, 1993, p.41–44. Ar. *Av.* 746. Eur. *Cr.* fr.472 (Nauck). Eur. *Hel.* 1301.
169 Gurôb Papyrus, 6. Derveni Papyrus Col.XXII.12. OR34/43/46/50. Euphorion fr.40. Also in the gold tablet from Pherae (2) we find Demeter Chthonia being mentioned alongside the Mountain Mother, another persona of Rhea and Kybele. Finally, in the Orphic Hymn (27) to Μητρὸς θεῶν we find the phrase: 'blessed one, who rejoices in the drum, all-taming, Phrygian, saviour' (11–12).

> δύσφημος πλάζοιτο δι' ἤέρος, ἥν ἔτι λαοὶ
> κηδείῃ βασιλῆος ἀνέστενον. ἔνθεν ἐσαιεὶ
> ῥόμβῳ καὶ τυπάνῳ 'Ρείην Φρύγες ἱλάσκονται.
>
> At the same time, upon Orpheus' command, the young men leapt as they danced the dance-in-armor and beat their shields with their swords, so that any ill-omened cry of grief, which the people were still sending up in lament for their king, would be lost in the air. Since then, the Phrygians have always propitiated Rhea with rhombus and tambourine.[170]

The ecstatic elements, and the use of *tympana* which were 'negatively stereotyped as 'Eastern' in the wake of the Persian wars, are most likely Greek developments originating in Krete'.[171] Furthermore, Strabo (1st B.C.) also mentions the Orphic rites in his discussion of the orgiastic Phrygian rites and notes that they originated among the Thracians. In this passage the Orphic rites are said to resemble several cults/rites – which admittedly have similarities, all being of an orgiastic/ecstatic nature – such as the Corybantic, Bacchic and Sabazian rites and the worship of Cybele:

> Τῷ δ' αὐλῷ καὶ κτύπῳ κροτάλων τε καὶ κυμβάλων καὶ τυμπάνων καὶ ταῖς ἐπιβοήσεσι καὶ εὐασμοῖς καὶ ποδοκρουστίαις οἰκεῖα ἐξεύροντο καί τινα τῶν ὀνομάτων, ἃ τοὺς προπόλους καὶ χορευτὰς καὶ θεραπευτὰς τῶν ἱερῶν ἐκάλουν, Καβείρους καὶ Κορύβαντας καὶ Πᾶνας καὶ Σατύρους καὶ Τιτύρους, καὶ τὸν θεὸν Βάκχον καὶ τὴν 'Ρέαν Κυβέλην καὶ Κυβήβην καὶ Δινδυμήνην κατὰ τοὺς τόπους αὐτούς. καὶ ὁ Σαβάζιος δὲ τῶν Φρυγιακῶν ἐστι καὶ τρόπον τινὰ τῆς Μητρὸς τὸ παιδίον παραδοὺς τὰ τοῦ Διονύσου καὶ αὐτός. Τούτοις δ'ἔοικε καὶ τὰ παρὰ τοῖς Θραξὶ τά τε Κοτύτια καὶ τὰ Βενδίδεια, παρ' οἷς καὶ τὰ Ὀρφικὰ τὴν καταρχὴν ἔσχε.
>
> They invented names appropriate to the flute, and to the noises made by castanets, cymbals, and drums, and to their acclamations and shouts of "ev-ah", and stampings of the feet; and they also invented some of the names by which to designate the ministers, choral dancers, and attendants upon the sacred rites, I mean "Cabeiri" and "Corybantes" and "Pans" and "Satyri" and "Tityri", and they called the god "Bacchos", and Rhea "Cybele" or "Cybebe" or "Dindymene" according to the places where she was worshipped. Sabazius also belongs to the Phrygian group and in a way is the child of the Mother, since he too transmitted the rites of Dionysus. Also resembling these rites are the Cotytian and the Bendideian rites practiced among the Thracians, among whom the Orphic rites had their beginning.[172]

The comparison of Orphic rites with the above orgiastic rites suggests that they were possibly also of an ecstatic nature. Strabo refers to Bacchos and Rhea, to

---

170 Ap. Rhod., *Argon*. I.1134–39 (Tr. Race) = OF526T.
171 Larson, 2007, p.171.
172 Strabo, X.3.15–16 (Tr. Jones) = OF528T.

cymbals and ecstatic dance and to the εὐασμοῖς. Euripides, through the mouth of Dionysos, also refers to these elements as part of the worship of Rhea and Dionysos, and he also links them to Phrygia:

1. ΔΙΟΝΥΣΟΣ: ... ἢν δὲ Θηβαίων πόλις
ὀργῇ σὺν ὅπλοις ἐξ ὄρους βάκχας ἄγειν
ζητῇ, ξυνάψω μαινάσι στρατηλατῶν.
ὧν οὕνεκ' εἶδος θνητὸν ἀλλάξας ἔχω
μορφήν τ' ἐμὴν μετέβαλον εἰς ἀνδρὸς φύσιν.
ἀλλ', ὦ λιποῦσαι Τμῶλον, ἔρυμα Λυδίας,
θίασος ἐμός, γυναῖκες ἃς ἐκ βαρβάρων
ἐκόμισα παρέδρους καὶ ξυνεμπόρους ἐμοί,
αἴρεσθε τἀπιχώρι' ἐν Φρυγῶν πόλει
τύπανα, Ῥέας τε μητρὸς ἐμά θ' εὑρήματα,
βασίλειά τ' ἀμφὶ δώματ' ἐλθοῦσαι τάδε
κτυπεῖτε Πενθέως, ὡς ὁρᾷ Κάδμου πόλις.
ἐγὼ δὲ βάκχαις, ἐς Κιθαιρῶνος πτυχὰς
ἐλθὼν ἵν' εἰσί, συμμετασχήσω χορῶν.

1. DIONYSOS: But if ever the city of Thebes should in anger seek to drive the Bacchae down from the mountains with arms, I, the general of the Maenads, will join battle with them. On which account I have changed my form to a mortal one and altered my shape into the nature of a man. But, you women who have left Tmolus, the bulwark of Lydia, my sacred band, whom I have brought from among the barbarians as assistants and companions to me, take your drums, native instruments of the city of the Phrygians, the invention of mother Rhea and myself, and going about this palace of Pentheus beat them, so that Kadmos' city may see. I myself will go to the folds of Kithairon, where the Bacchae are, to share in their dances.[173]

2. ΧΟΡΟΣ:
ὦ μάκαρ, ὅστις εὐδαί-
μων τελετὰς θεῶν εἰ-
δὼς βιοτὰν ἁγιστεύει
καὶ θιασεύεται ψυ-
χὰν ἐν ὄρεσσι βακχεύ-
ων ὁσίοις καθαρμοῖσιν,
τά τε ματρὸς μεγάλας ὄρ-
για Κυβέλας θεμιτεύων
ἀνὰ θύρσον τε τινάσσων
κισσῷ τε στεφανωθεὶς
Διόνυσον θεραπεύει.
ἴτε βάκχαι, ἴτε βάκχαι,
Βρόμιον παῖδα θεὸν θεοῦ

---

[173] Eur. *Bacch.* 50–63 (Tr. Buckley).

Διόνυσον κατάγουσαι
Φρυγίων ἐξ ὀρέων Ἑλλάδος εἰς εὐ-
ρυχόρους ἀγυιάς, τὸν Βρόμιον·

2. CHORUS: Blessed is he who, being
fortunate and knowing the rites of
the gods, keeps his life pure and has
his soul initiated into the Bacchic
revels, dancing in inspired frenzy
over the mountains with holy purifications,
and who, revering the mysteries of
great mother Kybele, brandishing the
thyrsos, garlanded with ivy, serves
Dionysus. Go, Bacchae, go, Bacchae,
escorting the god Bromius, child of a god,
from the Phrygian mountains to the
broad streets of Hellas – Bromius...[174]

Euripides' reference to an initiation of the soul and to keeping a pure life point to Orphic ideas, since as we have already seen non-Orphic sources refer to Orphic eschatological ideas of the soul and the afterlife related to ritual, and to the *Orphikos bios* which entailed the leading of a pure life. The passages from Euripides show the association of Dionysiac rites with Rhea and Phrygia, while later sources connecting these rites to Orpheus suggest that their formation was related to Orphic mythology and beliefs.

A similar passage combining various cults is the following one from Diodorus Siculus (1st B.C.) who relates Orpheus to the mysteries that the Kikones practice in Thrace:

τήν τε γὰρ παρ' Ἀθηναίοις ἐν Ἐλευσῖνι γινομένην τελετήν, ἐπιφανεστάτην σχεδὸν οὖσαν ἁπασῶν, καὶ τὴν ἐν Σαμοθρᾴκῃ καὶ τὴν ἐν Θρᾴκῃ ἐν τοῖς Κίκοσιν, ὅθεν ὁ καταδείξας Ὀρφεὺς ἦν, μυστικῶς παραδίδοσθαι, κατὰ δὲ τὴν Κρήτην ἐν Κνωσῷ νόμιμον ἐξ ἀρχαίων εἶναι φανερῶς τὰς τελετὰς ταύτας πᾶσι παραδίδοσθαι, καὶ τὰ παρὰ τοῖς ἄλλοις ἐν ἀπορρήτῳ παραδιδόμενα παρ' αὐτοῖς μηδένα κρύπτειν τῶν βουλομένων τὰ τοιαῦτα γινώσκειν.

The initiatory rite which is celebrated by the Athenians in Eleusis, the most famous, one may venture, of them all, and that of Samothrace, and the one practiced in Thrace among the Kikones, whence Orpheus came who introduced them – these are all handed down in the form of a mystery, whereas at Cnosus in Crete it has been the custom for ancient times that these initiatory rites should be handed down to all openly, and what is handed down

---

[174] Eur. *Bacch.* 73–87 (Tr. Buckley).

among other peoples as not to be divulged, this the Cretans conceal from no one who may wish to inform himself upon such matters.[175]

According to Diodorus, Orpheus introduced the Eleusinian and Samothracean mysteries and the ones practiced by the Kikones in Thrace. They also have another thing in common; they were handed down in secrecy. The Kikones lived at Ismaros, a town of the south coast of Thrace and are mentioned by Homer as allies of the Trojans.[176] They seem to disappear in historical sources from classical times onwards. This passage by Diodorus indicates once more the perception of Orpheus as the establisher of mysteries and his association with the Eleusinian ones.

Two scholia on Euripides refer to an oracle of Dionysos located in Thrace and associate it with Orpheus. The first, on *Alcestis*, identifies its source as 'the physicist Heraclides', possibly Heraclides Ponticus (4th B.C.):

> Ὀρφεία κατέγραψεν] καὶ ποιητὴς καὶ μάντις ἦν ὁ Ὀρφεύς. Φιλόχορος ἐν α' Περὶ μαντικῆς ἐκτίθησιν αὐτοῦ ποιήματα ἔχοντα οὕτως· 'οὗτοι ἀριστερός εἰμι θεοπροπίας ἀποειπεῖν, ἀλλά μοι ἐν στήθεσσιν ἀληθεύουσι μένοιναι'. ὁ δὲ φυσικὸς Ἡρακλείδης εἶναι ὄντως φησὶ σανίδας τινὰς Ὀρφέως, γράφων οὕτως· 'τὸ δὲ τοῦ Διονύσου κατεσκεύασται {ἐπὶ} τῆς Θράικης ἐπὶ τοῦ καλουμένου Αἵμου, ὅπου δή τινας ἐν σανίσιν ἀναγραφὰς εἶναι φασιν <Ὀρφέως>'.

> ...written down by the voice of Orpheus': Orpheus is a poet and a prophet. Philochorus in his work *Peri Mantikēs* (fr.191) sets out his poems in the following way: 'Indeed I am neither declaring an ill-omened oracle, but I am speaking truthfully from my heart'. And Herakleidis the physicist, attests writing the following, that there are indeed some boards by Orpheus: 'That [oracle] of Dionysos was built in Thrace, on the so called Haemus, where is said that there were some writings of Orpheus upon tablets'.[177]

The Euripidean passage refers to some 'Thracian tablets set down by the voice of Orpheus', which must have been considered to be very powerful since not even them were 'stronger than Necessity'.[178] This is a clear reference to a *written/inscribed* text which was supposed to be inspired or recited by Orpheus and which had 'curative' properties. Herodotus also refers to an oracle at Bessi in Thrace: 'It is they [the Satrae] who possess the place of divination sacred to Dionysus. This place is in their highest mountains; the Bessi, a clan of the Satrae, are the prophets of the shrine; there is a priestess who utters the oracle, as at Delphi; it is no

---

175 Diod. V.77.3 (Tr. Oldfather).
176 Hom. *Il.* 2.846–847; 17.70–74; Hom. *Od.* 9.39–61. Hdt. 7.110–111.
177 schol. In Eur. *Alc.* 968 Schwartz, Vol.2 p.239. Iliev, 2013, p.62.
178 Eur. *Alc.* 962–72.

more complicated here than there'.¹⁷⁹ Based on these references we can be fairly positive that this oracle was known to Athenians. The second scholion, on *Hecuba*, also links the oracle of Dionysos in Thrace to Orpheus:

> οἱ μὲν περὶ τὸ Πάγγαιον εἶναι τὸ μαντεῖόν φασι τοῦ Διονύσου, οἱ δὲ περὶ τὸν Αἷμον, οὗ εἰσι καὶ Ὀρφέως ἐν σανίσιν ἀναγραφαί, περὶ ὧν φησιν ἐν Ἀλκήστιδι· 'οὐδέ τι φάρμακον Θρῄσσαις ἐν σανίσιν, τὰς Ὀρφεία κατέγραψεν γῆρυς'. ὅτι δὲ καὶ Διόνυσος μάντις, καὶ ἐν Βάκχαις φησί· 'μάντις δ' ὁ δαίμων ὅδε· τὸ γὰρ βακχεύσιμον καὶ <τὸ> μανιῶδες μαντικὴν πολλὴν ἔχει'.
>
> Some say that the oracle of Dionysos is at Mt. Pangaion, while others say it is at Mt. Haemus, where are some tablets written by Orpheus, about which he says in *Alcestis:* 'nor is there any cure for it in the Thracian tablets set down by the voice of Orpheus' (966). And that Dionysos is a prophet, he says in the *Bacchae:* 'But this god is a prophet—for Bacchic revelry and madness have in them much prophetic skill' (298).¹⁸⁰

The source of the scholiast is unknown but the link to the previous scholion in *Alcestis* gives credibility to the argument that the oracle of Dionysos in Thrace was associated with tablets which were supposed to originate from Orpheus. We have also seen earlier that the author of *Rhesus* refers to an oracle of Dionysos in Mt. Pangaion in which a deified man 'the prophet of Bacchos dwelt'.¹⁸¹ A few lines earlier the Muse uttering these words has referred to an 'obligation' of Persephone to honour the friends of Orpheus.

Pausanias, in a passage already mentioned in relation to Orpheus' tomb, refers to an oracle given to the Leibethrans from an oracle of Dionysos in Thrace: 'In Larisa I heard another story, how that on Olympus is a city Leibethra, where the mountain faces Macedonia, not far from which city is the tomb of Orpheus. The Leibethrans, it is said, received out of Thrace an oracle from Dionysus, stating that when the sun should see the bones of Orpheus, then the city of Leibethra would be destroyed by a boar'.¹⁸² Once again, the Dionysiac oracle in Thrace is related to Orpheus. A final later passage referring to an oracle in relation to Orpheus is from Philostratus' (2nd A.D.) *Heroicus*. This time, the oracle is located on Lesbos, which is in close proximity to Thrace:

---

179 Hdt. 7.111. See also Ov. *Met.* X.77.
180 schol. in Eur. *Hec.* 1267, Schwartz Vol. 1, p.89.
181 Eur. *Rhes.* 967–74. For text see p.12.
182 Paus. IX.30.9: ἤκουσα δὲ καὶ ἄλλον ἐν Λαρίσῃ λόγον, ὡς ἐν τῷ Ὀλύμπῳ πόλις οἰκοῖτο Λίβηθρα, ᾗ ἐπὶ Μακεδονίας τέτραπται τὸ ὄρος, καὶ εἶναι οὐ πόρρω τῆς πόλεως τὸ τοῦ Ὀρφέως μνῆμα· ἀφικέσθαι δὲ τοῖς Λιβηθρίοις παρὰ τοῦ Διονύσου μάντευμα ἐκ Θρᾴκης, ἐπειδὰν ἴδῃ τὰ ὀστᾶ τοῦ Ὀρφέως ἥλιος, τηνικαῦτα ὑπὸ συὸς ἀπολεῖσθαι Λιβηθρίοις τὴν πόλιν.

χρῆσθαι μὲν γὰρ καὶ τοῖς οἴκοι μαντείοις τοὺς Ἀχαιούς, τῷ τε Δωδωναίῳ καὶ τῷ Πυθικῷ καὶ ὁπόσα μαντεῖα εὐδόκιμα Βοιωτιά τε ἦν καὶ Φωκικά· Λέσβου δὲ ὀλίγον ἀπεχούσης τοῦ Ἰλίου, στέλλειν ἐς τὸ ἐκεῖ μαντεῖον τοὺς Ἕλληνας. ἔχρα δέ, οἶμαι, ἐξ Ὀρφέως· ἡ κεφαλὴ γὰρ μετὰ τὸ τῶν γυναικῶν ἔργον ἐς Λέσβον κατασχοῦσα, ῥῆγμα τῆς Λέσβου ᾤκησε καὶ ἐν κοίλῃ τῇ γῇ ἐχρησμῴδει. ὅθεν ἐχρῶντό τε αὐτῇ τὰ μαντικὰ Λέσβιοί τε καὶ τὸ ἄλλο πᾶν Αἰολικὸν καὶ Ἴωνες Αἰολεῦσι πρόσοικοι, χρησμοὶ δὲ τοῦ μαντείου τούτου καὶ ἐς Βαβυλῶνα ἀνεπέμποντο. πολλὰ γὰρ καὶ ἐς τὸν ἄνω βασιλέα ἡ κεφαλὴ ᾖδε, Κύρῳ τε τῷ ἀρχαίῳ χρησμὸν ἐντεῦθεν ἐκδοθῆναι λέγεται· "τὰ ἐμά, ὦ Κῦρε, σά"· καὶ ὁ μὲν οὕτως ἐγίνωσκεν, ὡς Ὀδρύσας τε καὶ τὴν Εὐρώπην καθέξων, ἐπειδὴ Ὀρφεύς ποτε, μετὰ τοῦ σοφοῦ καὶ δυνατὸς γενόμενος, ἀνά τε Ὀδρύσας ἴσχυσεν ἀνά τε Ἕλληνας ὁπόσοι τελεταῖς ἐθείαζον...

He says the Greeks usually employed the oracles near their home, like Dodona, Delphi and other well-known oracles of Boeotia and Phocis; but since Lesbos was near Troy they sent to the oracle there. I suppose that the prophecy in this case came from Orpheus. For after the women had done their work, his head drifted to Lesbos, lodged in a chasm on Lesbos and sang its prophecies in an earthen chamber. Therefore it was used for prophecies not only by the Lesbians, but also by all the Aeolians and their neighbors the Ionians; oracles from this shrine were even sent to Babylon, and the head sang many prophecies relating to the king of Persia. And a prophecy from there is said to have been given to Cyrus the great: "What was mine, O Cyrus, will be yours." He understood by this that he was going to conquer the Odrysians and Europe, since Orpheus had been powerful as well as poetic, with authority among Odrysians and all the Greeks who were inspired by his rituals.[183]

An earlier passage from Phanocles (3rd B.C.) might reveal the mythological background of the Lesbian oracle:

τοῦ δ'ἀπὸ μὲν κεφαλὴν χαλκῷ τάμον, αὐτίκα δ'ὑπῆν.
εἰς ἅλα Θρηϊκίην ῥῖψαν ὁμοῦ χέλυϊ
ἥλῳ καρτύνασαι, ἵν'ἐμφορέοιντο θαλάσσῃ
ἄμφω ἅμα, γλαυκοῖς τεγγόμεναι ῥοθίοις
τὰς δ'ἱερῇ Λέσβῳ πολιὴ ἐπέκελσε θάλασσα
ἠχὴ δ'ὣς λιγυρῆς πόντον ἐπέσχε λύρης,
νήσους τ'αἰγιαλούς θ'ἁλιμυρέας, ἔνθα λίγειαν
ἀνέρες Ὀρφείην ἐκτέρισαν κεφαλήν
ἐν δὲ χέλυν τύμβῳ λιγυρὴν θέσαν...

The women cut off his head with their bronze and straightaway they threw it in the sea with his Thracian lyre of tortoiseshell, fastening them together with a nail, so that both would be borne on the sea, drenched by the grey waves. The hoary sea brought them to land on holy Lesbos [...] and thus the lyre's clear ring held sway over the sea and the islands and the sea-soaked shores, where the men gave the clear-sounding head of Orpheus its funeral rites.[184]

---

183 Philostr. *Her.* 28.8–11 (Tr. Rusten).
184 Stob. *Ecl.* 20.2.47, IV 461–2 = Phan. fr.1.10–17 Powell (Tr. Burges Watson).

There is a version of the story where the head continues to talk/sing even after it is cut off which is mentioned by some later writers such as Virgil, Conon, Lucian and Ovid.[185] Lucian (early 2nd A.D.) gives the additional information that the Lesbians buried Orpheus' head in the place where the Βάκχειον was later built, indicating a connection of Orpheus with the Bacchic cult at the island of Lesbos.[186] Pausanias might also be referring to this story, even though he does not identify the head as that of Orpheus, when he says that some fishermen in Lesbos picked up with their nets a head made of olive-wood which looked divine. After they inquired Pythia whose god it was, she told them to worship Dionysos Phallen (Διόνυσον Φαλλῆνα). Since then, 'the people of Methymna kept for themselves the wooden image out of the sea, worshipping it with sacrifices and prayers, but sent a bronze copy to Delphi'.[187] Bearing in mind these passages, some of a historical nature and others literary, it seems that there was at least from the 5th century B.C. oracle(s) of Dionysos in Thrace and possibly other areas such as Lesbos. These oracles appear to have been closely related to Orpheus, through texts being written through his voice or through his prophesying head, or through other ways. The possible existence of such oracles not only supports the close relation of Dionysiac practices to Orphic ideas, but also the perception of Orpheus as a religious authority.

Apart from Thrace, several authors point to a relation between Orphic and Phrygian practices. The following passage by Plutarch connects Orpheus and Phrygia not only in terms of the nature of the rites but also to a specific doctrine:

> εὖ μὲν οὖν λέγουσι καὶ οἱ λέγοντες ὅτι Πλάτων τὸ ταῖς γεννωμέναις ποιότησιν ὑποκείμενον στοιχεῖον ἐξευρών, ὃ νῦν ὕλην καὶ φύσιν καλοῦσιν, πολλῶν ἀπήλλαξε καὶ μεγάλων ἀποριῶν τοὺς φιλοσόφους· ἐμοὶ δὲ δοκοῦσι πλείονας λῦσαι καὶ μείζονας ἀπορίας οἱ τὸ τῶν δαιμόνων γένος ἐν μέσῳ θέντες θεῶν καὶ ἀνθρώπων καὶ τρόπον τινὰ τὴν κοινωνίαν ἡμῶν συνάγον εἰς ταὐτὸ καὶ συνάπτον ἐξευρόντες, εἴτε μάγων τῶν περὶ Ζωροάστρην ὁ λόγος οὗτός ἐστιν, εἴτε Θράκιος ἀπ' Ὀρφέως εἴτ' Αἰγύπτιος ἢ Φρύγιος, ὡς τεκμαιρόμεθα ταῖς ἑκατέρωθι τελεταῖς ἀναμεμειγμένα πολλὰ θνητὰ καὶ πένθιμα τῶν ὀργιαζομένων καὶ δρωμένων ἱερῶν ὁρῶντες.

> They put the case well who say that Plato, by his discovery of the element underlying all created qualities, which is now called 'Matter' and 'Nature' has relieved philosophers of many great perplexities; but, as it seems to me, those persons have resolved more and greater perplexities who have set the race of demigods midway between gods and men, and

---

185 Linforth, 1941, p.128–129; Verg. G. IV 523; Luc. Ind.11; Ov. Met. XI 50.
186 Luc. Ind.11. He also says that his lyre was kept as a relic in Apollo's temple at Lesbos. This perhaps indicates an Orphic connection of the two gods, which will be discussed more in Chapter 4.
187 Paus. X.19.3.

have discovered a force to draw together, in a way, and to unite our common fellowship - whether this doctrine comes from the wise men of the cult of Zoroaster, or whether it is Thracian and harks back to Orpheus, or is Egyptian, or Phrygian, as we may infer from observing that many things connected with death and mourning in the rites of both lands are combined in the ceremonies so fervently celebrated there.[188]

The doctrine which Plutarch refers to may be the one analysed a few lines later:

Ἕτεροι δὲ μεταβολὴν τοῖς τε σώμασιν ὁμοίως ποιοῦσι καὶ ταῖς ψυχαῖς, ὥσπερ ἐκ γῆς ὕδωρ ἐκ δ᾽ ὕδατος ἀὴρ ἐκ δ᾽ ἀέρος πῦρ γεννώμενον ὁρᾶται, τῆς οὐσίας ἄνω φερομένης, οὕτως ἐκ μὲν ἀνθρώπων εἰς ἥρωας ἐκ δ᾽ ἡρώων εἰς δαίμονας αἱ βελτίονες ψυχαὶ τὴν μεταβολὴν λαμβάνουσιν. ἐκ δὲ δαιμόνων ὀλίγαι μὲν ἔτι χρόνῳ πολλῷ δι᾽ ἀρετὴν καθαρθεῖσαι παντάπασι θειότητος μετέσχον· ἐνίαις δὲ συμβαίνει μὴ κρατεῖν ἑαυτῶν, ἀλλ᾽ ὑφιεμέναις καὶ ἐνδυομέναις πάλιν σώμασι θνητοῖς ἀλαμπῆ καὶ ἀμυδρὰν ζωὴν ὥσπερ ἀναθυμίασιν ἴσχειν.

Others postulate a transmutation for bodies and souls alike; in the same manner in which water is seen to be generated from earth, air from water, and fire from air, as their substance is borne upward, even so from men into heroes and from heroes into demigods the better souls obtain their transmutation. But from the demigods a few souls still, in the long reach of time, because of supreme excellence, come, after being purified, to share completely in divine qualities. But with some of these souls it comes to pass that they do not maintain control over themselves, but yield to temptation and are again clothed with mortal bodies and have a dim and darkened life, like mist or vapour.[189]

Plutarch refers in a negative way to the reincarnation of the unlawful souls as a vapour-like life. This is a strange simile since it is not clear why vapour/mist would be considered as dim and dark. However, as we will see in the following chapter, according to Orphic mythology, the mortal race came into existence from the vapours/smoke of the Titans after being blasted by Zeus' thunderbolt for dismembering infant Dionysos. The crime of the Titans has been interpreted as a primal guilt which the human race carries, condemning them to a mortal incarnated existence. Several other passages from Plutarch, as we will see, seem to allude to this Orphic myth. In any case, we can once more see the parallelism of Orphic ideas to rites taking place in Egypt and Phrygia. Herodotus identifies the Phrygians' ancestry to a tribe dwelling in Macedonia/Thrace which moved to Phrygia at some point: 'As the Macedonians say, these Phrygians were called Bryges as long as they dwelt in Europe, where they were neighbors of the Macedonians; but when they changed their home to Asia, they changed their name also

---

[188] Plut. *De def. or.* 10.414f–415a (Tr. Babbitt)= OF524T.
[189] Plut. *De def. or.* 10.415b–c (Tr. Babbitt).

and were called Phrygians'.[190] Whether or not there was historically a migration from Macedonia to Anatolia is discussed by Carrington who seems to lean on the latter possibility.[191] However, a more recent study by White Muscarella attests that: 'Recent excavations at Gordion have revealed below the destroyed Phrygian city (ca. 700 B.C.) an early Iron Age settlement with handmade coarse ware, which is followed by a settlement that contains the earliest Phrygian pottery forms. The handmade ware relates to that from Troy and the Balkans, and is considered firm evidence of the historically recorded migration of the Brygians into Anatolia'.[192] This could be the reason of the transmission of Orphic rites and beliefs into Phrygia through Macedonia and Thrace from early times. This could also explain mythological traditions in reference to the Phrygian king Midas in relation to Dionysos who gave him a pair of donkey ears after he captured Silenus, and Orpheus who is identified by Ovid as the one who showed Midas the Bacchic rites: 'And after they bound him in garlands, they led him to their king Midas, to whom with the Cecropian Eumolpus, Thracian Orpheus had shown all the Bacchic rites.'[193] The capture of Silenus by Midas is depicted in an Attic red-figure stamnos dated at mid-5th century B.C. on which Midas is shown with donkey ears, confirming that the myth was known at least as early as the 5th century B.C.[194]

2.3.3 Asia Minor – Cyzicus

I referred earlier to the cult of Kore Soteira in Sparta and to Pausanias' testimony that it was instituted by Orpheus. Kore Soteira was worshipped in only two other places, Megalopolis (in Lacedaemonia) and Cyzicus (modern Balikesir Province in Turkey), a Milesian colony founded towards the middle of the 7th century in Asia Minor.[195] The reason I am discussing this cult is because there is evidence

---

190 Hdt. 7.73.1: οἱ δὲ Φρύγες, ὡς Μακεδόνες λέγουσι, ἐκαλέοντο Βρίγες χρόνον ὅσον Εὐρωπήιοι ἐόντες σύνοικοι ἦσαν Μακεδόσι, μεταβάντες δὲ ἐς τὴν Ἀσίην ἅμα τῇ χώρῃ καὶ τὸ οὔνομα μετέβαλον ἐς Φρύγας (Tr. Godley).
191 Carrington, 1977.
192 White Muscarella, 2013, pp.549.
193 Ar. *Plut.* 288; Arist. fr.44 Rose; Ov. *Met.* XI.85–102 (Tr. More).
194 Captured Silenus in front of Midas who has donkey ears. Attic red-figure stamnos. c.440 B.C. Attributed to the Midas Painter. London, British Museum. E447 (1851,0416.9). *LIMC*: Midas (S) 38.
195 Paus. VIII.31.1–8.

from Cyzicus which indicates an association with Orphic ideas. There is an abundance of Cyzicus' coins representing Kore Soteira dating as early as the 4th century B.C. and they are very frequent in imperial times.[196] The youthful Dionysos is often depicted on the reverse, or a winged serpent siting on a cista. These might be references to the Orphic myth in which Persephone gives birth to Dionysos after copulating with a serpent-shaped Zeus.[197] The cista points to the Orphic myth of Dionysos' dismemberment since following his second birth from Zeus he was carried in a *liknon* encircled by a serpent.[198] Further depictions on the coins also point to a Dionysiac context. For example in one case we have Kore Soteira on the one side and on the reverse a *liknophoros*, Eros, a Maenad with a tympanum and Pan. The *liknon* in itself also points to an Eleusinian association but the presence of the Maenad and the serpent is what makes these coins Dionysiac in nature too. The association of Persephone with Dionysiac motifs can only make sense in an Orphic context through their relationship as mother and son.

Other evidence point to a familiarity of the people of Cyzicus with Orphic mythology. According to Apollonius Rhodius' (3rd B.C.) *Argonautika* the people of Cyzicus were the Doliones whom he calls 'earthborn' (Γηγενεές).[199] They were monsters who initially offered hospitality to the Argonauts but later attacked them; most were slain by Herakles. Considering the cult of Kore Soteira and its association with Dionysos, this might be a reference to the descent of the human race from the dead Titans' soot after being blasted by Zeus' thunderbolt for murdering Dionysos. The Titans are also *gēgenees*, and even though we cannot be sure why the Doliones were *gēgenees*, a link to Orphic mythology is possible. Finally, in relation to the mysteries of Kore Soteira at Cyzicus, several inscriptions contain terms such as ἐξηγητής, ἀφηγούμενος, ἱερομνημῶν which in other cases refer to religious officials.[200] This suggests that, as in the case of Phlya, Cyzicus might have also regulated the conduct of the mysteries and – if indeed Orphic in nature – puts them in contrast to mystery rites performed by itinerant priests. In one inscription we find the phrase: 'ἐξηγητὴς τῶν μεγάλων μυστηρίων τῆς Σωτείρας Κόρης' (interpreter of the great mysteries of Kore Soteira).[201] This phrase, along with the previous terms, indicates an oral 'indoctrination' into the meaning of the mysteries, something which as we saw might have taken place in Athens

---

196 Hasluck, 1910, p.211.
197 See p.148.
198 See p.87.
199 Ap. Rhod. *Argon*, I.989–1012. See also Hecataeus, *FGrHist* 1 F 219; Strabo, 12.4.4.
200 Hasluck, p.212–13.
201 *Ath. Mitth.* VI.42. Hasluck, p.213.

for Orphic works and beliefs. It appears to have a different function in this case than elsewhere, where the term ἐξηγητής usually refers to official interpreters of sacred law who would answer enquiries on how to act in a specific situation.[202] This type of official is mentioned in Eleusinian contexts too and the mysteries of Kore Soteira are possibly of an Eleusinian nature, but based on the above discussion, an Orphic or Orphic/Eleusinian influence is also probable or an interchange of elements between the two.[203] This might be implied in Pausanias' reference to a temple of Demeter Eleusinia in Sparta inside which a wooden image of Orpheus can be found.[204] If such an ἐξηγητής, thus, was responsible for explaining the nature of the mysteries to the initiates, then in this case this role acquires a civic capacity since he was appointed by the city.

In any case, the fact that in two out of the three places where Kore Soteira was worshipped we have Orphic links to the cult, strongly idicates that this cult's rites were Orphic in nature. As alredy mentioned, the epithet Soteira points to eschatological ideas of a blissful afterlife, which as we established were part of Orphism.

2.4 Orphic writings and their authors

Several sources attribute specific works to Orpheus, or identify some works as Orphic. We already saw references to hymns and poems, some of which were attested as being used during rites (for example, those at Phlya). Orpheus is often mentioned by many writers as a part of a canonical list of poets, consisting of Orpheus, Musaeus, Homer and Hesiod.[205] Clement of Alexandria quotes Hippias (5th B.C.) saying: 'Some of these things may have been said by Orpheus, some by

---

[202] Official exponents of sacred law: Pl. *Leg.* 6.759c–e, 6.775a. Also, Dem. 47.68. Isae. 8.39. Theophr. *Char.* 16.6.
[203] E.g. in Lysias, 6.10 (Tr. Lamb): 'Yet Pericles, they say, advised you once that in dealing with impious persons you should enforce against them not only the written but the unwritten laws also, which the Eumolpidae follow in their exposition, and which no one has yet had the authority to abolish or the audacity to gainsay, laws whose very author is unknown: he judged that they would thus pay the penalty, not merely to men, but also to the gods'. The Eumolpidae were the hereditary priests of Eleusis.
[204] Paus. III.20.5.
[205] Linforth, 1941, p.104–107.

Musaeus briefly in various places, some by Hesiod and Homer, some by other poets...'.²⁰⁶ These poets are mentioned in the same order in Plato's *Apology*: 'Or again, what would any of you give to meet with Orpheus and Musaeus and Hesiod and Homer?'²⁰⁷ Similarly in *Ion*, with Hesiod excluded: 'And from these first rings – the poets – are suspended various others, which are thus inspired, some by Orpheus and others by Musaeus; but the majority are possessed and held by Homer'.²⁰⁸ Also, in a fragment of Alexis' *Linus* (4th B.C.): '(Linus) Yes, go over and pick any papyrus roll you like out of there and then read it – (Heracles) Absolutely! (Linus) examining them quietly, and at your leisure, on the basis of the labels. Orpheus is in there, Hesiod, tragedies, Choerilus, Homer, Epicharmus, prose treatises of every type'.²⁰⁹ By the 5th–4th century B.C., thus, Orpheus was considered to be one of the 'classics' as well as one of the representatives of poetry. The above references also suggest that his works were widely known, easily accessible and thus not secret.

What could these Orphic works be about? From what we have already discussed we should expect them to deal with religious matters. Once more we have to rely on references to the mythical Orpheus since he was supposed to be their author. The theogony attributed to Orpheus in the Derveni Papyrus, clearly evidences the existence of Orphic religious poetry already from the 5th century B.C.²¹⁰ Isocrates, in his speech *Busiris* (composed c.390–385 B.C.) says that Orpheus was one of the poets who wrote all kind of preposterous and outrageous

---

206 Clem. Al. *Strom.* 15.2 (Tr. Gallop) = Hippias DK 6B: τούτων ἴσως εἴρηται τὰ μὲν Ὀρφεῖ τὰ δὲ Μουσαίωι, κατὰ βραχὺ ἄλλωι ἀλλαχοῦ, τὰ δὲ Ἡσιόδωι, τὰ δὲ Ὁμήρωι, τὰ δὲ τοῖς ἄλλοις τῶν ποιητῶν...
207 Pl. *Ap.* 41a: ἢ αὖ Ὀρφεῖ συγγενέσθαι καὶ Μουσαίῳ καὶ Ἡσιόδῳ καὶ Ὁμήρῳ ἐπὶ πόσῳ ἄν τις δέξαιτ' ἂν ὑμῶν.
208 Pl. *Ion* 536b: ἐκ δὲ τούτων τῶν πρώτων δακτυλίων, τῶν ποιητῶν, ἄλλοι ἐξ ἄλλου αὖ ἠρτημένοι εἰσὶ καὶ ἐνθουσιάζουσιν, οἱ μὲν ἐξ Ὀρφέως, οἱ δὲ ἐκ Μουσαίου· οἱ δὲ πολλοὶ ἐξ Ὁμήρου κατέχονταί τε καὶ ἔχονται (Tr. Lamb). See also Ar. *Ran.* 1031–1036: Aeschylus: 'That's the sort of thing that poets should practice. Just consider how beneficial the noble poets have been from the earliest times. Orpheus revealed mystic rites to us, and taught us to abstain from killings; Musaeus instructed us on oracles and cures for diseases; Hesiod on agriculture, the seasons for crops, and ploughing. And where did the godlike Homer get respect and renown if not by giving good instruction in the tactics, virtues, and weaponry of men?' (Tr. Henderson).
209 Ath. *Deipn.* IV 164b–c (Tr. Olson) = Alexis fr.135: βιβλίον | ἐντεῦθεν ὅ τι βούλει προσελθὼν γὰρ λαβέ, | ἔπειτ' ἀναγνώσει – (Ηρ.) πάνυ γε. (Λι.) διασκοπῶν | ἀπὸ τῶν ἐπιγραμμάτων ἀτρέμα τε καὶ σχολῇ. | Ὀρφεὺς ἔνεστιν, Ἡσίοδος, τραγῳδίαι, | Χοιρίλος, Ὅμηρος, † Ἐπίχαρμος, συγγράμματα | παντοδαπά.
210 For the date of the *Papyrus* and the *Theogony* see p.206.

tales about the gods and this is why he got punished by being torn to death.[211] More specifically, he says that these poets – he only mentions Orpheus by name – 'not only have they imputed to them <the gods> thefts and adulteries, and vassalage among men, but they have fabricated tales of the eating of children, the castrations of fathers, the fetterings of mothers, and many other crimes'.[212] In a passage from Athenagoras (2nd A.D.), Orpheus is said to be the one who invented (ἐξηῦρεν) the gods' names and their generation stories, something also mentioned in the Derveni Papyrus.[213] This enhances the argument that Orpheus was regarded as a religious authority in the classical period. Some scholars disagree. Edmonds argues that Orpheus' status as a religious figure was created by Christian Apologists and especially Clement's influence on the Church Fathers through his portrayal of Orpheus, and that he did not have the same status in classical times.[214] This position is unconvincing, since we have sources as early as the 5th century B.C. such as Aristophanes, Plato and Euripides among others, and the abundance of Classical sources discussed in the previous section, linking Orpheus to religious practices and poetry, and referring to him as the institutioner of the most sacred rites.

Orphic works must have been also of a mythological nature since as already mentioned, a passage from the *Parian Marble* notes that Orpheus wrote a poem about the rape of Persephone and Demeter's search for her daughter.[215] Such a poem might have been related to the institution of the Eleusinian Mysteries. Clement of Alexandria quotes from an Orphic poem, which as he says is related to the Eleusinian mysteries, referring at the same time to Orpheus as the μυσταγωγὸς who is better suited to give the 'official' version of the myth:

ὡς εἰποῦσα πέπλους ἀνεσύρετο, δεῖξε δὲ πάντα
σώματος οὐδὲ πρέποντα τύπον· παῖς δ' ἦεν Ἴακχος,
χειρί τέ μιν ῥίπτασκε γελῶν Βαυβοῦς ὑπὸ κόλποις·
ἡ δ' ἐπεὶ οὖν μείδησε θεά, μείδησ' ἐνὶ θυμῷ,
δέξατο δ' αἰόλον ἄγγος, ἐν ᾧ κυκεὼν ἐνέκειτο.

---

211 Van Hook, 1945, p.101.
212 Isoc. *Bus*. 11.38: οὐ γὰρ μόνον κλοπὰς καὶ μοιχείας καὶ παρ' ἀνθρώποις θητείας αὐτοῖς ὠνείδισαν, ἀλλὰ καὶ παίδων βρώσεις καὶ πατέρων ἐκτομὰς καὶ μητέρων δεσμοὺς καὶ πολλὰς ἄλλας ἀνομίας κατ' αὐτῶν ἐλογοποίησαν (Tr. Van Hook).
213 Athenagoras, *Leg. pro Christ*. 18.3. DP Col.XXII 1.
214 Edmonds, 2013, p.30–33.
215 *Marm. Par*. (*IG* 12 (5), 444.14–15) = OF513T and OF1096T. For text see fn.55–56. Linforth, 1941, p.193. Athenagoras, *Leg. pro Christ*. 18.3.

> This said, she (Baubo) drew aside her robes, and showed a sight of shame; child Iacchus was there, and laughing, plunged his hand below her breasts. Then smiled the goddess, in her heart she smiled, and drank the draught from out the glancing cup.[216]

We should not rule out the possibility that this quotation comes from the poem identified in the Parian Marble as written by Orpheus about the myth of Demeter and her search for her daughter Persephone/Kore, or at least that this was an episode included in the poem. The passage from the *Parian Marble* as we saw earlier (p.24) notes that Eumolpus instituted the Eleusinian mysteries and made known the works of his father, Musaeus.[217] Eumolpus was the founder of the family from which the *hierophant* for the Eleusinian mysteries came from and even though we have testimonies for poems of his we cannot date them.[218] In another passage from Plato's *Republic*, Adeimantus indicates that a poem by Musaeus' son Eumolpus related to blessings in the afterlife and as 'the story goes' (τῷ λόγῳ) referred to an everlasting drunk state for the pious.[219] Adeimantus, as discussed at the beginning of this chapter, goes on to describe the punishments, and relate the rewards to the just and the punishments to the unjust.[220] It is significant, thus, that we have testimonies about a specific poem by Musaeus and his son Eumolpus which referred to the blessings of the afterlife. The purpose of such a poem must have been without a doubt didactic and if we take into consideration the inscription from the *Parian Marble*, it is possible that a work attributed to Musaeus or Eumolpus provided an aetiology of the mysteries and perhaps was used in the indoctrination of the initiates. Concerning this matter and in relation to Plato's passage, Parker argues that: 'Very possibly then the underworld of flowery meadows and mud and sieve-carriers and a judgement on moral criteria was described in one or several poems ascribed to Orpheus or Musaeus or Eumolpus'.[221] An Orphic poem, thus, might have served as the *hieros logos* of the Eleusinian mysteries. This is in accordance with my earlier discussion of Orphic texts being related to the development of mysteries. It also seems that (some) Orphic writings were of a didactic nature.

In relation to Orphic works we have references which do not specify the title of the work and references that do. In the first category belong cases such as the ones discussed in the first half of this chapter: e.g. Aristotle referring to the Orphic

---

216 Clem. Al. *Protr.* 2.17 (Tr. Butterworth).
217 *Marm. Par.* (*IG* 12 (5), 444, 15). For text see fn.55.
218 Parker, 2007, p.361–362.
219 Pl. *Resp.* 2.363c–d.
220 See p.21 ff.
221 Parker, 2007, p.363.

poems which include a theory about the airy substance of the soul or Pausanias who mentions the short Orphic hymns that in poetic beauty come next to those of Homer.[222] We also have quoted verses from unspecified Orphic works such as the ones of the Derveni Papyrus whose author quotes verses – or paraphrases – from an Orphic theogonical poem which must have been in circulation from the 5th century B.C.[223] Also, Plato quotes Orpheus several times:

1. λέγει δέ που καὶ Ὀρφεὺς ὅτι "Ὠκεανὸς πρῶτος καλλίρροος ἦρξε γάμοιο, | ὅς ῥα κασιγνήτην ὁμομήτορα Τηθὺν ὄπυιεν".
2. "ἕκτῃ δ' ἐν γενεᾷ", φησὶν Ὀρφεύς, "καταπαύσατε κόσμον ἀοιδῆς"
3. γέλωτ' ἂν παρασκευάζοιεν τῶν ἀνθρώπων ὅσοις φησὶν Ὀρφεὺς "λαχεῖν ὥραν τῆς τέρψιος·"

1. 'Orpheus, too, says – "Fair-flowing Ocean was the first to marry and he wedded his sister Tethys, daughter of his mother."'
2. '"But with the sixth generation", says Orpheus, "cease the rhythmic song"'
3. ...would furnish a theme for laughter to all the men who, in Orpheus' phrase, "have attained the full flower of joyousness".[224]

The first two quotations are of a religious/theogonical nature; the third one is harder to define. Damascius also refers to an Orphic Theogony mentioned by Eudemus (c.370–300 B.C.) and one by Hieronymos and Hellanikos.[225] We can be sure, thus, that Orphic works were known at least from the 5th century B.C. and the variety in terms of genre and date of the authors quoting Orpheus, is perhaps indicative of their wide circulation. On the other hand, references to specific Orphic works are attested in the *Suda*, a quite late source (10th A.D.) and I have listed them in eight categories based on the sources and their titles, as shown in the table in the following page (p.75).[226]

What, then, were these works supposed to be about? Initially, we can see that these categories correspond to Orpheus' and Orphic practices' representation by the ancient authors discussed earlier in this chapter. The ritualistic, religious, divinatory and mythological categories all reflect Orpheus' persona as the establisher of mysteries and the writer of *hieroi logoi* as represented in our ancient

---

222 Arist. *De an.* A5 410b29–33. Paus. IX.30.12.
223 Discussed in Chapter 5.
224 1: Pl. *Cra.* 402b (Tr. Fowler). 2: Pl. *Phlb.* 66c. (Tr. Fowler). 3: Pl. *Leg.* 2.669d (Tr. Bury).
225 Damas. *De Princ.* 123–124 (III 160, 17–162, 19 Westerink). A work called ἐν ταῖς ἀστρολογικαῖς ἱστορίαις (*Astronomical Histories*) is attributed to Eudemus (fr.143; fr.144; fr.145 Wehrli).
226 Suda s.v. Ὀρφεύς. ο' 654–660.

sources, which also often refer to the oracles of Orpheus and to his curative practices such as the tablets mentioned in Euripides' *Alcestis*.[227] The categories of astronomy and philosophy, also reflect (yet again) the scientific/philosophical side of the Orphic works and beliefs; beliefs about the nature of the soul, about the origins of the universe and the human race and even astronomical observations such as the one mentioned by Heraclides Ponticus. In general, the majority of these Orphic works seem to have a didactic, explanatory or aetiological nature and as Edmonds argues: '...Orpheus' reputation for wisdom of all kinds ensured that didactic poems continued to be attributed to him'.[228] If we were to discover evidence tomorrow which proved that all of these works actually existed and were attributed to Orpheus, this would not be out of place with the Orphic image created by our ancient sources. Unfortunately, however, we do not have many verses surviving from these works and indeed not many ancient testimonies in general which would verify their existence, let alone help us define their contents and use. Nonetheless, the fact that their nature, as far as we can define it, corresponds to our ancient testimonies about Orpheus and Orphics, should validate that the ancient perception of Orphism was fairly consistent.

Tab. 1: List of Orphic works with a specific title along with sigla of Bernabé's edition

Astronomical	Δωδεκαετηρίδες (OF726T-OF752F)	= On the cycle of twelve years
	Ἐφημερίδες (OF753T-OF767F)	= Journals
	Περὶ σεισμῶν (OF778F)	= On earthquakes (shakings)
	Περὶ δραπετῶν (OF777F)	= On escaping
	Περὶ ἐμβάσεων (OF779F)	= On embarking
	Περὶ καταρχῶν (OF780T-OF781V)	= On beginnings
	Ἀστρονομία (OF782T)	= Astronomy
	Μετέωρα (OF836T)	= On those floating in mid-air
	Γεωργία (OF768T-OF776F)	= Georgics
Divinatory	Χρησμοί (OF806T-OF810F)	= Oracles
	Ἀμμοσκοπικά/Ἀμμοσκοπία (OF805)	= Divination by sand
	Ὠιοσκοπικά/Ὠιοθυτικά (OF811T)	= Divination by eggs
Nature	Λιθικά	= On stones (4th A.D.)

---

227 Eur. *Alc.* 962–72. See p.63.
228 Edmonds, 2013, p.147.

	Φυσικά (OF800T-OF803F) = On nature	
	Ἰδιοφυῆ (OF792T-OF794F) = On peculiar nature	
	Ἱεροστολικά (OF606T) = On Sacred Vestments	
Ritualistic	Καταζωστικὸν (OF608T) = Katazostikon (Girdles?)	
	Καθαρμοί (OF607T) = Purifications	
	Κλήσεις Κοσμικαὶ (OF609T) = Cosmic Calls	
	Νυκτέλια (OF613T) = Nocturnals	
	Ὅρκοι (OF614T-OF624V) = Oaths	
	Θυηπολικὸν (OF692T-OF694T) = Sacrificial	
	Τελετάς (OF840T) = On mysteries	
	Θρονισμοὺς Μητρῴους (OF602T-OF605T) = Enthronements of the Mother	
	Βακχικά (OF835T) = Bacchic matters	
	Ἐπιγράμματα (OF706F) = Epigrams	
Religious	Σωτήρια (OF839T) = Deliverances	
	Ὀνομαστικὸν (OF838T) = On naming (epic)	
	Εἰς Ἅιδου κατάβασις (OF707T-OF717) = Descent into Hades	
Mythological	Κορυβαντικὸν (OF610T-OF611T) = Korybantic	
	Τριασμούς/Τριαγμοῖς (OF506T and OF841T) = On Triads	
Philosophical	Εἰς τὸν Ἀριθμὸν Ὕμνος (OF695T-OF705F) = Hymn to the number	
	Κρατήρ (OF409T-OF412F) = Mixing vessel	
Various	Μικρότερος Κρατήρ (OF413F-OF416F) = Smaller mixing vessel	
	Λύρη (OF417F-OF420T) = Lyre	
	Πέπλον (OF406T-OF407F) = Robe	
	Σφαῖρα (OF408T) = Sphere	
	Δίκτυον (OF403T-OF405F) = Net	
	Νόμοι (OF837T) = Customs	
	Νεωτευτικὰ (OF612T)	
	Χωρογραφία (OF842T) = Maps	

The most extensive passage from the *Suda*, which refers to the majority of Orphic works, notes that these are considered to be written by Orpheus but also gives their supposed authors: Ion of Chios, Theognetos the Thessalian, the Pythagorean Kerkops, Onomakritos, Timockles the Syracusan, Persinos the Milesian, Zopyros of Heraklea, Nikias of Elea, Herodikos of Perinthos and Brontinos.[229] Edmonds, notes: 'Some of these attributions may go back to Epigenes in the fourth century BCE, but few firm conclusions can be drawn about the dates of any particular works'.[230] He also suggests that the Orphic works of the late archaic and classical period probably dealt with similar cosmological issues to other thinkers of the time. Some of the above authors are attested as Pythagoreans; this is one of the reasons which has led to the association of Orphism with Pythagoreanism. According to Clement of Alexandria (2nd–3rd A.D.), Ion of Chios (5th B.C.) stated that Pythagoras had attributed some of his works to Orpheus:

> καὶ τοὺς μὲν ἀναφερομένους εἰς Μουσαῖον χρησμοὺς Ὀνομακρίτου εἶναι λέγουσι, τὸν Κρατῆρα δὲ τὸν Ὀρφέως Ζωπύρου τοῦ Ἡρακλεώτου τήν τε Εἰς Ἅιδου κατάβασιν Προδίκου τοῦ Σαμίου. Ἴων δὲ ὁ Χῖος ἐν τοῖς Τριαγμοῖς καὶ Πυθαγόραν εἰς Ὀρφέα ἀνενεγκεῖν τινα ἱστορεῖ. Ἐπιγένης δὲ ἐν τοῖς Περὶ τῆς εἰς Ὀρφέα ποιήσεως Κέρκωπος εἶναι λέγει τοῦ Πυθαγορείου τὴν Εἰς Ἅιδου κατάβασιν καὶ τὸν Ἱερὸν λόγον, τὸν δὲ Πέπλον καὶ τὰ Φυσικὰ Βροντίνου.

And the *Oracles* ascribed to Musæus are said to be the production of Onomakritos, and the *Cratēres* of Orpheus the production of Zopyrus of Heraclea, and *The Descent to Hades* that of Prodicus of Samos. Ion of Chios relates in the *Triagmi*, that Pythagoras ascribed certain works [of his own] to Orpheus. Epigenes, in his book respecting the poetry attributed to Orpheus, says that *The Descent to Hades* and the *Sacred Discourse* were the production of Cercops the Pythagorean; and the *Peplus* and the *Physics* of Brontinus.[231]

Moreover, Iamblichus (3rd–4th A.D.) in his *Life of Pythagoras* suggests that Orpheus had influenced Pythagoras. He mentions that the Pythagorean theology based on numbers is to be found in Orphic writings and that Pythagoras composed his work *Concerning the Gods* based on Orphic ideas.[232] He also claims that Pythagoras worshipped the gods in a way similar to Orpheus: 'placing them in images and in brass, not conjoined to our forms, but to divine receptacles; because they comprehend and provide for all things, and have a nature and *morphē* similar to the universe'.[233] Epigenes (4th B.C.) – according to Clement's passage –

---

229 Suda s.v. Ὀρφεύς. ο' 654.
230 Edmonds, 2013, p.144–148.
231 Clem. Al. *Strom.* 1.21.131.3 (Tr. Alexander) The translations of *Stromata* by Clement are by Alexander, W.L. from Coxe *et al.* 1885.
232 Iambl. *VP* 28.145 and 28.146.
233 Iambl. *VP* 28.151: ὅλως δὲ φασὶ Πυθαγόραν ζηλωτὴν γενέσθαι τῆς Ὀρφέως ἑρμηνείας τε καὶ διαθέσεως καὶ τιμᾶν τοὺς θεοὺς Ὀρφεῖ παραπλησίως, ἱσταμένους αὐτοὺς ἐν τοῖς ἀγάλμασι καὶ τῷ χαλκῷ, οὐ ταῖς ἡμετέραις συνεζευγμένους μορφαῖς, ἀλλὰ τοῖς ἱδρύμασι τοῖς θείοις, πάντα περιέχοντας καὶ πάντων προνοοῦντας καὶ τῷ παντὶ τὴν φύσιν καὶ τὴν μορφὴν ὁμοίαν ἔχοντας.

and the *Suda* both attribute a work about an *Hieron Logon* to Cercops the Pythagorean. The title given by *Suda* suggests a work including many(?) *hieroi logoi*: Ἱεροὺς Λόγους ἐν ῥαψῳδίαις κδ'. The *Suda* also gives Theognetus the Thessalian as another possible author.[234] According to Cicero (1st B.C.), the Pythagoreans claimed that Cercops was the author of 'the Orphic poem which we possess'.[235] Cicero's description indicates the poem's survival since they have it in their possession at the time and it could have been the *Hieros Logos* mentioned by Epigenes and the *Suda* – or the *Descent to Hades* attributed to Cercops only by Epigenes. Rohde, commenting on the authorship of these Orphic poems, noted that many of the authors are from Southern Italy and suggested that Orphic societies must have already be in existence in those areas when Pythagoras arrived there around 530 and also that he must have been the one who was influenced by Orphic ideas and not the other way around.[236] In any case, a Pythagorean origin of some of the Orphic works cannot be excluded. Several scholars have discussed the relation between Orphism and Pythagoreanism since Rohde, an issue which is particularly difficult due to the paucity of Pythagorean writings.

It is worth discussing in more detail the work *Physika* because not only do we have some more evidence on this work but also the case of the *Physika* might be an example of how Orphic mythological works were used for aetiological purposes. In general, until the end of the 5th century B.C., most works of Greek literature – prose and verse – did not have a specific title and many of the works of the Pre-Socratic philosophers were labelled as Τὰ Φυσικὰ or Περὶ Φύσεως, while after Aristotle this specific title was attributed to Epicurean and Stoic investigations of the natural world.[237] According to Harpokration's lexicon: 'In Orpheus' *Physika* the Tritopatores were named Amalkeides, Protoklea and Protokreon, and they were the door-keepers and guardians of the winds'.[238] Phanodemus also says in his sixth book that only the Athenians sacrificed and prayed to them for the generation of children, when they were about to get married.[239] We get some information about the Tritopatores from some other Atthidographers, such as Philochorus, Demon and Clitodemus. As mentioned in the *Suda*, Philochorus said

---

Iamblichus is probably referring here to the sphere and points to the egg out of which Phanes sprung in the *Rhapsodies*.
234 *Suda* s.v. Ὀρφεύς (III 564,29 Adler).
235 Cic. *De Nat. Deo.* 1.107: '*et hoc Orphicum carmen Pythagorei ferunt cuiusdam fuisse Cercopis.*'
236 Rohde, 1894, p.337.
237 Gagné, 2007, p.8.
238 Harp. *Lex.* s.v. Τριτοπάτορες: 'ἐν δὲ τῷ Ὀρφέως Φυσικῷ ὀνομάζεσθαι τοὺς Τριτοπάτορας Ἀμαλκείδην καὶ Πρωτοκλέα καὶ Πρωτοκρέοντα, θυρωροὺς καὶ φύλακας ὄντας τῶν ἀνέμων'.
239 Phanodemus, DFHG p.367 F4 = *Suda* v. Τριτοπάτορες.

that the Tritopatores were the first of all beings and that men called them their ancestors and believed that they were the sons of the Earth and the Sun (whom Philochorus calls Apollon).[240] Clitodemus in his *Exēgētikon* makes them the children of Earth and Heaven and says that their names are Kottos, Briareus and Gyges, who in Hesiod's *Theogony* are the Hundred-handed ones.[241] Demon in the *Atthis* said that the Tritopatores were the winds.[242] It is very difficult to draw conclusions about the content of the *Physika* but based on the little evidence we have available, it must have dealt with the nature of the winds and mentioned the Tritopatores. This kind of cosmogonical mythical content would place this particular work in the first and earliest category of works labelled with the title *Physika*.

Based on the perception of the Tritopatores, it is possible that one of the subjects of the Orphic *Physika* was the generative force of air. As we saw, according to Clement the *Physika* were attributed to the Pythagorean Brontinus.[243] He is supposed to have lived in the 6th century B.C. and came from Metapontum, an Achaean colony situated on the gulf of Tarentum in southern Italy. Syrianus says that Brontinus said that there is a cause which surpasses intelligence and the *ousia*, in power and dignity – even though we do not know in which work he expressed this idea.[244] It might be that this 'cause' was air as a generative force. This is an idea which relates to Aristotle's attestation mentioned earlier that in the so-called Orphic poems it is said that the nature of the soul is airy and that it was born upon the winds.[245] One of the Orphic poems which Aristotle mentions could have been a work such as the *Physika*. If this is the case, a combination of cosmogonical mythology with philosophical/scientific theories might have been a trait of Orphic thought and philosophy. As we will see, similar ideas are present in the Derveni Papyrus whose author interprets an Orphic poem and equates Zeus with aer. He quotes the following verse from the poem: 'Zeus is the head, Zeus the middle, and from Zeus is everything fashioned.'[246] Here we see mythology being combined with elemental theories, with a cosmogonic aetiological purpose through the image of Zeus/aer as creator of the cosmos. Piano also argues that the airy constitution of the soul is one of the main ideas of the Derveni author and suggests that the Erinyes and daimons mentioned in the Derveni papyrus are a

---

240 Philochorus DFHG p.384 F2 = *Suda* v. Τριτοπάτορες.
241 Clitodemus, DFHG p.363 F19; Hes. *Th*. 148–150.
242 Demon, DFHG p.378 F2 = *Suda* v. Τριτοπάτορες.
243 Clem. Al. *Strom*. 1.21.131.
244 Syrianus, *In Arist. Met*. 165,33–166,6 Kroll.
245 Arist. *De an*. 410b–411a. See p.14.
246 DP, Col.XVII.12.

different kind of manifestation of the divine air, associating with this idea their perception as winged beings and their identification with souls.[247]

Apart from the Derveni Papyrus, surviving verses from the *Orphic Rhapsodies* show a preoccupation with both cosmogonical myth, and the nature of the soul/eschatology in relation to the element of aer. The following verses from the *Rhapsodies* are characteristic: 'Men's soul is rooted in the aether (OF436F) and as we draw in air, we collect the divine soul (OF422F)'.[248] This is a scientific statement which also has a religious explanatory purpose. The generative force of aer is also expressed in mythological terms in the *Rhapsodies* through the entity of Protogonos and its birth. Protogonos, the first divine entity and creator of the world was born from an egg which was generated by aether and chronos.[249] He is even called 'the son of enormous Aether' [Πρωτόγονος Φαέθων περιμήκεος Αἰθέρος υἱός], and he is the one who creates the cosmos and everything that is in it. If Protogonos is the son of aether/aer and he is the generator of the cosmos then this places aer at the beginning of all creation. Aristophanes in *Birds* might be alluding to this episode of the Orphic Theogony when he refers to the ὑπηνέμιον ᾠόν (wind-egg), an egg lifted by the wind which was produced by Night.[250] The comic effect of Aristophanes' Theogony, as Gagné notes, was the placing of a wind-egg, which is sterile, at the beginning of the world's generation.[251] Gagné also argues that another element of the comic effect might have been that this was a reference to a recognisable theogonical tradition of the time which did attribute to the winds a generative power; the comic effect would be enhanced if, as I argue, that tradition already included an egg born by the aer/aether. Such a theogonical tradition could be an Orphic one. If this is true, then the generative force of aer was a recognisable trait of Orphism or Orphic literature. The above ideas will be more evident when I discuss the major Orphic sources in Chapters 4–6 since the generative force of aer will be prominent. A conclusion which can be made based on the above is that Orphic cosmogonical ideas were religious/philosophical and expressed through allegorical mythology. In other words, there was perhaps a deeper meaning and interpretation of the Orphic myths and literature which was not immediately visible.

---

247 Piano, 2016, p.270–273.
248 OR89.
249 OR6–8. The *Rhapsodies* will be discussed in detail in Chapter 6.
250 Ar. *Av.* 695. More on this suggestion in Chapter 6.
251 Gagné, 2007, p.6.

In relation to specific authors mentioned in our sources, we should take a closer look to Ion of Chios (c.485–420 B.C).[252] Some fragments survive from his *Triagmos*, which could be the one mentioned in the *Suda*: ἔγραψε Τριαγμοὺς, λέγονται δὲ εἶναι Ἴωνος τοῦ τραγικοῦ.[253] A passage from Harpokration (2nd A.D.) quotes from this philosophical treatise:

> ΙΩΝ: ...ἔγραψε δὲ μέλη πολλὰ καὶ τραγῳδίας καὶ φιλόσοφόν τι σύγγραμμα τὸν Τριαγμὸν ἐπιγραφόμενον, ὅπερ Καλλίμαχος ἀντιλέγεσθαί φησιν ὡς Ἐπιγένους· ἐν ἐνίοις δὲ καὶ πληθυντικῶς ἐπιγράφεται Τριαγμοί, καθὰ Δημήτριος ὁ Σκήψιος καὶ Ἀπολλωνίδης ὁ Νικαεύς. ἀναγράφουσι δὲ ἐν αὐτῷ τάδε 'ἀρχὴ ἥδε μοι τοῦ λόγου. πάντα τρία καὶ πλέον οὐδὲν οὐδὲ ἔλασσον. τούτων τῶν τριῶν ἑνὸς ἑκάστου ἀρετὴ τριάς, σύνεσις καὶ κράτος καὶ τύχη.'

> ION: ...he composed many lyric poems and tragedies and some kind of philosophical treatise entitled *Triad* ('triagmos'). Callimachus says that its authorship is disputed, and in some copies it is entitled *Triads*, in the plural (according to Demetrius of Scepsis and Apollonides of Nicaea). They record in it the following: he says 'This is the beginning of my account. All things are three, and there is nothing more or less than these three. Of each one thing the excellence is a triad, intelligence and power and fortune'.[254]

Baltussen, in his chapter on Ion's *Triagmoi*, taking into consideration the most important previous works on him by West, Dover and Huxley, discusses only a possible Pythagorean influence, without considering a possible Orphic one.[255] This demonstrates the problems with many modern discussions of material which could be approached differently from an Orphic point of view. Various possibilities should be considered in this case. This work could be influenced by both Orphism and Pythagoreanism, or influenced by one or the other, or written by a Pythagorean but circulated as Orphic, or Pythagorean but with the same title as an Orphic work. Unfortunately, the fact that we do not have much written Pythagorean material and that very few verses survive from such specific Orphic works prevents us from drawing confident conclusions about their origin.

The names, however, with the strongest link to Orphism are Onomakritos and Musaeus. The first is mentioned by Herodotus (5th B.C.) as an Athenian diviner

---

252 Huxley, 1965, p.30–31.
253 *Suda* s.v. Ὀρφεύς (III 564.29 Adler) = OF841T.
254 Harp. s.v. Ἴων = DK 36A1, B1. See also Chapter 6, p.306 ff about Chios in relation to Orphic Phanes.
255 Baltussen, 2007, p.318: 'I therefore agree with Dover (1986, 30) that Ion wore his Pythagoreanism rather lightly, trying his hand at yet another mode of expression' (p.318).

who had put the oracles of Musaeus in order.[256] Musaeus, as we saw, was considered by some to be Orpheus' son, teacher or student.[257] He is frequently mentioned alongside Orpheus and in the Berlin Papyrus (1st–2nd A.D.) it is noted that Musaeus wrote down the hymns of Orpheus as he heard them from him.[258] A passage from Tatian (2nd A.D.) informs us that: '...all the works attributed to him (Orpheus) were composed by Onomakritos the Athenian, who lived during the reign of the Pisistratids, about the fiftieth Olympiad' and that 'Musaeus was a disciple of Orpheus'.[259] Onomakritos is related to Orphism in another passage from Pausanias, who notes that he took the name of the Titans from Homer, where they were gods in Tartarus, and 'in the orgies he composed for Dionysos made the Titans the authors of the god's sufferings'.[260] This can only point to the Orphic myth of the dismemberment of the infant Dionysos by the Titans, which will be discussed in Chapter 3.

Considering, the discussion in this section, we can see that very few firm conclusions can be extracted on the authorship of the Orphic works. We can, however, see that Orphic works were of a mythological, religious and scientific/cosmogonical nature and most probably had an allegorical interpretation. There was also an aetiological connection between Orphic mythology/works and Orphic rites and some Orphic works were in circulation at least from the 5th century B.C.

2.5 Conclusion

The non-Orphic sources we have examined in this chapter suggest the existence of people who 'were affiliated to Orpheus', and were defined by others in reference to their interpretation of Orphic texts and the performance of mysteries. The nature of the Orphic texts must have been complex and not simply theogonical/mythological since scientific/cosmogonical and eschatological ideas are associated to them, such as the airy nature of the soul which enters the body

---

256 Hdt. 7.6.2.
257 See Clem. Al., *Strom*. 1.21.107.4; Euseb., *Chron*. II 46 Schone.
258 OF383T = Pap. Berol. 44, ed. Buecheler. I have already referred to the passage from the Parian Marble mentioning that Eumolpus instituted the Eleusinian mysteries and made known the works of Musaeus. See p.73 and fn.55.
259 Tatianus, *Ad Gr*. 41.3: τὰ εἰς αὐτὸν ἐπεισφερόμενά φασιν ὑπὸ Ὀνομακρίτου τοῦ Ἀθηναίου συντετάχθαι, γενομένου κατὰ τὴν Πεισιστρατιδῶν ἀρχήν, περὶ τὴν πεντηκοστὴν Ὀλυμπιάδα; 41.4: τοῦ δ'Ὀρφέως Μουσαῖος μαθητής (Tr. Ryland in Coxe et al. 1885).
260 *Iliad*, 14.279. Paus. VIII.37.5: συνέθηκεν ὄργια καὶ εἶναι τοὺς Τιτᾶνας τῷ Διονύσῳ τῶν παθημάτων ἐποίησεν αὐτουργούς (Tr. Jones).

through breathing. This association of Orphic texts to eschatological matters is consistent in non-Orphic sources. Some preliminary ideas related to Orpheus, Orphic texts or those affiliated to him is a duality of body and soul and the perception of incarnation as something bad or a punishment, especially through the Orphic interpretation of the word *sēma* (body) as a tomb for the soul. Also, the release of the soul presupposes the payment of a penalty. Orphic texts, then, are related in non-Orphic sources with beliefs about the soul, reincarnation, the afterlife and post-mortem rewards or punishments which are linked to leading a just life.

The Orphic texts are often referred to as *logoi* or *hieroi logoi* and we also find the use of the term *bibloi*. There must have been a variety of them in circulation as well as forgeries. We have also established that there was a level of secrecy about the Orphic texts. This appears to have been not so much of the text themselves but of their interpretation or application in mysteries and rites. The secrecy might also have been due to them being highly revered and thus considered *arrēta*. We also established two different attitudes in our sources in relation to Orphic texts or rites. It was suggested that the negative attitude is not towards the Orphic texts or rites themselves but towards those who use them for the wrong purposes, namely itinerant priests who use a combination of religious elements and not exclusively Orphic ones. *Orpheotelestae* or itinerant priests, then, are just one strand of Orphism. Many non-Orphic sources also relate to Orpheus several Orphic rites performed in areas all around Mainland Greece, Magna Graecia and Asia Minor. In many cases these rites are also linked to texts, and are of an orgiastic, Dionysiac nature. They involve deities such as Demeter Chthonia and Kore Soteira, while in the majority of the cases they are in honour of chthonic deities. In some cases such as Phlya there must have been official religious personelle involved such as *dadouchoi* or *exēgētes*, which distinguishes them from the ones performed by itinerant priests. I also suggested the possible existence of oracles of Dionysos from at least the 5th century B.C. in Thrace and possibly other areas, and in several cases they were closely related with Orpheus through texts being written through his voice, or through his prophesying head, or through other ways. The association of Dionysos, then, with prophecy might have been due to an Orphic tradition.

We also established that the works attributed to Orpheus are thematically consistent with the representation of Orphism in non-Orphic sources, meaning that they deal with religious, ritualistic, mythological, philosophical and scientific matters. The fact that some of these Orphic texts were attributed to Pythagoreans demonstrates the close similarities between Orphic and Pythagorean ideas, through either interchange of ideas or direct influence. The particular example of the *Physika* that we examined shows how Orphic mythological texts might have been used for aetiological purposes for cosmological/eschatological ideas such as the airy nature of the soul. In general, considering the non-Orphic sources discussed so far, thus, I am more inclined to accept the existence of specific Orphic beliefs and mysteries which were closely related to Orphic texts, rather than deny such a possibility.

3 The Myth of Dionysos' Dismemberment

In the following chapters we will be discussing, as part of the analysis, Dionysos' Dismemberment myth, conventionally known and referred to by scholarship as the Zagreus myth. Getting familiar with the complexities and the scholarship behind the Zagreus myth is essential for the discussion of sources such as the gold tablets and the *Orphic Rhapsodies*. I will, thus, analyse it in detail before proceeding and this is why I have devoted a separate chapter for its discussion. Certainly, as we will proceed in the following chapters more information will become available which is relevant to this myth, but in the present chapter I will be confined to the material whose discussion does not relate to the gold tablets, Derveni Papyrus and the *Orphic Rhapsodies*. I will be concerned with matters such as the narrative of the myth, its date and interpretation, as well as with the various sources through which it survives. The way that scholarship has treated this myth has greatly affected the way Orphism has been defined. Some scholars place it at the centre of Orphic beliefs while others believe that some of its major components have been later additions or interpolations.[261] Before, however, proceeding to the discussion of this myth it is essential to get familiar with the narrative. The following table demonstrates the narrative of the Dismemberment myth and provides the sources along with their dates, through which each section of the myth has survived:[262]

Tab. 2: Sources of Dionysos' Dismemberment myth

Mythological Narrative	Sources	Date
Dionysos (Zagreus) as a child of Zeus and Persephone is declared by Zeus as the new king of the cosmos.	Callim. fr. 43, 117 Pf. = OF34V	3rd B.C.–6th A.D.
	Procl. *In Cra.* 306b, 55.5 = OF299F = OR79	
	Procl. *In Cra.* 396b, 52.26 = OF166F = OR79	
	Procl. *In Ti.* 42e, III.316.3 = OF300F = OR80	
	Olymp. *In Phd.* p.85.9 = OF299F = OR79	
	Diod. Sic. V.75.4 = OF283F	

---

[261] The representatives of these opposing views are Bernabé and Edmonds respectively.
[262] Information taken from: Guthrie, 1952, p.82–83; Graf and Johnston, 2013, p.67. The myth is also included in my reconstruction of the *Rhapsodies* [OR78-OR87]. In Bernabé's edition of the fragments the myth is included in the *Rhapsodies* and the relevant fragments are OF296F to OF331F.

Mythological Narrative	Sources	Date
The Titans, the sons of Gaia and Ouranos, who were jealous of Dionysos plot against him.	Diod. Sic. V.75.4 = OF283F Nonnus *Dion*. VI 169ff = OF308V = OR81 Luc. *Salt*. 39 = OF304F (IV) Dam. *De Princ*. 94 Olymp. *In Phd*. 1.3 = OF304F	1st B.C. – 6th A.D.
With the help of some toys and objects (a mirror, knucklebones, apples, a sphere, a bull-roarer, a spinning-top and a fleece) – and by painting their face white – the Titans distract Dionysos and take him away from his guardians, the *Kuretes*. They slay and then dismember him, cutting him into seven pieces.	Diod. Sic. V.75.4 = OF283F (See also Diod. III.62.2-8) Luc. *Salt*. 39 = OF311F(IX) Gurôb Papyrus, 29-30 = OF578F (Text in p.265) See also OF209-12 (Kern) Plut. *De esu carn*. I 7 996c = OF313F(I) Arn. *Adv. nat*. 5.19 = OF313F(III) Titans' white face: Harp. Lex. s.v. ἀπομάττων = OF308V(II) Nonnus *Dion*. VI 169ff = OF308V = OR81 Clem. Al. *Protr*. 2.17.2–18.1 = OF306F Phld. *On Piety* 192–3 (ll. 4956–4969) (ed. Obbink). Procl. *In Ti*. 35a, II.145.18ff = OF311F + OF314F = OR82 Procl. *In Ti*. 23d–e, I.142.24. Procl. *In Ti*. 29a-b, I.336.29. (Mirror made by Hephaestus). Procl. *In R*. I.94.5. Olymp. *In Phd*. 3.14. Plotinus, *Enn*. IV.3.12 = OF309F(I) Procl. *In Ti*. 33b, II.80.19 = OF309F(IV) Dam. *In Phd*. I.129 = OF309F(II) Procl. *In Ti*. II 146.9 = OF311F(I) (See also OF310F)	3rd B.C. – 4th A.D.
They then boil his limbs and taste them.	Euphorion (3rd B.C.), fr.14[263] Plut. *De esu carn*. 1.7 996c = OF313F(I)	3rd B.C. – 6th A.D.

---

[263] See p.91 for discussion of this passage.

Mythological Narrative	Sources	Date
	Clem. Al. *Protr.* 2.18.1-2 cf. Euseb. *Praep. Enag.* 2.3.25 = OF318F(I)[264]	
	Olymp. *In Phd.* I.3 = OF313F(II)	
Zeus orders Apollo to collect Dionysos' limbs (in some sources Dionysos is referred to as Wine – *Oinos*).[265]	Olymp. *In Phd.* 67c, p.43.14 = OF322F(III) = OR83	5th A.D. – 6th A.D.
	Procl. *In Ti.* 35b, II.198.2ff = OF322F(IV) = OR83	
	Procl. *In Cra.* 406c p.108.13 = OF321F = OR84	
The heart is saved by Athena (or Rhea) and taken to Zeus and the limbs are collected by Apollo and taken to Mount Parnassos at Delphi.	Olymp. *In Phd.* p.111.14 = OF209 (Kern) = OR83	2nd/1st B.C. – 6th A.D.
	Olymp. *In Phd.* 67c, p.43.14 = OF322F(III)	
	Procl. *In Ti.* 35b, II.198.2 = OF322F(IV) = OR83	
	Procl. *In Prm.* 130b, 808.25 = OF314F(II)	
	Procl. *In Ti.* 35a, II.145.18 = OF314F(I) = OR82	
	Procl. *In Cra.* 406c, 108.13 = OF321F = OR84	
	Procl. *In Alc.* 103a, p.344.31 = OF316F(I)	
	Dam. *In Phd.* 1.129 = OF322F(II)	
	Heart collected by Athena: Clem. Al. *Protr.* 2.18.1 = OF315F(I)	
	Parts collected by Rhea: Phld. *On Piety* 192-3 (ll. 4956–4969) ed. Obbink.	
	Clem. Al. *Protr.* 2.18.2 cf. Euseb. *Praep.Enag.*2.3.25 = OF322F	
Zeus brings back to life (gives birth to) Dionysos using his saved heart. Hipta receives the newborn Dionysos and places him in a *liknon* (winnowing-fan) encircled by a snake on her head.	Procl. *Hymn* 7.11-15 = OF327F(II)	2nd/1st B.C. – 5th A.D.
	Procl. *In Ti.* 30b, I.407.22ff = OF296F = OR85	
	Rebirth: Phld. *On Piety* 192-3 (ll. 4956–4969) ed. Obbink.	
	Brought to life by Zeus: Aristid. *Or.* 41.2 = OF328F(I).	
	Diod.Sic. III.62.2-10 = OF328F(V)	
	Hipta: Procl. *In Ti.* 30b, I.407.22ff = OF329F(I);	

---

[264] 'Later on Zeus appeared; perhaps, since he was a god, because he smelt the steam of the flesh that was cooking, which your gods admit they receive as their portion (γέρας λαχεῖν)' (Tr. Butterworth).
[265] For the location of Dionysos' tomb at Delphi see p.120.

Mythological Narrative	Sources	Date
	Procl. *In Ti.* 34b, II.105.28 = OF329F(II); Orphic Hymn XLVIII Ἵπτας	
As a punishment for their actions, Zeus throws a thunderbolt at the Titans and burns them. From their remaining ashes/smoke (sometimes blood), the human race comes to life.	Olymp. *In Phd.* 61c, p.2.21. = OF320F(I) = OR86	1st A.D. – 6th A.D.
	Clem. Al. Protr. 2.18.2 cf. Euseb. Praep. Enag.2.3.25 = OF318F(I)	
	Procl. In R. 2.74.26 = OF320F(II); Dam. In Phd. 1.7-8 = OF320F(IV)	
	Dio Chrys. Or. 30.10 = OF320F(VII)	
	Orphic Hymn XXXVI Τιτάνων = OF320(X)	
	Procl. In R. II.338.10 = OF338F. Also, see commentary on OR92.	
This is why we as humans have a twofold nature: a mortal and wicked Titanic one and a divine and heavenly Dionysiac one, since the Titans contained Dionysos inside them, by eating him.	Dionysiac Nature: Olymp. In Phdr. 1.3 = OF304F(I), OF318F(III), OF320F(I);	1st A.D. – 6th A.D.
	Olymp., In Phdr. 8.7 = OF320F(III);	
	Dam. *In Phdr.* 1.4-9 = OF299F(II)	
	Procl. *In Cra.* 400d1-5, 77.25-78.4	
	Titanic nature: Plut. *De esu carn.* 1.7, 996b = OF313F(I)	
	Relation to soul: Origen, *C. Cels.* 4.17 = OF326F(IV)	

As Gantz records, the earliest mention of the name Zagreus is in the lost Greek epic *Alkmaionis*, which is considered to be part of the Theban cycle, and he is not mentioned in Homer or Hesiod.[266] He is referred to in Aischylos' *Sisyphos* and the *Aigyptioi* as a personage of the Underworld, or Hades himself. By the time of Kallimachos he is identified with Dionysos, since he refers to the birth of Dionysos Zagreus.[267] An interesting passage referring to Zagreus is the one found in Euripides' *Cretans*:

> Φοινικογενοῦς τέκνον Εὐρώπης
> καὶ τοῦ μεγάλου Ζηνός, ἀνάσσων

---

[266] Fr.3 *PEG*: 'Mistress Earth, and Zagreus highest of all the Gods'. Gantz, 1993, p.118.
[267] *TrGF* Aes. fr.228 and fr.5. Kall. fr.43.117 Pf. Dionysos is identified with Hades in various earlier sources, e.g. Herakleitos B15 D-K: 'But Hades is the same as Dionysos, for whom they rave and perform the Lenaia'.

Κρήτης ἑκατομπτολιέθρου·
ἥκω ζαθέους ναοὺς προλιπών,
οὓς αὐθιγενὴς στεγανοὺς παρέχει
τμηθεῖσα δοκοὺς Χαλύβῳ πελέκει
καὶ ταυροδέτῳ κόλλῃ κραθεῖσ᾽
ἀτρεκεῖς ἁρμοὺς κυπάρισσος.
ἁγνὸν δὲ βίον τείνομεν ἐξ οὗ
Διὸς Ἰδαίου μύστης γενόμην
καὶ νυκτιπόλου Ζαγρέως βούτης
τὰς ὠμοφάγους δαῖτας τελέσας,
Μητρί τ᾽ ὀρείᾳ δᾷδας ἀνασχὼν
μετὰ Κουρήτων
βάκχος ἐκλήθην ὁσιωθείς.
πάλλευκα δ᾽ ἔχων εἵματα φεύγω
γένεσίν τε βροτῶν καὶ νεκροθήκας
οὐ χριμπτόμενος, τήν τ᾽ ἐμψύχων
βρῶσιν ἐδεστῶν πεφύλαγμαι.

Son of Phoenician-born Europa and of great Zeus –you who rule Crete and its hundred cities! I have come here from the most holy temple whose roof is provided from native cypress-wood cut into beams with Chalybean axe and bonded in exact joints with ox-glue. Pure is the life I have led since I became an initiate of Idaean Zeus and a servitor of night-ranging Zagreus, performing his feasts of raw [food]; and raising torches high to the mountain Mother among the Curetes, I was consecrated and named a celebrant. In clothing all of white I shun the birthing of men, and the places of their dead I do not go near; against the eating of animal foods I have guarded myself.[268]

Nilsson considers this fragment to be uncertainly Orphic because it 'offers a mixture of all kind of mystic cults' such as the Cretan Zeus, the Great Mother and Bacchos, but nevertheless important since it 'proves the identification of Zagreus and Dionysos in the 5th century B.C'.[269] Even though I will discuss this passage in more detail in the following chapters in relation to the Derveni Papyrus and the gold tablets, I can still note some significant points. This passage has a clear ritual context and the fact that Zagreus is mentioned alongside deities of mystery cults implies that he was also associated with mysteries. This is reinforced by the word *mystēs* which is a title of mystery initiates and in the case of the Eleusinian Mysteries it indicates the first initiation stage. This word is also found on several gold tablets, again indicating a ritual context.[270] Also, deities mentioned in the above passage, such as the Great Mother and Bacchos – and possibly Cretan

---

[268] Eur. *Cretans,* fr.472 (Tr. Collard).
[269] Nilsson, 1935, p.222.
[270] See fn.499.

Zeus – are also mentioned in the gold tablets.[271] The last verse is particularly important since the avoidance of eating 'living food' was a characteristic of the so-called *Ophikos Bios* as we saw in Chapter 2, and it thus gives an Orphic element to this passage as does the emphasis on purity.[272] By becoming an initiate of Idaean Zeus, Zagreus and the Mountain Mother, the person has become a βάκχος. The importance of this passage, then, is that it allows for an identification of Zagreus with Dionysos and his association with Dionysiac rites from the 5th century B.C.

We firstly need to determine whether or not the Zagreus myth can be called Orphic. Even though the available evidence is quite scarce, the little evidence we do have supports an Orphic identity for the myth. But what would the term Orphic identity mean? It would mean that the particular myth at some point became associated with Orpheus' name and was interpreted in a specific way which led to the formation of specific rituals which in turn became known to have been instituted by Orpheus. Would this allow us to 'label' the particular mysteries and their participants Orphic(s)? In my opinion, yes, in the same way we would identify the Eleusinian Mysteries as a single entity in the history of ancient Greek religion. Meaning, that the Eleusinian initiates interpreted a well-known myth in a particular way, performed mysteries based on the myth and expected specific outcomes from the performance of these mysteries. This would not exclude the possibility that the Zagreus myth was known in non-Orphic circles or interpreted in different ways by people not participating in such mysteries, or even that it inspired other mysteries or rites as well. It would, however, most probably mean that the Orphic interpretation which gave rise to mysteries was a specific one – as in the case of the Eleusinian Mysteries.

The most important source that links the Dismemberment Myth to Orphics or Orpheus is Philodemos (2nd–1st B.C.) who in his work *On Piety* refers to the three births of Dionysos:

[Διονύσωι δέ φασιν]
[εἶναι τρεῖς γενέ-]
[σεις, μίαν μὲν του]-
των 'τὴν ἐκ' τῆς μ[ητρός],
ἑτέραν δὲ τ[ὴν ἐκ]
τοῦ μηροῦ [Διός, τρί]-
την δὲ τὴ[ν ὅτε δι]-
ασπασθεὶς ὑ[πὸ τῶν]

---

[271] D4, D1, D2, D5.
[272] See p.28.

Τιτάνων Ῥέ[ας τὰ]
μέλη συνθε[ίσης]
ἀνεβίω{ι}. κἀν [τῆι]
Μοψοπία[ι] δ'Εὐ[φορί]-
ων [ὁ]μολογεῖ [τού]-
τοις. [οἱ] δ' Ὀρ[φικοὶ]
καὶ παντά[πασιν]
ἐνδιατρε[ίβουσιν].²⁷³

[They say that Dionysos had three births: one] of these is that from his m[other], another [that from] the thigh [of Zeus], and the third the one [when] he was torn apart by [the] Titans and came back to life after Rhea reassembled his limbs. (space) And in [his] *Mopsopia* Euphorion agrees with this (account); [the] Orph[ics] too dwell on (it) intensively.

The importance of this passage lies firstly to its early date and secondly to the reference to Orphics who dwell on this myth intensively. Henrichs argues that the term 'Orphics' was used by Hellenistic scholars such as Apollodorus of Athens 'for the authors of writings that circulated under Orpheus' name'.²⁷⁴ The word παντάπασιν translates as 'altogether', 'wholly' or 'absolutely' and this could signify that this myth had a central role in Orphism or Orphic writings.²⁷⁵ The two sources which Philodemos quotes in the above passage, namely Euphorion (3rd B.C.) and the writers of the Orphic works, push the date of the dismemberment of Dionysos and his restoration by Rhea – and also the association to Orphics – to the earliest Hellenistic period and further back.²⁷⁶ Euphorion is in fact quoted in another instance in relation to the Zagreus myth in Tzetzes' scholia to Lycophron:

ἐτιμᾶτο δὲ καὶ Διόνυσος ἐν Δελφοῖς σὺν Ἀπόλλωνι οὑτωσί· οἱ Τιτᾶνες τὰ Διονύσου μέλη σπαράξαντες Ἀπόλλωνι ἀδελφῷ ὄντι αὐτοῦ παρέθεντο ἐμβαλόντες λέβητι, ὁ δὲ παρὰ τῶι τρίποδι ἀπέθετο, ὥς φησι Καλλίμαχος (fr.643 Pf.) καὶ Εὐφορίων (fr.14) λέγων· 'ἐν πυρὶ Βάκχον δῖον ὑπερφίαλοι ἐβάλοντο'.

Dionysus, too, was honoured in Delphi together with Apollo, in the following way. The Titans tore asunder Dionysus' limbs, threw them into a cauldron, and set it before his brother Apollo. Apollo stowed it away beside his tripod, as we learn from Callimachus [fr.643 Pf]

---

273 Phld. *On Piet*. N 247 III (*HV²* II 44) 1–13 (Tr. Henrichs). Philodemos refers to the Dismemberment Myth again in a later part of *On Piety*: N 1088 XI 14–21 (*HV²* II 9) = OF59F.
274 Henrichs, 2011, p.65.
275 LSJ παντάπασιν.
276 Henrichs, 2011, p.66.

and Euphorion [fr.14], who says: 'In(to) the fire those arrogant beings [Titans] cast divine Bacchus'.[277]

The line quoted from Euphorion indicates that the Titans not only dismembered Dionysos but also cooked him. It seems, therefore, that Euphorion was familiar with this myth, and the detail of the Titans' tasting Dionysos' flesh could be dated back to the 3rd century B.C.[278]

Other authors also connect this myth to Orpheus. Diodorus refers to some *teletas* related to Dionysos in the following passage: 'This god was born in Crete, men say, of Zeus and Persephone, and Orpheus has handed down the tradition in the initiatory rites that he was torn in pieces by the Titans'.[279] According to Diodorus, not only were there rites related to the dismemberment of Dionysos by the Titans, but these rites were created by Orpheus. Also, Clement specifically refers to a Dionysiac rite based on the Zagreus myth and whose author was Orpheus. He even quotes two verses from the relevant Orphic work:

Τὰ γὰρ Διονύσου μυστήρια τέλεον ἀπάνθρωπα· ὃν εἰσέτι παῖδα ὄντα ἐνόπλῳ κινήσει περιχορευόντων Κουρήτων, δόλῳ δὲ ὑποδύντων Τιτάνων, ἀπατήσαντες παιδαριώδεσιν ἀθύρμασιν, οὗτοι δὴ οἱ Τιτᾶνες διέσπασαν, ἔτι νηπίαχον ὄντα, ὡς ὁ τῆς Τελετῆς ποιητὴς Ὀρφεύς φησιν ὁ Θράκιος·
"κῶνος καὶ ῥόμβος καὶ παίγνια καμπεσίγυια,
μῆλά τε χρύσεα καλὰ παρ' Ἑσπερίδων λιγυφώνων."

The mysteries of Dionysus are of a perfectly savage character. He was yet a child, and the Curetes were dancing around him with warlike movement, when the Titans stealthily drew near. First they beguiled him with childish toys, and then, – these very Titans – tore him to pieces, though he was but an infant. Orpheus of Thrace, the poet of the Initiation, speaks of the:
"Top, wheel and jointed dolls, with beauteous fruit
Of gold from the clear-voiced Hesperides".[280]

Also, we saw earlier that Pausanias claims that the dismemberment myth was created by Onomakritos who founded the *orgia* of Dionysos and 'made the Titans the authors of the god's sufferings'.[281] The possible existence of rituals based on

---

277 Euphorion fr.14 (Tr. Lightfoot) = Tzetz. In *Lycophr. Alex.* 208.
278 Edmonds, in his analysis of the myth, (2008a) mentions this verse by Euphorion only in the footnotes and gives a very different edition: Καλλίμαχος καὶ Εὐφορίων λέγων ἂν πυρὶ Βάκχαν δίαν ὑπὲρ φιάλην ἐβάλοντο – no information given on the edition of the text –.
279 Diod. Sic. V.75.4: τοῦτον δὲ τὸν θεὸν γεγονέναι φασὶν ἐκ Διὸς καὶ Φερσεφόνης κατὰ τὴν Κρήτην, ὃν Ὀρφεὺς κατὰ τὰς τελετὰς παρέδωκε διασπώμενον ὑπὸ τῶν Τιτάνων (Tr. Oldfather).
280 Clem. Al. *Protr.* 2.15 (Tr. Butterworth).
281 Guthrie, 1950, p.320; Paus. VIII.37.5–6. See p.82.

the Zagreus myth is corroborated by the fact that the toys which the Titans used to trick Dionysos are mentioned in the Gurôb Papyrus (dated to the 3rd century B.C.) in a Dionysiac context reminiscent of the Zagreus myth: ']and consume what has been given to you | put in]to the basket, | spinning-top, bull-roarer, knuckle-bones |]mirror'.[282] The toys are identified as *symbola* in a clearly ritualistic context. I will discuss, however, the Gurôb Papyrus in detail in Chapter 5. Finally, the Orphic identity of this myth is further supported by the fact that our non-Orphic sources do not provide anything more than brief allusions to the story.

But what is the modern scholarly approach to the Zagreus myth? Comparetti connected the gold tablets with the Zagreus myth as early as 1882, and this association has influenced scholarship ever since.[283] The idea of an original sin being a central component of Orphism, as it stems from the interpretation of the Zagreus myth, has travelled from Comparetti (1882) to Rohde (1894) and Harrison (1903) and is represented today by Bernabé and followed by several other scholars.[284] Gagné's is the most recent study on ancestral fault in general and it discusses the Zagreus' myth to some extent in relation to the belief to an original sin. He rejects the belief that there was a doctrine of ancestral fault or inherited guilt in ancient Greece but that it was instead 'the situational expression of a traditional idea' which became particularly popular with tragedians: 'Although there can be no doubt that some, and probably many, people during this time 'believed' in ancestral fault in one way or another, what we see in our sources is not merely a reflection of these beliefs, but adaptations of the idea to specific messages'.[285] Johnston considers that the above narrative – as outlined in the table – is the actual form of the myth composed by someone who took already existing mythic themes and recomposed them having as an *aition* to make them suit the Orphic cult or rituals.[286] Despite Johnston's excellent discussion, there is no certain way of knowing whether or not the myth was deliberately formed so that it would fit Orphic beliefs, and as we will see this myth was potentially used in other mysteries too, such as in Delphic rites.[287] If, though, the myth was especially composed to be used by Orphics alone, this would explain the limited circulation of the

---

[282] GP 27–30: καὶ ὃ σοι ἐδόθη ἀνήλωσαι | ε]ἰς τὸν κάλαθον ἐμβαλ<ε>ῖν | κ]ῶνος ῥόμβος ἀστράγαλοι |]η ἔσοπτρος. For text and discussion see p.264 ff.
[283] Comparetti, 1882, p.116–18; Graf and Johnston, 2013, p.54–55; Edmonds, 1999, p.38.
[284] Rohde, 1894, p.417ff and Appendix IX, p.596–98. Harrison, 1903, 573ff and Appendix, p.660ff. Graf and Johnston, 2013, p.54–56. Bernabé and Jiménez San Cristóbal, 2008, pp.41–42, pp.105–109 and p.188.
[285] Gagné, 2013, p.156–157; 438ff and 470.
[286] Graf and Johnston, 2013, p.70–73.
[287] See p.165.

myth in this form. As already noted though, the possibility that the myth was not composed by Orphics but that it was attributed to Orpheus and interpreted in a specific way by them seems more probable. Nilsson and Guthrie accept that the myth was part of Orphism from early years as well. Guthrie suggests that this myth was created or remodelled on previously existing religious elements by the Orphics in order to suit their own purposes.[288] Nilsson's argument for the myth being part of Orphism from early years is based on a Platonic passage where men's Titanic nature is used as a 'proverbial saying in the sense of an innate evil nature', which in his opinion cannot be explained by the common Titanic myth of their battle with the Olympian Gods, but only by the Orphic Titanic myth.[289] Linforth, in his discussion of the myth acknowledges that: 'there can be no doubt of the existence of an Orphic poem in which were told the successive incidents of the dismembering of Dionysos by the Titans, of their tasting his flesh, of the blasting of their bodies by the thunderbolt, and of the generation of men from the soot in the smoke which rose from them'.[290] Edmonds considers the myth to be 'a modern fabrication dependent upon Christian models that reconstruct the fragmentary evidence in terms of a unified 'Orphic' church, an almost Christian religion with dogma based on a central myth – specifically, salvation from original sin through the death and resurrection of the suffering god'.[291] He attempts to demonstrate that the evidence used for the construction of the myth 'fail(s) to support not only the centrality and early date of the myth' 'but even the existence of such a story before the modern era' (p.37). He considers that the myth has been wrongly reconstructed based on Christian religious models and played a role in the debates concerning the nature of the early Church.[292] Even though this suggestion might be attractive it is not based on any firm evidence and is not the prevalent position in recent scholarship. The idea of a god being resurrected is not exclusive to Christianity and it existed in ancient Greece from Archaic times, most importantly through the Cretan Zeus and the idea of the tomb of Dionysos being located at Delphi.[293] If we want to talk about the borrowing of a model, it would go the other way around, that is Christianity borrowing from Ancient Greek myths and not vice versa. Most importantly, Edmonds does not include the passage from Philodemus quoted above in the sources for the dismemberment myth

---

[288] Nilsson, 1935, p.203/224. Guthrie, 1952, p.120.
[289] Pl. *Leg.* 3.701b. Nilsson, 1935, p.203.
[290] Linforth, 1941, p.329. The myth is discussed by Linforth, 1941, p.307–364.
[291] Edmonds, 1999, p.36. See also Edmonds, 2008a.
[292] Edmonds, 1999, p.38.
[293] See p.120.

and as we have seen Philodemus draws a clear link of the myth to Orphics. This goes against Edmonds' argument that the myth did not give rise to specific beliefs for the Orphics. Henrichs, who draws attention to Edmonds' exclusion of this passage from his discussion, also correctly emphasises that the argument *ex silentio* which Edmonds uses to argue for a late date is 'an imprecise tool that doesn't prove anything', as Edmonds himself seems to admit: '...too many texts are missing from antiquity to make a simple argument from silence persuasive'.[294] I will, however, discuss Edmonds' arguments in more detail since he is the main opponent to an Orphic use or identity of this myth.

The interpretation of the last two parts of the myth – as found on the above table – has played an important role in the modern definition of Orphism and was the reason for attributing to Orphics the idea of a primal Titanic guilt that had to be redeemed in order for them to have a happy afterlife. The mortal race carries the guilt of the Titans – their ancestors – who have murdered Dionysos and as a punishment their souls become incarnated. However, the Titans tasted Dionysos and this is why humans also have a divine Dionysiac element which they need to cultivate in order to escape from the circle of reincarnations and return to their primal state. This interpretation has been the major issue of dispute about the Zagreus myth with the main opposing argument being that the last part of the myth, referring to the Dionysiac element in every human, is clearly attested only by Olympiodorus, a Neoplatonic philosopher of the 6th century A.D.[295] The passage in question is:

καὶ τούτους ὀργισθεὶς ὁ Ζεὺς ἐκεραύνωσε, καὶ ἐκ τῆς αἰθάλης τῶν ἀτμῶν τῶν ἀναδοθέντων ἐξ αὐτῶν ὕλης γενομένης γενέσθαι τοὺς ἀνθρώπους. οὐ δεῖ οὖν ἐξάγειν ἡμᾶς ἑαυτούς, οὐχ ὅτι, ὡς δοκεῖ λέγειν ἡ λέξις, διότι ἔν τινι δεσμῶι ἐσμεν τῶι σώματι (τοῦτο γὰρ δῆλον ἐστι, καὶ οὐκ ἄν τοῦτο ἀπόρρητον ἔλεγεν), ἀλλ'ὅτι οὐ δεῖ ἐξάγειν ἡμᾶς ἑαυτοὺς ὡς τοῦ σώματος ἡμῶν Διονυσιακοῦ ὄντος. Μέρος γὰρ αὐτοῦ ἐσμεν, εἴ γε ἐκ τῆς αἰθάλης τῶν Τιτάνων συγκείμεθα γευσαμένων τῶν σαρκῶν τούτου.

And Zeus, being angry with them (Titans) struck them with his thunderbolts, and from the soot coming from the vapours that transpired from them was produced the matter out of which men are created. Therefore we must not kill ourselves, not because, as the text appears to say, we are in the body as a kind of bond, for that is obvious, and Socrates would not call this a mystery; but we must not kill ourselves because our bodies are Dionysiac; we

---

[294] Henrichs, 2011, p.66. Edmonds, 2008a.
[295] Edmonds, 1999.

are, in fact, a part of him, if indeed we come about from the sublimate of the Titans who ate his flesh.²⁹⁶

Linforth suggests that the idea of humans having a Dionysiac nature that they inherited from the Titans, was a fabrication by Olympiodorus in order to explain a Platonic passage which is against suicide.²⁹⁷ Olympiodorus, then, comments on this passage because he also wants to make a point against suicide. Edmonds agrees with Linforth's view and claims that it does not seem that Olympiodorus linked this passage to an inherited guilt but simply that modern scholars interpreted the passage in this way.²⁹⁸ The suggestion that Olympiodorus might have altered the Orphic Theogony to make his point is supported by the fact that he only mentions four reigns instead of the six that were characteristic of Orphic theogonies, again because it is essential to his point.²⁹⁹ However, there are other authors, earlier than Olympiodorus who seem to relate the incarnation of humans to Dionysos. The first one is Proclus, who refers to this idea clearly:

> ταῦτα καὶ τῆς Ὀρφικῆς ἡμᾶς ἐκδιδασκούσης θεολογίας. ἢ οὐχὶ καὶ Ὀρφεὺς τὰ τοιαῦτα σαφῶς παραδίδωσιν, ὅταν μετὰ τὴν τῶν Τιτάνων μυθικὴν δίκην <u>καὶ τὴν ἐξ'ἐκείνων γένεσιν τῶν θνητῶν τούτων ζώιων</u> πρῶτον μὲν, ὅτι τοὺς βίους ἀμείβουσιν αἱ ψυχαὶ κατὰ δή τινας περιόδους καὶ εἰσδύονται ἄλλαι εἰς ἄλλα σώματα πολλάκις ἀνθρώπων. [OF338F = OR92] ἐν γὰρ τούτοις τὴν ἀπ'ἀνθρωπίνων σωμάτων εἰς ἀνθρώπινα μετοίκισιν αὐτῶν παραδίδωσιν ... ἔπειθ'ὅτι καὶ εἰς τὰ ἄλλα ζῶια μετάβασις ἐστι τῶν ψυχῶν τῶν ἀνθρωπίνων, καὶ τοῦτο διαρρήδην Ὀρφεὺς ἀναδιδάσκει, ὁπηνίκα ἄν διορίζεται [OF338F = OR92].

> And these are what the Orphic theology also teaches us. Or is it not true that Orpheus clearly gives these doctrines, when, after the mythical chastisement of the Titans and the generation of all mortal living beings out of them, he says first of all that all souls exchange lives according to certain periods of time, and that they enter into one another's human bodies many times: [OF338F = OR92] In this passage [Orpheus] teaches the transmigration from human bodies into human bodies. ... Following, Orpheus openly teaches, that there is also a transmigration of human souls into other kinds of living beings, when he declares: [OF338F = OR92]³⁰⁰

Proclus, not only clearly says that mortal beings were born from the Titans after they were punished according to Orphic mythology, but also relates this idea with

---

296 Olymp. *In Phd.* 61c, p.2.21 = OR86.
297 Linforth, 1941, p.359.
298 Edmonds, 2009, p.512/514.
299 Edmonds, 2009, p.516.
300 Procl. *In R.* II.338.10.

multiple re-incarnations and the transmigration of one being to the next, something which suggests that this endless cycle of reincarnation is directly connected to the Titans' punishment for their crime of murdering Dionysos. Since Proclus is earlier than Olympiodorus, Edmonds' argument that this part of the myth was fabricated by Olympiodorus cannot stand. Another author not mentioned by Edmonds and who seems to refer to this idea is Plotinus (3rd A.D.):

> Ἀνθρώπων δὲ ψυχαὶ εἴδωλα αὐτῶν ἰδοῦσαι οἷον Διονύσου ἐν κατόπτρῳ ἐκεῖ ἐγένοντο ἄνωθεν ὁρμηθεῖσαι, οὐκ ἀποτμηθεῖσαι οὐδ' αὗται τῆς ἑαυτῶν ἀρχῆς τε καὶ νοῦ. οὐ γὰρ μετὰ τοῦ νοῦ ἦλθον, ἀλλ' ἔφθασαν μὲν μέχρι γῆς, κάρα δὲ αὐταῖς ἐστήρικται ὑπεράνω τοῦ οὐρανοῦ. πλέον δὲ αὐταῖς κατελθεῖν συβέβηκεν, ὅτι τὸ μέσον αὐταῖς ἠναγκάσθη, φροντίδος δεομένου τοῦ εἰς ὃ ἔφθασαν, φροντίσαι. Ζεὺς δὲ πατὴρ ἐλεήσας πονουμένας θνητὰ αὐτῶν τὰ δεσμὰ ποιῶν, περὶ ἃ πονοῦνται, δίδωσιν ἀναπαύλας ἐν χρόνοις ποιῶν σωμάτων ἐλευθέρας, ἵν' ἔχοιεν ἐκεῖ καὶ αὗται γίνεσθαι, οὗπερ ἡ τοῦ παντὸς ψυχὴ ἀεὶ οὐδὲν τὰ τῇδε ἐπιστρεφομένη.

> But the souls of men see their images as if in the mirror of Dionysus and come to be on that level with a leap from above: but even these are not cut off from their own principle and from intellect. For they did not come down with Intellect, but went on ahead of it down to earth, but their heads are firmly set above in heaven. But they experienced a deeper descent because their middle part was compelled to care for that to which they had gone on, which needed their care. But Father Zeus, pitying them in their troubles, makes the bonds over which they have trouble dissoluble by death and gives them periods of rest, making them at times free of bodies, so that they too may have the opportunity of being there where the soul of the All always is, since it in no way turns to the things of this world.[301]

Plotinus refers to the incarnation of humans as a fallen state and draws a connection with infant Dionysos looking at himself in the mirror. The idea seems to be that just as Dionysos got tricked by the Titans through looking at the material image of his divine intellect, in the same way the human souls being drawn by materiality degrade from the 'soul of the All' and descend into the visible world through being incarnated. It cannot be said with certainty that Plotinus alludes to the idea of an original sin which led to the incarnation of the entirety of the human race but his reference to the Zagreus myth might indicate a connection of this myth to the incarnation of humans. He also says that the souls, despite descending into materiality, are still attached to their own principle and intellect since their 'heads are firmly set above in heaven'. This implies that there is a divine element in humans as incarnated beings. Whether or not this was the actual interpretation of the Zagreus myth we cannot be sure yet, but Plotinus connects the myth with the above ideas. Proclus, who is a century earlier than Olympiodorus, also interprets this myth in the same way. In his commentary on Plato's

---

[301] Plotinus, *Enn.* IV.3.12.1–13 (Tr. Armstrong).

Cratylus he clearly identifies our intellect as Dionysian and an image of Dionysos and links this idea to the Zagreus myth in a passage which is again not mentioned by Edmonds:

> ὅτι ὁ ἐν ἡμῖν νοῦς Διονυσιακός ἐστιν καὶ ἄγαλμα ὄντως τοῦ Διονύσου. ὅστις οὖν εἰς αὐτὸν πλημμελῇ καὶ τὴν ἀμερῆ αὐτοῦ φύσιν διασπᾷ Τιτανικῶς διὰ τοῦ πολυσχιδοῦς ψεύδους, οὗτος δηλονότι εἰς αὐτὸν τὸν Διόνυσον ἁμαρτάνει, καὶ μᾶλλον τῶν εἰς τὰ ἐκτὸς τοῦ θεοῦ ἀγάλματα πλημμελούντων, ὅσον ὁ νοῦς μᾶλλον τῶν ἄλλων συγγενής ἐστι τῷ θεῷ.

> The intellect in us is Dionysian and truly an image of Dionysos. Therefore, anyone that transgresses against it and, like the Titans, scatters its undivided nature by fragmented falsehood, this person clearly sins against Dionysos himself, even more than those who transgress against external images of the God, to the extent that the intellect more than other things is akin to the God.[302]

Proclus notes that whoever transgresses against their divine intellect, acting essentially like the Titans, performs an act of 'sin'. The human beings, then, should try and act according to their intellect which is Dionysiac and hence divine, and not go against it by acting in a Titanic way. This imposes a contrast between two opposing powers, but most importantly confirms the existence of a divine Dionysiac part in mortals, which Proclus essentially identifies as the intellect.

But can we trace this interpretation even further back? A passage from Plutarch (1st A.D.) might be relevant:

> οὐ χεῖρον δ' ἴσως καὶ προανακρούσασθαι καὶ προαναφωνῆσαι τὰ τοῦ Ἐμπεδοκλέους· (...) ἀλληγορεῖ γὰρ ἐνταῦθα τὰς ψυχάς, ὅτι φόνων καὶ βρώσεως σαρκῶν καὶ ἀλληλοφαγίας δίκην τίνουσαι σώμασι θνητοῖς ἐνδέδενται. καίτοι δοκεῖ παλαιότερος οὗτος ὁ λόγος εἶναι. τὰ γὰρ δὴ περὶ τὸν Διόνυσον μεμυθευμένα πάθη τοῦ διαμελισμοῦ καὶ τὰ Τιτάνων ἐπ' αὐτὸν τολμήματα, κολάσεις τε τούτων καὶ κεραυνώσεις γευσαμένων τοῦ φόνου, ᾐνιγμένος ἐστὶ μῦθος εἰς τὴν παλιγγενεσίαν. τὸ γὰρ ἐν ἡμῖν ἄλογον καὶ ἄτακτον καὶ βίαιον οὐ θεῖον ἀλλὰ δαιμονικὸν ὂν οἱ παλαιοὶ Τιτᾶνας ὠνόμασαν, καὶ τοῦτ' ἔστι κολαζομένου καὶ δίκην διδόντος.

> Yet perhaps it is not unsuitable to set the pitch and announce the theme by quoting some verses of Empedokles (...) By these lines he means, though he does not say so directly, that human souls are imprisoned in mortal bodies as a punishment for murder, the eating of animal flesh, and cannibalism.[303] This doctrine, however, seems to be even older, for the stories told about the sufferings and dismemberment of Dionysus and the outrageous assaults of the Titans upon him, and their punishment and blasting by thunderbolt after they had tasted his blood (γευσαμένων τοῦ φόνου) all this is a myth which in its inner meaning has to do with rebirth. For to that faculty in us which is unreasonable and disordered and

---

302 Procl. *In Cra.* 400d1–5, 77.25–78.4 (Tr. Duvick).
303 Some lines by Empedokles which have fallen out.

violent, and does not come from the gods, but from evil spirits, the ancients gave the name Titans, *and this faculty is punished and receives a penalty...*[304]

It is quite clear that Plutarch identifies a part in humans which does not come from the gods – in other words is not divine – as being Titanic. This part is punished and the punishment is related to rebirth. He not only relates this idea to the dismemberment myth and the tasting of Dionysos' flesh – which is attested by Euphorion (3rd B.C.) as we saw earlier – but also records that this Titanic part comes in contrast to the part that comes from the gods.[305] Despite the fact that it is clearly stated by Plutarch that this internal (ἐν ἡμῖν) lawless part was <u>named</u> by the ancients Titanic (οἱ παλαιοὶ Τιτᾶνας <u>ὠνομάσαν</u>), meaning it was identified as such and not simply allegorised as such, Edmonds rejects this idea and suggests that Plutarch is only referring to an allegory in this case and not to an aetiological myth. He argues that Plutarch uses the same vocabulary with which he introduces an allegory (ἠνιγμένος ἐστὶ μῦθος εἰς τὴν παλιγγενεσίαν) while earlier on he had criticised Bernabé for using the same argument for Plato, namely that the phrase λέγοι δή τις ἂν usually introduces an Orphic myth or idea. Plutarch claims that the human souls 'are imprisoned in mortal bodies' as a punishment for murder and cannibalism. Since it would hardly be possible that every human being's soul or one of its ancestors had committed murder or cannibalism in a previous life causing its incarnation or rebirth, then Plutarch must refer to a single event of cannibalism and murder, which has led to the rebirth (παλιγγενεσίαν) of the human race in mortal bodies. It is illogical to suggest that a soul could have committed murder, or cannibalism, without first being incarnated, since this is the reason which has led to its incarnation. The cannibalism, then, must be directly related to a Titanic descent. I would argue that the use of the word παλιγγενεσία instead of μετεμψύχωσις by Plutarch is important. The latter means the transmigration of souls from one material body to the next while the first one can also refer to the regeneration of a race apart from transmigration. If my interpretation of the above passage is correct this double meaning would allow Plutarch to refer to the Titanic deed as the one-off event which led to the 'fall' of the human souls to mortality but also to the continuation of rebirths whenever a mortal allows for the Titanic part to take over his/her intellect. Overall, in my opinion, Edmonds considers that the apparent meaning of the above passage which is clearly

---

304 Pl. *De esu carn.* 1.7, 996b–c (Tr. Cherniss). The English text between * is my own translation. The word δίκην when paired with the verb δίδωμι it is translated as: 'atonement', 'penalty', 'the object or the consequence of the action' according to LSJ. Wyttenbach: κολαζομένου καὶ δίκην διδόντος.
305 See p.91.

stated by Plutarch is less likely than another hidden meaning which is different than the one that the author himself states.

The same Platonic passage discussed by Olympiodorus in the disputed passage quoted earlier, is discussed by Damascius who also comments on the word φρουρᾷ in relation to the dismemberment myth. Damascius also cites Xenokrates (4th B.C.) who says that the soul is of 'the Titanic order and culminates in Dionysos'.[306] The Platonic passage in discussion is *Phaedo* 62b, where Socrates refers to a secret doctrine/*exēgēsis* (λόγος) which explains why humans should not kill themselves. The *logos* is that we are in a kind of prison (φρουρᾷ) from which we should not set ourselves free. Socrates goes on to say: 'but am confident there is something there for the dead and, as has long been said (ὥσπερ γε καὶ πάλαι λέγεται), it is better for those who are good than those who are bad'.[307] According to Socrates, then, there is an old doctrine which says that those that are good will have a better luck in the afterlife, in contrast to the evil ones. In my earlier discussion of the Eleusinian mysteries I have mentioned another Platonic passage from *Cratylus* (400b–c) which refers to the same idea of the soul being imprisoned in the body as a form of punishment, only this time this interpretation is identified as Orphic. In addition, the word φρουρᾷ is also mentioned by Dio Chrysostom (1st A.D.) in relation to the Titans. He indicates that the reason that humans are punished with mortality and incarnation is because they are descended from the Titans:

ὅτι τοῦ τῶν Τιτάνων αἵματός ἐσμεν ἡμεῖς ἅπαντες οἱ ἄνθρωποι. ὡς οὖν ἐκείνων ἐχθρῶν ὄντων τοῖς θεοῖς καὶ πολεμησάντων οὐδὲ ἡμεῖς φίλοι ἐσμέν, ἀλλὰ κολαζόμεθά τε ὑπ' αὐτῶν καὶ ἐπὶ τιμωρίᾳ γεγόναμεν, ἐν φρουρᾷ δὴ ὄντες ἐν τῷ βίῳ τοσοῦτον χρόνον ὅσον ἕκαστοι ζῶμεν. τοὺς δὲ ἀποθνῄσκοντας ἡμῶν κεκολασμένους ἤδη ἱκανῶς λύεσθαί τε καὶ ἀπαλλάττεσθαι.

It is to the effect that all we human beings are of the blood of the Titans. Then, because they were hateful to the gods and had waged war on them, we are not dear to them either, but are punished by them and have been born for chastisement, being, in truth, imprisoned in life for as long a time as we each live. And when any of us die, it means that we, having already been sufficiently chastised, are released and go our way.[308]

---

306 Dam. In *Phd.* I 84.22: Τιτανική ἐστιν καὶ εἰς Διόνυσον ἀποκρυφοῦται. Xen. fr.20 Heinze. Also, see the commentary on OR92.
307 Pl. *Phd.* 63c: ἀλλ' εὔελπίς εἰμι εἶναί τι τοῖς τετελευτηκόσι καί, ὥσπερ γε καὶ πάλαι λέγεται, πολὺ ἄμεινον τοῖς ἀγαθοῖς ἢ τοῖς κακοῖς (Tr. Emlyn-Jones).
308 Dio Chrys. *Or.* 30.10 (Tr. Cohoon).

Edmonds argues that Dio Chrysostom must be referring to the Titanomachy here and thus this passage cannot be used as evidence for the Zagreus myth.[309] However, the Titanomachy as found in sources such as Hesiod does not lead to the creation of the human race from the defeated Titans. Dio Chysostom says that the Titans were hateful and fought against the gods. This context can be applied to the Zagreus myth as well, since the Titans were hostile to Dionysos and Zeus and plotted to kill Dionysos and become in charge. Even though Dio Chrysostom does not refer directly to the Zagreus myth and he says that men are born from the Titans' blood instead of smoke/ashes, the terminology he uses is particularly Orphic. He also refers to humans' life as an imprisonment and even mentions the word φρουρᾷ as already noted. He also says that when we die we are released (λύεσθαί) from this τιμωρίᾳ being sufficiently punished. All these references would not make sense if Dio Chrysostom was referring to the Titanomachy which does not end with an anthropogony. The intertextual similarities between the Platonic passages, Damascius and Dio Chrysostom allow us to define the idea of incarnation as a punishment and imprisonment of the soul, as Orphic and relate it to the descent of mortals from the Titans. The quotation from Xenokrates could be evidence that this belief was formed and was in existence already in the 4th century B.C. As we saw, Edmonds, based on the argument that they are Olympiodorus' invention, rejects the concept of an 'original sin' which originates in the murdering of Dionysos by the Titans and is inherited by humans, and also the belief that humans have a divine/Dionysiac and an evil/Titanic nature. In the light of the above evidence, however, his rejection cannot be accepted since we find the same ideas in earlier sources such as Proclus, Dio Chrysostom, Plutarch and Xenokrates.

The idea of a primal guilt and of an innate Titanic and Dionysiac nature can be possibly traced further back through various Platonic passages which have been interpreted by scholarship in this way. One such passage is from *Laws* 3.701b–c:

ΑΘΗΝΑΙΟΣ:
Ἐφεξῆς δὴ ταύτῃ τῇ ἐλευθερίᾳ ἡ τοῦ μὴ ἐθέλειν τοῖς ἄρχουσι δουλεύειν γίγνοιτ' ἄν, καὶ ἑπομένη ταύτῃ φεύγειν πατρὸς καὶ μητρὸς καὶ πρεσβυτέρων δουλείαν καὶ νουθέτησιν, καὶ ἐγγὺς τοῦ τέλους οὖσι νόμων ζητεῖν μὴ ὑπηκόοις εἶναι, πρὸς αὐτῷ δὲ ἤδη τῷ τέλει ὅρκων καὶ πίστεων καὶ τὸ παράπαν θεῶν μὴ φροντίζειν, <u>τὴν λεγομένην παλαιὰν Τιτανικὴν φύσιν ἐπιδεικνῦσι καὶ μιμουμένοις</u>· ἐπὶ τὰ αὐτὰ πάλιν ἐκεῖνα ἀφικομένους, χαλεπὸν αἰῶνα διάγοντας μὴ λῆξαί ποτε κακῶν.

---

[309] Edmonds, 2008a.

ATHENIAN:
Next after this form of liberty would come that which refuses to be subject to the rulers; and, following on from that, the shirking of submission to one's parents and elders and their admonitions; then, as the penultimate stage, comes the effort to disregard the laws; while the last stage of all is to lose all respect for oaths or pledges or divinities,—wherein men display and reproduce the character of the Titans of story, who are said to have reverted to their original state, dragging out a painful existence with never any rest from woe.[310]

The key words here are ἐπιδεικνῦσι καὶ μιμουμένοις which have a different meaning but Plato uses them for the same action. ἐπιδεικνῦσι implies the projection of one's true self or of an innate quality, while μιμουμένοις implies that the person is imitating something external and foreign. The use of the word *mimoumenois* by Plato, however, might be due to his general argument entailing the notion of harmful or positive effects of *mimesis*.[311] As Edmonds has argued for other authors, Plato might be taking a mythic narrative as a point of departure and adjusting it to his argument. Also, it is important that Plato refers to the Titanic nature as λεγομένην, meaning that it is a term being told and used and not just a phrase which he has created. Bernabé argues that the phrase τὴν λεγομένην παλαιὰν resembles the way that Plato introduces other Orphic references.[312] This in itself, of course, does not constitute proof that this is an Orphic reference, but if we find further evidence, then this detail makes the possibility stronger. It is certain that Plato was aware of Orphic works since he cites 'Orpheus' on three occasions, in the *Laws* 669d, *Philebus* 66c and *Cratylus* 402b as we saw (p.74). The phrase μὴ λῆξαι ποτε κακῶν ('never any rest from woe') has a parallel to a phrase quoted by Proclus as being part of the *Rhapsodies*: κύκλου τ' ἂν λῆξαι καὶ ἀναπνεῦσαι κακότητος ('and to escape from the cycle and find respite from the misery').[313] Bernabé agrees with this but Edmonds suggests that there is no striking similarity here and rejects that this indicates Orphic influence. It is interesting

---

310 Tr. Bury.
311 For the notion of *mimesis* see Pl. *Resp.* 3.395bff.
312 Bernabé, 2003, p.37. Edmonds argues that this phrase is used in non-Orphic instances as well, giving one example from the *Statesman* 268e7. Since, however, the use of this phrase to introduce Orphic material is more frequent, it is more possible than not that in this case too it introduces Orphic material. In fact the other two instances Edmonds mentions might as well be Orphic references; 269b refers to the old tale that men were born from the earth which might be a reference to the Titanic descend and 274c to the old tale which refers to the gifts that were given to men by gods: the crafts and arts by Hephaestus and Aphrodite. This is a detail found in a verse from the *Rhapsodies* OR70-71 = Procl. *In. Ti.* 29a, I.327.23 and Hermias *In Phdr.* 247c, 149.9 = OF269F and Procl. *In Cra.* 389b, 21.13 = OF271F.
313 Procl. *In Ti.* 42c, III.297.3 = OF348F.

though, that Proclus quotes this phrase when commenting on the following passage from Plato's *Timaeus*:

μὴ παυόμενός τε ἐν τούτοις ἔτι κακίας, τρόπον ὃν κακύνοιτο, κατὰ τὴν ὁμοιότητα τῆς τοῦ τρόπου γενέσεως εἴς τινα τοιαύτην ἀεὶ μεταβαλοῖ θήρειον φύσιν, ἀλλάττων τε <u>οὐ πρότερον πόνων λήξοι</u>, πρὶν τῇ ταὐτοῦ καὶ ὁμοίου περιόδῳ τῇ ἐν αὑτῷ ξυνεπισπώμενος τὸν πολὺν ὄχλον καὶ ὕστερον προσφύντα ἐκ πυρὸς καὶ ὕδατος καὶ ἀέρος καὶ γῆς, θορυβώδη καὶ ἄλογον ὄντα λόγῳ κρατήσας εἰς τὸ τῆς πρώτης καὶ ἀρίστης ἀφίκοιτο εἶδος ἕξεως.

...and if, in that shape, he still does not refrain from wickedness he will be changed every time, according to the nature of his wickedness, into some bestial form after the similitude of his own nature; nor in his changings will he cease from woes, until he yields himself to the revolution of the Same and Similar that is within him, and dominating by force of reason that burdensome mass which afterwards adhered to him of fire and water and earth and air, a mass tumultuous and irrational, returns again to the semblance of his first and best state.[314]

Apart from the fact that the underlined phrase is very similar to the one from the *Laws* passage, Plato is here again referring to two different innate natures, a bestial one and a divine one. If a mortal wants to 'cease from <his> woes', to stop being reborn and return to his initial and perfect state then he has to refrain from evil and repress his/her bestial nature while complying to his/her divine nature. The use of the same wording for the notion of escaping woes in relation to the existence of two opposing innate natures in human beings indicates that Plato is influenced by the same work.

Another passage from *Laws* (2.672b–c) indicates that Plato was familiar with the Zagreus myth:

ΑΘΗΝΑΙΟΣ: Λόγος τις ἅμα καὶ φήμη ὑπορρεῖ πως, ὡς ὁ θεὸς οὗτος ὑπὸ τῆς μητρυιᾶς Ἥρας διεφορήθη τῆς ψυχῆς τὴν γνώμην, διὸ τάς τε βακχείας καὶ πᾶσαν τὴν μανικὴν ἐμβάλλει χορείαν τιμωρούμενος· ὅθεν καὶ τὸν οἶνον ἐπὶ τοῦτ' αὐτὸ δεδώρηται. ἐγὼ δὲ τὰ μὲν τοιαῦτα τοῖς ἀσφαλὲς ἡγουμένοις εἶναι λέγειν περὶ θεῶν ἀφίημι λέγειν, τὸ δὲ τοσόνδε οἶδα, ὅτι πᾶν ζῷον, ὅσον αὐτῷ προσήκει νοῦν ἔχειν τελεωθέντι, τοῦτον καὶ τοσοῦτον οὐδὲν ἔχον ποτὲ φύεται. ἐν τούτῳ δὴ τῷ χρόνῳ ἐν ᾧ μήπω κέκτηται τὴν οἰκείαν φρόνησιν, πᾶν μαίνεταί τε καὶ βοᾷ ἀτάκτως, καὶ ὅταν ἀκταινώσῃ ἑαυτὸ τάχιστα, ἀτάκτως αὖ πηδᾷ. ἀναμνησθῶμεν δὲ ὅτι μουσικῆς τε καὶ γυμναστικῆς ἔφαμεν ἀρχὰς ταύτας εἶναι.

ATHENIAN: There is a secret stream of story and report to the effect that the god <Dionysus' seat of intellect was dispersed> by his stepmother Hera, and that in vengeance therefore he brought in Bacchic rites and all the frenzied choristry, and with the same aim bestowed also the gift of wine. These matters, however, I leave to those who think it safe to say them about

---

[314] Pl. *Ti.* 42c–d.

deities; but this much I know,— that no creature is ever born in possession of that reason, or that amount of reason, which properly belongs to it when fully developed; consequently, every creature, during the period when it is still lacking in its proper intelligence, continues all in a frenzy, crying out wildly, and, as soon as it can get on its feet, leaping wildly. Let us remember how we said that in this we have the origin of music and gymnastics.[315]

It is almost certain that Plato has the dismemberment myth in mind here and he mentions that this is a secret, kind of 'underground', story. The result of Dionysos' death and vengeance was the formation of the Bacchic rites and the gift of wine. It also seems that he does not want to dwell on this story extensively or identify the source but rather leave it to those who would not impose risk on themselves by talking about it. The context of this reference seems to be relevant to an innate 'reasoning' nature of mortals. The Athenian in Plato seems to argue that every human has a frenzied nature from the moment of birth and that this frenzy can be turned into rhythm by Dionysos. This is obvious from what the Athenian says right after the above passage: 'Do we not also remember how we said that from this origin there was implanted in us men the sense of rhythm and harmony, and that the joint authors thereof were Apollo and the Muses and the god Dionysus?'.[316] This was also discussed earlier in 2.653d where a similar expression is used by Plato once again:

> ΑΘΗΝΑΙΟΣ: Καλῶς τοίνυν. τούτων γὰρ δὴ τῶν ὀρθῶς τεθραμμένων ἡδονῶν καὶ λυπῶν παιδειῶν οὐσῶν χαλᾶται τοῖς ἀνθρώποις καὶ διαφθείρεται τὰ πολλὰ ἐν τῷ βίῳ, θεοὶ δὲ οἰκτείραντες τὸ τῶν ἀνθρώπων ἐπίπονον πεφυκὸς γένος <u>ἀναπαύλας τε αὐτοῖς τῶν πόνων</u> ἐτάξαντο τὰς τῶν ἑορτῶν ἀμοιβὰς [τοῖς θεοῖς], καὶ Μούσας Ἀπόλλωνά τε μουσηγέτην καὶ Διόνυσον ξυνεορταστὰς ἔδοσαν, ἵν' ἐπανορθῶνται τάς γε τροφὰς γενόμενοι ἐν ταῖς ἑορταῖς μετὰ θεῶν.

> ATHENIAN: Very good. Now these forms of child-training, which consist in right discipline in pleasures and pains, grow slack and weakened to a great extent in the course of men's lives; so the gods, in pity for the human race thus born to misery, have ordained the feasts of thanksgiving as periods of *respite from their troubles*; and they have granted them as companions in their feasts the Muses and Apollo the master of music, and Dionysus, that they may at least set right again their modes of discipline by associating in their feasts with gods.

---

315 Tr. Bury. The text in < > is my own translation. διαφορέω is translated as 'disperse' or 'tear in pieces' and this is why Bury's translation as 'the god Dionysus was robbed of his soul's judgment' was not considered accurate.
316 Pl. *Leg.* 2.672d: Οὐκοῦν καὶ ὅτι τὴν ῥυθμοῦ τε καὶ ἁρμονίας αἴσθησιν τοῖς ἀνθρώποις ἡμῖν ἐνδεδωκέναι τὴν ἀρχὴν ταύτην ἔφαμεν, Ἀπόλλωνα δὲ καὶ Μούσας καὶ Διόνυσον συναιτίους γεγονέναι (Tr. Bury).

The fact that these theories about the existence of an innate nature in humans are mentioned in conjunction with the dismemberment myth indicates that the myth might have been interpreted in contemporary times in such a way.[317] If Plato is using the same expression in several passages related to this theory and if these passages refer to the Zagreus myth as well, then we should accept the possibility that Plato has in mind an Orphic work which referred to this myth and included a verse similar to the one quoted by Proclus and mentioned earlier. The specific phrase of respiting from troubles, is what connects all the above Platonic passages and allows us to identify the Zagreus myth as Plato's point of reference.

There is one final passage from the *Laws* in which Plato might be alluding to the Zagreus myth:

> λέγοι δή τις ἂν ἐκείνῳ διαλεγόμενος ἅμα καὶ παραμυθούμενος, ὃν ἐπιθυμία κακὴ παρακαλοῦσα μεθ' ἡμέραν τε καὶ ἐπεγείρουσα νύκτωρ ἐπί τι τῶν ἱερῶν ἄγει συλήσοντα, τάδε· Ὦ θαυμάσιε, οὐκ ἀνθρώπινόν σε κακὸν οὐδὲ θεῖον κινεῖ τὸ νῦν ἐπὶ τὴν ἱεροσυλίαν προτρέπον ἰέναι, <u>οἶστρος δέ σέ τις ἐμφυόμενος ἐκ παλαιῶν καὶ ἀκαθάρτων τοῖς ἀνθρώποις ἀδικημάτων</u>, περιφερόμενος ἀλιτηριώδης, ὃν εὐλαβεῖσθαι χρεὼν παντὶ σθένει.

> By way of argument and admonition one might address in the following terms the man whom an evil desire urges by day and wakes up at night, driving him to rob some sacred object – "My good man, the evil force that now moves you and prompts you to go temple-robbing is neither of human origin nor of divine, but it is some impulse bred of old in men from ancient wrongs unexpiated, which courses round wreaking ruin; and it you must guard against with all your strength..."[318]

The interesting word here is οἶστρος which is usually related to Bacchic mania: 'αὐτὸς ἐκ δόμων ᾤστρησ' ἐγώ | μανίαις', 'οἰστρηθεὶς Διονύσῳ', 'οἰστροπλῆγας' and it appears various times in the Orphic Hymns.[319] Plato says that this *oistros* is innate and rooted within (ἐμφυόμενος) all humans from some ancestral crimes. Edmonds argues that Plato could be referring to the Erinyes here and we do indeed find this word in association with the Erinyes, e.g. in Euripides' *Iphigeneia in Tauris* 1456: οἴστροις Ἐρινύων. However, I will argue why it is more probable that Plato's reference has Dionysiac connotations. Damascius, in his commentary on Plato's *Phaedo* quotes some verses from the *Orphic Rhapsodies* (OR95):

---

317 And possibly the role of wine in the Bacchic mysteries had something to do with the taming of this innate frenzy as well.
318 Pl. *Leg.* 9.854a–b (Tr. Bury).
319 Eur. *Bacch.* 32–33: 'I have goaded them from the house in frenzy', 119: 'goaded away by Dionysos', 1229: 'driven wild'. Orphic Hymns: OH11.23, OH71.11, OH32.6, OH70.9. See also Levaniouk, 2007, p.192.

ὁ Διόνυσος λύσεώς ἐστιν αἴτιος· διὸ καὶ Λυσεὺς ὁ θεός, καὶ ὁ Ὀρφεύς φησιν:
'πέμψουσιν πάσηισιν ἐν ὥραις ἀμφιέτηισιν
ὄργια τ'ἐκτελέσουσι λύσιν προγόνων ἀθεμίστων
μαιόμενοι· σὺ δὲ τοῖσιν ἔχων κράτος, οὕς κ'ἐθέλῃσθα,
λύσεις ἔκ τε πόνων χαλεπῶν καὶ ἀπείρονος οἴστρου.'

Dionysos is the cause of deliverance. And this is why this god is also called Lyseus, as Orpheus says:
'men will send you hecatombs of unblemished beasts and offer yearly sacrifices at all seasons, and they will perform your secret rites seeking deliverance from the lawless deeds of their ancestors. And you, *Dionysos*, having the power as far as these are concerned, shall deliver whomever you will be willing to, from grievous toil and endless agony'.[320]

Not only are these Orphic verses, but we find the same expression referring to a relief from pain as in the Platonic passages discussed above, and this time in conjunction with the word οἶστρος. The context of this quotation is the dismemberment myth since all the paragraphs preceding the above passage from the beginning of this section – namely 1–10 – have to do with the dismemberment myth. In section 7 Damascius says that according to the traditional myth – only a single myth (εἰ καὶ ὁ μῦθος μερίζει), and not many as Edmonds suggest – there are three punishments for the Titans: 'lightning-bolts, shackles, descents into various lower regions'.[321] Edmonds argues that: 'Different tales seem to have included different punishments according to the context of the tale; we cannot deduce the preceding crime from the punishment' and he argues that Damascius might also be referring to the Titanomachy and not just the Zagreus' myth.[322] However, in the previous paragraphs Damascius says:

Διὰ τί λέγονται οἱ Τιτᾶνες ἐπιβουλεύειν τῷ Διονύσῳ; - ἢ ὅτι δημιουργίας ἐξάρχουσιν οὐκ ἐμμενούσης τοῖς ὅροις τῆς Διονυσιακῆς πολυειδοῦς συνεχείας. ὅτι δίκας τίνουσιν ἐπεχόμενοι τὰς διαιρετικὰς ἐνεργείας. τοιοῦτον γὰρ πᾶσα κόλασις· ἀνακόπτειν βούλεται καὶ συστέλλειν τὰς ἁμαρτωλοὺς ἕξεις τε καὶ ἐνεργείας. ὅτι τριτταὶ παραδέδονται τῶν Τιτάνων κολάσεις· κεραυνώσεις, δεσμοί, ἄλλων ἀλλαχοῦ πρόοδοι πρὸς τὸ κοιλότερον.

Why are the Titans said to plot against Dionysus? – Because they initiate a mode of creation that does not remain within the bounds of the multiform continuity of Dionysos. Their punishment consists in the checking of their dividing activities. Such is all chastisement: it aims at restraining and reducing erroneous dispositions and activities. Tradition knows three

---

320 Dam. *In Phd.* I 87.11 = OF350F (Translation by the author).
321 Dam. *In Phd.* I 87.7: τριτταὶ παραδέδονται τῶν Τιτάνων κολάσεις· κεραυνώσεις, δεσμοί, ἄλλων ἀλλαχοῦ πρόοδοι πρὸς τὸ κοιλότερον ... δεῖ δὲ περὶ ἕκαστον τὰς τρεῖς θεωρεῖν, εἰ καὶ ὁ μῦθος μερίζει· (Tr. Westerink). Edmonds, 2008a.
322 Edmonds, 2008a.

kinds of punishments inflicted on the Titans: lightning-bolts, shackles, descents into various lower regions.[323]

The Titanomachy is not mentioned anywhere by Damascius but quite clearly only the dismemberment myth. Edmonds continues to say that Damascius links the anthropogony with the last punishment mentioned, namely the Tartarosis – and thus he must be referring to the Titanomachy.[324] However, in the paragraph following right after, Damascius says:

> πῶς ἐκ Τιτανικῶν θρυμμάτων οἱ ἄνθρωποι γίνονται; ἢ ἐκ μὲν τῶν θρυμμάτων, ὡς ἀπεστενωμένοι τὴν ζωὴν εἰς ἔσχατον μερισμόν· ἐκ δὲ τῶν Τιτανικῶν, ὡς ἐσχάτων δημιουργῶν καὶ τοῖς δημιουργήμασι προσεχεστάτων. ὁ μὲν γὰρ Ζεὺς 'πατὴρ ἀνδρῶν καὶ θεῶν', οἱ δὲ ἀνθρώπων μόνων ἀλλ' οὐχὶ καὶ θεῶν, καὶ οὐκέτι πατέρες ἀλλὰ αὐτοὶ ἁπλῶς ἀλλὰ τεθνεῶτες, καὶ οὐδὲ τοῦτο μόνον ἀλλὰ καὶ συντεθρυμμένοι· ὁ γὰρ τοιοῦτος τρόπος τῆς ὑποστάσεως εἰς τοὺς αἰτίους ἀναπέμπεται.

> In what sense are men created from the fragments of the Titans? – From the fragments, because their life is reduced to the utmost limit of differentiation; of the Titans, because they are the lowest of Creators and in immediate contact with their creation. For Zeus is the 'Father of men and Gods', the Titans of men only, not of Gods, and they cannot even be called fathers, but have become men themselves, and not simply themselves, but their dead bodies, and even of these only the fragments, the fragmentary condition of our existence being thus transferred to those who are its causes.[325]

It appears, thus, that Damascius has a single story in mind which includes all the punishments. Edmonds argues that the Orphic story ends with just the lightning punishment.[326] However, the Orphic Hymn to the Titans refers to the anthropogony by the Titans and the Tartarosis:

> Τιτῆνες, Γαίης τε καὶ Οὐρανοῦ ἀγλαὰ τέκνα,
> ἡμετέρων πρόγονοι πατέρων, γαίης ὑπένερθεν
> οἴκοις Ταρταρίοισι μυχῶι χθονὸς ἐνναίοντες,
> ἀρχαὶ καὶ πηγαὶ πάντων θνητῶν πολυμόχθων,
> εἰναλίων, πτηνῶν τε καὶ οἳ χθόνα ναιετάουσιν·
> ἐξ ὑμέων γὰρ πᾶσα πέλει γενεὰ κατὰ κόσμον.

> Titans, glorious children of Ouranos and Gaia,
> forbears of our fathers, who dwell down below
> in Tartarean homes, in the earth's bowels.

---

323 Dam. *In Phd.* I 85.5–86.7 (Tr. Westerink).
324 Edmonds, 2008a.
325 Dam. *In Phd.* I 86–87.8 (Tr. Westerink).
326 Edmonds, 2008a.

> From you stem all toiling mortals,
> the creatures of the sea and of the lands, the birds,
> and all generations of this world come from you...[327]

It can be argued that the Orphic myth included all three punishments, but only verses referring to the lightning punishment have survived. The Titans were possibly bound to Tartaros and then killed by lightning and from their remains the human race came into being. The section following the passage from Damascius quoted above refers to the Titanic mode of life which should be avoided if we wish to become *Dionysoi*:

> ὅτι ἡ Τιτανικὴ ζωὴ ἄλογός ἐστιν, ὑφ'ἧς ἡ λογικὴ σπαράττεται. κάλλιον δὲ πανταχοῦ ποιεῖν αὐτήν, ἀπὸ θεῶν γε ἀρχομένην τῶν Τιτάνων· καὶ τοίνυν τῆς λογικῆς τὸ δοκοῦν αὐτεξούσιον καὶ οἷον ἑαυτοῦ βουλόμενον εἶναι μόνου, οὔτε δὲ τῶν κρειττόνων οὔτε τῶν χειρόνων, τοῦτο ἡμῖν οἱ Τιτᾶνες ἐμποιοῦσιν, καθ' ὃ καὶ τὸν ἐν ἡμῖν Διόνυσον διασπῶμεν, παραθραύοντες ἡμῶν τὸ ὁμοφυὲς εἶδος καὶ οἷον κοινωνικὸν πρὸς τὰ κρείττω καὶ ἥττω. οὕτω δὲ ἔχοντες Τιτᾶνές ἐσμεν· ὅταν δὲ εἰς ἐκεῖνο συμβῶμεν, Διόνυσοι γινόμεθα τετελειωμένοι ἀτεχνῶς.

> The Titanic mode of life is the irrational mode, by which rational life is torn asunder. It is better to acknowledge its existence everywhere, since in any case at its source there are Gods, the Titans; then also on the plane of rational life, this apparent self-determination, which seems to aim at belonging to itself alone and neither to the superior nor to the inferior, is wrought in us by the Titans through it we tear asunder the Dionysus in ourselves, breaking up the natural continuity of our being and our partnership, so to speak, with the superior and the inferior. While in this condition, we are Titans; but when we recover that lost unity, we become Dionysus and we attain what can be truly called completeness.[328]

Considering all the above discussion by Damascius of the dismemberment myth, it becomes clear that the human race comes from the Titans and that there is a Titanic and Dionysiac nature in mortals who can become *Dionysoi* if they follow the non-Titanic rational life. These are not, then, ideas created by Olympiodorus as Edmonds has argued. Going back to the word *oistros*, a passage from Plutarch might be relevant:

> βαλάνου δὲ γευσάμενοι καὶ φαγόντες ἐχορεύσαμεν ὑφ' ἡδονῆς περὶ δρῦν τινα καὶ φηγόν, ζείδωρον καὶ μητέρα καὶ τροφὸν ἀποκαλοῦντες· ἐκείνην μόνην ὁ τότε βίος ἑορτὴν ἔγνω, τὰ δ' ἄλλα φλεγμονῆς ἦν ἅπαντα μεστὰ καὶ στυγνότητος. ὑμᾶς δὲ τοὺς νῦν τίς λύσσα καὶ τίς οἶστρος ἄγει πρὸς μιαιφονίαν, οἷς τοσαῦτα περίεστι τῶν ἀναγκαίων; τί καταψεύδεσθε τῆς γῆς ὡς τρέφειν μὴ δυναμένης; τί τὴν θεσμοφόρον ἀσεβεῖτε Δήμητρα καὶ τὸν ἡμερίδην καὶ μειλίχιον αἰσχύνετε Διόνυσον, ὡς οὐχ ἱκανὰ παρὰ τούτων λαμβάνοντες.

---

327 OH 37.1–6 Τιτάνων (Tr. Athanassakis).
328 Dam. *In Phd.* I 86–87.9 (Tr. Westerink).

When we had tasted and eaten acorns we danced for joy around some oak, calling it 'life-giving' and 'mother' and 'nurse'. This was the only festival that those times had discovered; all else was a medley of anguish and gloom. But you who live now, what madness, what frenzy drives you to the pollution of shedding blood, you who have such a superfluity of necessities? Why slander the earth by implying that she cannot support you? Why impiously offend law-giving Demeter and bring shame upon Dionysus, lord of the cultivated vine, the gracious one, as if you did not receive enough from their hands?[329]

Plutarch refers to the blood-spilling and the eating of flesh as being driven by *oistros*. I have discussed in Chapter 2 the sources referring to the so-called *Orphikos Bios* which instructed abstinence from blood-spilling and flesh-eating.[330] It can be suggested, considering the above passages from Plutarch, Damascius and Plato that the Bacchic frenzy (*oistros*) represented the Titanic nature from which Dionysos was the one to release. More on this matter, will be said in the following chapters were we will have more evidence available to support it.

The scholars who accept the interpretation of the Zagreus myth based on a primal guilt, assume that in order for mortals to be released from this ancestral crime they have to 'ask for forgiveness' through rituals and offerings from the gods and in particular Persephone – Dionysos' mother according to the Orphic version – and Dionysos himself. This was the key element which led several scholars to identify the gold tablets as Orphic and interpret them in this light, as we will see in Chapter 4. A relevant passage is that of Pindar in which he talks about Persephone receiving a penalty for an ancient grief:

οἷσι δὲ Φερσεφόνα ποινὰν παλαιοῦ πένθεος
δέξεται, ἐς τὸν ὕπερθεν ἅλιον κείνων ἐνάτῳ ἔτεϊ
ἀνδιδοῖ ψυχὰς πάλιν, ἐκ τᾶν βασιλῆες ἀγαυοί
καὶ σθένει κραιπνοὶ σοφίᾳ τε μέγιστοι
ἄνδρες αὔξοντ'· ἐς δὲ τὸν λοιπὸν χρόνον ἥροες ἁγνοὶ πρὸς ἀνθρώπων καλέονται.

But for those from whom Persephone accepts requital for the ancient grief, in the ninth year she returns their souls to the upper sunlight; from them arise proud kings and men who are swift in strength and greatest in wisdom, and for the rest of time they are called sacred heroes by men.[331]

This 'ancient grief' could be identified as a Titanic primal guilt for Dionysos' murder, but Edmonds believes that the phrase παλαιοῦ πένθεος could refer to any crime. In another work, he claims that: 'Persephone's πένθος is not grief over a

---

329 Plut. *De esu carn.* I, 1.2 (994a) (Tr. Cherniss).
330 See p.28 ff.
331 Pind. fr.133 (Tr. Race); Pl. *Meno*, 81b–c; Edmonds, 1999, p.48.

murdered son but rather her anguish over this turbulent passage from Kore to Queen of the Underworld'.[332] This interpretation presupposes, as Edmonds claims, that the word πένθεος does not have the usual meaning of mourning for a kin's death and also that the word ποινὰν does not have the usual meaning of 'bloodprice' or 'were-gild' but as Edmonds puts it 'ritual honors in recompense for her traumatic abduction to the underworld by Hades'.[333] Even if we accept that this is the case for the sake of the argument, another problem with this interpretation, which Edmonds notes in his discussion, is that there is no reason for the human race to be blamed for Persephone's abduction by Hades. He tackles this issue by suggesting that humans offer honours to Persephone to cheer her up and win a favourable position in the underworld. This does not seem plausible to me since, as Pindar says, these humans are reborn as kings and wise people who are eventually honoured by men as heroes. Humans, then, do not honour Persephone because they are obliged to, but to ask something in return. What they ask is not simply a favourable place in the underworld, but to be honoured as heroes. Finally, Edmonds' interpretation of the gold tablets as an attempt to cheer up Persephone overlooks details that cannot be explained based on Persephone's abduction myth such as the frequent phrases 'I am the child of Earth and Starry Heaven' and 'A bull/ram/kid you fell into milk', and the importance of Mnemosyne and the water of memory. I will address these matters, however, in the following chapter.

It would be particularly helpful to examine the Platonic context around the reference to Pindar in the above passage.[334] Right before this, Plato refers through Socrates to the ideas of wise men and women, priests and priestesses, which he finds true and admirable and notes that they have studied to be able to give a reasonable account of their ministry. These people talked about how the soul is immortal and is born again, and that is why one must live his life in the utmost holiness.[335] It is at this point that Plato references Pindar, and it seems that the

---

332 Edmonds, 2008a.
333 Edmonds, 2008a.
334 Pl. *Meno*, 81a–d.
335 Pl. *Meno*, 81a-b: ΣΩ: Ἔγωγε· ἀκήκοα γὰρ ἀνδρῶν τε καὶ γυναικῶν σοφῶν περὶ τὰ θεῖα πράγματα ΜΕΝ: Τίνα λόγον λεγόντων; ΣΩ: Ἀληθῆ, ἔμοιγε δοκεῖν, καὶ καλόν. ΜΕΝ: Τίνα τοῦτον, καὶ τίνες οἱ λέγοντες; ΣΩ. Οἱ μὲν λέγοντές εἰσι τῶν ἱερέων τε καὶ ἱερειῶν ὅσοις μεμέληκε περὶ ὧν μεταχειρίζονται λόγον οἵοις τ' εἶναι διδόναι· λέγει δὲ καὶ Πίνδαρος καὶ ἄλλοι πολλοὶ τῶν ποιητῶν, ὅσοι θεῖοί εἰσιν. ἃ δὲ λέγουσι, ταυτί ἐστιν· ἀλλὰ σκόπει, εἴ σοι δοκοῦσιν ἀληθῆ λέγειν. φασὶ γὰρ τὴν ψυχὴν τοῦ ἀνθρώπου εἶναι ἀθάνατον, καὶ τοτὲ μὲν τελευτᾶν, ὃ δὴ ἀποθνῄσκειν καλοῦσι, τοτὲ δὲ πάλιν γίγνεσθαι, ἀπόλλυσθαι δ οὐδέποτε· δεῖν δὴ διὰ ταῦτα ὡς ὁσιώτατα διαβιῶναι τὸν βίον: 'SOC: I can; for I have heard from wise men and women who told of things divine that –

way to pay the penalty for Persephone's ancient grief is by living a holy life. Plato goes on to refer to how the soul, after being born many times and after acquiring knowledge of everything, has the ability to recollect everything that it has learned about virtue and all the other things. The question is, then, why did Plato consider the Pindaric fragment relevant to his discussion and chose to quote it in this context? Not only does he relate it to a specific religious group, since he is referring to priests and priestesses, but it is also clear that the particular religious group places an emphasis on knowledge, rebirth and piety. Plato could possibly be referring to the Eleusinian initiates here, but as we saw the Eleusinian *mystai* participated in Demeter's grief for her daughter and not Persephone's for her abduction. What is more, as Bremmer notes: 'the actual performance of the Mysteries points only to agricultural fertility' and 'as noone seems to have put the fact of their Eleusinian initiation on his or her tombstone before the second century BC, most Greeks may well have looked forward more to the promise of wealth in this life than to a good afterlife'.[336] It is more plausible, thus, that Plato has in mind another religious group which might have been the Orphics. It has been suggested by scholarship, as we saw, that Orphism has influenced the formation of the Eleusinian mysteries or that there was an interchange of ideas and mythological background between the two. Orphic beliefs, mythology and rituals could have possibly filled in this 'gap' of afterlife expectations and beliefs in the Eleusinian initiations. Finally, in relation to the previous paragraphs about the 'original sin', since the word ποινὰν in Pindar's fragment is in the singular, it seems more plausible to talk about a single common crime for everyone. This is supported by the fact that according to Socrates there is a single way of paying the penalty and this is the acquiring of knowledge and living a holy life. It is reasonable to assume that if there was a variety in the quantity and the seriousness of the crimes then there would also be a variety in the way of paying the penalty. It is also interesting that in this case the rebirth is not considered as a punishment, since it seems that those who 'offer requital for the ancient grief' are still reborn after nine years. However, they are distinguished from other 'ordinary' people because they are strong and wise men who eventually become heroes. It seems,

---

MEN: What was it they said? SOC: Something true, as I thought, and admirable. MEN: What was it? And who were the speakers? SOC: They were certain priests and priestesses who have studied so as to be able to give a reasoned account of their ministry; and Pindar also and many another poet of heavenly gifts. As to their words, they are these: mark now, if you judge them to be true. They say that the soul of man is immortal, and at one time comes to an end, which is called dying, and at another is born again, but never perishes. Consequently one ought to live all one's life in the utmost holiness.' (Tr. Lamb).

336 Bremmer, 2014, p.16–20.

thus, that the process of 'repaying' the *poinan* is gradual and the ancient grief cannot be simply erased with a 'one-off payment'.

Conclusion

Based on the passages we have examined in this chapter it became evident that the myth of Dionysos' dismemberment was clearly associated to Orphics as early as the beginning of the Hellenistic period through sources such as Philodemus. The myth's association with rites is evidenced in the Gurôb Papyrus (3rd B.C.) and later authors repeatedly link the myth to Orpheus and the institution of mysteries. Based on all the evidence discussed in this chapter Edmonds' argument that this myth was wrongly reconstructed based on Christian religious models and that it did not give rise to specific beliefs cannot be accepted. Nor his argument of the anthropogony being fabricated by Olympiodorus since sources earlier than him, such as Proclus, refer to the anthropogony. Also, Plutarch and Plotinus link the incarnation of humans as a punishment, to the dismemberment myth and refer to two different human natures, a divine and a wicked one which Plutarch and Plato identify as Titanic.

It was mostly through juxtaposing several passages and establishing textual similarities between them which were Orphic in nature, that I was able to identify – where this was not stated explicitly – that ancient authors were indeed referring to the Orphic myth, beliefs or mysteries and not some other tradition such as the Eleusinian. The intertextual similarities between the passages from Plato, Damascius and Dio Chrysostom, allowed us to define as Orphic the idea of incarnation as a punishment and imprisonment of the soul, and relate it to the descent of mortals from the Titans. Moreover, several passages from Plato use Orphic terminology as found in the *Orphic Rhapsodies* in reference to an innate wicked and divine nature and we also established that the formulaic phrase of being delivered from pain/toil as found in Plato and elsewhere must have been Orphic. This demonstrates the importance of undertaking this textual comparison between our sources since it seems that, in some cases, references to the interpretation of Orphic mythology are not entirely straightforward.

4 The Gold Tablets – Practical and Eschatological Aspects

4.1 Introduction

The gold tablets constitute one of our major sources in defining Orphism. In this chapter, however, I will not take anything as a given and begin by examining whether they should actually be considered Orphic or not. There will be a four layered analysis of the tablets. First, I will discuss archaeological and geographical information in order to establish common elements between them. Second, a textual analysis will follow, including a comparison with Homeric epics and an attempt to answer the question of whether the texts have an archetype. Third, I will discuss the tablets from a ritual perspective, attempting to detect any performative and ritual elements. Fourth, I will attempt to define the eschatological and religious beliefs of the owners of the tablets, their possible relation to Orphic works and ideas established so far, and interpret the symbolism of important elements found in the tablets' narrative. Also, a comparison with a ritual from the Greek Magical Papyri which shows similarities to the gold tablets will be made. This chapter precedes the discussion of the Derveni Papyrus and the *Orphic Rhapsodies* since it is easier to determine specific religious practical activity first and then detect its possible relation to theogonical and cosmogonical material – if there is any relation at all. Modern scholarship has heavily based its interpretation of the tablets on the Zagreus myth, discussed in the previous chapter, considering it one of the major arguments for identifying the tablets as Orphic.

4.2 Archaeological and Geographical Information

What makes the gold tablets fascinating is their vast geographical and chronological dispersal. Around 40 tablets have been published so far which were found in areas such as Calabria, Sicily, Rome, Crete and various areas of mainland Greece such as Thessaly, Macedonia, Elis and Achaea.[337] Their chronology ranges from the 4th century B.C. to the 2nd century A.D. The following table (Table 3, p.115) provides information about the tablets' date, length and find-spot, and

---

[337] Three additional tablets are included in Edmonds' edition, two of which are also included in Bernabé/Jiménez's edition: F8 = -/S3a, F9 = -/S3b and F13. They have only names inscribed: F8: Ξεναρίστη – Xenariste, F9: Ἄνδρων – Andron, F13: Παλάθα – Palatha.

their *sigla* in the most recent editions. If we establish textual and other similarities between tablets chronologically and geographically distant from each other this might constitute evidence of a common religious background.

Let us focus on the non-textual similarities first. The tablets are all made of gold, a material that was traditionally connected with divinity and deification.[338] In the case of the Cretan lamellae and *epistomia* (a term referring to gold tablets which have the shape of a mouth), some scholars have suggested that they were descendants of the Mycenaean gold masks; a practical and cheaper replacement of covering the whole face with gold.[339] The gold tablets were found inside graves or cemetery areas and they belonged both to male and female deceased persons. Some of them were found placed on the mouth or the chest of the deceased while others were found inside cases such as an amulet, a terracotta lamp, a bronze hydria and a marble *osteotheke*.[340] In his recent edition of the tablets, Edmonds provides a list of archaeological information as taken from Tzifopoulos' edition of the Cretan gold tablets and *epistomia*.[341] Most of the tablets are rectangular and some of them were found folded, while others have the shape of an ivy or myrtle leaf and less often olive leaf.[342] One of the two tablets from Pelinna (D1/D2) was found unfolded inside the grave but appears to have been folded at an earlier time.[343] This might indicate that the tablet was in the possession of the deceased before he died and thus was not created by a priest specifically for the purposes of the burial; but this is just one of the possibilities. The cases where the tablets were folded might be related to secrecy, in the sense of hiding the text from those performing the burial or anyone else.[344] The tablet from Petelia (B1) which included one of the longest texts, is dated to the 4th century B.C. but was found inside a cylinder attached to a chain which is dated to the 2nd–3rd A.D. This means that someone retrieved the tablet from the grave, presumably read it, and then rolled it and placed it in the cylinder. Some reasons why someone would do that are either to know the text (though this does not explain why it was subsequently placed in a cylinder), or to protect the text from other potentially 'curious'

---

338 Brown, 1998, p.393.
339 Tzifopoulos, 2011, p.168.
340 Chest: B10, D1, D2, D4; Mouth: B6, F3. Probably E5 and F7. Amulet: B1. Lamp: B11. Hydria: B2, B9. Osteotheke: D5.
341 Detailed archaeological information about the tablets' shape and position found, and of burial and grave goods can be found in Tzifopoulos 2010 in Appendix 1 and Edmonds, 2011a, p.42–48.
342 Tzifopoulos, 2011, p.170; F2, F4, F5, F7, D1, D2, E4, F6.
343 Riedweg, 2011, p.221/fn.10.
344 Tzifopoulos, 2010, p.95–96.

people. The majority of the burials, where the method could be identified, were inhumations; only four cases were cremation. As Tzifopoulos records, the gold tablets were never placed in the pyre to be burned with the deceased, and they were placed in the urn after the cremation along with the human remains.[345] This is evidence that they were intended to be used in the underworld by the deceased and they should not be destroyed. This, along with the placement of the tablets on top of the mouth, indicates that they perhaps served the purpose of becoming the 'voice' of the deceased person in the underworld. Their physical use in the underworld is also indicated by their frequent placement on the hand.

Tab. 3: List of gold tablets with sigla of most recent editions.

Edmonds	Graf/Johnston	Bernabé/ Jiménez	Area Found	Date	No. of lines
A1	5 Thurii 3	488/L9	Lucania	4th B.C.	10
A2	7 Thurii 5	489/L10a	Lucania	4th B.C.	7
A3	6 Thurii 4	490/L10b	Lucania	4th B.C.	7
A4	3 Thurii 1	487/L8	Lucania	4th B.C.	6
A5	9 Rome	491/L11	Italy	2nd A.D.	4
B1	2 Petelia	476/L3	Calabria	4th B.C.	14
B2	25 Pharsalos	477/L4	Thessaly	350 – 300 B.C.	10
B3	10 Eleutherna 1	478/L5a	Crete	2nd – 1st B.C.	3
B4	11 Eleutherna 2	479/L5b	Crete	2nd – 1st B.C.	3
B5	12 Eleutherna 3	480/L5c	Crete	2nd – 1st B.C.	3
B6	16 Mylopotamos	481/L5d	Crete	2nd B.C.	3
B7	13 Eleutherna 4	482/L5e	Crete	2nd – 1st B.C.	3
B8	14 Eleutherna 5	483/L5f	Crete	2nd – 1st B.C.	3
B9	29 Unknown	484/L6	Thessaly	Mid. 4th B.C.	4
B10	1 Hipponion	474/L1	Calabria	5th B.C. (ca. 400 B.C.)	16
B11	8 Entella	475/L2	Sicily	3rd B.C.	21
B12	18 Rethymnon 2	484a/L6a	Crete	2nd – 1st B.C.	4
C1	4 Thurii 2	492/L12	Lucania	4th B.C.	10
D1	26 a Pellina	485/L7a	Thessaly	Late 4th B.C.	7
D2	26 b Pellina	486/L7b	Thessaly	Late 4th B.C.	7

---

345 Tzifopoulos, 2010.

Edmonds	Graf/Johnston	Bernabé/Jiménez	Area Found	Date	No. of lines
D3	27 Pherae 1	493/L13	Thessaly	350 – 300 B.C.	6
D4	30 Amphipolis	496n/L16n	Macedonia	4th– Early 3rd B.C.	4
D5	28 Pherae 2	493a/L13a	Thessaly	4th– Early 3rd B.C.	2
E1	38 Agios Athan.	495a/L15a	Macedonia	Hell. Period	3
E2	15 Eleutherna 6	495/L15	Crete	2nd – 1st B.C.	2
E3	37 Vergina (Aigai)	496k/L16k	Macedonia	Hell. Period	1
E4	31 Pella/Dion 1	496b/L16b	Macedonia	End of 4th B.C.	3
E5	17 Rethymnon 1	494/L16l	Crete	25 B.C.–40 A.D.	2
F1	23 Elis 1	496i/L16i	Elis		1
F2	20 Aigion 1	496e/L16e	Achaia	Hell. Period	1
F3	35 Methone	496h/L16h	Pieria/Macedonia	4th B.C.	1
F4	21 Aigion 2	496c/L16c	Achaia	Hell. Period	1
F5	22 Aigion 3	496d/L16d	Achaia	Hell. Period	1
F6	32 Pella/Dion 2	496a/L16a	Macedonia		1
F7	24 Elis 2	496j/L16j	Elis	3rd B.C.	1
F8 (Coin)	-	-/S3a	Pydna/Pieria	336 – 300 B.C.	1
F9 (Coin)	-	-/S3b	Pydna/Pieria	336 – 300 B.C.	1
F10	36 Europos	496g/L16g	Macedonia		1
F11	34 Pella/Dion 4	496f/L16f	Macedonia	Late 4th B.C.	1
F12	33 Pella/Dion 3	-/S5	Macedonia	Hell. Period	1
-	19 Lesbos	-	Lesbos	-	-
-	39 Uncertain	-	-	-	13

In terms of grave goods and offerings we have eight cases where the deceased has received burial offerings, *enagismoi* and sacrifices after the burial. Five come from Thurii in Lucania and three from various locations in Macedonia.[346] This could indicate that the burial offerings were a practice of the religious groups active in these two areas. On the other hand, there were no offerings at graves in other areas of Macedonia, so the offerings might indicate a special status of the deceased. In fact, one of the deceased from Thurii, appears to be the recipient of

---

346 Lucania: A1–A4; C1. Macedonia: D4 (Amphipolis), E5 (Agios Athanasios), F10 (Europos).

a local hero-cult.[347] The tumulus above this grave is comprised of eight strata consisting of 'ashes, carbon and burnt pottery sherds topped by earth above, a strong indication of rituals, sacrifices, and hero-worship of the dead buried inside'.[348] This case is unique because a gold tablet (A4) inscribed with 6 lines of text was found inside another gold tablet (C1) folded like an envelope and inscribed with a 10-line long text of what might be words in between nonsensical sequences of letters. Also, this tablet clearly states that the deceased has turned into a god from a mortal (θεὸς ἐγένου ἐξ ἀνθρώπου) as is also the case with tablet A1 from Thurii and a quite late tablet from Rome (A5 – 2nd A.D) for which we do not have any archaeological information.

Other grave goods appear to have Dionysiac connotations. The grave of D2 (Pelinna/Thessaly) included a figurine of a comic actor sitting on an altar and in the grave of F3 were found ivory fragments of the bier's decorations which included figures from the Dionysiac cycle. In several cases the owners were crowned with wreaths made out of gold or gilt clay or with a diadem.[349] Also, in the grave of the owner of tablet 19 Lesbos (Fritz-Graf) 'a gold diadem with Herakles' knot flanked by stylised Aeolic capitals' was found along with some gold olive leaves and the 'inscribed gold sheet with an Orphic text' which unfortunately has not been published yet.[350] The scarcity of wreaths found in the hundreds of tombs in Athens for example, in contrast to their frequent reference in literature and inscriptions as given to honoured citizens or initiates and then dedicated to the appropriate god, suggests that the crowned deceased 'would have certainly expected to attain eternal life among the blessed'.[351] We might not have any gold tablets found in Athens but, as we will see, other eschatological evidence present ideas similar to the gold tablets. The discovery of wreaths might indicate an initiation where the wreath was acquired, since it is a symbol often associated with mystic initiation, or with the symposium and the triumph at a competition.[352] As Bernabé and Jiménez San Cristóbal note, all these symbolic values of the wreath could appear simultaneously in this context.[353] In a tablet from Thurii (A1) we find the verse 'I came on with swift feet to the desired crown'.

---

347 A4 and C1.
348 Tzifopoulos, 2010, p.72.
349 Diadem: D2, F1. Gold or gilt-clay wreath: E4, F6, F5, F10 and an unincised tablet from Pella/Macedonia (200–150 B.C.). See Tzifopoulos for archaeological information (2011a, p.171 and Appendix for the unincised tablet) and Edmonds, 2011a, p.42–48.
350 Catling, 1989, p.93.
351 Despoini, 1996, p.28 as cited by Tzifopoulos, 2011a, p.171.
352 Tzifopoulos, 2011, p.172.
353 Bernabé and Jiménez San Cristóbal, 2008, p.126

Could this desired crown be the one with which the seven cases mentioned above were crowned? This possibility relates to the question of whether the tablets echo in any way a ritual, a matter which will be discussed further on.

As mentioned earlier and as outlined in Table 3 above, the tablets were found in various areas around Magna Graecia and mainland Greece. As Bernabé and Jiménez San Cristóbal mention, the majority of the places in which the tablets were found 'have a specific connection with Orpheus or with Orphism either because some episode of the myth of Orpheus was situated there, or because other texts of an Orphic character have appeared there'.[354] We have already discussed Macedonia in Chapter 2 analysing testimonies and evidence for Orphic rites taking place there. As far as Thessaly is concerned, there was a pan-Thessalian cult of Ennodia/Brimo from the 7th century B.C. which is especially well-documented for Pherai.[355] Thurii was a city established in 443 B.C. following Pericles' plea to all the Greek cities to participate in re-founding a Panhellenic colony at Sybaris in Calabria in Italy which had been destroyed in 510 B.C.[356] The coins from Thurii always had the head of Athena on the obverse as an allusion to her mother city and on the reverse there was a bull which might point to Dionysos due to the association he has with this animal.[357] Lesbos is related to one of the mythical versions of Orpheus' death, as we saw, in which after he was murdered by the Meanads, his severed head, which was still singing, was thrown into the Thracian river Hebros from which it travelled to Lesbos where it continued to dictate poems and was honoured by the Lesbian people.[358]

---

[354] Bernabé and Jiménez San Cristóbal, 2008, p.183. Bernabé and Jiménez San Cristóbal, 2011, p.72–74.
[355] Ferrari and Prauscello, 2007, p.200.
[356] Diod. Sic. XII.10ff; Astour, 1985, p.29. See also Rutter, 1973, p.161.
[357] Kraay & Hirmer, 1966, Plate 86–87–88, no.250–54. Sophocles calls him 'bull-eating' (Διονύσου τοῦ ταυροφάγου) (*Tyro* fr.668 Lloyd-Jones) and 'of the bull's horns' (Ἴακχος βούκερως) (fr.959 Lloyd-Jones). Plutarch, in a passage were he claims that Dionysos is identical to Osiris, making special reference to the fact that they are both dismembered, mentions the following: 'For the same reason many of the Greeks make statues of Dionysos in the form of a bull; and the women of Elis invoke him, praying that the god may come with the hoof of a bull; and the epithet applied to Dionysos among the Argives is 'Son of the Bull' (βουγενὴς) (Plut. *De Is. et Os.* 364e–f). Also, the followers of Dionysos are often depicted visually as having horns (Apulian crater. St. Petersburg, The State Hermitage Museum, 6 312 (1. Inv.), St 880 (2. Inv.). *LIMC*: Dionysos 870; Apulian bell crater, 350–340 B.C. Copenhagen, Glyptothèque Ny Carlsberg, 2249 (1. Inv.), H 46 (2. Inv.). *LIMC*: Dionysos 357). Lycoph. *Alex.* 209-10: θεοῦ Ταύρῳ ('bull-god'). See also p.164 ff and p.268.
[358] Bernabé and Jiménez San Cristóbal, 2008, p.184; Verg. *G.* 4.523; Ov. *Met.* 11.50; Hyg. *Poet. Astr.* 2.7; Philostr. *Her.* 5.3.

Many of the tablets were found in Crete which thus requires a more detailed discussion, especially since authors such as Diodorus claim that the Orphic *teletai* originated in Crete.[359] Six of the tablets were found at the ancient city of Eleutherna which is very close to the Idaean Cave, and one was found at nearby Mylopotamos. Two more tablets were found at Rethymnon which is also relatively close to Eleutherna. All the Cretan gold tablets were thus found around the same area. Apollo was one of the major divinities of Eleutherna. Its coins, dated from the mid 5th to the 2nd century B.C., depict Apollo laureate on the obverse and in the reverse either Apollo standing nude, holding a sphere and a bow, or Apollo with a bow and a sphere, seated on an omphalos with a lyre beside it. As Tzifopoulos argues, the necropolis at Orthi Petra at Eleutherna which dates from the 9th to the end of 6th century B.C. 'attests to a variety of burial practices which demonstrate a developing ideology and self-consciousness of the city's inhabitants during this period'.[360] At this cemetery there was also a public cenotaph or heroon inside which a baetyl – a sacred stone – was found and on whose roof the ten shield-bearing warriors, probably the Kouretes, stood as akroteria or cornices. Tzifopoulos suggests that Eleutherna's most prominent necropolis might have developed from 'an intra-mural monument of one or more aristocratic clan-members who claimed their ancestry from one or more of the Kouretes'.[361] According to an Euripidean fragment from the *Cretans*, discussed in Chapter 3, the *mystes* of Idaean Zeus were also *mystes* of Zagreus.[362] The Cretan myth referring to the daemons called Kouretes who danced around infant Idaean Zeus while clashing their shields so that his cries would not be heard by Kronos who wanted to swallow him, is similar to the Zagreus myth where the Kouretes were guarding infant Dionysos from the Titans.[363] In the same Euripidean passage, as we saw, the chorus refers to priests who seem to have many Orphic characteristics.[364]

---

[359] Diod. Sic. V.77.3: 'They also assert that the honours accorded to the gods and their sacrifices and the initiatory rites observed in connection with the mysteries were handed down from Crete to the rest of men, and to support this they advance the following most weighty argument, as they conceive it: The initiatory rite which is celebrated by the Athenians in Eleusis, the most famous, one may venture, of them all, and that of Samothrace, and the one practised in Thrace among the Cicones, whence Orpheus came who introduced them – these are all handed down in the form of a mystery...'; V.75.4: 'This god <Dionysos> was born in Crete, men say, of Zeus and Persephone, and Orpheus has handed down the tradition in the initiatory rites that he was torn in pieces by the Titans.' (Tr. Oldfather).
[360] Tzifopoulos, 2011, p.184–185.
[361] Tzifopoulos, 2011, p.184.
[362] Eur. *Cr.* fr.472; See p.88.
[363] Guthrie, 1952, p.117. See Table 2 at p.85.
[364] Eur. *Cr.* fr.472. See p.88 ff. Bernabé and Jiménez San Cristóbal, 2008, p.183.

The discovery of the baetyl inside this cenotaph might also relate the Cretan Zeus with Dionysos since the *omphalos* at Delphi has been associated with Dionysos. Tatian claims that the *omphalos* was in fact Dionysos' tomb and the dramatists associate the Delphic rock with Dionysos, Bacchic mysteries and initiates.[365] Dionysos' death is most probably associated with Orphics, since he dies in the Orphic myth of dismemberment, his parts are then collected by Apollo and taken to Delphi, on behalf of Zeus who resurrects him.[366] The earliest author attesting that there was a tomb of Dionysos at Delphi is Philochorus (3rd B.C.), who quotes the epitaph: Ἔστιν ἰδεῖν τὴν ταφὴν αὐτοῦ ἐν Δελφοῖς παρὰ τὸ Ἀπόλλωνα τὸν χρυσοῦν. Βάθρον δέ τι εἶναι ὑπονοεῖται ἡ σορὸς, ἐν ᾧ γράφεται "Ἐνθάδε κεῖται θανὼν Διόνυσος ὁ ἐκ Σεμέλης'.[367] Also, a great Bacchic festival was celebrated at Delphi every second year and it was believed that in the three winter months Apollo was absent and Dionysos took his place. This is attested by Plutarch, who was a priest at Delphi for many years, in a passage where he mentions Dionysos Zagreus and the myth of dismemberment in relation to Delphic rites of transformation, and he identifies Dionysos and Apollo as being the same entity.[368] These things, as he says, are only known to the enlightened (σοφώτεροι).[369] Furthermore, Pausanias refers to an *omphalos* being present in Phlious, a town near Sikyon, close to which there was a sanctuary of Dionysos and a sanctuary of Apollo.[370] Two Epimenidian verses survive where he denies that the *omphalos* was at Delphi while he is said to refer to the Cretan *omphalos* which is not the central point 'but the navel of the infant Zeus, which had fallen to the ground when he was being brought to Crete'.[371] If we take into consideration the mythological similarities of Zeus and Dionysos who have associations with motifs of death and rebirth, and the possibility that some aristocratic clan members at Eleutherna claimed to be descended from the Kouretes, as well as the baetyl and

---

365 Tatianus, *Ad Gr.* 8; Eur. *Ion* 550, 715; Soph. *Ant.* 1126; Ar. *Nub.* 603.
366 Plut. *De E.* 388c ff: He notes a connection with the myth of dismemberment too. Parke and Wormell, 1956, p.15 and p.335–46 for various links of Dionysos to Delphi.
367 Phil. FGrHist 22: 'His burial-place can be seen at Delphi next to golden Apollo. The funerary urn seems to be a kind of pedestral, on which it is inscribed: 'Here lies dead, Dionysos, born from Semele.' This however was possibly invented (Kerényi, 1996, p.232).
368 Plut. *De E.* 388f–389c, tr. Babbitt: (389c). Kerényi, 1996, p.214–15ff. For a discussion of evidence showing that the cult of Dionysos preceded the one of Apollo at Delphi see Kerényi, 1996, p.204ff. Parke and Wormell, 1956, p.336. See also Tzifopoulos, 2010, p.140–143.
369 Plut.*De E.* 389a.
370 Paus. II.13.7.
371 DK3B11: οὔτε γὰρ ἦν γαίης μέσος ὀμφαλὸς οὔτε θαλάσσης | εἰ δέ τις ἔστι, θεοῖς δῆλος, θνητοῖσι δ' ἄφαντος.

the associations of omphalos with Zeus, Dionysos and Apollo, and finally statements such as those from Diodorus and Epimenides, we can see how eschatological ideas about rebirth and divine descend might have travelled from one place to the next. Since Apollo and Zeus were not chthonic deities, a deity of the nature of Zagreus Dionysos would be particularly suitable to complete eschatological ideas of death and rebirth. It remains to see whether such ideas were also present in the gold tablets.

4.3 New Discoveries: New Theories

Comparetti (1835–1927) was the scholar who perhaps had the biggest influence on the subsequent scholarship on the tablets, since he was one of the first to provide serious discussion of the matter and his theories were adopted and used as a starting point for many years. He considered that the tablets belonged to 'the popular spread of Orphism', and argued that their verses 'are taken from the various books of the Orphic canon' and rejected any relationship to Pythagoreanism, with which Orphism has often been associated.[372] Comparetti furthermore identified the Euklēs mentioned in the Thurii tablets with 'the infernal Dionysos, or the Zagreus of the Orphics', and interpreted them based on his myth and the model of original sin.[373] Based on the six gold tablets available to him in 1882 he associated their eschatology with the Orphic anthropogony from the Titans and argued that the initiates claimed to be purified from the original guilt of Dionysos' murder by the Titans 'for which the human soul is excluded from the community of the other gods', 'condemned to a succession of births and deaths'.[374] His interpretation was picked up by Rohde and Harrison and through their influential studies *Psyche* (1894) and *Prolegomena to the Study of Greek Religion* (1903) continued to make an impact and lead many scholars to consider the Zagreus myth and the idea of an original sin as basic components of Orphism for many years following.[375] Rohde ascribed the gold tablets to Orphics and considered that their representation of the afterlife and the Underworld influenced Pindar's Victory Odes.[376] Harrison discussed them under the heading of 'Orphic eschatology' and for her

---

[372] Comparetti, 1882 p.117.
[373] Comparetti, 1882, p.116–118. Graf and Johnston, 2013, p.55; Edmonds 1999, p.39. Euklēs tablets: A1, A2, A3, A5.
[374] Tablets: B1, A4, C, A1, A3, A2. Comparetti, 1882, p.116.
[375] Graf and Johnston, 2013, p.56.
[376] Rohde, 1925, p.417ff and Appendix IX, p.596–98.

the texts were part of a reformed, more spiritual Dionysiac cult created by Orpheus, while the Orphic movement truly depicted the 'philosophical force of Greek religion before the rise of true philosophy'.[377] However, not everyone was convinced about the Orphic identity of the gold tablets and Linforth (1941) did not include the gold tablets in his chronological discussion of the evidence for Orphism.

In his edition, Zuntz (1971), with four more tablets to examine than previously, arranged the tablets in two groups: in group A the deceased addresses Persephone and mentions his divine origin as a means to be admitted among the privileged of the Underworld; in group B the deceased has to be aware of the guardians of the lake of Mnemosyne and instructions for an Underworld journey are given.[378] He considered them to belong to the Pythagorean tradition, based on the reincarnation motif found in one of the tablets of group A (A1) and denied any connection with Orpheus.[379] But a new find, the Tablet excavated in Hipponion which included the word βάχχοι, restored Comparetti's attribution of the Tablets to Dionysiac mysteries and overturned Zuntz's attribution of the Tablets to Pythagoreanism alone.[380] Pugliese-Caratelli (1993 and 2001) also distinguished the tablets in two groups, the Pythagorean 'Mnemosynial' ones and the Orphic ones where the fountain of Mnemosyne is absent.[381] Riedweg's (1998) edition followed Zuntz's classification. In another work – revised in Edmonds' edition (2011a) – he attempted to reconstruct an original text from which all the verses from the tablets came and to situate them in a ritualistic context. He argues that there are significant 'reasons to consider all gold leaves in the end as a unity, regardless of all differences concerning their individual form, their geographical, chronological, and socio-cultural provenance' and that 'even if there are numerous points of contact between Orphism and Pythagoreanism, as has been well known since antiquity <...> the attribution of the gold leaves to Pythagorean ritual <...> is unlikely to find a great number of followers nowadays' after the discovery of tablets which mention *mystai* and *Bacchoi*.[382] Graf and Johnston's edition (2007 and revised in 2013) arranged the tablets based solely on geographical criteria.[383] Bernabé and Jiménez San Cristóbal (2008) arranged the tablets according to a reconstructed narrative based on 'the soul's transition towards the other world, since most of

---

377 Harrison, 1903, 573ff and Appendix, p.660ff. Graf and Johnston, 2013, p.56–57.
378 Zuntz, 1971, p.277–393. B2, B7, B8, E2.
379 Graf and Johnston, 2013, p.62.
380 B10. Graf and Johnston, 2013, p.62.
381 Pugliese-Caratelli, 1993, p.11–16 and 2001, p.10–20.
382 Riedweg, 2011, p.221 and p.223/fn.23.
383 The text and translation in this book are taken from Edmonds 2011a.

the tablets refer to various stages of its journey', and discuss them in chapters.[384] They conclude that they belong to a single religious tradition based on 'the type of text (hexameters mixed with other meters or non-metrical formulas), the theme of the Beyond, the repetition of *topoi*, the consistent use of gold and their great dispersion in space and time'. They also argue that the users of the tablets could not be other than Orphics, using arguments related to 'authorship, geography, mystical environment, references to purity and justice, the characteristics of the gods cited and iconography'.[385] Their interpretation is heavily based on the Zagreus myth and they argue that 'the religious movement to which the leaves belong is a mystery cult'.[386] Herrero de Jáuregui also argues that 'the connection with the myth of Dionysos and the Titans is relevant to explain some crucial points', something which might label the tablets as Orphic. However, he notes that this does not mean that the owners of the tablets should be called 'Orphics' since he does not believe there was the 'uniformity of doctrine and practice' which would characterise a sect but that "Orphic' conceptions' were flexible and unsystematic.[387]

Tzifopoulos' edition (2010) includes only the gold tablets found in Crete along with some un-incised gold *epistomia* which are not included in any other edition; he discusses them in the Cretan context with a particular emphasis on archaeological details. He arranges the totality of the published tablets in seven groups, two of which are the same as Zuntz's. Group C which includes the 'so-called Orphic texts', comprises one gold tablet and, as Tzifopoulos suggests, it should also perhaps include other related texts such as the Derveni Papyrus, the Olbian Tablets and the Gurôb Papyrus, all of which will be discussed later on. His classification aims to project their similarities, since as he says the tablets' texts are interrelated, but also to emphasise their divergences.[388] As he argues:

> The context that produced these texts is not only a Bacchic-Orphic Panhellenic mystery cult, as the other texts denote from Italy, the Peloponnese, Thessaly, and Macedonia with which they share strong similarities. The Cretan examples argue in favour of a process by which the Bacchic-Orphic Panhellenic mystery cult which produced these texts underwent changes and adaptations in order to cater to local (or individual) cultic and ritual concerns

---

[384] Bernabé and Jiménez San Cristóbal, 2008, p.6. Bernabé had already included the gold tablets in his edition of the Orphic fragments (2004).
[385] Bernabé and Jiménez San Cristóbal, 2008, p.181–205.
[386] Bernabé and Jiménez San Cristóbal, 2011, p.73. Their arguments are summarised in Bernabé and Jiménez San Cristóbal, 2011, p.69ff.
[387] Herrero de Jáuregui, 2011, p.273.
[388] Tzifopoulos, 2010, p.100.

about the afterlife, a process that in all probability had also taken place in Italy, the Peloponnese, Thessaly, and Macedonia.[389]

The most recent edition of the gold tablets by Edmonds (2011a) arranges the tablets in six groups based on the typology of Zuntz, Riedweg and Tzifopoulos.[390] Edmonds' edition is very useful since it summarises the most recent scholarship and provides important archaeological information. Edmonds had earlier discussed the gold tablets in another work (2004) and concluded that:

> With cautionary quotes, however, the term 'Orphic' may be used to indicate the nature of religious cults such as those that produced the gold tablets, groups to whom the difference between themselves and the common herd was of primary importance, who emphasized their ritual purity and special divine connections over other qualifications more valued by the mainstream society.[391]

In my opinion, this interpretation is limiting, since it focuses on the social aspect of the matter, without taking psychological factors into consideration. Differentiation from others is not always appealing, while, on the other hand, a cult that promises a divine status and a happy post mortem existence as the gold tablets did, would – presumably – always be. Moreover, Edmonds' suggestion presupposes that not everyone could acquire these tablets, otherwise the distinction from the 'common herd' would not be of any importance.[392] However, there is no evidence that this is true. Despite the numerous editions and intensive scholarly discussion, questions about the ownership of the tablets and their exact purpose are still unresolved, a situation to which the continuing discovery of more tablets contributes.

4.4 Textual Analysis

Before proceeding to discuss the content of the tablets I must refer briefly to some information on the transcription of the text. One question is when were the tablets produced and by whom? Was it by the deceased persons themselves or by a professional inscriber or a priest? The text seems to have been transcribed rapidly, as the 'systematic recurrence of faulty or omitted letters indicates'.[393] We also

---

[389] Tzifopoulos, 2011, p.189.
[390] Edmonds, 2011a, p.10–11.
[391] Edmonds, 2004, p.103–104.
[392] Edmonds, 2004, p.108.
[393] Calame, 2011, p.208.

need to consider that the tablets were very small, not only for financial reasons (gold is an expensive material), but also perhaps because they were usually placed on top of the mouth, on the chest or the hand. For this reason, a complete text would not fit on the tablets and thus only the most important or relevant parts of the texts were chosen – since in most of the cases there are gaps in the narrative. As Jiménez San Cristóbal suggests, the fate of the profane is perhaps not mentioned not only because it was irrelevant, but also because it might have been considered a bad omen for the deceased.[394] There is, thus, a possibility that there was a longer text from which they derive. It is unclear whether the tablets were initially cut in their shape and then inscribed or the other way around. Tablet E2 seems to have been cut carelessly – or as if it was done in the dark – since the cut goes through the words (see Tzifopoulos 2010, Fig.7a/7b). In other instances, the letters seem to be crammed or too much space is unused. These may be minor details, but they might indicate that the tablets, or some of them, were not produced by professionals. On the other hand, on some tablets, the lettering is careful, with very few mistakes, which might indicate that they were inscribed by a professional.[395] It is, however, difficult to make suggestions based solely on this information, since the transcription and the lettering might be due to personal idiosyncrasies.

The use of the actual gold tablet as a 'symbol' of initiation, or someone's status, or a ticket to the Isles of the Blessed, might surpass the particular text inscribed on them. Perhaps it is not as important which phrases were used by the owner of the tablets, as that the tablet itself was placed in the tomb and existed as a material token which had an 'extra-textual function'.[396] In this sense, the fact that all the tablets were made out of gold, were inscribed with text and placed in the tomb in specific positions on the body, is perhaps the strongest indicator that they should be grouped together as part of the same religious phenomenon. A variety of people, chronologically and geographically distant from each other, felt the need to carry text inscribed on gold with them in the tomb and consequently the underworld. This not only shows the importance of *logos* (text) and memory for the owners of the tablets but also the existence of a collective belief between them that they would be able to use this text, this information and this knowledge in the afterlife for a better lot. Such a belief could not exist without a specific eschatological framework, since it is closely linked with matters such as the 'substance' of the soul, its identity and abilities after-death, with a specific

---

394 Jiménez San Cristóbal, 2015, p.113.
395 Tzifopoulos, 2010, p.59–60.
396 Tzifopoulos, 2010, p.96–97; p.108–109.

underworld topography and afterlife expectations, and with the importance of specific gods in the soul's afterlife bliss. The way, however, to discover who and what the generative force behind these tablets was, is exactly through analysing the inscribed text.

As mentioned in the previous section, the tablets have been arranged into groups by various scholars.[397] In four of them, including some of the longest inscribed texts, instructions for an underworld journey are given without a specific god or goddess being mentioned, while in fourteen of them, Persephone and other gods such as Brimo, Demeter, Zeus and Plouto are mentioned.[398] Twelve include the phrase Γῆς παῖς εἰμι καὶ Οὐρανοῦ ἀστερόεντος ('I am a child of Earth and starry Sky') as an answer to the questions 'Who are you? Where are you from?' and 'What are you seeking in Hades?', asked by the guardians of the lake of Memory.[399] In five the word Mnemosyne is mentioned. In A1 and A4 we find the phrase ἔριφος ἐς γάλ' ἔπετον ('a young goat you fell into milk') and in D1 and D2 the phrases ταῦρος εἰς γάλα ἔθορες, αἶψα εἰς γάλα ἔθορες and κριὸς εἰς γάλα ἔπεσες ('Bull, you jumped into milk, Quickly, you jumped into milk, Ram you fell into milk').[400] Those found in mainland Greece have only a few words inscribed on them which are either the name of the deceased alone, or the word μύστης accompanied by the name of the deceased, while two of them mention Persephone and another two mention Dionysos Baccheios.[401] Finally an unspecified number of gold tablets found in fifteen graves at Pella/Dion and dated to the 4th century B.C. are each inscribed with the name of the deceased and placed on the deceased's mouth.[402]

However, tablets with similar text were found in different areas. For example, tablets with the phrase 'I am the child of Earth and starry Heaven' (Group B) were found in Crete, Mainland Greece and Italy. Also, tablets with the salutation *chaire* to Plouton and Persephone (Group E) were found in both Crete and Macedonia, while a tablet from Group A from Thurii (A4) also includes the salutation *chaire*. Moreover, the tablets referring to Mnemosyne were found in Italy and mainland Greece, while one of these tablets found in Rome also includes the formula 'Pure I come from the pure' (Group A). In this way, tablets from Group A have common

---

[397] For the most recent one see Edmonds 2011a, p.41–48 which is followed in this chapter.
[398] B10, B1, B11, B2.
[399] B10, B1, B11, B3, B4, B5, B7, B8, B6, B12, B2, B9.
[400] B10, B1, B11, A5, B2.
[401] Persephone: E4, E3. Dionysos: D4, D1, D2.
[402] Graf and Johnston, 2013, p.46.

elements with Group B according to Edmonds' classification. Additionally, tablets from Group A which have the 'pure from the pure' formula are linked with tablets from Group D which mention Dionysos and Persephone, through the phrase of 'falling into milk'. Minor textual similarities also bring two different groups together, such as the words λειμῶνάς θ'{ε} ἱεροὺς (sacred meadows) from a Group A tablet (A4.6) which are also found in a tablet from Group D (D3.2): ἱερὸν λειμῶνα (sacred meadow). Finally, tablets from across all Groups apart from F, use nonsensical words and *symbola*, which is a strong indication of a common religious background and perhaps secrecy. Because of these textual similarities which entangle tablets classified in different groups by Edmonds and tablets geographically and chronologically distant from each other, it appears probable that they stem from the same religious background and could derive from a textual archetype, without this meaning that there was a central religious administration behind them.

Bernabé and Jiménez San Cristóbal suggest that the 'different types of texts refer to different moments of the soul's journey and have different functions'.[403] Tablets from Group B refer to the initial moments of the deceased's journey, tablets from Group A refer to the point where the soul must mention to Persephone the passwords which prove its purity, and tablets from Group D and tablet A4 are greetings made by another person to the dead. Tablets from Groups E and F are either salutations to the gods or for identifying the owner as a *mystēs*. In my opinion, the tablets from Group A, B, C, D and E have to do with an underworld journey and an encounter of the deceased with subterranean entities – whether they be gods or the guardians of fountains – to which they need to prove their special status. We cannot be absolutely sure that the tablets from Group F were part of the same journey, but they must have been intended for subterranean beings and to be used in the afterlife. In this sense, they are not much different than the rest of the tablets. Another similarity between the tablets of Group A, B, D and E is that they have a dialogic nature and the emphasis changes from an 'I' to a 'you'.[404] We also have a guiding voice which gives instructions to the deceased on where to go, what to avoid and what to say. This voice could not be the tablet itself, since on tablet B1 from Petelia and dated to the 4th century B.C. we find the words τόδε γράψ[, meaning 'write this'.[405] This suggests that the voice gave these instructions before the owner died which were at some later point inscribed on the tablet. In addition, the phrase on tablet D1 'Say to Persephone that Bacchios himself freed

---

403 Bernabé and Jiménez San Cristóbal, 2011, p.69–70.
404 Riedweg, 2011, p.225.
405 B1.13.

you' indicates that the particular tablet might constitute evidence for interpreting the tablets through the Zagreus myth and the anthropogony from the Titans, since Dionysos would have a reason to release the soul from the crime much to Persephone's delight.

4.4.1 Instructions for an underworld journey

Instructions are found in the tablets with the longest texts which are B1, B2, B10 and B11. They were discovered in Italy (Calabria, Sicily) and Mainland Greece (Thessaly). The length of the text varies from 10–21 lines and they date from the 5th (ca. 400 B.C.) to the 3rd century B.C. According to the instructions given by the Tablets, the deceased is advised emphatically not to approach the spring that is located at the right – and in one case the left – side with a white cypress by it, but approach instead the spring of Memory which is watched over by some guards.[406] The deceased will be asked by the guards what he/she is seeking in the darkness of Hades; the deceased must reply that he/she is the child of Earth and starry Heaven and then ask to drink water from the spring of Memory because he/she is parched with thirst and dying.[407] Then the guardians will announce the deceased to the Chthonian King or Persephone and allow him/her to drink from the Lake of Memory and he/she will have his/her rightful and glorious place among the other initiates.[408] In one of these tablets the soul is said to march along

---

406 Right: B10, B11, B2. Left: B1. Lake of Memory: B1: Εὑρήσ{σ}εις ⟨δ'⟩ Ἀΐδαο δόμων ἐπ' ἀριστερὰ κρήνην, | πὰρ δ' αὐτῆι λευκὴν ἑστηκυῖαν κυπάρισσον· | ταύτης τῆς κρήνης μηδὲ σχεδὸν ἐμπελάσειας. | εὑρήσεις δ' ἑτέραν, τῆς Μνημοσύνης ἀπὸ λίμνης | ψυχρὸν ὕδωρ προρέον· φύλακες δ' ἐπίπροσθεν ἔασιν: 'You will find in the halls of Hades a spring on the left, | and standing by it, a glowing white cypress tree; | Do not approach this spring at all. | You will find another, from the lake of Memory | refreshing water flowing forth. But guardians are nearby.'

407 B10: οἳ δέ σε εἰρήσονται ἐν⟨ὶ⟩ φρασὶ πευκαλίμαισι | ὅτ⟨τ⟩ι δὴ ἐξερέεις Ἄϊδος σκότος ὀρφ⟨ν⟩ήεντος | εἶπον· Γῆς παῖ⟨ς⟩ ἠμι καὶ Οὐρανοῦ ἀστερόεντος. | δίψαι δ' εἰμ' αὖος καὶ ἀπόλλυμαι· ἀλ⟨λ⟩ὰ δότ' ὦκα | ψυχρὸν ὕδωρ πιέναι τῆς Μνημοσύνης ἀπὸ λίμνης⟩: 'They will ask you, with sharp minds, | why you are seeking in the shadowy gloom of Hades. | Say: "I am the child of Earth and starry Heaven; | I am parched with thirst and I perish; but give me quickly | refreshing water to drink from the lake of Memory.'

408 B10: καὶ δή τοι ἐρέουσιν ὑποχθονίωι βασιλῆι· | καὶ {δή τοι} δώσουσι πιεῖν τᾶς Μναμοσύνας ἀπ[ὸ] λίμνας, | καὶ δὴ καὶ σὺ πιὼν ὁδὸν ἔρχεα⟨ι⟩ ἄν τε καὶ ἄλλοι | μύσται καὶ βάχχοι ἱερὰν στείχουσι κλε⟨ε⟩ινοί: 'And then they will speak to the underworld ruler, | and then they will give you to drink from the lake of Memory, | and you too, having drunk, will go along the sacred road that the | other famed initiates and bacchics travel.'

the sacred path of the other initiates and *Bacchoi*.[409] This was one of the decisive elements which compelled scholars to reconsider an Orphic rather than a Pythagorean identity for the tablets. It is an important affirmation that this text was used by followers of Dionysos. But did the followers of Dionysos have any reason to claim a special status on the Isles of the Blessed in the afterlife, or that their soul is of a heavenly race? We have to assume that these initiates were not the 'typical' followers of Dionysos but that they had a special perception for the fate of the soul in the afterlife and a specific topography for the underworld. In addition, they made use of texts. These are attributes of what we identified as Orphic in Chapter 2 based on ancient sources.

The text of these four tablets discussed above demonstrates slight variations. Some examples are found in the following table:

Tab. 4: Textual divergences between tablets from group B.

	B1 – Petelia (Italy) 4th B.C.	B2 – Pharsalos (Thessaly) 350 -300 B.C.	B10 – Hipponion (Italy) 5th B.C.	B11 – Entella (Italy) 3rd B.C.
1.	<δ'> Ἀίδαο	Ἀίδαο	εἰς Ἀίδαο	Ἀίδαο
2.	δόμων	δόμοις	δόμους	δόμοις
3.	ἀριστερὰ	ἐνδέξια	ἐπὶ δ<ε>ξιά	ἐπὶ]δεξιὰ
4.	κρήνην	κρήνην	κρήνα	λίμνην
5.	σχεδὸν ἐμπελάσειας	σχεδόθεν πελάσηισθα	σχεδὸν ἐνγύθεν ἔληις	σχέδον ἐ<μ>πέλασ<ασ>θαι
6.	δ'ἐπίπροσθεν ἔασιν	δ'ἐπύπερθεν ἔασιν	δ'ἐπύπερθεν ἔασι	θ' ὑποπέθασιν

We can see that the textual variations do not add anything in terms of style or plot. It can be suggested that the text was not copied from a written source but written down from memory. This indicates that the text was transmitted orally; which is supported by the fact that, as we will see, epic formulas can be distinguished. If the text was written down from memory then the omission of some phrases can be explained. For example, the phrase οἳ δὲ σε εἰρήσονται ἐνὶ] φρασὶ πευκαλίμῃσιν from tablet B11 is also found in B10, but the phrase τόδε δ'ἴστε καὶ αὐτοὶ in tablet B11 is also found in B1 but is absent from B10.[410] Tablet B11, thus,

---

409 See previous footnote.
410 'They will ask you, with sharp minds...'; 'And this you know yourselves.'

contains both phrases, tablet B1 one phrase, tablet B10 one phrase and tablet B2 neither of these phrases. It appears probable that the person responsible for the inscription of tablet B11 had the best memory and the one for tablet B2 the worst one. In this case, the suggestion that only the parts of the text which were necessary were included does not apply because these two phrases are part of the same 'scene' or 'phase' and are indeed included both in B11. So either the owner of B11 thought it was necessary to include these phrases in addition or the text was inscribed from memory and the others forgot some of the text.

Tablets B10 and B11 include the phrase: ἔνθα κατερχόμεναι ψυχαὶ νεκύων ψύχονται.[411] As the instructor informs the owner of B10/B11, the souls of other dead people, presumably the un-initiated ones, make the mistake of drinking water from the wrong fountain which the initiates are emphatically warned not to approach. This phrase makes it clear that the owners of the tablets distinguished themselves from the rest of the souls and that the main means to avoid the same mistake as the other souls is *knowledge*. As Jiménez San Cristóbal suggests: 'It has generally been interpreted that the unnamed fountain is the fountain of Lethe, that is of Forgetfulness. The tablets indicate that the soul which drinks this water forgets what it has learned in the initiation and other earlier experiences, so it can come back to the earth for a new incarnation.'[412] The knowledge necessary to avoid this fate was communicated to the tablets' owner by someone who knew the underworld and the nature of the soul very well. In other words, the souls of the un-initiated could have reached the Isles of the Blessed as well, if they had the same information and knowledge as the tablets' owners. What distinguishes the tablets' owners, thus, and gives them an advantage is not a special status but knowledge. This knowledge is not confined in directions for an underworld journey, but also relates to matters of the soul.

How did the tablets' owners understand the importance of Mnemosyne? Why did they proclaim that they are the children of Earth and starry Heaven and that their race is heavenly? These concepts demand background information in order to be understood. Edmonds suggests that the tablets identify the deceased 'as someone who stands out from the mainstream of society, marked by her special qualifications of divine lineage and religious purity'. He interprets this as a 'rejection of normal means of identification with human society such as family, city, or occupation' which 'locates the deceased within the countercultural religious currents that provided an alternative to normal polis religion'.[413] This argument

---

411 B10.4: '...there the descending souls of the dead refresh themselves'. B11.6.
412 Jiménez San Cristóbal, 2011, p.165.
413 Edmonds, 2009, p.75.

is implausible since we cannot be sure that the owners of the tablets did not participate in 'normal' polis religion too – it would be hard to define normal polis religion in any case – in the same way that for example, the Eleusinian initiates did, or that such special knowledge about the afterlife was not available to anyone who wanted to get initiated.[414] The only straightforward distinction we can make between the owners of the tablets and the rest of the Greeks is that not everyone would be interested in a good fate in the afterlife. This notion was not popular during archaic and classical times and it was more probable that someone would chose a good present life rather than a good afterlife.[415] The tablets' owners, thus, were people who either cared more about the afterlife or wanted to have both a good present life and a good afterlife. The very positive representation of the afterlife as found in the tablets and the representation of death as a rebirth (e.g. D1 and D2: 'Now you have died and now you have been born, thrice blessed one, on this very day.'), corroborates the first possibility.[416] This, in turn, does not mean that these were people of low status, or non-elites – people who would have a reason to long for a better afterlife since they were not distinguished in this one: the richness of the grave goods in many cases demonstrates the opposite.[417] Nor does it mean that the tablets' owners necessarily rejected other polis practices.

4.4.2 Purity and divine lineage

In the tablets from Group A the deceased claims to be 'Pure from the pure' and in the tablets from Group B the deceased claims to be 'A child of Earth and starry Heaven'. Through these two main formulas being used by the deceased for self-identification we can understand what was mentioned in the previous section. Both phrases indicate a special purity and that the deceased is aware of his/her divine status. He/She is the purest of the pure and has a divine linage. These self-identification formulas are almost identical on tablets dating from the 5th century B.C. to the 2nd century A.D. and in areas such as Calabria, Lucania, Sicily, Crete

---

414 Tzifopoulos, 2010, p.121-122: 'Although Edmonds readily admits the problem in 'defining countercultural religion in the context of a religious system like the ancient Greek, which had not real orthodoxy as it is understood in the Judaeo-Christian tradition', it is not only the term *countercultural religion* that is problematic. Equally problematic are terms like *polis religion* (behind which usually lies Athens) and *marginal*'.
415 Bremmer, 2014, p.20.
416 Bernabé, 2009. D1 and D2: νῦν ἔθανες καὶ νῦν ἐγένου, τρισόλβιε, ἄματι τῶιδε. The topography of the underworld of the gold tablets will be discussed in a following section.
417 Tzifopoulos, 2010, p.75.

and Thessaly. They also have a dialogic nature: 'I am a child of Earth and starry Heaven' is the answer to questions from the guards of the Mnemosyne fountain such as 'who are you?', 'what are you looking for in Hades?', 'where do you come from?'. The phrase appears to have the function of convincing the guards to offer the soul cold water from the fountain of Mnemosyne and announce the initiate to the chthonic gods. 'Pure I come from the pure' seems to be addressed to Persephone or the chthonic gods as an affirmation of the initiates' right to dwell with the other blessed ones. Both phrases have similar functions in terms of revealing that the initiate has some knowledge about his/her descent and secondly that he/she is extremely pure. They are, however, used in different locations of the underworld and uttered to different entities.

The expression 'Pure I come from the pure' indicates a purificatory background, whether through rituals or other means such as a specific way of life. We saw earlier that purity was an important element in the ancient references to Orphics. We can refer back to Theseus' description of Hippolytus as someone who has made Orpheus his lord, engaging in mystic rites and following vegetarianism, and his questions to the latter: 'Are you, then, the companion of the gods, as a man beyond the common? Are you the chaste one, untouched by evil?'[418] These accusations may well have been thrown against the owners of the gold tablets. What was it that made them so pure and worthy to dwell with the gods? Moreover, Theseus also refers to the use of texts by those who resort to *baccheuein* and make Orpheus their lord.[419] The relation of the tablets to *baccheuein* is evident from the reference to the Isles of the Blessed as the place where *mystes* and *Bacchoi* dwell. The same goes for the use of texts, since as already said, it is very probable that the text of the tablets has an archetype. I am not suggesting that Euripides knew about the practice of the gold tablets – no gold tablets were found in Athens – even though we cannot exclude this possibility. The fact, however, that he relates all these elements of extreme purity, the use of texts, the right to dwell with the gods and the *baccheuein* with Orpheus indicates that the combination of these elements characterised Orphism; and if all these elements are found combined in the gold tablets, this is one reason to suggest they should be considered Orphic. Hippolytus sees the gates of the underworld when he is about to die and when Theseus pledges to him to wait and not leave him, Hippolytus' answer is: 'My

---

418 Eur. *Hipp.* 948–949: σὺ δὴ θεοῖσιν ὡς περισσὸς ὢν ἀνὴρ | ξύνει; σὺ σώφρων καὶ κακῶν ἀκήρατος; (Tr. Kovacs).
419 Eur. *Hipp.* 953–955.

struggle is over, father: I am gone. Cover my face, and quickly, with my garments!'[420] This enigmatic answer suggests that Hippolytus longs to go to Hades, as if the afterlife is better and this life is the struggle in between. This is also the case with the tablets' owners who are blessed, ὄλβιοι and μάκαρες when they arrive in the afterlife: ὄλβιε καὶ μακαριστέ, θεὸς δ'ἔσηι ἀντὶ βροτοῖο.[421] It has to be said, however, that just because tablets were not found in Athens, this does not mean that they might not be found in the future or that they were made out of a different, perishable material. From over 200 hundred Attic epitaphs, a handful from the 4th century B.C. declare that the deceased 'is now enjoying the reward for piety or justice in Persephone's realm', in two cases the soul 'has gone to the chamber of the pious', and the soul of an *isoteles* (equally taxed foreigner) is 'honoured among the chthonian gods'.[422] We can see, thus, that similar ideas were expressed in Athens too, publicly for everyone to see; we cannot be sure if there were others who did not wish to express such ideas publicly. In any case, what matters most are the common elements of Euripides' description of an Orphic, and the owners of the tablets. Orphic practices may have varied in different areas but it becomes increasingly probable that there was a specific nucleus of ideas, beliefs and/or texts.

Another passage from Plato's *Phaedo* might be related to the ideas behind the gold tablets. Socrates quotes a verse which is uttered in the mysteries:

> καὶ κινδυνεύουσι καὶ οἱ τὰς τελετὰς ἡμῖν οὗτοι καταστήσαντες οὐ φαῦλοί τινες εἶναι, | ἀλλὰ τῷ ὄντι πάλαι <u>αἰνίττεσθαι</u> ὅτι ὃς ἂν ἀμύητος καὶ ἀτέλεστος εἰς Ἅιδου ἀφίκηται ἐν <u>βορβόρῳ</u> κείσεται, ὁ δὲ κεκαθαρμένος τε καὶ τετελεσμένος ἐκεῖσε ἀφικόμενος μετὰ θεῶν οἰκήσει. εἰσὶν γὰρ δή, ὥς φασιν οἱ περὶ τὰς τελετάς, "ναρθηκοφόροι μὲν πολλοί, βάκχοι δέ τε παῦροι·" οὗτοι δ' εἰσὶν κατὰ τὴν ἐμὴν δόξαν οὐκ ἄλλοι ἢ οἱ πεφιλοσοφηκότες ὀρθῶς.

> And I fancy that those men who established the mysteries were not unenlightened, but in reality had a hidden meaning when they said long ago that whoever goes uninitiated and unsanctified to the other world will lie in the mire, but he who arrives there initiated and purified will dwell with the gods. For as they say in the mysteries, "the thyrsus-bearers are many, but the mystics few"; and these mystics are, I believe those who have been true philosophers.[423]

---

420 Eur. *Hipp.* 1456–1458: ΘΗΣΕΥΣ: μή νυν προδῷς με, τέκνον, ἀλλὰ καρτέρει. | ΙΠΠΟΛΥΤΟΣ: κεκαρτέρηται τἄμ'· ὄλωλα γάρ, πάτερ. | κρύψον δέ μου πρόσωπον ὡς τάχος πέπλοις (Tr. Kovacs).
421 A1.10: 'Happy and most blessed one, a god you shall be instead of a mortal'.
422 Parker, 2007, p.336.
423 Pl. *Phd.* 69c–69d (Tr. Fowler). The word αἰνίττεσθαι entails the same meaning as the Derveni author's saying that Orpheus' texts were αἰνι[γμ]ατώδης [Col.VII].

Plato does not make a clear association with Orphism, but according to Olympiodorus' commentary, Plato is referring to τὰ Ὀρφέως and quotes from an 'Orphic epic' (ἔπος Ὀρφικὸν).[424] In this passage also, we find the notion of a purified initiate dwelling with the gods in the afterlife. Here too, the idea is related to *Bacchoi*, so Plato is not referring to Eleusinian initiates. He also gives evidence that specific phrases were uttered at the Bacchic mysteries. In Plato's passage we find ideas present in the gold tablets, ideas of purity and *baccheuein* being the means to dwell with the gods. This notion seems once again to be associated with Orphism, since Dionysiac mysteries – as far as we know – did not make promises of dwelling with the gods. More importantly, the verse quoted by Socrates is ostensibly simple but it must have had a deeper meaning. If not everyone who held a thyrsus – and thus was initiated in Dionysiac mysteries – could dwell with the gods, what more did it take to achieve that? Perhaps the answer lies in Plato's parallel between the mystics and true philosophers. The true *Bacchoi* were only those who acquired and practised the knowledge behind the mysteries. If this knowledge was related to the necessity of living a pure life in order to avoid punishments in the afterlife as mentioned by Plato, it could be related to the Zagreus myth and the necessity to oppress the Titanic nature in order to be able to acclaim in the afterlife that you are the child of Earth and Heaven but your race is heavenly. Jiménez San Cristóbal also sees a connection between the phrase quoted by Plato and the Zagreus myth: '…among the many thyrsus-bearers, only a few are or will become bacchoi. In the same way, the Titanic heritage is carried by the whole of humanity, which includes not only the profane, but also the initiates who try to free themselves from it in this life'.[425] If we can trust Olympiodorus saying that Plato is here quoting this verse from an Orphic epic and if this verse, as Socrates says, was uttered during mysteries, we return to the importance of *legomena* and the use of texts in mysteries in Orphism as analysed in Chapter 2. The ideas expressed in this and Euripides' passage fit very well with the gold tablets and thus corroborate their Orphic identity.

The belief in underworld judgement as portrayed in the gold tablets is mentioned in a passage from Plato's *Republic*:

"Ἀλλὰ γὰρ ἐν Ἅιδου δίκην δώσομεν ὧν ἂν ἐνθάδε ἀδικήσωμεν, ἢ αὐτοὶ ἢ παῖδες παίδων."
Ἀλλ᾽, ὦ φίλε, φήσει λογιζόμενος, αἱ τελεταὶ αὖ μέγα δύνανται καὶ οἱ λύσιοι θεοί, ὡς αἱ μέγισται πόλεις λέγουσι καὶ οἱ θεῶν παῖδες ποιηταὶ καὶ προφῆται τῶν θεῶν γενόμενοι, οἳ ταῦτα οὕτως ἔχειν μηνύουσιν. Κατὰ τίνα οὖν ἔτι λόγον δικαιοσύνην [ἂν] πρὸ μεγίστης ἀδικίας

---

424 Olymp. *in Phaed.* 69c, 48.20 = OF576F. Orphic epic: See OF576F(V). Bernabé and Jiménez San Cristóbal, 2011, p.9: Bernabé suggests that this passage has a clearly Orphic context.
425 Jiménez San Cristóbal, 2009, p.48.

αἱροίμεθ' ἄν, ἢν ἐὰν μετ' εὐσχημοσύνης κιβδήλου κτησώμεθα, | καὶ παρὰ θεοῖς καὶ παρ' ἀνθρώποις πράξομεν κατὰ νοῦν ζῶντές τε καὶ τελευτήσαντες, ὡς ὁ τῶν πολλῶν τε καὶ ἄκρων λεγόμενος λόγος;

> But the fact is that we shall pay for the misdeeds done in this world in Hades: either we ourselves or our children's children. "But, my friend," will come the considered reply, "again, initiation rites and gods who give absolution are very powerful, as the greatest cities affirm, and the children of gods who have become poets and prophets of the gods reveal that these things are so." Well then, by what argument might we still prefer justice instead of the greatest injustice, which, if we acquire it with a counterfeit elegance, we shall be able to practice as we like among gods and men, in this world and the next, as the argument of the majority of the acutest minds goes?[426]

Adeimantus (the speaker) criticises those people who are unjust and are acquitted of their wrong-doings through prayers and rites of the dead which combined with a 'counterferit elegance' offer prosperity with gods and men, in life and death. Adeimantus could be referring to practices such as the gold tablets but the fact that he refers to a 'counterfeit elegance' suggests that apart from being initiated, these people also had to be modest or graceful. It seems, though, that not everyone was. His criticism, thus, might not be of the practices themselves but of those who fail to follow them through and still expect to enjoy a happy afterlife. A similar view might explain the phrase 'many are the thyrsus-bearers, but few the *Bacchoi*' quoted above and the use of the perfect participles κεκαθαρμένος and τετελεσμένος which, as Jiménez San Cristóbal claims, suggest a 'lasting condition reached by the initiates who have performed the rites and have purified themselves'.[427] Adeimantus' critique might also relate to Plato's understanding of knowledge, goodness and justice and the difference between being good for its own sake *vs* being good because it is most advantageous. However, the reference to these mysteries being hailed by 'the greatest cities' and declared by 'the prophets of the gods' indicates that perhaps Plato has the Eleusinian mysteries in mind, which also promised a happy afterlife and, as we have seen, an Orphic poem about Demeter's wandering might have been their *hieros logos*.[428] This could also be conceived as a fundamental difference between the Eleusinian and the Orphic-Dionysiac mysteries, the first consisting of solely the performance of rites and the second being a way of life. In any case, we can see that there seemed to have been a distinction between those bearing the thyrsus – any *mystēs* – and those actually becoming *Bacchoi* – the *mystēs* who became a god in the sense of identifying with

---

426 Pl. *Resp.* 2.366a–b (Tr. Emlyn-Jones).
427 Jiménez San Cristóbal, 2009, p.75.
428 *Marm. Par.* (*IG* 12 (5), 444.14–15). See p.72.

Dionysos after a constant lifelong effort –. The reference in the Hipponion tablet (B10) to both μύσται and βάχχοι supports such a distinction. Similarly, in the passage from Euripides' *Hippolytus* discussed above, Theseus refers to those who use texts, make Orpheus their king, follow vegetarianism, stay pure and abstain from sex as performing what he calls *baccheuein*. The owners of the gold tablets could belong to either group, but the inscription of text which seems to require some background information for its understanding, and the fact that they had a specific perception about the nature of the soul, suggest they were not mere performers of rites but that they belonged to the second group.

The phrase Γῆς παῖς εἰμι καὶ Οὐρανοῦ ἀστερόεντος is often followed by αὐτὰρ ἐμοὶ γένος οὐράνιον, meaning 'But my race is heavenly'. This, as Janko notes, can only make sense if 'the writers of these versions considered that all mortals were descended from Earth and Heaven (i.e. via the Titans), but that in initiates the heavenly side predominated', a sign that they deserved to dwell with the gods.[429] The anthropogony of the human race from the Titans as found in the Zagreus myth would be a good reason why the deceased says he/she is the child of Earth and Heaven, the parents of the Titans. Other elements of Dionysos' dismemberment myth would also explain why the deceased says that Dionysos has freed him/her: εἰπεῖν Φερσεφόναι σ'ὅτι Β<άκ>χιος αὐτὸς ἔλυσε [D1, D2].[430] In D3 we find the phrase ἄποινος γὰρ ὁ μύστης which means that the initiate is free from the penalty (ποινή). The word ποινή has a very specific meaning which is a penalty being paid by the slayer to the kinsmen of the slain. This would correspond to the human race carrying the crime of dismembering Dionysos – Persephone's son according to the Orphic mythology – through their Titanic ancestry. Some scholars have combined the *Republic* passage with a reference elsewhere in Plato to Pindar's *Threnoi*. This passage was discussed in Chapter 3 and refers to Persephone receiving requital for the ancient grief: [Φερσεφόνα ποινὰν παλαιοῦ πένθεος δέξεται] by men who for the rest of the time 'are called sacred heroes by men' [ἥροες ἀγνοὶ πρὸς ἀνθρώπων καλέονται].[431] It was suggested in Chapter 3 that this 'ancient grief' could be identified as a Titanic primal guilt and a particular *penthos* fixed in the past.[432] Based on the Platonic context discussed it was suggested that the way to pay the penalty for Persephone's ancient grief is by living a holy life, an idea also present in the gold tablets through the emphasis on purity. This

---

429 Janko, 1984, p.95.
430 'Say to Persephone that Bacchios himself freed you.'
431 Pind. fr.133 (Tr. Race); Pl. *Meno*, 81b–c; Edmonds, 1999, p.48. See p.109 for text.
432 See p.109.

was based on the context of the Pindaric quotation in Plato and Socrates' reference to priests and priestesses who have studied to give a reasonable account of their ministry about how the soul is immortal and is born again and that for this reason one must live his life in holiness.[433] Plato also says that the soul after being born many times and acquiring knowledge of everything, has the ability to recollect everything that it has learned about virtue and all the other things. Since Plato refers to the idea of re-incarnation, one might say that he means the Pythagoreans. The reference to Persephone, however, and to priests and priestesses count against this and point towards Orphism where reincarnation was also a central idea and Persephone was a prominent deity.

We cannot be sure that the deceased really means that he/she is a child of goddess Gaia and god Ouranos when saying 'I am the child of Earth and starry Heaven', but he/she might literally mean earth as soil and heaven as air/aether (and a link to the stars). We do find the epithet ἀστερόεντος for god Ouranos in the Homeric Hymn to 'Gaia Mother of All', so it is an epithet that was used in relation to him.[434] The expression, however, 'but my race is heavenly', suggests an 'aetherial' understanding of the soul's substance. There is also the possibility that both notions coexist and that the Titanic anthropogony was a mythical allegory of an elemental explanation of the soul's substance, identity and place of abode. The idea that the soul returns to the aether after death is inscribed on an Attic public inscription, an official war monument for the souls of Athenian soldiers dated at 432 B.C. which says: αἰθὴρ μὲμ φσυχὰς ὑπεδέχσατο, σόμ[ατα δὲ χθὸν] (aether received our souls, and the earth our bodies).[435] As Parker notes, 'this return of the soul to the aether was apparently a happy destiny that permitted the continuance of consciousness, not a blowing away on the wind'.[436] Additionally, the notion that the soul's place of abode is the aer/aether is expressed repeatedly in Euripides. In the *Suppliants* Theseus says:

> ἐάσατ' ἤδη γῇ καλυφθῆναι νεκρούς,
> ὅθεν δ' ἕκαστον ἐς τὸ φῶς ἀφίκετο
> ἐνταῦθ' ἀπελθεῖν, πνεῦμα μὲν πρὸς αἰθέρα,
> τὸ σῶμα δ' ἐς γῆν· οὔτι γὰρ κεκτήμεθα
> ἡμέτερον αὐτὸ πλὴν ἐνοικῆσαι βίον,
> κἄπειτα τὴν θρέψασαν αὐτὸ δεῖ λαβεῖν.

---

433 Pl. *Meno* 81a–d.
434 HH 30.17.
435 *IG* I³ 1179.
436 Parker, 2007, p.336.

> Now let the dead be buried in the earth, and let each element return to the place from whence it came into the light of day, the spirit to the upper air, the body to the earth. We do not possess our bodies as our own: we live our lives in them, and thereafter the earth, our nourisher, must take them back.[437]

In *Helen*, Theonoe says: 'The mind of the dead does not live, yet it has eternal thought as it falls into eternal aether'.[438] In *Melanippe the Wise* we learn that aether is the dwelling place of Zeus: 'I swear by sacred aether, Zeus' dwelling'.[439] In the following fragments from *Bellerophon*, Euripides seems to create the same imagery as the gold tablets: σπεῦδ', ὦ ψυχή | *** | πάρες, ὦ σκιερὰ φυλλάς, ὑπερβῶ | κρηναῖα νάπη· τὸν ὑπὲρ κεφαλῆς | αἰθέρ' ἰδέσθαι σπεύδω, τίν' ἔχει | στάσιν εὐοδίας.[440] These words are uttered by Bellerophon before he flies on Pegasus towards the heavens and he is wishing that his soul will have a good journey upwards and towards the aether after firstly going through a valley with springs. The word σπεῦδ' shows Bellerophon's excitement for his soul's journey into the aether. This journey of the soul from water to the aetherial heavenly divine state is reminiscent of the gold tablets' journey. Another fragment from *Melanippe the Wise*, suggest that Euripides was familiar with religious ideas similar to the ones found in the gold tablets:

> ΜΕΛΑΝΙΠΠΗ:
> κοὐκ ἐμὸς ὁ μῦθος, ἀλλ' ἐμῆς μητρὸς πάρα,
> ὡς οὐρανός τε γαῖά τ' ἦν μορφὴ μία,
> ἐπεὶ δ' ἐχωρίσθησαν ἀλλήλων δίχα,
> τίκτουσι πάντα κἀνέδωκαν εἰς φάος,
> δένδρη, πετεινά, θῆρας, οὕς θ' ἅλμη τρέφει,
> γένος τε θνητῶν.
>
> MELANIPPE: The account is not my own, but comes from my mother, that Heaven and Earth were once a single form, but when they were parted from each other into two, they bore and

---

437 Eur. *Supp.* 531–536 (Tr. Kovacs).
438 Eur. *Hel.* 1015-1017: ὁ νοῦς | τῶν κατθανόντων ζῇ μὲν οὔ, γνώμην δ' ἔχει | ἀθάνατον εἰς ἀθάνατον αἰθέρ' ἐμπεσών.] (Tr. Coleridge).
439 Eur. *Mel. Wise* fr.487: ὄμνυμι δ' ἱερὸν αἰθέρ', οἴκησιν Διός.
440 Eur. *Beller.* fr.307a, 308.3: '(307a) Hurry, my [soul]! . . . (308) Give way, shadowy foliage! Let me cross the valleys with their springs! I hurry to see what state the sky overhead has for a good journey.' (Tr. Collard). Except the text in brackets; I have replaced Collard's 'heart' with 'soul' as it is more accurate. See Dixon, 2014, p.498–499.

delivered into the light all things – trees, winged things, beasts, creatures of the sea, and the race of mortals.[441]

What is particularly important here is the reference to the creation of the human race, which is not found explicitly outside Orphism and the tracing of their lineage back to Heaven and Earth, in the same way as it is found in the gold tablets. As we will see in subsequent chapters, such an idea of the totality of the world, including the human race, being created by gods is found in Orphic theogonical texts.

The gold tablets' reference to being a child of Earth and Heaven, then, could be interpreted as an expression of dualism into earthly body and heavenly soul. Betz wonders if by the denomination 'I am' it is an earthly-human or a divine soul which is meant or a soul at all, since he notes that 'It is remarkable that the deceased initiates do not introduce themselves in the after-life simply as souls who have left their bodies behind on Earth, but as men and women, some of them even with their names'.[442] In my opinion, however, we can be sure that it is the deceased's soul which is travelling in the underworld because some of the deceased were cremated, and thus thought they would not need their mortal body in the afterlife. The fact that in some tablets the name of the deceased is inscribed is a sign of individualisation, a need to maintain the earthly identity until the deceased drinks the water of memory and proceeds to universalisation. It is through having the specific earthly and mortal identity that the initiate is able to get initiated and acquire knowledge so that he/she would be able to acclaim in front of Persephone that he/she is the child of Earth and starry Heaven. In other words, without the individualisation, universalisation would not be possible.

4.4.3 Epic Formulas

The suggestion that the gold tablets have an archetype which was transmitted orally is supported by parallels to the Homeric epics and the use of Homeric formulas. These are phrases that predominantly have to do with the special status of the deceased and they appear in the tablets of Group A, Group B and Group E. In general, the journey of the deceased in the underworld, the questions about the identity of the deceased by the guards, the request and offering of water and

---

[441] Eur. *Mel. Wise* fr.484 (Tr. Cropp). Lopez-Ruiz, p.36. Mayhew, p.97 refers to this passage having an Orphic or Hesiodic ring to it.
[442] Betz, 2011, p.110.

the final admission to the locus amoenus, are strongly reminiscent of Homeric scenes of *xenia*. There is also a similarity to the Homeric dialogues of heroes who wish to assert their special *genos* and acquire their rightful *kleos*. Much in the same way, the owners of the tablets' main issue is to prove they are worthy to dwell with the gods through referring to a divine lineage (Group B) or references to their *genos* (Group A).

Herrero de Jáuregui (2011) discusses this matter in reference to dialogues from the *Iliad* between heroes when they are about to fight and either win and achieve *kleos*, or lose and die in which case their enemy will achieve *kleos*. Such examples are the dialogues between Diomedes and Glaucos (*Il.* 6.121–236), Achilles and Aeneas (*Il.* 20.177–352) and Achilles and Asteropaeus (*Il.* 21.149–160, 182–199).[443] Before the fight, both heroes emphasise their *genos*. The questions to Glaucos and Asteropaeus by Diomedes and Achilles respectively are: τίς δὲ σύ ἐσσι; (*Il.* 6.122) τις πόθεν εἰς ἀνδρῶν; (*Il.* 21.150). These questions are similar to the ones the guards of the fountain of Memory ask the deceased: τὶς δ'ἐσσί; πῶ δ'ἐσσί; τίς δ' εἶ ἤ πῶ δ' εἶ. This similarity is not sufficient evidence of epic parallels since such questions would be expected when inquiring someone's identity. However, there are more similarities: in the gold tablets found in Thurii we find the verb εὔχομαι: καὶ γὰρ ἐγὼν ὑμῶν γένο<ς> εὔχομαι ὄλβιον εἶναι ('For I also claim that I am of your blessed race.').[444] This word has a twofold nature. In Homer, it is used to 'assert one's place and rightful claims in social space as well as to assert one's relation to and claims on a god'.[445] On the other hand: 'In a religious context it means "pray (loudly)", mostly in the sense of "addressing a god with a request"'.[446] It could be said, in the case of the gold tablets, that elements of a long epic tradition are being amalgamated with the practice of uttering a prayer and put to a practical religious use. In the *Iliad* we find it being used by a hero to declare his lineage: ταύτης τοι γενεῆς τε καὶ αἵματος εὔχομαι εἶναι (*Il.* 6.211; 20.241: 'this is my generation and the bloodline I claim to be born from'); in the gold tablets it is used to define the initiates' divine descent.[447] Our interest in the verb *euchomai* could go even further in regards to Homer since in the Shield of Achilles it is used in a legal/juridical context:

---

[443] Herrero de Jáuregui, 2011, p.272.
[444] A1, A2, A3.
[445] Depew, 1997, p.232. Examples in Homer: *Il.*: 2.82, 4.405, 5.172–73, 5.246–248, 6.211, 9.161, 13.54, 14.113, 20.209, 21.186–87; *Od.*: 1.180, 1.187, 9.263, 9.519, 14.199, 14.204, 15.426, 16.63, 17.373, 21.335, 24.269. See also Muellner's comprehensive study on the use of this verb in Homer (1976).
[446] Versnel, 2015, p.447–48.
[447] Herrero de Jáuregui, 2011, p.275.

λαοὶ δ'εἰν ἀγορῇ ἔσαν ἀθρόοι, ἔνθα δὲ νεῖκος
ὠρώρει, δύο δ'ἄνδρες ἐνείκεον εἴνεκα ποινῆς
ἀνδρὸς ἀποφθιμένου· ὃ μὲν εὔχετο πάντ' ἀποδοῦναι
δήμῳ πιφαύσκων, ὃ δ' ἀναίνετο μηδὲν ἑλέσθαι.

But the people were gathered in the place of assembly; for there a strife had arisen, and two men were striving about the blood price of a man slain; the one claimed that he had paid all, declaring his cause to the people, but the other refused to accept anything...[448]

The verb *euchomai* is used by the murderer pleading that he has paid the 'bloodmoney'. In gold tablet A3 the initiate says: καὶ γὰρ ἐ‹γ›ὼ‹ν› ὑ‹μῶν› γένος εὔχομαι ὄλβιον‹ ε‹ἶ›να‹ι› {ὄλβιο} | ποινὰν ‹δ'› ἀνταπέτε‹ισ'› ἔργω‹ν› ἔνεκ'› ο‹ὔ›τι δικα‹ί›ων ('For I also claim that I am of your blessed race. Recompense I have paid on account of deeds not just').[449] In this case we find a combination of all three uses of this verb as found in Homer and even earlier texts; the initiate prays to the chthonian gods and claims that he/she has a divine linage and that he/she has paid the bloodprice of unjust deeds. This might indicate that the crime for which the tablets' owners have paid the bloodprice was related to Dionysos' dismemberment by the Titans, inherited to them through the Titanic anthropogony. By repaying the crime, the deceased's divine side, the *ouranion genos*, has prevailed, through which they can claim deification by asserting it to Persephone. Similarly, the heroes in the *Iliad* also refer to the past crimes of their ancestors before achieving *kleos*.[450]

The use of the word *euchomai* corroborates the argument that the text of the gold tablets stems from an orally transmitted poem. A passage from Proclus' commentary on Plato's *Timaeus* brings together the use of this particular verb with Orphic practices related to Dionysos, Persephone and the soul:

Τὴν οὖν πρώτην ἕξιν κατὰ τὴν σχέσιν ἀφεῖσα τὴν πρὸς πᾶσαν τὴν γένεσιν καὶ τὸ ἄλογον τὸ ποιοῦν αὐτὴν γενεσιουργόν, λόγωι μὲν κρατοῦσα τὸ ἄλογον, νοῦν δὲ χορηγοῦσα τῆι δόξηι, πᾶσαν δὲ τὴν ψυχὴν εἰς τὴν εὐδαίμονα περιάγουσα ζωὴν ἀπὸ τῆς περὶ τὴν γένεσιν πλάνης, ἧς καὶ οἱ παρ''Ορφεῖ τῶι Διονύσωι καὶ τῆι Κόρηι τελούμενοι τυχεῖν <u>εὔχονται 'οἷς ἐπέταξεν | κύκλου τε λῆξαι καὶ ἀναψῦξαι κακότητος'</u>].

---

[448] *Il.*18.497–501 (Tr. Murray).
[449] A3.3–4. See also A2.5. It might be relevant that verses from the *Rhapsodies* as we will see in Chapter 6 are also found in the Homeric Shield of Achilles.
[450] Herrero de Jáuregui, 2011, p.280: 'so did Glaucos proclaim that his grandfather Bellerophon 'also became hateful to the gods' (*Il.* 6.200).

> Dismissing therefore, her first habit which subsists according to an alliance to the whole of generation, and, laying aside the irrational nature which connects her with generation, likewise governing her irrational part by reason, and extending opinion to intellect, she will be circularly led to a happy life, from the wanderings about the regions of sense; which life those that are initiated by Orpheus in the mysteries of Bacchus and Proserpine, pray that they obtain, together with the allotments of the sphere, and a cessation of evil. [451]

Proclus might have chosen to use the particular word by chance, but the context suggests otherwise. He refers to mysteries (τελούμενοι) performed by Orphics in honour of Dionysos and Kore which relate to obtaining a happy afterlife (εὐδαίμονα περιάγουσα ζωήν). Since it is not very probable that Proclus knew about the practices of the gold tablets he either had a source which referred to these Orphic practices or he was familiar with the text behind them. A phrase from tablet A1 suggest the latter possibility:

> καὶ γὰρ ἐγὼν ὑμῶν γένος ὄλβιον εὔχομαι εἶμεν.
> ἀλ‹λ›ά με Μο‹ῖ›ρ'{α} ἐδάμασ‹σ›ε {καὶ ἀθάνατοι θεοὶ ἄλλοι}
> καὶ ἀσ{σ}τεροβλῆτα κ‹ε›ραυνῶι.
> κύκλο‹υ› δ' ἐξέπταν βαρυπενθέος ἀργαλέοιο. [452]

> For I also claim that I am of your blessed race.
> But Fate mastered me and the thunderer, striking with his lightning.
> I flew out of the circle of wearying heavy grief...

The words κύκλο‹υ› δ'ἐξέπταν are essentially the same as οἷς ἐπέταξεν κύκλου in Proclus which he says are uttered during these Orphic *teletae*. It also becomes possible, then, that there was an initiation behind the gold tablets with specific *legomena*. Considering these textual similarities, Proclus can be considered as a reliable source of the text behind the gold tablets. His identification of these practices as Orphic is significant because he also gives information about the religious eschatological philosophy of these Orphics: before quoting the Orphic phrase he refers to the necessity of governing the irrational part of the soul in order to obtain a happy afterlife. The Platonic passage on which Proclus is commenting could be referring to Orphic ideas of reincarnation and the divine descent of the human race as discussed in Chapter 3:

---

[451] Procl. *In Ti.* 42c, III.297 = OF348F (Tr. Taylor).
[452] A1.3–5; In these particular verses we also have another Homeric formula, namely the phrase ἀλ‹λ›ά με... κ‹ε›ραυνῶι which is found in other tablets too: A.2; A3; *Il*.18.119. Obbink, 2011, p.304.

καὶ ὁ μὲν εὖ τὸν προσήκοντα χρόνον βιούς, πάλιν εἰς τὴν τοῦ ξυννόμου πορευθεὶς οἴκησιν ἄστρου, βίον εὐδαίμονα καὶ συνήθη ἕξοι· σφαλεὶς δὲ τούτων εἰς γυναικὸς φύσιν ἐν τῇ δευτέρᾳ γενέσει μεταβαλοῖ· μὴ παυόμενός τε ἐν τούτοις ἔτι κακίας, τρόπον ὃν κακύνοιτο, κατὰ τὴν ὁμοιότητα τῆς τοῦ τρόπου γενέσεως εἴς τινα τοιαύτην ἀεὶ μεταβαλοῖ θήρειον φύσιν, ἀλλάττων τε οὐ πρότερον πόνων λήξοι, πρὶν τῇ ταὐτοῦ καὶ ὁμοίου περιόδῳ τῇ ἐν αὑτῷ ξυνεπισπώμενος

And he that has lived his appointed time well shall return again to his abode in his kindred star, and shall gain a life that is blessed and congenial but whoever has failed shall be changed into woman's nature at the second birth; and if, in that shape, he still shall not refrain from wickedness he shall be changed every time, according to the nature of his wickedness, into some bestial form after the similitude of his own nature; nor in his changings shall he cease from woes until he yields himself to the revolution of the Same and Similar that is within him.[453]

Timaeus refers to a series of reincarnations until the soul escapes and returns to its place of abode, which is according to him a star. The fact that the way to escape from this cycle of rebirths is through developing the 'Same and Similar' within him, which is his divine aspect, can be associated with what has been discussed so far about the tablets and the Zagreus myth as justification for apotheosis. Timaeus' identification of the blessed abode of the soul in the afterlife as a star relates this particular eschatology to astrological ideas. The Orphic fragment from Heraclides Ponticus comes to mind where he says that the Orphic writings 'make a world out of each of the stars'.[454] Moreover, I have discussed in Chapter 2 the Orphic works and based on the surviving titles and testimonies many of them must have been related to astronomy.[455] There are, then, reasons to believe that the Orphic religious eschatology and philosophy was elemental and related to astronomy. One important reason to suggest this, is the Orphic idea, mentioned in ancient sources such as Aristotle, that the soul is rooted in the aether/aer. We will develop this idea more in a following section in relation to another phrase found in the gold tablets, and in the following chapters in relation to the Derveni Papyrus and the *Orphic Rhapsodies*.

The final *kleos* achieved by the tablets' owners is similar to the *kleos* gained by the Homeric heroes who will be remembered forever. In the same way, the deceased can proceed to the Isles of the Blessed after drinking from the fountain of Mnemosyne.[456] Such parallels are probably not only related to the text behind

---

453 Pl. *Ti*. 42b–c (Tr. Lamb).
454 Heraclid. Pont. fr.75 Schütrumpf (= ps.-Plut. 2.13 888 F = Euseb. 15.30.8 = ps.-Gal. 52.). For text see p.15.
455 See Table 1 in p.75.
456 B10.16: μύσται καὶ βάχχοι ἱερὰν στείχουσι κλε‹ε›ινοί.

the gold tablets being orally transmitted or the use of formulas out of tradition, but also to the fact that the owners of the tablets are often proclaimed as heroes or gods.[457] In this way, they legitimate their right to deification in a way that no one familiar with epic poetry could dispute. If my *genos* is divine, then I must be too, we can imagine the initiates realizing at some point of their initiation. However, this is where it becomes crucial that this lineage is justified somehow, and the most probable means of justification is a divine anthropogony. This is why, apart from everything else discussed so far which suggests that the gold tablets were related to the Zagreus myth, we must now seriously consider this possibility. That the tablets' owners could claim that they are pure and released from a crime is not surprising, but their claim that they have become a god from a mortal or that they should dwell at the Isles of the Blessed, a place reserved for the heroes of the distant past and unreachable by a mere mortal, is a different story; a story that needs justification: a justification which comes in the form of divine descent. The religious eschatology and philosophy, thus, of the tablets might have resulted from the transformation of traditional forms of heroisation into an explanation of the soul's incarnation due to a previous crime and the justification of its eventual deification through its divine lineage.

4.4.4 Stemmatological Approach – In search of an Archetype

Considering everything that has been discussed so far, it can be argued that there was an archetype behind the gold tablets. Janko and Riedweg have attempted to reconstruct an archetype of the tablets with the long text (B10, B1, B2, B9, B3, B4, B5, B7, B8). Janko examines these tablets in order to show: '...how the metre and diction, with peculiar mock-epic forms, Homeric epithets misused, repetitions and inconcinnities, is the product of memorisation, neither word for word nor excessively free, repaired and 'improved' from time to time, showing a half-educated grasp of the epic style, but with an underlying archetype'.[458] On the other hand, Betz argues that the 'comparatively strong variability of the texts' does not allow for a fixed written source.[459] He considers it more probable that there is a close connection to rituals and that some sentences are quotations from rituals. He finally attributes the textual similarities to an 'implied mythological and ritual

---

[457] B1.11: καὶ τότ'ἔπειτα [τέλη σὺ μεθ'] ἡρώεσσιν ἀναξει[ς]: 'And then you will celebrate [rites with the other] heroes'.
[458] Janko, 1984, p.91; Riedweg, 2011. See also Ferrari, 2011d, p.206/210.
[459] Betz, 2011, p.103.

frame of reference' which is rooted in oral traditions that were later written down.⁴⁶⁰ Betz's argument does not really exclude the existence of an archetype, since it could have been orally transmitted, especially considering the earlier discussion about epic formulas. Also, not all the verses must necessarily come from such an archetype. We have a combination of hexameters mixed with other types of meter and un-metrical formulas. It is possible that there was an archetype of some of the verses while others come from a ritual. This is the view of Riedweg, who has attempted to reconstruct an archetype and argues that: 'a considerable number of leaves seem to be composite units, made up of mainly two heterogeneous ingredients: (1) a hexametrical poem about the underworld, and (2) cultic acclamations evocative of ritual actions...'.⁴⁶¹ However, the evidence for oral transmission of whatever text was behind the tablets makes it doubtful that there were many texts in circulation at the same time.⁴⁶² The text's orality would also explain the divergences which Tzifopoulos attributes to 'local influences' or 'individual choices from the Bacchic-Orphic discourse of afterlife', since variations are expected in the process of oral transmission.⁴⁶³ Riedweg also suggests that at least some of the engravers worked from memory, while writing errors and metric violations suggest that their engravers were not the most 'erudite'.⁴⁶⁴ However, this might be another indication that the tablets were not engraved by professionals and we must not rule out the possibility that they were engraved by the initiates themselves.

As we saw in Chapter 2 one of the works attributed to Orpheus was titled Εἰς Ἅιδου κατάβασις (*Descent into Hades*).⁴⁶⁵ Edmonds argues against the existence of such an autobiographical poem based on the argument that no Orphic fragments quoted about the soul 'show any signs of coming from a first person, autobiographical account'.⁴⁶⁶ This in itself, does not eliminate the existence of such a text since it could have been about someone else's descent: for example, Herakles.⁴⁶⁷ Even if it was narrated in the third person, then, such a story would still

---

460 Betz, 2011, p.104.
461 Riedweg, 2011, p.220.
462 On this matter see also Tzifopoulos, 2011, p.179 and Torjussen, 2014, p.37.
463 Tzifopoulos, 2011, p.179.
464 Riedweg, 2011, p.221.
465 See Table 1 in p.75.
466 Edmonds, 2011b, p.259.
467 See Bernabé OF713T-OF716T for the testimonies of an Orphic *katabasis* of Heracles.

qualify Orpheus as an expert on Underworld travel.[468] In Euripides' *Alcestis* already from the mid-5th century B.C., Admetus – the king of Pherae in Thessaly, the finding place of some of our tablets – refers to Orpheus' ability to charm Persephone with his song and music:

εἰ δ' Ὀρφέως μοι γλῶσσα καὶ μέλος παρῆν,
ὥστ' ἢ κόρην Δήμητρος ἢ κείνης πόσιν
ὕμνοισι κηλήσαντά σ' ἐξ Ἅιδου λαβεῖν,
κατῆλθον ἄν, καί μ' οὔθ' ὁ Πλούτωνος κύων
οὔθ' οὑπὶ κώπῃ ψυχοπομπὸς ἂν Χάρων
ἔσχ' ἄν, πρὶν ἐς φῶς σὸν καταστῆσαι βίον.

If I had the voice and music of Orpheus so that I could charm Demeter's daughter or her husband with song and fetch you from Hades, I would have gone down to the Underworld, and neither Pluto's hound nor Charon the ferryman of souls standing at the oar would have kept me from bringing you back to the light alive.[469]

Admetus wishes to postpone his death but someone else must die in his place and his wife is the only volunteer. In this passage he wishes he could descend into Hades and bring her back; it is, eventually, Herakles who fights with Death on Admetus' behalf and brings Alcestis back from the dead. The fact that, as Admetus says, Orpheus could charm Persephone with his song is an indication that there was either an Orphic myth or work referring to a *katabasis* into Hades. It is Orpheus' song in itself which would help him enchant Persephone and perform a successful *katabasis*. Orphic songs/texts, thus, must have been related to the ability to overcome death or to deal with the underworld challenges and chthonic deities such as Persephone. Moreover, it is in this same work that the Chorus refers to the Thracian tablets mentioned in the first chapter: 'I have found nothing stronger than Necessity, nor is there any cure for it in the Thracian tablets set down by the voice of Orpheus'.[470] The writings supposedly dictated by Orpheus offered cures for unknown 'conditions'. They must have been considered very powerful and perhaps had eschatological connotations since the chorus emphasises that *not even* these Orphic texts could provide a cure for death. Admetus, who curses his life and envies the dead, referring to his birth as ill-fated, says:

---

[468] Pl. *Symp.* 179d; Diod., IV.25.1–4; Heracl. *Paradox.* 21; Apollo. *Bibliot.* 1.3.2; Apollod. *Bibliot.* 2.5.12; Ps.Moschus, 3.115–125; Cono ap. Phot. Bibli. 186, 140a 24; Paus. IX.30.6; 982T = Isoc. *Bus.* 11.8: 'But Orpheus led the dead back from Hades'; OF980T = Eur. *Alc.* 357–362; OF985T = Hermesian. Leont. fr.7.1–14. Bernabé and Jiménez San Cristóbal, 2011, p.71.
[469] Eur. *Alc.* 357–363 (Tr. Kovacs).
[470] Eur. *Alc.* 965–969: κρεῖσσον οὐδὲν Ἀνάγκας | ηὗρον οὐδέ τι φάρμακον | Θρήσσαις ἐν σανίσιν, τὰς | Ὀρφεία κατέγραψεν | γῆρυς. See p.63.

'My friends, I think my wife's lot is happier than my own, though it may not appear so. For she will never be touched by any grief and has ended her many troubles with glory'.[471] We once again have the idea that the present life is an ordeal and the afterlife is something better which is found in the gold tablets. We also find similar terminology found in other Orphic references, where death is considered a respite from pain/trouble/grief. The existence of an Orphic katabatic poem, or eschatological texts which could provide means to deal with mortality, becomes more plausible.

Let us now focus on a single tablet (A1) to demonstrate how poetic and ritualistic verses might have been mingled:

1 Ἔρχομαι ἐκ κοθαρῶ‹ν› κοθαρά, χθονί‹ων› βασίλεια,
Εὐκλῆς Εὐβο‹υ›λεύς τε καὶ ἀθάνατοι θεοὶ ἄλλοι·
καὶ γὰρ ἐγὼν ὑμῶν γένος ὄλβιον εὔχομαι εἶμεν.
ἀλ‹λ›ά με Μο‹ῖ›ρ'{α} ἐδάμασ‹σ›ε {καὶ ἀθάνατοι θεοὶ ἄλλοι}
καὶ ἀσ{σ}τεροβλῆτα κ‹ε›ραυνῶι.
5 κύκλο‹υ› δ' ἐξέπταν βαρυπενθέος ἀργαλέοιο,
ἱμερτο‹ῦ› δ' ἐπέβαν στεφάνο‹υ› ποσὶ καρπαλίμοισι,
δεσ{σ}ποίνας δ'{ε} ὑπὸ κόλπον ἔδυν χθονίας βασιλείας·
{ιμερτοδαπεβανστεμανοποσικαρπασιμοισι}
ὄλβιε καὶ μακαριστέ, θεὸς δ' ἔσηι ἀντὶ βροτοῖο.
ἔριφος ἐς γάλ' ἔπετον.

1 Pure I come from the pure, Queen of those below the earth,
and Eukles and Eubouleus and the other immortal gods;
For I also claim that I am of your blessed race.
But Fate mastered me and the thunderer, striking with his lightning.
5 I flew out of the circle of wearying heavy grief;
I came on with swift feet to the desired crown;
I passed beneath the bosom of the Mistress, Queen of the Underworld,
"Happy and most blessed one, a god you shall be instead of a mortal."
A kid I fell into milk.

In my opinion, the text: 'Pure I come from the pure … with his lightning' comes from a poem of eschatological/mythological nature while the rest of the text includes phrases uttered during a ritual, such as 'A kid I fell into milk', and phrases

---

[471] Eur. *Alc.* 864–869: 'I wish I could die! It was to an ill fate that my mother bore me. I envy the dead, I long for their state, I yearn to dwell in those halls below. For I take no joy in looking on the light or in walking about on the earth.' (Tr. Kovacs); 935–938: φίλοι, γυναικὸς δαίμον' εὐτυχέστερον | τοὐμοῦ νομίζω, καίπερ οὐ δοκοῦνθ' ὅμως. τῆς μὲν γὰρ οὐδὲν ἄλγος ἅψεταί ποτε, | πολλῶν δὲ μόχθων εὐκλεῆς ἐπαύσατο.

which might relate to the *dromena* of the initiation which the initiate has experienced. An initial indication is that the first half of the poem up to the point where lightning has struck the initiate, takes place in the present while the rest of the poem refers to events which have happened in the past: 'I flew', 'I came', 'I passed', 'I fell'. Verses 3–4 ('For I also claim ... his lightning') are epic formulas, as discussed in the previous section, while verses 1–2 constitute a direct salutation to Persephone and the Chthonian gods. We cannot rule out the possibility that the poetic versers were also uttered during a ritual – if it had the form of a *katabasis* – at the time the initiate saw Persephone. Even in this case, however, their epic character suggests that they come from a poem. The verse 'I flew out of the circle of wearying heavy grief', as mentioned earlier, is said by Proclus to be the wish of those participating in the Orphic mysteries of Dionysos and Kore: this supports the supposition that it was uttered during a ritual. The phrase δεσ{σ}ποίνας δ'{ε} ὑπὸ κόλπον ἔδυν χθονίας βασιλείας alludes a practice of the Sabazian mysteries described by Clement of Alexandria, where the phrase διὰ κόλπου θεός was also used as a password:

> Σαβαζίων γοῦν μυστηρίων σύμβολον τοῖς μυουμένοις ὁ διὰ κόλπου θεός· δράκων δέ ἐστιν οὗτος, διελκόμενος τοῦ κόλπου τῶν τελουμένων, ἔλεγχος ἀκρασίας Διός.

> At any rate, in the Sabazian mysteries the sign given to those who are initiated is "the god over the breast" this is a serpent drawn over the breast of the votaries, a proof of the licentiousness of Zeus.[472]

Clement relates this and the Sabazian rites to the Orphic myth of Dionysos' birth from Zeus' copulation with Persephone in the form of a snake. Clement's testimony supports the suggestion that this is a ritual phrase, as does the fact that this phrase is also found in the Gurôb Papyrus, which has ritual connotations (see Chapter 5, section 5.2). This phrase comes right before the tablet's owner proclaims that he has become a god instead of a mortal and might refer to the initiate identifying himself with Dionysos if we interpret *kolpos* as 'womb'. In the context of the passage mentioned above, Clement specifically refers to a Dionysiac rite based on the Zagreus myth and whose author was Orpheus.[473] He also relates the Thesmophoria to the murdered Dionysos and the Korybantic and Kabeiric rites with the castrated phallus of Bacchos being carried in a box.[474] Since he is discussing all these rites in the same section in relation to this myth, the Sabazian

---

472 Clem. Al. *Protr.* 2.14 (Tr. Buterworth).
473 Clem. Al. *Protr.* 2.15.
474 Clem. Al. *Protr.* 2.16.

rites might also have been related to it. Clement also says that Dionysos is called Attes because he was mutilated. This word is found in a passage from Demosthenes discussed in Chapter 2 where he accuses Aeschines of performing private Bacchic rites with his mother, where he uses books and performs purifications uttering phrases such as: ἔφυγον κακόν, εὗρον ἄμεινον ('I have escaped the bad, I have found the better') and shouting εὐοῖ σαβοῖ and ὑῆς ἄττης ἄττης ὑῆς while leading *thiasoi* and squeezing and brandishing snakes.[475] Similar rites may have been behind the gold tablets since we have several parallels. Going back to the last phrases of tablet A1, the phrase 'a kid I fell into milk' is reminiscent of similar phrases using verbs in the aorist which were uttered during mysteries such as the phrase mentioned above (ἔφυγον κακόν, εὗρον ἄμεινον). In any case, we can clearly see how poetic and ritual phrases are mingled in the gold tablets.

Apart from a hexametric katabatic poem there is another possible type of archetype for the gold tablets as suggested by Edmonds and Tzifopoulos who argue for an oracular type of poem. Edmonds argues that an oracular text 'fits better with the model of itinerant ritual specialists adapting their materials to serve a varied clientele, and a number of such texts, devised by craftsmen in different areas, would better explain the variety of types of texts among the corpus of tablets'.[476] Edmonds and Tzifopoulos refer to some textual similarities between oracles and the gold tablets such as the words: ἀλλ'ὅταν which is often found in oracles.[477] However, the multiple references to *mystes* in the tablets, especially in the case of B10 where *mystai* and *Bacchoi* are mentioned, suggests that it was an *hieros logos* of a rite and not an oracle that was the archetype. Many elements found in the tablets cannot be explained with an oracular archetype, such as the epic formulas discussed earlier or the ritualistic aspects of the tablets and phrases such as 'a kid you fell into milk', or the use of symbols and passwords; nor would an oracle justify the right of the tablets' owners to claim deification. Edmonds also thinks that various texts were used by ritual practitioners in different areas; to support this he notes that 'the only tablet that contains material from both A and B texts is the late A5, which seems to be several centuries later than all of the others'.[478] This argument, however, disregards all the other textual points of contact between all the groups (according to Edmonds' classification) as outlined at

---

475 Dem. 18.259–260. See p.35.
476 Edmonds, 2011b, p.258ff.
477 Edmonds, 2011b, p.264; Tzifopoulos, 2010, p.133ff. See also Betegh, 2004, p.360–370 discussing the oracular hermeneutic attitude of the Derveni Papyrus' author interpretation.
478 Edmonds, 2011b, p.265.

the beginning of this chapter, which strongly suggest a common archetype.[479] Moreover, Edmonds himself notes that there is no record of an inquiry to an oracle about the afterlife, even though he attributes this to the fact that they would be personal and thus not of interest to others.[480] It is nonetheless almost certain that such inquiries took place, as is evident from other ancient sources such as the Derveni Papyrus' author who refers to those who seek oracular answers about the afterlife. But in this case, how would personal inquiries end up inspiring ritual practitioners across Mainland Greece and Magna Graecia for six centuries? Also, if in any case the archetype of the gold tablets was an oracle this would not go against an Orphic identity since Orpheus was famous for writing oracles. There is no reason to exclude the possibility that a supposed archetypal oracle was of an Orphic identity. The example given by Edmonds from Plutarch who describes Timarchus' experience at Trophonius' oracle has many Orphic elements as established so far: an airy nature for the soul (ἐς αἰθέρα πᾶσα φορεῖται αἰὲν ἀγήραος οὖσα), the idea that the body is the soul's 'prison' (ψυχὴ μὲν, μέχρις οὗ δεσμοῖς σῶμα κρατεῖται), the reference to a first-born divine providence which is the root of soul's aetheral immortality (πρωτόγονος πρόνοια), an idea which is similar to the Protogonos of the *Rhapsodies* who was born in the aether and created the totality of the cosmos, including mortals.[481] These are distinctively Orphic ideas according to all the ancient sources examined so far, which might indicate an affiliation of the oracle of Trophonios with Orphic ideas. There are several similarities between the descending experience of an inquirer at the oracle of Trophonios as described by Pausanias and some elements of the gold tablets, such as the fountains of Mnemosyne and Lethe.[482] However, there are also significant differences, such as that the inquirer had to drink water from both fountains while in the gold tablets drinking water from the first fountain is strictly prohibited.[483] Also, some elements of the gold tablets cannot be explained by the case of the Trophonios oracle: for example, the self-identification as a *mystēs* and Bac-

---

479 See p.126.
480 Edmonds, 2011b, p.268.
481 Plut. *De gen.* 21 (590a ff). OR8-OR24.
482 Paus. IX.39.3ff.
483 Paus. IX.39.8: ἐνταῦθα δὴ χρὴ πιεῖν αὐτὸν Λήθης τε ὕδωρ καλούμενον, ἵνα λήθη γένηταί οἱ πάντων ἃ τέως ἐφρόντιζε, καὶ ἐπὶ τῷδε ἄλλο αὖθις ὕδωρ πίνειν Μνημοσύνης· ἀπὸ τούτου τε μνημονεύει τὰ ὀφθέντα οἱ καταβάντι: 'Here he must drink water called the water of Forgetfulness, that he may forget all that he has been thinking of hitherto, and afterwards he drinks of another water, the water of Memory, which causes him to remember what he sees after his descent.' (Tr. Jones).

chos, and part of a *thiasos* which indicate Dionysiac initiations. For these reasons, even though it is likely that there was some common inspiration between the gold tablets and Trophonios' oracle, I do not think it probable that the gold tablets resulted from their owners' visit there. Tzifopoulos argues more plausibly that 'If Homeric rhapsodizing provided a context, 'prophesying' and oracular poetry influenced the technique and composition of the texts on the lamellae and *epistomia*'.[484] The oracular examples discussed by Tzifopoulos demonstrate some similarities with the gold tablets in form and structure but there are also significant differences, such as that none of them refers to actions to be taken in the afterlife. His suggestion, however, about a common influence seems plausible.

Since Riedweg has proposed an elaborate reconstruction of the archetype there is no need to recreate this in this book, but merely make it clear that I also follow the argument that we can trace an archetype behind the gold tablets.[485] This was most probably of the nature of a poem dealing with a *katabasis* in the underworld and various obstacles that the descending person had to overcome to reach the chthonian gods and make their request. This poem most probably included additional narrative elements, absent from the gold tablets, such as the fate of the non-initiated. We only get a hint of their path in the underworld from tablet B10 where we are told that the descending souls of the dead drink water from the first fountain – assumed to be that of Lethe – which is to be avoided. We can also not exclude that the punishments in Hades as described in Plato and other authors, were part of the katabatic poem.[486]

4.5 Ritualistic Analysis

We have established that the gold tablets' texts are a combination of poetic verses stemming from an archetype, and ritualistic acclamations or performative elements. In this section I will examine any ritualistic/performative elements found in the tablets, with particular emphasis on the enigmatic phrase of 'falling into milk'. I will also make some suggestions about a ritual behind the tablets and draw a comparison to a ritual outlined in a text from the Greek Magical Papyri.

---

484 Tzifopoulos, 2010, p.132. Oracular examples: p.132–137.
485 Riedweg, 2011: The reconstructed poem along with a translation can be found in pages 248–252.
486 Bernabé and Jiménez San Cristóbal, 2008, p.232.

4.5.1 Performative Aspects of the Gold Tablets

First of all, what do I mean by the word 'performative'? One way to identify a text (not necessarily a written text) as performative would be if it is actually spoken out loud during a ritual or a mystery. Such would be a hymn sung or a prayer recited to a deity. The supplicant would make a claim to the god, after first recalling an occasion where devotion was portrayed, which would 'oblige the deity to come to their aid'.[487] These elements, as we saw, are also present in some of the gold tablets where the deceased emphasises his/her purity and repayment of a debt in order to be turned into a god or join the other blessed ones. However, the texts of the gold tablets are much more complicated than a prayer. In some we have a very dramatic, lively instruction for an underworld journey, in others we have various versions of an enigmatic phrase about 'falling into milk', and other ambiguous phrases which need to be explained. It is possible, thus, that the gold tablets belong in another kind of a performative text which could echo the performance of a ritual, maintain some elements of a mystery, or even include some verses uttered during a mystery.[488]

Do we have any other examples where a mystery was based on a text? One such example would be the Eleusinian mysteries. Several authors refer to a 'sacred drama' taking place at the *dromena* of the Eleusinian Mysteries during which an impersonation of the deities by priestly personnel would take place, while Cosmopoulos claims that the 'initiates actually took part in the re-enactment of the story, rather than being mere spectators'.[489] This sacred drama would re-enact a story close to the *Homeric Hymn to Demeter*, including elements such as Persephone's abduction, Demeter's withdrawal and mourning, and their final reunion, probably accompanied by music, singing and perhaps dancing.[490] As Parker argues: 'In all probability the initiates thought that at certain stages in the ritual they were in some sense re-enacting and participating in Demeter's grief for her

---

[487] Graf, 1991, p.189.
[488] Seaford, 2006, p.82: 'The funerary leaves from Hipponion and Pelinna record formulae, almost certainly uttered in mystic ritual, that embody instructions to Dionysiac initiates on what to do in the underworld'.
[489] Sourvinou-Inwood, 2003, p.29. She cites, among other, Tert., *Ad Nat.* II.7, Gr. Nazia., *Orat.* 39.4 and Clem. Al., *Protr.* 2.12: Δηὼ δὲ καὶ Κόρη δρᾶμα ἤδη ἐγενέσθην μυστικόν, καὶ τὴν πλάνην καὶ τὴν ἁρπαγὴν καὶ τὸ πένθος αὐταῖν Ἐλευσὶς δᾳδουχεῖ: 'Demeter and Persephone have come to be the subject of a mystic drama (δρᾶμα ἤδη ἐγενέσθην μυστικόν), and Eleusis celebrates with torches the rape of the daughter and the sorrowful wandering of the mother' (Tr. Butterworth). Cosmopoulos, 2015, p.22. Larson, 2007, p.76.
[490] Cosmopoulos, 2015, p.23.

lost daughter, and the joy of her recovery'.[491] Parker actually argues that the *Homeric Hymn to Demeter* itself was written based around the Mysteries and falls to pieces if taken out of the Eleusinian context. He suggests that all the stages of initiation are echoed in the poem, such as *myesis* and *epopteia*.[492] The initiates would search for Persephone and celebrated by throwing their torches when they had found her.[493] According to some sources the initiates would see the phantoms (φάσματα) of the goddesses in bright light once the *hierophant* would announce the arrival of the Kore and her reunion with Demeter.[494]

Re-enacting myths, then, could be part of rituals and as Burkert argues: '...the importance of the myths of the gods lies in their connection with the sacred rituals for which they frequently provide a reason, an aetiology, which is often playfully elaborated'.[495] Re-enacting a myth during an initiation or ritual is different to using written text as part of the *teletē*. Both cases, however, have performative connotations. It would not be unprecedented, thus, if the gold tablets' text also echoed a mystery or if some of its verses were uttered during a ritual. In the case of the Eleusinian mysteries a very important component, about which we have no information, were the *legomena* (the things said). Despite the lack of evidence, scholars seem to agree that the *legomena* were not 'long religious discourses, but short liturgical statements and explanations, and perhaps invocations'.[496] It was again the *hierophant* who revealed the *legomena* which might have been explanations of what took place in the *dromena*. We know that the knowledge imparted to the initiates was an essential part of the mysteries since 'it was a common belief in ancient Greece that without the *legomena* the initiation ceremony was incomplete'.[497] It is also possible that knowledge was transmitted at earlier stages or even prior to the mysteries. As Bremmer argues: 'Prospective initiates will have been introduced into the secret teachings of the Mysteries by so-called mystagogues, friends and acquaintances who were already initiated'.[498]

Can it be argued, then, that the gold tablets' owners were initiated in a mystery which had an *hieros logos*? And did such a mystery have *legomena*? And what kind of *dromena* could it be constituted of? Firstly, we can say that at least some

---

491 Parker, 1991, p.4–5.
492 Parker, 1991, p.13. For general information on the Eleusinian Mysteries see also Larson, 2007, p.73–76.
493 Sourvinou-Inwood, 2003, p.31.
494 Cosmopoulos, 2015, p.23.
495 Schaps, 2011, p.318. Burkert, 1985, p.8.
496 Mylonas, 1961, p.272.
497 Cosmopoulos, 2015, p.23.
498 Bremmer, 2014, p.3.

of the owners of the tablets – which as a result of the discussion so far are now treated as belonging to the same religious tradition – must have gone through an initiation. This is evident from the word *mystes* which is often inscribed on the tablets, but also from other words such as *Bacchoi*, *thiasos* and *orgia*.[499] Other, minor textual details also point to a prior initiation such as the future tense of the verb in this phrase from A1: ὄλβιε καὶ μακαριστέ, θεὸς δ'ἔσηι ἀντὶ βροτοῖο ('Happy and most blessed one, a god you shall be instead of a mortal'). The future tense might indicate that this phrase was uttered to the initiate by a priest at an initiation during his lifetime since it refers to the future; especially since in other tablets such as A4 it is found in the past tense: θεὸς ἐγένου ἐξ ἀνθρώπου ('A god you have become from a man'). It is also possible that this phrase was uttered by a priest during a funerary rite. Apart from textual indications of a ritual, we also have other indications. As Betz notes about the decision of Persephone to send the initiates to the Isles of the Blessed: 'We have to assume that the initiates knew about the decision already before their deaths, or it would not have been put into their graves in order to remind them. They must have learned of the *makarismos* while they were still alive, so that the decision of the goddess only represents the redemption of a promise given earlier'.[500] Such knowledge about the justification of the *makarismos* and the right to deification must have been communicated to the initiates before or during an initiation – or even after. Also, some of the initiates proclaim that Baccheios himself has delivered them from their crimes; this deliverance must have taken place in an initiation during their lifetime.[501]

More specifically there are several elements in the gold tablets which could be identified as performative indications of a ritual or initiation:
- The interchange of hexameters with rhythmic prose:
  D1 + D2: τα{ι}ῦρος εἰς γάλα ἔθορες. | αἶψα εἰς γ‹ά›λα ἔθορες. | κριὸς εἰς γάλα ἔπεσ‹ες›: 'A bull you rushed to milk. Quickly, you rushed to milk. A ram you fell into milk'.
- The use of words and phrases such as 'now' (νῦν), 'quickly' (αἶψα), 'as soon as' (ὁπόταν) and 'at the time' (ἐπεὶ ἄν) which make better sense in a context referring to an action (without being able to exclude that this action took place in the afterlife):
  A2/A3: νῦν δ' ἱκέτι‹ς› ἥκω: 'Now I come, a suppliant'. D1: νῦν ἔθανες καὶ νῦν ἐγένου: 'Now you have died and now you have been born'. B11: ἐπεὶ ἄμ μέλ]ληισι θανεῖσθαι: 'When you are about] to die...'

---

[499] B10.16, D1.2, D2.2, D3.2, D4, D5, E3, F2, F4.
[500] Betz, 2011, p.114.
[501] D1.2, D2.2; Also D3.2: ἄποινος γὰρ ὁ μύστης: 'For the initiate is without penalty'.

- The dialectic nature of the text with quick interchange of questions and answers:
  B12: τίς δ' εἶ ἦ πῶ δ' εἶ; Γᾶς ἡμ{ο}ὶ μάτηρ {πωτιαετ} ‹κ›αὶ ‹Ο›ὐρανῶ ‹ἀ›στε‹ρόε-ντος›: '"Who are you? From where are you?" Earth is my mother and starry Heaven'.
- Repetition:
  D1 + D2.
- The use of nonsensical words:
  B12: '{τισδιψαιτοιατοιιυτοοπασρατανηο}'. Especially C1.
- The word symbola-passwords which must have been given to the initiate at an earlier stage:
  B11: σύμβολα φ[. D3: σύμβολα· Ἀν‹δ›ρικεπαιδόθυρσον. Ἀνδρικεπαιδόθυρσον. Βριμώ. | Βριμώ. εἴσιθ‹ι› ἱερὸν λειμῶνα. ἄποινος γὰρ ὁ μύστης. ΓΑΠΕΔΟΝ: 'Passwords: Man-boy-thyrsos, Man-boy-thyrsos. Brimo, Brimo. Enter the sacred meadow. For the initiate is without penalty.'
- Words such as *mystēs*, *thiasos*, *orgia* which are found in several tablets indicating that their owners have been initiated into mysteries:
  D5: πέμπε με πρὸς μυστῶ‹ν› θιάσους· ἔχω ὄργια [ἰδοῦσα] | Δήμητρος Χθονίας, τε ‹τέ›λη καὶ Μητρὸς Ὀρεί[ας]. 'Send me to the *thiasos* of the initiates; I have seen the festivals of Demeter Chthonia and the rites of the Mountain Mother'.[502] B10: ὁδὸν ἔρχεα‹ι› ἄν τε καὶ ἄλλοι | μύσται καὶ βάχχοι ἱερὰν στείχουσι κλε‹ε›ινοί: '...will go along the sacred road that the other famed initiates and Bacchoi travel'.
- The fact that the instructions are narrated by someone to the deceased person. It could be, thus, that the verbs which are in the second person singular, point to the active participation of the initiate in a ritual:
  B1: Εὑρήσ{σ}εις ‹δ'› Ἀίδαο δόμων ἐπ' ἀριστερὰ κρήνην, | πὰρ δ' αὐτῆι λευκὴν ἑστηκυῖαν κυπάρισσον· | ταύτης τῆς κρήνης μηδὲ σχεδὸν ἐμπελάσειας: 'You will find in the halls of Hades a spring on the left, and standing by it, a glowing white cypress tree; Do not approach this spring at all'.
- Finally, in some cases, such as the tablets B, there is a sense of urgency and danger at the beginning of the texts which leads to the reassuring confirmation that the initiate is now part of the blessed ones. This is similar to the nature of initiations which initially caused fear and confusion to the initiate, only for the restoration of order to come at the end.

---

[502] For alternative editions of this tablet in terms of the word *orgia* see Bernabé and Jiménez San Cristóbal, 2008, p.53ff.

As Riedweg suggests, we have two kinds of rhythmical prose: 'one *originating from ritual actions and acclamations* and showing a certain tendency to adjust to its hexametric surroundings by assuming versified form (A1.8f; A4.3–5a; D1–2.1; D1–2.3–5; cf.A5.4a)' and one which 'results from an *adaptation of the poetic narration in order to be used as a libretto* within the frame of a performance of the events narrated' which was most likely part of the *mystai* initiation (B3–9.3; D3; cf.E2 and E5).[503] Considering the discussion so far, it is probable that the owners of the gold tablets went through an initiation during their lifetime which included *legomena*, *dromena* and an interpretation of the meaning of the mystery at which time the significant mystic knowledge was communicated to them.

4.5.2 'A ram/bull/kid you fell into milk'

Apart from all the performative/ritual elements mentioned above, one formulaic phrase is particularly puzzling. This is the phrase of falling, or perhaps leaping, into milk as a ram, a bull or a kid. There have been a few interpretations of what it could mean, mostly in relation to a ritual.[504] This phrase is found on two tablets from Lucania and two from Thessaly, all dated to the 4th century B.C. The text of the tablets is the following:

> A1.9–11: {ιμερτοδαπεβανστεμανοποσικαρπασιμοισι}
> ὄλβιε καὶ μακαριστέ, θεὸς δ' ἔσηι ἀντὶ βροτοῖο.
> ἔριφος ἐς γάλ' ἔπετον.
>
> A4.4:
> θεὸς ἐγένου ἐξ ἀνθρώπου· ἔριφος ἐς γάλα ἔπετες.[505]
>
> D1 + D2:
> νῦν ἔθανες καὶ νῦν ἐγένου, τρισόλβιε, ἄματι τῶιδε.
> εἰπεῖν Φερσεφόναι σ' ὅτι Βάκ‹χ›ιος αὐτὸς ἔλυσε.
> τα{ι}ῦρος εἰς γάλα ἔθορες.
> αἶψα εἰς γ‹ά›λα ἔθορες. (Only D1)
> κριὸς εἰς γάλα ἔπεσ‹ες›.

---

503 Riedweg, 2011, p.245.
504 See Bernabé and Jiménez San Cristóbal, 2008, p.76–83.
505 A1.9–11: '"Happy and most blessed one, a god you shall be instead of a mortal." A kid I fell into milk.'; A4.4: 'A god you have become from a man. A kid you fell into milk'.

οἶνον ἔχεις εὐδ‹αι›ίμονα τιμή‹ν›
καὶ σὺ μὲν εἶς ὑπὸ γῆν τελέσας ἅπερ ὄλβιοι ἄλλοι. (Only D1).[506]

We can already see many of the performative or ritual elements mentioned above such as nonsensical words, words denoting the present, repetition and the interchange of hexameters with rhythmic prose.[507] Also, as we have seen, the archaeological evidence might indicate that the owners of the tablets were initiated. In the case of the Pelinna tablets we have elements of a Dionysiac nature: the tablets were ivy-leaf shaped, a wreath and a maenad statue were found alongside. In the case of the Thurii tablets we have evidence of ritual activity and possible worship of the deceased, which suggests that there was an active religious community at the place. Also, the aorist verbs 'you fell' or 'rushed to milk' recall the assertions of initiates in other mystery-rites, which in turn usually refer back to a status-transforming ritual performed by the speaker. Some examples would be the phrase 'I drank the *kukeon*, I took from the *kistes*' uttered at the Eleusinian mysteries, the phrase 'I ate from the *tumpanon*, I drank from the *kumbalos*' uttered at the Attis and Kybele mysteries and the phrase 'I escaped the bad; I found the better' uttered in the Sabazios mysteries.[508] Segal emphasises that in the tablets from Thessaly, the urgent tone of the words 'now' and 'quickly' contrasts with the calmer mood of the last line, the assurance of the bliss that awaits the addressee. This progression from 'intensity to reassurance constitutes the dynamics or the implicit drama of the represented event'.[509] Such dynamics were characteristic of mystery-rites such as the Eleusinian. In general, mystery cults usually have three components: 1) the existence of mystai, 2) a death-like or suffering experience for the mystai and 3) a promise of a happy afterlife and present prosperity. It is possible, thus, that the milk phrase was either uttered or related to a ritual and that this ritual was related to motifs of death and 'renewal'. In the case of the tablets this 'renewal' or change of status is a rebirth or an *apotheosis* since the phrase follows assertions such as 'Now you have died and now you have been born' [D1+D2] and '...a god you shall be instead of a mortal/man' [A1+A4].

---

[506] D1: 'Now you have died and now you have been born, thrice blessed one, on this very day. Say to Persephone that Bacchios himself freed you. A bull you rushed to milk. Quickly, you rushed to milk. A ram you fell into milk. You have wine as your fortunate honor. And you will go beneath the earth, having celebrated rites just as the other blessed ones'.
[507] Riedweg, 2011, p.240.
[508] Clem. Al. *Protr.* 21.2. Obbink, 2011, p.295.
[509] Segal, 1990, p.414.

Faraone argues that these verses refer to ritual movements during which the devotee imitates the actions of the god himself or his divine companions in mythology, for example in a dance or through jumping into the foam of the sea.[510] Graf emphasised the importance of the verbal actions of rushing, referring to the repetition of the word.[511] Zuntz suggested that these expressions were similar to secular proverbs of happiness such as 'a donkey into hay' or 'water to a frog'.[512] This interpretation is implausible since it does not explain the alternation between different animals, or why a grown bull would feel happiness jumping into milk in the same way as a kid (young goat) would. I argue instead that this phrase might have astronomical references and that the milk here refers to the Milky Way which was in antiquity called *gala/galaxias*.[513] Already in the 5th century B.C. Parmenides refers to the Milky Way in his poem *On Nature*:

(D11) – ⏑ ⏑ | – πῶς γαῖα καὶ ἥλιος ἠδὲ σελήνη
αἰθήρ τε ξυνὸς <u>γάλα τ' οὐράνιον</u> καὶ Ὄλυμπος
ἔσχατος ἠδ' ἄστρων θερμὸν μένος ὡρμήθησαν
γίγνεσθαι ⏑ ⏑ | – ⏑ ⏑ | – ⏑ ⏑ | – ⏑ ⏑ | – –
(D12) εἴσῃ δ' αἰθερίαν τε φύσιν τά τ' ἐν αἰθέρι πάντα
σήματα καὶ καθαρᾶς εὐαγέος ἠελίοιο
λαμπάδος ἔργ' ἀίδηλα καὶ ὁππόθεν ἐξεγένοντο,
ἔργα τε κύκλωπος πεύσῃ περίφοιτα σελήνης
καὶ φύσιν, εἰδήσεις δὲ καὶ οὐρανὸν ἀμφὶς ἔχοντα
ἔνθεν ἔφυ τε καὶ ὥς μιν ἄγουσ' ἐπέδησεν Ἀνάγκη
πείρατ' ἔχειν ἄστρων. ⏑ ⏑ | – ⏑ ⏑ | – ⏑ ⏑ | – –

(D11) How the earth, the sun and the moon, the aether in common and the heavenly milk, farthest Olympus and the hot strength of the stars strove to be born and he teaches the origin of the things that are born and are destroyed, all the way to the parts of animals.
(D12) You will know the aethereal nature, and in the aether all the signs, and of the pure torch of the brilliant sun the blinding works, and from where they are born, and you will learn the wandering works of the round-eyed moon and its nature, and you will also know from where the sky, which is on both sides, was born and how Necessity led and enchained it to maintain the limits of the heavenly bodies.[514]

---

510   Faraone, 2011, p.310ff, p.313/321.
511   Graf, 1993, p.249–250.
512   Zuntz, 1971, p.322–327.
513   Torjussen, 2014, p.41. Torjussen, however, concludes that milk does not refer to the Milky Way but to a blissful afterlife 'regardless of where this was enjoyed' (42). E.g. Arist. *Mete*. 1.8 (345a 11): Ὅπως δὲ καὶ διὰ τίν' αἰτίαν γίγνεται καὶ τί ἐστι τὸ γάλα, λέγωμεν ἤδη: 'Let us now explain how the Milky Way is formed, and what is its cause and nature.' (Tr. Lee).
514   Prm. *On Nature*, D11, D12 (ed. and tr. Laks and Most).

Initially, I should mention that *ekthrōskō* in general can also refer to leaping up into the air.[515] So on a semantic level such an expression would still make sense if it referred to the soul rushing to the stars. There is evidence that the belief that the soul went to the stars after death was established at least as early as the 5th century B.C.[516] The conncection of the soul to the heavens is in any case a part of pre-Socratic philosophical theories and evident in e.g. the Pythagorean cosmic music of the spheres.[517] What is of my particular interest, however, is the possibility that such a belief was specifically related to not just philosophical theories but also religious beliefs and practices, especially in connection to Orphic circles and texts. In Aristophanes' *Peace* the servant asks Trygaeus who has just returned from his journey in the sky if it is true that men are turned into stars after death:

ΟΙΚΕΤΗΣ: τί δ' ἔπαθες;
ΤΡΥΓΑΙΟΣ: ἤλγουν τὼ σκέλει μακρὰν ὁδὸν διεληλυθώς.
ΟΙΚΕΤΗΣ: ἴθι νυν, κάτειπέ μοι—
ΤΡΥΓΑΙΟΣ: τὸ τί;
ΟΙΚΕΤΗΣ: ἄλλον τιν' εἶδες ἄνδρα κατὰ τὸν ἀέρα πλανώμενον πλὴν σαυτόν;
ΤΡΥΓΑΙΟΣ: οὔκ, εἰ μή γέ που
ψυχὰς δύ' ἢ τρεῖς διθυραμβοδιδασκάλων.
ΟΙΚΕΤΗΣ: τί δ' ἔδρων;
ΤΡΥΓΑΙΟΣ: ξυνελέγοντ' ἀναβολὰς ποτώμεναι
τὰς ἐνδιαεριαυρονηχέτους τινάς.
ΟΙΚΕΤΗΣ: οὐκ ἦν ἄρ' οὐδ' ἃ λέγουσι, κατὰ τὸν ἀέρα ὡς ἀστέρες γιγνόμεθ', ὅταν τις ἀποθάνῃ;
ΤΡΥΓΑΙΟΣ: μάλιστα.
ΟΙΚΕΤΗΣ: καὶ τίς ἐστιν ἀστὴρ νῦν ἐκεῖ;
ΤΡΥΓΑΙΟΣ: Ἴων ὁ Χῖος, ὅσπερ ἐποίησεν πάλαι ἐνθάδε τὸν Ἀοῖόν ποθ'· ὡς δ' ἦλθ', εὐθέως
Ἀοῖον αὐτὸν πάντες ἐκάλουν ἀστέρα.
ΟΙΚΕΤΗΣ: τίνες γὰρ εἰσ'οἱ διατρέχοντες ἀστέρες,
οἳ καόμενοι θέουσιν;
ΤΡΥΓΑΙΟΣ: ἀπὸ δείπνου τινὲς
τῶν πλουσίων οὗτοι βαδίζουσ' ἀστέρων
ἰπνοὺς ἔχοντες, ἐν δὲ τοῖς ἰπνοῖσι πῦρ.

SERVANT: What has happened to you?
TRYGAEUS: My legs pain me; it was such a dammed long journey.
SERVANT: Oh! tell me ...

---

515 E.g. in Aesch. *Cho.* 845: ἀληθῆ καὶ βλέποντα δοξάσω, | ἦ πρὸς γυναικῶν δειματούμενοι λόγοι | πεδάρσιοι θρῴσκουσι: 'Should I regard it as the living truth, or are these just the frightened words of women that leap high in the air'.
516 Avagianou, 2002, p.82ff. Torjussen, 2014, p.41–42.
517 Burkert, 1972, p.350–368.

TRYGAEUS: What?
SERVANT: Did you see any other man besides yourself strolling about in heaven?
TRYGAEUS: No, only the souls of two or three dithyrambic poets.
SERVANT: What were they doing up there?
TRYGAEUS: They were seeking to catch some lyric exordia as they flew by immersed in the billows of the air.
SERVANT: Is it true, what they tell us, that men are turned into stars after death?
TRYGAEUS: Quite true.
SERVANT: And who is the star over there now?
TRYGAEUS: Ion of Chios. The one who once wrote a poem about the dawn; as soon as he got up there, everyone called him the Morning Star.
SERVANT: And those stars like sparks, that plough up the air as they dart across the sky?
TRYGAEUS: They are the rich leaving the feast with a lantern and a light inside it.[518]

The reference to dithyrambic poets suggests that this idea was related to Dionysiac circles and that it was expressed through poetic works. Ion of Chios was perhaps one of the people referring to such ideas and we saw in Chapter 2 that he was familiar with Orphic works. Trygaeus' reference to a feast of the rich taking place at the stars is reminiscent of Plato's reference to the symposium of the holy (συμπόσιον τῶν ὁσίων).[519] Plato says that these blessings from the gods for the righteous are told by Musaeus and his son who lead them with their speech into Hades (εἰς Ἅιδου γὰρ ἀγαγόντες τῷ λόγῳ): 'For the story goes that when they have conducted them to Hades they sit them down to a wine party for the pious that they have laid on, and have them pass the whole time drinking with garlands on their heads in the belief that the finest reward of virtue is to be drunk for all eternity.'[520] To this might be related that in the Pelinna tablets (D1+D2), the phrase about falling into milk is followed by οἶνον ἔχεις εὐδ‹α›ίμονα τιμή‹ν› ('You have wine as your fortunate honour'). Could this 'symposium' take place in the stars?

Many of the Orphic writings outlined in Chapter 2 dealt with astronomical matters. We mentioned Heraclides Ponticus according to which the Orphic writings make a world out of each star; he elsewhere refers to the Milky Way as a road

---

518 Ar. *Peace*, 825–841 (Tr. O'Neill).
519 Pl. *Resp.* 2.363c–d.
520 Pl. *Resp.* 2.363c–d: Μουσαῖος δὲ τούτων νεανικώτερα τἀγαθὰ καὶ ὁ ὑὸς αὐτοῦ παρὰ θεῶν διδόασιν τοῖς δικαίοις· εἰς Ἅιδου γὰρ ἀγαγόντες τῷ λόγῳ καὶ | κατακλίναντες καὶ συμπόσιον τῶν ὁσίων κατασκευάσαντες ἐστεφανωμένους ποιοῦσιν τὸν ἅπαντα χρόνον ἤδη διάγειν μεθύοντας, ἡγησάμενοι κάλλιστον ἀρετῆς μισθὸν μέθην αἰώνιον: 'But Musaeus and his son sing of still more splendid rewards that the just can expect from the gods. For the story goes that when they have conducted them to Hades they sit them down to a wine party for the pious that they have laid on, and have them pass the whole time drinking with garlands on their heads in the belief that the finest reward of virtue is to be drunk for all eternity.'

which leads the souls from the Earth to the stars.[521] There are also several references in Macrobius' *Saturnalia* linking Orpheus to astronomical observations.[522] Also, a funerary epigram from Pherai in Thessaly dated to the early Hellenistic period, reads:

Ζηνὸς ἀπὸ ῥίζης μεγάλου Λυκόφρων ὁ Φιλίσκου
δόξηι, ἀληθείαι δὲ ἐκ πυρός ἀθανάτου
καὶ ζῶ ἐν οὐρανίοις ἄστροις ὑπὸ πατρὸς ἀερθείς
σῶμα δὲ μητρὸς ἐμῆς μητέρα γῆν κατέχει.

I, Lykophron, the son of Philiskos, seem sprung from the root of great Zeus, but in truth am from the immortal fire; and I live among the heavenly stars uplifted by my father; but the body born of my mother occupies mother-earth.[523]

This epigram is another indication that such an idea was present in Thessaly where two of the tablets with the milk formula were found. Lykophron expresses belief in a duality of body and soul, that he descends from Zeus and that the soul lived in the stars after death. The association of this idea with Zeus and the element of aether (πυρός ἀθανάτου) gives it a secular character which brings it closer to Orphic ideas of the soul being of an airy nature, as expressed in the Derveni Papyrus and the *Orphic Rhapsodies*.[524] In the Derveni Papyrus everything comes from Zeus who is equated with air and in the *Orphic Rhapsodies* we have verses such as: 'Men's soul is rooted in the aether' (Ψυχὴ δ' ἀνθρώποισιν ἀπ' αἰθέρος ἐρρίζωται) and 'the immortal and un-aging soul comes from Zeus' (ψυχὴ δ' ἀθάνατος καὶ ἀγήρως ἐκ Διός ἐστιν).[525] The textual similarity between Ζηνὸς ἀπὸ ῥίζης from Lycophron's epigram and αἰθέρος ἐρρίζωται from the *Rhapsodies* is notable

---

521 Heraclid. Pont. fr.75 Schütrumpf. For text see p.15. Milky Way: Heraclid. Pont. fr.50 Schütrumpf: διατρίβειν μὲν γὰρ αὐτὴν εἰς μοῖράν τινα τοῦ αἰσθητοῦ, καθήκειν γε μὴν εἰς τὸ στερεὸν σῶμα ἄλλοτε ἀπ' ἄλλων τοῦ παντὸς τόπων. καὶ τούτους Ἡρακλείδην μὲν τὸν Ποντικὸν ἀφορίζειν περὶ τὸν γαλαξίαν...: 'For it [the soul] supposedly resides in a certain portion of the perceptible realm, and it arrives back into a solid body at various times from varius regions of the universe. Heraclides Ponticus marked off these regions around the Milky Way.' Heraclid. Pont. fr.52: ὁ Δαμάσκιος τὴν Ἐμπεδοτίμου περὶ τοῦ γάλακτος (scil. ὑπόθεσιν) οἰκειοῦται, ἔργον αὐτὴν οὐ μῦθον καλῶν. φησὶ γὰρ ἐκεῖνος ὁδὸν εἶναι ψυχῶν τὸ γάλα τῶν τὸν Ἅιδην τὸν ἐν οὐρανῷ διαπορευομένων: 'Damascius appropriates the hypothesis of Empedotimus concerning the Milky Way, calling it a fact and not a myth. For he says that the Milky Way is the path of souls that travel through the Underworld in the sky.' Dam. 117.9–12 Hayduck.
522 See p.185–187, p.216–218.
523 Avagianou, 2002, p.75.
524 For immortal fire being aether see Avagianou, 2002, p.79–80, fn.25.
525 OR89 = OF436F, OF426F: Vettius Valens, *Anthol.* IX 1, p.330.23.

and could show a familiarity of Lykophron with Orphic texts. As Avagianou argues the entire fourth verse of Lykophron's epigram which identifies the mortal body with earth 'clearly echoes the initiate's confession of the Orphic texts 'Γῆς παῖς εἰμι" [in the gold tablets].[526] In any case, the astral immortality of the gold tablets' owners might be hinted at through the phrase Γῆς παῖς εἰμὶ καὶ] Οὐρανοῦ ἀστερόεντος and the self-identification as a child of 'starry heaven'. It might also be relevant that the reborn initiate and owner of the gold tablet B2 says that his name is Starry (Ἀστέριος).

The so-called Palaikastro Hymn might offer some insights on the use of the verb θρῴσκω as an almost technical term in hymnic /religious poetry. The fragmentary inscription was discovered at Palaikastro during the excavation of the sanctuary of Dictaean Zeus and even though it dates to c. 200 A.D. according to Alonge the hymn is typically dated to the 3rd century B.C. or earlier.[527] This text is controversial and it is not certain if the god mentioned in the hymn is in fact Zeus but it seems that the god must have been a youthful one.[528] In the hymn which is sung by a chorus around the altar, the expression θόρε κές and θόρ'ές is repeated several times as an invitation for abundancy and an invocation to the god to leap to the cities, the seafaring ships, the new citizens, the fleecy flocks, the houses and the fruits.[529] The way this expression is used in this hymn creates the image of a god filling with his presence the world bringing prosperity. Tzifopoulos discusses this hymn and argues that the verb is here used to invite the god to rush towards the world 'with the same energy that a newborn would, or in the manner that a bull or ram might charge, in order to effect fertility and growth'.[530] I believe, however, that there might be another explanation. The god, who is called bright, is repeatedly invited to come to Dicte at a specific time – 'at the turn of the year' – and we have a reference to the beautiful dawn. These elements might suggest that the god's arrival/epiphany is associated with the appearance of a star and the verb θρῴσκω refers to the 'leaping' of the star above the horizon at a time of the year associated with the rejuvenation of nature/life. Especially, since as Tzifopoulos notes the verb θρῴσκω is particularly used in relation to birth or rebirth while he defines it as an almost technical term that describes the first movements and birth of a god or a hero.[531] A good example related

---

526 Avagianou, 2002, p.87; p.84: Avagianou connects the ideas of the epigram with Orphic ideas and texts.
527 Alonge, 2005, p.1.
528 See Alonge, 2005, p.15–17.
529 *IC* III.2.2.
530 Tzifopoulos, 2010.
531 Tzifopoulos, 2010.

to this is the birth of the heliacal Oprhic god Protogonos/Phanes in the *Orphic Rhapsodies*: ἐξέθορε πρώτιστος ἀνέδραμε ('he sprang upwards first of all').[532] This concept fits particularly well with the renewed divine/heroic status that the owners of the gold tablets claim to have. MacGillivray and Sackett identified the Palaikastro Kouros – a Minoan chryselephantine statuette which was discovered near the find-place of the hymn – as the god of the hymn: 'the youthful male god who arrived from the Underworld to herald the beginning of the Harvest: Diktaian Zeus, associated with Egyptian Osiris and immortalized as Orion'.[533] They also associate its worship and display of the statuette with the heliacal setting and rising of a star, namely Orion, which signified the death and rebirth of the god and the beginning of the ploughing or the harvest season accordingly. Sources such as the Hibeh papyri (3rd B.C.), which record astronomical movements associated with religious festivals of Athena, Prometheus, and Hera evidence the important role of the astral sphere to religious practices.[534] Boutsika and Ruggles for example, suggest that Alcman's *Partheneion* ode (mid 7th B.C.) might describe a rite in honour of Artemis Orthia in Sparta performed at night, during the heliacal rising of the Pleiades star cluster as evidenced by verses such as: 'For the Pleiades as we carry the robe to (the) *orthia* [are] rising through the ambrosial night like the star Sirius and fight against us'.[535] A Hymn to Dionysos of the women of Elis which is usually dated to archaic times might have been performed under similar circumstances since Dionysos is invited to appear being called worthy bull, a possible reference to the Taurus constellation which is associated to him.[536] Perhaps this is why Pindar calls Dionysos 'the holy light at summer's end' [ἁγνὸν φέγγος ὀπώρας] that brings joy and fosters the trees.[537] Plato, in the *Cratylus*, refers through Socrates to the etymology of the word θεός as deriving from the word θέω, explaining that the earliest men in Greece believed that the sun, moon, earth, stars and sky were gods and thus they named them θεούς because of their constant running (θεῖν) celestial course.[538] We have to seriously start considering

---

[532] OR10.
[533] MacGillivray and Sackett, 2000, p.169.
[534] Grenfell and Hunt, 1906, p.138–157.
[535] Alcm. *PMG* 1.60–63; Boutsikas and Ruggles, 2011, pp.60–66.
[536] *PMG* 871: ἐλθεῖν, ἥρω Διόνυσε, Ἀλίων ἐς ναὸν ἁγνὸν σὺν Χαρίτεσσιν ἐς ναὸν τῷ βοέῳ ποδὶ θύων. ἄξιε ταῦρε, ἄξιε ταῦρε: 'Come here Dionysos, to the holy temple of the Eleans along with the Graces, to the temple, raging with your bovine foot, worthy bull, worthy bull.'
[537] Pind. fr.153 Race: δενδρέων δὲ νομὸν Διώνυσος πολυγαθὴς αὐξάνοι, | ἁγνὸν φέγγος ὀπώρας: 'may Dionysus, bringer of joy, foster the grove of trees, the holy light at summer's end'.
[538] Pl. *Crat.* 397c–d: ΣΩ: Τοιόνδε τοίνυν ἔγωγε ὑποπτεύω· φαίνονταί μοι οἱ πρῶτοι τῶν ἀνθρώπων τῶν περὶ τὴν Ἑλλάδα τούτους μόνους τοὺς θεοὺς ἡγεῖσθαι, οὕσπερ νῦν πολλοὶ τῶν

the possibility that such hymns, must have been related to nocturnal practices which involved the astral sphere in the action and the rising or setting of specific stars/constellations which were associated with specific gods and motifs of death and rebirth.

Going back to the gold tablets, if we accept that *gala* refers to the Milky Way, I suggest that the bull, the ram and the kid could refer to constellations. The ἔριφος, ταῦρος and κριός, according to ancient sources, would correspond to the constellations of Auriga (referred to as Ἔριφοι in ancient sources), Taurus (Bull), and Aries (Ram) respectively. These three constellations are next to each other and located on the Milky Way. Jakob also believes that the animals refer to 'stars' indicating that the soul transforms into a star after death but he argues that we are not in a position to answer the question as to why these particular stars were selected and that in fact 'no one at that time understood the puzzling phrase about "milk" which they repeated mechanically.[539] However, I disagree with the argument that the initiates were not aware of the meaning of these verses and I believe that the references to these constellations relate to their associations with Dionysos and Zeus. The constellation Taurus is related to Zeus but also to Dionysos since as already said the bull was Dionysos' persona. Diodorus Siculus quotes some relevant verses:

> τῶν δὲ παρ' Ἕλλησι παλαιῶν μυθολόγων τινὲς τὸν Ὄσιριν Διόνυσον προσονομάζουσι καὶ Σείριον παρωνύμως· ὧν Εὔμολπος μὲν ἐν τοῖς Βακχικοῖς ἔπεσί φησιν· 'ἀστροφαῆ Διόνυσον ἐν ἀκτίνεσσι πυρωπόν', Ὀρφεὺς δὲ 'τούνεκά μιν καλέουσι Φάνητά τε καὶ Διόνυσον'

> And of the ancient Greek writers of mythology some give to Osiris the name Dionysus or, with a slight change in form, Sirius. One of them, Eumolpus, in his *Bacchic Hymn* speaks of "Our Dionysus, shining like a star, with fiery eye in every ray", while Orpheus says: "And this is why men call him Shining One and Dionysus".[540]

βαρβάρων, ἥλιον καὶ σελήνην καὶ γῆν καὶ ἄστρα καὶ οὐρανόν· ἅτε οὖν αὐτὰ ὁρῶντες πάντα ἀεὶ ἰόντα δρόμῳ καὶ θέοντα, ἀπὸ ταύτης τῆς φύσεως τῆς τοῦ θεῖν θεοὺς αὐτοὺς ἐπονομάσαι· ὕστερον δὲ κατανοοῦντες τοὺς ἄλλους, πάντας ἤδη τούτῳ τῷ ὀνόματι προσαγορεύειν. ἔοικέ τι ὃ λέγω τῇ ἀληθείᾳ ἢ οὐδέν; EPM: Πάνυ μὲν οὖν ἔοικε: 'SOC: Something of this sort, then, is what I suspect: I think the earliest men in Greece believed only in those gods in whom many foreigners believe to-day – sun, moon, earth, stars, and sky. They saw that all these were always moving in their courses and running, and so they called them gods (θεούς) from this running (θεῖν) nature; then afterwards, when they gained knowledge of the other gods, they called them all by the same name. Is that likely to be true, or not? HER: Yes, very likely.'; See also Pl. *Epin.* 981d ff.

539 Jakob, 2010, p.71/74.
540 Diod. Sic. 1.11.3 (Tr. Oldfather).

We can see, thus, an association of the Orphic Dionysos-Phanes with the stars. The constellation of Taurus was formed from the Pleiades and the Hyades. In Sophocles' *Antigone* the chorus of Theban elders addresses Dionysos which is identified with the Eleusinian Iacchos:

ἰὼ πῦρ πνεόντων
χοράγ' ἄστρων, νυχίων
φθεγμάτων ἐπίσκοπε,
Ζηνὸς γένεθλον, προφάνηθ',
ὦναξ, σαῖς ἅμα περιπόλοις
Θυίασιν, αἵ σε μαινόμεναι πάννυχοι
χορεύουσι τὸν ταμίαν Ἴακχον.

> O leader of the chorus of the stars with the fiery breath, overseer of the nocturnal chants, child begotten of Zeus, come to light, my king, with your attendants the Thyiades, who in night-long frenzy dance for Iacchus the giver![541]

Also, in Aristophanes' *Frogs* the chorus says: Ἴακχ' ὦ Ἴακχε, νυκτέρου τελετῆς φωσφόρος ἀστὴρ φλογὶ φέγγεται δὲ λειμών ('Iacchos, Oh Iacchos, the light-bringing star of our nocturnal rite. Now the meadow brightly burns').[542] These passages give a clear identification of Dionysos-Iackhos as a star leading a chorus of stars and most importantly relate this notion to nocturnal rites. In the passage from Sophocles, the chorus refers to the Thyiades who were the ones performing rites at Delphi to bring back to life Dionysos. Their rite must have been important since the west pediment of the classical temple of Apollo at Delphi depicted Dionysos and the Thyiades, while the east pediment depicted Apollo's arrival with Leto, Artemis and the Muses.[543] The rites of the Thyiades took place in November and February and the Taurus constellation is most visible in November. Perhaps the resurrection of Dionysos was associated with the specific location of the constellation Taurus in the sky, which also marked the beginning of the new cycle of the grape season which ended in October with the harvest of the grapes. Aratus (3rd B.C.) refers to the constellations and other celestial bodies in his *Phaenomena*. He notes that the Pleiades were used for marking agricultural and seasonal cycles: 'Small and dim are they all alike, but widely famed they wheel in heaven

---

541 Soph. *Ant.* 1146-1154.
542 Ar. *Ran.* 342-344 (Tr. Dillon). For the connection between Iacchos and Dionysos: Eur. *Bacch*.725; Soph. *Ant.* 1146-1154; ΣAr. *Ran.* 479; Bremmer, 2014, p.6; Soph. fr.959 Lloyd-Jones, 1996; Bremmer, 2104, p.5 and p.10-11; Parker, 2007, p.327; Lada-Richards, 1999, p.49. Also, *LIMC* Dionysos 531 (Attic krater 4th century B.C.) represents Dionysos/Iacchos as a son of Persephone or Demeter wrapped in a fawnskin on her lap. Edmonds, 2013, p.244, fn.158.
543 Tzifopoulos, 2010, p.142.

at morn and eventide, by the will of Zeus, who bade them tell of the beginning of summer and winter and of the coming of the ploughing-time.'[544] We can see, thus, that the constellation of Taurus was associated with motifs of death and rebirth. It would not be surprising, then, if the owners of the gold tablets connected Taurus with eschatological beliefs of immortality and its location in the Milky Way with the Isles of the Blessed where they could dwell with the gods for all eternity. By uttering the *makarismos* of falling into milk as a bull, the initiates proclaimed their ultimate union with Dionysos and their new immortal state in the stars where Dionysos was also forever fixed as the constellation of Taurus and the leader of a chorus of stars (souls?), as the Theban elders in *Antigone* proclaim.

But what about the *eriphos* falling into milk? According to Aratus, the Auriga (Ἔριφοι) constellation is associated with the Charioteer and one of the kids he holds are identified with Amaltheia who suckled young Zeus.[545] He notes:

Πὰρ ποσὶ δ' Ἡνιόχου κεραὸν πεπτηότα ΤΑΥΡΟΝ
μαίεσθαι. [...]
καὶ λίην κείνων ὄνομ' εἴρεται, οὐδέ τοι αὔτως
νήκουστοι ΥΑΔΕΣ. ταὶ μέν ῥ' ἐπὶ παντὶ μετώπῳ
Ταύρου βεβλέαται· λαιοῦ δὲ κεράατος ἄκρον
καὶ πόδα δεξιτερὸν παρακειμένου Ἡνιόχοιο
εἷς ἀστὴρ ἐπέχει· συνεληλάμενοι δὲ φέρονται,
ἀλλ' αἰεὶ Ταῦρος προφερέστερος Ἡνιόχοιο
εἰς ἑτέρην καταβῆναι, ὁμηλυσίῃ περ ἀνελθών

At the feet of the Charioteer seek for the crouching horned Bull [Taurus]. [...]
Often spoken is their name and famous are the Hyades. Broadcast are they on the forehead of the Bull. One star occupies the tip of his left horn and the right foot of the Charioteer, who

---

544 Aratus, *Phaen.* 264–268: αἱ μὲν ὁμῶς ὀλίγαι καὶ ἀφεγγέες, ἀλλ' ὀνομασταί | ἦρι καὶ ἑσπέριαι, Ζεὺς δ' αἴτιος, εἰλίσσονται, | ὅ σφισι καὶ θέρεος καὶ χείματος ἀρχομένοιο | σημαίνειν ἐκέλευσεν ἐπερχομένου τ' ἀρότοιο (Tr. Mair). Hes. *Op.* 618ff.
545 Aratus, *Phaen.* 156–164: Εἰ δέ τοι ΗΝΙΟΧΟΝ τε καὶ ἀστέρας Ἡνιόχοιο | σκέπτεσθαι δοκέει, καί τοι φάτις ἤλυθεν ΑΙΓΟΣ | αὐτῆς ἠδ' ΕΡΙΦΩΝ, οἵ τ' εἰν ἁλὶ πορφυρούσῃ | πολλάκις ἐσκέψαντο κεδαιομένους ἀνθρώπους, | αὐτὸν μέν μιν ἅπαντα μέγαν Διδύμων ἐπὶ λαιᾷ | κεκλιμένον δήεις· Ἑλίκης δέ οἱ ἄκρα κάρηνα | ἀντία δινεύει. σκαιῷ δ' ἐπελήλαται ὤμῳ | αἲξ ἱερή, τὴν μέν τε λόγος Διὶ μαζὸν ἐπισχεῖν, | Ὠλενίην δέ μιν Αἶγα Διὸς καλέουσ' ὑποφῆται: 'But if it be <your> wish to mark Charioteer [Auriga] and his stars, and if the fame has come to you of the Goat herself and the Kids, who often on the darkening deep have seen men storm-tossed, you will find him in all his might, leaning forward at the left hand of the Twins. Over against him wheels the top of Helice's head, but on his left shoulder is set the holy Goat <Amaltheia>, that, as legend tells, gave the breast to Zeus.' (Tr. Mair).

is close by. Together they are carried in their course, but ever earlier is the Bull than the Charioteer to set beneath the West albeit they fare together at their rising.⁵⁴⁶

In Plato's *Timaeus*, Socrates refers to the idea that each star is assigned a soul which rides the star as a chariot; the number of souls is equal to the number of stars in the sky:

> 41d–e: ξυστήσας δὲ τὸ πᾶν διεῖλε ψυχὰς ἰσαρίθμους τοῖς ἄστροις ἔνειμέ θ' Εἑκάστην πρὸς ἕκαστον, καὶ ἐμβιβάσας ὡς ἐς ὄχημα τὴν τοῦ παντὸς φύσιν ἔδειξε, νόμους τε τοὺς εἱμαρμένους εἶπεν αὐταῖς, ὅτι γένεσις πρώτη μὲν ἔσοιτο τεταγμένη μία πᾶσιν, ἵνα μήτις ἐλαττοῖτο ὑπ' αὐτοῦ [...] 42b: καὶ ὁ μὲν εὖ τὸν προσήκοντα χρόνον βιούς, πάλιν εἰς τὴν τοῦ ξυννόμου πορευθεὶς οἴκησιν ἄστρου, βίον εὐδαίμονα καὶ συνήθη ἕξοι· σφαλεὶς δὲ τούτων εἰς γυναικὸς φύσιν ἐν τῇ δευτέρᾳ γενέσει μεταβαλοῖ· μὴ παυόμενός τε ἐν τούτοις ἔτι κακίας, τρόπον ὃν κακύνοιτο, κατὰ τὴν ὁμοιότητα τῆς τοῦ τρόπου γενέσεως εἴς τινα τοιαύτην ἀεὶ μεταβαλοῖ θήρειον φύσιν, ἀλλάττων τε οὐ πρότερον πόνων λήξοι, πρὶν τῇ ταὐτοῦ καὶ ὁμοίου περιόδῳ τῇ ἐν αὑτῷ ξυνεπισπώμενος...

> 41d–e: And having made it he divided the whole mixture into souls equal in number to the stars, and assigned each soul to a star; and having there placed them as in a chariot, he showed them the nature of the universe, and declared to them the laws of destiny, according to which their first birth would be one and the same for all, no one should suffer a disadvantage at his hands[...] 42b: He who lived well during his appointed time was to return and dwell in his native star, and there he would have a blessed and congenial existence. But if he failed in attaining this, at the second birth he would pass into a woman, and if, when in that state of being, he did not desist from evil, he would continually be changed into some brute who resembled him in the evil nature which he had acquired, and would not cease from his toils and transformations until he followed the revolution of the same and the like within him...⁵⁴⁷

According to Socrates, each soul has to be incarnated due to the law of destiny but it can eventually return to its native star. Socrates says that these things have been said a long time ago by those who claim to be children of gods. Significantly, Plato relates these ideas to the belief in multiple reincarnations and to an innate divine nature of the soul which needs to be cultivated in order for the soul to escape this cycle of rebirths. These are ideas related to Plato's notion of controlling the tripartite soul, but they are nonetheless ideas expressed through this mythological motif found in the words of old storytellers. The idea of a cycle of rebirths from which you can escape through living a just and pure life is an idea that according to the examination of the evidence so far is found in Orphism and the

---

546 Aratus, *Phaen.* 167–178 (Tr. Mair).
547 Pl. *Ti.* 41d–e;42b (Tr. Jowett). See also Pl. *Leg.* 10.899a–899c.

gold tablets. This Platonic passage, thus, corroborates the suggestion that the Orphic belief of the soul being rooted in the aether had astronomical connotations. How better could we explain Heraclides Ponticus' attestation that the Orphic writings make a world out of each star?

An epigram from Miletus which includes ideas found in the gold tables and is dated to the 1st century A.D. locates the Isles of the Blessed at the exact same place that I have suggested:

> οὐ Λήθης, Ἑρμα[ῖε, ποτὸν πίες,] οὐδέ σ' ἔκρυπτε
> [Τάρταρα καὶ] στυγνῆς δώματ[α Περσεφόν]ης,
> ἀλλά σ' ἔχων ἐς "Ολυμπον ἀν[ήγαγεν] εὔσφυρος Ἑρμῆς,
> ἐκ χαλεπ[οῦ] μερόπων ῥυσάμενος βιότου·
> αἰθέρα δ' ὀκταέτης κατιδὼν ἄστροις ἅμα λάμπεις
> πὰρ κέρας Ὠλενίης Αἰγὸς ἀνερχόμενος
> παισί τε νῦν ἐπαρωγὸς ἐνὶ σθεναραῖσι παλαίστραις
> φαίνῃ, σοὶ μακάρων τοῦτο χαριζομένων.

> You have not drunk the water from Lethe, Hermaios, and neither Tartarus nor the abode of hateful Persephone is hidden to you. But Hermes, of the beautiful ankles, led you up to Olympus and he saved you from the painful life of human beings. At the age of eight, you have seen the aether and now you sparkle among the stars, beside the horn, in the constellation of the Goat, and next to the elbow of the Charioteer. You shine now to protect the strong boys in the wrestling school and thus the blessed show you their favour.[548]

Hermaios' blissful afterlife is dependent on the fact that he did not drink from the water of Lethe, just as in the gold tablets. Another similar idea is that mortal life is perceived as painful which I have argued to be Orphic religious terminology. The divine celestial substance is aether and Hermaios now sparkles among the stars located between the constellation of the Goat and the Charioteer. Even though this epigram comes from an area where no gold tablets have been found, it still lends support to my suggestion of locating the Isles of the Blessed in the Milky Way near the constellations of *Eriphos* and the Bull – although this need not mean that Hermaios was an Orphic. Whether or not his family was influenced by Orphic ideas and how these ideas reached Miletus is not possible to know, but we can now locate the blessed meadows of the gold tablets among the stars with more confidence. It also becomes clearer that there is an astronomical association of the soul's immortality in Orphism and even elsewhere, which was probably related to its elemental 'composition' out of divine aether/aer. The identification

---

[548] *IMilet.* 755 Herrmann. Jiménez San Cristóbal, 2011, p.166.

of aether as the purer divine essence seems to be evoked in other religious circumstances too. In Euripides' *Helen* the prophetess Theonoe appears on the scene singing in prophetic strain (θεσπιῳδὸς Θεονόη), accompanied by handmaidens carrying torches and performing a ritual while she says the following:

> ἡγοῦ σύ μοι φέρουσα λαμπτήρων σέλας
> θείου τε σεμνὸν θεσμὸν αἰθέρος μυχούς,
> ὡς πνεῦμα καθαρὸν οὐρανοῦ δεξώμεθα·

> Please lead the way with blazing torches, and purify, according to the sacred law, the inmost corners of the aether, so I may receive the pure breath of heaven.[549]

The fact that Theonoe is concerned here with extreme purity and performs a purification rite according to the sacred law while invoking aether and the pure heavenly πνεῦμα, corroborates the connection of such elemental and scientific ideas to various types of religious practices.

In relation to Aratus, the proem of his work *Phenomena* shows similarities with the Derveni Papyrus' Orphic Theogony, which was found in Macedonia, the home place of Aratus. The most interesting similarity is the idea that humans are the off-spring of Zeus and the way that Aratus expresses this notion:

> Ἐκ Διὸς ἀρχώμεσθα, τὸν οὐδέποτ' ἄνδρες ἐῶμεν
> ἄρρητον· μεσταὶ δὲ Διὸς πᾶσαι μὲν ἀγυιαί,
> πᾶσαι δ' ἀνθρώπων ἀγοραί, μεστὴ δὲ θάλασσα
> καὶ λιμένες· πάντη δὲ Διὸς κεχρήμεθα πάντες.
> τοῦ γὰρ καὶ γένος εἰμέν·

> From Zeus let us begin; whom we mortals never leave unnamed; full of Zeus are all the streets and all the market-places of men; full is the sea and the harbours; and we proclaim everything to come from Zeus. For we also descent from his race.[550]

This passage creates the same imagery and expresses the same ideas as the ones found in the following Orphic verses quoted in the Derveni Papyrus (1) and slightly variant in the *Rhapsodies* (2):

> (1) "Πρωτογόνου βασιλέως αἰδοίου· τῶι δ' ἄρα πάντες
> ἀθάνατοι προσέφυν μάκαρες θεοὶ ἠδὲ θέαιναι
> καὶ ποταμοὶ καὶ κρῆναι ἐπήρατοι ἄλλα τε πάντα,
> ἄσσα τότ' ἦν γεγαῶτ', αὐτὸς δ' ἄρα μοῦνος ἔγεντο".

---

549 Eur. *Hel.* 865–867 (Tr. Coleridge).
550 Aratus, *Phaen.* 1–6 (My translation).

(2) καὶ ποταμοὶ καὶ πόντος ἀπείριτος ἄλλα τε πάντα
πάντες τ' ἀθάνατοι μάκαρες θεοὶ ἠδὲ θέαιναι,
ὅσσα τ' ἔην γεγαῶτα καὶ ὕστερον ὁπόσσ' ἔμελλεν,
ἐνγένετο, Ζηνὸς δ' ἐνὶ γαστέρι σύρρα πεφύκει

"Of the First-born king, the reverend one; and upon him all the immortals grew, blessed gods and goddesses and rivers and lovely springs and everything else that had then been born and he himself became the sole one". (DP Col.XVI.3–6)

...and rivers and the inaccessible deep, and everything else and all the immortal and blissful Gods and Goddesses and all that has already happened and all that will in the future became one, tangled inside the belly of Zeus and were brought forth again (OR59).

It can be argued that Aratus was familiar with Orphic texts or ideas, especially since as it becomes more and more evident, Macedonia was an important centre of Orphic activity, and also bearing in mind that it is the finding place of the Derveni Papyrus. Apart from Dionysos and Persephone – the deities who appear to be the most significant in the gold tablets – I would also argue for the presence of Zeus. This is supported by the reference to Eukles and Eubouleus, both deities mentioned in A1, A2, A3 and A5, and who are sometimes identified as Dionysos and sometimes as the Chthonic Zeus.[551] Zeus might also be mentioned in tablet C which was folded in the shape of an envelope and inside which the Thurii tablet (A4) was found which includes the falling into milk phrase. This tablet has been

---

551 A1.2–3: Εὐκλῆς Εὐβο‹υ›λεύς τε καὶ ἀθάνατοι θεοὶ ἄλλοι· | καὶ γὰρ ἐγὼν ὑμῶν γένος ὄλβιον εὔχομαι εἶμεν: 'Eukles and Eubouleus and the other immortal gods; For I also claim that I am of your blessed race'. Bremmer, 2013, p.37ff: 'Yet it is clear that Zeus Eubouleus originally belonged to a very limited part of Greece, the Cyclades, from where he was perhaps exported to a few other places. Zeus Eubouleus (Z.E) was particularly popular on Delos where his cult is attested from the middle of the third Century BC onwards, mainly in the context of the Thesmophoria. Usually he is worshipped together with Demeter (D) and Kore (K), but sometimes only Demeter.'. *IG* XI 2.287 A.69 (mid 3rd B.C.). *IG* XII 7.76: Δήμητρι Κόρηι | Διὶ Εὐβουλεῖ (4th B.C.). See also *IG* I³ 78a.38–40 (422/1 B.C.), the Athenian First Fruits decree on the Eleusinian mysteries. Tzifopoulos, 2010, p.129: 'He considers that the reference to these deities becomes 'the mortal initiate's *symbolon* for attaining immortality the 'Orphic' way: through *Eukles* ('beautiful *kleos*'), Hades' euphemistic epithet, and through *Eubouleus* ('beautiful *boule*'), a euphemism for Zeus/Dionysos (and perhaps also Hades), a way which transforms the epic symbols of immortal *kleos* into a more concrete immortality: the *mystes* is reborn and acquires the status of a hero/god in the afterlife.'. Hades is also sometimes identified with Dionysos: Herakleitos, fr.D16 (Laks-Most): ὡυτὸς δὲ Ἅιδης καὶ Διόνυσος, ὅτεῳ μαίνονται καὶ ληναΐζουσιν: '...but Hades is the same as Dionysus, for whom they go mad and celebrate maenadic rites'. Plut. *Quaest. conv.* 7.714c: 'And in very ancient times, men regarded Dionysus as not even needing the help of Hermes; they spoke of him as *Eubuleus* (Good Counsellor), and on his account they termed night *euphrone* (good thinking).' (Tr. Minar).

heavily debated because it is very different from the other ones. The text is made up of letters which at first glance seem to make no sense. However, scholars such as Bernabé have identified some words in between the random letters.[552] Bernabé's transliteration of the tablet is published in Edmonds' most recent publication of the tablets and accepted by many scholars. I agree with Bernabé's suggestions, some of which are hard to deny; for example, 'Prōtogonos' is the very first word on the tablet and 'Kybeleia' is too characteristic to attribute its presence to chance. In this tablet, Zeus is mentioned alongside Persephone and Prōtogonos, the deity found in the *Rhapsodies* and the Derveni Papyrus as already mentioned. In lines 2–3 we can read the words Ζεῦ / ἀέρ / Ἥλιε, πῦρ δὴ πάντα / νικᾶι / Τύχα / Φάνης, πάμνηστοι Μοῖραι.[553] If we accept Bernabé's reading then many of the ideas discussed in this section can be found in this tablet's text: the fiery aer (aether); the sun which shines on everything and is perhaps Phanes/Prōtogonos who as we saw was identified with the Orphic Dionysos by Diodorus Siculus, and the association of Zeus with aer, the divine substance of the soul which underlays the cosmos (as expressed in the DP). Many of the words identified by Bernabé allude to other Orphic texts such as the Derveni Theogony and the *Orphic Rhapsodies* as we will see (Chapters 5 and 6). The presence of Zeus in this tablet would be another way to identify them as Orphic since the combination of Zeus, Dionysos and Persephone can be explained through the Orphic myth of Dionysos' birth from Zeus and Persephone and it would support that Persephone's 'judgement' has something to do with Dionysos' dismemberment. The transformation of Zeus into a snake to mate with Persephone in the Orphic myth attributes a chthonic aspect to him which would justify the references to Eukles and Eubouleus and Zeus' association with an eschatological context such as the one found in the gold tablets.

Bernabé disagrees with the identification of *gala* with the Milky Way, arguing that it comes in contrast with the expression: καὶ σὺ μὲν εἶς ὑπὸ γῆν τελέσας ἅπερ ὄλβιοι ἄλλοι.[554] This phrase is translated by Bernabé as 'and you will go under the earth, once you have accomplished the same rites as the other happy ones' and by Edmonds as 'And you will go beneath the earth, having celebrated rites just as the other blessed ones'. Edmonds and Bernabé, however, do not explain why the deceased soul would perform rites in the underworld and in the afterlife. There is no hint of such underworld *teletae* in the other tablets or indeed in any other

---

552 Bernabé and Jiménez San Cristóbal, 2008, p.137ff. See also Betegh, 2011, p.219–225.
553 C1.2.
554 D1.7. The same reason Torjussen rejects this idea. (See fn.513).

source for initiations (*teletae*) being performed in the afterlife.⁵⁵⁵ For this reason, I disagree with both translations and suggest the following one: 'and you too shall proceed just as the other blessed ones, having performed rites under the earth'. This is as plausible a translation as Edmonds' and Bernabé's, especially if the ritual performed by the tablets' owners was of a katabatic nature. There is no doubt that the souls of the tablets' owners had to perform a journey into the underworld. From the moment of their death until they reached the guards of the fountain of Memory and addressed Persephone in order to convince her of their special status, they were as ordinary as any other uninitiated soul. This journey was essential in order to be admitted to the Isles of the Blessed. Where exactly Persephone's meadow was is not specified in the tablets and there is no reason to reject an upward journey of the soul as soon as they became gods.⁵⁵⁶

4.5.3 Similarities between the Gold Tablets and the *Eighth Book of Moses*

The *Eighth Book of Moses* (part of the *Greek Magical Papyri*), is one of the most valuable sources of incantations. It comes from Leiden Papyrus J 395 dated to the 3rd century A.D. I have identified some striking similarities between the text of the *Eighth Book of Moses* and the gold tablets and specifically to the 'falling into milk' formula. The text explicitly constitutes instructions for an initiation:

> πρότερον δὲ συνιστάνου οἷα δήποτ' οὖν νεομηνίᾳ κατὰ θεὸν τοῖς ὡρογενέσιν θεοῖς, οἷς ἔχεις ἐν τῇ 'Κλειδί'. τελεσθήσῃ δὲ αὐτοῖς οὕτως· ποίησον ἐκ σεμιδάλεως ζῴδια γ'· ταυροπρόσωπον, τραγοπρόσωπον, κριοπρόσωπον, ἓν ἕκαστον αὐτῶν ἐπὶ πόλου ἑστῶτα, μάστιγας ἔχοντα Αἰγυπτίας, καὶ περικαπνίσας κατάφαγε λέγων τὸν λόγον τῶν ὡρογενῶν, τὸν ἐν τῇ 'Κλειδί', καὶ τὸν ἐπάναγκον αὐτῶν καὶ τοὺς ἐφεβδοματικοὺς τεταγμένους, καὶ ἔσῃ <τε>τελεσμένος αὐτοῖς.

---

555 Odysseus' sacrifice to the dead in the *Nekyia* would not constitute an initiation (*teletē*).
556 See also Obbink, 2011, p.300 and fn.35. Passages such as this one from Diodorus Siculus suggest the place of the souls' punishment was different from the sacred meadows: Ὀρφέα μὲν γὰρ τῶν μυστικῶν τελετῶν τὰ πλεῖστα καὶ τὰ περὶ τὴν ἑαυτοῦ πλάνην ὀργιαζόμενα καὶ τὴν τῶν ἐν ᾅδου μυθοποιίαν ἀπενέγκασθαι. [...] τὰς δὲ τῶν ἀσεβῶν ἐν ᾅδου τιμωρίας καὶ τοὺς τῶν εὐσεβῶν λειμῶνας καὶ τὰς παρὰ τοῖς πολλοῖς εἰδωλοποιίας ἀναπεπλασμένας παρεισαγαγεῖν μιμησάμενον τὰ γινόμενα περὶ τὰς ταφὰς τὰς κατ' Αἴγυπτον: 'Orpheus, for instance, brought from Egypt most of his mystic ceremonies, the orgiastic rites that accompanied his wanderings, and his fabulous account of his experiences in Hades. [...] and the punishments in Hades of the unrighteous, the Fields of the Righteous, and the fantastic conceptions, current among the many, which are figments of the imagination – all these were introduced by Orpheus in imitation of the Egyptian funeral customs'. (Diod. Sic. I.96.4–6. Tr. Oldfather).

First, however, present yourself, on whatever auspicious new moon occurs, to the gods of the hours of the day, whose names you have in the *Key*. You will be made their initiate as follows: Make three figures from the flour, one bull-faced, one goat-faced, one ram-faced, each of them standing on the celestial pole and holding an Egyptian flail. And when you have censed them, eat them, saying the spell for the gods of the hours (which is in the *Key*) and the compulsive formula for them and the names of the gods set over the weeks. Then you will have been made their initiate.[557]

Despite having this combination of a bull, a goat and a ram this does not necessarily mean that this is related to the gold tablets' formula or Orphism. We do, however, have more parallels between the two. Firstly, Orpheus himself is mentioned as one of the revealer of the information given in the *Eighth Book of Moses*: 'As the revelatory Orpheus handed down in his private note'.[558] The words 'private note' suggest that 'Orpheus' made a note in his book and that the instructor was in possession of or familiar with such a book. This is supported by the following lines where the instructor gives a quotation from the *Orphica* which is a series of nonsensical words similar to the ones we occasionally find in the gold tablets (especially tablet C): 'Erotylos, in his *Orphica*: 'ΥΟΕΕΟΑΙ ΟΑΙ ΥΟΕΕΑΙ ΥΟΕΕΟ ΕΡΕΠΕ ΕΥΑ...'"[559] Secondly, the instructor says:

> ἔχε δὲ πινακίδα, εἰς ἣν μέλλεις γράφειν, ὅσα σοι λέγει, καὶ μαχαῖρι, ἵνα ἂν τὰ θύματα θύῃς, καθαρὸς ἀπὸ πάντων, καὶ σπονδήν, ἵνα σπείσῃς. πάντα δέ σοι παρακείσθω ἑτοῖμα. σὺ δ' ἐν λίνοις ἴσθι καθαροῖς, ἐστεμμένος ἐλαΐνῳ στεφάνῳ

> Have a tablet in which you will write what he says to you and a two-edged knife, all of iron, so that, clean from all [impurities], you may kill the sacrifices, and a libation (a jug of wine and a flask full of honey) that you pour. Have all these ready nearby you. And you be in clean linens, crowned with an olive wreath.[560]

This means that the initiate must write down what the god will tell him when the epiphany takes place. The initiate is then instructed to wash the tablet with wine and dip it into a bowl containing milk and wine and then drink it. In line 890 we are informed that the tablet is gold: 'This initiation is performed to the suns of the thirteenth day of the month, when the gold lamella is licked off and one says over it...'.[561] The instructor says that the seven vowels are written on the gold tablet to

---

[557] *PGM* XIII.29–37 (All translations by Smith in Betz).
[558] *PGM* XIII.935: ὡς ὁ θεολ<ό>γος Ὀρφεὺς παρέδωκεν διὰ τῆς παραστιχίδος τῆς ἰδίας·.
[559] *PGM* XIII.940–950: Ἐρώτυλος ἐν τοῖς Ὀρφικοῖς· 'υοηεωαι ωαι υοηεαι υοηεω ερεπε, ευα...'
[560] *PGM* XIII.646–651.
[561] *PGM* XIII.890–892: τελεῖται ἡλίοις τῆς ιγ' αὕτη ἡ τελετὴ τοῦ χρυσοῦ πετάλου ἐκλειχομένου τε καὶ ἐπιλεγομένου· See also *PGM* XIII.129–147.

be licked off and are repeated six times and on another silver tablet the seven vowels are inscribed as a phylactery.[562] Finally, in lines 1051–52 the instructor says: 'Having said these words thrice, lick off the leaf, and have the lamella with you. And if things come to hand to hand fighting, wear it on your hand'.[563] We can see that in this initiation a gold tablet has to be inscribed with the god's words during the epiphany, that the tablet is used physically during the initiation, that formulas and text are being uttered, that milk and wine is involved and that the same or a secondary tablet is kept as a phylactery. So far we have several similarities with the gold tablets, which are also inscribed, include formulas and nonsensical words, are kept as phylacteries, in the sense that they have a protective purpose in the afterlife of reminding the initiate of important information, and a practice with milk is mentioned.

Apart from the identification of Orpheus as one of the revealers of the initiation it could be argued that we have more similarities with Orphic texts. From lines 163 to 205 the instructor refers to a Theogony that has parallels to the *Orphic Rhapsodies*. In this 'laughing Theogony' every time the god laughs a divine entity is created. The first divine entity created is Phos (Light), to whom Kairos hands over a sceptre:

> *PGM* XIII.164–167: κακχάσαντος πρῶτον αὐτοῦ ἐφάνη Φῶς (Αὐγή) καὶ διηύγασεν τὰ πάντα. ἐγένετο δὲ θεὸς ἐπὶ τοῦ κόσμου καὶ τοῦ πυρός, Βεσσυν βεριθεν βεριο.
> *PGM* XIII.186–190: ἐκάκχασε τὸ ἕκτον καὶ ἱλαρύνθη πολύ. καὶ ἐφάνη Καιρὸς κατέχων σκῆπτρον, μηνύων βασιλείαν, καὶ ἐπέδωκεν τῷ θεῷ <u>τῷ πρωτοκτιστῷ</u> τὸ <u>σκῆπτρον</u>, καὶ λαβὼν ἔφη· 'σὺ τὴν δόξαν τοῦ Φωτὸς περιθέμενος, ἔσῃ μετ' ἐμέ'...

> *PGM* XIII.164–167: When he laughed first, <u>Phōs</u> – *Augē* [Light-Radiance] appeared and irradiated everything and became god over the cosmos and fire, BESSYN BERITHEN BERIO.
> *PGM* XIII.186–190: He laughed the sixth time and was much gladdened, and Kairos [Season] appeared holding a sceptre, indicating kingship, and he gave over the <u>sceptre</u> to the <u>first-created</u> god, who receiving it, said, 'You, wrapping yourself in the glory of *Phōs* [Light] will be with me'...

This is similar to the *Orphic Rhapsodies* where the first god, the Protogonos, is called Phanes, a name which derives from φαίνω and means the one who came forth into the light from an egg that Time (Chronos) had made: 'Then Phanes

---

562 *PGM* XIII.898–901: ἐν τελετῇ ταῦτα ἐξάκις λέγεται σὺν τοῖς πᾶσι. γράφεται δὲ ἐν τῷ χρυσῷ πετάλῳ πρὸς τὸ ἐκλε<ί>ξαι τὰ ζ', ἐν δὲ τῷ ἀργυρῷ τὰ ζ' πρὸς τὸ φυλακτήριον: 'In [the] initiation these things are said six times with all [the rest?], and the seven vowels are written on the gold lamella to be licked off, and on the silver lamella the seven vowels for the phylactery'.
563 *PGM* XIII.1052–1054: ταῦτα εἴπας γ' ἔκλειξον τὸ φύλλον καὶ ἔχε μετὰ σεαυτοῦ τὸ πέταλον, ἐὰν δὲ διὰ χειρῶν, ἐπὶ τῇ χειρί.

(Φάνης) broke through the clouds (ἐξέθορε) his bright tunic and from the divided shell of the great-encompassing egg he sprang upwards first of all, the hermaphrodite and highly-honoured Protogonos.'⁵⁶⁴ Phanes, too, was also in a possession of a sceptre which he himself had made and which was handed over from one ruler to the next.⁵⁶⁵ The significant thing about the sceptre is that it does not appear in any other theogonies. Also, personifications of time as a god, are very little attested in classical or earlier sources.⁵⁶⁶ It can be argued, thus, that both are particularly characteristic Orphic elements. The verb used in the *Orphic Rhapsodies* to describe the birth of Phanes is ἐξέθορε. This is the same verb used in the milk formula in the gold tablets discussed earlier (e.g. τα{ι}ῦρος εἰς γάλα ἔθορες). This textual similarity could corroborate the connection of the gold tablets to Orphic texts. Could this mean that in the same way that Phanes – who represents the sun – broke through the clouds in the sky, the souls of the initiates of the gold tablets leapt into the night sky as stars? Let us not forget that the name Phanes is possibly inscribed on tablet C where the words *Prōtogonos* and *Hēlie* (Sun) are also found. Finally, another possibly Orphic element in the *Eighth Book of Moses* is the deity Zagourē, who is mentioned four times (lines 80, 146, 452 and 590) and might be an anagram of the name Zagreus, whose myth has been closely associated with the interpretation of the gold tablets by many scholars as we have seen. This ZAGOURĒ in the *Eighth Book of Moses* has the same attributes as the Orphic Phanes:

> 'ἐπικαλοῦμαί σε πάσῃ φωνῇ, τὸν τὰ πάντα περιέχοντα, καὶ πάσῃ διαλέκτῳ. ὑμνῶ σε ἐγώ, ὡς πρώτως ὕμνησέ σ'| ὁ| ὑπὸ| σοῦ ταχθεὶς καὶ πάντα πιστευθεὶς τὰ αὐθεντικά, Ἥλιος· Ἀχεβυκρωμ (ὃ μηνύει τοῦ δίσκου τὴν φλόγα καὶ τὴν ἀκτῖνα), οὗ ἡ δόξα· ααα ηηη ωωω, ὅτι διὰ σ' ἐνεδοξάσθη (εἶθ', ὡς ἄλλως· ἀγλαομορφούμενος) τοὺς ἀστέρας ἱστὰς καὶ τῷ φωτὶ τῷ ἐνθέῳ κτίζων τὸν κόσμον, ἐν ᾧ διέστησας τὰ πάντα· ιιι· ααα· ωωω· Σαβαώθ, Ἀρβαθιάω, Ζαγουρη.
>
> 'I call on you, you who surround all things, in every language, and in every dialect, I hymn you, / as he first hymned you who was by you appointed and entrusted with all authorities, Helios ACHEBYKRŌM' (which signifies the flame and radiance of the disk) 'whose is the glory AAA ĒĒĒ ŌŌŌ, because he was glorified by you' (or, as other [texts read], 'was given glorious form') – '[you] who set [in their places] the stars/and who, in divine light, create the cosmos, in which you have set in order all things III AAA ŌŌŌ. SABAŌTH, ARBATHIAŌ ZAGOURĒ'.⁵⁶⁷

---

564 OF121F. OR1–OR9. See reconstruction of the *Orphic Rhapsodies* in Ch.6.
565 OR26–OR27 = OF98T(III).
566 See Chapter 6, p.299.
567 *PGM* XIII.443–452.

Zagourē here is the creator of the cosmos and all things, in the same way Orphic Phanes was the creator of everything that exists.[568] Also, Zagourē has glorified Helios and has entrusted him with all authority, as Phanes has also done according to the *Orphic Rhapsodies:* 'And he created <the Sun> to be a guardian, and ordered him to rule over everything' (καὶ φύλακ' αὐτὸν ἔτευξε κέλευσέ τε πᾶσιν ἀνάσσειν).[569] If Zagourē is indeed Zagreus, then, and if the instructor was familiar with an Orphic Theogony, Zagreus would be identified here with Phanes. Perhaps, thus, Bernabé is right to suggest that Dionysos is identified with Phanes in Tablet C based on the text by Diodorus quoted in p.164 (1.11: τούνεκά μιν καλέουσι Φάνητά τε καὶ Διόνυσον): 'Judging by this parallel, we would have in our tablet, approximately contemporary with the text cited by Diodorus, a new case of the use of the epithet Phanes to refer to Dionysus, identified with the Sun'.[570] Also, Helios has a very prominent role in the Derveni Papyrus, too, as this quoted Orphic verse shows: 'For without the sun it is not possible for the beings (ὄντα) to become such...'[571] These parallels support the suggestion that the gold tablets stem from an Orphic text. They also show that Orphic texts demonstrate a relative consistency in their ideas and are of a religious cosmogonical/eschatological nature.

But what about other, more generic similarities between the gold tablets and the *Eighth Book of Moses*? Instructive religious texts such as the Greek Magical Papyri were circulated by itinerant magicians to be practised out loud by whoever would pay them.[572] The more elaborate incantation texts comprised various oral, instructive and performative elements such as the uttering of verses or passwords, the invocation of deities, or the description of an action. In this sense they seem to have a lot in common with the gold tablets. The difference is that the text of the gold tablets was supposed to be used in the afterlife, irrespective of whether there was an *hieros logos* behind them and whether it was used one way or another during rituals. Symbols and passwords, the so-called *voces magicae* as found in the magical papyri, were used as credentials of the revealed knowledge which the practitioner possessed and did not appear in the Greek curse tablets of Classical and Hellenistic times, in contrast to the abundant use of such words from the 1st century A.D. onwards. The presence, then, of the word 'symbola' and of nonsensical words in some of the gold tablets dating to the 4th and 3rd century

---

568 OR19-OR24.
569 OR22 = OF158F: Procl. in Pl. *Ti.* 41c, III.227.31.
570 Bernabé and Jiménez San Cristóbal, 2008, p.144.
571 DP Col.XIII.
572 Gager, 2006, p.72.

B.C. is in itself significant in the sense that it portrays the interchange of techniques between various religious practices. It seems, that this practice is used in different ways through time; in the gold tablets the nonsensical words do not appear to have a magic power and purpose other than hiding the meaningful words, while in the magical papyri the nonsensical words become *voces magicae*, words with a concealed meaning and special power.[573] It is probable that the instructor of this initiation was influenced by Orphic initiations and texts. This does not mean that this particular initiation can be identified as Orphic. Such religious practitioners were creating their rituals through the process of bricolage and through combining several religious elements from various cults and beliefs. The *Eighth Book of Moses* does not only include Orphic religious motifs but also Egyptian, Hebraic and more. Nonetheless, such a source is very important, because it can help us better understand the nature of the gold tablets and it further supports their Orphic identity based on the fact that practices and ideas which can be found in the gold tablets are attributed to Orpheus in the *Eighth Book of Moses*.

4.5.4 A katabatic mystery?

Any attempt to define the nature of mystic initiations which took place more than two millennia ago is bound to be speculative. That being said we have several ancient sources, many of them already mentioned, which can help us get a glimpse of such mystic initiations. So what could have been the religious practices behind the gold tablets? They must have included purificatory elements and practices which would help the initiate to identify himself with god and come to the realisation of his/her 'heavenly race'. A re-enactment of a *katabasis* into the underworld might also have taken place since the motif of death-rebirth is strongly present in the tablets. Also, since I have argued that the Zagreus myth is part of the ideological background of the tablets it is possible that rites were influenced by this myth. Finally, considering the discussion so far, texts must have been involved in the ritual, either in the form of phrases being uttered by the initiate or of an *hieros logos* underlying the initiation.

In relation to the gold tablets, current scholarly opinion favours funeral rites, though this is based mainly on the fact that the texts were all found in burials, together with the eschatological imagery of the texts.[574] However, the performative elements of the tablets as discussed above and the frequent use of the word

---

[573] Betegh, 2011, p.220.
[574] Obbink, 2011, p.297.

mystēs – as well as words such as *thiasos, telē* and *orgia* – indicate that we have to do with an initiation ritual. We cannot exclude the possibility that there were both initiations and funerary rites. Graf, for example, argues that the Pelinna text refers specifically to Bacchic initiation and funerary rituals: on his reading, the milk and wine in the text recall a ritual in which the initiate may have poured three libations of milk followed by one of wine.[575] However, Graf's suggestion disregards that in one of the tablets (A1) the subject changes into the first person: ἔριφος ἐς γάλ'ἔπετον (A kid I fell into milk); this suggests an acclamation of the initiate during the initiation.

In general, modern scholarship denominates two kinds of rituals, both with a transitional nature: 1) initiation rites, usually referred to by the Greeks as *muēsis* or *teletē*, through which the initiate had access to secret knowledge and practices, such as the Eleusinian Mysteries, and 2) rituals signifying the transition from childhood to an adult status.[576] Both types provide comparative evidence, even though type (1) is more obviously analogous to the gold tablets. Initiation mysteries often include the concept of death and rebirth and after the experience of *muēsis* the initiate comes out as a brand new person. Binary oppositions such as life/death, male/female, sterile/fertile etc. are considered to have had a vital part in the formation of cultic systems, apart from other factors such as local idiosyncrasies or historical contingencies. We should keep in mind that cultic systems that have grown and evolved blindly over long periods of time do not always display order and symmetry but we surely have to do with complex systems and not random accretions.[577]

Some ancient Greek rituals would begin with the creation of temporary fear, disorder or uncertainty and eventually lead to the restoration of order. In general, mystery cults usually have three components: 1) the existence of *mystai*, 2) a death-like or suffering experience for the *mystai* and 3) a promise of a happy afterlife and present prosperity.[578] The notion of death and rebirth is present in the gold tablets since not only their narrative takes place in Hades, but many of them refer to their owner's death and rebirth: e.g. νῦν ἔθανες καὶ νῦν ἐγένου, τρισόλβιε, ἄματι τῶιδε.[579] As Larson argues: 'Often, a rite had to be performed as expiation for an ancient offence against a god (thus, the Attic Arkteia appeased Artemis' anger at the slaughter of her sacred bear)' which corresponds to the second type

---

[575] Graf, 1993, p.248–249.
[576] Larson, 2007, p.5; Graf, 2003, p.4–5.
[577] Larson, 2007, p.3.
[578] Clinton, 2003, p.55.
[579] D1: 'Now you have died and now you have been born...'; B10: 'When you are about to die...'

of initiation mentioned above.[580] We can see that many of the initiation elements are found in the gold tablets such as expiating an offence, death and rebirth motifs, disorder and uncertainty leading to restoration and the promise of a happy afterlife. But the initiates of the tablets must have been very different from the Eleusinian initiates who gathered at Athens and Eleusis to perform the mysteries, in other words at specific places. The gold tablets were found in an abundance of places geographically distant from each other. This suggests either the existence of wandering religious practitioners or the existence of several places of initiation around Greece, without this excluding the – admittedly improbable – scenario that there was a single place of initiation as in the case of Eleusis or that the initiation was performed in a more closed domestic environment. In any case, we have seen in Chapter 2 evidence for katabatic mysteries being associated with Orpheus in ancient sources which could support the existence of main locations of initiation.[581]

In the following fragment, Plutarch describes what 'men who are undergoing initiation into great mysteries' would experience:

> ἐνταῦθα δ' ἀγνοεῖ, πλὴν ὅταν ἐν τῷ τελευτᾶν ἤδη γένηται· τότε δὲ πάσχει πάθος οἷον οἱ τελεταῖς μεγάλαις κατοργιαζόμενοι. διὸ καὶ τὸ ῥῆμα τῷ ῥήματι καὶ τὸ ἔργον τῷ ἔργῳ τοῦ τελευτᾶν καὶ τελεῖσθαι προσέοικε. πλάναι τὰ πρῶτα καὶ περιδρομαὶ κοπώδεις καὶ διὰ σκότους τινὲς ὕποπτοι πορεῖαι καὶ ἀτέλεστοι, εἶτα πρὸ τοῦ τέλους αὐτοῦ τὰ δεινὰ πάντα, φρίκη καὶ τρόμος καὶ ἱδρὼς καὶ θάμβος· ἐκ δὲ τούτου φῶς τι θαυμάσιον ἀπήντησεν καὶ τόποι καθαροὶ καὶ λειμῶνες ἐδέξαντο, φωνὰς καὶ χορείας καὶ σεμνότητας ἀκουσμάτων ἱερῶν καὶ φασμάτων ἁγίων ἔχοντες· ἐν αἷς ὁ παντελὴς ἤδη καὶ μεμυημένος ἐλεύθερος γεγονὼς καὶ ἄφετος περιιὼν ἐστεφανωμένος ὀργιάζει καὶ σύνεστιν ὁσίοις καὶ καθαροῖς ἀνδράσι, τὸν ἀμύητον ἐνταῦθα τῶν ζώντων καὶ ἀκάθαρτον ἐφορῶν ὄχλον ἐν βορβόρῳ πολλῷ καὶ ὁμίχλῃ πατούμενον ὑφ' ἑαυτοῦ καὶ συνελαυνόμενον, φόβῳ δὲ θανάτου τοῖς κακοῖς ἀπιστίᾳ τῶν ἐκεῖ ἀγαθῶν ἐμμένοντα. ἐπεὶ τό γε παρὰ φύσιν τὴν πρὸς τὸ σῶμα τῇ ψυχῇ συμπλοκὴν εἶναι καὶ σύνερξιν ἐκεῖθεν ἄν συνίδοις.

> In this world it <the soul> is without knowledge, except when it is already at the point of death; but when that time comes, it has an experience like that of men who are undergoing initiation into great mysteries; and so the verbs *teleutân* (die) and *teleisthai* (be initiated), and the actions they denote, have a similarity. In the beginning there is straying and wandering, the weariness of running this way and that, and nervous journeys through darkness that reach no goal, and then immediately before the consummation every possible terror, shivering and trembling and sweating and amazement. But after this a marvellous light meets the wanderer, and open country and meadow lands welcome him; and in that place there are voices and dancing and the solemn majesty of sacred music and holy visions. And

---

[580] Larson, 2007, p.7.
[581] See p.50.

amidst these, he walks at large in new freedom, now perfect and fully initiated, celebrating the sacred rites, a garland upon his head, and converses with pure and holy men; he surveys the uninitiated, unpurified mob here on earth, the mob of living men who, herded together in mirk and deep mire, trample one another down and in their fear of death cling to their ills, since they disbelieve in the blessings of the other world. For the soul's entanglement with the body and confinement in it are against nature, as you may discern from this.[582]

Sourvinou-Inwood refers to this passage in her elaborate discussion of the Eleusinian Mysteries' *dromena* suggesting that it refers to the Eleusinian search for Persephone.[583] However, in my opinion, this passage seems to have Dionysiac rather than Eleusinian connotations and even includes Orphic allusions.[584] The term *orgia* and derivative words most commonly refer to Dionysiac mysteries.[585] We already saw Pausanias mentioning this word in an Orphic context: παρὰ δὲ Ὁμήρου Ὀνομάκριτος παραλαβὼν τῶν Τιτάνων τὸ ὄνομα Διονύσῳ τε συνέθηκεν ὄργια καὶ εἶναι τοὺς Τιτᾶνας τῷ Διονύσῳ τῶν παθημάτων ἐποίησεν αὐτουργούς.[586] The same goes for Herodotus who also associates the Orphic *orgia* with an *hieros logos* as we saw in Chapter 2:

> ὁμολογέουσι δὲ ταῦτα τοῖσι Ὀρφικοῖσι καλεομένοισι καὶ Βακχικοῖσι, ἐοῦσι δὲ Αἰγυπτίοισι καὶ Πυθαγορείοισι· οὐδὲ γὰρ τούτων τῶν ὀργίων μετέχοντα ὅσιον ἐστὶ ἐν εἰρινέοισι εἵμασι θαφθῆναι. ἔστι δὲ περὶ αὐτῶν ἱρὸς λόγος λεγόμενος.
>
> They agree in this with practices called Orphic and Bacchic, but in fact Egyptian and Pythagorean: for it is impious, too, for one partaking of these rites to be buried in woollen wrappings. There is a sacred <discourse> about this.[587]

According to the Plutarch fragment, what is being imitated during the initiation is the experience of death through possibly a symbolic *katabasis*. The initiating experience described is very similar to what is narrated in the gold tablets and

---

[582] Plut. fr.178 Sandbach (Tr. Sandbach): Stob. *Ecl.* iv. 52.49. Cosmopoulos' (2015, p.22) translation of this phrase as 'those who have been initiated into the great Mysteries' is not entirely accurate and it implies that the reference is to the Eleusinian Great Mysteries. The reference here is not definitive but generic so it should not be translated as 'into *the* great Mysteries' but 'into great mysteries'. Cosmopoulos considers that this is a reference to the Eleusinian mysteries (p.22–23).
[583] Sourvinou-Inwood, 2003, p.33–34.
[584] On this passage see also Jiménez San Cristóbal, 2015, p.118. Bernabé, 2009, p.105–107.
[585] Eur. *Bacch.* 32–34.
[586] Paus. 8.37.5: 'From Homer the name of the Titans was taken by Onomacritus, who in the orgies composed for Dionysus made the Titans the authors of the god's sufferings' (Tr. Jones).
[587] Hdt. 2.81.2 (Tr. Godley adapted).

such *dromena* could very well be associated with them. At the end of the fragment, Plutarch says that the confinement of the soul to the body is against nature and refers to those who disbelieve in the blessings of the afterlife. As we have seen, the perception that the afterlife was better than this life was most probably Orphic, while in the case of the Eleusinian mysteries a happy afterlife was promised but it did not overshadow this one. Moreover, another Plutarch fragment (1) refers to the etymology of the word 'body' and corresponds to the Platonic passage from the *Cratylus* (400c) (2) discussed in Chapter 2, which refers to the meaning that the Orphic poets have given to this word. I quote the two passages for comparison:

(1) ἀπολύεσθαι γὰρ τὸν ἀποθνήσκοντα καὶ τὴν τελευτὴν ἀπόλυσιν καλοῦσιν, ἂν δὲ ἔρῃ, καὶ τοῦ σώματος. τοῦτο γὰρ 'δέμας' ὀνομάζουσιν, ὡς 'δεδεμένης' ὑπ' αὐτοῦ τῆς ψυχῆς ἐνταῦθα παρὰ φύσιν· οὐδὲν γὰρ ἐν ᾧ πέφυκεν εἶναι κατέχεται βίᾳ, καὶ τὸ δεδέσθαι τήν τε 'βίαν' ταύτην παραγαγόντες ὠνόμασαν 'βίον'...

(2) καὶ γὰρ σῆμά τινές φασιν αὐτὸ εἶναι τῆς ψυχῆς, ὡς τεθαμμένης ἐν τῷ νῦν παρόντι· καὶ διότι αὖ τούτῳ σημαίνει ἃ ἂν σημαίνῃ ἡ ψυχή, καὶ ταύτῃ σῆμα ὀρθῶς καλεῖσθαι. δοκοῦσι μέντοι μοι μάλιστα θέσθαι οἱ ἀμφὶ Ὀρφέα τοῦτο τὸ ὄνομα, ὡς δίκην διδούσης τῆς ψυχῆς ὧν δὴ ἕνεκα δίδωσιν· τοῦτον δὲ περίβολον ἔχειν, ἵνα σῴζηται, δεσμωτηρίου εἰκόνα· εἶναι οὖν τῆς ψυχῆς τοῦτο, ὥσπερ αὐτὸ ὀνομάζεται, ἕως ἂν ἐκτείσῃ τὰ ὀφειλόμενα, τὸ σῶμα, καὶ οὐδὲν δεῖν παράγειν οὐδὲ γράμμα.

(1) ...men say that the dying man 'is released' and call his end 'a release', and if you ask them, they in fact mean thereby a release from the body, which they name the 'frame' (δέμας), because the soul is unnaturally imprisoned (δεδεμένης) within: for nothing is forcibly detained in a place where it is natural for it to be. To this forcible (βίαν) imprisonment they have by a change of termination given the name of life (βίον)...[588]

(2) ...for some say it is the tomb (σῆμα) of the soul, their notion being that the soul is buried in the present life; and again, because by its means the soul gives any signs which it gives, it is for this reason also properly called "sign" (σῆμα). But I think it most likely that <those affiliated to Orpheus> (οἱ ἀμφὶ Ὀρφέα) gave this name, with the idea that the soul is undergoing punishment for something; they think it has the body as an enclosure to keep it safe, like a prison, and this is, as the name itself denotes, the safe (σῶμα) for the soul, until the penalty is paid, and not even a letter needs to be changed.[589]

---

588 Plut. fr.177 (Sandbach).
589 Pl. *Cra.* 400b (Tr. Fowler). See also Iambl. *Protr.* 77.27 = Arist. fr.60 Rose = OF430(V): τίς ἂν οὖν εἰς ταῦτα βλέπων οἴοιτο εὐδαίμων εἶναι καὶ μακάριος, εἰ πρῶτον εὐθὺς φύσει συνίσταμεν, καθάπερ φασὶν οἱ τὰς τελετὰς λέγοντες, ὥσπερ ἂν ἐπὶ τιμωρίαι πάντες. τοῦτο γὰρ θεῖον οἱ ἀρχαιότεροι λέγουσι τὸ φάναι διδόναι τὴν ψυχὴν τιμωρίαν καὶ ζῆν ἡμᾶς ἐπὶ κολάσει μεγάλων τινῶν ἁμαρτημάτων· 'So who could consider himself successful and happy, looking at these things for

Additionally, the phrase: καὶ ἀκάθαρτον ἐφορῶν ὄχλον ἐν βορβόρῳ πολλῷ ('...herded together in mirk and deep mire...') from Plutarch (fr.178, quoted in p.179) describes the same afterlife 'punishment' for the uninitiated ones as another passage from Plato we discussed in p.133:

> καὶ κινδυνεύουσι καὶ οἱ τὰς τελετὰς ἡμῖν οὗτοι καταστήσαντες οὐ φαῦλοί τινες εἶναι, | ἀλλὰ τῷ ὄντι πάλαι αἰνίττεσθαι ὅτι ὃς ἂν ἀμύητος καὶ ἀτέλεστος εἰς Ἅιδου ἀφίκηται ἐν βορβόρῳ κείσεται, ὁ δὲ κεκαθαρμένος τε καὶ τετελεσμένος ἐκεῖσε ἀφικόμενος μετὰ θεῶν οἰκήσει. εἰσὶν γὰρ δή, ὥς φασιν οἱ περὶ τὰς τελετάς, "ναρθηκοφόροι μὲν πολλοί, βάκχοι δέ τε παῦροι·" οὗτοι δ' εἰσὶν κατὰ τὴν ἐμὴν δόξαν οὐκ ἄλλοι ἢ οἱ πεφιλοσοφηκότες ὀρθῶς.

> And I fancy that those men who established the mysteries were not unenlightened, but in reality had a hidden meaning when they said long ago that whoever goes uninitiated and unsanctified to the other world will lie in the mire, but he who arrives there initiated and purified will dwell with the gods. For as they say in the mysteries, 'the thyrsus-bearers are many, but the mystics few'; and these mystics are, I believe, those who have been true philosophers.[590]

Some scholars, such as Clinton, claim that it is the Eleusinian mysteries being mentioned here, arguing that ἡμῖν (for us) which signifies mysteries established for the Athenians could 'hardly not refer to the Eleusinian Mysteria'.[591] However, we find the same word in Aristophanes' *Frogs* in which Aeschylus specifically refers to Orpheus as the establisher of *teletas*: Ὀρφεὺς μὲν γὰρ τελετάς θ'ἡμῖν κατέδειξε φόνων τ'ἀπέχεσθαι ('Orpheus revealed mystic rites to us, and taught us to abstain from killings').[592] In the same work Heracles warns Dionysos about the location in the underworld where there is 'a great slough of ever-flowing dung' in which lie all those who acted wrongly (εἶτα βόρβορον πολὺν | καὶ σκῶρ ἀείνων: ἐν δὲ τοῦτο κειμένους...).[593] The word βόρβορος connects all three passages from Plutarch, Plato and Aristophanes suggesting that they all draw from the same tradition or text. Aristophanes relates this punishment to an impious life which is what the *Orphikos bios* opposed to in order to avoid afterlife punishments. Heracles goes on to say that 'Next a breath of pipes will surround you, you'll see a shining light, just like up here, then myrtle groves, and happy *thiasoi* of men and

---

which we have been composed right from the beginning by nature, as if for punishment – all of us – as they say the mysteries relate? For the ancients express this in an inspired way by saying the soul 'pays a punishment' and we live for the atonement of certain great failings'. See discussion in p.9.
590 Pl. *Phd.* 69c–d (Tr. Fowler).
591 Clinton, 2003, p.56. Graf, 1974, p.100–101.
592 Ar. *Ran.*, 1032 (Tr. Henderson).
593 Ar. *Ran.* 145–150 (Tr. Dillon).

women mixed who loudly clap their hands' whom he defines as those who have gone under mystic initiation: the μεμυημένοι.[594] Additionally, the verse in *italics* quoted by Plato, is also quoted by Olympiodorus as a verse from the *Orphic Rhapsodies*, and Plato specifically refers to *bacchoi*; all these elements suggest that these ideas are Dionysiac and most probably Orphic.[595] These intertextual points of contact suggest that Plato, Plutarch and Aristophanes had Bacchic mysteries in mind and not the Eleusinian ones. It therefore seems more probable that a Bacchic and perhaps Orphic *teletē* is described by Plutarch and not an Eleusinian one. And this specific *teletē* was of a performative nature involving a journey in the darkness in imitation of a *katabasis*. This journey could have taken place either inside a cave, or subterranean location, or at a superterranean location with the use of a blindfold. A similar initiation might have been performed by the owners of the gold tablets.

A katabatic mystery would not only serve as 'practice' for the actual afterlife journey but also symbolise the initiate's death and rebirth as a purified member of the holy *thiasos*. The *katabasis* would eventually lead to an epiphany (through the mystic light) which would lead to an ascent to an open meadow. According to Plutarch fr.178, quoted above, after the journey into the darkness the initiate would be crowned with a garland, join in the revel of dance and music with the other initiates and converse with 'pure and holy men'. This is parallel to the communal perception of the afterlife in the gold tablets where the initiate asks to be sent to the *thiasoi* of the blessed. It is not hard to imagine an initiation such as the one described in Plutarch being performed by the gold tablets' owners where *legomena* such as the *makarismoi* of the tablets or a dialogue between the hierophant pretending to be Persephone and the initiate were also involved.[596] The author of *Rhesus* (5th or 4th B.C.) refers to the 'dark mysteries with their torch processions' which were revealed by Orpheus (μυστηρίων τε τῶν ἀπορρήτων φανὰς ἔδειξεν Ὀρφεύς).[597] Also, we saw that Pausanias refers to a *dadouchos* (Torchbearer) who showed him the secret Orphic hymns used in the rites of the

---

594 Ar. *Ran.* 154–159: ΗΡΑΚΛΗΣ: ἐντεῦθεν αὐλῶν τίς σε περίεισιν πνοή, | ὄψει τε φῶς κάλλιστον ὥσπερ ἐνθάδε, | καὶ μυρρινῶνας καὶ θιάσους εὐδαίμονας | ἀνδρῶν γυναικῶν καὶ κρότον χειρῶν πολύν (Tr. Dillon).
595 OR96 = OF576F: Olympiodor. In Pl. *Phaed.* 69c, p.48.20.
596 See also Tzifopoulos, 2011, p.195–197. Riedweg, 2011, p.227: 'It is not entirely to be excluded that the dactylic verses and the insertions or rhythmical prose were uttered by the τελέστης or by fellow initiates at the initiation, for we can assume with some plausibility that such an initiation also included a ritual enactment of death which thus was symbolically anticipated'. Herrero de Jáuregui, 2011, p.281. Obbink, 2011, p.295–297.
597 *Rhesus*, 942–944. For *Rhesus*' date and authorship see fn.24.

Lykomidae at Phlya (see Chapter 2).[598] Seaford argues that in Aeschylus' *Bassarai* there are hints of an eschatological mystic rite involving a mystic light which represents Helios, based on a pre-Aeschylean Orphic poem of Orpheus' *katabasis*.[599] Similarly, perhaps the Orphic initiates would follow a mystic light representing a Heliadic deity such as Phanes or Apollo during the *katabasis* in order to reach the blessed meadows. In this way they would imitate how they would follow the 'sun' in the afterlife through their circular motion in the celestial sphere – since the system was believed to be geocentric at those times. Perhaps this is what Pindar meant when he said that the good men in the afterlife have the sun by night as much as by day, in a passage where he says that 'it is a brilliant star, a man's true light' (ἀστὴρ ἀρίζηλος, ἐτυμώτατον | ἀνδρὶ φέγγος·) and refers to rewards and punishments in the afterlife.[600] In the same passage, Pindar uses what I have identified to be Orphic religious terminology when he refers to the unbearable toil that the unjust have to endure (τοὶ δ' ἀπροσόρατον ὀκχέοντι πόνον).

In a pottery fragment from an Attic red-figure Kalpis in Malibu (c.480 B.C.) a sun-struck satyr is represented looking at the sky and hiding his face from the sunlight, while next to him there is the inscription ΔΥΕΛΙΟ (δυ'ἥλιο), which means two suns.[601] This brings to mind the double vision of Pentheus in Euripides' *Bacchae* when under frenzy he sees Dionysos turning into a bull and says: 'I

---

598 Paus. 9.27.2. For text see p.46.
599 Seaford, 2005, p.602–606. Based on a new edition of the text by West who argued that the story of Orpheus being torn apart by the Bassarai who were sent by Dionysos being angry with him for worshipping Apollo (Helios) as the superior god, was part of the original *Bassarai* and not a later addition, since it is found in both Greek and Latin traditions of the text.
600 Pind. *Ol.* 2.55–68 (Tr. Svarlien): ἀστὴρ ἀρίζηλος, ἐτυμώτατον | ἀνδρὶ φέγγος· εἰ δέ νιν ἔχων τις οἶδεν τὸ μέλλον, | ὅτι θανόντων μὲν ἐνθάδ' αὐτίκ' ἀπάλαμνοι φρένες | ποινὰς ἔτεισαν - τὰ δ' ἐν τᾷδε Διὸς ἀρχᾷ | ἀλιτρὰ κατὰ γᾶς δικάζει τις ἐχθρᾷ | λόγον φράσαις ἀνάγκᾳ· | ἴσαις δὲ νύκτεσσιν αἰεί, | ἴσαις δ' ἁμέραις ἅλιον ἔχοντες, ἀπονέστερον | ἐσλοὶ δέκονται βίοτον, οὐ χθόνα ταράσσοντες ἐν χερὸς ἀκμᾷ | οὐδὲ πόντιον ὕδωρ | κεινὰν παρὰ δίαιταν, ἀλλὰ παρὰ μὲν τιμίοις | θεῶν οἵτινες ἔχαιρον εὐορκίαις | ἄδακρυν νέμονται | αἰῶνα, τοὶ δ' ἀπροσόρατον ὀκχέοντι πόνον: '…it is a brilliant star, a man's true light, at least if one has and knows the future, that the reckless souls of those who have died on earth immediately pay the penalty – and for the crimes committed in this realm of Zeus there is a judge below the earth; with hateful compulsion he passes his sentence. But having the sun always in equal nights and equal days, the good receive a life free from toil, not scraping with the strength of their arms the earth, nor the water of the sea, for the sake of a poor sustenance. But in the presence of the honored gods, those who gladly kept their oaths enjoy a life without tears, while the others undergo a toil that is unbearable to look at'.
601 See Lissarrague, 2000, p.190–197, fig.1 and 4.

see two suns' to which Dionysos replies 'Now, you see what you should'.⁶⁰² Typically, it would be Apollo who would be identified with the sun but we often see Dionysos and Apollo to be perceived as one, as was also discussed earlier in this chapter in relation to the Delphic rites. Aeschylus refers to Apollo as: ὁ κισσεὺς Ἀπόλλων, ὁ βακχεύς, ὁ μάντις ('Apollo, the ivy-crowned, the reveller, the seer') and Euripides says: δέσποτα φιλόδαφνε Βάκχε, παιὰν Ἄπολλον εὔλυρε ('Lord Bacchos who loves the laurel, Paean Apollo skilled with the lyre…').⁶⁰³ It might be, thus, that the two suns that were related to Dionysiac beliefs and mysteries were a nocturnal 'sun' and the actual sun. A deity such as Apollo represented through an Orphic heliadic deity such as Protogonos/Phanes could personify the actual sun (creative light/present life) and Dionysos/Zagreus could represent the eschatological nocturnal 'sun' (death/afterlife). Cleanthes refers to the sun with the mystic term *dadouchos*: καὶ δᾳδοῦχον ἔφασκε εἶναι τὸν ἥλιον, καὶ τὸν κόσμον μυστήριον καὶ τοὺς κατόχους τῶν θείων τελεστὰς ἔλεγε.⁶⁰⁴ He also identifies Dionysos with the sun; the fragment comes form Macrobius' *Saturnalia* who quotes an Orphic passage where the sun is identified with both Phanes and Dionysos:

> Orpheus quoque solem volens intellegi ait inter cetera:
> τήκων αἰθέρα δῖον ἀκίνητον πρὶν ἐόντα
> ἐξανέφηνε θεοῖσιν ὁρᾶν κάλλιστον ἰδέσθαι,
> ὃν δὴ νῦν καλέουσι φάνητά τε καὶ Διόνυσοντ'
> Εὐβουλῆα τ' ἄνακτα καὶ Ἀνταύγην ἀρίδηλον·
> ἄλλοι δ' ἄλλο καλοῦσιν ἐπιχθονίων ἀνθρώπων.
> πρῶτος δ' ἐς φάος ἦλθε, Διώνυσος δ' ἐπεκλήθη,
> οὕνεκα δινεῖται κατ' ἀπείρονα μακρὸν Ὄλυμπον·
> ἀλλαχθεὶς δ' ὄνομ' ἔσχε, προσωνυμίας πρὸς
> ἑκάστων παντοδαπὰς κατὰ καιρὸν ἀμειβομένοιο
> χρόνοιο.

---

602 Eur. *Bacch.* 918–924: ΠΕΝΘΕΥΣ: καὶ μὴν ὁρᾶν μοι δύο μὲν ἡλίους δοκῶ, | δισσὰς δὲ Θήβας καὶ πόλισμ'ἑπτάστομον· | καὶ ταῦρος ἡμῖν πρόσθεν ἡγεῖσθαι δοκεῖς | καὶ σῷ κέρατα κρατὶ προσπεφυκέναι. | ἀλλ' ἦ ποτ' ἦσθα θήρ; τεταύρωσαι γὰρ οὖν. | ΔΙΟΝΥΣΟΣ: ὁ θεὸς ὁμαρτεῖ, πρόσθεν ὢν οὐκ εὐμενής, | ἔνσπονδος ἡμῖν· νῦν δ' ὁρᾷς ἃ χρή σ' ὁρᾶν: PENTHEUS: Look, I seem to see two suns in the sky! The seven-gated city of Thebes—I see two of them! And you seem to be going before me as a bull, and horns seem to have sprouted upon your head! Were you an animal before now? Certainly now you have been changed into a bull. DIONYSUS: The god has made a truce and is with us now, though before he was our enemy. And now you see as you ought to see (Tr. Kovacs).
603 Aeschylus: fr.341 Nauck. Euripides: fr.477 Nauck. See also Tzifopoulos, 2010, p.139–140.
604 Cleanthes: *SVF* fr. I.538: 'He called the sun *dadouchos*, and the world a mystery, and he called *telestas* the ones that understood the holy things.

Φάνητα *dixit solem* ἀπὸ τοῦ φωτὸς καὶ φανεροῦ, *id est lumine atque inluminatione, quia cunctis visitur cuncta conspiciens.* Διόνυσος, *ut ipse vates ait,* ἀπὸ τοῦ δινεῖσθαι καὶ περιφέρεσθαι, *id est quod circumferatur in ambitum. unde Cleanthes ita cognominatum scribit* ἀπὸ τοῦ διανύσαι, *quia cotidiano impetu ab oriente ad occasum diem noctemque faciendo caeli conficit cursum*

Orpheus too, intending a reference to the sun to be understood, says (among other things): 'Melting the bright aether that was before now unmoved, he revealed to the gods the fairest sight to be seen, the one they now call both Phanês and Dionysos, sovereign Euboulês and Antaugês seen from afar: among men who dwell on earth, some give him one name, others another. First he came into the light, and was named Dionysos, because he whirls along the limitless length of Olympos; but then he changed his name and took on forms of address of every sort from every source, as suits the alternating seasons'.
He called the sun Phanês from "light and illumination," because in seeing all he is seen by all, and Dionysus, as the inspired singer himself says, from "whirling about in a circle." Cleanthes writes that he is so named from "bringing to completion," because as he hastens every day from east to west he completes the course of heaven by creating day and night.[605]

Apart from being identified with Phanes and the sun, Dionysos is also connected with creation. The latter is also proposed by Plutarch who suggests that Dionysos' dismemberment represents the creation of the world through him:

κρυπτόμενοι δὲ τοὺς πολλοὺς οἱ σοφώτεροι τὴν μὲν εἰς πῦρ μεταβολὴν Ἀπόλλωνά τε τῇ μονώσει Φοῖβόν τε τῷ καθαρῷ καὶ ἀμιάντῳ καλοῦσι. τῆς δ' εἰς πνεύματα καὶ ὕδωρ καὶ γῆν καὶ ἄστρα καὶ φυτῶν ζῴων τε γενέσεις τροπῆς αὐτοῦ καὶ διακοσμήσεως <u>τὸ μὲν πάθημα καὶ τὴν μεταβολὴν διασπασμόν τινα καὶ διαμελισμὸν αἰνίττονται</u>· Διόνυσον δὲ καὶ Ζαγρέα καὶ Νυκτέλιον καὶ Ἰσοδαίτην αὐτὸν ὀνομάζουσι, καὶ φθοράς τινας καὶ ἀφανισμοὺς εἶτα δ'ἀναβιώσεις καὶ παλιγγενεσίας, οἰκεῖα ταῖς εἰρημέναις μεταβολαῖς αἰνίγματα καὶ μυθεύματα περαίνουσι· καὶ ᾄδουσι τῷ μὲν διθυραμβικὰ μέλη <u>παθῶν</u> μεστὰ καὶ μεταβολῆς πλάνην τινὰ καὶ διαφόρησιν ἐχούσης·

The more enlightened, however, concealing from the masses the transformation into fire, call him <Dionysus> Apollo because of his solitary state, and Phoebus because of his purity and stainlessness. And as for his turning into winds and water, earth and stars, and into the generations of plants and animals, and his adoption of such guises, they speak in a deceptive way of what he undergoes in his transformation as a tearing apart as it were, and a dismemberment. They give him the names of Dionysus, Zagreus, Nyctelius, and Isodaetes; they construct destructions and disappearances, followed by returns to life and regenerations – riddles and fabulous tales quite in keeping with the aforesaid transformations. To this god they also sing the dithyrambic strains laden with emotion and with a transformation that includes a certain wandering and dispersion.'[606]

---

605 Macrob. *Sat.* I.18.12–14 (Tr. Kaster). Orpheus: PEGr fr. 237. Cleanthes: *SVF* fr. I.546.
606 Plut. *De E.* 388f–389a (Tr. Babbitt).

In this passage Plutarch says that Zagreus' dismemberment is an allegorical representation of creation through the flowing of the light/aether throughout the cosmos. The myth is just an αἴνιγμα used by the enlightened ones to conceal the truth. According to Plutarch, this dismemberment is recreated during transformative rites accompanied by the dithyramb. The rite is defined through the word παθῶν, which echoes Dionysos' πάθημα of being dismembered. In gold tablet A4 we find the phrase: χαῖρε παθὼν τὸ πάθημα τὸ δ' οὔπω πρόσθ'{ε} ἐπεπόνθεις· | θεὸς ἐγένου ἐξ ἀνθρώπου· ('Hail, you having experienced the experience you had not experienced before. A god you have become from a man.'). This πάθημα might be referring to an initiation which led to the transformation from a mortal into a god. Macrobius interprets the Orphic verses quoted above and the epithet Eubouleus – a deity mentioned in the gold tablets – as referring to Zeus' good counsel and equates the sun with the mind of the cosmic order; he quotes the following Orphic verse: εἷς Ζεὺς εἷς Ἀίδης εἷς Ἥλιος εἷς Διόνυσος ('Zeus is one, Hades is one, the sun is one, Dionysus is one').[607] These ideas might be exactly what we find in gold tablet C in the words: Ζεῦ/ ἀέρ/ Ἥλιε, πῦρ δὴ πάντα/ Φάνης, πάμνηστοι Μοῖραι/ νύξ/ ἡμέρα/ φάος ἐς φρένα/ ἀέρ/ ἐς φρένα. If Phanes – who is also called Metis (Counsel) in the *Rhapsodies* – is the counsel of Zeus which disperses through the light of the sun and leads to the creation of material things such as humans, then the fire could be identified with materiality and aer with the nature of the soul. In this case we can interpret the opposites day ≠ night and 'light in the mind' ≠ 'aer in the mind' as referring to life and death/afterlife. These suggestions might seem far-fetched, because they require us to accept that some ancient religious practices were based on abstract interpretations of the cosmos. There is no reason, though, to reject such a possibility since it is supported by literary sources; more will be said in Chapters 5 and 6. The more we examine the evidence, then, the more it seems that Orphic writings were allegorical αἰνίγματα that had to be interpreted through elemental and scientific ideas, as already mentioned in Chapter 2.

If my earlier astronomical interpretation is correct, this nocturnal 'sun' represented by the mystic light could in reality be the Auriga star, the point of contact between the Charioteer constellation and the Taurus constellation.[608] This would explain why the 'good ones' according to Pindar enjoy the sun during the night, too, in the afterlife. A katabatic mystery, then, where the initiates would follow

---

607 Macrob. *Sat.* I.18.17–18. For Eubouleus see also Bremmer, 2013, pp.37–40.
608 In fact we have very early representations of a bull with a star between its horns, in the same way it is found in the Taurus constellation such as the famous Minoan bull rheton which might have been the forerunner of representations of Dionysos in the same way.

the mystic light to ascend into the light and the meadows from the darkness might have represented the journey of the soul from the underworld to become a star and dwell with the gods at the blessed meadows, where the Taurus constellation is located in the Milky Way. This suggestion is based on the previous discussion and is of course not the only possibility. It is, nonetheless, again supported by literary evidence. These might have been the beliefs of the owners of the gold tablets and the fact that no gold tablets were found in Athens does not make it improbable that these ideas would be mentioned in Athenian sources, since it is not necessary for them to be 'translated' into the same religious practices all around Greece. We already referred to Attic epitaphs referring to the return of the soul to aether. Moreover, several Attic funerary stelae represent the deceased as a hero, either participating in a symposium, much like the one mentioned by Plato and discussed earlier, or being naked and crowned, or being honoured by his/her relatives alongside another god represented on the stele such as Hermes or Aphrodite.[609] They represent, thus, the same heroic perception of the deceased in the afterlife as the one found in the gold tablets.

According to Aristophanes' *Frogs* 341–343 quoted earlier, Dionysos-Iacchos was the 'light-bringing star' of the nocturnal rite which brightly burned at the meadow (λειμών).[610] The word λειμών, which is also mentioned in Plutarch's passage about mystic initiation (fr.178 quoted in p.179), finds a parallel in the gold tablet A4 from Lucania: λειμῶνάς θ'{ε} ἱεροὺς καὶ ἄλσεα Φερσεφονείας and D3 from Thessaly: εἴσιθ‹ι› ἱερὸν λειμῶνα. ἄποινος γὰρ ὁ μύστης.[611] This word is also found in the *Orphic Rhapsodies*:

οἳ μέν κ' εὐαγέωσιν ὑπ' αὐγὰς ἠελίοιο,
αὖτις ἀποφθίμενοι μαλακώτερον οἶτον ἔχουσιν
ἐν καλῶι λειμῶνι βαθύρροον ἀμφ' Ἀχέροντα,
οἳ δ' ἄδικα ῥέξαντες ὑπ' αὐγὰς ἠελίοιο
ὑβρισταὶ κατάγονται ὑπὸ πλάκα Κωκυτοῖο
Τάρταρον ἐς κρυόεντα. ‿ – ◡◡ – ◡◡ – ◡

And from men, the ones who dwell purely under the rays of the sun, when they in turn perish, they have a more gentle fate in the beautiful meadow around deep-flowing Acheron,

---

609 Himmelmann, 2000, p.136–144; See also Sourvinou-Inwood, 1996.
610 See p.165.
611 A4: 'The sacred meadows and groves of Phersephoneia.' D3: 'Enter the sacred meadow. For the initiate is without penalty.'

but the ones who acted unjustly under the rays of the sun, the insolent, are led down under the surface of Kokytos to chilly Tartaros.⁶¹²

The word εὐαγέωσιν is also found in the gold tablets describing the ones who gain access in the sacred meadow just as in the above passage: ὥς {λ} με ‹π›ρόφ‹ρων› πέ[μ]ψ‹η›ι› {μ} ἕδρας ἐς εὐ‹α›γ‹έων› (A2+A3 from Lucania) and εὐαγὴς ἱερὰ Διονύσου Βακχίου εἰμί (D4 from Macedonia).⁶¹³ Could it be that the *hieros logos* of the gold tablets was part of or inspired by this Orphic work? The content of the above verses and the textual similarities to the gold tablets make this plausible. The specification that the unjust are led *downwards* to Tartaros suggests that the beautiful meadows were not situated underground, despite the reference to river Acheron which was one of the underworld rivers. In fact, the use of the term 'underworld' might not be accurate since it is not certain, as we saw, that the topography of the afterlife was subterranean in its totality for all ancient Greeks.

If there was an *hieros logos* or sacred text behind the gold tablets, it can be argued that it was communicated or explained to the initiates prior to the initiation, without excluding the possibility that it was communicated during or after the initiation. As Riedweg notes: '...the *mystai* most likely got acquainted with this Logos at the παράδοσις of the initiation'.⁶¹⁴ The initiates would need background knowledge to understand the *dromena* of the mystery, the meaning of the *legomena* of the mystery and the religious eschatology behind them. They would need to know why it was Dionysos who 'released them', what was the *poinē* they were released from, why their afterlife bliss was dependent on Persephone, what 'cycle' they had escaped from, why Mnemosyne was so important, why it was a bull, a ram and a kid falling into milk, why milk, why they had the right to claim apotheosis and the answers to many more questions. They would also need to know the topography of the netherworld and what to say to Persephone and the chthonic gods when they confronted them through the hierophant during the initiation, and which mystic symbols and passwords to utter. In other words, the background knowledge was specific/practical on the one hand and analytical/ideological on the other. In the same way that today a Christian would wear a cross as a protective cult object but also know its meaning and the reason it has

---

612 OR88 = OF340F: Procl. in Pl. *R.* II.340.11.
613 A2 + A3: 'That she, gracious, may send me to the seats of the blessed.' D4: 'Holy priestess of Dionysos Bacchios am I...'
614 Riedweg, 2011, p.238. Bremmer, 2014, p.73.

power. Also, the fact that we have a variation in the texts of the tablets demonstrates the ability of the initiates to identify the important elements which had to be included; that in turn demonstrates their background knowledge.

The possibility that the gold tablets were used in the performance of funerary rites cannot be excluded, especially since the tablets were located on specific spots on the body, which indicates a specific procedure followed. However, I find it implausible that text from the tablets was uttered by a priest during the funerary rite. Calame suggests that the command to address Persephone most probably relates to the voice of the priest performing the burial ceremony, who would help the deceased perform his/her journey.[615] The presence of passwords, symbols, nonsensical words and formulaic phrases on the gold tablets indicates a secrecy about their contents. If these were given as a privilege to the initiates then a funerary rite would require all of the people attending the funeral to be initiated or anyone could use the same formulas and claim to be the 'Child of earth and starry heaven'. It is possible that the priest performed the funeral alone, but it also seems unlikely that the owners of the tablets would have spent their lives trusting that the priest would perform what is necessary during their burial for them to secure a happy afterlife without acquiring any special knowledge during their lifetime or feeling the security of performing a rite. Most importantly, many phrases are in the first person and this interpretation is incompatible with instructive phrases such as: ἀλλ' ὁπόταν ψυχὴ προλίπῃι φάος ἀελίοιο (A4) and ἐπεὶ ἄμ μέλ]ληισι θανεῖσθαι (B11) which indicate that the instructions were given to the initiate *before* he/she died.[616] It is also incompatible with the alternation between the first person and the third person in phrases such as: Ἔρχομαι ἐ‹κ› καθαρῶ‹ν› καθ‹αρά (A1,A2,A3) as opposed to Ἔρχεται ἐκ καθαρῶν καθαρά (A5) or τα{ι}ῦρος εἰς γάλα ἔθορες. αἶψα εἰς γ‹ά›λα ἔθορες. κριὸς εἰς γάλα ἔπεσ‹ες› (D1+D2) in contrast to ἔριφος ἐς γάλ' ἔπετον (A1).[617] Also, the use of phrases such as θεὸς ἐγένου ἐξ ἀνθρώπου (A4) and νῦν ἔθανες καὶ νῦν ἐγένου (D1+D2) does not necessarily mean that they refer to the specific time of actual death because they could be phrases uttered by the priest during the symbolic death of a katabatic ritual.[618] We do not need to assume that such phrases can be used only after death when

---

615 Calame, 2011, p.218.
616 A4: 'But when the soul leaves the light of the sun...' B11: 'When you are about to die...'
617 A1,A2,A3: 'Pure I come from the pure, Queen of those below the earth.' A5: 'Pure she comes from the pure.' D1+D2: 'A bull you rushed to milk. Quickly, you rushed to milk. A ram you fell into milk.' A1: 'A kid I fell into milk.'
618 A4: 'A god you have become from a man.' D1+D2: 'Now you have died and now you have been born.' Riedweg, 2011, p.228: He argues that words denoting present 'point at the actual moment of the burial'.

the initiate actually became a god, because the arrival of the initiate at the sacred meadows during the initiation – as was also the case in the Eleusinian mysteries – imitated the bliss of the afterlife existence. Riedweg agrees to this idea when he argues that the phrase ἔριφος ἐς γάλ' ἔπετον could be the response of the *mystēs* to the priest's *makarismos* of 'you have become a god instead of a mortal'.[619] Also, as Obbink notes, there is a similarity between funeral rites and procedures for initiation since due to the symbolic death that the initiate undergoes 'rites of initiation often take on the trappings, actions and language of death rites – and vice versa'.[620] In any case, we cannot exclude that some phrases were uttered by a priest during the funeral and some during an initiation as Riedweg seems to argue, but what is most important is the meaning and power of the phrases.[621]

4.6 Mnemosyne – Memory

A final matter to be addressed is the references to Mnemosyne. They are of two kind: ἀλλὰ δέχεσθε Μνημοσύνης τόδε δῶρον ἀοίδιμον ἀνθρώποισιν (A5), or εὑρήσεις δ'ἑτέραν, τῆς Μνημοσύνης ἀπὸ λίμνης ψυχρὸν ὕδωρ προρέον (B1 and slightly variant B2 and B11), while tablet B10 includes both phrases.[622] The tablets come from Sicily, Rome, Calabria and Thessaly and date from as early as the 4th century B.C. to the 2nd century A.D. Agreeing with Riedweg's suggestion we can be fairly confident that the short B tablets' textual background included the Mnemosyne phrases but were not inscribed by their owners who had instead adapted a poetic narrative into '*a kind of libretto for* δρώμενα'.[623] We can trace, thus, the emphasis on Mnemosyne/Memory in tablets of both group A and B and the majority of the tablets with the long texts. Riedweg also includes the Mnemosyne phrase in his archetype/*hieros logos*.[624] The initiate drinks the water of Memory in order to be sent to the blessed meadows and the owner of tablet B11 is called a hero that has remembered (μ]εμνήμε<ν>ος ἥρως). The word τόδε in Μνημοσύνης τόδε δῶρον (A5)/ ἔργον (B1, B10) also suggests that the actual tablet or its text, or

---

[619] Riedweg, 2011, p.239.
[620] Obbink, 2011, p.297. See also Torjussen, 2014, p.40.
[621] Riedweg, 2011, p.230, 236, 238–239.
[622] A5:'But receive this gift of Memory, famed in song among men.' B1: 'You will find another, from the lake of Memory refreshing water flowing forth.'
[623] Riedweg, 2011, p.243.
[624] Riedweg, 2011, p.248.

the ability to perform the underworld journey is a gift/work of memory.[625] The souls of the initiates are contrasted with the uninitiated souls who drink from the other fountain, which as mentioned has been generally identified as the lake of Lethe (Oblivion). Remembering, then, was very important for securing a blessed afterlife/apotheosis.[626] In tablet B2 after the initiate finds the Lake of Memory he is urged to tell the whole truth to the guards of the lake: τοῖς δὲ σὺ εὖ μάλα πᾶσαν ἀληθείην καταλέξαι | εἰπεῖν 'Γῆς παῖς εἰμι καὶ Οὐρανοῦ ἀστ<ερόεντος>.[627] The word *alētheia* etymologically refers to the 'lack of oblivion' (a+*lēthē*).[628] In this case, the initiate remembers the necessary knowledge which will grant him water from the lake of memory; namely that he is the child of earth and starry heaven. His acknowledgement of his divine ancestry is the ultimate proof that he has been initiated. This knowledge, as I have suggested, must have been communicated to the initiate prior to and/or during, or after the mysteries.

Based on tablet A5 it seems that the knowledge inscribed on the gold tablets was a gift of memory which has been 'famed in song among men'. It might not have been, thus, only a result of the initiate's memory of the story but also of the survival of such a text/*hieros logos* through time – indicated also by the great chronological dispersal of the tablets – through memorisation.[629] The initiate recollects his/her divine descent through listening to stories with cosmogonical/elemental themes and their interpretation. The belief that the soul is made of sacred aether and ideas such as rebirth, the location of the Isles of the Blessed in the stars and the prospect of apotheosis, as discussed so far, are all ideas which require background knowledge and an allegorical understanding of mythology. Such mythological stories in general survived through storytellers and contain a past wisdom recollected by the poet through divine inspiration, which is the reason that Homer and Hesiod pray to the Muses for inspiration at the beginning of

---

625 Bernabé and Jiménez San Cristóbal, 2011, p.75. Bernabé and Jiménez San Cristóbal (2008), Graf and Johnston (2013), Pugliese-Caratelli (1993; 2001) all give ἔργον, contrary to Edmonds (2011a) who gives ἔριον.
626 OH76.9–10: 'Awaken in the initiates the memory of the pious ritual and send forgetfulness far from them'. Riedweg, 2011, p.255. Herrero de Jáuregui, 2011, p.289: 'Heroic immortality is granted by *kleos*, the memory the living keep of the dead; in the leaves, however, it is granted by Mnemosyne, personification of the memory the soul must keep of its divine origin. The memory of the dead as object has been transformed into memory of the dead as subject...'
627 B2: 'to them you should relate very well the whole truth; Say: "I am the child of Earth and starry Heaven.'
628 Betz, 2011, p.104: 'In that sense forgetting is the real death, the death within death'. Jiménez San Cristóbal, 2011, p.165–166. Bernabé and Jiménez San Cristóbal, 2011, p.75.
629 Bernabé and Jiménez San Cristóbal, 2008, p.15.

their story. It is this memory which is invoked in the initiate during the mysteries. As Obbink argues, the composers of the gold tablets 'were engaged in a deliberate re-mythologizing' of Orpheus' original insight.[630] But memory also had another level of meaning. We have seen that the text of the tablets includes epic formulas of heroic *kleos*. The whole essence of heroic *kleos* is the remembrance of the heroic deeds of the heroes. They live on forever in the memories of the people *through* the stories told by the storytellers. Similarly, the initiates' 'divine past' lives on through the stories of storytellers like Orpheus. In the same way that the mythological story behind the tablets preserves the *kleos* of the gods, the initiates secure their own *kleos* of immortality through reiterating and remembering this story which reveals the divine descent of men. On a metapoetic level the initiate imitates the storyteller through uttering the formulaic phrases. He/She participates in the continuation of memory. This is perhaps one of the reasons that Orphic writings and mythology were so important. In the Derveni Papyrus, as we will see in Chapter 5, the importance of uttering and of understanding Orphic texts in relation to mysteries is particularly emphasized.

The importance of memory and ideas similar to the ones found in the gold tablets are mentioned by Plato in his much-discussed Myth of Er in the *Republic*, and the similarities are too many to overlook.[631] This myth has been associated with a variety of traditions, including Orphic ideas.[632] Socrates says that this *mythos* is a *logos* because it has truth value. The story is about Er's 'near-death' experience and his afterlife journey. It says that once the soul leaves the body it goes to a blessed place – a meadow – with two chasms connected to the underworld and two which offer entrance and exit from *ouranos*. We notice here that, as suggested earlier, the topography of the afterlife is not necessarily subterranean in its totality. There, the souls are judged by judges who decide if the soul will go left and down if unjust or right and upward if just. The judges also give 'signs' to the souls to mark them as just or unjust. At this place the souls would 'camp' for seven days and discuss their experiences. They would then move on to another place where Socrates says they could see the light which holds together the entire revolving vault:

---

630 Obbink, 2011, p.308.
631 Pl. *Resp.* 10.614a–621d.
632 Horky (2006, p.394, fn.31) also considers how Orphic should we consider this story to be. Halliwell notes that the Myth of Er weaves numerous strands of Greek philosophy, science, religion, poetry, histroriography and visual art (2007, p.445). For specifically a relation to 'Bacchic-Orphic mystery religion': p.458, 461. See also Edmonds, 2004, p.51–52, 88–89. For relation to Orphic-Pythagorean ideas: Adam, 1963, p.378–80.

καὶ ἀφικνεῖσθαι τεταρταίους ὅθεν καθορᾶν ἄνωθεν διὰ παντὸς | τοῦ οὐρανοῦ καὶ γῆς τεταμένον φῶς εὐθύ, οἷον κίονα, μάλιστα τῇ ἴριδι προσφερές, λαμπρότερον δὲ καὶ καθαρώτερον· εἰς ὃ ἀφικέσθαι προελθόντες ἡμερησίαν ὁδόν, καὶ ἰδεῖν αὐτόθι κατὰ μέσον τὸ φῶς ἐκ τοῦ οὐρανοῦ τὰ ἄκρα αὐτοῦ τῶν δεσμῶν τεταμένα – εἶναι γὰρ τοῦτο τὸ φῶς σύνδεσμον τοῦ οὐρανοῦ, οἷον τὰ ὑποζώματα τῶν τριηρῶν, οὕτω πᾶσαν συνέχον τὴν περιφοράν.

After four days they arrived at a place from where they could see clearly a straight shaft of light stretched out from above through the whole of the sky and the earth like a pillar, closely resembling the rainbow, but brighter and purer. They reached this after a day's journey and there they saw in the center of the light the ends of its bonds stretched from the sky: for this light was what bound the sky together, like the braces of triremes, so holding together the whole revolution.[633]

The spindle of Necessity stretched from the edges of this vault and the souls were guided by a prophet before Lachesis where he would ask them to choose their lot in the next life; there were lives of all kinds, of animals and all sorts of human beings to chose from (10.617d–618b).[634] Socrates says that the souls which came from the heavens chose 'bad' lives despite the prophet's warnings because they were unfamiliar with suffering (πόνων ἀγυμνάστους) – notice the pain terminology–, while the ones who came from the earth did not chose hastily having suffered down to earth (πεπονηκότας) (10.619d). If a soul choses wisely every time it arrives at this place, then 'his journey from here to there and back again will not be a rough one through the earth, but a smooth one through the sky' (10.619e).[635] According to Socrates, Er saw the soul of Orpheus choosing the life of a swan (10.620a). After their choice, their lot was 'woven' by the Moirai and then send to the 'plain of Lethe' and the 'river of Forgetfulness' where they all had to drink 'a measure of this water' and 'each one, as he drank, forgot everything' (10.621a).[636]

---

633 Pl. *Resp.* 10.616b–c (Tr. Emlyn-Jones).
634 Pl. *Resp.* 10.618a: ζῴων τε γὰρ πάντων βίους καὶ δὴ καὶ τοὺς ἀνθρωπίνους ἅπαντας.
635 Pl. *Resp.* 10.619e: ἐπεὶ εἴ τις ἀεί, ὁπότε εἰς τὸν ἐνθάδε βίον ἀφικνοῖτο, ὑγιῶς φιλοσοφοῖ καὶ ὁ κλῆρος αὐτῷ τῆς αἱρέσεως μὴ ἐν τελευταίοις πίπτοι, κινδυνεύει ἐκ τῶν ἐκεῖθεν ἀπαγγελλομένων οὐ μόνον ἐνθάδε εὐδαιμονεῖν ἄν, ἀλλὰ καὶ τὴν ἐνθένδε ἐκεῖσε καὶ δεῦρο πάλιν πορείαν οὐκ ἂν | χθονίαν καὶ τραχεῖαν πορεύεσθαι, ἀλλὰ λείαν τε καὶ οὐρανίαν: Yet if an individual, whenever he arrived at the life in this world, constantly practiced sound philosophy and the lot he chose did not fall out among the last, there is a chance, from all that has been reported from the other world, that not only he may be happy here, but also that his journey from here to there and back again will not be a rough one through the earth, but a smooth one through the sky (Tr. Emlyn-Jones).
636 Pl. *Resp.* 10.621a–b: πορεύεσθαι ἅπαντας εἰς τὸ τῆς Λήθης πεδίον διὰ καύματός τε καὶ πνίγους δεινοῦ· καὶ γὰρ εἶναι αὐτὸ κενὸν δένδρων τε καὶ ὅσα γῆ φύει. | σκηνᾶσθαι οὖν σφᾶς ἤδη ἑσπέρας γιγνομένης παρὰ τὸν Ἀμέλητα ποταμόν, οὗ τὸ ὕδωρ ἀγγεῖον οὐδὲν στέγειν. μέτρον μὲν οὖν τι τοῦ ὕδατος πᾶσιν ἀναγκαῖον εἶναι πιεῖν, τοὺς δὲ φρονήσει μὴ σῳζομένους πλέον πίνειν

There they fell asleep and there was 'a thunderbolt and an earthquake, and then suddenly they were taken up, one this way, another that, to their birth, like shooting stars' (10.621b).[637] Socrates ends the story saying that if we believe it, it will save us (ἡμᾶς ἂν σώσειεν) and we will receive our reward just like victors in games if we pursue righteousness and wisdom (10.621c-d).

Such a story could have been behind the text of the gold tablets. Firstly, their owners' souls are judged by the chthonic gods and Persephone just like the souls in the Myth of Er are judged by judges. Secondly, the gold tablets themselves have a function similar to the marks fastened on the souls in the Myth of Er that signify whether they have been just or unjust, since they also evidence their owner's pureness and worthiness to be admitted in the Isles of the Blessed. Thirdly, the girdle of the celestial vault as described in the Myth of Er could be the Milky Way appearing in the night sky as a bright rainbow stretching around the earth, the planets, the moon and the stars, which would agree with my suggestion that the gold tablet's owners final and desired destination was the Milky Way. We also have the idea of being reincarnated as a human or an animal, which can be considered an Orphic idea and the water of forgetfulness which is drunk by the souls that are reborn again and which the souls of the gold tablets are told to avoid at any cost. Also, Socrates says that whoever lives a righteous life will be saved and receive a reward; the same idea is expressed through the gold tablets where the souls proclaim their release, their purity and ask to be send to the Isles of the Blessed. Moreover, after multiple rebirths, if a soul chooses wisely then its journey will be not underground but smooth and through the heavens which corresponds to the double topography argued for the gold tablets. The 'weaving' of the lot of the returning souls by the Moirai and their subsequent description of rebirth as if they were 'shooting stars' is strikingly similar to the expression found in the gold tablets (A1, A2, A3): ε⟨ὖτ⟨ε⟩ με Μοῖρα ⟨ἐδάμασσ'⟩ ε⟨ἴτε ἀσ⟩τεροπῆτα {κη}

τοῦ μέτρου· τὸν δὲ ἀεὶ πιόντα πάντων ἐπιλανθάνεσθαι: they all made their way to the plain of Lethe through terrifying choking fire: for the place was empty of trees and anything else that grows in the earth. So as evening was already approaching they encamped beside the river of Forgetfulness, whose water no vessel can hold. Now they all had to drink a measure of this water, but those who did not have enough sense to be moderate drank more than their measure, while each one, as he drank, forgot everything (Tr. Emlyn-Jones).

637 Pl. *Resp.* 10.621b: ἐπειδὴ δὲ κοιμηθῆναι καὶ μέσας νύκτας γενέσθαι, βροντήν τε καὶ σεισμὸν γενέσθαι, καὶ ἐντεῦθεν ἐξαπίνης ἄλλον ἄλλῃ φέρεσθαι ἄνω εἰς τὴν γένεσιν, ἅττοντας ὥσπερ ἀστέρας (Tr. Emlyn-Jones).

κεραυνῶ‹ν› ('Either Fate mastered me or the lightning bolt thrown by the thunderer').[638] Plato might be drawing from a common 'pool' of eschatological ideas. But the combination of several elements found in the gold tablets and ideas which have so far been identified as Orphic indicates that this posthumous experience of Er was inspired by Orphic beliefs and texts. Plato's reference to Orpheus in this myth, and his choice to be reborn as a swan, certainly makes this more plausible since in an indirect way Orpheus' persona is related to these ideas.

If Plato is inspired by a common source with the compilers of the gold tablets then we can at least be confident that such ideas about an astral immortality of the soul at the Milky Way were related to a journey in the underworld, a posthumous judgement of how just each soul was during its lifetime, the importance of Mnemosyne, and the dangers of the fountain of oblivion. A final reward would be given to the just, according to Plato, as if they were victors in games, an image similar to the initiate of tablet A1 who approaches swiftly the desired crown (ἱμερτο‹ῦ› δ' ἐπέβαν στεφάνο‹υ› ποσὶ καρπαλίμοισι), an expression evoking athletic victory through the crown. According to Plutarch's *De Sera* – which deals with the late punishment of the wicked and its scene is Delphi where Plutarch was one of the two priests of Apollo – when Orpheus descended to the underworld he arrived at a place where there was a great chasm resembling a great *krater* with some streams stretching from it, and where he saw three daimons sitting in a triangular shape.[639] Plutarch's description of the afterlife scene through the myth of Arideus which left his body, refers to the place of emergence where all the pure and impure souls are gathered and where the three kinds of punishment are explained to him, to the chasm of Lethe, the crater of dreams, and the place of punishment.[640] Plutarch also describes the topography of the afterlife in elemental terms, meaning that, as he says, the place of emergence is the sublunary region where air gives way to fire or aether.[641] The stage of emergence, which suggests prior submergence, e.g. *katabasis*, is in fact described in this way:

---

[638] Pinchard (2012) relates to the gold tablets another idea about the soul found in Plato's Phaedrus: 'SOCRATES: When the soul is perfect and endowed with feathers, it travels through sky, and administers the whole world.' Pinchard sees a connection with the phrase καὶ τότ' ἔπειτ'ἄ[λλοισι μεθ'ἡρώεσσιν ἀνάξεις ('And thereon you will rule among the other heroes') from tablet B1. Imagining a soul to 'rule' in the afterlife among other deified souls is indeed a peculiar idea if taken literally, but if I am right that the owners of the gold tablets believed that the soul returns to the divine aether if it manages to escape the cycle of rebirths, then the soul would participate in the ruling of the cosmos through the divine aether which underlays everything.
[639] Plut. *De Sera*, 566a–c. Henderson, 1959, p.173–174.
[640] Pl. *De Sera*, 563e ff; Henderson, 1959, p.177.
[641] Henderson, 1959, p.177.

Ἐπεὶ γὰρ ἐξέπεσε τὸ φρονοῦν τοῦ σώματος οἷον ἄν τις ἐκ πλοίου κυβερνήτης εἰς βυθὸν ἀπορριφεὶς πάθοι τὸ πρῶτον, οὕτως ὑπὸ τῆς μεταβολῆς ἔσχεν· εἶτα μικρὸν ἐξαρθεὶς ἔδοξεν ἀναπνεῖν ὅλος καὶ περιορᾶν πανταχόθεν, ὥσπερ ἑνὸς ὄμματος ἀνοιχθείσης τῆς ψυχῆς. ἑώρα δὲ τῶν πρότερον οὐθὲν ἀλλ' ἢ τὰ ἄστρα παμμεγέθη καὶ ἀπέχοντα πλῆθος ἀλλήλων ἄπλετον, αὐγήν τε τῇ χρόᾳ θαυμαστὴν ἀφιέντα καὶ τόνον ἔχουσαν, ὥστε τὴν ψυχὴν ἐποχουμένην λείως πλοῖον ὥσπερ ἐν γαλήνῃ τῷ φωτὶ ῥᾳδίως πάντῃ καὶ ταχὺ διαφέρεσθαι.

He said that when his intelligence was driven from his body, the change made him feel as a pilot might at first on being flung into the depths of the sea; his next impression was that he had risen somewhat and was breathing with his whole being and seeing on all sides, his soul having opened wide as if it were a single eye. But nothing that he saw was familiar except the stars, which appeared very great in size and at vast distances apart, sending forth a marvellously coloured radiance possessed of a certain cohesion, so that his soul, riding smoothly in the light like a ship on a calm sea, could move easily and rapidly in all directions.[642]

We should keep this in mind, since in Chapter 6 more will be said on a possible elemental transformation of the soul. Most importantly, Plutarch says that at this place nothing that he saw was familiar except the stars, which appeared very great in size and at vast distances apart, while the soul appeared to become one with the light being able to move in all directions. This description, places the blessed meadows once again at the astral sphere. Considering the similarities of Plutarch's story and the similarities of Plato's story with the afterlife topography of the gold tablets, it is possible that Plato was inspired by the same story that the gold tablets' compilers were, and which might after all have been a story of Orpheus' journey in the afterlife. Plato was certainly aware of Orpheus' journey since he refers to it in the *Symposium*.[643] Plutarch must have been familiar with Plato's story but his description of the afterlife in elemental terms suggests that he was also familiar with a cosmological eschatology related to such a story which is not mentioned by Plato. Even if we cannot be sure that Plato was influenced by Orphic beliefs and texts, we can now be more confident about the suggestion that it was an astral immortality which was expected by the gold tablets' initiates and that this was directly dependent on their ability to recall and acknowledge their divine essence and descent, and on living a just life.

Pinchard interprets these ideas on a philosophical level. He defines Orphism as 'the cultural process – neither a fixed doctrine nor an organised church – that

---

642 Plut. *De Sera*, 563f (Tr. De Lacy). More will be said in relation to why this journey might have began with a *katabasis* in Chapter 6, p.222ff. The great distance of the stars is also mentioned by the DP author (Col.XXV).
643 Pl. *Symp.*179d.

led from the positive valuation of an external memory concerning epic or old theogonical patterns, working as a condition of the *kleos aphthiton* for heroes and poets, toward the positive valuation of the internal memory which is conceived of as bringing the philosopher's soul in touch with eternal realities'.[644] I, too, have been arguing for an allegorical interpretation of the text of the gold tablets. The initiates of the gold tablets did not perform rites 'empty of meaning' such as those perhaps offered by the *Orpheotelestae* and mocked by Plato, but accepted the interpretation of mythological and cosmogonical stories through a scientifical/elemental lens. This allowed them to trace their origin to a single divine substance of which everything was made, the sacred aether which was materialised through the sun and heat in the present life and transformed into star-matter in the afterlife. An afterlife *kleos* and immortality was not, thus, exclusive to the Homeric heroes of the distant past but became available to anyone who recollected the *alētheia* and recognised their divine ancestry. Based on the many references by ancient sources to the belief that the soul turned into aether and became a star post-mortem it is improbable that such ideas were 'marginal' or 'peripheral' to conventional religion – a problematic term in itself – but personal, esoteric and 'supplementary'.[645] There is a shift, thus, from the collective to the self, which nonetheless becomes part of the collective divine soul. This is not to suggest that all the owners of the tablets were under a single religious administration but that these ideas travelled in space and time *through* the Orphic texts and were practiced in mysteries. Perhaps the mystic initiation was not exactly the same for all the tablets' owners – if there were not main places of intiation – but the knowledge they acquired and the justification for afterlife *kleos* and *apotheosis* remained the same. In the same way that our bodies change as we get older but our essence – whether it is consciousness or soul – remains the same, the surface of Orphism was fluid but its essence, its cosmological and elemental interpretation of the human existence, remained the same.[646]

4.7 The Olbian Bone Tablets

I will now be examining the Olbian Bone Tablets which constitute material of a similar nature to the gold tablets, meaning that they are also inscribed tablets

---

[644] Pinchard, 2012, p.1. He also argues that: 'Orphism might be the analogy-generating tradition in which Plato found the first connection between different kinds of memory and different levels of immortality' (p.1).
[645] Tzifopoulos, 2010, p.121–124.
[646] See also Pinchard, 2012, p.2, fn.3.

used for religious purposes. In 1951 several bone tablets were found in Olbia and three of them that were inscribed were published in 1978. Olbia was one of the largest and well-known Greek colonies located on the right bank of river Hypanis (Bug) in modern Ukraine and founded in the 7th century by Milesian colonists. The tablets were found in the central *temenos* precinct where there was an Ionic temple of Apollo Delphinios and various other buildings such as altars, a cistern, a treasury and a workshop.[647] In the Western *temenos* area sanctuaries were found of Apollo Iatros, Hermes, Aphrodite, Zeus, the Dioskouroi, and the Mother of the Gods.[648]

The tablets are around five to six centimetres long, their shape is almost rectangular and they are dated to the early 5th century B.C. All three of them have the word Dio(nysos) inscribed on the one side, the letter A, the word ἀλήθεια (truth) and a zigzag line. Tablet A has the words βίος – θάνατος – βίος and ἀλήθεια inscribed on the upper half and Διό(νυσος) Ὀρφικ- and some illegible letter(s) towards the bottom of the lower half. The word Ὀρφικ- could be read as Ὀρφικῶι, Ὀρφικοῦ, Ὀρφικός or Ὀρφικοί. These tablets are an important source, since they are among the earliest pieces of evidence referring explicitly to the characterisation Orphic. Tablet C which has the words Διό(νυσο), ἀλήθεια, σῶμα – ψυχή inscribed on the one side and a drawing on the other side refer to the duality of body and soul which is clearly related to eschatological beliefs of the soul being a separate entity from the body, an idea attested as Orphic in other sources too. Tablet B has the words εἰρήνη – πόλεμος, ἀλήθεια – ψεύδος and Διό(νυσος) inscribed on the one side and on the other side a drawing of a rectangle divided into seven parts, each of them having a circle in the middle. I would argue against West's suggestion that the drawing might represent a 'tray or table with offerings (possibly eggs, or some kind of musical instrument)' since it is difficult to imagine why an initiate would draw the offerings instead of simply making the offering, or what kind of musical instrument this would be.[649] I know of no parallels for a *drawing* of offerings, although sculptural representations of animal and other offerings are not uncommon in some cults. The instrument traditionally associated with Orpheus is the lyre, and the drawing seems nothing like a lyre. However, I suggest that the drawing might be related to Orpheus' lyre indirectly. The fact that the drawing is divided into *seven* sections might be the element to which we

---

647 EOAG, 510.
648 EOAG, 510; Rusjaeva, 2003, p.93. Rusjaeva suggests that 'from the very beginning of the colonisation, an important role was also played by the cult of the Mother of the Gods' (p.97).
649 West, 1983, p.23.

should pay attention. Considering the discussion above of an astronomical interpretation of the eschatology of the gold tablets, the seven spheres might be the seven planets known at the time. What would this have to do with Orpheus' lyre? West refers to a scholium on Virgil where it is noted that some say that the seven strings of Orpheus' lyre corresponded to the seven circles of heaven (the planets).[650] This idea is also found in Lucian (2nd A.D.):

> Ἕλληνες δὲ οὔτε παρ' Αἰθιόπων οὔτε παρ' Αἰγυπτίων ἀστρολογίης πέρι οὐδὲν ἤκουσαν, ἀλλὰ σφίσιν Ὀρφεὺς ὁ Οἰάγρου καὶ Καλλιόπης πρῶτος τάδε ἀπηγήσατο, οὐ μάλα ἐμφανέως, οὐδὲ ἐς φάος τὸν λόγον προήνεγκεν, ἀλλ' ἐς γοητείην καὶ ἱερολογίην, οἵη διανοίη ἐκείνου. πηξάμενος γὰρ λύρην ὄργιά τε ἐποιέετο καὶ τὰ ἱερὰ ἤειδεν· ἡ δὲ λύρη ἑπτάμιτος ἐοῦσα τὴν τῶν κινεομένων ἀστέρων ἁρμονίην συνεβάλλετο.

> The Greeks did not learn astrology either from the Ethiopians or the Egyptians; it was Orpheus, son of Oeagra and Calliope, who revealed to them the first principles. He did not, however, make them public; he did not teach this science in broad daylight, but enveloped it with enchantments and mysteries to second his views. He made a lyre and instituted orgies in which he sang his sacred teachings. His lyre with seven strings rendered a harmony which was like that of the moving stars.[651]

Lucian says that the Greeks learned about astronomy from Orpheus and that through playing his lyre he created *orgia* and mysteries. Varro also claims that there was an Orphic work about summoning the soul, called the *Lyre*.[652] If he is correct, then the lyre's astronomical nature was used to invoke the aetheral/astral nature of the initiate's soul. As Lucian says, through playing the seven strings of his lyre Orpheus imitated the harmony of the planetary spheres and that is why the Greeks turned his lyre into the constellation Lyra. Lyra is next to the constellation of the Swan (Cygnus) which according to some sources represented Orpheus who was turned into the constellation after being torn apart by Maenads. Perhaps this is why Plato notes that Orpheus chose to be reborn as a swan in the myth of Er, indicating that he was not in fact reborn but gained eternal bliss in the stars, this being a subtle indication of Orpheus' connection with such ideas. In any case, astronomy must have been an important part of Orphic beliefs as we established so far and it is possible that the seven circles on the Olbian Tablet represent the seven planets or 7 stars such as the Pleiades, the 7 stars which were part of the Taurus' constellation indicating the location of the Isles of the Blessed as argued in this chapter.

---

650 Servius *in Vergil Aeneid*. VI 645. West, 1983, p.30–33.
651 Lucian, *De astr*. 10 (Tr. Harmon).
652 Suda o654.

The words βίος – θάνατος – βίος can refer either to the idea of reincarnation or to the idea that the life after death is the true life, both ideas found in Orphism.[653] The word ἀλήθεια must be the most significant, since it is found in all the tablets. This does not come as a surprise considering the discussion of Mnemosyne and recollection and the importance of knowing the truth about life and death and humans' true identity. The truth expressed in these bone tablets also has to do with rebirth and death as a way of rebirth which leads to the true life. The contrast to ψεύδος entails the same 'urgency' as the gold tablets and the warning against the fountain of *lethe*. Not knowing the truth can have devastating outcomes in the gold tablets such as staying forever trapped in the cycle of rebirths. The zigzag symbol could be an allusion to lightning, which is also found in some of the gold tablets in the form of star-striking lightning possibly as the means which leads humans to their mortal existence. This idea will be explored more in Chapter 6, since there is evidence that the lightning was a symbol of incarnation. Alternatively, it might be argued that the zig-zag lines could represent a serpent, a symbolic animal closely related to the cult of Dionysos and his Orphic birth but I consider this less likely. Finally, the letter A might be a representation of the head of a bull – one of Dionysos' personas as mentioned earlier – an interpretation supported by a drawing found on another Olbian bone tablet, which represents an animal (a cow or a bull?) whose head is made out of the letter A.[654] The Greek letter alpha (A) is in fact a development of the Phoenician aleph which means bull. If this suggestion is true, then this could be another astronomical reference since as I suggested earlier, the Isles of the Blessed in the gold tablets were possibly located near the horns of the bull on the Taurus constellation which is marked by the star common to the Eriphoi constellation. The opposites *eirēnē – polemos* are reminiscent of the language used by Herakleitos and other Pre-Socratic philosophers and the early date of these tablets presents the possibility of drawing from a common pool of eschatological ideas. This matter will be discussed in more detail in the following two chapters.

There is also further evidence of Bacchos being worshipped at Olbia from early times. For example, a c.500 B.C. inscription on a mirror found in a grave reads: 'Demonassa daughter of Lenaeos, *euai* and Lenaeos, son of Demoklos, *euai*!'[655] The *euai* proclamation is Bacchic as is attested by several authors such

---

653 Graf, 2011, p.56.
654 See West, 1983, p.20.
655 Graf and Johnston, 2013, p.216.

as Sophocles and Aristophanes.[656] Also, Herodotus refers to the story of the Skythian king Skyles who around 460 B.C. wished to become initiated into the ecstatic cult of Dionysos Baccheios at Olbia.[657] Finally, a vase-stand of the 5th century B.C. found in Olbia bears a later Bacchic inscription (c.300 B.C.) written in two concentric circles, naming several males as 'members of the northern thiasos' in the outer circle, and in the inner circle: βίος βίος Ἀπόλλων Ἀπόλλων, ἥλιος ἥλιος κόσμος κόσμος φῶς φῶς ('Life life, Apollo Apollo, sun sun, order order (or cosmos), light light').[658] We can see that the style of this inscription is similar to that of the Bone Tablets, with the word βίος, the pairing and repetitions. The *thiasos* was the ecstatic entourage of Dionysos and we find this term in the gold tablets, too, as we saw. Also, we have already seen how Apollo might have been perceived as Helios and alter-ego of Dionysos in Orphism. His reference here in combination to a Dionysiac thiasos supports this suggestion, bearing in mind the similarities of this inscription to the Orphic Bone tablets. The combination of the two gods in this Olbian vase and the associations to Helios as the source of life and creator of the world give it an Orphic ring according to the interpretation of the Orphic eschatology I have given so far. The reference to a thiasos makes it possible that mystic rites such as the ones practised by the gold tablets' owners, and formed around the same ideas, were practised by the owner of this vase.

It appears, thus, that an Orphic 'community' was already active in Olbia in the 5th century B.C. and had specific eschatological beliefs which might have been associated with astronomy and to which the notion of truth was closely related. They certainly show similarities to the gold tablets in terms of content in a very 'minimalistic' way. Perhaps this minimalism is due to the fact that they were offered as dedications, since the ones we have were found in the Olbian sanctuary area. Their dedicatory context is different than the funerary find-context of the gold tablets which suggests their post-mortem use. The Olbian Bone Tablets,

---

656 Soph. *Trach.* 218–20: ἰδού μ' ἀναταράσσει, | εὐοῖ, | ὁ κισσὸς ἄρτι Βακχίαν | ὑποστρέφων ἄμιλλαν: 'See, the ivy excites me – Euoi! – whirling me around in the Bacchic rush!' (Tr. Lloyd-Jones). Soph. *Ant.* 1131–36: καί σε Νυσαίων ὀρέων | κισσήρεις ὄχθαι χλωρά τ' ἀκτὰ | πολυστάφυλος πέμπει | ἀμβρότων ἐπέων | εὐαζόντων Θηβαΐας | ἐπισκοποῦντ' ἀγυιάς: 'And the ivycovered slopes of the hills of Nysa and the green coast with many grapes send you here, while voices divine cry "euhoe," as you visit the streets of Thebes.' (Tr. Lloyd-Jones). Ar. *Thesm.* 986–91: ἡγοῦ δέ γ' ὧδ' αὐτὸς σύ, | κισσοφόρε Βακχεῖε | δέσποτ'· ἐγὼ δὲ κώμοις | σε φιλοχόροισι μέλψω | Εὔιε, ὦ Διός σὺ | Βρόμιε, καὶ Σεμέλας παῖ: 'This way, Lord Bacchus crowned with ivy,do personally be our leader: and with revels I will hymn you,who love the dance!Euius, you Noisemaker,son of Zeus and Semele...' (Tr. Henderson). Bremmer, 2013, p.71.
657 Bremmer, 2013, p.72; Hdt. 4.79.
658 Graf and Johnston, 2013, p.216–217.

thus, did not have to include passwords or formulaic phrases or lengthy instructions for an underworld journey, but merely to show that their dedicator knew the truth.

4.8 Conclusion

The textual similarities between the gold tablets across all different groups, evidence that they have the same religious background and textual archetype. This does not mean that there was a central religious administration behind them but that these ideas travelled in space and time through the Orphic texts and were practiced in mysteries which were fluid in their formation. Perhaps the mystic initiation was not exactly the same for all the tablets' owners but the knowledge they acquired and the justification for afterlife *kleos* and apotheosis remained the same. Grave-goods and terms such as *thiasos, orgia, mystēs, bacchos* and the reference to deities such as Dionysos, Mountain Mother, Persephone and Demeter Chthonia indicate the Dionysiac/Orphic character of the tablets and reject a Pythagorean. Their archetype could be a katabatic Orphic poem, while their dialogic nature and several other practical elements indicate that some of the text derives from ritualistic language. Slight variations of the text which do not add anything in terms of style or plot also suggest that the text was orally transmitted. This is also suggested by the use of epic formulas and the verb *euchomai* in relation to heroic motifs of affirming divine lineage. Since a divine lineage available to all has to be justified somehow, the Titanic anthropogony must be the means for this justification. This is also evident from the phrase 'I am the child of Earth and starry Heaven' and the reference to lighnitng as a form of punishment.

The phrase I am the child of earth and starry heaven was consider to have a double connotation of expressing both a Titanic descent and an elemental division of body and soul to earth and astral aether. This is also supported by the interpretation of the formulaic phrase 'A kid/bull/ram you fell into milk' as a reference to astral immortality where the milk is the *galaxias* (Milky Way) and the animals correspond to the constellations of the Bull and the Charioteer which were established as the location of the Isles of the Blessed. It was suggested that the afterlife topography of the gold tablets is dual and the afterlife journey includes two stages. At first, the souls descend along with the other uninitiated souls and are warned to avoid the fountain of Lethe and proceed to the fountain of Mnemosyne instead. After the initiates demonstrate their status as pure initiates and their mystic knowledge through the utterance of formulaic enigmatic phrases and passwords they are given water from the fountain of memory and are admitted into the astral Isles of the Blessed. An astral immortality was also supported by external literary references relating Dionysos and the soul to the stars while the eschatology and topography we find in the gold tablets is perhaps alluded to by Plato and Plutarch.

It was also suggested that the afterlife journey was re-enacted during katabatic mysteries ending with an ascend into the meadows of Persephone corresponding to the Isles of the Blessed. This perhaps included torch procession signifying the nocturnal sun, *dromena* and *legomena* with some of the phrases found on the gold tablets uttered during the mysteries. Background knowledge was essential: the initiates would need to know the cosmological eschatology, the topography of the netherworld and what to say to Persephone and the chthonic gods. The background knowledge, then, was specific/practical on the one hand and analytical/ideological on the other. This knowledge does not appear to be exclusive but open to anyone who would get initiated.

The Olbian Bone tablets are essentially of the same nature as the gold tablets since they are inscribed tablets evidencing their owner/dedicator's status as initiate and indicating the mystic knowledge he/she has. Their use, however, is different since the one is a dedication and the other is to be used in the afterlife by the initiate. They express eschatological ideas in a very minimalistic way and specifically relate them to Orphism through the inscribed term Orphic-. Their language shows similarities with Pre-Socratic language which might indicate a common traditional background.

5 Papyrological Evidence: The Derveni Papyrus and the Gurôb Papyrus

5.1 The Derveni Papyrus

5.1.1 Introduction

The Derveni Papyrus was found in 1962 at Derveni, around ten kilometres to the north of Thessalonika. It was discovered in one of the seven graves which were found in the area, in which a soldier was buried; the quantity of the grave goods and the construction of the graves is indicative of the high social and economic status of the deceased.[659] The soldier was cremated on an elaborate structure and buried around the end of the fourth century B.C.; the Derveni Papyrus was burned on the funeral pyre and was found carbonised among the pyre's debris. Tsantsanoglou argues that the burning of the papyrus on the funeral pyre might be related to the contents of the book and that the cremated man was an initiate, based on the proximity of the grave to the shrine of Demeter and Kore.[660] The use of the papyrus during the funeral might indeed point to its significance in relation to eschatological beliefs, and it is something we need to take into consideration. The fact that the seven tombs were all together in an isolated area outside of the city's cemetery supports the hypothesis that the deceased was an initiate. The same can be said for funerary findings in the other tombs, such as the Derveni krater, which is adorned with Dionysiac imagery: a bearded man next to a woman which could be Dionysos and Ariadne, a woman holding a child over her shoulders in the air and another one tearing apart a goat – images which point to maenadism.[661] Inside the crater a gold ring and a coin of Philip II were found, and on top there was a gold olive wreath, items often found in the tombs where the gold tablets were discovered.

In order, however, to define the identity of the Derveni author I will examine the contents of the papyrus. The restoration of almost two hundred fragments has given us twenty-six columns of text. Although intensive scholarly discussion of the papyrus has shed new light on Orphism, the text remains one of the most

---

659 For a detailed description of the tombs and the objects that were found in the tombs see Betegh, 2004, p.56–59.
660 KPT, 2006, p.3–4.
661 For discussion and a different view see Carpenter, 2000.

controversial that has ever concerned the academic community, since it comprises an allegorical interpretation of an Orphic poem in relation to Pre-Socratic physics.[662] The Derveni Papyrus is one of the most important texts to have been discovered during the last decades, not only because it is one of the few that have been found in Greece itself, but also because it is one of the oldest literary papyri ever found.[663] Most papyrologists date it to the second half of the 4th century; Kouremenos, Parássoglou and Tsantsanoglou date it more specifically to a period from 340 to 320 B.C.[664] However, the text itself may be earlier, while it is safe to assume that the Orphic poem which is discussed by the author was of an even earlier date again (perhaps as early as the 6th century B.C.), placing the author's treatise in the late 5th century B.C. as argued by many scholars.[665]

The bottom part of the Derveni papyrus was burned; the remaining seven or eight centimetres of the top half give us fifteen to seventeen lines of text in the columns which are better preserved. The first ten to eleven lines of the columns have an almost continuous text, while in the bottom lines just a few letters are readable. From the first badly damaged columns we only have small fragments, with nearly no readable letters, of nine to ten lines. We cannot be sure about how much of the original papyrus has survived, since we do not know how many columns there were before the first column on the roll, but considering the usual length of papyri it is possible that we only have 1/3 of the total papyrus. The regular length of a column was usually twenty-one to thirty-one lines, making it possible that we have about half of the lines for each column of the Derveni papyrus. The text is easy to read, since the handwriting is clear and can be compared to the lapidary style of inscriptions of the 4th century B.C.[666] The first published edition of the text, and the only one available for a long time, was the one by Kapsomenos (1964), which was quite incomplete. In 1982, an anonymous unauthorised transcript was included in *Zeitschrift für Papyrologie und Epigraphik* 47, on

---

[662] See e.g. Tsantsanoglou, 1997, p.93–128; Betegh, 2004.
[663] Most, 1997, p.117.
[664] Betegh, 2004, p.61.
[665] Janko, 2002, p.1: Janko suggests that the treatise that the papyrus contains was composed in late 5th century B.C. KPT, 2006, p.10: Tsantsanoglou also seems to agree with the suggestion that the work preserved by the papyrus was composed around the turn of the 5th century. Sider, 2014; Tzifopoulos, 2014, p.137 and Burkert, (1997) consider possible the poem being dated at the 6th century B.C.
[666] Betegh, 2004, p.60–61.

separate numbering after page 300.[667] This transcript was used by scholars in the following years, and it was the basis for the first English translation of the text, published by Laks and Most in 1997. Their volume contains a detailed commentary on the first seven columns by Tsantsanoglou where he suggested some important amendments to the text. In 2002, Janko published the first critical edition with a translation and index of words, while he attempted to use words quoted by the author to reconstruct some of the verses of the Orphic poem which are commented on by the Derveni author but are not given in the text. Later, Betegh (2004) presented a critical edition of the text with a translation, and a reconstruction and interpretation of the Orphic poem through isolating the lemmata given by the Derveni author and putting them all together. The first official edition is that of Kouremenos, Parássoglou and Tsantsanoglou (2006), with a translation and commentary as well as a list of unplaced fragments. This is the edition I will be using in this chapter and throughout the book. Some additional suggestions for the first six columns of the Papyrus have been made by Ferrari but a complete edition has not been published.[668] Bernabé and Piano (2016) have also given an edition of the columns VII–XXVI which can be found online along Ferrari's and Kouremenos-Parássoglou-Tsantsanoglou edition at the CHS-iMouseion Project website. Piano, has also published an edition of the first six columns of the papyrus which is different than that of Janko and Ferrari, offering stimulating suggestions and several alternatives.[669] Laks and Most (2016a) have also included the Derveni Papyrus in their sixth Loeb volume of *Early Greek Philosophy, Vol.VI: Later Ionian and Athenian Thinkers (Part 1)* where they indicate in the introduction that they relied on Piano's edition for columns up to and including Col.VI and on the edition of Kouremenos-Parássoglou-Tsantsanoglou for columns VII–XXVI.[670] The editions of Betegh, Janko, Ferrari, Kouremenos-Parássoglou-Tsantsanoglou and Bernabé-Piano do not seem to differ significantly in their restorations of words missing from the papyrus, nor are the various translations substantially different in meaning. In the few cases where a passage is ambiguous, it is discussed in the following sections. A more recent edition was published in March 2017 by Kotwick in association with Janko as a result of new and advanced technologies

---

667 The scholar(s) entrusted with producing the editio princeps failed to produce it in a reasonable time: so an anonymous scholar decided (with the connivance of the editors of *ZPE*) to override the normal scholarly convention and pre-empt the right of first publication.
668 Ferrari's edition (2012) of the text can be found online at the CHS-iMouseion Project website. See also Ferrari 2011a,b,c and 2010.
669 Piano, 2016.
670 Laks and Most, 2016a, p.374.

to photograph papyri.⁶⁷¹ Janko notes that the KPT edition is reliable but there are a few helpful additions to the text.

We have already established, based on the discussion in the previous chapters, that Macedonia must have been an important centre of Orphic activity and we should bear this in mind when discussing the Derveni Papyrus. It is also important that several tombs were found in Macedonia whose paintings point to a combination of eschatological ideas and philosophical interests, which I have identified to be a trait of Orphism, and might support the suggestion that the Derveni papyrus was important to the deceased and the funeral rite.⁶⁷² Of particular interest is the so-called 'Tomb of the Philosophers' (300 B.C) whose paintings represent the deceased as a war hero and a philosopher surrounded by five men reading papyrus rolls and one of them pointing to a celestial globe and which might refer to a Platonic school.⁶⁷³ The so-called 'Tomb of Judgement' (late 4th B.C.) shows the deceased soldier being led by Hermes Psychopompos to the judges of the netherworld, Aiakos and Rhadamanthys just like in the myth of Er in Plato's *Republic* discussed in p.193ff and argued to be influenced by Orphic ideas, and in a way reminiscent of the gold tablets owners having to prove their worthiness to Persephone. Finally, we have several tombs found in Vergina and Amphipoli depicting Hades and Persephone and some tombs depicting a symposium with Dionysos being the central figure, which recall the eschatological imagery of the gold tablets. We should also, thus, juxtapose the contents of the Orphic poem commented on by the Derveni author and his interpretation of them to the Orphic picture painted so far based on non-Orphic sources and the gold tablets. I will not dwell at length on matters of authorship, since not only do I believe this is an impossible task, but unconfirmed guesses are pointless if they do not influence the interpretation of the text, and potentially misleading if they do.⁶⁷⁴

---

671 Kotwick, 2017.
672 For a discussion of these tombs see Piano, 2016, p.35–58. Piano also suggests that the papyrus' use as a funerary object was motivated by the deceased's interest in cosmology and his eschatological expectations.
673 Piano, 2016, p.36–39.
674 KPT, 2006, p.59.

5.1.2 What does the Orphic poem say?

The Derveni author quotes verses from a poem which he attributes to Orpheus and offers his interpretation of it. We have, thus, two levels of text: the actual Orphic text and the author's interpretation. We have around 30 hexameter verses quoted from the Orphic poem, some of which are specified by the Derveni author to have been consecutive in the text.[675] We cannot be sure in what order the rest were found in the poem, but we can still get an outline of some of the episodes discussed in it: Zeus becomes king not by forcibly taking power from Kronos but according to an oracle. He cooperates with Kronos and is advised by Night who prophesies everything which it is legitimate for Zeus to do for his reign. Zeus then – on Night's advice? – swallows αἰδοῖον, which is either the Orphic deity Protogonos/Phanes or Ouranos' genitalia. This is a much debated matter and will be discussed later on. Following the swallowing episode, Zeus becomes the creator of the world and the whole cosmos 'grows' from him. Several verses refer to Zeus' supremacy as the first and last, the beginning, middle and end, and king of all. The remaining verses refer to Peitho, Harmonia, Aphrodite Ourania, Okeanos and Acheloos with its silver swirls. Finally, the last verses before the papyrus' abrupt end seem to refer to Zeus committing incest with his mother. Apart from the verses from the Orphic poem, the Derveni author also quotes a verse from some Orphic Hymns, some Homeric verses and a verse from Herakleitos. He was, thus, familiar with various Orphic works and with Pre-Socratic works. The latter is in any case obvious from the close similarity of his ideas with Pre-Socratic perceptions of the cosmos as we will see.

At first glance, it seems that the Derveni author focuses on the episodes involving Zeus, at least in the part of the papyrus we have available. His attempt to portray Zeus as the ultimate divine entity is evident. Verses such as "Ζεὺς κεφα[λή, Ζεὺς μέσ]σα, Διὸς δ' ἐκ [π]άντα τέτ[υκται" and "Ζεὺς βασιλεύς, Ζεὺς δ' ἀρχὸς ἀπάντων ἀργικέραυνος", indicate that according to this Orphic text Zeus was the entity which was the beginning, middle and end, the creator and supreme king.[676] This is what the actual verse denotes and not the Derveni author, and we can assume based on this passage that this Orphic text referred to Zeus as the creator of the cosmos, an idea not found in other theogonies. The Orphic verses describing the creation of the cosmos are also given by the Derveni author:

---

675 KPT, 2006, p.20–21.
676 Col.XVII.12: 'Zeus is the head, Zeus the middle, and from Zeus is everything fashioned.' Col.XIX.10: 'Zeus the king, Zeus the ruler of all, he of the bright bolt.'

Πρωτογόνου βασιλέως αἰδοίου· τῶι δ' ἄρα πάντες
ἀθάνατοι προσέφυν μάκαρες θεοὶ ἠδὲ θέαιναι
καὶ ποταμοὶ καὶ κρῆναι ἐπήρατοι ἄλλα τε πάντα,
ἄσσα τότ' ἦν γεγαῶτ', αὐτὸς δ' ἄρα μοῦνος ἔγεντο.

Of the First-born king, the reverend one; and upon him all the immortals grew, blessed gods and goddesses and rivers and lovely springs and everything else that had been born; and he himself became the sole one. [677]

There is, thus, an apparent monism and pantheism in this Orphic text and Zeus is portrayed as the force that keeps everything together as can be deduced by the fact that after he created the world upon him, 'he became the sole one'. According to these verses, thus, the totality and multiplicity of the cosmos is included in and is a part of the whole, which is Zeus. It is not, thus, that different entities did not exist, but that all entities were underlain by immanent Zeus. We can identify this monism in another verse quoted by the Derveni author from a different Orphic work: "Δημήτηρ ['Ρ]έα Γῆ Μήτηρ Ἑστία Δηιώι".[678] According to this Orphic Hymn Demeter is equated with Rhea, Gaia, Mother and Hestia as if the different names are just different facets of the same goddess and we do not need the Derveni author's help to infer this. Even though the Derveni author's cosmo-theogony is focused on Zeus, we can discern a succession of divine entities in the surviving part of the Orphic poem in the following order: Night, Ouranos, Kronos and Zeus. To this we may add the *aidoion* whose identity remains to be examined later on.

The emphasis on Zeus has led Torjussen to put forth the argument *ex silentio* that Dionysos and metempsychosis were not mentioned in the Derveni Papyrus and we cannot juxtapose it with or use other Orphic texts to fill in the gaps.[679] This argument, however, is not plausible, since not only is a large part of the papyrus missing, so that there is no way for us to know what its contents were, but there are also textual and contextual similarities to other Orphic works such as the *Orphic Rhapsodies* which suggest that they belong to the same mythological tradition. Yet again, even if we had the whole of the papyrus available we could still not be sure that the Derveni author referred to the totality of the Orphic poem. The verses we do have available, however, reveal episodes which are distinctively

---

677 Col.XVI.3–6.
678 Col.XXII.12: 'Demeter, Rhea, Ge, Meter, Hestia, Deio.'
679 Torjussen, 2005, p.10–12. Jiménez San Cristóbal, on the other hand, notes that the allusion to 'mother' and 'sister' at the end of Col.XX, which refers to rituals, could indicate that Dionysos' conception, a frequent ritual motif, might have been included in this particular Orphic poem (Jiménez San Cristóbal, 2018, p.139).

different to other theogonies such as the Hesiodic one: these are e.g. the swallowing of the *aidoion*, the oracular and important role of Night, the creation of the entire world by Zeus and the peaceful acquiring of power by Zeus. In the next chapter we will be able to see if these episodes are also to be found in the *Orphic Rhapsodies*. For the moment I would refer to Kouremenos' suggestion that if the Derveni author's commentary closely follows the Orphic poem, the latter seems to have been 'a very condensed, partial 'summary' of the *Orphic Rhapsodies*'.[680]

5.1.3 What does the Derveni author say?

The Derveni author is heavily preoccupied with the meaning of words and names; his allegorical interpretation is based on etymological arguments and is truly remarkable. One of the main ideas he discusses is that Zeus is essentially air, the primal substance of the cosmos. He then suggests that gods such as Ouranos and Kronos represent different stages in the process of creation and that they are also essentially different manifestations of Zeus/Nous. He explains the workings of the cosmos through opposing powers such as love and strife, and hot and cold guided by the divine intelligence of Mind/Nous. The style of the Derveni author is somewhat polemical in the sense that he often opposes himself to 'the others' who do not know or understand the real meaning of the Orphic poem. He urges his audience to go beyond the poem's obvious and literal meaning.[681]

The Derveni author identifies the divine Nous in both Ouranos and Kronos. He interprets Kronos as the stage in creation during which the Mind *krouei* (strikes) the *eonta* (particles) towards and against each other; a process which leads to the formation of the first entities. This process is also driven by heat ('So he says that this Kronos was born from Helios to Ge, because it was on account of the sun that (the ἐόντα) were induced to be struck against each other' Col.XIV.2–4):

> "ἐκ τοῦ δὴ Κρόνος αὖτις, ἔπειτα δὲ μητίετα Ζεύς"·
> λέγει τι 'ἐκ τοῦδε [ἀ]ρχή ἐστιν, ἐξ ὅσου βασιλεύει ἥδε
> ἀρχή'. διηγεῖται Ν[οῦς τ]ὰ ὄντα κρούων πρὸς ἄλληλα
> διαστήσας τε [πρὸς τὴ]ν νῦν μετάστασιν οὐκ ἐξ ἑτέρ[ων]
> ἕτερ' ἀλλ' ἑτε[ροῖα ποεῖν.]

> "following him in turn was Kronos, and then Zeus the contriver" He means something like 'from that time is the beginning, from which the magistracy reigns'. It has (already) been

---

680 KPT, 2006, p.24. See also Brisson, 2003, p.19–22.
681 Bossi, 2011, p.15.

related that Mind, striking the ὄντα to one another and setting them apart toward the present transformative stage, [created] from different things not different ones but diversified ones.[682]

The Derveni author argues that Orpheus gave the name Kronos to the creation stage where the *eonta* were being struck against each other by Nous (Col.XIV.7). He then says that Ouranos represents the stage in creation where Nous defines the nature of the *eonta*:

[τῶν ἐ]όντων γὰρ ἁπάντ[ω]ν [οὔπω κρουομέ]νων
[ὁ Νοῦ]ς ὡς ὁρ[ίζω]ν φύσιν [τὴν ἐπωνυμίαν ἔσχε]ν

For when all the *eonta* [were not yet being struck, Mind,] as determining the creation, [received the designation Ouranos].[683]

Perhaps if we had the remaining papyrus, we would find the Derveni author explaining Dionysos' name as the Nous of Zeus (*Dios Nous*) which is distributed to all beings through its *diairesis* (division); an idea which could have nicely been allegorised through Dionysos' dismemberment. Since we do not have the remaining papyrus this will remain mere speculation.

The Derveni author says that Zeus was not born but his name just denominates a stage of the creation procedure and that some mistakenly believe that he was born when he was given a name.[684] The Derveni author's cosmogony proclaims that there was no generation of things because the divine matter pre-existed since forever and the formation of beings was the arrangement of the little particles which he calls *eonta*.[685] The particles move, or more precisely 'jump around' and similar particles are drawn together forming entities:

[...] "θόρ[ν]ηι" δὲ λέγ[ων] δηλοῖ
ὅτι ἐν τῶι ἀέρι κατὰ μικρὰ μεμερισμένα ἐκινεῖτο
καὶ ἐθόρνυτο, θορνύμενα δ' ἕκα[σ]τα συνεστάθη
πρὸς ἄλληλα. μέχρι δὲ τούτου ἐθόρνυτο, μέχρι
ἕκαστον ἦλθεν εἰς τὸ σύνηθες.

---

[682] Col.XV.6–10. Col.XIV.2–4: τοῦτον οὖν τὸν Κρόνον | γενέσθαι φησὶν ἐκ τοῦ Ἡλίου τῆι Γῆι, ὅτι αἰτίαν ἔσχε | διὰ τὸν ἥλιον κρούεσθαι πρὸς ἄλληλα.
[683] Col.XIV.11–12.
[684] Col.XVII.
[685] Col.XVI.

By saying 'to jump' he makes it clear that (the *eonta*), divided into small particles, moved and jumped in the air, and by jumping all and each severally were set together with one another. And they continued jumping until each came to its like.[686]

The particular verb *throskō* emphasised here, and quoted from the poem, is the same we saw being used in the gold tablets as a mystic formula and I have suggested that it signifies the return of the soul to its divine abode which is aether located among the stars in the Milky Way. An argument like the one made by the Derveni author would be in accordance with this interpretation since the initiate would refer, at an allegorical level, to this 'leaping forward' in imitation of the *eonta*'s movement prior to them coming together. They would perform this movement wishing to go back εἰς τὸ σύνηθες since they jump as a bull, a ram and a kid all of which I have identified as constellations related to Zeus and Dionysos. The same verb, as already mentioned, is also found in the *Orphic Rhapsodies* describing the birth of Phanes/Protogonos, the son of aether, bursting out of the cosmic egg into the aether.[687] This verb, thus, appears to have an important meaning in Orphic texts and practices. The Derveni author also says that the goddesses Aphrodite Ourania, Peitho, Harmonia, and *aphrodisiazein* and *thornusthai* are just different names for Zeus' functions: Aphrodite refers to the *eonta* being brought into contact with each other, Peitho refers to the *eonta* yielding to each other and Harmonia refers to many *eonta* being closely attached (ἁρμόζειν) by god.[688] We could describe this perception of cosmos as a dual-faceted monism, where everything is one but we also have manifestations of matter which are underlaid by Nous without which nothing would exist:

[ἀεὶ] τὸν Νοῦν πάντων ἄξιον εἶναι μόν[ο]ν ἐόντα,
[ὥσπερ]εἰ μηδὲν τἆλλα εἴη· οὐ γὰρ [οἷόν τε δι' α]ὐτὰ εἶναι
[τὰ νῦν] ἐόντα ἄγ[ε]υ τοῦ Νοῦ.

Mind, being alone, is always worth everything, as if the rest were nothing. For it is not [possible] for the present *eonta* to exist [because of] them without Mind.[689]

---

686 Col.XXI.1–5.
687 OR8: Πρωτόγονος Φαέθων περιμήκεος Αἰθέρος υἱός: 'And Protogonos Phaethon the son of enormous Aether'. OR10: ^'Ῥῆξε δ' ἔπειτα Φάνης νεφέλην, ἀργῆτα χιτῶνα, | <ἐκ δὲ> σχισθέντος κρανίου πολυχανδέος ᾠοῦ | ἐξέθορε πρώτιστος ἀνέδραμε τ' ἀρσενόθηλυς | Πρωτόγονος πολυτίμητος^: 'Then Phanes broke through the clouds his bright tunic and from the divided shell of the great-encompassing egg he sprang upwards first of all the hermaphrodite and highly-honoured Protogonos....'
688 Col.XXI.5–12.
689 Col.XVI.10–12.

This is very clearly expressed through the last phrase of the passage quoted in the previous page: '[created] from different things not different ones but diversified ones'.[690]

The process of creation is regulated through temperature. If the heat is low, the particles are in a state of floating in the air; if the heat is too high the particles strike against each other (the Kronos stage); when the heat comes to the right level through the cooling effect of Zeus/*aer*/Mind, then creation takes place (the Zeus stage). One could, thus, conceive *aer* as the life-giving element or soul. In the same spirit the Derveni author explains that Night is called *trophos* in the Orphic poem because: 'those things which the sun thaws by heating, night congeals by making cold'.[691] This delicate balance between heat and cold is why the Sun is situated precisely in the middle of the sky, not too far from and not too close to the earth: 'For when the sun is separated and confined in the middle, it (sc. Mind) holds fast, having fixed them, both those above the sun and those below'.[692] And even though the Sun has this central role in the creative process, it is still an entity created by Zeus/Nous: 'If the god did not wish the present *eonta* to exist, he would not have made the sun. But he made it of such a form and size as <he recounts at the beginning of the *logos*>'.[693] There is, thus, an emphasis on fire and *aer* as primal substances of the creation of the cosmos. There is also a hint of astronomy in the Derveni author's commentary since he refers to the stars which float away in the distance far away from each other, due to Necessity, and an explanation of why they cannot be seen during daytime, being overshadowed by the light of the Sun:

καὶ λαμπρό[τ]ητα· τὰ δ' ἐξ ὧν ἡ σελήνη [λ]ευκότατα μὲν
τῶν ἄλλων κατὰ τὸν αὐτὸν λόγον μεμερισμένα,
θερμὰ δ' οὐκ ἔστι. ἔστι δὲ καὶ ἄλλα νῦν ἐν τῶι ἀέρι ἑκὰς
ἀλλήλων α[ἰ]ωρούμεν', ἀλλὰ τῆς μὲν ἡμέρης ἄδηλ' ἐστὶν
ὑ[π]ὸ τοῦ ἡλίου ἐπικρατούμενα, τῆς δὲ νυκτὸς ἐόντα
δῆλά ἐστιν, ἐπικρατεῖται δὲ διὰ σμικ[ρ]ότητα.
αἰωρεῖται δ' αὐτῶν ἕκαστα ἐν ἀνάγκηι, ὡς ἂν μὴ συνίηι
πρὸς ἄλληλα·

---

690 Col.XV.9–10.
691 Col.X.11–13: "τροφ[ὸν] δὲ λέγων αὐ]τὴν αἰγί[ζε]ται ὅτι [ἄ]σσα | ὁ ἥλι[ος θερμαίνων δι]αλύει ταῦτα ἡ νὺξ ψύ[χουσα] | συ[νίστησι........]
692 Col.XV.3–5: χωρ[ι]ζομένου γὰρ τοῦ ἡλίου καὶ ἀπολαμβανομένου | ἐν μέσωι πήξας ἴσχει καὶ τἄνωθε τοῦ ἡλίου | καὶ τὰ κάτωθεν.
693 Col.XXV.10–12: ὁ θεὸς εἰ μὴ ἤθελεν εἶναι, οὐκ ἂν ἐπόησεν ἥλιον. ἐπόησε δὲ | τοιοῦτον καὶ τ[ο]σοῦτον γινόμενον οἷος ἐν ἀρχῆι τοῦ λόγου | διηγεῖτᾳι. The translation in < > is my own since it was considered more accurate.

and brightness; but those out of which the moon (is composed) are the whitest of all, distributed according to the same principle, but are not hot. There are also others now in the air floating at a great distance from each other, but during the day they are invisible because they are overcome by the sun, while during the night they are visible but are overcome because of (their) smallness. Each of these is floating of necessity so as not to come together with one another...[694]

It can be suggested, based on Col.XVII, that the 'Zeus stage' was not the last one but that another stage followed after this where the *eonta* would return to their initial floating state:

καὶ "ὕστατον" ἔφησεν ἔσεσθαι τοῦτον, ἐπείτ'
ὠνομάσθη Ζεὺς καὶ τοῦτο αὐτῶι διατελεῖ ὄνομα ὄγ,
μέχρι εἰς τὸ αὐτὸ εἶδος τὰ νῦν ἐόντα συνεστάθη
ἐν ὧιπερ πρόσθεν ἐόντα ἠιωρεῖτο.

He also said that it will be 'last', after it was named Zeus and this continues being its name until the present *eonta* were set together into the same state in which they were floating as former *eonta*.[695]

It is tempting to suggest that this will happen through a different cosmological stage actualised through a different manifestation of Zeus, which could be Dionysos. This might be the meaning of the enigmatic phrase from the *Orphic Rhapsodies*: 'And so father Zeus formed all things, and Bacchos completed them.'[696] The role of Dionysos, thus, would have been to bring the materialised *eonta* back to their initial aetherial state; the astral immortality of the gold tablets might be a symbolic understanding of this return, and the transformation of mortals into *bacchoi*, the way to get back.

It can be argued that the Derveni author's interpretation is not so 'out of character' of our understanding of Orphism so far, as established in the previous chapters. We have seen that the airy nature of the soul was identified as an Orphic belief, that astronomy might have underlain the gold tablet's practice, that the nature of some Orphic texts must have been cosmogonical/scientific, theological and in some cases astronomical, that a creative intelligence was a central part of Orphic theogonical texts, and that gods were often interchanged, as for example Apollo with Dionysos, Dionysos with Zeus, Dionysos with Hades, or Dionysos

---

694 Col.XXV.1–8.
695 Col.XVII.6–9.
696 OR80: Κραῖνε μὲν οὖν Ζεὺς πάντα πατήρ, Βάκχος δ' ἐπέκραινε.

with Phanes. The next step, then, must be to establish whether the Derveni author's interpretation was a personal/arbitrary one or one that was followed by other Orphics.

5.1.3.1 How unique was the Derveni author's interpretation?

Firstly, I have already referred in the previous chapter to an abundance of sources referring to the aetherial nature of the soul and its re-unification with aether after death. The Derveni author's interpretation of the Orphic text, though, is more elaborate and complicated than a perception of the soul as made of divine aether; nonetheless, such a perception still requires background knowledge and justification. We also have authors such as Aristotle, Plato, Plutarch and others referring to allegorical interpretation of myth in relation to religion. If allegorical interpretations such as the Derveni author's are related to religion in other ancient sources, it becomes more probable that such an interpretation was related to Orphism and that perhaps it was not as arbitrary as assumed.

A passage from Aristotle's *De anima* refers to those who suppose that the first principle, and similarly the soul, is one and made of a pair of opposites such as hot and cold:

> διὸ καὶ τοῖς ὀνόμασιν ἀκολουθοῦσιν, οἱ μὲν τὸ θερμὸν λέγοντες, ὅτι διὰ τοῦτο καὶ τὸ ζῆν ὠνόμασται, οἱ δὲ τὸ ψυχρὸν διὰ τὴν ἀναπνοὴν καὶ τὴν κατάψυξιν καλεῖσθαι ψυχήν. τὰ μὲν οὖν παραδεδομένα περὶ ψυχῆς, καὶ δι' ἃς αἰτίας λέγουσιν οὕτω, ταῦτ' ἐστίν.

> Thus they appeal to etymology also; those who identify the soul with heat derive ζῆν (to live) from ζεῖν (to boil), but those who identify it with cold maintain that soul (ψυχή) is so called after the cooling process (κατάψυξις) associated with respiration. These, then, are the traditional views about the soul and the grounds upon which they are held.[697]

This is a theory very similar to the one found in the Derveni Papyrus and also based in etymological arguments. It might be of importance that a few paragraphs later on, Aristotle refers to the theory found in the Orphic texts already discussed, that the soul is airy and inhaled through breathing.[698] Iamblichus comments on this passage from Aristotle and gives some additional details of the Orphic beliefs about the soul:

---

697 Arist. *De an.* 405b28–31 (Tr. Hett).
698 Arist. *De an.* 410b28–411a3: 'The theory in the so-called poems of Orpheus presents the same difficulty; for this theory alleges that the soul, borne by the winds, enters from the universe into animals when they breathe' (Tr. Hett). For ancient text see p.14.

Τινὲς δὲ τῶν φυσικῶν σύνοδον τῶν ἐναντίων συνυφαίνουσι, οἷον θερμοῦ καὶ <ψυχροῦ>, ξηροῦ καὶ ὑγροῦ. Καὶ γὰρ τὸ ζῆν ἀπὸ τοῦ ἀναζεῖν ὑπὸ τοῦ θερμοῦ καὶ τὴν ψυχὴν ἀπὸ τοῦ ἀναψύχεσθαι ὑπὸ τοῦ ψυχροῦ ὠνομάσθαι ἀποφαίνονται, καὶ ἅμα ἐπ' ἀμφοτέρων <ἐτυμολογοῦσι πρὸς τὴν οἰκείαν δόξαν· ἢ γὰρ ψυχὴν τὸ πῦρ λέγουσιν> ἢ τὸν ἀναπνεόμενον ἀέρα ψυχὴν νομίζουσιν· ὥσπερ Ἀριστοτέλης μὲν ἐν τοῖς Ὀρφικοῖς ἔπεσι φησι λέγεσθαι τὴν ψυχὴν εἰσιέναι ἐκ τοῦ ὅλου ἀναπνεόντων ἡμῶν φερομένην ὑπὸ τῶν ἀνέμων· ἔοικέ γε μὴν αὐτὸς ὁ Ὀρφεὺς χωρὶς ὑπολαμβάνειν εἶναι καὶ μίαν τὴν ψυχήν, ἀφ' ἧς πολλὰς μὲν εἶναι διαιρέσεις, πολλὰς δὲ καὶ μέσας ἐπιπνοίας καθήκειν ἐπὶ τὰς μεριστὰς ψυχὰς ἀπὸ τῆς ὅλης ψυχῆς.

Certain of the physical philosophers make the soul a union woven together from opposites, such as hot and dry and wet. For they derive the word "live" from "to boil up" due to heat, and the word "soul" from "to cool down" due to cold, and in both cases <they produce etymologies to accord with their beliefs; for either they say that fire is the substance of the soul,> or they consider that the air breathed into the body is soul, as, according to Aristotle, it is said in the Orphic poems that the soul enters into us from the Universe, borne by the winds, when we breathe; and it seems certainly that Orpheus himself considered that the soul was separate and one, and that out of it there spring many divisions, and that many intermediary "breaths" descended to the individual souls from the universal soul.[699]

The idea that there is one individual soul which is airy and participated in individual beings is expressed in the DP since Zeus/air/Nous is the element that leads to the creation of beings through the cooling effect. Air, thus, as already mentioned, is the essential component which gives life and could be identified as soul. The expression τὸν ἀναπνεόμενον ἀέρα ψυχὴν νομίζουσιν is similar to what is said in the DP about Moira, the divine *phronēsis* of god dwelling in the air: καὶ τἆλλα πάν[τ]α εἶναι | ἐν τῶι ἀέρι [πνε]ῦμα ἐόν. τοῦτ' οὖν τὸ πνεῦμα Ὀρφεὺς | ὠνόμασεν Μοῖραν.[700] Macrobius in his *Saturnalia* also relates the generating power of the sun through heat to Orpheus' words:

> Apollinem Πατρῷον cognominaverunt non propria gentis unius aut civitatis religione sed ut auctorem progenerandarum omnium rerum, quod sol umoribus exsiccatis ad progenerandum omnibus praebuit causam, ut ait Orpheus, πατρὸς ἔχοντα νόον καὶ ἐπίφρονα βουλήν. unde nos quoque Ianum patrem vocamus, solem sub hac appellatione venerantes.

> They named Apollo Patroios ('Ancestral'), not because of a belief specific to a single nation or community, but as the source of generation for all things, because the sun dried up moisture and so began the general process of propagation, "having" as Orpheus says "a father's

---

[699] Iambl. *De An.* 1.8 (Tr. Dillon). Supplement < > by Festugière.
[700] Col.XVIII.2-3: '...and all else are in the air, being breath. It is this breath that Orpheus called Moira.' For the supremacy of Zeus in mythologists in relation to unity as a first principle see also Arist. *Metaph.* 14.4: 1091b.

good sense and shrewd counsel'". For that reason we call Janus father, worshipping the sun under that form of address.[701]

Once more, Orpheus' words are associated with cosmological interpretations and in reference to the generative force of the sun/heat. In this case the sun is identified with Apollo, who as I suggested in previous chapters must have been closely associated with Dionysos for Orphics and worshipped through a deity such as Protogonos/Phanes. A few lines later [1.17.46] Macrobius gives the epithet Ἐλελεὺς to Apollo and in 1.18.1 he says that Apollo and Dionysos are essentially the same. The epithet Ἐλελεὺς is otherwise attested only by Ovid and as an epithet of Dionysos: 'father Eleleus'.[702] Macrobius says that the epithet refers to the circular movement of the sun around the earth and he gives a verse from Euripides' *Phoenissae* to demonstrate this: Ἥλιε, θοαῖς ἵπποισιν εἱλίσσων φλόγα ['Sun, who on swift steeds whirl your blaze in an arc…'].[703] Macrobius also singles out *nous* and *boulēn* as important elements of the creative process just as we see the Derveni author doing.

Orphic mythology is associated with cosmology in Plutarch, too. A passage already discussed from *De E apud Delphos* says that:

> ἀκούομεν οὖν τῶν θεολόγων τὰ μὲν ἐν ποιήμασι τὰ δ' ἄνευ μέτρου λεγόντων καὶ ὑμνούντων ὡς ἄφθαρτος ὁ θεὸς καὶ ἀΐδιος πεφυκώς, ὑπὸ δή τινος εἱμαρμένης γνώμης καὶ λόγου μεταβολαῖς ἑαυτοῦ χρώμενος ἄλλοτε μὲν εἰς πῦρ ἀνῆψε τὴν φύσιν πάνθ' ὁμοιώσας πᾶσιν, ἄλλοτε δὲ παντοδαπὸς ἔν τε μορφαῖς καὶ ἐν πάθεσι καὶ δυνάμεσι διαφόροις γιγνόμενος, ὡς γίγνεται νῦν ὁ κόσμος.

Now we hear the theologians affirming and reciting, sometimes in verse and sometimes in prose, that the god is deathless and eternal in his nature, but, owing forsooth to some predestined design and reason, he undergoes transformations of his person, and at one time enkindles his nature into fire and makes it altogether like all else, and at another time he

---

701 Macrob. *Sat.* 1.17.42 (Tr. Kaster). See also Macrob. *Sat.* 1.17.52–56 where he describes a cosmology similar to the Derveni one.

702 Ov. *Met.* IV.9–17: *parent matresque nurusque | telasque calathosque infectaque pensa reponunt | turaque dant Bacchumque vocant Bromiumque | Lyaeumqu eignigenamque satumque iterum solumque bimatrem; | additur his Nyseus indetonsusque Thyoneus | et cum Lenaeo genialis consitor uvae | Nycteliusque Eleleusque parens et Iacchus et Euhan, | et quae praeterea per Graias plurima gentes | nomina, Liber, habes*: 'The matrons and young wives all obey, put by weaving and work-baskets, leave their tasks unfinished; they burn incense, calling on Bacchus, naming him also Bromius, Lyaeus, son of the thunderbolt, twice born, child of two mothers; they hail him as Nyseus also, Thyoneus of the unshorn locks, Lenaeus, planter of the joy-giving vine, Nyctelius, father Eleleus, Iacchus, and Euhan, and all the many names besides by which thou art known, O Liber, throughout the towns of Greece.' (Tr. Miller).

703 Macrob. *Sat.* 1.17.46. Eur. *Phoen.* 3 (Tr. Kovacs).

undergoes all sorts of changes in his form, his emotions and his powers, even as the universe does to-day.[704]

He then says, in a passage already discussed in Chapter 4, that for the transformation of the god into 'winds and water, earth and stars, and into the generations of plants and animals', the theologians 'speak in a deceptive way of what he undergoes in his transformation as a tearing apart, as it were, and a dismemberment' and call him Dionysos, Zagreus, Nyctelius and Isodaetes.[705] These theologians, thus, interpret mythology in an allegorical way to describe a cosmology, in much the same way as the Derveni author – and not just any mythology, but Orphic mythology such as the Zagreus myth. This pantheistic description of the cosmos' creation is similar to Zeus' creation after the swallowing episode as described in the DP. Plutarch may allude to this in *De communibus notitiis adversus Stoicos*, again in relation to cosmogonical and theological ideas and the opposites of vice and good:

> οὐκοῦν ἐν θεοῖς ἀγαθὸν οὐδὲν ἔστιν, ἐπεὶ μηδὲ κακόν· οὐδέ, ὅταν ὁ Ζεὺς εἰς ἑαυτὸν ἀναλύσας τὴν ὕλην ἅπασαν εἷς γένηται καὶ τὰς ἄλλας ἀνέλῃ διαφοράς, οὐδέν ἐστιν ἀγαθὸν τηνικαῦτα, μηδενός γε κακοῦ παρόντος.

> So then, among the gods there is nothing good, since there is nothing evil either; and, whenever Zeus, having reduced all matter to himself, becomes one and abolishes all difference else, then, there being nothing evil present, there is nothing good either.[706]

Even though this work is dealing with Stoics, the absorption of all matter by Zeus can only refer to a mythological episode such as the one found in the Orphic Theogony. Also, in his work *De Defectu Oraculorum*, Plutarch says: 'I hear this from many persons, and I observe that the Stoic 'Conflagration,' just as it feeds on the verses of Heracleitus and Orpheus, is also seizing upon those of Hesiod'.[707] Some of the ideas found in the DP are also close to Stoic ideas. The central idea of Zeus/aer being the divine denominator of the whole cosmos is the same as the Stoic theory of *Heimarmenē* and *Theios Logos*, the eternal divine breath which was Zeus himself and which underlies and unites everything.[708] As Cleanthes

---

704 Plut. *De E.* 388f (Tr. Babbitt).
705 Plut. *De E.* 389a (Tr. Babbitt). For text see p.186.
706 Plut. *Comm. not.* 1065b (Tr. Cherniss).
707 Plut. *De def. or.* 415f–416a: "ἀκούω ταῦτ'," ἔφη, "πολλῶν καὶ ὁρῶ τὴν Στωικὴν ἐκπύρωσιν ὥσπερ τὰ Ἡρακλείτου καὶ Ὀρφέως ἐπινεμομένην ἔπη οὕτω καὶ τὰ Ἡσιόδου καὶ συνεξάπτουσαν (Tr. Babbitt). Cleombrotus is the speaker.
708 West, 1983, p.238.

said: 'the soul extends throughout the cosmos, and we partake of it as animate beings'.[709] Plutarch also says that Chrysippus believed that when a baby is born, the *pneuma* 'cooled and tempered by the air' is transformed into a living being.[710] This process is similar to the one described by the Derveni author to be performed by Zeus/air.

Some scholars, such as Brisson, Casadesús and Jourdan have argued for a Stoic identity of the Derveni text, based on similarities such as the importance of etymology and allegory, the existence of a rational god who determines how things are and how they will be at the centre of a cosmic theology, pantheistic elements and the importance of air and fire.[711] However, as we saw, physical allegory and etymology was not specific to the early Stoics and as Betegh notes physical allegory was practiced much earlier from authors such as Theagenes of Rhegium (6th B.C.), Stesimbrotus of Thasos (5th B.C.) and Metrodorus of Lampascus (5th B.C.).[712] It is also evident in the Derveni Papyrus, that even though fire/heat has a cosmogonical importance, the prevalent element is aer which always existed and always will and which underlays everything that exists. This comes in contrast to one of the main Stoic ideas, that of *ekpyrosis* which supports that the whole cosmos is engulfed by fire every now and then. As Betegh argues, the cosmogonical roles that fire and aer have in the Derveni papyrus and the 'relative hierarchy established between them, create a strong constrast that render the assumed similarity rather superficial.'[713] Piano also argues that it is not necessary to resort to the Stoics to justify distinctive ideas of the Derveni text such as the importance of air as a divine element, which she considers to be more related to the Pre-Socratic ideas of authors such as Anaximenes, Philolaus and Diogenes

---

[709] *SVF* I 495: τὴν δὲ ψυχὴν δι'ὅλου τοῦ κόσμου διήκειν, ἧς μέρος μετέχοντας ἡμᾶς ἐμψυχοῦσθαι.

[710] Plut. *De Stoic. Rep.* 1052f = *SVF* II 806A: Τὸ βρέφος ἐν τῇ γαστρὶ φύσει τρέφεσθαι νομίζει καθάπερ φυτόν· ὅταν δὲ τεχθῇ, ψυχόμενον ὑπὸ τοῦ ἀέρος καὶ στομούμενον τὸ πνεῦμα μεταβάλλειν καὶ γίνεσθαι ζῷον· ὅθεν οὐκ ἀπὸ τρόπου τὴν ψυχὴν ὠνομάσθαι παρὰ τὴν ψῦξιν: 'He believes that the foetus in the womb is nourished by nature like a plant but that at birth the vital spirit, being chilled and tempered by the air, changes and becomes animal and that hence soul has not inappropriately been named after this process.' (Tr. Cherniss).

[711] Betegh, 2007, p.137. Brisson, 2009, p.28. Jourdan, 2003. Casadesús, 2010, p.196/200/202/204/209-210/218/221/224-225/232/237-239: 'En definitiva, dado que el Papiro de Derveni anticipa algunos de los principales rasgos del estoicismo antiguo, estamos autorizados a considerarlo como un documento "protoestoico", que refleja la labor tanto exegética como especulativa desarrollada en un ambiente ilustrado por un autor anónimo interesado en interpretar los poemas de Orfeo.'

[712] Betegh, 2007, p.138–139. Piano, 2016, p.286–295.

[713] Betegh, 2007, p.144.

of Apollonia.[714] Similarly, Megino Rodríguez in his discussion on the similarities between the daimons in the Derveni Papyrus and in early Stoicism argues that: 'It seems clear that the philosophical universe of the DA is mainly related to authors such as Heraclitus, Democritus or Anaxagoras' but that based on the similarities with early Stoicism he can be called a pre-Stoic in the same way he is pre-Socratic or pre-Platonic.[715] Indeed, as we will see in the following section, the Derveni author has several similarities to Pre-Socratic philosophers and considering matters of dating it is more probable that he belongs in that sphere of influence or theoretical narrative. I would argue, thus, that Stoicism, which developed in the 3rd century B.C., was influenced by allegorical interpretations of Orphic texts such as the one of the Derveni author, or that they interpreted Orphic texts in this way themselves and formed their own cosmology. It is probable, though, that the latter case would still require an existing point of departure.

Plato in the *Cratylus* also discusses the etymological interpretation of gods' names and interprets Zeus as the one 'through whom (δι' ὄν) all living beings have the gift of life (ζῆν)' and Kronos as 'the purity (καθαρόν) and unblemished nature of his <Zeus'> mind (τοῦ νοῦ)'.[716] Even though this is similar to the Derveni author's commentary, since the name of Kronos is related to Nous and the interpretation of Zeus' name is similar to the life-giving air of the DP, we are more interested in what Hermogenes says straight afterwards:

ΕΡΜ: Καὶ μὲν δή, ὦ Σώκρατες, ἀτεχνῶς γέ μοι δοκεῖς ὥσπερ οἱ ἐνθουσιῶντες ἐξαίφνης χρησμῳδεῖν.
ΣΩ: Καὶ αἰτιῶμαί γε, ὦ Ἑρμόγενες, μάλιστα αὐτὴν ἀπὸ Εὐθύφρονος τοῦ Προσπαλτίου προσπεπτωκέναι μοι. ἕωθεν γὰρ πολλὰ αὐτῷ συνῆ καὶ παρεῖχον τὰ ὦτα. κινδυνεύει οὖν ἐνθουσιῶν οὐ μόνον τὰ ὦτά μου ἐμπλῆσαι τῆς δαιμονίας σοφίας, ἀλλὰ καὶ τῆς ψυχῆς ἐπειλῆφθαι.

HER: Indeed, Socrates, you do seem to me to be uttering oracles, exactly like an inspired prophet.
SOC: Yes, Hermogenes, and I am convinced that the inspiration came to me from Euthyphro the Prospaltian. For I was with him and listening to him a long time early this morning. So

---

[714] See Piano, 2016, p.309-347: 'Dovremo allora concludere che tutti questi punti di contatto anche terminologici con il nostro testo rafforzano l'ipotesi che πνεῦμα vada inteso come sinonimo di ἀήρ, alla stregua del pensiero fisico di area milesia riecheggiato da Filolao, con il quale l'Autore condivide anche l'idea della massa infuocata al centro del cosmo' (p.346).
[715] Megino Rodríguez, 2018, p.43.
[716] Pl. *Cra.* 396b: συμβαίνει οὖν ὀρθῶς ὀνομάζεσθαι οὗτος ὁ θεὸς εἶναι, δι' ὃν ζῆν ἀεὶ πᾶσι τοῖς ζῶσιν ὑπάρχει. […] κόρον γὰρ σημαίνει οὐ παῖδα, ἀλλὰ τὸ καθαρὸν αὐτοῦ καὶ ἀκήρατον τοῦ νοῦ (Tr. Fowler). See Pl. *Cra.* 396a–397a.

he must have been inspired, and he not only filled my ears but took possession of my soul with his superhuman wisdom.[717]

We can see, thus, that such etymological interpretation was a practice of 'inspired prophets', and it is possible that the Derveni author was one of them, especially since, as we will see, the verb χρη[στη]ριαζομ[is used in Col.V, and the author also says: '...for them we enter the oracle in order to ask'.[718] What is more, a few paragraphs later Socrates discusses the etymology of body and soul and refers specifically to those around Orpheus (οἱ ἀμφὶ Ὀρφέα) explaining why they called the body σῆμα giving etymological reasons. Socrates uses the word δοκοῦσι which means that 'the followers of Orpheus' 'have the opinion' or 'they suppose/consider' that this is the meaning of the word (δοκοῦσι μέντοι μοι μάλιστα θέσθαι οἱ ἀμφὶ Ὀρφέα τοῦτο τὸ ὄνομα).[719] This suggests that there was deliberate etymological interpretation of Orphic works by a group of people. I have already discussed this passage in depth but what I would like to emphasise here is that Orphic works are related to etymological interpretations during Plato's time, which suggests that this was a usual practice followed by Orphics, or at least not out of the ordinary.[720] The interpretation that Socrates gives of the word ψυχή (soul) in the previous paragraph, is related to breathing as a life-force:

ΣΩ: Ὡς μὲν τοίνυν ἐκ τοῦ παραχρῆμα λέγειν, οἶμαί τι τοιοῦτον νοεῖν τοὺς τὴν ψυχὴν ὀνομάσαντας, ὡς τοῦτο ἄρα, ὅταν παρῇ τῷ σώματι, αἴτιόν ἐστι τοῦ ζῆν αὐτῷ, τὴν τοῦ ἀναπνεῖν δύναμιν παρέχον καὶ ἀναψῦχον.

SOC: To speak on the spur of the moment, I think those who gave the soul its name had something of this sort in mind: they thought when it was present in the body it was the cause of its living, giving it the power to breathe and reviving it.[721]

This is again similar to what the Derveni author says when he identifies Zeus/air with the divine breath and substance which cools down (ψύχειν) and gives life to the *eonta*.

Two passages from Diodorus Siculus refer to cosmological ideas through the mythological vehicle and in relation to etymological analysis in reference to Orphic ideas. I have already referred to the first one in Chapter 4, where Diodorus refers to Dionysos' name and quotes Orpheus: 'And this is why (τούνεκά) men

---

[717] Pl. *Cra.* 396d (Tr. Fowler).
[718] Col.V.3–4: χρησ[τ]ηριάζον[ται].[.]......[..]ι | αὐτοῖς πάριμεν [εἰς τὸ μα]ντεῖον ἐπερ[ω]τήσ[οντες]
[719] Pl. *Cra.* 400c. For text see p.9. LSJ δοκέω: think; suppose; have or form an opinion.
[720] See p.9 ff and p.97–98 for discussion.
[721] Pl. *Cra.* 399d–e. See also 404c.

call him Phanes and Dionysos'.[722] The word τούνεκά is explanatory and it implies that some of the Orphic texts could be dealing with the explanation of the gods' names' meaning. In this case, according to what Diodorus has said earlier, the explanation that the Orphic texts gave for the name Phanes and Dionysos was through Dionysos' identification with the Sun. Once again, we can see not only that Orphic texts dealt with etymological analysis, but that the Sun was indeed a prominent figure personified as Phanes. What is more, Phanes was conceived to be the same as Dionysos, which is in line with the monotheistic element of the DP. A few paragraphs later, Diodorus quotes another Orphic verse which relates to the name of Demeter:

> καὶ τοὺς Ἕλληνας δὲ ταύτην παραπλησίως Δήμητραν καλεῖν, βραχὺ μετατεθείσης διὰ τὸν χρόνον τῆς λέξεως· τὸ γὰρ παλαιὸν ὀνομάζεσθαι γῆν μητέρα, καθάπερ καὶ τὸν Ὀρφέα προσμαρτυρεῖν λέγοντα "Γῆ μήτηρ πάντων, Δημήτηρ πλουτοδότειρα."
>
> ...and in like manner the Greeks also call it Demeter, the word having been slightly changed in the course of time; for in olden times they called her Ge Meter (Earth Mother), to which Orpheus bears witness when he speaks of: "Earth the Mother of all, Demeter giver of wealth".[723]

The Derveni author also quotes an Orphic verse from a hymn which gives the same origin of Demeter's name: 'She was named Demeter like Ge-Meter, one name from both; for it was the same. It is also said in the Hymns: "Demeter, Rhea, Ge, Meter, Hestia, Deio"'.[724] In this case, we see the etymological interest, but also the monotheistic element which the Derveni author presents in his commentary. Finally in Book 5, Diodorus refers to Zeus in a manner reminiscent of the DP:

> 70.1: Περὶ δὲ τῆς τοῦ Διὸς γενέσεώς τε καὶ βασιλείας διαφωνεῖται· καί τινες μέν φασιν αὐτὸν μετὰ τὴν ἐξ ἀνθρώπων τοῦ Κρόνου μετάστασιν εἰς θεοὺς διαδέξασθαι τὴν βασιλείαν, οὐ βίᾳ κατισχύσαντα τὸν πατέρα, νομίμως δὲ καὶ δικαίως ἀξιωθέντα ταύτης τῆς τιμῆς·
>
> 72.2: διόπερ αὐτὸν προσαγορευθῆναι Ζῆνα μὲν ἀπὸ τοῦ δοκεῖν τοῖς ἀνθρώποις αἴτιον εἶναι τοῦ <u>ζῆν</u>, ταῖς ἐκ τοῦ περιέχοντος εὐκρασίαις τοὺς καρποὺς ἀνάγοντα πρὸς τέλος, πατέρα δὲ διὰ τὴν φροντίδα καὶ τὴν εὔνοιαν τὴν εἰς ἅπαντας, ἔτι δὲ καὶ τὸ δοκεῖν ὥσπερ ἀρχηγὸν εἶναι τοῦ γένους τῶν ἀνθρώπων, ὕπατον δὲ καὶ βασιλέα διὰ τὴν τῆς ἀρχῆς ὑπεροχήν, <u>εὐβουλέα δὲ καὶ μητιέτην</u> διὰ τὴν ἐν τῷ βουλεύεσθαι καλῶς σύνεσιν.

---

[722] Diod. Sic. 1.11.3. For text see p.164.
[723] Diod. Sic. 1.12.4 (Tr. Oldfather).
[724] Col.XXII.9–12: ... Δημήτηρ [δὲ] | ὠνομάσθη ὥσπερ ἡ Γῆ Μήτηρ, ἐξ ἀμφοτέρων ἓ[ν] ὄνομα·_| τὸ αὐτὸ γὰρ ἦν. ἔστι δὲ καὶ ἐν τοῖς "Ὕμνοις εἰρ[η]μένον· | "Δημήτηρ ['Ρ]έα Γῆ Μήτηρ Ἑστία Δηιώι".

> 70.1: Some say that he succeeded to the kingship after Cronus passed from among men into the company of the gods, not by overcoming his father with violence, but in the manner prescribed by custom and justly, having been judged worthy of that honour...
>
> 72.2: It is for this reason also that names have been given him; Zêna, because in the opinion of mankind he is the cause of life (ζῆν) bringing as he does the fruits to maturity by tempering the atmosphere (εὐκρασίαις); Father, because of the concern and goodwill he manifests toward all mankind, as well as because he is considered to be the first cause of the race of men; Most High and King, because of the preeminence of his rule; Good Counsellor and All-wise, because of the sagacity he manifests in the giving of wise counsel.[725]

Firstly, Diodorus refers to a version of the succession myth where Zeus has taken the power from Kronos justly and so there is a good chance that he has in mind the Orphic poem, since the Derveni author emphasises that Zeus took power according to the prophecies as it was just. He then analyses etymologically Zeus' name in the same way as the Derveni author, meaning as the generative force which gives life to the *eonta* through the process of cooling down. Finally, Diodorus also gives the epithets μητιέτην which is also an epithet for Zeus in the DP explained etymologically as representing Zeus' devising mind from *mētis* (counsel/wisdom), and εὐβουλέα which in the gold tablets is evoked as a chthonic deity and where as suggested it represented chthonic Zeus and was often identified with Dionysos too.[726]

Considering all of the above, it seems that etymological analysis of Orphic texts in scientifical and cosmogonical terms was not out of the ordinary. In my opinion, then, we need to consider the Derveni author's commentary as a phenomenon not external to Orphism, but as an internal one. By this I mean that the Derveni author was probably not someone who gave an arbitrary commentary on the Orphic poem because he was fascinated by Pre-Socratic philosophy but someone who analysed the text according to Orphic ideas using practices common to Orphic circles and popular in general at the time, such as etymology and physical theories.

---

[725] Diod. Sic. 5.70.1/72.2 (Tr. Oldfather).
[726] Col.XV. See p.170.

5.1.4 The Derveni Papyrus and Pre-Socratic Philosophy

Throughout the Derveni author's commentary we find Pre-Socratic parallels, especially with Thales, Anaximander, Anaximenes, Herakleitos, Parmenides, Anaxagoras and Diogenes of Apollonia.[727] The prevalent view on the matter is that there is a Pre-Socratic influence on the Derveni commentator, based on two key points: the absence of any direct reference to Plato and the citation of Herakleitos.[728] Even though the term 'Pre-Socratic' is a modern one, and we can assume that the Derveni author would not have Socrates in mind as a turning-point in philosophical thinking, he is likely to have conceived of the above philosophers as a group, since they all had the same approach to the matter of explaining the cosmos. For the Pre-Socratics, it was no longer satisfying to explain the workings of the cosmos through the actions of anthropomorphic gods, but they attempted instead to give an explanation based on observation and rational thought. As Guthrie puts it, philosophy started with the belief that 'not caprice but an inherent *orderliness* underlies the phenomena, and the explanation of nature is to be sought within nature itself'.[729] We need to bear in mind, however, that the Pre-Socratics had not yet rejected all the previous mythical and anthropomorphic conceptions about the cosmos through the inquiry into whether this orderliness had a divine nature. What the Pre-Socratics introduced was that the divine was 'subject to the uniformity of impersonal power' – which is characteristic of the Derveni author's interpretation since, as we saw, he equated Zeus with *aer* and Nous.[730] On a more general level, the discussion of the connection between the Derveni Papyrus and Pre-Socratic philosophy reveals the development and interaction between ideas through time and space, allowing us to see how Orphism fits into the wider world of ideas. It could be that this different way of explaining the world, which was characterised by systematisation and generalisation, was interesting to the Derveni author, and since in many cases it was not yet detached from divine causation it could, through parallelism with Orphic

---

727 The translations for the Pre-Socratic passages are taken from the KRS edition.
728 Brisson, 2009, p.34. As mentioned earlier, Brisson argues for a Stoic influence and the slightly later dating for the composition of the commentary c.300 B.C. (p.28). His interpretation of the last column of the DP is interesting, but in terms of dating I believe that the argument of the absence of any Platonic reference is quite strong. As mentioned in the discussion in p.220 ff it is more probable that the Derveni author was earlier than the Stoics and that they might have been interested in Orphic ideas, as Brisson also suggests (p.36; Cic. *De natura deorum* 2.141; SVF II 906,1077 and 1078).
729 Guthrie, 1962, p.44.
730 Seaford, 2004, p103.

writings, move Orphism to a more universal sphere. As far as the Orphic text in itself is concerned, there is the possibility that it contributed to the evolution from mythos to logos, or that there was a parallel development of philosophy and Orphic beliefs. This matter will be discussed more in Chapter 6.

In Col.IV.7–9, the Derveni author quotes a Herakleitean passage which presents the Erinyes as guardians of justice who will prevent any transgression of boundaries by the sun regarding its size.[731] The notion of Δίκη in Col.IV is closely related to that of ἀνάγκη (Necessity) evident in Col.XXV.7–12, which refers to the stars floating at a distance from each other out of Necessity and explains the reasons for the size of the sun:

αἰωρεῖται δ' αὐτῶν ἕκαστα ἐν ἀνάγκηι, ὡς ἂν μὴ συνίηι
πρὸς ἄλληλα· εἰ γὰρ μή, συνέλθοι [ἂν] ἀλέα ὅσα τὴν αὐτὴν
δύναμιν ἔχει, ἐξ ὧν ὁ ἥλιος συνεστάθη. τὰ νῦν ἐόντα
ὁ θεὸς εἰ μὴ ἤθελεν εἶναι, οὐκ ἂν ἐπόησεν ἥλιον. ἐπόησε δὲ
τοιοῦτον καὶ τ[ο]σοῦτον γινόμενον οἷος ἐν ἀρχῆι τοῦ λόγου
διηγεῖται.

Each of these is floating of necessity so as not to come together with one another; for otherwise all those that have the same property as those from which the sun was composed would come together in a mass. If the god did not wish the present *eonta* to exist, he would not have made the sun. But he made it of such a form and size as is related at the beginning of this account.

The sun has its specific size out of Necessity, and as we are told in Col.IV if it transgresses its size then divine justice will prevail (Col.IV.7–9). Justice and Necessity as important factors in maintaining order and harmony in the universe are also part of Parmenides' theory:

τῶν δὲ συμμιγῶν τὴν μεσαιτάτην ἁπάσαις <ἀρχήν> τε καὶ <αἰτίαν> κινήσεως καὶ γενέσεως
ὑπάρχειν, ἥντινα καὶ δαίμονα κυβερνῆτιν καὶ κληδοῦχον ἐπονομάζει Δίκην τε καὶ Ἀνάγκην.

The middlemost of the mixed rings is the [primary cause] of movement and of coming into being for them all, and he calls it the goddess that steers all, the holder of the keys, Justice and Necessity.[732]

For Parmenides these two forces drive movement and generation; in the DP they maintain order in the universe. Their association with heat and the sun suggests

---

[731] For text and translation see p.245–246. The case of Herakleitos will also be discussed in p.245 ff.
[732] Parmenides, KRS 307 = DK 28A37. Tsantsanoglou, 1997, p.110.

that on a scientifical level they regulate temperature so that the continuation of the generative process is ensured.

In Col.XXI.3-4, the world is formed when the particles θορνύμενα δ' ἕκα[σ]τα συνεστάθη | πρὸς ἄλληλα ('by jumping all and each severally were set together with one another'), an idea that can also be found in Anaxagoras: τὰ συγγενῆ φέρεσθαι πρὸς ἄλληλα.[733] In order for these particles to come together, they have to be triggered to move by Νοῦς (Mind), which strikes them against one another as is noted in Col.XIV.7: 'Because Mind was striking (the *eonta*) against each other, he named it Kronos (i.e. Striking Mind)' (κρούοντα τὸν Νοῦν πρὸς ἄλληλ[α] Κρόνον ὀνομάσας). This once again points to Anaxagoras: 'And when Mind (νοῦς) initiated motion (κινεῖν), from all that was moved Mind was separated, and as much as Mind moved was all divided off'.[734] Further similarities between Anaxagoras' and the Derveni author's Mind, can be identified through comparing the following Anaxagorean passage with Col.XVI:

> τὰ μὲν ἄλλα παντὸς μοῖραν μετέχει, νοῦς δέ ἐστιν ἄπειρον καὶ αὐτοκρατὲς καὶ μέμεικται οὐδενὶ χρήματι, ἀλλὰ μόνος αὐτὸς ἐφ'ἑαυτοῦ ἐστιν [...] ἔστι γὰρ λεπτότατόν τε πάντων χρημάτων καὶ καθαρώτατον, καὶ γνώμην γε περὶ παντὸς πᾶσαν ἴσχει καὶ ἰσχύει μέγιστον· καὶ ὅσα γε ψυχὴν ἔχει [...] καὶ τὰ συμμισγόμενά τε καὶ ἀποκρινόμενα καὶ διακρινόμενα πάντα ἔγνω νοῦς. καὶ ὁποῖα ἔμελλεν ἔσεσθαι καὶ ὁποῖα ἦν καὶ ὅσα νῦν ἔστι καὶ ὁποῖα ἔσται, πάντα διεκόσμησε νοῦς
>
> All other things have a portion of everything, but Mind is infinite and self-ruled, and is mixed with nothing but is all alone by itself [...] For it is the finest of all things and the purest, it has all knowledge about everything and the greatest power; and Mind controls all things, both the greater and the smaller, that have soul [...] And the things that are mingled and separated and divided off, all are known by Mind. And all things that were to be – those that were and those that are now and those that shall be – Mind arranged them all...[735]

The similarities with Col.XVI are not only conceptual but also textual. The Derveni author mentions that Mind alone, is worth everything and that all the things (*eonta*) exist because of Mind who 'is king of all and always will be':

[ἐ]ν τούτοις σημαίνει ὅτι τὰ ὄντα ὑπῆ[ρ]χεν ἀεί, τὰ δὲ
νῦν ἐόντα ἐκ τῶν ὑπαρχόντων γίγ[ε]ται. τὸ δὲ
"[αὐ]τὸς δὲ ἄρα μοῦνος ἔγεντο"· τοῦτο δὲ [λ]έγων δηλοῖ
[ἀεὶ] τὸν Νοῦν πάντων ἄξιον εἶναι μόν[ο]ν ἐόντα,

---

733 KRS 492 = DK 59A41: '...things of a like kind tend together...'
734 KRS 477: καὶ ἐπεὶ ἤρξατο ὁ νοῦς κινεῖν, ἀπὸ τοῦ κινουμένου παντὸς ἀπεκρίνετο, καὶ ὅσον ἐκίνησεν ὁ νοῦς πᾶν τοῦτο διεκρίθη.
735 KRS 476.

[ὥσπερ]εἰ μηδὲν τἆλλα εἴη· οὐ γὰρ [οἷόν τε δι' α]ὐτὰ εἶναι
[τὰ νῦν] ἐόντα ἄν[ε]υ τοῦ Νοῦ. [καὶ ἐν τῶι ἐχ]ομένωι
[ἔπει τούτ]ου ἄξιον πάντων [τὸν Νοῦν ἔφησεν ε]ἶναι·
"[νῦν δ' ἐστὶ]ν βασιλεὺς πάντ[ων καί τ' ἔσσετ' ἔ]πειτα".
[δῆλον ὅτι] Νοῦς καὶ π[άντων βασιλεὺς ἐστι τα]ὐτό

In these verses he indicates that the *eonta* always existed, and that the present *eonta* come to be from the existing ones. As for the phrase "and he himself became the sole one", by saying this he makes it clear that Mind, being alone, is always worth everything, as if the rest were nothing. For it is not [possible] for the present *eonta* to exist [because of] them (sc.the excisting ones) without Mind. [Also in the verse] after this [he said that Mind] is worth everything: "[And now he is] king of all [and will be] afterwards". [It is clear that] 'Mind' and ['King of all' are the] same thing...'.[736]

Laks argues that the Derveni Mind is not an independent entity, as we can conclude from the identification of Zeus and his intelligent air in Col.XVIII-XIX, and therefore that this is a doctrine of Diogenes of Apollonia.[737] According to the Derveni author, though, the Mind *is* Zeus and Zeus *is* air and thus the divine power behind the generative process is indeed one independent entity. The fact that Mind is Zeus is noted by the Derveni author in a quotation from the Orphic poem in Col.XV.11-12: τὸ δ' "ἔπειτ[α δὲ μητίετα Ζεὺ]ς"· ὅτι μὲν οὐχ ἕτερ[ος] | ἀλλὰ ὁ αὐ[τὸς δῆλον, which means that the Orphic phrase "and then Zeus the contriver" shows that Zeus is actually Mind, since the previous column is referring to the workings of Mind.[738] The same conclusion can be drawn from the intense presence of the pantheistic element in the hymn and the commentary, with the constant connection of the name Zeus with deities such as Okeanos and concepts such as Metis, and from the fact that, as we saw, Aphrodite Ourania, Zeus, Peitho and Harmonia are names given to the same god.[739] The fact that air is Zeus is denoted by the phrase in Col.XIX.1-4:

---

736 Col.XVI.7-15.
737 Laks, 1997, p.131.
738 This reconstruction of the text is given by all the latest editions of Janko (2002), Betegh (2004) and KPT (2006). Janko gives the following translation: 'The phrase 'and next contriving Zeus' reveals that he is not different (from Mind), but the same'. KPT translation: 'As for the phrase 'and then Zeus the contriver', that he is not a different one but the same is clear'.
739 Col.XXIII.3: "Ὠκεανός" ἐστιν ὁ ἀήρ, ἀὴρ δὲ Ζεύς.: "Okeanos" is the air and that air is Zeus' → A=B, B=C therefore A=C. Col.XIX.4-7: 'Μοῖραν' δ' 'ἐπικλῶσαι'| λέγοντες τοῦ Διὸς τὴν φρόνησιν ἐπικυρῶσαι | λέγουσιν τὰ ἐόντα καὶ τὰ γινόμενα καὶ τὰ μέλλοντα, | ὅπως χρὴ γενέσθαι τε καὶ εἶναι κα[ὶ] παύσασθαι: 'So when they say that 'Moira spun' they are saying that the thought of Zeus ratified in what way what exists and what comes to be and what will come to be must come to be and be and cease'. Col.XXI.5-7: Ἀφροδίτη Οὐρανία | καὶ Ζεὺς καὶ ἀφροδισιάζειν καὶ θόρνυσθαι

ἐκ [τοῦ δ]ὲ̣ [τ]ὰ̣ ἐόντα ἓν [ἕκ]αστον κέκ[λητ]αι ἀπὸ τοῦ
ἐπικρατοῦντος, Ζεὺ[ς] πάντα κατὰ τὸν αὐτὸν
λόγον ἐκλήθη· πάντωγ γὰρ ὁ ἀὴρ ἐπικρατεῖ
τοσοῦτον ὅσον βούλεται.

...since the time when the *eonta* were given names, each after what is dominant (in it), all things were called Zeus according to the same principle. For the air dominates all things as much as it wishes.

The above can be related to the Pre-Socratics' concern to find the *archē*, the first principle from which *ta onta*, 'the beings', have their origin. The *archē* is the 'unifying principle of all reality'; it does not come into being neither does it cease to be, in contrast to the beings that are finite and eventually perish.[740] I have already mentioned that the Derveni author argues that Zeus was not born but always existed, since Mind/aer always existed. The problem of explaining how one principle can be the origin of everything that exists, commonly known as the One-Many problem, seems to have a counterpart in the Derveni papyrus with Zeus' act of swallowing and recreation of the world. Everything becomes one inside of him and is then recreated as many again. The One-Many problem was treated by some Pre-Socratic philosophers, such as Anaximenes and Thales, diachronically as well as synchronically, meaning that while the One was developed into Many, the essence of the One continued to underlie the Many up to the point of the reduction back to One again, while as we are informed by Aristotle, the first principle for Thales was water and for Anaximenes air.[741] We find the same idea in the DP in Col.XVI.7–15 quoted in p.228, where the author describes how the beings which are now came to be from subsisting things which, as we saw above, would not be possible without the Mind who is the king of all and always will be.

The fact that Zeus/Mind/air representing the *archē* was not born but always existed also reminds us of the Parmenidean idea that nothing can be created from

---

καὶ Πειθὼ | καὶ Ἁρμονία τῶι αὐτῶι θεῶι ὄνομα κεῖται: 'Ouranian Aphrodite, Zeus, aphrodising, jumping, Peitho, Harmonia are established names for the same god.'
740 Roochnik, 2004, p.18–19.
741 KRS 139 = Arist. *Metaph*. 984a6-7: Ἀναξιμένης δὲ ἀέρα καὶ Διογένης πρότερον ὕδατος καὶ μάλιστ' ἀρχὴν τιθέασι τῶν ἁπλῶν σωμάτων: 'Anaximenes and Diogenes make air, rather than water, the material principle above the other simple bodies'. Finkelberg, 1986, p.324. KRS 85 = Arist. *Metaph*. 983b19–23: ἀεὶ γὰρ εἶναί τινα φύσιν ἢ μίαν ἢ πλείους μιᾶς, ἐξ ὧν γίγνεται τἆλλα σωζομένης ἐκείνης. τὸ μέντοι πλῆθος καὶ τὸ εἶδος τῆς τοιαύτης ἀρχῆς οὐ τὸ αὐτὸ πάντες λέγουσιν, ἀλλὰ Θαλῆς μὲν ὁ τῆς τοιαύτης ἀρχηγὸς φιλοσοφίας ὕδωρ φησὶν εἶναι: '...for there must be some natural substance, either one or more than one, from which the other things come-into-being, while it is preserved. Over the number, however, and the form of this kind of principle they do not all agree; but Thales, the founder of this type of philosophy, says that it is water...'

nothing because 'nothing' or 'non-being' cannot be imagined, and thus does not exist.[742] The elimination of 'non-being' also eliminates the process of becoming, since 'becoming' presupposes 'non-being'. Therefore, we have the idea of One eternal Being which can be related to the Orphic notion found in the DP that everything can be named Zeus because Zeus is the underlying principle of everything and thus from one aspect everything becomes One.[743] Ferella, plausibly argues that Parmenides' conception of *what-is* might have been shaped by the Orphic idea of monism as found in the DP which maintains as she argues 'that Zeus is μοῦνος because he encloses the whole of reality' and that Parmenides' μουνογενές might be echoing the orphic verse quoted by the Derveni author: αὐτὸς δ'ἄρα μοῦνος ἔγεντο.[744] The Derveni author continues in Col.XVII.1–9 by saying that 'air' has always existed before the things that are now, something that shows that for the Derveni author 'air' was the first principle, while it is also named 'Zeus'; this will be its name until the things that are now set together into the same form in which they were before.[745] Similarly, Anaximenes, as we saw, also considered 'air' to be the primary substance. The notion of the underlying primary substance

---

742 Col.XVI.7–15. For text see p.227–228. KRS 295: ταύτῃ δ'ἔπι σήματ'ἔασι | πολλὰ μάλ', ὡς ἀγένητον ἐὸν καὶ ἀνώλεθρον ἐστιν, | οὖλον μουνογενές τε καὶ ἀτρεμὲς ἠδὲ τέλειον· 'On this way there are very many signs, that being uncreated and imperishable it is, whole and of a single kind and unshaken and perfect.' KRS 296: οὐδέ ποτ' ἦν οὐδ' ἔσται, ἐπεὶ νῦν ἔστιν ὁμοῦ πᾶν, | ἕν, συνεχές· τίνα γὰρ γένναν διζήσεαι αὐτοῦ; | πῇ πόθεν αὐξηθέν; οὔτ' ἐκ μὴ ἐόντος ἐάσσω | φάσθαι σ' οὐδὲ νοεῖν· οὐ γὰρ φατὸν οὐδὲ νοητόν | ἔστιν ὅπως οὐκ ἔστι. τί δ' ἄν μιν καὶ χρέος ὦρσεν | ὕστερον ἢ πρόσθεν, τοῦ μηδενὸς ἀρξάμενον, φῦν; | οὕτως ἢ πάμπαν πέλεναι χρεών ἐστιν ἢ οὐχί· 'It never was, not will be, since it is now, all together, one, continuous. For what birth will you seek for it? How and whence did it grow? I shall not allow you to say nor to think from not being: for it is not to be said nor thought that it is not; and what need would have driven it later rather than earlier, beginning from the nothing, to grow? Thus it must either be completely or not at all.'
743 Roochnik, 2004, p.41. Col.XIX.1–3.
744 Ferella, 2018, p.67–69.
745 Col.XVII.1–9: π[ρ]ότερον ἦν πρ[ὶν ὀν]ομασθῆναι, ἔπ[ει]τα ὠνομάσθη· | ἦν γὰρ καὶ πρόσθεν 'ὢν' ἢ τὰ νῦν ἐόντα συσταθῆναι | ἀὴρ καὶ ἔσται ἀεί· οὐ γὰρ ἐγένετο, ἀλλὰ ἦν. δι' ὅ τι δὲ | ἀὴρ ἐκλήθη δεδήλωται ἐν τοῖς προτέροις. γενέσθαι δὲ | ἐνομίσθη ἐπείτ' ὠνομάσθη Ζεύς, ὡσπερεὶ πρότερον | μὴ ἐών. καὶ "ὕστατον" ἔφησεν ἔσεσθαι τοῦτον, ἐπείτ' | ὠνομάσθη Ζεὺς καὶ τοῦτο αὐτῶι διατελεῖ ὄνομα ὄν, | μέχρι εἰς τὸ αὐτὸ εἶδος τὰ νῦν ἐόντα συνεστάθη | ἐν ὧιπερ πρόσθεν ἐόντα ἠιωρεῖτο· '...it (sc.air) existed before it was named; then ti was named. For air both existed before the present *eonta* were set together and will always exist. For it did not come to be but existed. And why it was called air has been made clear earlier in this book. But after it had been named Zeus it was thought that it was born, as if it did not exist before. He also said that it will be "last", after it was named Zeus, and this continues being his name until the present *eonta* were set together into the same state in which they were floating as former *eonta*.'

can be clearly seen in the following Orphic verse quoted by the Derveni author in Col.XVII.12: "Ζεὺς κεφα[λή, Ζεὺς μέσ]σα, Διὸς δ' ἐκ [π]άντα τέτ[υκται".] ("Zeus is the head, Zeus the middle, and from Zeus is everything fashioned."). The fact that for the Derveni author 'air' was the primary substance is similar to the belief which Aristotle attributes to Orphics, namely the airy nature of soul which enters the body through breathing.[746] In the *Orphic Rhapsodies* too, as we will see, the soul floats in the air and enters the body through breathing.[747] Perhaps this is indicated in the DP in Col.XVIII.1-2 where the Derveni author equates Zeus with Moira: `[τὴν δὲ Μοῖρα]ν" φάμενος [δηλοῖ]´ | τήνδ[ε γῆν] καὶ τἆλλα πάν[τ]α εἶναι | ἐν τῶι ἀέρι [πνε]ῦμα ἐόν ('And by saying ['Moira' he makes it clear] that this [earth] and all else are in the air, being breath.'). The notion of breath being the life-substance, the importance that the Derveni author gives to *air*, and its equation to Zeus find a parallel in Diogenes of Apollonia, since for him air *is* god: a god who is eternal, who steers all things and exists in everything as everything is made out of air. Diogenes' *air* is both intelligence and soul, as can be seen in the following passages:

(1). ἔτι δὲ πρὸς τούτοις καὶ τάδε μεγάλα σημεῖα· ἄνθρωποι γὰρ καὶ τὰ ἄλλα ζῷα ἀναπνέοντα ζώει τῷ ἀέρι καὶ τοῦτο αὐτοῖς καὶ ψυχή ἐστι καὶ νόησις...
(2). καί μοι δοκεῖ τὸ τὴν νόησιν ἔχον εἶναι ὁ ἀὴρ καλούμενος ὑπὸ τῶν ἀνθρώπων, καὶ ὑπὸ τούτου πάντας καὶ κυβερνᾶσθαι καὶ πάντων κρατεῖν· αὐτὸ γάρ μοι τοῦτο θεὸς δοκεῖ εἶναι καὶ ἐπὶ πᾶν ἀφῖχθαι καὶ πάντα διατιθέναι καὶ ἐν παντὶ ἐνεῖναι. καὶ ἔστιν οὐδὲ ἓν ὅ τι μὴ μετέχει τούτου·

(1). Men and the other living creatures live by means of air, through breathing it. And this is for them both soul and intelligence...[748]
(2). And it seems to me that that which has intelligence is what men call air, and that all men are steered by this and that it has power over all things. For this very thing seems to me to be a god and to have reached everywhere and to dispose all things and to be in everything. And there is no single thing that does not have a share of this.[749]

These ideas are once again, strongly comparable to the Derveni author equating Zeus with Mind and air which 'dominates all things as much as it wishes' and which is why all things were called Zeus (Col.XIX.1–4 quoted in p.229).

As we saw, in the DP, 'heat' has a role in maintaining a cosmic balance and the generating quality of the sun is eminent since it is noted that the things that

---

746 Arist. *De an*. A5 410b29 – 411a3. See Chapter 2, p.14.
747 OR89 = OF436F, OF422F, OF426F, OF425F.
748 KRS 602.
749 KRS 603.

are, could not have become such without the sun; as the author notes: if the god had not wished for things that are now to exist, he would not have made the sun.⁷⁵⁰ The predominant role of air and fire/heat in the generative cosmogonical process in the DP is similar to Anaxagoras' theory that all the things in the primal state of cosmos were held by *aether* and air.⁷⁵¹ In the Anaxagorean cosmogony, the generative process took place through a separation of the primitive mixture of things.⁷⁵² This is parallel to the Derveni author's belief that Zeus/aer, the primal and ruling substance which underlies everything was not born but always existed. That everything was one is expressed in Col.XXI.13–15, where the Derveni author notes that:

ἦν μὲν γ[ὰρ καὶ π]ρόσθεν, ὠγομάσθη δὲ γενέσθ[αι] ἐπεὶ
διεκρίθ[η·......δι]ακριθῆναι δηλοῖ οτ[.]..[.....] τεις
κ]ρατεῖ ὥστε δι...

For they existed even before, but the term 'being born' was used for them after they had been separated. [For] 'being separated' is clearly... prevails (?) so that they separate (?)

According to Anaximander the genesis of the world took place with the separation from the primeval state of a generative entity of heat and cold called ἄπειρον, which was the ἀρχὴ of all things and was in constant movement. The earth was

---

750 Col.IX.5–10: γινώσκ[ω]ν οὖν τὸ πῦρ ἀναμεμειγμένον τοῖς | ἄλλοις ὅτι ταράσσοι καὶ κ[ωλ]ύοι τὰ ὄντα συνίστασθαι | διὰ τὴν θάλψιν ἐξαλλάσ[ει ὅσ]ον τε ἱκανόν ἐστιν | ἐξαλλαχθὲν μὴ κωλύ[ειν τὰ] ὄντα συμπαγῆναι. | ὅσα δ' ἂ[ν] ἀφθῆι ἐπικρα[τεῖται, ἐπικ]ρατηθὲν δὲ μίσγεται | τοῖς ἄλ[λ]οις: 'So, knowing that fire, when mixed with the other things, agitates the things that are (the *eonta*) and prevents them from coming together because of the heat, he removes it to such a distance as to render it unable, once removed, to prevent the ὄντα from condensing. For whatever is ignited is subdued, and having been subdued it is mixed with the others'. Col.XIII.10–11: ἄνευ [γὰρ τοῦ ἡ]λ[ίο]υ τὰ ὄντα τοιαῦτα οὐχ οἷόν [τε] | γίγ[εσθαι: 'For without the sun it is not possible for the ὄντα to become such...'. Col.XXV.7–10: For text see p.226.
751 KRS 467 = DK 59B1: καὶ πάντων ὁμοῦ ἐόντων οὐδὲν ἔνδηλον ἦν ὑπὸ σμικρότητος· πάντα γὰρ ἀήρ τε καὶ αἰθὴρ κατεῖχεν ἀμφότερα ἄπειρα ἐόντα· ταῦτα γὰρ μέγιστα ἔνεστιν ἐν τοῖς σύμπασι καὶ πλήθει καὶ μεγέθει: '...And while all things were together, none of them were plain because of their smallness; for air and aither held all things in subjection, both of them being infinite; for these are the greatest ingredients in the mixture of all things, both in number and size'.
752 KRS 468: πρὶν δὲ ἀποκριθῆναι ταῦτα πάντων ὁμοῦ ἐόντων οὐδὲ χροίη ἔνδηλος ἦν οὐδεμία: 'But before these things were separated off, while all things were together, there was not even any colour plain...'. See also KRS 488–490.

surrounded by a sphere of flame that was brought forth out of this generative entity and from the pieces of fire that were split from this sphere, the sun, the moon and the stars were created:

> φησὶ δὲ τὸ ἐκ τοῦ ἀιδίου γόνιμον θερμοῦ τε καὶ ψυχροῦ κατὰ τὴν γένεσιν τοῦδε τοῦ κόσμου ἀποκριθῆναι καί τινα ἐκ τούτου φλογὸς σφαῖραν περιφυῆναι τῷ περὶ τὴν γῆν ἀέρι ὡς τῷ δένδρῳ φλοιόν· ἧστινος ἀπορραγείσης καὶ εἴς τινας ἀποκλεισθείσης κύκλους ὑποστῆναι τὸν ἥλιον καὶ τὴν σελήνην καὶ τοὺς ἀστέρας.

> He says that <the seed of the> hot and cold was separated off at the coming-to-be of this world, and that a kind of sphere of flame from this was formed round the air surrounding the earth, like bark round a tree. When this was broken off and shut off in certain circles, the sun and the moon and the stars were formed.[753]

The above can be related to the generative power of fire in the DP as discussed so far, and Col.XXV.1–9 where the author describes the creation of the moon from a white, cold substance of which presumably the stars which float at a distance from each other are also made.[754] The elements of movement, heat and cold are, thus, essential components to the beginnings of the cosmos for the Derveni author too. The passage from Anaximander also has textual similarities to the beginning of the *Orphic Rhapsodies* and the figure of Phanes, characterised as *aidios*, who broke out of an aetherial egg and created the cosmos. This will be discussed in Chapter 6.

Based on the above, we can see that several Pre-Socratic theories have parallels to the Derveni author's allegorical interpretation of the Orphic text. It is not yet clear why this is the case since we have not touched on the matter of the Derveni author's identity. I have deliberately not discussed the case of Herakleitos, the only Pre-Socratic philosopher who is quoted by the Derveni author, since he will be discussed more closely in section 5.1.7.

5.1.5 Religious Elements and the Derveni Author

The first columns of the papyrus, deal with eschatological rites and beliefs and they offer some clues about the identity of the Derveni author. The knowledge and recounting of religious information, for example, show his interest in these matters. In Col.V.4–8 the Derveni author says:

---

[753] KRS 121 = DK 12A10. The translation in < > is from Laks and Most's edition.
[754] See p.214–215 for text.

αὑτοῖς πάριμεν [εἰς τὸ μα]ντεῖον ἐπερ[ω]τήσ[οντες,]
τῶν μαντευομένων [ἕν]εκεν, εἰ θέμι[...].. ηδα[
ἆρ' Ἅιδου δεινά τί ἀπιστοῦσι; οὐ γινώσ[κοντες ἐ]γύπνια
οὐδὲ τῶν ἄλλων πραγμάτων ἕκαστ[ον], διὰ ποίων ἂν
παραδειγμάτων π[ι]στεύοιεν;

> ...for them we enter the oracle in order to ask, with regard to those seeking a divination, whether it is proper...Why do they disbelieve in the horrors of Hades? Without knowing (the meaning of) dreams or any of the other things, by what kind of evidence would they believe?

The Derveni author includes himself amongst those who enter the oracle in order to obtain answers for the afterlife since the verb is in the first person plural. He must, then, have been a religious figure, presumably a prophet who interpreted oracles, without other possibilities being excluded. Kouremenos argues that 'There is no reason to assume that the speaker here is the Derveni author', but in the absence of any substantial reasons to support the case for a different speaker I agree with Betegh's argument that it is indeed the Derveni author speaking.[755] However, I disagree with Betegh's suggestion that the Derveni author is to be identified with the *magoi* he refers to in the previous columns: the fact that he names them and refers to them as external suggests that he saw them as a distinct group, of which he was not a member.[756] It is possible that the Derveni author was a prophet interpreting dreams and divinations such as the ones mentioned by Plato in the *Timaeus*:

> ἀλλὰ ξυννοῆσαι μὲν ἔμφρονος τά τε ῥηθέντα ἀναμνησθέντα ὄναρ ἢ ὕπαρ ὑπὸ τῆς μαντικῆς τε καὶ ἐνθουσιαστικῆς φύσεως, καὶ ὅσα ἂν φαντάσματα ὀφθῇ, πάντα λογισμῷ διελέσθαι [...] ὅθεν δὴ καὶ τὸ τῶν προφητῶν γένος ἐπὶ ταῖς ἐνθέοις μαντείαις κριτὰς ἐπικαθιστάναι νόμος· οὓς μάντεις αὐτοὺς ὀνομάζουσί τινες, τὸ πᾶν ἠγνοηκότες ὅτι τῆς δι' αἰνιγμῶν οὗτοι φήμης καὶ φαντάσεως ὑποκριταί, καὶ οὔ τι μάντεις, προφῆται δὲ μαντευομένων δικαιότατα ὀνομάζοιντ' ἄν.

> But it belongs to a man when in his right mind to recollect and ponder both the things spoken in dream or waking vision by the divining and inspired nature, and all the visionary forms that were seen, and by means of reasoning to discern about them all [...] Wherefore also it is customary to set the tribe of prophets to pass judgement upon these inspired divinations; and they, indeed, themselves are named "diviners" by certain who are wholly ignorant of the truth that they are not diviners (μάντεις) but interpreters of the mysterious

---

755 KPT, 2006, p.162, 53-54; Betegh, 2004, p.82.
756 Betegh, 2004, p.82. The identity of the *magoi* will be considered shortly.

voice and apparition, for whom the most fitting name would be "prophets (προφῆται) of things divined".[757]

Some scholars, however, disagree. Janko suggested that the Derveni author is speaking sarcastically in the previous passage, with the general meaning being that the people who disbelieve in the terrors of Hades would still disbelieve even if we asked the oracle if it is right to disbelieve (based on his supplement εἰ θεμι[ς ἀπ]ιστεῖν [Col.V.5] and the translation of τῶν μαντευομένων as passive with a neuter subject).[758] I agree, however, with Betegh who finds Janko's supplement unlikely, while Kouremenos takes the phrase τῶν μαντευομένων [ἕν]εκεν to mean either 'for the sake of those who consult the oracle' or 'with regard to those who consult the oracle'.[759] The Derveni author's 'respect' towards oracles and divination might also be indicated by the emphasis that Zeus took the power from Kronos according to the prophecies, which suggests that prophecies should be followed and considered valid.

From the above passage we can also see that the Derveni author believed in the existence of punishments in the afterlife. He also suggests that dream interpretation and some other unspecified things provide evidence for the punishments in Hades. I do not believe, however, that the Orphic poem was of an oracular nature – and interpreted by the author in this capacity – since the author refers to it as a hymn:

[..ὕ]μνον [ὑγ]ιῆ καὶ θεμ[ι]τὰ λέγο[ντα· ἱερουργεῖ]το γὰρ
[τῇ]ι ποήσει. [κ]αὶ εἰπεῖν οὐχ οἷόν τ[ε τὴν τῶν ὀ]νομάτων
[λύ]σιν καίτ[οι] ῥηθέντα. ἔστι δὲ ξ[ένη τις ἡ] πόησις
[κ]αὶ ἀνθρώ[ποις] αἰνι[γμ]ατώδης, [κε]ὶ [Ὀρφεὺ]ς αὐτ[ὸ]ς
[ἐ]ρίστ' αἰν[ίγμα]τα οὐκ ἤθελε λέγειν, [ἐν αἰν]ίγμασ[ι]ν δὲ
[μεγ]άλᾳ. ἱερ[ολογ]εῖται μὲν οὖν καὶ ἀ[πὸ το]ῦ πρώτου
[ἀεὶ] μέχρι οὗ [τελε]υτα[ίου ῥήματος.

[...a hymn saying sound and lawful words. For [a sacred rite was being performed] through the poem. And one cannot state the solution of the (enigmatic) words though they are spoken. This poem is strange and riddling to people, though [Orpheus] himself did not intend to say contentious riddles but rather great things in riddles. In fact he is speaking mystically <or speaking a holy discourse>, and from the very first word all the way to the last.[760]

---

757 Pl. *Ti.* 71e–72b (Tr. Bury).
758 Janko, 2010, p.182–184.
759 Betegh, 2004, p.90 and n.48. KPT, 2006, p.162.
760 Col.VII.2–8.

As is quite evidently the case here and as we saw elsewhere, the Orphic texts were often associated with the word αἴνιγμα (riddle) and its derivatives which indicates that they were in need of interpretation, without this presupposing an oracular nature. The Derveni author, then, is not interpreting oracular poetry but a hymn which was related to the performance of a sacred rite. Another reading of the first line of the passage above by Bernabé and Piano give ἱερολογεῖ]το instead of ἱερουργεῖ]το, a term which is in any case repeated by the Derveni author in the same column in line 7.[761] This would mean that the Orphic poem was an *hieros logos*, which again suggests its use in rites. This comes in accordance with my suggestions in Chapters 2 and 4 about the importance of texts in Orphism and their use in Orphic rites. In this case, the Derveni author might have been an *exēgētēs*, who would explain the meaning of the Orphic texts and rites as part of the initiation process. In a passage from Lucian discussed in a previous chapter, the word ἱερολογία is associated with Orpheus in terms of astrological knowledge, mystic rites through poetry and theology through song.[762] As Kouremenos suggests the verb ἱερολογεῖ]το could mean 'to recount in verse a story about gods as a vehicle for communicating allegorically scientific knowledge'.[763] This is certainly what the Derveni author argues through his interpretation and his characterisation of Orpheus' words as αἰνι[γμ]ατώδης.[764]

On the other hand, we have seen in Chapter 2 that there is evidence for the existence of oracles of Dionysos in Thrace and Lesbos which ancient sources associate with Orpheus; Heraclides Ponticus in fact, as we saw, refers to tablets written by Orpheus located at an oracle of Dionysos in Thrace.[765] It is possible, thus, that some Orphic texts might have been traditional poetic oracles which had to be interpreted.[766] As Fontenrose notes:

> 'Authentic verse oracles differ in style and content from the traditional oracles of folk narrative, poetry, chresmologues' compositions, and oracle collections. [...] traditional oracles are a genre of poetry. The original composition of this kind purported to be the pronouncements of seers, who were also poets'.[767]

---

761 Bernabé-Piano, 2016.
762 Luc. *Astr.* 10. For text see p.200.
763 KPT, 2006, p.172.
764 Col.VII.5.
765 See p.63. schol. In Eur. *Alc.* 968 Schwartz, Vol.2 p.239.
766 Pl. *Prot.* 316d: τοὺς δὲ αὖ τελετάς τε καὶ χρησμωιδίας τοὺς ἀμφί τε Ὀρφέα καὶ Μουσαῖον: 'sometimes of mystic rites and soothsayings, as did Orpheus, Musaeus and their sects.'. Clem. Al. *Strom.* 1.21.134.
767 Fontenrose, 1978, p.195.

The oracles that the Derveni author and his like enter – as suggested by his own words – must have been of the kind found in Thrace and not the Delphic oracle for example for which no records of inquiries for the afterlife survive – apart from one case from the 3rd century A.D. of Amelios asking: 'where has the soul of Plotinos gone?'[768] Oracular questions concerning the dead were only related to establishing a cult to the dead, appeasing the dead or proper burial.[769] On the other hand, the oracles of Dionysos in Thrace were associated with curative purposes, according to the scholia on Euripides' *Alcestis* for example, which might have something to do with the soul.[770] The association of Dionysos with mantic attributes might seem paradoxical since the opposition between ecstatic Dionysos and prophetic Apollo has been a dominant part of western thought since Nietzsche.[771] However, we already referred to the double occupation of the Delphic oracle by Dionysos and Apollo and, as Tzifopoulos argues, the common ground between the two 'seems to have been *mania*': Apollo would prophesy through the mantic/manic Pythia and Dionysiac initiates experience *mania* in order to become *bacchoi* during their *teletai*.[772] This is nicely expressed in Euripides' *Bacchae* by Teiresias:

> μάντις δ' ὁ δαίμων ὅδε· τὸ γὰρ βακχεύσιμον
> καὶ τὸ μανιῶδες μαντικὴν πολλὴν ἔχει·
> ὅταν γὰρ ὁ θεὸς ἐς τὸ σῶμ' ἔλθῃ πολύς,
> λέγειν τὸ μέλλον τοὺς μεμηνότας ποιεῖ.

> The god <Dionysos> is also a prophet: for the ecstatic and the manic have mantic powers in large measure. When the god enters someone in force, he causes him in madness to predict the future'.[773]

Tzifopoulos identifies a distinction between *mantis* and *prophētēs* in this passage which is also evident in Plato's *Timaeus* passage (71e-72b) quoted above in p.234 and suggests that a *mantis* would be the one possessed by the god and speaking the future, while a *prophētēs* would interpret the words uttered by a *mantis*.[774] It

---

768 Fontenrose, 1978, p.39–40; 164–165. Edmonds, 2011b, p.268. Plut. *De gen.* 21 (590a).
769 Tzifopoulos, 2010, p.150; fn.161. On the matter of the consultation of Greek oracles see also Bowden, 2013.
770 schol. In Eur. *Alc.* 968 Schwartz, Vol.2 p.239.
771 Tzifopoulos, 2010, p.139–140.
772 Tzifopoulos' elaborate discussion on the matter demonstrates the merging of the two through mania (2010, p.139–165).
773 Eur. *Bacch.* 298–301 (Tr. Kovacs).
774 Tzifopoulos, 2010, p.143–146.

might be that oracles of Dionysos 'specialised' in matters of eschatology and the afterlife, in the sense that they constituted the post-mortem future, and that the Derveni author was a *prophētēs* in the capacity described above.[775]

Columns I–VI of the papyrus refer to religious practices. The first column is too damaged to be of any use. The second column refers to libations, to a ritual involving a bird, and to some hymns adapted to music. Suggestions have been made about the nature of the ritual involving a bird. The reading of KPT [δαίμοσι δ'] ἑκάστο[ι]ς ὀρνίθειόν τι κα[ίειν] suggests the burning of a bird in honour of daimons. Bernabé suggests that a bird was being set free in relation to the soul being set free.[776] The text is quite damaged in this case too and so any proposed restoration might be far from the original text. For example, Calvo-Martínez suggests that perhaps the souls are attempting to exit Hades to contact those who request mantic revelations and thus the offerings might aim at appeasing the daimons impeding them from getting out.[777] Bernabé suggests that in the same way the Derveni author interprets the Orphic text, he also interprets the meaning of the rites. As he says, this is more clearly shown in the reading [τούτων δὲ] τὰ σημαι[νόμενα ('And their meaning...') of Col.II.9.[778] Unfortunately, the text stops right after this phrase and due to the damaged nature of the available text it is impossible to reach reliable conclusions. Col.III is also quite corrupted but we can infer that it deals with eschatological entities such as daimons and their role in the afterlife. Piano's edition of the text suggests that the Derveni author 'embraces a double conception of δαίμων': a personal daimon and chthonic daimons:

δαίμ]ων γίνεται[ι ἑκά]στωι ἵλε[ως] ἢ ἄλ[λως ἀλάστω]ρ, ἡ
γὰρ Δί]κη ἐξώλεας. [οὐ μ]έτεισι ἐκ[ὰς] Ἐρινύψ[ν· εἰσὶν] δὲ
δ]αίμονες οἳ κατὰ [γῆς ο]ὐδέκοτ[(ε)....] ροὐσι [?
θεῶν ὑπηρέται δ[..(.)]ι πάντας υ[.............Ω]ι
εἰσὶν ὅπωσπερ ἀ[νδρὸς] ἀδίκου θ.[.............( )]νοι
αἰτίην [τ' ἔ]χουσι [

[...] a daimon becomes for each person benevolent or [otherwise vindictive (?)]. [For Dike] does not pursue people who are utterly destroyed far from (or independently of?) the Erinyes; [there are] daimons under the earth who never [withdraw (or delay) ?, but as ?] servants

---

775 See also the three works of divinatory nature which have been attributed to Orpheus as outlined in Chapter 2, Table 1 in p.75: Χρησμοί, Ἀμμοσκοπικά, Ὠιοσκοπικά.
776 Bernabé, 2005b. Bernabé's edition of the text: [χ]ρὴ) ἑκάστο[ι]ς ὀρνίθειον τι κλ[εισθὲν (2010, p.83).
777 Calvo-Martínez, 2011, p.374.
778 Bernabé, 2010, p.82–84.

of gods [justly (or for Dike)? ...] they all [...] they are like an unjust man's [...] they have the responsibility (or the guilty) [...].[779]

These chthonic daimons, thus, were the servants of the gods ensuring that justice is maintained and they could be 'benevolent or vindictive in accordance with the behaviour displayed by humans in their lifetime'.[780] This would be in accordance with the Orphic picture created so far which involved rewards or punishments in the afterlife depending on whether or not the deceased followed a just life.

By contrast, the text of Column VI is far more extensive. It refers to some rituals performed by the *magoi* and the *mystai* and it seems that the two are not identical but juxtaposed. This is suggested by Jourdan, who also argues that the Derveni author might reject the practices performed by the *magoi*, based on the word ὡσπερεί (just as if).[781] In my opinion, this is insufficient evidence for us to be sure that the Derveni author rejects the practices of the *magoi*, but I also suggest that the Derveni author refers to the *magoi* for purposes of comparison and so he is not one of them. Bernabé also *a priori* assumes that a causal explanation by the Derveni author must be his own intervention, arguing that 'rites, as such, were not interpreted'.[782] But it is very difficult to reject the Derveni author's interpretations based on such an incomplete text, and the fact that we have a papyrus in which the meaning of rites is explained should be enough evidence that rites *could* be explained. Considering what was argued in Chapter 4 about the gold tablets, a person like the Derveni author could be the one giving the background knowledge necessary to justify their claims to immortality. The aetherial nature of the soul, for example, as was identified in an abundance of ancient sources, had to be somehow justified. And I do not believe that we have substantial reasons to deny that the initiates were aware of the meaning of things such as, for example, the fire carried by the *dadouchos* as outlined in the previous chapter. In addition, a person like the Derveni author could be the one giving background information necessary to successfully complete the afterlife journey in the netherworld with information about the daimons, the Eumenides and the punishments which took place there. The punishments would also promote the necessity for leading a just life such as the *Orphikos Bios*. The combination of these two types of background information in the face of the Derveni author, supports the

---

779 Piano, 2018, p.22ff. Col.III.3–4 (Tr. Piano).
780 Piano, 2018, p.23–25.
781 Jourdan 2003, p.37ff as cited by KPT, 2006, p.168–169.
782 Bernabé, 2010, p.83: 'When they are, the reason of the rite was simply described as an aetiological myth explaining the reason of its existence, but the aim that each part of the rite might have had was left unstated'.

argument that this kind of *exēgētes* existed and corroborates the argument for religious groups that combined practical mythological religious theology with theoretical and scientifical eschatology based on cosmogonical and elemental theories.

But who could the *magoi* be then? The word *magos* had a double connotation at the time when the papyrus was written: a negative one relating to charlatans who could practice dark magic and a positive one relating specifically to Persian religious experts.[783] Since the word is mentioned in our passage in a positive way, the author is presumably referring to Persian practices, revealing his familiarity with religious matters.[784] Regarding the identity of the *magoi* referred to in the Derveni Papyrus Bernabé plausibly argues that they were Orphic officiates similar to or equated with the *Orpheotelestae* and possibly had duties such as those mentioned in the Derveni Papyrus: sacrifice, divination, healing, purification.[785] However, I disagree with Bernabé's suggestion that in general the *magi/Orpheotelestae* were not charlatans and that they instructed the Orphic *mystae* on how to act and informed them about the mythological significance of the mysteries. As already argued, Orphic officiates which dealt with exegesis and non-practical matters certainly must have existed, but it is difficult to place them under the general label of *Orpheotelestae* which occurs only twice in ancient sources in general, and only once in classical sources specifically, and which we have seen to have both negative and non-negative connotations.[786] Most probably the kind of person who would instruct and guide the Orphic *mystai* would be someone like the Derveni author, who clearly distinguishes himself from these *magoi* referring to them as something external and also has a polemical stance against those who perform rites without any further knowledge of their meaning clearly evident in Col.XX, which comes closer to the services offered by the itinerant priests mentioned by Plato and who scholarship tends to identify with the so-called *Orpheotelestae*. Jiménez San Cristóbal also compares the officials being criticized by the DA in Col.XX with the *magoi* of Col.VI arguing that the DA: 'describes and explains the activities of the *magoi*, but they do not amaze him, and he does not even censure them because they provide no competition for his own interests.'[787] The contrast is also evident from the fact that the Derveni author is claiming to

---

[783] Betegh, 2004, p.78–79. Kouremenos, 2006, p.166. See also Ferrari, 2014.
[784] To this might corroborate Ferrari's reading of Col.IV where he reads Π]έρσαι θύου[σι(ν) (2011c, p.367). Betegh, 2004, p.78–79.
[785] Bernabé, 2014.
[786] See discussion in p.24 ff.
[787] Jiménez San Cristóbal, 2018, p.131.

offer true and substantial knowledge, whilst the *magoi* are presented as being related to more practical issues. It is also possible that the Derveni author is referring alternately both to Greek *magoi* such as the *Orpheotelestae* and Persian *magoi* with the purpose of comparing them. If this would be the case, however, then it must follow that the *Orpheotelestae* were presented in a negative light, consistent with the negative use of the term at the time when referring to Greek magoi. The above support my argument that the *Orpheotelestae* were an external part of Orphism and must be distinguished from Orphic religious *exēgētes* or *prophētes* like the Derveni author.

5.1.6 Identifying αἰδοῖον in Col.XIII.4–9

Col.XIII has caused the most controversy, the debate concerning the identity of the *aidoion* which Zeus swallows. One side argues that it is Ouranos' phallus and the other that it is Protogonos/Phanes/Metis, a motif which can also be found in the *Orphic Rhapsodies*.[788] The Derveni author quotes the relevant verse from the Theogony and then explains that the *aidoion* is actually the sun:

> "αἰδοῖον κατέπινεν, ὃς αἰθέρα ἔκθορε πρῶτος".
> ὅτι μὲν πᾶσαν τὴν πόησιν περὶ τῶν πραγμάτων
> αἰνίζεται κ[α]θ' ἔπος ἕκαστον ἀνάγκη λέγειν.
> ἐν τοῖς α[ἰδοίο]ις ὁρῶν τὴν γένεσιν τοὺς ἀνθρώπου[ς]
> νομίζογ[τας ε]ἶ̓ναι τούτωι ἐχρήσατο, ἄνευ δὲ τῶν
> αἰδοίων [οὐ γίν]εσθαι, αἰδοίωι εἰκάσας τὸν ἥλιο[ν·]

> ..."the reverend one he swallowed, who first sprung out of the aither". Since he is speaking through the entire poem allegorically about the real things, it is necessary to speak about each word in turn. Seeing that people consider all birth to depend on the genitals and that without the genitals there can be no birth, he used this (word) and likened the sun to a genital organ (αἰδοῖον) [789]

In my opinion, the word αἰδοῖον should in fact be taken here as the accusative singular of the masculine adjective αἰδοῖος (reverend), and not of the neuter noun αἰδοῖον (sexual organ).[790] The relative pronoun ὅς and the denominative adjective

---

[788] Phallus: Bernabé (2007, p.107–109; 2013, p.9–19), Betegh (2004), p.29/154–158). Protogonos/Phanes: Brisson (2003, p.23–29), Laks and Most (1997, p.15), KPT (2006, 133), West (1983, p.85).
[789] Col.XIII.4–9.
[790] KPT, 2006, p.27. See also Sider, 2014.

πρῶτος which are masculine singular – and the reading of which is indisputable – and refer to αἰδοῖον support this reading, since if they referred to a neuter noun it should have been ὄν and πρῶτον. This should be enough evidence that the αἰδοῖον is in fact a separate male entity. Sider also supports the reading of the word as masculine, pointing out that the word in its singular form was rarely used to refer to the male genitalia, first appearing only at the end of the 5th century.[791] On the other hand, Bernabé suggests that ὅς refers to the owner of the αἰδοῖον who is Ouranos, the first god.[792] It is, thus, Ouranos' genitals which Zeus swallows, in order to become a kind of father to him and the first in the hierarchy and genealogical order of all the gods. This argument in itself is not adequate, since the same thing could be achieved by Zeus by swallowing Protogonos, the first divine entity. Bernabé suggests that 'Sky's penis must have been left in space after the castration' and that *Aither* 'was interpreted as Sky's ejaculation'.[793] For this argument to stand, we need to accept that the verb ἔκθορε means ejaculate, which is not its usual meaning; its usual meaning is leap or spring forward.[794] Even if we accept this meaning, however, Bernabé's suggestion does not explain why it needs to be specified that Ouranos ejaculated the aether *first* since this would indicate that other deities ejaculated aether after him and there is no evidence for this. We know that certainly Zeus did not create through ejaculation since the creative process is quoted by the Derveni author in Column XVI. The verb ἔκθορε most probably, thus, refers to a male entity who sprung into the aether first.

The Derveni author notes that Orpheus in his poem likens the sun to an αἰδοῖον because the latter constitutes the reproductive organ and thus is connected with the generative power of the sun. This is further evidence that *aidoion* is a separate *heliadic* entity since it is the sun which is likened to genitalia and not genitalia to the sun. This is clearly stated by the Derveni author: ἄνευ δὲ τῶγ | αἰδοίων [οὐ γίν]εςθαι, αἰδοίωι εἰκάσας τὸν ἥλιο[ν·] ('and that without the genitals there can be no birth, he used this (word) and likened the sun to a genital organ').[795] The author's interest is in the use of the word *aidoios* by Orpheus as an epithet for the Sun. If it was the other way around, the Derveni author should have said αἰδοῖον εἰκάσας τῷ ἡλίῳ. Kouremenos, too, suggests that αἰδοῖον refers to Protogonos/Phanes and notes that this becomes more plausible if the relevant

---

791 Sider, 2014.
792 Bernabé, 2007, p.107–108.
793 Bernabé, 2007, p.108.
794 See also Brisson, 2003, p.23.
795 Col.XIII.9.

verse of the Orphic poem follows the quotation from Col.VIII.4–5 which would give: "Ζεὺς μὲν ἐπεὶ δὴ πα[τρὸς ἐο]ῦ πάρα θέ[σ]φατον ἀρχὴν | [ἀ]λκήν τ' ἐν χείρεσσι ἔ[λ]αβ[εν κ]α[ὶ] δαίμον[α] κυδρόν | αἰδοῖον κατέπινεν, ὃς αἰθέρα ἔκθορε πρῶτος".[796] If this is the case, it could indicate that this *aidoios daimon* signified the generative power and was passed or taken from one ruler to the next. It would be, in any case, peculiar to call genitalia, an illustrious god (δαίμον[α] κυδρόν). What is more, the Derveni author explicitly says that 'If the god did not wish the present *eonta* to exist, he would not have made the sun. But he made it of such a form and size as is related at the beginning of this account'.[797] It is harder to imagine how god would create a phallus and suspend it in the air, than accepting that *aidoion* is a separate divine entity and the Derveni author's discussion is about Orpheus using the word *aidoion* in reference to Protogonos/Phanes. The phrase 'at the beginning of this account' could mean, as Betegh argues, 'at the beginning of Orpheus' poem', which would support the identification of *aidoion* with Protogonos/Phanes who was the first divine entity and creator of the world.[798]

In the *Orphic Rhapsodies*, as we will see, Protogonos/Phanes is the Mind (Metis) and the world is filled with his light while he has the seed of the gods within him.[799] From him a series of deities are generated and he also creates the sun and the moon.[800] He is a *heliadic* and generative deity. He leaps forth from an Egg which Chronos fabricated with aether and the verses describing his birth in the *Rhapsodies* are similar to the DP verses referring to *aidoion*:

– ᴗ ἔπειτα δ'ἔτευξε μέγας Χρόνος Αἰθέρι δίωι
ᾤεον ἀργύφεον. ᴗᴗ – ᴗᴗ – ᴗᴗ – ᴗ
Πρωτόγονος Φαέθων περιμήκεος Αἰθέρος υἱός,
ὡρμήθη δ'ἀνὰ κύκλον ἀθέσφατον. – ᴗᴗ – ᴗ (OR7-9)
...ἐξέθορε πρώτιστος ἀνέδραμε τ' ἀρσενόθηλυς
Πρωτόγονος πολυτίμητος (OR10)
χάσμα δ'ὑπ' ἠέριον καὶ νήνεμος ἐρράγη αἰθήρ

---

796 Col.VIII.4-5 + Col.XIII.4: 'Zeus then, when from his father the prophesied rule and power in his hands had taken, and the glorious daimon the reverend one he swallowed, who first sprung out of the aither'. KPT, 2006, p.23–28. See also discussion in KPT, 2006, p.197–201 on why we do not need to assume the presence of Ouranos' castrated genitals to explain why the Derveni author considers the Sun to be the father of Cronus.
797 Col.XXV.10–12: ὁ θεὸς εἰ μὴ ἤθελεν εἶναι, οὐκ ἂν ἐπόησεν ἥλιον. ἐπόησε δὲ | τοιοῦτον καὶ τ[ο]σοῦτον γινόμενον οἷος ἐν ἀρχῆι τοῦ λόγου | διηγεῖται.
798 Betegh, 2004, p.327–329.
799 OR17 = OF140F; OR25 = OF123F.
800 OR19-OR24 = OF167F, OF152F, OF158F, OF160F, OF155F-OF157F, OF138F.

ὀρνυμένοιο Φάνητος ᴗ - ᴗᴗ - ᴗᴗ - ᴗ (OR13)
- ᴗᴗ - ᴗᴗ - ᴗᴗ πρῶτον δαίμονα σεμνόν,
Μῆτιν σπέρμα φέροντα θεῶν κλυτόν... (OR17)

Then great Chronos created a shining egg along with the divine Aether. And the son of enormous Aether, the shining Protogonos began to move in an incredible circle (OR7–9) ...he sprang upwards first of all, the hermaphrodite and highly-honoured Protogonos ... (OR10) And at the time of Phanes' birth, the misty chasm below and windless Aether were separated...(OR13) the immaculate daemon called Metis who bore the famous seed of the gods...(OR17).[801]

The same verb as in the DP, ἐξέθορε, is used to describe Protogonos/Phanes' birth into the aither. He is also called *daimon* as in the DP. It is Protogonos/Phanes that Zeus' swallows in the *Orphic Rhapsodies* and with him the whole world which he later on re-creates:

καὶ ποταμοὶ καὶ πόντος ἀπείριτος ἄλλα τε πάντα
πάντες τ'ἀθάνατοι μάκαρες θεοὶ ἠδὲ θέαιναι
ὅσσα τ'ἔην γεγαῶτα καὶ ὕστερον ὁππος'ἔμελλεν,
ἐνγένετο, Ζηνὸς δ'ἐνὶ γαστέρι σύρρα πεφύκει.

and rivers and the inaccessible deep, and everything else and all the immortal and blissful Gods and Goddesses and all that has already happened and all that will in the future, became one, tangled inside the belly of Zeus and were brought forth again.[802]

These verses which describe what was inside Zeus' belly after the swallowing of Protogonos are very similar to a quotation from the Orphic poem in Col.XVI.3–6, which describes what happens after the act of swallowing, namely the creation of gods and goddesses, rivers and springs:

"Πρωτογόνου βασιλέως αἰδοίου· τῶι δ' ἄρα πάντες
ἀθάνατοι προσέφυν μάκαρες θεοὶ ἠδὲ θέαιναι
καὶ ποταμοὶ καὶ κρῆναι ἐπήρατοι ἄλλα τε πάντα,
ἄσσα τότ' ἦν γεγαῶτ', αὐτὸς δ' ἄρα μοῦνος ἔγεντο".

'Of the First-born king, the reverend one; and upon him all the immortals grew, blessed gods and goddesses and rivers and lovely springs and everything else that had then been born; and he himself became the sole one'.[803]

---

[801] OR7-OR17 = OF114F, OF125F, OF118F, OF121F, OF132F, OF136F, OF122F, OF130F, OF134F, OF144F, OF140F.
[802] OR59 = OF241F; OR60-62 = OF243F, OF245V.
[803] Col.XVI.3–6.

We can see that in the DP *aidoios* is also called Protogonos in verses quoted from the Orphic poem, as is the case in the *Orphic Rhapsodies*. The narrative points of contact between these two passages support the contention that it is indeed Phanes/Protogonos who is being swallowed in the DP.[804] The similarities of Phanes to the primary divine generative substance of the Orphic poem in the Derveni papyrus are striking, and even though the *Orphic Rhapsodies* are subsequent to the Orphic poem, this does not exclude the possibility that they preserved elements of a very old tradition. Thus, it does not seem so plausible that the word αἰδοῖον in the Orphic poem refers to genitals; more probably, it is related to the primeval deity described above, whether we want to call it Phanes or Protogonos. Torjussen argues that we should not use external evidence such as the *Orphic Rhapsodies* in order to define *aidoion* since 'there is no need to make the text fit the 'Orphic context' since this 'context' is not fixed'.[805] However, the argument that there is no Orphic fixed context also constitutes a kind of context and ignoring strong textual similarities might stem from an attempt to adjust the text to the context of 'no fixed context'.

5.1.7 The case of Herakleitos

The case of Herakleitos, who was active at the end of the 6th century B.C., differs from the other Pre-Socratic philosophers because similarities have been identified between Herakleitean and Orphic ideas and sources in general.[806] The Herakleitean column (Col.IV) has been a subject of discussion among many scholars especially because Herakleitos is the only author that the Derveni author quotes and names. The Herakleitean passage that is quoted is related to Justice (Dikē):

[.]ου ε.[.........ὥ]ς περ φυσικ[ὸς μετ]ὰ δίκης ἐὼν
ὁ κείμ[ενα] μεταθ[εὶς] μὲν ἃ εὐχα[ῖς χρὴ] ἐκδροῦναι,
μᾶλλ[ον ἃ] σίνεται [ἢ ὡ]ς ἀνημμέ[να εἰς] τὰ τῆς τύχης π[ῶς
οὐκ εἴ[α λα]μμάνειν ἄρ' οὐ ταῦ[τα κρατεῖ ο]ὐδε κόσμος;
κατὰ [ταὐτ]ὰ Ἡράκλειτος μα[ρτυρόμενος] τὰ κοινὰ
κατ[αστρέ]φει τὰ ἴδ[ι]α, ὅσπερ ἴκελα [τῶι ἱερο]λόγωι λέγων
'ἥλι[ος κόσ]μου κατὰ φύσιν ἀνθρω[πηΐου] εὖρος ποδός [ἐστι
τὸ μ[έγεθο]ς οὐχ ὑπερβάλλων εἰκ[ότας οὔ]ρους ε[ὔρους
ἐοῦ· εἰ δὲ μ]ή, Ἐρινύε[ς] νιν ἐξευρήσου[σι, Δίκης ἐπίκουροι'.

---

804 See also Morand (2010, p.162) who discusses the etymology of divine names in Orphic texts and comments on the link between Phanes and light as evident in the Orphic Hymns.
805 Torjussen, 2005, p.14.
806 The fragments and translations of Herakleitos are from Laks and Most 2016b.

...<even as righteously, being a natural philosopher>, having altered the rudiments that should be attached to prayers, why did he not allow to consider what harms us more than whatever depends on chance? Isn't it not true that not even the universe is able to control these powers? §In the same manner, Herakleitos, invoking common truths, presents his own views upside down, he who said, speaking like§ the author of [sacred] tales (sc. Orpheus): "The sun, according to the nature of <the world>, is a human foot in width, not exceeding [in size] the proper limits [of its width. Or else,] the Erinyes, [assistants of Dike,] will find it out."[807]

The author's purpose in referencing Herakleitos' passage about the Erinyes being the guardians of Justice, who make sure that the sun will not transgress its size, is to strengthen his argument about cosmic order. There is a contrast between order and cause – which is the desirable state – and chance, which only brings harm in the development of the world, a notion which is found in other Pre-Socratic philosophers as well, such as the Atomists Democritus and Leucippus.[808] The Derveni author, thus, seems to go against ideas such as the ones put forth by Herakleitos that everything depends on chance, by using a quotation from Herakleitos to prove his point and by saying that Herakleitos himself seems to be overturning his own views.[809] I suggest that the first lines of the text also refer to Herakleitos as does the accusation: 'why did he not allow to consider what harms

---

807 Col.IV.7–9. This reading of the text is a combination of Ferrari (2012) and KPT's reading. One significant difference is that KPT have [ἀστρο]λόγωι instead of [τῶι ἱερο]λόγωι. I also accept Janko's (2016) and Piano's (2016) edition of ἥλι[ος κόσ]μου. The translation is Ferrari's (2012) [Except text in < > is my alteration and text in §§ is KPT's translation as it was considered more accurate]. Herakleitos D89: ἥλιος γὰρ οὐχ ὑπερβήσεται μέτρα, φησὶν ὁ Ἡράκλειτος· εἰ δὲ μή, Ἐρινύες μιν Δίκης ἐπίκουροι ἐξευρήσουσιν: 'The sun will not overstep measures', says Heraclitus; 'otherwise, the Erinyes, Justice's helpers will find it out.' Janko interprets τὰ κοινὰ as the 'shared world' perceived when we are awake and τὰ ἴδ[ι]α as 'the individual one' which we perceive when dreaming (2010, p.183). I find this suggestion unconvincing.

808 Tsantsanoglou, 1997, p.108. Leukippus, KRS569: "οὐδὲν χρῆμα μάτην γίγνεται, ἀλλὰ πάντα ἐκ λόγου τε καὶ ὑπ᾽ ἀνάγκης.": "Nothing occurs at random but everything for a reason and by necessity.". Democritus, D74 (Laks-Most) (Not in KRS) = Arist. *Gen. An.* 5.789b2–4: Δημόκριτος δὲ τὸ οὗ ἕνεκα ἀφεὶς λέγειν, πάντα ἀνάγει εἰς ἀνάγκην οἷς χρῆται ἡ φύσις: 'Democritus, neglecting to speak of the final cause, refers to necessity everything of which nature makes use'.

809 See Herakleitos D60: ὥσπερ †σάρξ† εἰκῇ κεχυμένων ὁ κάλλιστος ὁ κόσμος: 'Like †flesh† of things spread out at random, the most beautiful order (kosmos).' D65: ποταμοῖσι τοῖσιν αὐτοῖσιν ἐμβαίνουσιν ἕτερα καὶ ἕτερα ὕδατα ἐπιρρεῖ: 'It is always different waters that flow toward those who step into the same rivers.' D76: αἰών παῖς ἐστι παίζων, πεσσεύων· παιδὸς ἡ βασιληίη: 'A lifetime (aiōn) is a child playing, playing checkers: the kingship belongs to a child.' Ferrari (2014) suggests that the latter famous quotation by Herakleitos (D76) is included in the last line of this column, namely αἰ]ῴν ἐστι πα]ῖσ π[αίζων, πεσσεύων· παιδὸς ἡ βασιληίη. This would support my

us more than whatever depends on chance?' We have already established that the location of the Sun at the precisely correct distance is crucial to the maintenance of the generative process. The Derveni author, then, makes a point about the importance of knowing the limits and acting justly, and thus not leaving everything to chance, by giving an example where if limits are transgressed the consequences would be of cosmic proportions. The Derveni author, then, refers to Herakleitos to make his point that the cosmic order did not arise by chance and it is preserved because of Nous.[810]

It is important that Herakleitos also refers to mythological entities such as the Erinyes, in this way demonstrating how Pre-Socratic philosophy had not yet de-associated from mythological motifs and how it most probably emerged through mythological language and the re-interpretation of myth. As Granger suggests, it is perhaps better if we move away from Aristotle's definition of Pre-Socratic philosophers as 'natural philosophers' since they are ,as much 'natural theologians' as they are 'natural philosophers''.[811] Herakleitos' language is in general riddling and enigmatic, a word which the Derveni author uses to characterise the Orphic poem as well, as was mentioned earlier.[812] Several scholars have discussed Herakleitean fragments in relation to Orphism and some have identified parallels. Sider and Bossi argue that Herakleitos used, adopted and adapted many of the Orphic writings for his own purposes but he is not to be identified as an Orphic.[813] The above fragment could be an example of that. Herakleitos and Orpheus are also juxtaposed in Plato's *Cratylus* which deals with etymological analysis. In 402a-c he quotes two verses from Orpheus ['Fair-flowing Ocean was the first to marry, and he wedded his sister Tethys, daughter of his mother'] and says that on this he agrees with Homer, Hesiod, and Herakleitos' theory of eternal flux and the likening of the universe to a river. Later authors such as Clement over-emphasise an Orphic influence on Herakleitos:

Ὀρφέως δὲ ποιήσαντος· "ἔστιν ὕδωρ ψυχῆι θάνατος, χὔδάτεσσι δὲ γαῖα· ἐκ δ'ὕδατος <πέλε> γαῖα, τὸ δ'ἐκ γαίας πάλιν ὕδωρ, ἐκ τοῦ δὴ ψυχὴ ὅλον αἰθέρα ἀλλάσσουσα." Ἡρακλεῖτος ἐκ

---

suggestion that the Derveni author is particulary interested in rejecting the notion of chance, but since a lot of the text is missing we cannot be confident about this reading of the text.
810 KPT, 2006, p.270.
811 Granger, 2013, p.163.
812 Col.VII.4–5: ἔστι δὲ ξ[ένη τις ἡ] πόησις | [κ]αὶ ἀνθρώ[ποις] αἰνι[γμ]ατώδης: 'This poem is strange and riddling to people...'
813 Sider, 1997, p.147–148; Bossi, 2011, p.15. Casadesús also discusses the relation between Herakleitos and Orphism (1995).

τούτων συνιστάμενος τοὺς λόγους ὧδέ πως γράφει "ψυχῆισιν θάνατος ὕδωρ γενέσθαι, ὕδατι δὲ θάνατος γῆν γενέσθαι, ἐκ γῆς δὲ ὕδωρ γίνεται, ἐξ ὕδατος δὲ ψυχή."

And Orpheus having said: "And water is death for the soul and for the water the same requital applies. From water comes into existence earth, and from earth water once again, and from that, soul, becoming aether in its entirety"; and Herakleitos, putting together the expressions from these lines, writes thus: 'For souls it is death to become water, for water it is death to become earth; but out of earth, water comes to be, and out of water, soul.'"[814]

These verses are part of the *Orphic Rhapsodies* and they have an eschatological/scientifical meaning which is very close to the one expressed in the DP since we have an alteration of the divine substance through the elements, while aether is the underlying constant element. This cycle of imperishable reformation of the cosmos constitutes the Derveni author's interpretation of the Orphic text since Zeus/aer/Nous always existed and transforms the particles into beings through fire (heat) and *aer* (cold). One could argue that the ψυχρὸν ὕδωρ προ<ρέον> which is offered to the souls by the guards in the gold tablets has something to do with these scientific ideas. This can be seen from the emphasis on the coldness of the water through the word ψυχρὸν which might also be a word-play on the word ψυχή. In a sense the water needs to be cold so the souls cool down and become part of the aether/air. The final return of the soul to divine air/aether would come in accordance with my suggestion that Orphic initiates believed in an astral immortality. Also, the Derveni author says that the moon and the stars are made of the brighter, clearest and purest particles. Considering that the animating substance which is essentially the divine soul is Zeus/air, it can be suggested that the sphere of the stars is where the purest kind of air abides.

In another fragment Herakleitos says that: '…for souls it is a pleasure, and not death to become moist' [D101] and in D67 Herakleitos says: 'Cold things become warm, warm becomes cold, wet becomes dry, parched becomes moist'. [815] These Herakleitean and the above Orphic verses could be perceived as a cycle of transmigration where beginning and end was the same, namely aether/air. Other relevant Herakleitean fragments are D54: 'For on the circumference of a circle, the beginning and the end are in common, according to Herakleitos' and D51:

---

814 Clem. Al. *Strom.* 6.2.17; Herakleitos D100. Translation of the Orphic fragment by the author and of the Herakleitean fragment by Laks-Most. Bernabé (2004b, p.61–62) argues that this is a late passage inspired by Herakleitos. See also West, 1983, p.223.
815 D101: ὅθεν καὶ Ἡράκλειτον ψυχῇσι φάναι τέρψιν μὴ θάνατον ὑγρῇσι γενέσθαι. D67: τὰ ψυχρὰ θέρεται, θερμὸν ψύχεται, ὑγρὸν αὐαίνεται, καρφαλέον νοτίζεται. On the other hand D103: αὔη ψυχή, σοφωτάτη καὶ ἀρίστη: 'A dry soul, is the wisest and best'. This phrase is transmitted in different ways by various authors so its exact form is uncertain.

'The way upward and downward: one and the same'.[816] In other fragments of Herakleitos the role of the Sun and the sacred fire is emphasised: D85: 'The world order (*kosmos*), the same for all, none of the gods or humans made it, but it always was and is and will be: fire ever-living, kindled in measures and extinguished in measures'.[817] This is very close to the Derveni author's theory of everything being connected through the divine substance Zeus, who always existed, and the formation of beings through the regulation of temperature. In D90 Plutarch says that Herakleitos believed that: 'the sun, which is the overseer and observer of these things [i.e. limits and periods], becomes the collaborator of the god who leads and is first, by limiting, judging, revealing, and illuminating the changes and seasons that bring all things'.[818] This is not only related to the fragment quoted by the Derveni author but also to the fact that Zeus takes the 'Sun' in his hands from Kronos, which (as we will see) is an essential element of his kingship.

But there are more specific textual similarities between Herakleitos and Orphic texts. As we saw in Chapter 4, the pairs of opposites inscribed in the Orphic Olbian Bone Tablets (early 5th century) included the words εἰρήνη – πόλεμος (peace-war) alongside words such as life-death, body-soul and Orphic Dio(nysos). The notion of peace and war, or Love and Strife, are related to life and death, to corporeality and incorporeality. Herakleitos was heavily preoccupied with pairs of opposites; around 35 fragments refer to the opposites, the unity of opposites or anthithetical concepts.[819] Two fragments are particularly relevant to the bone tablets and the Derveni Papyrus:

> D48: ὁ θεὸς ἡμέρη εὐφρόνη, χειμὼν θέρος, πόλεμος εἰρήνη, κόρος λιμός· ἀλλοιοῦται δὲ ὅκωσπερ <πῦρ>, ὁκόταν συμμιγῇ θυώμασιν, ὀνομάζεται καθ' ἡδονὴν ἑκάστου.
> D63: εἰδέναι χρὴ τὸν πόλεμον ἐόντα ξυνόν, καὶ δίκην ἔριν, καὶ γίνομενα πάντα κατ' ἔριν καὶ χρεών.

---

816 D54: ξυνὸν γὰρ ἀρχὴ καὶ πέρας ἐπὶ κύκλου περιφερείας, κατὰ τὸν Ἡράκλειτον. D51: ὁδὸς ἄνω κάτω μία καὶ ωὐτή.
817 D85: κόσμον τόνδε, τὸν αὐτὸν ἁπάντων, οὔτε τις θεῶν οὔτε ἀνθρώπων ἐποίησεν, ἀλλ' ἦν ἀεὶ καὶ ἔστιν καὶ ἔσται, πῦρ ἀείζωον, ἁπτόμενον μέτρα καὶ ἀποσβεννύμενον μέτρα. See also Herakleitos D84, D86, D87.
818 D90: [. . .] ὧν ὁ ἥλιος ἐπιστάτης ὢν καὶ σκοπὸς ὁρίζειν καὶ βραβεύειν καὶ ἀναδεικνύναι καὶ ἀναφαίνειν μεταβολὰς καὶ ὥρας αἳ πάντα φέρουσι καθ' Ἡράκλειτον τῷ ἡγεμόνι καὶ πρώτῳ θεῷ γίγνεται συνεργός.
819 Herakleitos D47–D81.

D48: God: day night, winter summer, war peace (πόλεμος εἰρήνη), satiety hunger. He changes just as <fire>, when it is mixed together with incense, is named according to the scent of each one.

D63: One must know that war (πόλεμον) is in common, that justice is strife, and that all things come about by strife and constraint.

The notion of opposites or opposing powers which are nonetheless part of the whole is found not only in the Olbian Bone Tablets but also in the Derveni author's description of the formation of the cosmos through particles coming together or being struck against each other, through the alteration between hot and cold, between fire and air, under the workings of the unifying principle of Nous. Also, Herakleitos says that 'All these things the thunderbolt (κεραυνός) steers', which reminds us of the gold tablets' initiates' proclamation that they have been mastered by Moira and the thunderbolt, in reference to the necessity for mortal corporeality.[820] Herakleitos' κεραυνός could be perceived as a mythological motif representing the transformation of the incorporeal divine essence into corporeal matter.[821]

Two fragments of Herakleitos appear to attack traditional practices of initiation and purification by blood and criticise Dionysiac rites during which a hymn is sung to *aidoia*:

D15: καθαίρονται δ' ἄλλως αἵματι μιαινόμενοι οἷον εἴ τις εἰς πηλὸν ἐμβὰς πηλῷ ἀπονίζοιτο. μαίνεσθαι δ' ἂν δοκοίη εἴ τις αὐτὸν ἀνθρώπων ἐπιφράσαιτο οὕτω ποιέοντα. καὶ τοῖς ἀγάλμασι δὲ τουτέοισιν εὔχονται, ὁκοῖον εἴ τις δόμοισι λεσχηνεύοιτο, οὔ τι γινώσκων θεοὺς οὐδ' ἥρωας οἵτινές εἰσι.

D16: εἰ μὴ γὰρ Διονύσῳ πομπὴν ἐποιοῦντο καὶ ὕμνεον ᾆσμα αἰδοίοισιν, ἀναιδέστατα εἴργαστ' ἄν· ὡυτὸς δὲ Ἅιδης καὶ Διόνυσος, ὅτεῳ μαίνονται καὶ ληναΐζουσιν.

D15: They are purified in vain, because they are polluted by blood, just as if someone who had stepped into mud cleaned himself with mud; if any [*scil.* other] human noticed him doing this, he would think that he was mad. And they pray to these statues, just as if someone were to converse with houses, not knowing who the gods and heroes are.

D16: If it were not for Dionysus that they performed the procession and sang the hymn to the shameful parts, most shamefully would they be acting; but Hades is the same as Dionysus, for whom they go mad and celebrate maenadic rites.

---

820 Herakleitos D82: τάδε πάντα οἰακίζει κεραυνός. GT: A1.4–5; A2.5; A3.5.

821 It is perhaps relevant that one of the Orphic verses quoted by the Derveni author refers to: Ζεὺς βασιλεύς, Ζεὺς δ'ἀρχὸς ἁπάντων ἀργικέραυνος: 'Zeus the king, Zeus the ruler of all, he of the bright bolt.' [Col.XIX.10]

Herakleitos makes a play between the word Ἅιδης, αἰδοῖον and ἀναιδέστατα and says that Dionysos is the same as Hades.[822] In the first fragment he ridicules purifications of bloody deeds with blood saying that is the same as if someone covered in mud tried to clean himself with mud (πηλῷ). We have already seen that lying in the mire was considered by Orphics a punishment in the afterlife, based on non-Orphic sources such as Plato and Aristophanes.[823] Herakleitos also uses the word βορβόρῳ, which I suggested constitutes Orphic religious terminology, saying that ὕες βορβόρῳ ἥδονται μᾶλλον ἢ καθαρῷ ὕδατι.[824] Even though Herakleitos is earlier than the sources in which this belief is associated with Orphics, it is likely that his accusations go against groups such as the performers of Orphic rites. Clement, who is also the source of D16, suggests that Herakleitos was criticising Dionysiac initiates:

> D18: τίσι δὴ μαντεύεται Ἡράκλειτος ὁ Ἐφέσιος; νυκτιπόλοις, μάγοις, βάκχοις, λήναις, μύσταις· τούτοις ἀπειλεῖ τὰ μετὰ θάνατον, τούτοις μαντεύεται τὸ πῦρ· τὰ γὰρ νομιζόμενα κατὰ ἀνθρώπους μυστήρια ἀνιερωστὶ μυεῦνται.
>
> D18: To whom does Herakleitos of Ephesus address his prophesies? To night-wanderers, Magi, Bacchants, Maenads, and initiates. It is to these that he threatens what comes after death, to these that he prophesies the fire. For they are initiated impiously into the mysteries that are recognised among men.

Granger, who considers that the assimilation of deities was a characteristic of early and late Orphic poetry, interprets D16 as Herakleitos suggesting that when the Dionysiac initiates perform the rites 'their pursuit of life in Dionysos in sex and wine is their pursuit of death in Hades, since it is death for souls to become wet (B77)'.[825] Herakleitos' prophecy against the Dionysiac initiates is that there is no individual immortality in the afterlife such as the one suggested in the gold tablets, but that the soul returns to the sacred fire post-mortem.[826]

---

822 Granger, 2013, p.190.
823 For discussion see p.179–183 and p.21 ff. Pl. *Resp.* 1.363d; 7.533d; Pl. *Phd.* 69c: 'And I fancy that those men who established the mysteries were not unenlightened, but in reality had a hidden meaning when they said long ago that whoever goes uninitiated and unsanctified to the other world will lie in the mire [ἐν βορβόρῳ κείσεται]'. Ar. *Av.* 145–152; 268–276. See also Aesch. 680–696.
824 D80: 'Pigs take greater pleasure in mire than in pure water'.
825 Granger, 2013, p.194. B77 = D101 (For text see fn.815).
826 See also Herakleitos D120: ἀνθρώπους μένει ἀποθανόντας ἄσσα οὐκ ἔλπονται οὐδὲ δοκέουσιν: 'What awaits humans after they have died is everything that they do not expect nor suppose.'

Considering all the above, I would argue that the Derveni author is responding to Herakleitos' accusations against Orphic initiates or texts and his commentary is an attempt to show that Herakleitos' theories were firstly expressed in the Orphic texts; in other words that Herakleitos 'appropriated' his theories from Orpheus.[827] This would not necessarily mean that this was the sole purpose of the Derveni author. Admittedly, this is a suggestion which cannot be verified but it is nonetheless supported by the close similarities between Herakleitean ideas and the Derveni author's commentary, and the fact that Herakleitos is the only pre-Socratic philosopher to be explicitly quoted. What is more, he is not just quoted, but the Derveni author suggests that Herakleitos presents his views upside-down or appears to go against his own views (κατ[αστρέ]φει τὰ ἴδ[ι]α) and so his words need to be properly understood. In a similar way, the Derveni author often stresses that Orpheus' words need to be re-arranged in order to be understood, which could be perceived as an indirect accusation that Herakleitos has not understood the real meaning of Orpheus' words. Secondly the Derveni author focuses on the word *aidoion* and tries to justify why the sun has been characterised in this way by Orpheus. He also constantly stresses Orpheus' ability to name the gods in such a profound way.[828] Thirdly, the beginning of the papyrus refers to some religious practices including offerings to the Erinyes and daimones, justifying the reasons that they take place. Finally, as we will see, the Derveni author emphasises the importance of seeing, hearing and understanding, which is also an idea stressed in the Herakleitos' fragments.[829] Certainly we might imagine that the person who used the Derveni Papyrus during his funeral in an isolated place, who followed specific funerary rites and was apparently concerned with pollution, would be deeply offended by Herakleitos' words that νέκυες κοπρίων ἐκβλητότεροι [D119: 'Corpses are more to be thrown out than manure']. It is very difficult to know if an Orphic text inspired Herakleitos, or if Herakleitean ideas influenced the interpretation of Orphic texts in mystic circles, but perhaps this is not as important as the possibility that the Derveni papyrus might constitute a genuine philosophical discourse between two theological philosophies.

---

[827] See also Obbink, who suggested that the Derveni author is perhaps answering a criticism of Orphic *teletae* (1997, p.52).
[828] Emphasised throughout the papyrus. See also Col.XXII.1–2.
[829] See Herakleitos D1–D8 and D31–D34.

5.1.8 A sacred cosmology? The usage of the Derveni text and the role of the Derveni author

I have suggested that the Derveni author was most probably a religious figure such as a prophet or a theologian. Scholars such as West, Tsantsanoglou, Laks and Most have suggested that he was a *mantis*, an Orphic priest, or a 'theologian' and that his interpretation of the Orphic poem was a part of an initiation procedure, while others such as Obbink and Edmonds have suggested that we cannot be sure that he was an Orphic.[830] According to Flower, a *mantis* was 'a professional diviner, an expert in the art of divination'.[831] A *mantis* would deal with a variety of religious and prophetic activities, from dream interpreting and purifications, to being a medium at oracles and accompanying generals on campaign. He would be considered to have a higher state of inspiration and consciousness than ordinary men and 'be the most authoritative expert on religious matters'; the word can be translated as 'diviner', 'prophet' or 'soothsayer'.[832] As far as priests/priestesses are concerned, they could be religious personnel of the state public cults or private initiators and performers of rites. Even though the *polis* was in control of selecting many priesthoods, the most respected and old ones were inherited, such as the Eumolpidae at Eleusis or the Lykomidae, performers of Orphic rites at Phlya, as was mentioned in Chapter 2.[833] There was a variety of religious specialists, such as purifiers and oracle-sellers who operated independently and could occasionally be reproached by the public or local authorities.[834] As already said, it seems more probable that if the Derveni author was a religious figure, he must have been a prophet or theologian or a combination of the two.

---

830 West,1997, p.83: *theologos*. Tsantsanoglou, 1997, p.99: *mantis*. Laks, 1997, p.123: Orphic. Most, p.1997, 121: An Orphic who 'claims a special and restrictive position within Orphism' and who 'is, or would like to be, the leader of a particular grouping or sect within Orphism which considers itself Orphic and stands in opposition to non-Orphics, but at the same time distinguishes itself by its doctrine from other Orphic groups'. Obbink, 1997, p.52; Edmonds, 2008b, p.29. On the other hand, Janko suggested that the Derveni author was the 'atheist' Diagoras of Melos (2010, p.180). For an extensive analysis of Janko's arguments and an outline of reasons why this suggestion is not possible see Winiarczyk, 2016, p.117–126 and Betegh, 2004, p.373–380.
831 Flower, 2008, p.22.
832 Flower, 2008, p.23–24.
833 See discusson in p.45. See Larson, 2007, p.13.
834 Larson, 2007, p.13.

This begs the question of under what circumstances the Derveni text might have been used. There are some important passages of the papyrus' text which I have not yet discussed and which will help with this question. In Col.VII.8–11 the Derveni author refers to the following Orphic verse which he does not quote directly but paraphrases:

> ... ὡ[ς δηλοῖ] καὶ ἐν τῶι
> [εὐκ]ρινήτῳ[ι ἔπει· "θ]ύρας" γὰρ "ἐπιθέ[σθαι" κελ]εύσας τοῖ[ς]
> ["ὠσὶ]ν" αὐτ[οὺς οὔτι νομο]θετεῖν φη[σιν τοῖς] πολλοῖς
> [ἀλλὰ διδάσκειν τοὺς τὴ]ν ἀκοὴν [ἁγνεύο]ντας κατ[ὰ]

> As he also makes clear in the well recognizable verse: for, having ordered them to "put doors to their ears" he says that he is not legislating for the many [but <instructing> those] who are pure in hearing.[835]

This might have been an introduction to an *hieros logos* which was secret, or it could be perceived as a warning against un-pure listeners, or that what was about to be said could not be understood by everyone. We find this phrase – or a variation of it – in some other instances which are associated with Orphic or Dionysiac elements. In *Quaestiones Convivales* Plutarch says:

> "Τὸ δ' ἐπὶ τούτοις," ἔφη γελάσας, "'ἀείσω ξυνετοῖσι' τὸν Ὀρφικὸν καὶ ἱερὸν λόγον, ὃς οὐκ ὄρνιθος μόνον τὸ ᾠὸν ἀποφαίνει πρεσβύτερον, ἀλλὰ καὶ συλλαβὼν ἅπασαν αὐτῷ τὴν ἁπάντων Ἐομοῦ πρεσβυγένειαν ἀνατίθησιν.

> "What is more," he added with a laugh, "'I shall recite for men of understanding' the sacred Orphic tenet which not only declares the egg older than the hen, but also attributes to it the absolute primordiality over all things together without exception.[836]

According to Plutarch this phrase must have introduced a cosmological or mythological story. The fact that he emphasises the relevance of this story to the primordial element suggests that such a story was perhaps understood at an allegorical level, but we cannot be sure about this. Plutarch also says that this Orphic *hieros logos* is suitable only for those who understand, which would bring the meaning of this phrase closer to the third possibility suggested above, which means that perhaps the story was not secret in itself but it required interpretation to be understood. The listener, thus, would need to have the right attitude to the story and for this reason it was not suitable for imprudent ears which would take the story literally and misunderstand episodes such as the swallowing of *aidoios*,

---

835 v.11 [ἀλλὰ διδάσκειν τοὺς τὴ]ν Bernabé-Piano. Translation in < > by the author.
836 Plut. *Quaest. Conv.* 636d (Tr. Clement).

as perhaps Herakleitos did in referring to the shameful hymn to *aidoia*.[837] What is more, this story is about an Egg being at the beginning of creation which is the egg out of which Protogonos/Phanes came and which as we argued is the *aidoios* mentioned in the DP. It seems, thus, that this phrase was used for introducing an Orphic cosmology which required a specific understanding from 'prudent' minds and consequently an exegesis.

So far we have seen that the phrase was associated with the introduction of a cosmological poem, but can we say that this was part of religious activity instead of just a regular poetical recitation in front of an audience? Another allusion to this phrase comes from Plato's *Symposium*:

> καὶ ὁρῶν αὖ Φαίδρους, Ἀγάθωνας, Ἐρυξιμάχους, Παυσανίας, Ἀριστοδήμους τε καὶ Ἀριστοφάνας· Σωκράτη δὲ αὐτὸν τί δεῖ λέγειν, καὶ ὅσοι ἄλλοι; πάντες γὰρ κεκοινωνήκατε τῆς φιλοσόφου μανίας τε καὶ βακχείας· διὸ πάντες ἀκούσεσθε· συγγνώσεσθε γὰρ τοῖς τε τότε πραχθεῖσι καὶ τοῖς νῦν λεγομένοις· οἱ δὲ οἰκέται, καὶ εἴ τις ἄλλος ἐστὶ βέβηλός τε καὶ ἄγροικος, πύλας πάνυ μεγάλας τοῖς ὠσὶν ἐπίθεσθε.

> I have only to look around me, and there is a Phaedrus, an Agathon, an Eryximachus, a Pausanias, an Aristodemus, and an Aristophanes – I need not mention Socrates himself – and all the rest of them; every one of you has had his share of philosophic frenzy and transport, so all of you shall hear. You shall stand up alike for what then was done and for what now is spoken. But the domestics, and all else profane and clownish, must clap the heaviest of doors upon their ears.[838]

It is peculiar that Plato compares philosophy with *mania* and *baccheia*. This might be due to the perception of philosophy as an outcome of an altered state of mind. Similarly, however, the reference to the particular phrase in relation to *mania* and *baccheia* might indicate that it was uttered during an initiation, meaning that the explanation of the Orphic cosmology was part of an initiation procedure.[839] Such an initiation procedure must have been associated with a philosophical approach to religion.[840] The reference to *mania* also suggests that this

---

837 See p.250.
838 Pl. *Symp*. 218b (Tr. Lamb).
839 Obbink, 1997, p.40: Obbink suggests that 'the Derveni author might have seen his elucidation of cosmology as possible instruction for mystic initiates'.
840 There is also the possibility that this phrase is alluded to in Euripides' *Bacchae*, 471–475 in relation to *baccheuein*: ΠΕΝΘΕΥΣ: τὰ δ' ὄργι' ἐστὶ τίν' ἰδέαν ἔχοντά σοι; | ΔΙΟΝΥΣΟΣ: ἄρρητ' ἀβακχεύτοισιν εἰδέναι βροτῶν. | ΠΕΝΘΕΥΣ: ἔχει δ' ὄνησιν τοῖσι θύουσιν τίνα; | ΔΙΟΝΥΣΟΣ: οὐ θέμις ἀκοῦσαί σ', ἔστι δ' ἄξι' εἰδέναι. | ΠΕΝΘΕΥΣ: εὖ τοῦτ' ἐκιβδήλευσας, ἵν' ἀκοῦσαι θέλω: 'Pentheus: These rites—what is their nature? Dionysus: They may not be told to the uninitiated. Pentheus: But those who perform them—what kind of benefit do they get? Dionysus: You are not allowed

phrase might have been uttered by a *prophētēs* in relation to eschatological matters and in the sense discussed earlier on. This is corroborated by the following passage by Clement, who also quotes the verse in question as part of an Orphic text:

ὁ δὲ Θράκιος ἱεροφάντης καὶ ποιητὴς ἅμα, ὁ τοῦ Οἰάγρου Ὀρφεύς, μετὰ τὴν τῶν ὀργίων ἱεροφαντίαν καὶ τῶν εἰδώλων τὴν θεολογίαν, παλινῳδίαν ἀληθείας εἰσάγει, τὸν ἱερὸν ὄντως ὀψέ ποτε, ὅμως δ' οὖν ᾄδων λόγον·
"φθέγξομαι οἷς θέμις ἐστί· θύρας δ' ἐπίθεσθε βέβηλοι
πάντες ὁμῶς· σὺ δ' ἄκουε, φαεσφόρου ἔκγονε Μήνης,
Μουσαῖ', ἐξερέω γὰρ ἀληθέα, μηδέ σε τὰ πρὶν
ἐν στήθεσσι φανέντα φίλης αἰῶνος ἀμέρσῃ.
εἰς δὲ λόγον θεῖον βλέψας τούτῳ προσέδρευε,
ἰθύνων κραδίης νοερὸν κύτος· εὖ δ' ἐπίβαινε
ἀτραπιτοῦ, μοῦνον δ' ἐσόρα κόσμοιο ἄνακτα ἀθάνατον."
εἶτα ὑποβὰς διαρρήδην ἐπιφέρει·
"εἷς ἔστ', αὐτογενής, ἑνὸς ἔκγονα πάντα τέτυκται·
ἐν δ' αὐτοῖς αὐτὸς περινίσσεται, οὐδέ τις αὐτὸν
εἰσοράᾳ θνητῶν, αὐτὸς δέ γε πάντας ὁρᾶται."

And the Thracian interpreter of the mysteries, who was a poet too, Orpheus the son of Oeagrus, after his exposition of the orgies and account of the idols, brings in a recantation consisting of truth. Now at the very last he sings of the really sacred Word:
"My words shall reach the pure; put bars to ears all ye profane together. But hear thou, Child of the Moon, Musaeus, words of truth; Nor let past errors rob thee now of life. Behold the word divine, to this attend, Directing mind and heart aright; tread well The narrow path of life, and gaze on Him, The world's great ruler, our immortal king."
Then, lower down, he adds explicitly:
"One, self-begotten, lives; all things proceed From One; and in His works He ever moves: No mortal sees Him, yet Himself sees all."[841]

The way that Clement introduces the quoted Orphic verses suggest that such a text might have been related to religious practices. We see Clement referring to Orpheus as the hierophant who wrote a theology of the gods and an *hieron logon*, his description being in accordance with our established image of Orpheus as the writer of *hieroi logoi*, as someone who instituted mysteries and gave a reasoned account about the nature of the gods. The verse instructing the imprudent to put doors to their ears once again seems to be introducing a *logon* which must be rightly understood. The word παλινῳδία used by Clement to describe this Orphic

---

to hear—though the rites are well worth knowing. Pentheus: A clever counterfeit answer this, to pique my curiosity!' (Tr. Kovacs).
841 Clem. Al. *Protr.* 7.63.

text was first used for an ode by Stesichorus who recanted his attack upon Helen and is typically understood as an ode which retracts a previously held belief.[842] The use of this particular word by Clement might imply that the expression 'put doors in your ears' introduced a text which offered a necessary exegesis of the true meaning of the Orphic theology which might have been otherwise misunderstood but since this is only found in Clement, it might constitute only his own view or used here for his own purposes. It is also important that the verses quoted from this Orphic work convey the same ideas found in the DP about a single creator and ruler of the cosmos who oversees everything, and they are textually close to verses quoted in the DP such as: "[αὐ]τὸς δὲ ἄρα μοῦνος ἔγεντο" [Col.XVI.9], "Ζεὺς κεφα[λή, Ζεὺς μέσ]σα, Διὸς δ' ἐκ [π]άντα τέτ[υκται" [Col.XVII.12], "Ζεὺς πρῶτος | [γέν]ετο"· [Col.XVIII.12–13].

The most interesting case, however, is the possible allusion to this phrase in Pindar's *Ode for Theron of Acragas* (476 B.C.):

> ... πολλά μοι ὑπ'
> ἀγκῶνος ὠκέα βέλη
> ἔνδον ἐντὶ φαρέτρας
> φωνάεντα συνετοῖσιν· ἐς δὲ τὸ πᾶν ἑρμανέων
> χατίζει. σοφὸς ὁ πολλὰ εἰδὼς φυᾷ
>
> I have many swift arrows under my arm in their quiver that speak to those who understand, but for the whole subject, they need interpreters. Wise is he who knows many things by nature...[843]

The word συνετοῖσιν does not constitute enough evidence that this is an allusion to the Orphic phrase, even if the reference to interpreters for those who are not initiated is also significant since it suggests that there is a hidden allegorical meaning to what Pindar is saying which requires background knowledge. However, I have also discussed this passage in the previous chapter in relation to the eschatology of the gold tablets and especially the idea of astral immortality. I argued that Pindar's reference to the just souls having the sun by night as much by

---

842 Isoc. *Disc.* 10.64: Ἐνεδείξατο δὲ καὶ Στησιχόρῳ τῷ ποιητῇ τὴν αὑτῆς δύναμιν· ὅτε μὲν γὰρ ἀρχόμενος τῆς ᾠδῆς ἐβλασφήμησέ τι περὶ αὐτῆς, ἀνέστη τῶν ὀφθαλμῶν ἐστερημένος, ἐπειδὴ δὲ γνοὺς τὴν αἰτίαν τῆς συμφορᾶς τὴν καλουμένην παλινῳδίαν ἐποίησε, πάλιν αὐτὸν εἰς τὴν αὑτὴν φύσιν κατέστησεν: 'And she displayed her own power to the poet Stesichorus also; for when, at the beginning of his ode, he spoke in disparagement of her, he arose deprived of his sight; but when he recognized the cause of his misfortune and composed the Recantation, as it is called, she restored to him his normal sight.' (Tr. Van Hook). See also Pl. *Phdr.* 243b. Plut. *Alex.* 53. Paus. III.19.13–20.1. Pl. *Epistles* 3.319e.
843 Pind. *Oly.* 2.83–85 (Tr. Race). See also Bremmer, 2011, p.2.

day might be relevant to an astral immortality and katabatic initiations. The particular Pindaric *Ode* has many parallels to Orphic eschatology with references to punishments of reckless souls being judged in the afterlife and rewards given to the just souls who get to dwell with the gods in the Isles of the Blessed. It also has many astrological references which could be perceived as allusions to an astral immortality such as referring to the ability of remaining uncorrupted by wealth and live a just life as 'a conspicuous lodestar, a man's true light'.[844] As Pindar says, those who know the future [εἰ δέ νιν ἔχων τις οἶδεν τὸ μέλλον (56)] will be aware why they need to act justly, which again implies that these eschatological ideas about rewards and punishments were given by inspired prophets. He also refers to the idea of the soul's reincarnation saying the following:

> ὅσοι δ' ἐτόλμασαν ἐστρίς
> ἑκατέρωθι μείναντες ἀπὸ πάμπαν ἀδίκων ἔχειν
> ψυχάν, ἔτειλαν Διὸς ὁδὸν παρὰ Κρόνου τύρσιν·
> ἔνθα μακάρων
> νᾶσον ὠκεανίδες
> αὖραι περιπνέοισιν· ἄνθεμα δὲ χρυσοῦ φλέγει,

> But those with the courage to have lived three times in either realm, while keeping their souls free from all unjust deeds, travel the road of Zeus to the tower of Cronus, where ocean breezes blow round the Isle of the Blessed, and flowers of gold are ablaze...[845]

The 'road of Zeus which leads to the tower of Cronus' is not an idea found elsewhere and it certainly does not correspond to any known image of the underworld. The idea of ocean breezes blowing around the Isles of the Blessed corresponds to the Derveni author's equation of Okeanos with *aer*:

> τοῦτο τὸ ἔπος πα[ρα]γωγὸν πεπόηται καὶ το[ῖς] μὲν
> πολλοῖς ἄδηλόν ἐστιν, τοῖς δὲ ὀρθῶς γινώσκουσιν
> εὔδηλον ὅτι "Ὠκεανός" ἐστιν ὁ ἀήρ, ἀὴρ δὲ Ζεύς.
> οὔκουν "ἐμήσατο" τὸν Ζᾶνα ἕτερος Ζεύς, ἀλλ' αὐτὸς
> αὑτῶι "σθένος μέγα". οἱ δ' οὐ γινώσκοντες τὸν
> Ὠκεανὸν ποταμὸν δοκοῦσιν εἶναι ὅτι "εὐρὺ ῥέοντα"

> This verse is composed so as to be misleading; it is unclear to the many but quite clear to those who have correct understanding, that "Oceanus" is the air and that air is Zeus. Therefore

---

844 Pind. *Oly.* 2.55–56: ἀστὴρ ἀρίζηλος, ἐτυμώτατον | ἀνδρὶ φέγγος (Tr. Race).
845 Pind. *Oly.* 2.68–73 (Tr. Race). See also lines 7–9. A similar idea expressed in Hsch. ω 108–109: Ὠκεανοῖο πόρον· τὸν ἀέρα, εἰς ὃν αἱ ψυχαὶ τῶν τελευτώντων ἀποχωροῦσιν. Ὠκεανός· ἀήρ. θάλασσα, καὶ ποταμὸς ὑπερμεγέθης. φασὶ δὲ καὶ ὁμώνυμον αὐτοῦ ἐν Κρήτῃ. See also KPT, 2006, p.256.

it was not another Zeus who "contrived" Zeus, but the same one (contrived) for himself "great might". But the ignorant ones think that Oceanus is a river, because he added "wide-flowing".[846]

This idea would also be compatible with the location of the Isles of the Blessed in the Milky Way as already suggested. It is clear that in Pindar there is a division of locale for the unjust and for the just who will dwell with the gods. Pindar also says that there are fiery gold flowers on the Isles of the Blessed, which is a peculiar idea but could be understood as a reference to stars. The possibility that Pindar has in mind Dionysiac eschatological ideas is supported by the fact that he refers to two examples of immortalisation which are Semele, Dionysos' mother, and her sister Ino, Dionysos' nurse, both related to maenadism.[847] Semele is struck by Zeus' thunderbolt, which has parallels to the gold tablets, and the mythology around Ino is related to kin-killing and madness.[848] Furthermore, Pindar refers to Chronos as the father of all [Χρόνος ὁ πάντων πατὴρ (17)] and as we will see, according to the *Orphic Rhapsodies* he is at the beginning of creation. If Pindar was indeed familiar with Orphic ideas and an Orphic *hieros logos*, and if I am right in identifying in this *Olympian Ode* ideas present both in the gold tablets and the Derveni Papyrus, this would push back the interpretation of the Orphic text in a cosmological way to an even earlier date – as early as the late sixth century B.C. This was already implicit in my argument about Herakleitos being familiar with and potentially criticising such Orphic ideas.

It would not be beyond belief if the following Herakleitos' fragments allude to the Orphic phrase under discussion too:

D1: τοῦ δὲ λόγου τοῦδ' ἐόντος ἀεὶ <u>ἀξύνετοι</u> γίνονται ἄνθρωποι, καὶ πρόσθεν ἢ ἀκοῦσαι, καὶ ἀκούσαντες τὸ πρῶτον·
D4: ἀξύνετοι ἀκούσαντες κωφοῖσιν ἐοίκασι·

D1: And of this account (*logos*) that is – always – humans are uncomprehending, both before they hear it and once they have first heard it.
D4: Being uncomprehending, when they have heard they resemble deaf people...[849]

---

846 Col.XXIII.1–6.
847 Pind. *Oly.* 2.21–30: 'This saying befits Cadmus' fair-throned daughters, who suffered greatly; but grievous sorrow subsides in the face of greater blessings. Long-haired Semele lives among the Olympians after dying in the roar of a thunderbolt; Pallas loves her ever and father Zeus; and her ivy-bearing son loves her very much. They say, too, that in the sea Ino has been granted an immortal life.' Their father Kadmos is also included in those dwelling with the gods (67–80).
848 Gantz, 1993, p.112, 176–179, 472, 478, 705.
849 See also West, 1983, p.110.

These phrases are textually close to the Orphic phrase and the rest of the passages discussed through the word ἀξύνετοι. Moreover, Herakleitos' criticism is conceptually close to the Derveni author's criticism of those who get initiated without understanding the rituals or what they see and hear during their initiation, which in turn shows the importance of knowledge:

ἀνθρώπω[ν ἐν] πόλεσιν ἐπιτελέσαντες [τὰ ἱ]ερὰ εἶδον,
ἔλασσόν σφας θαυμάζω μὴ γινώσκειν· οὐ γὰρ οἷόν τε
ἀκοῦσαι ὁμοῦ καὶ μαθεῖν τὰ λεγόμενα· ὅσοι δὲ παρὰ τοῦ
τέχνην ποιουμένου τὰ ἱερά, οὗτοι ἄξιοι θαυμάζεσθαι
καὶ οἰκτε[ί]ρεσθαι· θαυμάζεσθαι μὲν ὅτι δοκοῦντες
πρότερον ἢ ἐπιτελέσαι εἰδήσειν ἀπέρχονται ἐπι–
τελέσαντες πρὶν εἰδέναι οὐδ' ἐπανερόμενοι ὥσπερ
ὡς εἰδότες τέων εἶδον ἢ ἤκουσαν ἢ ἔμαθον· [οἰ]κτε[ί]ρεσθαι δὲ
ὅτι οὐκ ἀρκεῖ σφιν τὴν δαπάνην προανηλῶσθαι, ἀλλὰ
καὶ τῆς γνώμης στερόμενοι πρὸς ἀπέρχονται

> [As for those men who believe that they learned] when they witnessed the rites while performing them [together with other] people in the cities, I wonder less that they do not understand; for it is not possible to hear and simultaneously comprehend what is being said. But those (who believe that they learned) from someone who makes a profession of the rites deserve to be wondered at and pitied: wondered at because, although they believe before they perform the rites that they will learn, they go away after performing them before having learned, without even asking further questions, as if they knew something of what they saw or heard or were taught; and pitied because it is not enough for them that they paid the fee in advance – they also go away devoid even of their belief.[850]

The Derveni author criticises those who perform rites along with other people in the cities, saying it is not possible for them to perform/witness/hear the rites and simultaneously understand them. This implies that for the Derveni author it was essential that the meaning of the rites and of the *legomena* was explained at some other time so that the initiation procedure would be completed. The reference to *polis* rites also suggests that the rites in which he was involved were performed in smaller groups. The fact that he also heavily criticises those who 'make a profession of the rites', which clearly means those who make money out of it, should be a clear indication that he is not one of the itinerant priests using the books of Orpheus criticised by Plato. He must belong, thus, to a different type of Orphic religious figure which placed grave emphasis on understanding the meaning of the *dromena* and *legomena* of Orphic rites. This suggestion is in accordance with what I have argued so far that there were two different strands of Orphism, and

---

850 Col.XX.1-10. See also Bossi, 2011, p.15 and fn.12.

for the importance of Orphic texts. This is perhaps why the Derveni author argues that what he says is the true meaning of Orpheus' words, which in turn will lead to a correct understanding of the cosmos. As Obbink notes, 'In the Derveni author's view, the world of Orpheus' narrative, understood correctly (ὀρθῶς), mirrors our cosmos'.[851] In this sense, the Derveni author could be one of those priests mentioned by Socrates in Plato's *Meno* who have studied so they can give a 'reasoned account of their ministry'.[852] The Orphic overtones of this Platonic passage have already been discussed.[853]

As Ranzato notes, and is evident from the above discussion about Herakleitos and Pindar, the quality of thought of old sages 'was closely related to the obscurity of their speech'.[854] It has become evident that this is also the case with texts associated with the name of Orpheus. The Orphic texts in general were of a riddling and enigmatic nature in need of an exegesis; texts whose meaning was not immediately evident. The Derveni author makes this explicit when he says that from the first up to the last word Orpheus talked in riddles [αἰνίγματα]; a word we often came across in relation to Orphic matters.[855] For example, Plutarch as discussed in Chapter 4 says that the more enlightened speak in riddles [αἰνίττονται] about the creation of the world through Dionysos' dismemberement myth.[856] In the same way, the gold tablets include enigmatic phrases such as the 'falling into milk' phrase or the acclamation 'I am the child of earth and starry heaven', while their archetype might have been influenced by oracular language as was mentioned.[857] The *Orphic Rhapsodies* begin with a plea to divine inspiration and an invocation, not to the Muses as it was usual, but to Apollo, the par excellence oracular deity. The obscurity of the Orphic texts seems to be presupposed by external *exēgētes* who claim to know the real meaning, while on the other hand philosophers such as Herakleitos, for example, seem to obscure their language deliberately following an oracular pattern.[858] This might indicate that, as argued

---

851 Obbink, 1997, p.42.
852 Pl. *Me.* 81a: ΣΩ: Οἱ μὲν λέγοντές εἰσι τῶν ἱερέων τε καὶ ἱερειῶν ὅσοις μεμέληκε περὶ ὧν μεταχειρίζονται λόγον οἵοις τ' εἶναι διδόναι· (Tr. Lamb).
853 See p.109 ff.
854 Ranzato, 2018, p.102.
855 Col.VII.2–8: For text see p.235. Col.X.11–12: "τροφ[ὸν] δὲ λέγων αὐ]τὴν αἰγί[ζε]ται ὅτι [ἅ]σσα | ὁ ἥλι[ος θερμαίνων δι]αλύει ταῦτα ἡ νὺξ ψύ[χουσα] | συ[νίστησι: 'And by calling her "nurse" he is saying in an enigmatic way that those things which the sun thaws by heating, night congeals by making cold.'
856 Plut. *De E.* 389a–b. For text and discussion see p.186 ff.
857 See discussion in p.149.
858 Ranzato, 2018, p.102.

earlier in this chapter, deciphering the true meaning of Orphic texts was a common practice and considering the fact that the archaic nature of Orphic texts is increasingly established, it can be argued that the 'obscurity = quality' tendency was a development of the obscurity of Orphic texts deeming them highly inspired and revered; a phenomenon derived from the notion that true knowledge should be concealed so that only the wise could understand it. At later times, this notion persists with the Neoplatonists referring to Orpheus as the *theologos* and Lucian saying that he did not plainly 'bring the science forth into illucidation but unto ingannation and pious fraude [ἀλλ' ἐς γοητείην καὶ ἱερολογίην]'.[859] The Derveni author also says that Orpheus ἱερολογεῖται, a term which, as was discussed earlier, Kouremenos suggests to mean the communication of allegorical scientific knowledge through poetry about the gods.[860] In Plato's *Cratylus*, Hermogenes tells to Socrates that he talks as if uttering oracles like an 'inspire prophet' [χρησμῳδεῖν] when explaining the etymology of the gods' names, to which Socrates answers that his inspiration came from listening all morning to Euthyphro who 'not only filled <his> ears but took possession of <his> soul with his superhuman wisdom'.[861] The boundaries between divine inspiration, μανία, philosophy, theology, χρησμῳδία and scientific discourse were blurry and tangent, making the role of a prophet or *exēgētēs* essential. The necessity, then, that these sacred texts be interpreted perhaps culminates in the expression that warns the audience that they address only the prudent and which dictates the profane to put doors to their ears. This formulaic phrase, thus, not only highlights the importance of understanding the correct meaning but also the danger of misinterpretation by imprudent minds which could lead to scorn or even condemnation.

---

859 Luc. *Astr.* 10: οὐ μάλα ἐμφανέως, οὐδὲ ἐς φάος τὸν λόγον προήνεγκεν, ἀλλ' ἐς γοητείην καὶ ἱερολογίην, οἵη διανοίη ἐκείνου: '...but not at all plainly, nor did he bring the science forth unto illucidation but unto ingannation and pious fraude, such being the humour of the man.' (Tr. Harmon). For more extensive text see p.200. More on the term *theologos* will be discussed in Chapter 6.
860 Col.VII.7. See discussion in p.235-236.
861 Pl. *Cra.* 396d: ΕΡΜ: Καὶ μὲν δή, ὦ Σώκρατες, ἀτεχνῶς γέ μοι δοκεῖς ὥσπερ οἱ ἐνθουσιῶντες ἐξαίφνης χρησμῳδεῖν. ΣΩ: Καὶ αἰτιῶμαί γε, ὦ Ἑρμόγενες, μάλιστα αὐτὴν ἀπὸ Εὐθύφρονος τοῦ Προσπαλτίου προσπεπτωκέναι μοι. ἕωθεν γὰρ πολλὰ αὐτῷ συνῆ καὶ παρεῖχον τὰ ὦτα. κινδυνεύει οὖν ἐνθουσιῶν οὐ μόνον τὰ ὦτά μου ἐμπλῆσαι τῆς δαιμονίας σοφίας, ἀλλὰ καὶ τῆς ψυχῆς ἐπειλῆφθαι: 'Her: Indeed, Socrates, you do seem to me to be uttering oracles, exactly like an inspired prophet. Soc: Yes, Hermogenes, and I am convinced that the inspiration came to me from Euthyphro the Prospaltian. For I was with him and listening to him a long time early this morning. So he must have been inspired, and he not only filled my ears but took possession of my soul with his superhuman wisdom.' (Tr. North-Fowler).

On the other hand, it has been argued that the author is attempting to connect a traditional Orphic poem to the most recent philosophical theories so it will retain its authority and validity and become more appealing to its receivers. If the wise words of a mythical figure such as Orpheus are 'verified' by natural philosophers, then they become more generalised and well-grounded.[862] This would mean that his allegorical interpretation of the Orphic poem was not one circulated in Orphic circles but simply a 'marketing technique'. However, we have already seen many reasons why the Derveni author cannot be included amongst those itinerant priests who wander around and take money from people through offering all kind of rites to them. His intense pre-occupation with the correct understanding of the poem and his criticism of those who make a profession out of the rites goes against this possibility. Also, it does not necessarily mean that this scientifical and allegorical approach would make the Derveni author more popular with an audience which presumably was after a 'quick fix' of religious salvation. Most argues that if the author is an Orphic he cannot ignore Pre-Socratic thought, since he 'believes that both Orpheus' revelation and contemporary physics are true'; this is why he attempts to combine them in a way that is close to 'secular theology', a religious movement that accommodates a sacred text to science.[863] However, we do not necessarily need to assume that the Orphic theological ideas were not of a cosmological nature. We have established through the analysis of other ancient sources that an allegorical interpretation such as the one by the Derveni author was not out of the ordinary, and would in fact be expected if ideas such as the airy nature of the soul could be justified. As Laks claims, the Derveni author is only interested in the physical world and the stars and the sun and the moon, because 'they are the work of intelligence'.[864] In other words, the author is not using Orpheus to benefit Pre-Socratic philosophy, but Pre-Socratic philosophy to exalt Orphism. The similarities to Pre-Socratic philosophy, however, does not necessarily mean that Orphic ideas were not of a cosmological nature too.

Based on the above, it seems that the Derveni text – meaning the allegorical interpretation of the Orphic poem – was secret and only revealed to initiates. This is supported by the Derveni author's constant opposition of those who understand the true meaning of the poem to those who do not: τοῖς] πολλοῖς (Col.VII.10), οἱ δὲ οὐ γινώσκον[τες] (Col.IX.2; Col.XXIII.5; Col.XXVI.8), μὴ γινώ-

---

862 Considering of course that the recepients accepted these natural theories.
863 Most, 1997, p.122.
864 Laks, 1997, p.132.

σκειν (Col.XX.2). Such an opposition would not make sense if the correct understanding of the poem according to the Derveni author was circulated openly, since nothing would prevent 'the many' from getting familiar with the true meaning. This does not mean that only certain people could get initiated, since we do not have evidence that suggests this. I propose, thus, that at some point during the Orphic initiation procedure the involvement of an expert who would give guidance in the understanding of Orphic literature through his teaching was essential, and it involved the analysis of Orphic religious text(s). It is difficult based on the available evidence to decide whether this exegesis took place before, during or after the practical part of the initiation procedure but perhaps this is not of particular importance since what matters is the fact that it was necessary and not when exactly it took place. Also, texts such as the Derveni Papyrus were probably owned and used by the Orphic initiates and the Orphic theogony was a key text that had to be understood and interpreted. This brings us back to what was mentioned in the introduction of this chapter, since we need to consider why the papyrus was used in the funeral pyre. If the text was a copy of Orphic teaching constituting knowledge transferred to the initiates through an interpreter, then the burning of the papyrus during the funeral might have had a double function. On the one hand, it could have had a ritual function similar to the one actualised by the gold tablets, meaning the transferring of knowledge in the afterlife through a physical object. On the other hand, if the interpretation of the text was secret and revealed only to initiates as suggested, the burning of the papyrus would ensure that the mystic knowledge would remain secret. Betegh also favours the hypothesis that the papyrus did have a function in the ritual, based on the Orphic concern with eschatology, the Orphic custom of 'equipping the dead with texts', the presence of other valuable objects in the pyre and possibly the important role of fire in the text.[865]

5.2 The Gurôb Papyrus

The Gurôb Papyrus' is dated to the mid-3rd century B.C. and it was found at Gurôb, an Egyptian town at the entry to the Fayûm. Only a part of a larger text is saved on the papyrus and since it is badly damaged we do not have any contextual information apart from that the text itself refers to the rituals of a cult group of Greek-speaking people in Ptolemaic Egypt.[866] Hordern notes that the script is

---

[865] Betegh, 2004, p.65–68.
[866] Graf and Johnston, 2013, p.150.

'a rather messy book-hand, roughly bilinear'.[867] As Graf and Johnston record, the language is liturgical, combining direct quotation with discursive text which perhaps constitutes directions for a ritual:

[ἔκ]αστα ἔ[χ]ων ἃ εὕρηι	1
τὰ] ὠμὰ δὲ συνλεγέ[τω	
] ..διὰ τὴν τελετήν.	
δῶρον δέξ]ατ'ἐμὸν ποινὰς πατ[έρων ἀθεμίστων.	
σῶισόν με Βριμὼ με[γάλη	5
Δημήτηρ τε 'Ρέα [	
Κούρητές τ'{ε} ἔνοπλοι [	
]ωμεν.	
ἵ]να ποιῶμεν ἱερὰ καλά	
].νηι κριός τε τράγος τε	10
] ἀπερ<ε>ίσια δῶρα.	
]..ου καὶ ἐπὶ ποταμοῦ νομῶι	
λαμβ]άνων τοῦ τράγου	
] τὰ δὲ λοιπὰ κρέα ἐσθιέτω	
]ος μὴ ἐφοράτω	15
]χου ἀναθεὶς εἰς τὸ ἀνηιρε[	
]αλων εὐχή·	
Πρωτόγο]νον καὶ Εὐβουλῆα καλῶ[	
]...εὑρήας κικλήσκω[	
... τε φίλους· σὺ ἀπαυάνας	20
Δ]ήμητρος καὶ Παλλάδος ἡμῖν	
Εὐβου]λεῦ Ἰρικεπαῖγε	22a
σῶισόν με [Ἀστεροπ]ῆτα	22b/23a
] εἷς Διόνυσος. σύμβολα	23b
]υρα θεὸς διὰ κόλπου	
ο]ἶν[ο]ν ἔπιον ὄνος βουκόλος	25
]..ιας σύνθεμα ἄνω κάτω τοῖς	
] καὶ ὃ σοι ἐδόθη ἀνήλωσαι	
ε]ἰς τὸν κάλαθον ἐμβαλ<ε>ῖν	
κ]ῶνος ῥόμβος ἀστράγαλοι	
]η ἔσοπτρος	30

....] having everything that he finds	1
....let him] collect the raw (meat)	
....] on account of the ritual.	
'[Receive my gift] as the payment for law[less ancestors...	
]Save me, Brimo, gr[eat	5
]and Demeter [and] Rhea [	
]and the armed Kouretes [...]	

---

[867] Hordern, 2000, p.131.

```
]that we ...
]so that we will perform beautiful rites
]....ram and he-goat                                    10
]immense gifts'.
] and along the river...
ta]king of the he-goat
]...let him eat the rest of the meat
]...let him not watch                                   15
]... dedicating the chosen
]....Prayer
'I call [Protogo]nos and Eubouleus,
]I call the wide
]...the dear ones. You, having parched...               20
of De]meter and Pallas
to us Eubou]leus, Irikepaios,                           22a
save me Hurler of lightn]ing...                         22b/23a
one Dionysos. Passwords                                 23b
]...god through the bosom
]... I drank [wine], donkey, herdsman                   25
]...token: above below for the...
]and consume what has been given to you
put in]to the basket,
spinning-top, bull-roarer, knucklebones
]mirror.[868]                                           30
```

Let us start with the specific deities which are also found in the gold tablets: Dionysos (Bacchos) is found in the tablets from Pelinna (D1, D2) dated to the early 3rd century B.C. and one from Amphipolis (D4) dated in the 4th century B.C. Brimo, Demeter and Rhea, mentioned in lines 5 and 6, are also mentioned in the two tablets found at Pherae (D3, D5) dated to the 4th century B.C. We have also seen that Demeter and Rhea were important deities in Orphism, as they have been associated with Orphic rites in ancient sources.[869] Protogonos and Eubouleus, who are mentioned in lines 18 and 22a, are also found in the gold tablets from Thurii (A1, A2, A3, A5) dated to the 4th century B.C. and tablet A5 from Rome (2nd

---

868 OF578F Bernabé. Bernabé (2005a) has plurar verbs in lines 18–19 but in my opinion plural is not compatible with the rest of the papyrus where we have singular. Hordern also reads singular verbs and points to με at line 22b (2000, p.138). Line 18: Πρωτόγο]νον Smyly. Line 22b/23a: [Ἀστεροπ]ῆτα West. Tr. Graf and Johnston, 2013, p.217 (Appendix: 3); apart from lines 27–30 translated by the author. Graf and Johnston, 2013, p.150.
869 See Chapter 2, p.48 ff.

A.D.). Also, the name Irikepaios in line 22a is another name for Phanes in the *Orphic Rhapsodies*.[870] Significantly, we find the word σύμβολα (passwords) which is also found in the tablet from Pherae (D3), in which case the passwords are Ἀνδρικεπαιδόθυρσον and Βριμώ. The last one, as already said, is also found in the Gurôb Papyrus and the first one could be perceived as a different form of Irikepaios combined with the word *thyrsos*. The gods are invoked through two prayers which are distinguished by the fact that they are in hexametres – in bold – and one of the two is introduced with what seems to be a heading.[871] Such headings were characteristic of the magical papyri too, such as the one discussed in Chapter 4.[872] The prayers were probably recited during or after an offering of sacrificial meat to the above mentioned gods as a payment for lawless ancestors (line 4). The animals must have been a ram and a goat which echo the formula uttered in the gold tablets or this could be due to the fact that the ram is often sacrificed to Persephone and the goat to Dionysos.[873] The fact that a sacrifice and consumption of meat is clearly stated in the papyrus in lines 2 and 14 is an important divergence from the Orphic avoidance of bloodshed and vegetarianism – as described in ancient sources such as Plato (Pl. *Leg.* 6.782c–d) – and the belief in the soul's transmigration.[874] The word ποινὰς mentioned in line 4 is also found in the gold tablets and its semasiological implications have already been discussed.

An identification of the lawless deed with Dionysos' dismemberment by the Titans is even more probable in the Gurôb Papyrus. In a passage from the *Protrepticus*, already discussed in Chapter 4, Clement specifically refers to a Dionysiac rite based on the Zagreus myth where Dionysos' toys are used as the symbols of the rite and whose author was Orpheus.[875] The final two verses of the Gurôb Papyrus mention the words 'spinning-top', 'bull-roarer', 'knuckle-bones' and 'mirror'. These are the toys which, as we saw, were used by the Titans to trick

---

870 As a variant of Erikepaios. OR15 = OF134F. See also OF139F, OF140F(XI). Hordern, 2000, p.133.
871 Smyly, 1921.
872 See section 4.5.3.
873 Graf and Johnston, 2013, p.151.
874 Pl. *Leg.* 6.782c–d: 'Ath: The custom of men sacrificing one another is, in fact, one that survives even now among many peoples; whereas amongst others we hear of how the opposite custom existed, when they were forbidden so much as to eat an ox, and their offerings to the gods consisted, not of animals, but of cakes of meal and grain steeped in honey, and other such bloodless sacrifices, and from flesh they abstained as though it were unholy to eat it or to stain with blood the altars of the gods; instead of that, those of us men who then existed lived what is called an "Orphic life," keeping wholly to inanimate food and, contrariwise, abstaining wholly from things animate. Clin: Certainly what you say is widely reported and easy to credit.' (Tr. Bury).
875 Clem. Al. *Protr.* 2.15.

Dionysos into his death and away from his guardians, the Kuretes, who are also mentioned in the Gurôb Papyrus in line seven. In the same context, Clement says that the phrase διὰ κόλπου θεός was a σύμβολον of the Sabazian mysteries and this phrase is also included in the Gurôb Papyrus (24).[876] A similar phrase is also found in gold tablet A1: δεσ{σ}ποίνας δ'{ε} ὑπὸ κόλπον ἔδυν χθονίας βασιλείας· ('I passed beneath the bosom of the Mistress, Queen of the Underworld'). This appears to be a statement of the initiate identifying himself with Dionysos born from Persephone, since one of the meanings of the word *kolpos* is 'womb'. In this case we would have the same password in both the GT and the Gurôb Papyrus. Moreover, the phrase ο]ἶν[ο]ν ἔπιον ὄνος in line 25 evokes the acclamations of the Eleusinian mysteries: ἐνήστευσα, ἔπιον τὸν κυκεῶνα, ἔλαβον ἐκ κίστης, ἐργασάμενος ἀπεθέμην εἰς κάλαθον καὶ ἐκ καλάθου εἰς κίστην.[877] The last part is also similar to the action described next in the Gurôb Papyrus, where the initiate is instructed to put some items back into the basket. If we accept West's reading of line 22b/23a, the phrase 'save me, hurler of lightn]ing ... | one (?) Dionysos', also has a parallel to the gold tablets and the Zagreus myth since we have seen that the lightning is associated with materialisation: in the gold tablets it is related to incarnation and in the Zagreus myth it constitutes the means of punishment of the Titans for killing Dionysos, and through their death the human race is created.[878] Finally, Clement refers to the word *boukolos* which is also found in the Gurôb Papyrus and is related to Dionysos' followers, the bull and Orphic initiates.[879] Jiménez San Cristóbal refers to the fact that the term βουκόλοι is occasionally used for Orphic officiates, which is a denomination characteristic of Dionysos with bull's horns and Graf notes that *boukolos* was a term designating a mid-range Bacchic initiate.[880] It should be mentioned that Clement does not directly identify as Orphic all of the above, but he does refer to Orpheus as the authority behind the rite related to the Zagreus myth and calls him 'the originator of the mysteries' (μυσταγωγόν).[881]

---

[876] Clem. Al. *Protr.* 2.14. See p.148. 'At any rate, in the Sabazian mysteries the sign (σύμβολον) given to those who are initiated is "the god over the breast" (ὁ διὰ κόλπου θεός·') this is a serpent drawn over the breast of the votaries, a proof of the licentiousness of Zeus'. Graf and Johnston, 2013, p.151.
[877] Clem. Al. *Protr.* 2.18: "I fasted; I drank the draught; I took from the chest; having done my task, I placed in the basket, and from the basket into the chest." (Tr. Butterworth).
[878] Gurôb Papyrus, 23–24.
[879] Hordern, 2000, p.134.
[880] Jiménez San Cristóbal, 2009, p.52; Eur. *Antiope* fr.203 Collard-Cropp. Aesch. *Edon. TrGF* fr.57.8–11. Graff and Johnston, 2013, p.151.
[881] Clem. Al. *Protr.* 2.17.

Considering all these similarities to other Orphic sources and texts, but also the important divergences, we need to establish what exactly the Gurôb Papyrus was and by whom it was used. The text of the papyrus appears to constitute instructions given to the initiate for the performance of a rite by the initiate himself/herself or instructions possessed by a priest for the performance of a rite. This can be adduced by the imperative of several verbs in prose text which seems to give instructions in between prayers which the initiate must utter to the gods during an offering. That the prayers are uttered by the performer of the ritual can be deduced from the verbs who are in the first person singular such as: σῶισόν με, καλῶ[, κικλήσκω[and phrases such as δῶρον δέξ]ατ'ἐμὸν. Such a text, thus, can be identified as an *hieros logos* in the sense that it gives instructions for a ritual. However, bearing in mind the discussion in Chapter 2 about the circulation of forgeries of *hieroi logoi*, we need to examine this possibility considering the eating of meat, which goes against the Orphic vegetarianism. The fact that the author of the papyrus combines various elements of the Orphic tradition leads me to the suggestion that he could be one of those wandering priests mentioned by Plato and who used books by Orpheus and Musaeus. As was discussed already, this kind of priests formed their texts and rituals through a process of *bricolage* combining various religious elements. I would even say that the compiler of this ritual text is almost trying too hard with all the *euchai* (17), *symbola* (23b) and *synthemata* (26) he includes.[882] We may recall Pausanias mentioning the Orphic Hymns possessed and used by the Lycomidae at Phlya which a *dadouchos* showed to him in secret.[883] Pausanias' comment on their genuineness suggests that most of the hymns in circulation were forgeries or copies of the original ones which might have been composed by a figure such as Onomakritos. The Gurôb Papyrus' ritual use of phrases such as θεὸς διὰ κόλπου and ο]ἶν[ο]ν ἔπιον ὄνος during a private initiation such as this one, is also perhaps incompatible with the usual use of such phrases in mysteries in which a group of people participated, such as the Eleusinian and the Sabazian ones. It does not seem probable that this is a Sabazian ritual, since neither Sabazios nor Kybele are mentioned, even though we have several different denominations of Dionysos. Moreover, the references to Demeter, Brimo and Pallas Athena count against this possibility, despite the inclusion of Rhea who was identified with Kybele. The presence of Pallas Athena who did not have a predominant role in other Orphic texts or Orphic beliefs, corrobates even more the suggestion that this text was a result of bricolage by an itinerant priest.

---

[882] For the meaning of the last two words see Graf and Johnston, 2013, p.154–155.
[883] For the discussion of this passage see p.46 ff.

If we refer back to the passage by Plato criticizing the itinerant priests performing private rituals we can see many elements which can be identified in the Gurôb Papyrus:[884]

- 'These they actually call initiations' [ἃς δὴ τελετὰς καλοῦσιν]:
  Line 3 of the Gurôb Papyrus identifies what is instructed as a *teletē* (διὰ τὴν τελετήν).
- 'through sacrifices and playful delights' [διὰ θυσιῶν καὶ παιδιᾶς ἡδονῶν]:
  A sacrifice might be usual practice during a ritual but it is significant that we also have toys used in the Gurôb Papyrus ritual.
- 'atonement and purification for their wrongdoing' [λύσεις τε καὶ καθαρμοὶ ἀδικημάτων]: This is clearly stated in the Gurôb Papyrus: δῶρον δέξ]ατ'ἐμὸν ποινὰς πατ[έρων ἀθεμίστων.

I would argue, therefore, that the Gurôb Papyrus belonged to an itinerant priest who offered purifications and rituals through a compilation of religious elements, but especially Orphic ones. The papyrus can certainly be identified as Orphic and be considered as part of Orphism. However, as I already argued in the previous chapters we need to distinguish at least two different strands in Orphism, and the Gurôb Papyrus would belong to the strand which is not exclusively Orphic. This is because it is a ritual influenced by Orphic ideas but it must be distinguished from the cosmological and scientific understanding of the Orphic texts which underlies other Orphic sources we have discussed so far. Even though we cannot be sure of how much text we are missing or that a religious philosophy was not outlined before or after the rite, the highly informal nature of the text, the comparative nature of the papyrus – characteristic of *bricolage* – the sacrifice and consumption of meat and the private character of the text – meaning that this ritual seems to have been performed one on one – and even its similarity to subsequent magical papyri distinguish it from the Orphic picture we have formed so far. Even though the text already has an exegetical – or rather instructive – nature its instructions go only as far as describing the ritual to be performed, in contrast to the DP or even the gold tablets which include traces of a theological narrative. It can be added that the absence of terms such as *pyr*, *aer*, *Helios* which are found in the DP, the gold tablets and other sources referring to Orphism also support the above suggestion, even though arguments *ex silentio* are not as potent. In addition, there is nothing in the Gurôb Papyrus as it stands to indicate that the person performing the ritual has a claim to purity, special status or special knowledge of truth which are characteristic of Orphic texts and

---

[884] Pl. *Resp.* 2.364e–365a. For text see p.21.

particularly important for being admitted to the Isles of the Blessed and for escaping the cycle of rebirths. There is also no clear indication that this *teletē* related to avoiding rebirth but rather that the ritual performed was primarily concerned with atonement from wrongdoings which was the main 'service' offered by the itinerant priests. This comes in contrast to the nature of the gold tablets and the depiction of Orphism in ancient sources as generally perceiving the afterlife as being better than the present life. The absence of Persephone might be related to this, as is the reference to Eubouleus who even though is a chthonic deity and also found in the GT, he was also associated with the Eleusinian mysteries and the Thesmophoria festival.[885] He is mentioned in the 'First Fruits Decree' (422/1 B.C.), a law about the Eleusinian mysteries which refers to sacrifices to Demeter, Kore, the God, the Goddess, Triptolemus and Eubouleus.[886] Clinton suggests that his role in the Eleusinian mysteries was to guide Kore back from the underworld which might indicate his association to life/rebirth rather than death, as perhaps also does his association to the Thesmophoria which related to matters of fertility and the renewal of nature.[887] On the other hand, the allusions to the Zagreus myth might indicate that this ritual offered an atonement from the crime of the Titans. If, however, we are dealing with a text used by an itinerant priest, it might be the case that the atonement aimed at the avoidance of punishments in the afterlife, rather than at deification, bearing in mind Plato's words who says that the so-called initiations performed by the itinerant priests 'free us from evils in the next world, while terrible things await those who neglect their sacrifices.'[888]

As Hordern observes, even though the Gurôb Papyrus might be an *hieros logos*, 'we may have here to do with a text belonging to a lower social and literary level as suggested by the somewhat messy script, occasional errors and perhaps by the irregular line-lengths'.[889] An itinerant priest was able to offer purifications and atonement of wrong-doings with a simple ritual – something much easier than living the *Orphikos Bios*, which demanded abstinence from killing, vegetarianism, the conduct of a just life and the acquiring of knowledge, as outlined by non-Orphic sources and the DP. As Nilsson notes, the purifications '...came to take a most important place for the many who, as man's nature is, were not able

---

[885] See fn.551.
[886] *IG* I³ 78.38–40.
[887] Clinton, 2007, p.351.
[888] Pl. *Resp.* 2.364e: ἃς δὴ τελετὰς καλοῦσιν, αἳ τῶν ἐκεῖ κακῶν ἀπολύουσιν ἡμᾶς, μὴ θύσαντας δὲ δεινὰ περιμένει.
[889] Hordern, 2000, p.132.

to take up an ascetic life but were impressed by the mystic doctrine or afraid of the consequences of their wrong-doings'.[890] It therefore seems plausible that the Gurôb Papyrus was an *hieros logos* written by an itinerant priest and used during purification rituals for people who wanted to be free of wrongdoings without necessarily living the demanding *Orphikos Bios*. The Gurôb Papyrus also makes evident how widespread Orphic myths, rites and ideas were and how, perhaps, the element which was common in all their various applications through rites or philosophical/scientific knowledge, was their curative capacity. Whether they offered the means to escape the cycle of rebirths and achieve deification through the acquiring of knowledge and 'waking' of the memory, or whether they offered the atonement of wrongdoings to avoid punishments, the Orphic texts and practices had the power to 'heal' and 'restore'.

5.3 Conclusion

In this chapter I argued that the Derveni author's interpretation of the Orphic poem is in accordance with Orphic ideas as have been established so far. The allegorical and cosmological understanding of Orphic texts was evidenced to be a common practice based on external sources which interpret Orphic ideas in the same way and using the same techniques as the Derveni author. This was evident in authors such as Macrobius, Plato, Plutarch, Diodorus, Iamblichus and others. Elements of the Orphic poem which the Derveni author interprets are distinctively different than other theogonical traditions, such as the swallowing of the *aidoion*, the subsequent creation of the whole cosmos by Zeus, the oracular and important role of Night and the peaceful and rightful acquiring of power by Zeus. It was established that the *aidoion* swallowed by Zeus is in fact the Protogonos of the *Orphic Rhapsodies*. Several more textual and conceptual similarities were also identified between the DP and the *Orphic Rhapsodies*.

The Derveni author identifies a primal entity which is ever-existing and manifested through the different rulers. This entity is Nous/Mind/Counsel. Every ruler represents a different cosmological stage where Nous is manifested in a different way. Zeus is equated with *aer* which underlies everything and generates life through a cooling process. There is a delicate balance between heat and cold and in this sense the importance of the Sun being at the right distance form the Earth is crucial. The creative process is driven by love and strife between the *eonta*, and the powers of heat and cold. This perception of cosmos can be perceived as a

---

890 Nilsson, 1935, p.220.

dual-faceted monism, where everthing is one but we also have manifestations of matter which are underlaid by Nous.

Several conceptual and textual parallels to Pre-Socratic philosophers were also established. The Derveni author's interpretation entails elements such as the no state of non-existence of Parmenides, the Mind of Anaxagoras or the air of Diogenes of Apollonia. The similarity with the totality of the Pre-Socratic philosophy comes down to the notion of the divine, being subject to the uniformity of impersonal power – which in the Derveni author's case would be Nous – and the solution to the One-Many problem. As far as the Orphic text in itself is concerned, there is the possibility that it contributed to the evolution from *mythos* to *logos*, or that there was a parallel development of philosophy and Orphic beliefs. It was also suggested that the Derveni author might be answering to a critique of the Orphic beliefs and mysteries by Herakleitos as evidenced in his fragments. This was based mostly on: the Derveni author's quoting Herakleitos to prove the opposite point and his insistence on proving that the use of the word *aidoion* – a word specifically targeted in Herakleitos' criticism – by Orpheus is not licentious.

The Derveni author appears to be a religious figure, most probably an Orphic *prophētēs* or *exēgētēs* who would explain the meaning of the Orphic texts and rites as part of the initiation procedure, as was argued. His critique against those who make a profession out of the rites, those who do not understand the correct meaning of the texts, and perform rites without gaining knowledge of their meaning, suggests that he is not one of the itinerant priests who used Orphic texts and were scorned by Plato. Neither does his interpretation constitute a marketing technique, since such a scientifical theology would not necessarily be appealing to the clientele persona of the itinerant priests, who were after quick and easy purifications.

On the other hand, the Gurôb Papyrus most probably constitutes one of the texts used by such itinerant priests since it is a highly comparative text and product of bricolage which combines several religious elements. The reference to a sacrifice also evidences that this rite goes against the Orphic practice of vegetarianism and of avoiding bloodshed. The papyrus' text also indicates that the myth of Dionysos' dismemberment influenced the formation of rites since Dionysos' toys are used during this ritual. Even though the Gurôb Papyrus can be considered Orphic it belongs to the same Orphic strand of the itinerant priests using books of Orpheus, since it combines some Orphic elements but it is not exclusively Orphic.

6 *Hieroi Logoi in 24 Rhapsodies*

6.1 Introduction

In this chapter I will discuss the so called *Hieroi Logoi in 24 Rhapsodies* which survives mainly through the works of Neoplatonists such as Proclus (mid 5th A.D.), Damascius (5th A.D.) and Olympiodorus (6th A.D.). These authors often include direct quotations of Orpheus in their commentaries on the Platonic dialogues, referring to Orpheus as 'the theologian'. When I began studying this work, I realised how difficult it was to make sense of it without having a continuous narrative available, but rather through disentagling hundreds of fragments. This is why I have attempted a reconstruction of the text, which is included in this chapter along with a translation, through analysing all the Orphic fragments related to the *Orphic Rhapsodies* published by Bernabé in 2004 and originally by Kern in 1922.[891]

The *Rhapsodies* are mentioned in the *Suda* under the name of Orpheus as the *Hieroi Logoi in 24 Rhapsodies*.[892] Before analysing the content and nature of the *Rhapsodies*, it would be helpful to say something about the Neoplatonists through whom this work has mainly survived. Olympiodorus was the pupil of Ammonius – who in his turn was a pupil of Proclus – in Alexandria. Olympiodorus is most discussed in relation to his references to the myth of the dismemberment of Dionysos by the Titans and as the only one who mentions the Dionysiac element in humans due to the anthropogony of the Titans, who had tasted Dionysos' flesh. This matter has been discussed extensively in Chapter 3 and so it will not be addressed in this chapter. In general, it is evident that the Neoplatonic commentators at some points interpreted the *Rhapsodies* in a way that would suit their own purposes. This can be seen in their constant attempts to form triads in the Theogony, and to interpret gods and elements by separating them into intelligible and sensible entities, and in their use of words such as 'mundane' and 'super-mundane', 'celestial' and 'super-celestial'. One example would be the Neoplatonic interpretation of the age of Zeus as the world of sense and matter and the age of Phanes as the intelligible world of the Platonic Ideas, which does not appear to be a part of the Orphic ideas as discussed so far.[893] Also, the similarities with Christian ideas that they found in the Orphic poems made them ideal for supporting Greek paganism through questioning Christianity's originality, and

---

[891] From now on I will be using the term *Rhapsodies* for convenience.
[892] West, 1983, p.226.
[893] Guthrie, 1952, p.76.

naturally the Neoplatonists achieved their results through forcing specific meanings in their reading of the *Rhapsodies*.[894] However, it does not follow that they also altered the verses that they quote. Of course, interpolations might exist in the text but this needs to be decided via close examination of the individual surviving verses themselves rather than being presupposed.

West argued that 'there is nothing in the fragments of the *Rhapsodies* which is evidently post-Hellenistic on grounds of metre, prosody, style, or philosophical or religious content' and maintains that they were in circulation soon after 100 B.C.[895] It must be pointed out though that this date is not so much based on the *Rhapsodies*' contents but on West's theory that Theognetus the Thessalian, who is given as the author by *Suda* – which also gives Cercops the Pythagorean – compiled the *Rhapsodies* 'at Pergamum when Athenodorus was there', whom he considers one of the sources of the story.[896] Gruppe, on the other hand, suggested that the study of language and metre have not been helpful in deciding a date of compilation, that the *Rhapsodies* do not contain any traces of late doctrines and that their antiquity cannot be clearly disproven.[897] Even though this work is treated as being a result of the compilation of earlier works, West, Gruppe and Guthrie suggest that the compiler recomposed a Theogony based on earlier Orphic theogonies, which presupposes that the *Rhapsodies* comprise a single continuing theogonical narrative, as evident from these scholars' use of the term 'theogony'. However, this might not be true, and we will need to examine the verses themselves to establish if their content is only theogonical or also exegetical. Even if the latter was the case there might still have been a thematic continuance in the narrative – if for example theogonical/cosmogonical material was followed by a hymn to a deity or exegetical verses about the meaning of myths. Also, if this work is a compilation of earlier works which were not recomposed, then the date that the *Rhapsodies* were compiled might not be as significant as the content of the *Rhapsodies* or the date of individual works. Similarly, Guthrie argued that the date of an archetypal Orphic Theogony, or even of the Rhapsodic one, 'is bound to be a date of compilation' which 'reduces considerably the importance of the question'.[898] He also notes that it is more important to 'consider each single feature or element in the theogony' and if possible discuss the similarities with other Orphic material and the probable date of introduction (p.78). Gruppe, who also

---

[894] Guthrie, 1952, p.72.
[895] West, 1983, 229.
[896] West, 1983, p.2
[897] Gruppe, 1890. Guthrie, 1952, p.77.
[898] Guthrie, 1952, p.78.

argues for a re-composition, maintains that the content and main doctrines of the *Rhapsodies* can be dated to the beginning of the 5th century and that a 6th century origin is possible, even though the date at which they were composed cannot be decided.[899] He also argues that behind this reconciliation of the Orphic tradition, which was conservative, there is no attempt to present a specific consistent system of religious philosophy, and that the attempt to integrate various Orphic sources has produced a high degree of inconsistency in the *Rhapsodies*.[900] If this is the case, I agree with Gruppe that we need to distinguish between the date of the 'individual concepts' in the *Rhapsodies* and the date that it was written down, since the Orphic works compiled were presumably in circulation before they were written down. After establishing the contents of the *Rhapsodies* I will also attempt to define their use. Their title as *hieroi logoi* already indicates their relation to religion and initiations since as we saw *hieroi logoi* constituted a kind of 'script' or aetiology of a rite.[901] To this is related Guthrie's argument that there is a basic difference between the Hesiodic Theogony and the *Rhapsodies* since 'the one could never be made the doctrinal basis of a religious life; the other both could be and in fact was'.[902] Again, this is something which needs to be decided after examining the verses themselves.

As already mentioned, it is evident from the scholarly approach to the question of the nature of the *Rhapsodies* that it is assumed that we have to do with a single continuous theogonical narrative. The early existence of Orphic *hieroi logoi*, often of a cosmogonical and theogonical nature, has been established by the discussion in the previous chapters where the importance of Orphic texts in Orphism was identified. As we saw in Chapter 2, already in the late fifth and fourth centuries, Orpheus' name is cited next to those of Homer and Hesiod as the most famous poets in a way that indicates that this was a canonical list; so poems under the name of Orpheus were already in circulation, as is in any case evidenced by the Orphic Theogony in the DP.[903] It is, thus, very probable that theogonical/cosmogonical poem(s) were part of the *Rhapsodies* as the surviving fragments also affirm. Damascius, who is one of the main sources, uses the following expression before proceeding to give the outline of a Theogony: ἐν μὲν τοίνυν ταῖς

---

899 Gruppe's position is summarised in Guthrie, 1952, p.74–9.
900 Guthrie, 1952, p.77.
901 See section 2.2, p.20.
902 Guthrie, 1952, p.84.
903 Linforth, 1941, p.67, p.105–107. Ar. *Ran.* 1031–1036. Alexis fr.135 Kock = Ath. *Deipn.* IV. 164b–c. Pl. *Ap.* 41a. See p.70 ff for discussion and texts.

φερομέναις ταύταις ῥαψωιδίαις Ὀρφικαῖς ἡ θεολογία.[904] In the same paragraph he specifies that this was the usual/customary Orphic Theogony: τοιαύτη μὲν ἡ συνήθης Ὀρφικὴ θεολογία.[905] This suggests that a Theogony was included in the *Rhapsodies*, but it was not the only poem/text since some sources distinguish between the Theogony and the totality of the *Rhapsodies*. The term θεολογία and the fact that Orpheus is referred to as the θεολόγος by the sources, also suggests that this work was of an exegetical nature since a θεολογία is different from a θεογονία. For example, Clement of Alexandria mentions the two terms side by side, which indicates the difference between them: 'Cleanthes of Pedasis, the Stoic philosopher, sets forth no genealogy of the gods (θεογονίαν), after the manner of poets, but a true theology (θεολογίαν).'[906] The term θεολογία is also often used in relation to Orpheus in other ancient sources and refers to a 'science of things divine'.[907] Menander Rhetor (3rd B.C.) classifies the hymns by Orpheus along with the poems of Empedokles and Parmenides under the category of 'scientific hymns' (ὕμνοι φυσικοί) since they deal with the nature of the gods and not

---

904 Dam. *De princ.* 123: 'In the *Rhapsodies* that are circulated under the name *Orphic*, the following is the theology...' (Tr. Ahbel-Rappe).
905 Dam. *De princ.* 123.
906 Clem. Al. *Protr.* 6.61: Κλεάνθης δὲ ὁ Πηδασεύς, ὁ ἀπὸ τῆς Στοᾶς φιλόσοφος, οὐ θεογονίαν ποιητικήν, θεολογίαν δὲ ἀληθινὴν ἐνδείκνυται (Tr. Butterworth).
907 Diod. Sic. I.23.6: ἐν δὲ τοῖς ὕστερον χρόνοις Ὀρφέα, μεγάλην ἔχοντα δόξαν παρὰ τοῖς Ἕλλησιν ἐπὶ μελῳδίᾳ καὶ τελεταῖς καὶ θεολογίαις: 'Now at a later time Orpheus, who was held in high regard among the Greeks for his singing, initiatory rites, and instructions on things divine...'; IV.25.3: περὶ δὲ παιδείαν ἀσχοληθεὶς καὶ τὰ περὶ τῆς θεολογίας μυθολογούμενα μαθών, ἀπεδήμησε μὲν εἰς Αἴγυπτον, κἀκεῖ πολλὰ προσεπιμαθὼν μέγιστος ἐγένετο τῶν Ἑλλήνων ἔν τε ταῖς θεολογίαις καὶ ταῖς τελεταῖς καὶ ποιήμασι καὶ μελῳδίαις: 'And after he had devoted his entire time to his education and had learned whatever the myths had to say about the gods, he journeyed to Egypt, where he further increased his knowledge and so became the greatest man among the Greeks both for his knowledge of the gods and for their rites, as well as for his poems and songs.' (Tr. Oldfather). Clem. Al. *Protr.* 7.63: ὁ δὲ Θρᾴκιος ἱεροφάντης καὶ ποιητὴς ἅμα, ὁ τοῦ Οἰάγρου Ὀρφεύς, μετὰ τὴν τῶν ὀργίων ἱεροφαντίαν καὶ τῶν εἰδώλων τὴν θεολογίαν, παλινῳδίαν ἀληθείας εἰσάγει: 'And the Thracian interpreter of the mysteries, who was a poet too, Orpheus the son of Oeagrus, after his exposition of the orgies and account of the idols, brings in a recantation consisting of truth.' (Tr. Butterworth). Philostr. *Imag.* 6.16–21: Ὁ δὲ κάθηται ἀρτίχνουν μὲν ἐκβάλλων ἴουλον ἐπιρρέοντα τῇ παρειᾷ, τιάραν δὲ χρυσαυγῆ ἐπὶ κεφαλῆς αἰωρῶν τό τε ὄμμα αὐτῷ ξὺν ἁβρότητι ἐνεργὸν καὶ ἔνθεον ἀεὶ τῆς γνώμης εἰς θεολογίαν τεινούσης: 'Orpheus sits there, the down of a first beard spreading over his cheeks, a tiara bright with gold standing erect upon his head, his eye tender, yet alert, and divinely inspired as his mind ever reaches out to divine themes.' See also Pl. *Resp.* 2.379a.

narrative action.⁹⁰⁸ This again suggests that Orphic texts were of a more complex nature than theogonical poetry, as was also evident from the previous chapters where we established that Orphic works were also of a cosmogonical and philosophical/scientific nature and required exegesis.

Edmonds has suggested that the *Rhapsodies* could contain a variety of poems 'that had been composed and reworked over the centuries by a number of different *bricoleurs*' and he compared them to the *Sibylline Oracles*.⁹⁰⁹ However, the problem with this analysis, as with other suggestions being made for the nature of the *Rhapsodies*, is that it makes assumptions rather than a systematic analysis of the verses. This problem is exacerbated by the absence of a reconstruction of the text, no matter how fragmentary and lacunose it might be, since an attempt to arrange the verses would create a clearer picture of the whole. Edmonds, thus, argues that the contents of the *Rhapsodies* have been recomposed and reworked – which might well be the case – without analysing the ancient text itself. Instead, he seems at times to overly rely on the nature of the *Sibylline Oracles* to define the *Rhapsodies*.⁹¹⁰ For example he argues that the preoccupations of the sources may skew a reconstruction of the *Rhapsodies*, through giving mostly examples of Lactantius' biased use of the *Sibylline Oracles* (p.155). In a similar manner, Edmonds says that the focus of the Neoplatonists on the creation of the world from first principles, or the many from one in relation to Dionysos' dismemberment, may distort our view of the content of the *Rhapsodies*, which may have included more about Demeter's wanderings and Persephone's grief (p.154). However, assuming what was and was not in the *Rhapsodies* based on the interpretation of the verses' sources is dangerous and it could constitute another case of assumptions based on the interpreter's pre-occupations. A reconstruction does not have to take into consideration the interpretation of the sources, other than for the placement of the verse(s) in the narrative, and a misinterpretation does not mean that the verse has been misquoted or altered. The quoted verses alone should be our safe guide for reconstructing and interpreting the *Rhapsodies* and determining their status.

The nature of the work is also affected by the length implied by its division into 24 rhapsodies. The Homeric classification into 24 rhapsodies most probably

---

908 Men. *Rhet*. 1.333: φυσικοὶ δὲ οἵους οἱ περὶ Παρμενίδην καὶ Ἐμπεδοκλέα ἐποίησαν, τίς ἡ τοῦ Ἀπόλλωνος φύσις, τίς ἡ τοῦ Διός, παρατιθέμενοι. καὶ οἱ πολλοὶ τῶν Ὀρφέως τούτου τοῦ τρόπου: 'Philosophical are the kind composed by Parmenides and Empedocles, explaining the nature of Apollo or Zeus. Most of the hymns of Orpheus are of this type.' (Tr. Race). Edmonds, 2013, p.146.
909 Edmonds, 2013, p.149.
910 Edmonds, 2013, p.150–159.

took place in Hellenistic times and the same is likely to be true for the *Orphic Rhapsodies*. The first appearance of the term rhapsody is in the 5th century B.C. but the practice and name may be older.[911] It is generally thought that the word comes from the verb ῥάπτειν which means to sew or stitch together. Definitions in Plutarch and Lucian, however, of a rhapsody as a 'portion of an epic poem fit for recitation' must be due to the later Hellenistic perception of these poems as books.[912] A rhapsody would be a poem to be recited and not sung and it does not necessarily mean that rhapsodes recited and composed only epic poems of great length such as the Homeric ones.[913] Plato, for example refers to Hesiod as a rhapsode in which case a rhapsody might refer to the idea of a poet's creative weaving of a text.[914] As Pavese argues, rhapsody 'is a formally unitary genre, which comprehends various species'.[915] One of Pavese's species is the 'theological' in which Hesiod's *Theogony* and the Homeric Hymns are included and is defined in the following way: 'Whereas the heroic and the antiquarian poems are historical and anthropocentric, the theological poem is theocentric and philosophic. The rhapsodic hymns are *prooimia* whose function is to introduce a following rhapsody. Their themes are Proposition and Dismission, Birth, Virtues, Abode, and Deeds of the gods'.[916] Some of the contents of the *Rhapsodies* could follow this model and if this is the case, it would not mean that the *Rhapsodies* should be dated to

---

911 Arist. *Poet.* 1447b.21–23: ὁμοίως δὲ κἂν εἴ τις ἅπαντα τὰ μέτρα μιγνύων ποιοῖτο τὴν μίμησιν καθάπερ Χαιρήμων ἐποίησε Κένταυρον μικτὴν ῥαψῳδίαν ἐξ ἁπάντων τῶν μέτρων, καὶ ποιητὴν προσαγορευτέον: 'Equally, even if someone should produce mimesis in a medley of all the metres (as Chaeremon did in composing his *Centaur*, a hybrid rhapsody containing all the metres), he ought still to be called a poet.' (Tr. Halliwell). Pl. *Leg.* 2.658b: ΑΘ: Εἰκός που τὸν μέν τινα ἐπιδεικνύναι, καθάπερ Ὅμηρος, ῥαψῳδίαν, ἄλλον δὲ κιθαρῳδίαν, τὸν δέ τινα τραγῳδίαν, τὸν δ' αὖ κωμῳδίαν: 'Ath: The natural result would be that one man would, like Homer, show up a rhapsody, another a harp-song, one a tragedy and another a comedy...' (Tr. Bury). Soph. *OT* 391–92. Hdt. 5.67.1. Ford, 1988, p.300.
912 Ford, 1988, p.300.
913 Pavese, 1998, p.63–64.
914 Pl. *Resp.* 10.600d–e: Ὅμηρον δ' ἄρα οἱ ἐπ' ἐκείνου, εἴπερ οἷός τ' ἦν πρὸς ἀρετὴν ὀνι(νά)ναι ἀνθρώπους, ἢ Ἡσίοδον ῥαψῳδεῖν ἂν περιιόντας εἴων, καὶ οὐχὶ μᾶλλον ἂν αὐτῶν ἀντείχοντο ἢ τοῦ χρυσοῦ καὶ ἠνάγκαζον παρὰ σφίσιν οἴκοι εἶναι, ἢ εἰ μὴ ἔπειθον, αὐτοὶ ἂν ἐπαιδαγώγουν ὅπῃ ᾖσαν, ἕως ἱκανῶς παιδείας μεταλάβοιεν: 'But if Homer was able to benefit his fellow men by promoting their virtue, would his contemporaries have allowed him or Hesiod to go round reciting and not have held on to them more tightly than to their gold, and have compelled them to live among them, or if they couldn't persuade them, they themselves would have followed them round wherever they went until they had received a sufficient level of education?' (Tr. Emlyn-Jones).
915 Pavese, 1998, p.84.
916 Pavese, 1998, p.86.

the 8th–6th century, but that some of its contents might have been transmitted to Hellenistic times while maintaining their nature. The few testimonies about specific rhapsodies refer to the episode of Phanes being narrated in the 4th rhapsody and the generation of the Giants in the 8th. If this is true it seems improbable that the rhapsodies were as long as Homer's since these two episodes are relatively close in terms of narrative – even though this is not adequate reason to exclude lengthy rhapsodies. Edmonds agrees that there is no reason to suppose that each Orphic rhapsody was as long as Homer's and so does West.[917]

6.2 West's Reconstruction of the Orphic theogonies

It is necessary to refer to any previous attempts to reconstruct the *Rhapsodies*. Essentially, West is the main scholar who has dealt with the *Rhapsodies* in general and in a detailed way – approaching them as a Theogony as already mentioned – and the importance of his contribution to the study of Orphism is unquestionable.[918] In his *Orphic Poems*, West has followed a stemmatological approach and reconstructed six different Orphic theogonies: the Protogonos Theogony which is the oldest and an archetype, the Derveni Theogony, the Eudemian Theogony, the Hieronymian Theogony, the Cyclic Theogony and the Rhapsodic Theogony. West assumes that the compiler of the Rhapsodic Theogony used the other Orphic theogonies he has reconstructed, with the aim of producing one Theogony assimilating all the earlier traditions. However, this becomes problematic for several reasons. Firstly, as will become evident, the *Rhapsodies'* contents varied and were not just theogonical. Secondly, the Protogonos Theogony and the Cyclic Theogony are West's own conception and not mentioned by any source; the Eudemian Theogony and the Hieronymos and Hellanikos Theogony are only referenced by Damascius and Athenagoras and there are very few details and testimonia about them.[919] West's reconstructions are particularly problematic in the Eudemian, Hieronymian and Cyclic cases. Even though the only information we have for the Eudemian theogony is that it begins with Night, West has reconstructed a detailed storyline that does not have strong foundations and is based on assumptions. For example, West reconstructs the beginning of the Eudemian theogony based on a passage from the *Timaeus* where Plato mentions a

---

[917] Edmonds, 2013, p.149–150. West, 1983, p.248.
[918] West, 1983.
[919] Dam. *De Princ.* 123–124. Athenagoras, *Leg. pro Christ.* 18–20. Hier. and Hell.: OF69T–OF89F. Eudemian: OF20F–OF27V.

theogony referring to the offspring of Ge and Ouranos, namely Oceanus and Tethys who beget Phorkys, Kronos and Rhea who beget Zeus and Hera.[920] Nowhere does Plato mention Night, but West considers that this should not be an obstacle to identifying this theogony with the Eudemian one, although, as mentioned, the only information we have for the Eudemian theogony is that it began with Night.[921] Furthermore, his reconstruction of the Eudemian theogony, which he dates to the 4th century B.C., is heavily dependent on the argument that it constitutes a source of the Cyclic Theogony, an argument that is not very strong considering that the Cyclic theogony is not mentioned in any sources and is West's hypothetical construction.[922] Its existence is inferred from West's comparison of a theogony in Apollodorus' *Library* with the reconstructed narrative of the Rhapsodic Theogony, and his assumption that this theogony must have been a different one, which was part of the Epic Cycle, based on the premise that Apollodorus was using the Epic Cycle as a source.[923] However, almost all of the similarities can be found in Hesiod as well, and so it is not clear why this Theogony should be considered to be an Orphic one. The same methodology is followed for the Hieronymian Theogony and Protogonos Theogony which constitutes a sort of archetype and understandably is bound to be speculative.

In relation to the Rhapsodic Theogony, West has not attempted a reconstruction of the ancient text with the actual verses surviving as in my case, but only of the narrative. West argues that: 'The *Rhapsodic Theogony* was a composite work, created in the late Hellenistic period by conflating earlier Orphic poems, in particular the Hieronymian (a descendant of the Protogonos), Eudemian, and Cyclic Theogonies'.[924] West's methodology, in my opinion, has several deficiencies and contradictions. The main one is that he used the Orphic fragments referring to the *Rhapsodies* to reconstruct the Protogonos, the Cyclic, the Eudemian and the Hieronymos and Hellanikos theogonies, even though he considered the Rhapsodic Theogony to be the latest of them.[925] For example he uses verses from the *Rhapsodies* to reconstruct the ancient text of the Derveni theogony which is the oldest one and for which we have direct evidence.[926] However, he considers that the

---

[920] Pl. *Tim.* 40e.
[921] West, 1983 p.117–118.
[922] West, 1983, p.123–26.
[923] Apollod. *Bibl.* 1.1.1–1.2.1.4. West, 1983, p.121–126.
[924] West, 1983, p.69–70.
[925] This is obvious from statements such as: 'The above reconstruction <of the Derveni Theogony> assumes that the Derveni poem in its latter parts contained everything that I have inferred (on the basis of the *Rhapsodies*) that the Protogonos Theogony contained' p.101.
[926] West, 1983, p.114–115: these are namely the following lines: 9 = OF112F and 38–40 = OF155F.

compiler of the *Rhapsodies* did not have the Derveni Theogony as a source, even though, as we will see, identical verses present in both of them make it plausible that they were somehow related.[927] He has also reconstructed the narrative of the *Rhapsodies* using ideas and entities found in other Orphic sources such as the *Argonautika*, the *Orphic Hymns*, Nonnus' *Dionysiaca* and Apollodorus' *Bibliotheca* even though as he says 'this source does not reflect the Rhapsodies directly but the Cyclic Theogony which the Rhapsodies incorporated'.[928]

6.3 Methodology of the Reconstruction of the *Orphic Rhapsodies*

I must make clear why I considered this reconstruction necessary, as well as what exactly its status is. Firstly, there has been no attempt so far to reconstruct the actual text: this in itself makes it worthwhile. Contrary to West – who has reconstructed only the narrative – I have based my reconstruction solely on the Rhapsodic fragments in order to not presuppose the presence of earlier ideas regardless of the actual text available. The narrative, thus, is based on the verses surviving and not any external evidence. Firstly, the reconstruction was a challenge in itself since Kern claimed that it is impossible to arrange the Orphic fragments of the *Rhapsodies* in a proper order; he emphasised this by placing OF63 (Kern), which is cited as coming from the fourth Rhapsody, at the beginning of his collection of the Orphic Fragments related to the *Rhapsodies*.[929] Bernabé also says that there are few helpful sources for organising the fragments.[930] However, even though there are some difficulties in the process of putting the fragments into a narrative order, the majority of the sources do provide information that can be used as a basis for this procedure. Some of them note that the quoted verses were at the beginning of the Rhapsodic Theogony or in a specific Rhapsody while others inform us about the basic storyline and structure of the Rhapsodic Theogony. This will be evident, since I have divided the text into sections and given a detailed justification for the arrangement of the verses in the specific order for each section.[931]

---

927 For West's stemma of the Orphic theogonies see p.264 (1983).
928 West, 1983, p.70–74.
929 Kern, 1922, p.141.
930 Bernabé, 2004, p.99.
931 See Apendix.

The outcome of the reconstruction constitutes the surviving text – as much as we have available – of the *Rhapsodies* at the time it was written down. I am not attempting to recreate an archetype of Orphic theogonies, neither is my approach stemmatological. The reconstruction of the text of the *Rhapsodies* is a necessary step towards grasping its content and narrative in a much clearer way than is possible when having to go through innumerable fragments. This will make it possible to distinguish patterns and motifs such as the regular use of epithets for example. Furthermore, the reconstruction of specific episodes allows for more elaborate, detailed and substantial connections to be made with other Orphic sources, mainly the Orphic Theogony of the Derveni Papyrus and the text of the gold tablets. It must be acknowledged that this attempt required speculation, so there is room for changes and improvements and it is in no way a perfect reconstruction. Even so, this text could benefit Orphic studies since approaching the *Rhapsodies* as a whole instead of through a warren of fragments can change how we see the work itself, while the fragments become more intelligible when they are a part of a story. This process is also essential in order to establish if there was a continuous storyline or thematic coherence in the *Rhapsodies* or if its contents varied.

The methodology for the reconstruction was primarily a careful examination of all the Orphic fragments related to the *Rhapsodies* in order to establish which were giving actual quotations of the text. Thereafter, the quoted verses were extracted from the text and placed in an order which was determined by following indications provided by the ancient sources who quoted the fragments. For example, some sources indicate the order of the gods' successions which helped organise the content in thematic episodes. Then, at a more detailed level some sources indicated that the quoted verses came from a specific point in the narrative, which helped in arranging the verses within each thematic episode. I have also attempted to incorporate a small number of paraphrases by the sources where this could make the narrative clearer: these are given in *italics* and with the symbol ~. I have avoided reconstructing ancient verses of my own based on passages that refer to the story, since this would be excessively speculative.[932] However, I have included an English paraphrase of what the hypothetical verses would have said, again to make the narrative clearer and include as many details as possible. These are given with the symbol *. The reconstruction, then, consists of a majority of poetic verses with some paraphrases. There are two cases where I incorporated text taken from other works, considering that it would help fill the

---

[932] I have, however, with some hesitation included Bernabé's reconstruction of OR10 (= OF121F). I have used the symbol ^ to mark the reconstructed nature of OR10.

gaps in the storyline; these are given with the symbol §. The first case is OR1 (OF1F) which I have suggested to be an Orphic verse in the previous chapter and a canonical beginning of Orphic *hieroi logoi*.[933] The other case is a passage from Nonnus (OR81 = OF308V) which refers to Dionysos' dismemberment myth and it was only used to fill gaps of an episode we already know from other sources that it was part of the *Rhapsodies*; it was not, thus, used to add a myth or episode not already part of the *Rhapsodies*.

Difficulties included the relatively late date of the sources and the possibility that their representation of the verses and story was biased and manipulated for the sake of the Neoplatonic context. I was particularly aware of that and did not overly rely on the sources' explanation or interpretation of the verses but only on their indications about their location in the narrative. Finally, the following table includes the sources used for the reconstruction in ascending chronological order so we can have a chronological frame and keep in mind that we have sources as early as the 1st century A.D. – not including Plato, whom most of our sources are commenting on when quoting verses from the *Rhapsodies*.

Tab. 5: Sources of the *Orphic Rhapsodies*

5th B.C.	1st A.D.	2nd A.D.	3rd A.D.	4th A.D.	5th A.D.	6th A.D.
Plato	Plutarch	Vettius Valens	Lactantius	Syrianus	Proclus	Simplicius
		Clement of Alexandria	Porphyry	Nonnus	Hermias	Ioannis Malalas
					Damascius	Olympiodorus
					Aristocritus Manichean	Tzetzes (12th A.D.)

What is the status of this reconstruction? Considering that apart from verses it also includes some paraphrases and in two cases, as I said, texts from other works, it should be clear that I do not suggest that the totality of the text was the actual form of the ancient text of the *Rhapsodies*. I suggest that the quoted verses were part of the text and anything else part of the narrative of the *Rhapsodies*. This text does not in any way constitute an archetype of the nature of West's Pro-

---

[933] See discussion in p.254 ff.

togonos Theogony. It includes as much text as survives and a fairly complete narrative of the *Rhapsodies*, and the purpose is to analyse its contents in the same way I have analysed other Orphic sources such as the Derveni Papyrus and the gold tablets. Any textual, semasiological and narrative similarities between the *Rhapsodies* and Orphic ideas or sources I have discussed so far will be pointed out, as well as any divergences. Common ideas and similarities will have to be explained in terms of the nature of the Orphic texts. Furthermore, the matter of variations, amendments and additions that occurred through time and throughout its transmission is a matter which requires the analysis of each verse and fragment individually. We can, however, rely on West's suggestion that there is nothing post-Hellenistic in the *Rhapsodies;* in the few cases there was any suspicion of post-Hellenistic elements these were excluded from the reconstruction.

6.4 Reconstruction of the Orphic Rhapsodies

The Beginning: Chronos, Aether and the Egg

(1) § Ἀείσω ξυνετοῖσι· θύρας δ' ἐπίθεσθε, βέβηλοι §	(1) § I will sing for those who are wise, cover your ears, you profane §
(2) ὦναξ, Λητοῦς υἱ᾽, ἑκατηβόλε, Φοῖβε κραταιέ, πανδερκές, θνητοῖσι καὶ ἀθανάτοισιν ἀνάσσων, Ἠέλιε, χρυσέαισιν ἀειρόμενε πτερύγεσσιν, δωδεκάτην δὴ τήνδε παραὶ σέο ἔκλυον ὀμφήν, σεῦ φαμένου· σὲ δέ γ' αὐτόν, ἑκηβόλε, μάρτυρα θείην.	(2) O master Apollo, son of Leto, you who shoot with your rays from afar, radiant and mighty; you who oversee everything and rule over mortals and immortals; Sun raised up in the air with golden wings. You have addressed me with your god-like voice twelve times; and since you have spoken to me, you who shine from afar I have made my witness...
(3) ~ τὴν πρώτην πάντων αἰτίαν Χρόνον καλεῖ. ~	(3) ~ Time was the pre-existing cause of all things. ~
(4) Αἰθέρα μὲν Χρόνος οὗτος ἀγήραος ἀφθιτόμητις γείνατο καὶ μέγα χάσμα πελώριον ἔνθα καὶ ἔνθα, οὐδέ τι πεῖραρ ὑπῆν, οὐ πυθμήν, οὐδέ τις ἕδρα.	(4) From Chronos, the one that never gets old and has imperishable counsel, Aether was born and a great Chasm stretching from this side to the other and it did not have an end, nor a bottom and neither any foundation.
(5) ~ Ἀδιακρίτων πάντων ὄντων ~ κατὰ σκοτόεσσαν ὀμίχλην	(5) ~ And everything was undivided ~ in the dark mist
(6) Νὺξ ζοφερά ~ πάντα κατεῖχε καὶ ἐκάλυπτε τὰ ὑπὸ τὸν Αἰθέρα. ~	(6) ~ and everything was held together by ~ gloomy Night ~ who covered what was under Aether. ~
(7) ~ ⏑ ἔπειτα δ᾽ ἔτευξε μέγας Χρόνος Αἰθέρι δίωι ὤεον ἀργύφεον. ⏑⏑ – ⏑⏑ – ⏑⏑ – ⏑	(7) ... Then great Chronos created a shining egg along with the divine Aether.
(8) Πρωτόγονος Φαέθων περιμήκεος Αἰθέρος υἱός,	(8) And Protogonos Phaethon the son of enormous Aether,
(9) ὡρμήθη δ᾽ ἀνὰ κύκλον ἀθέσφατον. – ⏑⏑ – ⏑	(9) began to move in an incredible circle.

The birth of Phanes: the First Ruler

(10) ^Ῥῆξε δ' ἔπειτα Φάνης νεφέλην, ἀργῆτα χιτῶνα, ‹ἐκ δὲ› σχισθέντος κρανίου πολυχανδέος ᾠοῦ ἐξέθορε πρώτιστος ἀνέδραμε τ' ἀρσενόθηλυς Πρωτόγονος πολυτίμητος^ ⏑⏑ – ⏑⏑ – ⏑	(10) ^Then Phanes broke through the clouds his bright tunic and from the divided shell of the great-encompassing egg he sprang upwards first of all, the hermaphrodite and highly-honoured Protogonos.^
(11) τετράσιν ὀφθαλμοῖσιν ὁρώμενος ἔνθα καὶ ἔνθα	(11) with four eyes looking all around
(12) χρυσείαις πτερύγεσσι φορεύμενος ἔνθα καὶ ἔνθα	(12) with golden wings moving all around.
(13) χάσμα δ' ὑπ' ἠέριον καὶ νήνεμος ἐρράγη αἰθὴρ ὀρνυμένοιο Φάνητος ⏑ – ⏑⏑ – ⏑⏑ – ⏑	(13) And at the time that Phanes sprung up, the misty chasm below and windless Aether were separated.
(14) βρίμας ταυρείους ἀφιεὶ‹ς› χαροποῦ τε λέοντος	(14) *He had the heads* of a fierce bull and of a lion with incandescent look
(15) θῆλυς καὶ γενέτωρ κρατερὸς θεὸς Ἠρικεπαῖος.	(15) female and father, all-mighty God Erikepaios.
(16) ποιμαίνων πραπίδεσσιν ἀνόμματον ὠκὺν Ἔρωτα,	(16) Cherishing in his heart swift and eyeless Eros,
(17) – ⏑⏑ – ⏑⏑ – ⏑⏑ πρῶτον δαίμονα σεμνόν, Μῆτιν σπέρμα φέροντα θεῶν κλυτόν, ὅν τε Φάνητα πρωτόγονον μάκαρες κάλεον κατὰ μακρὸν Ὄλυμπον,	(17) ...the immaculate daemon called Metis, who bore the famous seed of the gods, and which the blessed on long Olympus call Phanes the firstborn,
(18) οἷσιν ἐπεμβεβαὼς δαίμων μέγας αἰὲν ἐπ' ἴχνη.	(18) in whose tracks, the mighty daemon forever trod.

The First Creation of the World by Phanes

(19) τὸν τόδ' ἑλὼν διένειμε θεοῖς θνητοῖσί τε κόσμον, / οὗ πρῶτος βασίλευσε περικλυτὸς Ἠρικεπαῖος.

(19) After taking hold of the world over which renowned Erikepaios was the first to rule he distributed it to gods and mortals.

(20) ἔκτισεν ἀθανάτοις δόμον ἄφθιτον, – ⏑⏑ – ⏑

(20) He built for the immortals an imperishable house,

(21) – ⏑⏑ – ⏑⏑ – Διώρισε δ' ἀνθρώποισι / χωρὶς ἀπ' ἀθανάτων ναίειν ἕδος, ᾗ μέσος ἄξων / ἠελίου τρέπεται ποτινεύμενος οὔτε τι λίην / ψυχρὸς ὑπὲρ κεφαλῆς οὔτ' ἔμπυρος, ἀλλὰ μεσηγύς.

(21) ... But for men he determined an abode to live in, that is far away from the gods, where the axle of the Sun turns in a moderate way, and it is neither too cold nor too fiery over the head, but something in between.

(22) καὶ φύλακ' αὐτὸν ἔτευξε κέλευσέ τε πᾶσιν ἀνάσσειν.

(22) And he created *the Sun* to be a guardian, and ordered him to rule over everything.

(23) μήσατο δ' ἄλλην γαῖαν ἀπείριτον, ἥν τε σελήνην / ἀθάνατοι κλῄζουσιν, ἐπιχθόνιοι δέ τε μήνην, / ἣ πόλλ' οὔρε' ἔχει, πόλλ' ἄστεα, πολλὰ μέλαθρα (OF155F). / ~ *Γῆ αἰθερία ἡ σελήνη* ~ (OF155F(I)) / ὅσσ' ἐν μηνὶ τρέπηι ὅπερ ἥλιος εἰς ἐνιαυτόν (OF156F).

(23) And he created a different world, which is inaccessible and which the immortals call Selene and the people living on earth Mene; a world that has many mountains, many cities, many houses (OF155F). / ~ *And the moon is a celestial earth* ~ (OF155F(I)) which changes in a month as much as the sun does in a year (OF156F).

(24) ταῦτα νόωι πεφύλαξο, φίλον τέκος, ἐν πραπίδεσσιν, / εἰδὼς περ μάλα πάντα παλαίφατα κἀπὸ Φάνητος.

(24) These words that were spoken long ago you should keep in mind my dear child and know in your heart very well that everything comes from Phanes.

The Second Ruler: Night

(25) Πρωτόγονον γε μὲν οὔτις ἐσέδρακεν ὀφθαλμοῖσιν, / εἰ μὴ Νὺξ ἱερὴ μούνη, τοὶ δ' ἄλλοι ἅπαντες / θαύμαζον καθορῶντες ἐν αἰθέρι φέγγος ἄελπτον / τοῖον ἀπέστραπτε χροὸς ἀθανάτοιο Φάνητος.

(25) The Firstborn none saw with their eyes, except the holy Night alone. All the others marvelled when they gazed on the unlooked-for light in the Aether; in such way gleamed the body of immortal Phanes.

(26) – ⏑⏑ – σκῆπτρον δ' ἀριδείκετον εἷο χέρεσσιν / θῆκε θεᾶς Νυκτός, ⟨ἵν' ἔχηι⟩ βασιληΐδα τιμήν.

(26) He (Phanes) put the glorious sceptre in goddess Night's hands, giving her royal honour.

(27) σκῆπτρον ἔχουσ᾽ ἐν χεροῖν ἀριπρεπὲς Ἠρικεπαίου,	(27) And as she was holding in her hands the magnificent sceptre of Erikepaios,
(28) μαντοσύνην δ᾽ οἱ δῶκεν ἔχειν ἀψευδέα πάντῃ.	(28) he granted to her to have the art of prophesying always the truth.
(29) ταῦτα πατὴρ ποίησε κατὰ σπέος ἠεροειδές	(29) These things the father made in the dark and misty cave,
(30) αὐτὸς ἑῆς γὰρ παιδὸς ἀφείλετο κούριον ἄνθος.	(30) *where* he himself took from his daughter the flower of her maidenhood.

The Third Ruler: Ouranos

(31) ἣ δὲ πάλιν Γαῖάν τε καὶ Οὐρανὸν εὐρὺν ἔτικτε· δεῖξέν τ᾽ ἐξ ἀφανῶν φανεροὺς οἵ τ᾽ εἰσὶ γενέθλην.	(31) She (Night) in her turn bore Gaia and broad Ouranos and she brought to light making visible those that were invisible and of which descent they were.
(32) – ᴗᴗ – ᴗᴗ – οὖρος πάντων καὶ φύλαξ	(32) ... (Ouranos) who defines and protects all,
(33) ὃς πρῶτος βασίλευσε θεῶν μετὰ μητέρα Νύκτα.	(33) who was the first to rule over the gods after his mother Night.
(34) ~ τίκτει γὰρ ἡ Γῆ λαθοῦσα τὸν Οὐρανόν ~ ἑπτὰ μὲν εὐειδεῖς κούρας ἑλικώπιδας, ἁγνάς, ἑπτὰ δὲ παῖδας ἄνακτας ἐγείνατο λαχνήεντας· θυγατέρας μὲν <τίκτε> Θέμιν καὶ εὔφρονα Τηθὺν Μνημοσύνην τε βαθυπλόκαμον Θείαν τε μάκαιραν, ἠδὲ Διώνην τίκτεν ἀριπρεπὲς εἶδος ἔχουσα Φοίβην τε Ῥείην τε, Διὸς γενέτειραν ἄνακτος· Κοῖόν τε Κρεῖόν τε μέγαν Φόρκυν τε κραταιὸν καὶ Κρόνον Ὠκεανόν θ᾽ Ὑπερίονα τ᾽ Ἰαπετόν τε.	(34) ~ *And Gaia secretly bore from Ouranos*, ~ seven beautiful pure virgins with swift rolling eyes, and seven royal sons with fine hair. And the daughters <she bore> were Themis, and joyous Tethys, Mnemosyne with the long thick hair, and blessed Thea and she also bore Dione, who had a magnificent appearance, and Phoebe, and Rhea, who was king Zeus' mother. She also gave birth to Koeus and great Kroeus, and powerful Phorkys, and also Kronos, Okeanos, Hyperion and Iapetos.
(35) οὓς καλέουσι Γίγαντας ἐπώνυμον ἐν μακάρεσσιν οὕνεκα Γῆς ἐγένοντο καὶ αἵματος Οὐρανίοιο.	(35) Who they call Giants among the blessed, because they were created from Gaia and the blood of Ouranos.
(36) ~ ἀπὸ δὲ τούτων δευτέρα δυάς, Ὠκεανός καὶ Τηθύς ~	(36) ~ *And out of them the second pair Okeanos and Tethys*.~

Ouranos' Castration by Cronos

(37) ἐκ πάντων δὲ Κρόνον Νὺξ ἔτρεφεν ἠδ' ἀτίταλλεν,	(37) Night nurtured and took care of Kronos from among them all,
(38) – ⏑⏑ – ⏑ θεῶν τροφὸς ἀμβροσίη Νύξ·	(38) since Night is the immortal nurse of the gods.
(39) Τιτῆνες κακομῆται, ὑπέρβιον ἦτορ ἔχοντες,	(39) The ill-counselled Titans, who had a violent heart,
(40) καὶ κρατεροί περ ἐόντες ἀμείνονος ἀντιάσαντες, ὕβριος ἀντ' ὀλοῆς καὶ ἀτασθαλίης ὑπερόπλου.	(40) even though they were powerful, they were against a mightier opponent, due to their disastrous arrogance and malicious pride.
(41) ὡς δ' αὐτοὺς ἐνόησεν ἀμείλιχον ἦτορ ἔχοντας, καὶ φύσιν ἔκνομίην ⏑⏑ – ⏑⏑ – ⏑ ῥίψε βαθὺν γαίης ἐς Τάρταρον ⟨Οὐρανὸς εὑρύς⟩.	(41) For as soon as ⟨far-reaching Ouranos⟩ realised that they had an unrelenting heart and a disobedient nature, he threw them into Tartarus, the profundity of Gaia.
(42) ἔνθ' αὖτ' Ὠκεανὸς μὲν ἐνὶ μεγάροισιν ἔμιμνεν ὁρμαίνων, ποτέρωσε νόον τράποι, ἢ πατέρα ὃν γυι⟨ώσηι⟩ τε βίης καὶ ἀτάσθαλα λωβήσαιτο σὺν Κρόνωι ἠδ' ἄλλοισιν ἀδελφοῖς, οἳ πεπίθοντο μητρὶ φίλῃ, ἢ τούς γε λιπὼν μένοι ἔνδον ἔκηλος, πολλὰ δὲ πορφύρων μένεν ἥμενος ἐν μεγάροισιν, σκυζόμενος ἦι μητρί, κασιγνήτοισι δὲ μᾶλλον.	(42) However, Okeanos stayed at the place of his dwelling, contemplating in which way to direct his reasoning and whether he should deprive his father of strength and unjustly mutilate him along with Kronos and his other brothers, who were convinced by their beloved mother; or abandoning them stay unconcerned inside his abode. After being much tormented by his thoughts, however, he remained at home, being frustrated with his mother and even more with his brothers.
(43) – ⏑⏑ – ⏑⏑ – ⏑ ὁ ἀγκυλομήτης (OF181F) ... τέμνων καὶ τεμνόμενος ~ (OF225F). ἔστ' ἂν Ῥείηι παῖδα τέκηι Κρόνωι ἐν φιλότητι (OF251F).	(43) *Yet only Cronos (OF225F)* with the crooked heart (OF181F) *takes from Ouranos the kingship* ~ *castrating and being castrated* ~ (OF225F). Until Rhea would give birth to a child after copulating with Kronos *as Night foretold*(OF251F).
(44) μήδεα δ' ἐς πέλαγος πέσεν ὑψόθεν, ἀμφὶ δὲ τοῖσι λευκὸς ἐπιπλώουσιν ἑλίσσετο πάντοθεν ἀφρός· ἐν δὲ περιπλομένας ὥραις Ἐνιαυτὸς ἔτικτεν παρθένον αἰδοίην, ἣν δὴ παλάμαις ὑπέδεκτο γεινομένην τὸ πρῶτον ὁμοῦ Ζῆλός τ' Ἀπάτη τε.	(44) (Ouranos') genitals fell into the ocean from high above and white foam wrapped them all around as they floated. But as the seasons went by, the year brought forth a modest maiden (Aphrodite) who was first received in the hands of Jealousy along with Deception.

The Fourth Ruler: Kronos' Succession by Zeus

(45) πρώτιστος μὲν ἄνασσεν ἐπιχθονίων Κρόνος ἀνδρῶν· ἐκ δὲ Κρόνου γένετ' αὐτὸς ἄναξ, μέγας εὐρύοπα Ζεύς

(46) Ῥείη τὸ πρὶν ἐοῦσα, ἐπεὶ Διὸς ἔπλετο μήτηρ, Δημήτηρ γέγονε. ∪∪ – ∪∪ – ∪∪ –

(47) ‹ἣ› μήσατο γὰρ προπόλους ‹τε› καὶ ἀμφιπόλους καὶ ὀπαδούς, μήσατο δ' ἀμβροσίην καὶ ἐρυθροῦ νέκταρος ἁρμόν, μήσατο δ' ἀγλαὰ ἔργα μελισσάων ἐριβόμβων.

(48) – ∪∪ – ∪∪ – ὑπὸ Ζηνὶ Κρονίωνι ἀθάνατον ‹τ'› αἰῶνα λαχεῖν καθαροῖο γενείου ‹οὗ› διερᾶς χαίτας, εὐώδεας, οὐδέ ‹κάρητος γήραος ἠ›πεδανοῖο μιγήμεναι ἄνθεϊ λευκῷ, ἀλλὰ ‹περὶ κροτάφοισιν ἔχειν› ἐριθηλέα λάχνην.

(49) ~ ... καταπίνει τὰ οἰκεῖα γεννήματα κατὰ τὸν ἀμείλικτον. ~

(50) Ἴδη τ' εὐειδὴς καὶ ὁμόσπορος Ἀδρήστεια (OF208F) χάλκεα ῥόπτρα λαβοῦσα καὶ τύπανον λιγυηχές, (OF212F).

(51) ἔνθα Κρόνος μὲν ἔπειτα φαγὼν δολόεσσαν ἐδωδὴν

(52) κεῖτ' ἀποδοχμώσας παχὺν αὐχένα, κὰδ δέ μιν ὕπνος ᾕρει πανδαμάτωρ. ∪∪ – ∪∪ – ∪

(53) 'εὖτ' ἂν δή μιν ἴδηαι ὑπὸ δρυσὶν ὑψικόμοισιν ἔργοισιν μεθύοντα μελισσάων ἐριβόμβων, δῆσον'. ∪ – ∪∪ – ∪∪ – ∪∪ – ∪

(45) Kronos was the first to rule over the men living on earth and from Kronos, was born the great far-seeing king Zeus

(46) and though she was Rhea before, after she became Zeus' mother, she also became Demeter.

(47) She created attendants and priestesses and followers, and also ambrosia and the flow of red nectar, and she also devised the magnificent works of loud-murmuring bees.

(48) .... *the race* under Kronian Zeus was allotted an immortal lifetime, having fresh sweet-smelling flowing hair on their pure chin and neither their aged head bloomed mixed with white hair but on its sides had soft hair growing, such as of the first beard.

(49) *And Kronos, as having the lawless nature of the Titans* ~...was swallowing his own children without any remorse. ~

(50) However, beautiful Ide and Adrasteia who came from the same seed (OF208F) *guarded Zeus* by taking in their hands bronze cymbals and a clear-sounding drum *to produce loud noise in order to keep all the gods away* (OF212F). *While Rhea gave to Kronos a stone wrapped in clothes instead of Zeus, and Kronos swallowed it* (OF214F).

(51) At that moment and after Kronos ate the food given to him deceitfully

(52) he lay down, bending his thick neck to the side, and Sleep, who tames all, seized him.

(53) *And Night says to Zeus*, 'As soon as you see him getting drunk from the work of noisy bees, under the oaks with the high foliage, bind him'.

Zeus' Becomes the Fifth Ruler

(54) *ὄρθου δ' ἡμετέρην γενεήν, ἀριδείκετε δαῖμον'.	(54) *And Zeus says*, 'Guide our generation, most illustrious daemon'.
(55) ᾿μαῖα, θεῶν ὑπάτη, Νὺξ ἄμβροτε, πῶς, τάδε φράζε, πῶς χρή μ' ἀθανάτων ἀρχὴν κρατερόφρονα θέσθαι;	(55) *Zeus then asked Night*, 'Mother, supreme of the gods and immortal Night, tell me this: How is it fitting for me to establish my mighty rule over the immortals?
(56) πῶς δέ μοι ἕν τε τὰ πάντ' ἔσται καὶ χωρὶς ἕκαστον; 'αἰθέρι πάντα πέριξ ἀφάτωι λαβέ, τῶι δ' ἐνὶ μέσσωι οὐρανόν, ἐν δέ τε γαῖαν ἀπείριτον, ἐν δὲ θάλασσαν, ἐν δὲ τὰ τείρεα πάντα τά τ' οὐρανὸς ἐστεφάνωται,	(56) How can everything become one unto me and at the same time each separate?' *Night therefore says to him*: 'Surround all things with ineffable aether, and in the middle of it place the heaven and amidst that place infinite earth and in that the sea, and in that all of the constellations with which the sky is crowned,
(57) αὐτὰρ ἐπὴν δεσμὸν κρατερὸν περὶ πᾶσι τανύσσηις σειρὴν χρυσείην ἐξ αἰθέρος ἀρτήσαντα	(57) but as soon as you will expand a strong bond through all things, after hanging a golden chain from the aether
(58) ἀθανάτων βασιλῆα θεῶν πέμπτον σε γενέσθαι'.	(58) you will become the fifth king of the immortal gods'.

The Swallowing of Phanes by Zeus and the Second Creation of the World

(59) ὣς τότε πρωτογόνοιο χαδὼν μένος Ἠρικεπαίου [I.324.14] τῶν πάντων δέμας εἶχεν ἑῆι ἐνὶ γαστέρι κοίληι, μεῖξε δ' ἑοῖς μελέεσσι θεοῦ δύναμίν τε καὶ ἀλκήν, τοὔνεκα σὺν τῶι πάντα Διὸς πάλιν ἐντὸς ἐτύχθη, [I.325.3=313.9] αἰθέρος εὐρείης ἠδ' οὐρανοῦ ἀγλαὸν ὕψος, [I.313.10] πόντου τ' ἀτρυγέτου γαίης τ', Ἐρικυδέος ἕδρη, ὠκεανός τε μέγας καὶ νείατα Τάρταρα γαίης καὶ ποταμοὶ καὶ πόντος ἀπείριτος ἄλλα τε πάντα πάντες τ' ἀθάνατοι μάκαρες θεοὶ ἠδὲ θέαιναι, ὅσσα τ' ἔην γεγαῶτα καὶ ὕστερον ὁπόσσ' ἔμελλεν, ἐν γένετο, Ζηνὸς δ' ἐνὶ γαστέρι σύρρα πεφύκει. [I.313.16]	(59) Thus at that time after engulfing the power of the firstborn Erikepaios, he contained inside the hollow of his own belly the body of all things and he joined with his own limbs the strength and valence of the god. Hence, everything was created anew inside Zeus, and along with the universe, the wide aether and also the bright heights of the sky, the infertile sea and the foundations of glorious Gaia, and the great ocean, and earthly Tartarus anew and rivers and the inaccessible deep, and everything else and all the immortal and blissful Gods and Goddesses and all that has already happened and all that will in the future, became one, tangled inside the belly of Zeus and were brought forth again.

(60) πάντα τάδε κρύψας αὖθις φάος ἐς πολυγηθὲς μέλλεν ἀπὸ κραδίης προφέρειν πάλι θέσκελα ῥέζων.	(60) For having concealed all these things, he would bring them forth again from his heart into joyful light through a wondrous deed.

The Hymn to Zeus: the One, the Beginning and End

(61) Ζεὺς πρῶτος γένετο, Ζεὺς ὕστατος ἀργικέραυνος· Ζεὺς κεφαλή, Ζεὺς μέσσα, Διὸς δ' ἐκ πάντα τέτυκται· Ζεὺς ἄρσην γένετο, Ζεὺς ἄμβροτος ἔπλετο νύμφη· Ζεὺς πυθμὴν γαίης τε καὶ οὐρανοῦ ἀστερόεντος· Ζεὺς βασιλεύς, Ζεὺς αὐτὸς ἁπάντων ἀρχιγένεθλος, ἓν κράτος, εἷς δαίμων γενέτης, μέγας ἀρχὸς ἁπάντων ἓν δὲ δέμας βασίλειον, ἐν ὧι τάδε πάντα κυκλεῖται, πῦρ καὶ ὕδωρ καὶ γαῖα καὶ αἰθήρ, νύξ τε καὶ ἦμαρ, καὶ Μῆτις, πρῶτος γενέτωρ καὶ Ἔρως πολυτερπής· πάντα γὰρ ἐν Ζηνὸς μεγάλωι τάδε σώματι κεῖται,	(61) Zeus was the first, Zeus the last bright-thundering king, Zeus the head, Zeus the middle and from Zeus everything is created. Zeus was male and Zeus a divine maiden, Zeus the foundation of earth and starry heaven, Zeus the king, Zeus alone the superior cause of all things, One power, One begetter daimon, great ruler of all, One regal form, in whom everything is encircled, fire and water and Gaia and aether, night and day and also Metis, the first creator and much-delighting Eros, for all these lie inside Zeus' mighty body,
(62) πάντα μόνος δὲ νοεῖ πάντων προνοεῖ τε θεουδῶς· πάντηι δὲ Ζηνὸς καὶ ἐν ὄμμασι πατρὸς ἄνακτος ναίουσ' ἀθάνατοί τε θεοὶ θνητοί τε ἄνθρωποι, ὅσσα τ' ἔην γεγαῶτα καὶ ὕστερον ὁππόσ' ἔμελλεν θῆρές τ' οἰωνοί θ'ὁπόσα πνείει τε καὶ ἕρπει οὐδέ ἔ που λήθουσιν ἐφήμερα φῦλ' ἀνθρώπων, ὅσσ' ἀδίκως ῥέζουσί περ, οὐδ' εἰν οὔρεσι θῆρες ἄγριοι, τετράποδες, λασιότριχες, ὀμβριμόθυμοι.	(62) and he alone observes everything and for everything he provides in a way that brings awe. The entirety belongs to Zeus and under the gaze of their father, the king, dwell the immortal gods and mortal men, and all things that have come to be and such as will come to be in the future, and wild animals and birds and everything that breaths and crawls, and there is nowhere that the ephemeral races of men can escape his attention, not even those who act unjustly, nor in the mountains wild animals, savage, four-legged, shaggy, strong tempered.
(63) τῶι δὲ Δίκη πολύποινος, ἐφέσπετο πᾶσιν ἀρωγός.	(63) In the same way Dike (Justice) the abundant punisher and protector of all, follows (Zeus).

The generation of Gods from Zeus

(64) – ⏑⏑ – Βρόμιός τε μέγας καὶ Ζεὺς ὁ πανόπτης,	(64) *And then*, great Bromios and Zeus who sees everything,

(65) ... ὅπλοις λαμπομένην χαλκήιον ἄνθος ἰδέσθαι,

(66) – ∪∪ – ∪∪ – Ἀρετῆς τ' ὄνομ' ἐσθλὸν κλήιζεται – ∪∪ – ∪∪ – ∪∪ – ◡ (OF266F), ὄφρ' αὐτῶι μεγάλων ἔργων κράντειρα πέλοιτο (OF264F),

(67) δεινὴ γὰρ Κρονίδαο νόου κράντειρα τέτυκται.

(68) ~ ἡγεμὼν τῶν Κουρήτων, ~

(69) ~ καὶ γὰρ οἱ πρώτιστοι Κουρῆτες τά τε ἄλλα τῆι τάξει τῆς Ἀθηνᾶς ἀνεῖναι καὶ περιεστέρθαι λέγονται τῶι θαλλῶι τῆς Ἐλάας, ~

(70) οἳ Ζηνὶ βροντήν τε πόρον τεῦξέν τε κεραυνόν, πρῶτοι τεκτονόχειρες, ἰδ' Ἥφαιστον καὶ Ἀθήνην δαίδαλα πάντ' ἐδίδαξαν, ὅσ' οὐρανὸς ἐντὸς ἐέργει,

(71) ἥδε γὰρ ἀθανάτων προφερεστάτη ἐστὶν ἁπάσεων ἱστὸν ἐποίχεσθαι ταλασήϊά τ' ἔργα πινύσσειν.

(72) τὸν δὲ πόθος πλέον εἷλ', ἀπὸ δ' ἔκθορε πατρὶ μεγίστωι αἰδοίων ἀφροῖο γονῆι ὑπέδεκτο δὲ πόντος σπέρμα Διός, μεγάλου· περιτελλομένου δ' ἐνιαυτοῦ ὥρας καλλιφύτοις, τέκ' ἐγερσιγέλωτ' Ἀφροδίτην ἀφρογενῆ. ∪∪ – ∪∪ – ∪∪ – ◡

(73) – ∪∪ ἀτελής ⟨τε⟩ γάμων καὶ ἄπειρος ἐοῦσα παιδογόνου λοχίης πάσης ἀνὰ πείρατα λύει (OF257F). ἣ δ' ἄρα ὅτ' Ἑκάτη παιδὸς μέλη αὖθι λιποῦσα Λητοῦς εὐπλοκάμοιο κόρη προσεβήσατ' Ὄλυμπον (OF317F).

(65) *gave birth to Athena from his head*, glowing with her armour like a brazen flower to see,

(66) ...also praised with the noble name Arete (OF266F)... so that she would become for him the fulfiller of great deeds (OF264F)

(67) for she became the fearful accomplisher of the will of Kronos' son.

(68) *Athena is also called* ~ *the leader of the Kouretes,* ~

(69) ~ *and this is why the very first Kouretes are otherwise devoted in the order of Athena and said to be crowned with a young olive-branch.* ~

(70) *And the father created the Cyclopes*, the first craftsmen who offered to Zeus the thunder and created the lightning, and also taught Hephaestos and Athena all the kinds of elaborate works, as many as the heaven encloses,

(71) for this goddess is the most excellent of all the immortals in weaving on the loom and in teaching the works related to wool-spinning.

(72) *And then Zeus produced Aphrodite when* great desire filled him completely, and from the genitals of all-mighty Father sprang forth the foamy seed and the sea received under its surface the seed of mighty Zeus and after a year went by with the seasons bringing beauty to birth, it bore laughter-rousing Aphrodite, born from the foam.

(73) *Afterwards Artemis came into existence*, who without the fulfilment of marriage and being inexperienced in reproduction, she cut loose the bonds of all that belongs to begetting children (OF257F). And so Hekate (Artemis), abandoning the prospect of having children, the fair-haired daughter of Leto proceeded to Olympus (OF317F).

(74) ~ ἡ Δημήτηρ ἐγχειρίζουσα τῆι Κόρηι τὴν βασιλείαν φησίν, ~
'αὐτὰρ Ἀπόλλωνος θαλερὸν λέχος, εἰσαναβᾶσα
τέξεαι ἀγλαὰ τέκνα πυρὶ φλεγέθοντα πρόσωπος'.

(75) ἱστὸν ἐποιχομένην ἀτελῆ πόνον ἀνθεμόεσσαν, ~

(76) ~ ἀτελεῖς τε καταλείπειν τοὺς ἱστούς καὶ ἁρπάζεσθαι καὶ ~

(77) ~ ζεύγνυτο τῶι Ἅιδηι καὶ συναπογεννήσατο τὰς ἐν τοῖς ὑποχθονίοις Εὐμενίδας, ~ (OF292F)
ἐννέα θυγατέρας γλαυκώπιδας ἀνθεσιουργούς (OF293F).

(74) ~And as Demeter handed over to Kore the kingdom she said:~
'But after climbing to Apollo's vigorous bed you will give birth to glorious children blazing with fiery faces'.

(75) While weaving an unfinished work full of flowers, ~

(76) ~ she was seized, leaving the rest of the fabric unfinished, ~

(77) ~ and mated with Hades, with whom she bore the Eumenides who dwell in the underworld, ~ (OF292F)
the nine daughters with the bright eyes who create flowers (OF293F).

Zeus hands over the Reign to Dionysos who becomes the Sixth Ruler

(78) καίπερ ἐόντι νέωι καὶ νηπίωι εἰλαπιναστῆι,

(79) ~ ὁ γὰρ πατὴρ ἰδρύει τε αὐτὸν ἐν τῶι βασιλείωι θρόνωι καὶ ἐγχειρίζει τὸ σκῆπτρον ~ (OF299F)
ὄρθιον ἑξαμερὲς πισύρων καὶ εἴκοσι μέτρων (OF166F)
'κλῦτε, θεοί, τόνδ' ὕμμιν ἐγὼ βασιλῆα τίθημι' (OF299F).

(80) κραῖνε μὲν οὖν Ζεὺς πάντα πατήρ, Βάκχος δ' ἐπέκραινε.

(78) And even though he was young and only an infant compared to his symposiasts,

(79) ~ the father establishes him on the regal throne and entrusts in his hands the sceptre ~ (OF299F)
straight in six parts and of twenty-four measures (OF166F)
*'Listen Gods, him I proclaim as your king' (OF299F).

(80) And so father Zeus formed all things, and Bacchos completed them.

Dionysos' Dismemberment by the Titans and his following Rebirth

(81) § οὐδὲ Διὸς θρόνον εἶχεν ἐπὶ χρόνον· ἀλλά ἑ γύψωι
κερδαλέηι χρισθέντες, ἐπίκλοπα κύκλα προσώπου
δαίμονος ἀστόργοιο χόλωι βαρυμήνιος, "Ηρης § (OF308V)
Οἴνωι ἀγαιομένη κούρωι Διός, – ‿‿ – (OF303F)
§ Ταρταρίηι Τιτῆνες ἐδηλήσαντο μαχαίρηι

(81) § However, he did not hold Zeus' throne for a long time, because the Titans, having smeared cunningly their round faces with deceitful chalk, due to the heartless hatred of enraged goddess' Hera § (OF308V) being indignant at Oinos, the son of Zeus (OF303F).

ἀντιτύπωι νόθον εἶδος ὁπιπεύοντα κατόπτρωι § (OF308V).	§ and while he observed his elusive image being reflected in a mirror *made by Hephaestos* they destroyed him with a horrible knife § (OF308V).
(82) ἑπτὰ δὲ πάντα μέλη κούρου διεμοιρήσαντο (OF311F) μούνην γὰρ κραδίην νοερὴν λεῖπον ‿ ‿ ‿ (OF314F)	(82) They divided all of the limbs of the boy into seven equal parts (OF311F), leaving only the intellectual heart *preserved by Athena* (OF314F).
(83) ~ ὁ δὲ Ἀπόλλων συναγείρει τε αὐτὸν καὶ ἀνάγει… ~	(83) ~ Apollo then gathers and takes him up to the sky ~ *according to the will of the father*
(84) "Οἴνου πάντα μέλη κόσμωι λαβὲ καί μοι ἔνεικε'.	(84) *Who said to him*: 'Take hold of all the parts of Oinos in the world and bring them to me'.
(85) ‿ ‿ ‿ γλυκερὸν δὲ τέκος Διὸς ἐξεκαλεῖτο. (OF296F) ~ καὶ συλλαμβάνειν ἡ "Ιπτα λέγεται τίκτοντι τῶι Διί, λίκνον ἐπὶ τῆς κεφαλῆς θεμένη καὶ δράκοντι αὐτὸ περιστρέψασα τὸν κραδίαῖον ὑποδέχεται Διόνυσον. ~ (OF329F)	(85) *Afterwards, Zeus produced Dionysos from his thigh*, and that is why he is called the sweet child of Zeus. (OF296F) ~ And it is said that Ipta received Dionysos that came from the heart when he was brought forth from Zeus, and took in charge as a nurse by placing him in a winnowing-fan on her head and encircling it with a snake. ~ (OF329F)
(86) ~ καὶ τούτους ὀργισθεὶς ὁ Ζεὺς ἐκεραύνωσε, καὶ ἐκ τῆς αἰθάλης τῶν ἀτμῶν τῶν ἀναδοθέντων ἐξ αὐτῶν ὕλης γενομένης γενέσθαι τοὺς ἀνθρώπους. ~	(86) ~ And Zeus, being angry with them (Titans) struck them with his thunderbolts *into Tartarus*, and from the soot coming from the vapours that transpired from them was produced the matter out of which men are created. ~
(87) Ἄτλας δ' οὐρανὸν εὐρὺν ἔχει κρατερῆς ὑπ' ἀνάγκης, πείρασιν ἐν γαίης. ‿ ‿ ‿ ‿ ‿	(87) Atlas, however, out of strong necessity, holds up wide sky at the limits of the earth.

The Afterlife, the Soul and the Cycle of Rebirth

(88) οἱ μέν κ' εὐαγέωσιν ὑπ' αὐγὰς ἠελίοιο, αὖτις ἀποφθίμενοι μαλακώτερον οἶτον ἔχουσιν ἐν καλῶι λειμῶνι βαθύρροον ἀμφ' Ἀχέροντα, οἱ δ' ἄδικα ῥέξαντες ὑπ' αὐγὰς ἠελίοιο	(88) *And from men*, the ones who dwell purely under the rays of the sun, when they in turn perish, they have a more gentle fate in the beautiful meadow around deep-flowing Acheron, but the ones who acted unjustly

under the rays of the sun, the insolent, are led down under the surface of Kokytos to chilly Tartaros.

(89) Men's soul is rooted in the aether (OF436F) and as we draw in air, we collect the divine soul (OF422F) since the immortal and unaging soul comes from Zeus (OF426F), and for all things, the soul is immortal, but the bodies mortal (OF425F).

(90) And water is death for the soul and for the water the same requital applies. From water comes into existence earth, and from earth water once again, and from that, soul, becoming aether in its entirety.

(91) And when the souls of beasts and winged birds flit away and divine life abandons them, no one leads their soul to the house of Hades, but instead it flutters without a purpose in the same place, until another one would snatch it away being intermingled with the blasts of wind. But whenever a man leaves the sunlight, then Kyllenios Hermes leads the immortal souls down into the vast nether world.

(92) And fathers and sons in the halls, and graceful wives and mothers and also daughters, become the same through exchanging generations among one another,
because the soul of humans moves from one place to another with the circulation of time through exchanging with other animals. At one time it becomes a horse, at another ⟨.....⟩ now a sheep and then a bird, dreadful to see, at other times once more the form of a dog with a deep bark and the race of cold snakes which crawls on divine earth.

(93) Out of all the blooming things which mortals take care of on the earth, none of them has one and the same destiny upon their existence, but all

ὑβρισταὶ κατάγονται ὑπὸ πλάκα Κωκυτοῖο
Τάρταρον ἐς κρυόεντα. ∪ − ∪∪ − ∪ − ∪

(89) ψυχὴ δ' ἀνθρώποισιν ἀπ' αἰθέρος ἐρρίζωται (OF436F)
ἀέρα δ' ἔλκοντες, ψυχὴν θείαν δρεπόμεσθα (OF422F)
ψυχὴ δ' ἀθάνατος καὶ ἀγήρως ἐκ Διός ἐστιν (OF426F),
ψυχὴ δ' ἀθάνατος πάντων, τὰ δὲ σώματα θνητά (OF425F).

(90) ἔστιν ὕδωρ ψυχῆι θάνατος, δ' ὑδάτεσ⟨σ⟩ιν ἀμοιβή,
ἐκ δὲ ὕδατος ⟨πέλε⟩ γαῖα, τὸ δ' ἐκ γαίας πάλιν ὕδωρ,
ἐκ τοῦ δὴ ψυχὴ ὅλον αἰθέρα ἀλλάσσουσα.

(91) αἱ μὲν δὴ θηρῶν τε καὶ οἰωνῶν πτερόεντων
ψυχαὶ ὅτ' ἀίξωσι, λίπηι δέ μιν ἱερὸς αἰών,
τῶν οὔ τις ψυχὴν παράγει δόμον εἰς Ἀίδαο,
ἀλλ' αὐτοῦ πεπότηται ἐτώσιον, εἰς ὅ κεν αὐτὴν
ἄλλο ἀφαρπάζηι μίγδην ἀνέμοιο πνοιῆισιν·
ὁππότε δ' ἄνθρωπος προλίπηι φάος ἠελίοιο,
ψυχὰς ἀθανάτας κατάγει Κυλλήνιος Ἑρμῆς
γαίης ἐς κευθμῶνα πελώριον. − ∪∪ − ∪

(92) οἱ δ' αὐτοὶ πατέρες τε καὶ υἱέες ἐν μεγάροισιν
εὔκοσμοί τ' ἄλοχοι καὶ μητέρες ἠδὲ θύγατρες
γίνοντ' ἀλλήλων μεταμειβομένηισι γενέθλαις,
οὕνεκ' ἀμειβομένη ψυχὴ κατὰ κύκλα χρόνοιο
ἀνθρώπων ζώιοισι μετέρχεται ἄλλοθεν ἄλλοις·
ἄλλοτε μὲν ἵππος, τότε γίνεται ⟨− ∪∪ − ⟩,
ἄλλοτε δὲ πρόβατον, τότε δ' ὄρνεον αἰνὸν ἰδέσθαι,
ἄλλοτε δ' αὖ κυνέον τε δέμας φωνῇ τε βαρεία,
καὶ ψυχρῶν ὀφίων ἕρπει γένος ἐν χθονὶ δίῃ.

(93) θαλλῶν δ' ὅσσα βροτοῖσιν ἐπὶ χθονὸς ἔργα μέμηλεν,
οὐδὲν ἔχει μίαν αἶσαν ἐπὶ φρεσίν, ἀλλὰ κυκλεῖται

πάντα πέριξ, στῆναι δὲ καθ' ἓν μέρος οὐ θέμις ἐστίν, ἀλλ' ἔχει, ὡς ἤρξαντο, δρόμου μέρος ἴσον ἕκαστος.

(94) κύκλου τ' ἂν λῆξαι καὶ ἀναπνεῦσαι κακότητος,

(95) ‒ ‿‿ ἄνθρωποι δὲ τελήξαντες ἑκατόμβας πέμψουσιν πάσῃσιν ἐν ὥραις ἀμφιέτῃσιν ὄργια τ' ἐκτελέσουσι λύσιν προγόνων ἀθεμίστων μαιόμενοι· σὺ δὲ τοῖσιν ἔχων κράτος, οὕς κ' ἐθέλῃσθα, λύσεις ἔκ τε πόνων χαλεπῶν καὶ ἀπείρονος οἴστρου.

(96) πολλοὶ μὲν ναρθηκοφόροι, παῦροι δέ τε βάκχοι.

(97) θῆρές τε οἰωνοί τε βροτῶν τ' ἀετώσια φῦλα, ἄχθεα γῆς, εἴδωλα τετυγμένα, μηδαμὰ μηδὲν εἰδότες, οὔτε κακοῖο προσερχομένοιο νοῆσαι φράδμονες, οὔτ' ἄποθεν μάλ' ἀποστρέψαι κακότητος, οὔτ' ἀγαθοῦ παρεόντος ἐπιστρέψαι <τε> καὶ ἔρξαι ἴδριες, ἀλλὰ μάτην ἀδαήμονες, ἀπρονόητοι.

move around in a circle, and it is not right to stand still at each one's turn, but as they begun it, each has an equal part in this course.

(94) And to escape from the cycle and find respite from the misery,

(95) men will send you hecatombs of unblemished beasts and offer yearly sacrifices at all seasons, and they will perform your secret rites seeking deliverance from the lawless deeds of their ancestors. And you, *Dionysos*, having the power as far as these are concerned, shall deliver whomever you will be willing to, from grievous toil and endless agony,

(96) for many are the thyrsus-bearers, but few the Bacchoi.

(97) Wild beasts and birds, the races of mortals that have no purpose, a burden of the earth, created forms without a substance, neither having the intelligence to recognise or observe approaching evil, nor to avoid evil by staying completely away from it, nor being experienced in how to turn their attention towards the good next to them and achieve it, but they stay idly ignorant and imprudent.

6.5 Analysis of the Orphic Rhapsodies

6.5.1 The Beginning: OR1 – OR9

The first verses follow the common practice of theogonical poetry, of seeking inspiration from a god or foreshadowing the words which will follow as a divine revelation and not the poets' own conception; the same can be seen in Hesiod and Homer.[934] In this case, 'Orpheus' asks for inspiration from Helios who is identified with Apollo through the epithet *Phoibos*. Hesiod and Homer place greater emphasis on the Muses as source of inspiration and the idea of Apollo, an oracular deity, being the inspiration behind Orpheus' poem might be related to the fact that his poem is riddling and requires interpretation, as the DP author suggests.[935] It is notable that there is an emphasis on aether as a primal substance of the cosmos which brings the *Rhapsodies* closer to Pre-Socratic cosmogonies. The same can be said about OR5 (OF106F) since it implies that everything was one at the beginning, a common prerequisite of Pre-Socratic philosophies. We can observe that the beginning of the OR is abstract and could be paralleled to Pre-Socratic theories. Everything is one in the darkness, over time a great chasm and aether are formed of which the cosmic egg is created. In general, this initial state of the cosmos is imagined through cosmological philosophy, meaning through conceiving the universe as a whole and distinguishing its conceptual components: Time, Chaos, Aether, Night and the Sun.

The perception of time as a god was not common among Greeks and we do not have a representation of Chronos in Archaic or Classical Greek art.[936] Out of *LIMC*'s mere four entries for Chronos, three date to the Roman imperial period and one to the late 2nd century B.C. In terms of literary evidence, one of the earliest personifications of Time is found in Pindar who calls him the father of all: 'Once deeds are done, whether in justice or contrary to it, not even Time, the father of all, could undo their outcome'.[937] This is the poem which was discussed in relation to the Derveni Papyrus and as suggested it has several similarities to Orphic eschatology, especially as expressed in the gold tablets.[938] Euripides also

---

934 Hes. *Theog.* 1–35; *Op.* 1–10. Hom. *Od.* 1.1–12.
935 Even though Apollo is also mentioned in Hesiod in reference to poets in general: ἐκ γάρ τοι Μουσέων καὶ ἑκηβόλου Ἀπόλλωνος ἄνδρες ἀοιδοὶ ἔασιν ἐπὶ χθόνα καὶ κιθαρισταί (*Theog.* 94–95).
936 Guthrie, 1952, p.85. *LIMC* v.3/1: Bendala Galan, p.278.
937 Pind. *Ol.*2.17: τῶν δὲ πεπραγμένων | ἐν δίκᾳ τε καὶ παρὰ δίκαν ἀποίητον οὐδ' ἄν | Χρόνος ὁ πάντων πατὴρ | δύναιτο θέμεν ἔργων τέλος· (Tr. Race). See also Pind. *Ol.*10.50–55 where Chronos is personified and distinguished from Kronos.
938 See p.257 ff.

mentions Aion as being Chronos' son [Αἰών τε Χρόνου παῖς] and Sophocles refers to Chronos as 'a god who brings ease' [Χρόνος γὰρ εὐμαρὴς θεός].[939] Chronos as a first entity is also present in the Theogony of Pherekydes of Syros (6th century B.C.), since according to him in the beginning there was Zas, Chthoniē and Chronos who they always existed.[940] It is possible that the personification of Chronos as a primal deity was particularly Orphic since we can see that even though not widely attested in some of the cases where it is mentioned, such as Pindar, the context is characteristically Orphic. Notably, Chronos is not identified as one of the first entities by the DP author but he argues that when Orpheus refers to Olympos he means Chronos based on the epithet μακρὸς which he uses for Olympos in contrast to the epithet εὐρὺς which he uses for Οὐρανὸς.[941] The phrase μακρὸν Ὄλυμπον is also found in OR17 (OF140F) and Οὐρανὸν εὐρὺν in OR31 (OF149F) which might suggest textual continuity between the OR and an earlier Orphic Theogony such as the one found in the DP, which is supported by other textual similarities as we will see.[942] Similar phrases are found in Hesiod too, which supports poetic interchange and perhaps oral transmission.[943] In a sense, Chronos as a denomination of time constitutes the framework of the abstract entities, meaning that even though some of these abstract entities are also present in Hesiod, they are described through a spatial framework and not as cosmic sub-

---

939 Eur. *Heracl.* 900. Soph. *El.* 179.
940 Purves, 2010, p.101. Schibli 14 (= 7B1DK): σώζεται δὲ τοῦ Συρίου τό τε βιβλίον ὃ συνέγραψεν, οὗ ἡ ἀρχή· Ζὰς μὲν καὶ Χρόνος ἦσαν ἀεὶ καὶ Χθονίη ἦν· Χθονίῃ δὲ ὄνομα ἐγένετο Γῆ ἐπειδὴ αὐτῇ Ζὰς γῆν γέρας διδοῖ: 'The book that the one from Syros wrote has been preserved. Here is the beginning of it: "Zas and Chronos and Chthoniē always were. But Chthoniē was named Gē, when Zas gave her the earth (*gē*) as a gift"'.
941 Col.XII.3–10: Ὄλυμπ[ος καὶ χ]ρόνος τὸ αὐτόν. οἱ δὲ δοκοῦντες | Ὄλυμπ[ον καὶ] οὐρανὸν [τ]αὐτὸ εἶναι ἐξαμαρ|τάν[ουσ]ι[ν, οὐ γ]ι̣νώσκοντες ὅτι οὐρανὸν οὐχ οἷόν τε | μακ[ρό]τερον ἢ εὐρύτε[ρο]ν εἶναι, χρόνον δὲ μακρὸν | εἴ τις [ὀνομ]άζο[ι] οὐ̣κ ἂ̣ν [ἐξα]μαρτάνοι. ὁ δὲ ὅπου μὲν | 'οὐρανὸν' θέ[λοι λέγειν, τὴν] προσθήκην 'εὐρὺν' | ἐποιεῖτο, ὅπου [δ' 'Ὄλυμπον', το]ὐ̣γαντίον 'εὐρὺν' μὲν | οὐδέποτε, 'μα̣[κρὸν' δέ: 'Olympus and time are the same. Those who think that Olympus and heaven are the same are mistaken, because they do not realize that heaven cannot be long rather than wide, while if someone were to call time long, he would not be mistaken. Wherever he wanted to say "heaven" he added "wide", but wherever (he wanted to say) "Olympus" he did the opposite, he never (added) "wide" but "long".'
942 These epithets, are also used by Hesiod and Homer, which could suggest a common epic tradition.
943 Hes. *Theog.* 110: ἄστρά τε λαμπετόωντα καὶ οὐρανὸς εὐρὺς ὕπερθεν·: '...and the shining stars and the broad sky above.'

stances. The absence of spatial definition is characteristically evident in the description of Chaos/Chasm in the OR as having no 'end, nor a bottom and neither any foundation' (OR4 = OF111F).

6.5.2 The birth of Phanes from the Egg and the first creation of the world: OR10 – OR24

In this section too, aether has a prominent presence which supports the cohesiveness of the surviving verses and aether's importance as a first substance. This is also evident from the fact that the egg out of which the first divine entity and creator is born, is made out of aether. It is essential to discuss how far back we can trace this cosmic egg since it is a very distinctive part of the *Rhapsodies*. I have already referred briefly to a Theogony in Aristophanes' *Birds* including an egg, where I argued that the comic effect of placing a sterile egg at the beginning of the generation of the whole cosmos could be enhanced if the audience was familiar with a theogonical tradition where an egg was at the beginning of generation, such as an Orphic Theogony. Let us discuss in more detail the passage from *Birds* (produced in 414 B.C.):

> Χάος ἦν καὶ Νὺξ Ἔρεβός τε μέλαν πρῶτον καὶ Τάρταρος εὐρύς·
> Γῆ δ' οὐδ' Ἀὴρ οὐδ' Οὐρανὸς ἦν· Ἐρέβους δ' ἐν ἀπείροσι κόλποις
> τίκτει πρώτιστον ὑπηνέμιον Νὺξ ἡ μελανόπτερος ᾠόν,
> ἐξ οὗ περιτελλομέναις ὥραις ἔβλαστεν Ἔρως ὁ ποθεινός,
> στίλβων νῶτον πτερύγοιν χρυσαῖν, εἰκὼς ἀνεμώκεσι δίναις.
> οὗτος δὲ Χάει πτερόεντι μιγεὶς νύχιος κατὰ Τάρταρον εὐρὺν
> ἐνεόττευσεν γένος ἡμέτερον, καὶ πρῶτον ἀνήγαγεν εἰς φῶς.
> πρότερον δ' οὐκ ἦν γένος ἀθανάτων, πρὶν Ἔρως ξυνέμειξεν ἅπαντα·
> ξυμμειγνυμένων δ' ἑτέρων ἑτέροις γένετ' Οὐρανὸς Ὠκεανός τε
> καὶ Γῆ πάντων τε θεῶν μακάρων γένος ἄφθιτον. ὧδε μέν ἐσμεν
> πολὺ πρεσβύτατοι πάντων μακάρων ἡμεῖς. ὡς δ' ἐσμὲν Ἔρωτος
> πολλοῖς δῆλον·

In the beginning were Chaos and Night and black Erebus and broad Tartarus, and no Earth, Air, or Sky. And in the boundless bosom of Erebus did black-winged Night at the very start bring forth a wind egg, from which as the seasons revolved came forth Eros the seductive, like to swift whirlwinds, his back aglitter with wings of gold. And mating by night with winged Chaos in broad Tartarus, he hatched our own race and first brought it up to daylight. There was no race of immortal gods before Eros commingled everything; then as this commingled with that, Sky came to be, and Ocean and Earth, and the whole imperishable race of blessed gods. Thus we're far older than all the blessed gods, and it's abundantly clear that we're the offspring of Eros.⁹⁴⁴

The chorus says the above in order to prove that they are entitled to the power they have acquired, since their ancestry is older than the gods, and one might argue that the use of the egg is just a way for the chorus of Birds uttering these verses to prove their primal status. However, if we can establish textual and other similarities between the two texts, the suggestion that Aristophanes knew an Orphic Theogony, which he used for a comic effect through the sterile egg, becomes more plausible. The word τίκτει which Aristophanes uses for the egg is the same one used in the OR (ἔτευξε) for the creation of the egg by Chronos (OR7 = OF114F). Also, in Aristophanes' passage graceful Eros sprang from the Egg in 'swift whirlwinds' with 'his back aglitter with wings of gold'. There is an iconographic resemblance between this line and the one found in the OR where Protogonos, after coming out of the Egg 'began to move in an incredible circle', with his 'golden wings moving all around'.⁹⁴⁵ Eros, like Protogonos, has golden wings and moves in a swift circular motion, the two images being very close iconographically and textually. The epithet ὑπηνέμιον can be translated as wafted by the air, something that is in accordance with the creation of the egg by Chronos with aether (airy substance).⁹⁴⁶ The fact that the Egg is laid by Night is not in accordance with the Rhapsodic narrative since the Egg is fashioned by Chronos, but the same is true of the whole of the beginning of the Theogony mentioned by Aristophanes which is more similar to the Hesiodic one. This might indicate that Aristophanes combined the well-known Hesiodic beginning of a Theogony with the specific Orphic theogonical element that suited him the most in making his point about the supremacy of the Birds and the comic effect of a sterile egg. Finally, the fact that in Aristophanes, Eros who came out of the egg 'brought to light' the first beings is also in accordance with the emphasis in light at Phanes' birth in the OR (OR7: ὠέον ἀργύφεον, OR10 (OF121F): ἀργῆτα χιτῶνα, OR25 (OF123F): φέγγος ἄελπτον/ ἀπέστραπτε χροός). Apart from Phanes, Helios is also described as having χρυσαίεσιν πτερύγεσσιν (OR2 = OF102F) which suggests an identification of Phanes/Protogonos with Helios, who is also identified with Apollo. There is, thus, a sense of monotheism as expressed in the DP. I have also mentioned in Chapter 4 that Diodorus Siculus quotes a verse which identifies Dionysos with Phanes.⁹⁴⁷

---

944 Ar. *Av.* 693–704 (Tr. Henderson).
945 OR9 (OF118F): ὡρμήθη δ'ἀνὰ κύκλον ἀθέσφατον. OR12 (OF136F): χρυσείαις πτερύγεσσι φορεύμενος ἔνθα καὶ ἔνθα.
946 OR7 (OF114F).
947 Diod. Sic. 1.11.3. For text see p.164 and also p.222–223.

Considering this double identification of Phanes with Helios/Apollo and Dionysos this might be reflected in the Delphic omphalos whose association with both Apollo and Dionysos has already been discussed; if the omphalos was Dionysos' tomb perhaps it was also Apollo's place of birth. The omphalos resembles an egg and usually the bottom half is submerged in the earth which could represent the divine and the chthonic sphere, life and death represented by Apollo and Dionysos respectively.

On the other hand, it is possible that Aristophanes had in mind the Epimenidian Theogony in which the Egg also appears and Night is one of the first principles, even though she is not the creator of the Egg but two Titans instead:

> τὸν δὲ Ἐπιμενίδην δύο πρώτας ἀρχὰς ὑποθέσθαι Ἀέρα καὶ Νύκτα ... ἐξ ὧν γεννηθῆναι Τάρταρον ... ἐξ ὧν δύο Τιτᾶνας ... ὧν μιχθέντων ἀλλήλοις ᾠὸν γενέσθαι ... ἐξ οὗ πάλιν ἄλλην γενεὰν προελθεῖν.
>
> Epimenides posited two first principles, Air and Night... From these two arise Tartarus... And from these are the two Titans... which when they mix with each other become an egg... from which, again, another race arises.[948]

Guthrie dates this theogony to the 7th–6th century B.C. and Kirk et al place its origin in the 6th century B.C.[949] Plato records Epimenides being active in 500 B.C. but later authors, including Aristotle, place him in the 6th century B.C.[950] Fowler notes that Epimenides' inspiration for making Night a first principle surely came from an Orphic Theogony.[951] The presence of Aer as coeval with Night in Epimenides also links to the Derveni Papyrus, where Aer is considered the primal substance and the OR, where aether is emphasised at the beginning of the Theogony.[952] Since, however, it is not possible to know if Epimenides was inspired by Orphic texts or the other way around, or if they drew from a common tradition, we can at least locate the mythic motif of the egg as a primordial entity at the time of Epimenides.[953] I would suggest, however, in view of the textual and iconographical similarities between Aristophanes' passage and the OR, that it is more probable that Aristophanes has in mind an Orphic Theogony in this occasion.

---

948 *FGrHist* III B457 F4b (=DK 3B5). Dam. *De Principiis*, 124 (Tr. Ahbel-Rappe).
949 Guthrie, 1952, p.93; KRS, 1983, p.23/n.2 and p.44–45.
950 KRS, 1983, p.45; DK 3 A 1–5.
951 Fowler, 2013, p.7.
952 Fowler refers to the parallel to the DP and gives some other possible inspirations of Epimenides (2013, p.7). Col.XIX.1–3, Col.XVIII.1–3, Col.XVII.2–3.
953 About Epimenides' activity and reputation in relation to Crete see discussion in Tzifopoulos, 2010, Ch. 4.

We have also discussed in Chapter 1 a passage from Plutarch's *Table-talk* where he deals with the question of 'Which came first: the chicken or the egg?'[954] As already mentioned, he refers to an Orphic *hieros logos* where an egg was the primal agent of generation as proof that the egg came first: '"What is more," he added with a laugh, ["I will sing for those who are wise" the sacred discourse of Orpheus] ("ἀείσω ξυνετοῖσι' τὸν Ὀρφικὸν καὶ ἱερὸν λόγον") which not only declares the egg older than the hen, but also attributes to it the absolute primordiality over all things together without exception'.[955] It furthermore, supports the placement of OR1 (OF1F) at the beginning of the *hieros logos* in the *Rhapsodies* since Plutarch associates it with the theogonical elements we find in the *Rhapsodies*. The fact that Plutarch refers to this Orphic work, which makes the egg the primal entity, as an *hieros logos*, corroborates that it was one of the *Hieroi Logoi in 24 Rhapsodies*. He also relates the poem to mysteries without revealing any details apart from the following: 'It is therefore not inappropriate that in the rites of Dionysus the egg is consecrated as a symbol of that which produces everything and contains everything within itself'.[956] The use of the *hieros logos* in relation to mysteries would be consistent with what I have maintained throughout this book about the importance of Orphic texts in Orphic mysteries. In the same work, Plutarch notes that he was accused of being affiliated with Orphic or Pythagorean beliefs because he refused to eat an egg:

> ὑπόνοιαν μέντοι παρέσχον, ἑστιῶντος ἡμᾶς Σοσσίου Σενεκίωνος, ἐνέχεσθαι δόγμασιν Ὀρφικοῖς ἢ Πυθαγορικοῖς καὶ τὸ ᾠόν, ὥσπερ ἔνιοι καρδίαν καὶ ἐγκέφαλον, ἀρχὴν ἡγούμενος γενέσεως ἀφοσιοῦσθαι·

> But my companions at one of Sossius Senecio's dinners suspected me of being committed to beliefs of the Orphics or the Pythagoreans and holding the egg taboo, as some hold the heart and brain, because I thought it to be the first principle of creation.[957]

Plutarch, then, relates the theogonical motif of the egg being the beginning of generation with a specific habit of the Orphics. This confirms that the content of Orphic texts was transformed into religious practice, and in this case it was in the form of a lifelong habit, as in an *Orphikos bios*. It is finally worth mentioning that one of the works attributed to Orpheus is titled: Ὠιοσκοπικά/Ὠιοθυτικά (OF811T: 'Divination by eggs').

---

954 For text and discussion see p.17–18.
955 Plut. *Quaest. conv.* 2.3.2, 636d–636e (Tr. Clement). Translation in brackets [ ] is by the author.
956 Plut. *Quaest. conv.* 2.3.2, 636e (Tr. Clement).
957 Plut. *Quaest. conv.* 2.3.1, 635e (Tr. Clement).

In the case of Protogonos we can be more confident of his presence in Classical and other Orphic sources since we already saw that he is at least mentioned in the DP Theogony and in Tablet C from Thurii (4th B.C). Tablet C also includes words such as Φάνης, ἀέρ, Ἥλιε, νύξ, φάος, κλυτὲ δαίμον, all of which are related to the figure of Protogonos or the beginning of the OR in the following ways: Phanes is another denomination of Protogonos in the *Rhapsodies* (OR10/17/25 = OF121F/140F/123F), Night is a primal entity and the only one who can see Phanes (OR6/25 = OF107F/123F), Protogonos springs out of the egg made of aether into the light and he is also denominated as daimon (OR17 = OF140F). Some of these words are also found in fr.57 (Bond) of Euripides' *Hypsipyle* where there seems to be a description of a Theogony closely resembling the beginning of the OR: ὦ] πότνια θεῶ[ν | φ]άος ἄσκοπον [| αἰθ]έρι πρωτόγονο[| .]θελ' Ἔρως ὅτε νὺ[ξ ('O mistress of the gods ... invisible light ... of the aether firsborn ... Eros when Night').[958] It is suggested by Morel that πότνια θεῶν is goddess Earth, while Dodds prefers Rhea, both of them based on other Euripidean dramas.[959] These goddesses have been related to Orphic rites and it is mentioned in the *Rhapsodies* than when Rhea gave birth to Zeus she turned into Demeter (OR46 = OF206F). Protogonos, Eros and Night are all important deities found at the beginning of the Orphic theogonical myth and more importantly Protogonos/Phanes is a deity not found in other theogonies. Additionally, both suggested readings of φ]άος ἄσκοπον or χ]άος ἄσκοπον correspond to the beginning of the *Rhapsodies*. The first could refer to the 'invisible' light shining at the moment of Phanes' birth when he sprang through aether; this becomes even more plausible if we accept the reading αἰθ]έρι πρωτόγονο[. The second one could refer to chaos generated from Chronos alongside aether. Kern compares these lines to OF86 (Kern) and a quotation from the Orphic theogony by Hermias that refers to the ἐν αἰθέρι φέγγος ἄελπτον coming from Phanes, meaning 'the unlooked-for light in the aether'.[960] These verses, thus, have an Orphic context and overtone and it is probable that Euripides is referring to an Orphic theogony here.[961] FInally, Phanes' epithet Erikepaios (OR15 = OF134F) is found in the Gurôb Papyrus (mid-3rd century B.C.) and discussed in

---

[958] The most important work on Euripides' *Hypsipyle* is Bond's edition (1963) with a reconstruction of the narrative through the arrangement of the available fragments along with a commentary, while scholarship on this play is indeed limited.
[959] Bond, 1963, p.121: Morel parallels ὦ πότνια Χθών found in *Hec.* 70. Dodds, 1960, pp.76–77/85: Dodds compares μάτηρ θεῶν referring to Rhea found in *Helen* (1301 ff) and the *Bacchae* (120–134) and who is linked to Dionysos' cult (*Hel.* 1364).
[960] Kern, 1922, p.81 and p.158–159 (OF2 Kern/OF86 Kern). See OR25 (OF123F).
[961] Bremmer also suggest the possibility (2014, p.78).

is found in the Gurôb Papyrus (mid-3rd century B.C.) and discussed in the previous chapter.[962] I suggest, then, that as an entity Protogonos can be traced as early as the 5th century B.C. based on the Derveni Papyrus but we cannot be sure that the name Phanes was used as early as the name Protogonos. Also, the fact that Diodorus Siculus (1st B.C.), as mentioned earlier (p.302), quotes an Orphic verse which identifies Dionysos with Phanes, clearly places the name of Phanes in an Orphic context rather earlier than the Neoplatonic commentaries.

However, the figure of Phanes can perhaps be located in south-east Chios, near the modern village of Kato Phana, and the temple of Apollo Phanaeus dating to the end of the 7th century B.C., a case which has not been much discussed by scholarship due to the fact that the archaeological site has not yet been fully excavated.[963] Sherds inscribed with the word Φαναίο evidence that the site was dedicated to Apollo Phanaeus.[964] This would agree with my earlier suggestion that Phanes was essentially a persona of Apollo. Around the area of Kato Phana in Chios inscriptions have been found most of which, according to Forrest, almost certainly came originally from the sites at Emporio and Phanai.[965] Several of the inscriptions seem to reflect Orphic ideas and refer to Orphic deities. One inscription bears the names of Herakles and Dionysos [[Ε]ὔκ[ρ]ιτος | ['Η]ρακλ[εῖ] | καὶ Διονύσωι | ε[ὐχήν] and another reads σωτηρίην αἰωνίην Ο(ἰ)νοπίων[......]γενε]ὴν | [---] Ἐὐ[κ]λέων Δημητρίου Ἡρακλεῖ | [---] Σωτῆρι καθ'ὅραμα.[966] These two inscriptions could be interpreted together as referring to the people of Chios regarded as descendants of Oinopoion, who was the son of Dionysos, and they might relate to hero cult and divine descent.[967] Another inscription reads Ἀπόλλωνος | Ἀγρέτεω and the epithet could mean 'the assembler' from the verb ἀγείρω, or 'the hunter'.[968] In the first case this could be related to Dionysos' dismemberment myth and the assembling of his pieces by Apollo, which was part of the *Rhapsodies*. Another inscription reads Εὀήνωρ Ἡραγόρεω | Μητρὶ Κυβελείῃ(ι) | τὰ πρὸ

---

[962] See p.265. GP 22.
[963] Beaumont *et al.*, 1999, p.286; Payne, 1934.
[964] IChiosMcCabe 107. IChiosMcCabe 108. IChiosMcCabe 109. IChiosMcCabe 110. Payne, 1934.
[965] Forrest, 1963, p.53. Based on the fact that in the south-east corner of Chios there are traces of several other ancient sites but they 'appear to have been little more than isolated farmhouses or small sanctuaries'.
[966] IChiosMcCabe 124. IChiosMcCabe 121. Forrest: Ἐὐ[κ]λέων.
[967] Forrest, 1963, p.58.
[968] IChiosMcCabe 226. This might be related to the constellation of Orion which will be discussed later on.

area based on three other dedications to Meter.⁹⁷⁰ As was discussed in Chapter 4 these are deities mentioned in the gold tablets and as shown in Chapter 2, associated by ancient authors with Orphic rites – the same goes for Ἐὐ[κ]λέων found in the inscription mentioned above –.⁹⁷¹

The most interesting sherd/inscription, however, is the one that says Θεῶν πάντων | καὶ πασῶν and dating at the 2nd or 1st century B.C.⁹⁷² It has a drawing underneath the inscription of what Forrest identifies as two caps of the Dioskouroi with an eight-pointed star on top of each and encircled with a bay-leaf wreath.⁹⁷³ These could be the caps of the Dioskouroi – Castor and Pollux – sometimes portrayed with a star on top. However, considering Apollo's epithet Phanaeus it could be that the caps represent the Orphic egg signifying the totality of the cosmos, since Phanes holds inside him the seed of all the gods (OR17 = OF140F: σπέρμα φέροντα θεῶν κλυτόν). A connection between the Dioskouroi and Phanes should be explored since their caps are often perceived as the remaining shells of the egg out of which they were born.⁹⁷⁴ There might also be an astronomical connection since Castor and Pollux were considered to be the stars on the Gemini constellation which were visible for only 6 months each year, which in turn could be related to elements of rebirth and apotheosis, that are also evident in the story that only one of the brothers was made immortal by Zeus, who then nonetheless offered them alternate immortality.⁹⁷⁵ They are often referred to as saviours of men and the following verses from the *Homeric Hymn to the Dioskouroi* use the 'release from pain' vocabulary which is evident in the gold tablets, as we saw and in the *Rhapsodies*, as we will see: '...and release from travail; the sailors rejoice at the sight, and their misery and stress are ended' [πόνου

---

970 Forrest, 1963, p.43.
971 Euklēs: A1, A2, A3, A5. Cybele: C. Mētēr: C, D5. See section 2.3. in p.43.
972 IChiosMcCabe 232.
973 Forrest, 1963, p.61 and Plate 17.
974 Gantz, 1993, p.323–328.
975 Pind. *Pyth.* 11.61–64: καὶ Κάστορος βίαν, | σέ τε, ἄναξ Πολύδευκες, υἱοὶ θεῶν, | τὸ μὲν παρ' ἆμαρ ἕδραισι Θεράπνας, | τὸ δ' οἰκέοντας ἔνδον Ὀλύμπου: '...and mighty Castor, and you, lord Polydeuces, sons of the gods, you who spend one day in your homes at Therapna, and on the next dwell in Olympus.' (Tr. Race). Pind. *Nem.* 10.49–51: Κάστορος δ' ἐλθόντος ἐπὶ ξενίαν πὰρ Παμφάη | καὶ κασιγνήτου Πολυδεύκεος, οὐ θαῦμα σφίσιν | ἐγγενὲς ἔμμεν ἀεθληταῖς ἀγαθοῖσιν·: 'But given that Castor and his brother Polydeuces came for hospitality to the home of Pamphaës, it is no wonder that they have inborn ability to be good athletes.' (Tr. Race). Alcm. fr.2 Campbell: π[ᾶσι κἀνθρώποισί τ' αἰδ]οιεστάτοι ν[αί]ο̣ισι νέ[ρθεν γᾶς ἀειζώοι σι]όδματο[ν τ]έγος Κά[στωρ τε πώλων ὠκέων] δματῆ[ρε]ς̣ [ἱ]ππόται̣ σοφοὶ καὶ Πωλυδεύκης] κυδρός: 'Most worthy of reverence from all gods and men, they dwell in a god-built home (beneath the earth, always alive?), Castor – tamers of swift steeds, skilled horsemen – and glorious Polydeuces.'. Lycoph. *Alex.* 564ff.

<ἀπονό>σφισιν· οἳ δὲ ἰδόντες | γήθησαν, παύσαντο δ' ὀϊζυροῖο πόνοιο].⁹⁷⁶ This is related to their role as protectors of sea-farers but their connection with motifs of death and rebirth and the association of the word *ponos* with mortality, suggest that their roles as saviours might have been eschatological.⁹⁷⁷ It is not possible to cover in depth in this chapter the complicated matter of the Dioskouroi but the possible connection with Phanes – and his double identification with Dionysos and Apollo – in this evidence from Chios is nonetheless worth identifying for future research.⁹⁷⁸ In general, the fact that many elements from the findings from Kato Phana correspond to Orphic ideas and deities found elsewhere suggest that this very early temple of Apollo Phanaeus might have been in honour of Phanes or at least that there was Orphic activity on the island in relation to Apollo Phanaeus.

Another case is the Greek colony Phanagoria which is located very close to Olbia where the earliest Orphic evidence has been found, namely the Olbian Bone Tablets. This colony was founded by inhabitants of Teos in Ionia in the mid-6th century B.C. and the archaeological material 'attests the typical Hellenic nature of the Phanagorian *polis* throughout antiquity'.⁹⁷⁹ The name in itself could be an indication of a relation with the figure of Phanes, or Apollo Phanaeus for that matter.⁹⁸⁰ Kuznetsov suggests that their major deities were Apollo and Aphrodite Ourania, who is mentioned in the Derveni Papyrus where she is identified with Peitho, Harmonia and the act of procreation.⁹⁸¹ The earliest coins of Phanagoria,

---

976 *Hom.Hymn* 33.16–17 (Tr. West). See also Alc. fr.34 Campbell.
977 Based on evidence I have collected as early as Homer and Pindar, there is scope for future research which I intend to pursue, which suggests that the sea-faring trip might in fact be an allegorical representation of the soul's return back to its divine abode and that it is in this sense that the Kabeiroi and Dioskouroi are protectors of sea-farers. A good starting point would be Euripides' *Andromeda* (*TrGF* fr.124): ΠΕΡΣΕΥΣ: ὦ θεοί, τίν' εἰς γῆν βαρβάρων ἀφίγμεθα | ταχεῖ πεδίλῳ; διὰ μέσου γὰρ αἰθέρος | τέμνων κέλευθον πόδα τίθημ' ὑπόπτερον | ὑπέρ τε πόντου χεῦμ' ὑπέρ τε Πλειάδα, | Περσεύς, πρὸς Ἄργος ναυστολῶν, τὸ Γοργόνος | κάρα κομίζων: 'Perseus: (flying in above the stage) 'O gods, to what barbarians' land has my swift sandal brought me? Through middle heaven (διὰ μέσου γὰρ αἰθέρος) I cut my path, setting winged foot over flowing sea and Pleiad – I, Perseus, as I voyage for Argos bearing the Gorgon's head' (Tr. Collard-Cropp).
978 See Bowden (2015) for a discussion of an interchange of elements between the Dioskouroi, the Kabeiroi and Theoi Megaloi. He argues: 'Representations of the Kabeiroi as the Dioskouroi, or of Kabeiros as Dionysus, are, I would argue, attempts to clothe in meaningful garb gods who have no iconography of their own' (p.36).
979 Kuznetsov, 2016, p.43. All the information about Phanagoria are taken from Kuznetsov (ed.) (2016).
980 Kuznetsov, 2016, p.85.
981 Kuznetsov, 2016, p.129. DP.Col.XXI.5–10: Ἀφροδίτη Οὐρανία | καὶ Ζεὺς καὶ ἀφροδισιάζειν καὶ θόρνυσθαι καὶ Πειθὼ | καὶ Ἁρμονία τῶι αὐτῶι θεῶι ὄνομα κεῖται. ἀνὴρ | γυναικὶ μισγόμενος

dating to the late 5th century B.C. according to Kuznetsov, always depict on the one side a beardless head with long hair, wearing a *pilos* – sometimes laureate –, and on the obverse a bull and an ear of corn with the letters ΦΑΝΑ or ΦΑ.[982] The *pilos*, as mentioned earlier is the same cup worn by the Dioskouroi sometimes taken to be the egg out of which they were born. The same could apply to the deity of the Phanagoria coins too. Even if the word ΦΑΝΑ might be due to the name of the colony we need to wonder about the combination of these figures. It is mentioned in the *Rhapsodies* that Phanes is a bisexual deity (OR10 = OF121F: ἀρσενόθηλυς) and he is also called 'female and father' (OR15 = OF134F: θῆλυς καὶ γενέτωρ). He is also Eros, who is usually found alongside Aphrodite, while he is said to have the head of a bull (OR14 = OF130F). I would argue that it is very probable that it is Phanes who is depicted in these coins since not only do we have a beardless entity which could be due to its bisexuality, but the bull and the corn could represent the double identity of Phanes as Dionysos/Zeus – as identified elsewhere – and Ge Meter who in the DP is equated with Demeter, Hestia, Hera and Rhea. In other words it could represent the first generative deity, encompassing all male and female deities and having the power to generate everything by itself. This is furthermore supported by the fact that an abundance of coins minted in Pantikapaion were circulating in Phanagoria depicting the head of Pan bow and arrow, which entails both elements of Phanes encompassing the cosmos and Apollo with the bow and arrow which typically refer to the rays of the sun shooting from afar on mortals. We also have later coins depicting Dionysos and a thyrsus and in other cases Apollo with a thyrsus or Dionysos, thyrsus and a tripod. Phanagoria coinage remained inactive from the early 4th century to the beginning of the 2nd century B.C. and when resumed it struck silver *tetrobols* with the head of Artemis on the one side and a rose or a stag on the other with the word ΦΑΝΑΓΟΡΙΤΩΝ under it. A series of Greek coins that are the earliest known inscribed issue might be related to Artemis and the stag; they date to the late 7th-early 6th century B.C. and were found in western Asia Minor, where the idea of coinage first started developing in the second half of the 7th century, and more specifically in Ephesus in Ionia where the colonists of Phanagoria were from.[983]

ἀφροδισιάζειν λέγεται κατὰ | φάτιν· τῶν γὰρ νῦν ἐόντων μιχθέντων ἀλλ[ή]λοις | Ἀφροδίτη ὠνομάσθη: 'Ouranian Aphrodite, Zeus, aphrodising, jumping, Peitho (i.e. Persuasion), Harmonia are established names for the same god. A man having sexual contact with a woman is said in everyday usage to be 'aphrodising'. So, because the *eonta* were brought into contact with each other, it (or: the god) was called Aphrodite.'

982 Kuznetsov, 2016, p.108. Coin examples in p.109–115.
983 Guthrie, 1952, p.99. CM BMC Ephesus 1 (BNK.950); Kraay & Hirmer, 1966, no.585 (Plate 177) and p.354–55.

The inscription is Φάνος ἐμὶ σῆμα, written retrograde, and a stag is portrayed, an animal traditionally related to Artemis. In the *Rhapsodies*, Artemis is another deity who has a double identity, since she is equated with Hecate and even Persephone (OR73 = OF317F/OF257F). The practice of inscribing the name of the issuer, or highest political power of the city that issued the coin, was not common at the earliest stage of the development of coinage; this supports the suggestion that the name Phanes did not belong to an official or actual person.[984] The phrase inscribed on one of the coins can be translated in many ways such as: 'I am the tomb of Phanes', 'I am the sign of Phanes (or light)' or 'I am the badge of Phanes'.[985] The first two translations are consistent with the hypothesis of Phanes being a deity, something that is further supported by the fact that the coins were found in the excavations of the temple of Artemis in Ephesus, which makes the cultic associations of the coins stronger.[986] This is of course also supported by the coins of Phanagoria. If the deity depicted and mentioned on the Phanagoria and Ephesus coins is Phanes then this entity can be located as early as the 7th century B.C.

In the *Rhapsodies* the creation of the world by Phanes/Erikepaios is characterised by astronomical and cosmological elements. Selene is referred to as 'a celestial earth' which rotates around its axis and changes four times in a month while the sun does the same in a year. It is furthermore noted that the earth, the abode of humans, was located far away from the home of the gods and at a specific distance from the sun so it was not too hot or too cold but something in between. This makes us imagine the earth, the moon and the sun floating in space while it is suggested that the heaven which is the gods' house is located far away from the earth. We would not expect to find such a cosmological representation of the world in a Theogony, which suggests that this poem is not solely concerned with theogonical ideas. Moreover, the importance of the position of the sun is related to the DP. I have discussed in Chapter 5 the important role of the sun in the creation of life in DP since heat and cold are two essential components for the *eonta* to come together.[987] It is also stressed in the DP that the sun was located in

---

[984] Kraay & Hirmer, 1966.
[985] If the Phanes of the coins is the Orphic Phanes, the heliadic primal deity who created the world and was born out of the aether, which as established so far was the divine substance of the soul according to Orphic beliefs, it is possible that in a very minimalistic way the dedicator of the coins acknowledges his/her divine ancestry, bearing in mind that according to Plato the Orphics gave the word σῶμα to the body thinking that it is the tomb (σῆμά) of the soul which undergoes a punishment (Pl. *Cra.* 400c). See p.9–10 for text and discussion.
[986] Kraay & Hirmer, 1966, p.354.
[987] Col.IX/X/XXI. See p.214.

the middle (ἐν μέσωι πήξας ἴσχει καὶ τἄνωθε τοῦ ἡλίου | καὶ τὰ κάτωθεν) and that if it ever trespassed its size it would be punished because the world order would be disrupted.[988] Similarly, in the OR it is said that Erikepaios created the sun to be a guardian and ruler over everything which is reminiscent of the Derveni author's words that god would not have created the sun if he did not want the *eonta* to exist. The emphasis on the sun, which is also evident from the previous sections of the *Rhapsodies* through the figure of Phanes/Protogonos and Orpheus' invocation for inspiration to the sun, is something very clearly different from other theogonical traditions. The fact that we find striking similarities with the DP suggests that the sun was important for the Orphics since it is consistently found through our sources. The presence of cosmogonical and astronomical ideas in the OR is also consistent with the suggestion made so far that the Orphic texts were of a religious scientific, cosmogonical and allegorical nature.

6.5.3 The Second and Third Ruler: Night and Ouranos: OR25 – OR34

The prominent place which Night has in the OR is different from the Hesiodic theogony, where Night is one of the first principles, but does not have the key role that she has in the *Rhapsodies*. In Hesiod she is the begetter of a number of deities while she is even called evil, deadly and murky.[989] She gives birth to a series of dreadful entities most of which bring suffering to mortals and which beget further horrible creatures: Doom, Death, Sleep, Black Fate, Blame, Distress, Nemesis, Deceit, Old Age and Strife.[990] As Strauss Clay notes, the catalogue of Night's offspring is strategically placed by Hesiod at the point of 'entrance of evil into the cosmos'.[991] This is very different from the motherly ruler described in the OR as: 'Mother, supreme of the gods and immortal Night' and who gives birth to Ouranos and Gaia.[992] Night is called holy and nurturer, and becomes the second ruler who reigns after Phanes gives her his sceptre and the gift of prophecy.[993] Furthermore, she has an important role as nurturer of the gods and adviser of Zeus on how to overthrow Kronos and establish his rule among the mortals.[994] She also advises Zeus prior to the fabrication of the world on how to have all things one and each

---

988 Col. XV.4–5. See also Col.IV/XIII. See p.245.
989 Hes. *Theog.* 124–126, 211–225, 745–760. Evil: 757, 223: ὀλοή. Murky: 744: ἐρεβεννῆς.
990 Hes. *Theog.* 211–226.
991 Strauss Clay, 2003, p.96.
992 OR55 (OF237F): μαῖα, θεῶν ὑπάτη, Νὺξ ἄμβροτε.
993 Holy: OR25. Nurturer: OR38. Sceptre: OR26–28. OR28: 'the gift of prophecy'.
994 OR38/53/55 (OF112F/220F/237F).

one separate.⁹⁹⁵ She has a fundamental and positive impact on the unfolding of events which lead to Zeus' supremacy.

West suggests that the reign of Night is a construction of the *Rhapsodies*' compiler because she is the only female sovereign and her reign is eventless.⁹⁹⁶ However, as we said, in the OR Ouranos is considered to be Night's son (ὅς (Ouranos) πρῶτος βασίλευσε θεῶν μετὰ μητέρα Νύκτα) and the same thing is said in a verse quoted by the Derveni author: "Οὐρανὸς Εὐφρονίδης, ὃς πρώτιστος βασίλευσεν".⁹⁹⁷ Ouranos is given the epithet Εὐφρονίδης (i.e. the son of Euphrone), which is an epithet of Night.⁹⁹⁸ This suggests that Night was one of the primal entities in Orphic theogonical texts from early times, and it does not follow that her reign was interpolated in the *Rhapsodies*, since in the DP verse it is clearly said that Ouranos' reign was after the reign of his mother Night. Apart from the fact that both poems regard Ouranos as the son of Night the similarity between the two verses is evident and one might say that the Derveni verse could be followed by the verse found in the OR: θεῶν μετὰ μητέρα Νύκτα. Moreover, both verses refer to Ouranos being one of the first rulers and so we know that the succession Night – Ouranos was part of the beginning of an early Orphic theogony. One might say that since in the OR the same expression is used for Phanes (κόσμον, οὗ πρῶτος βασίλευσε περικλυτὸς Ἠρικεπαῖος), there is an inconsistency as to who was the first ruler.⁹⁹⁹ However, the verse identifies Phanes as the first ruler of the *whole cosmos* – including the gods and mortals that he has created – since the cosmos did not exist before him.¹⁰⁰⁰ Ouranos, on the other hand is identified as the first ruler of the *gods*. This suggestion is also supported by the fact that the same verse is mentioned for Kronos in the OR: πρώτιστος μὲν ἄνασσεν ἐπιχθονίων Κρόνος ἀνδρῶν.¹⁰⁰¹ In this case, Kronos is said to be the first to rule over *mortals*. The repetition of this verse, I would suggest, is due to the fact that with every ruler the sphere of ruling changes and seems to have a gradual hierarchical degradation, until we reach Zeus who swallows Phanes deliberately so he can become the ruler of the whole cosmos again and it is perhaps significant that inside Zeus, as we will see, everything is mixed, mortal and immortal become

---

995 OR56–58 (OF237F/219F).
996 West, 1983, p.234.
997 OR33 = OF174F. Col.XIV.6.
998 Sider, 2014, p.560: An epithet found as early as Hesiod's *Works and Days*: μακραὶ γὰρ ἐπίρροθοι εὐφρόναι εἰσίν (560).
999 OR19 = OF167F.
1000 For a different opinion see Edmonds, 2013, p.153.
1001 OR45 = OF363F.

one. In reference to the epithet Εὐφρονίδης, matronymics are not common in ancient Greek, the patronym being far more common, especially in poetry.[1002] The fact, then, that we have the same unusual theogonical element and two very similar verses supports that the importance of Night as a primal deity was part of the early Orphic tradition and was most probably not invented by the *Rhapsodies'* compiler.[1003]

Apart from the fact that Night is Ouranos' mother in both the OR and the DP, we have further similarities which reside in her role as nurturer and prophet, roles which are both distinctive compared with other theogonical traditions. In the DP, as in the OR, she is called nurse/nurturer: 'By saying that she is "nurse", he (Orpheus) expresses in riddling form that whatever the sun dissolves by heating, the night unites by cooling'.[1004] We can see, thus, that the perception of Night as a nurse in the DP is also related to heat and the sun, which as we saw are also important in the OR for the generation of life. In the OR it is also mentioned that Night nurtured Kronos the most out of all the gods who, as the Derveni author notes, was the one who struck the *eonta* to one another with the heat of the sun. It was only when the *eonta* cooled down that they were able to come together and form beings. Could it be that this is the reason for Night's preferential treatment of Kronos? In this case there would be another point of contact between the OR and the DP. Moreover, it is evident that Night has an important role as prophet and advisor in the OR after receiving the gift of prophecy from Phanes: she prophesies the coming of Zeus, she advises Zeus on how to bind Kronos and establish his rule and also how to bring all things of the cosmos together.[1005] In the DP the Derveni commentator notes that Night had prophetic powers and that she had proclaimed an oracle in order to assist Zeus:

[τ]ῆς Νυκτός. "ἐξ ἀ[δύτοι]ο" δ' αὐτὴν [λέγει] "χρῆσαι"
γνώμην ποιού[με]νος ἄδυτον εἶναι τὸ βάθος
τῆς νυκτός· οὐ γ[ὰρ] δύνει ὥσπερ τὸ φῶς, ἀλλά νιν
ἐν τῶι αὐτῶι μέ[νο]γ αὐγὴ κατα[λ]αμβάνει.
χρῆσαι δὲ καὶ ἀρκέσαι ταὐτὸ [δύ]ναται.
σκέψασθαι δὲ χρὴ ἐφ' ὧι κεῖτα[ι τὸ] ἀρκέσαι
καὶ τὸ χρῆσαι.

1002 Sider, 2014.
1003 See also the earlier discussion about the possible Aristophanic reference to the Orphic egg in p.301.
1004 Col.X.11–12: "τροφ[ὸν] δὲ λέγων αὐ]τὴν αἰγί[ζε]ται ὅτι [ἅ]σσα | ὁ ἥλι[ος θερμαίνων δι]αλύει ταῦτα ἡ νὺξ ψύ[χουσα].
1005 Coming of Zeus: OR43 = OF251F. How to bind Kronos: OR53/55 = OF220F/237F. How to bring all things together: (OR56–58 = OF237F/219F).

'χρᾶν τόνδε τὸν θεὸν νομίζοντ[ες ἔρ]χονται
πευσόμενοι ἅσσα ποῶσι'. τὰ δ' [ἐπὶ τούτ]ωι λέγει·
"[ἡ δὲ] ἔχρησεν ἅπαντα τά οἱ θέ[μις ἦν ἀνύσασ]θαι".

...of Night. He says that 'she prophesied from the innermost shrine meaning to say that the depth of night is unsetting; for it does not set as the light does, but daylight occupies it as it remains in the same place. And 'prophesying' and 'availing' mean the same. One has to consider what 'availing' and 'prophesying' are applied to: 'Believing that such and such a god prophesies/avails they go to inquire what they should do'. And after this he says: "And he prophesied everything that was proper for him to accomplish".[1006]

In this passage Night is portrayed, according to the Orphic verses, as a deity that prophesies from an innermost shrine and who has proclaimed an oracle for a male deity about all that was right for him to accomplish.[1007] This male deity is most probably Zeus since in Col. VIII the Derveni author quotes a verse which says that Zeus took the 'prophesied rule and power' from Kronos and following stresses that these verses might be misunderstood as denoting that Zeus did not take the kingship lawfully: '[In the other] word order the impression would be given that he took the power contrary to the prophecies'.[1008] In other words, in both the OR and the DP the prophecies of Night are used to legitimise Zeus' kingship.

This must be an innovation of the Orphic tradition since in the OR the kingship is handed willingly from one ruler to the next in all cases apart from Kronos, who castrates his father, and Zeus who binds Kronos. Through Night's prophecies, though, Zeus' actions are legitimised and the only lawless ruler is Kronos, a Titan. As a result, the Titanic race, who will later on also dismember Dionysos, are portrayed as the only lawless race of rulers. We have, therefore, a strong narrative parallel between the DP and the OR concerning the important role of Night for the establishment of Zeus' kingship which moreover is not present in other theogonical traditions. The lawless nature of the Titans is furthermore emphasised in the OR by the use of epithets such as κακομῆται and ἀγκυλομήτης which means they have bad counsel (*mētis*).[1009] *Mētis* is actually an epithet of Protogonos and Zeus, while Chronos is said to be ἀφθιτόμητις (the one with imperishable counsel).[1010] Mētis/Protogonos is also called *daimon* in the OR and after Kronos'

1006 Col.XI.1–10.
1007 Night abodes in a 'dark and misty cave' in the OR too (OR29 = OF163F).
1008 Col.VIII.11-12: [ἄλλως δ' ἔ]χοντα παρὰ θέσφατα δ[όξειεν ἂν λαβεῖ]ν | [τὴν ἀλκήν·. Sider, 2014.
1009 OR39 = OF301F: κακομῆται. OR43 = OF181F: ἀγκυλομήτης.
1010 Protogonos: OR17 = OF140F. Zeus: OR61 = OF243F. Kronos: OR4 = OF111F.

binding from Zeus, the latter says: 'Guide our generation, most illustrious daimon (ἀριδείκετε δαῖμον)'.[1011] Proclus, who quotes this verse, notes that it is said when Zeus binds Kronos, and he says that Zeus calls his father daimon, suggesting that the daimon refers to Kronos. However, the epithet 'illustrious' suggests that perhaps this daimon is in fact Metis which is passed from one ruler to the next. This suggestion might be supported by the following Orphic verses quoted in the DP:

> Ζεὺς μὲν ἐπεὶ δὴ πα[τρὸς ἑο]ῦ πάρα θέ[σ]φατον ἀρχὴν
> [ἀ]λκήν τ' ἐν χείρεσσι ἔ[λ]αβ[εν κ]α[ὶ] δαίμον[α] κυδρόν.
>
> Zeus then, when from his father the prophesied rule and power in his hands had taken, and the glorious daimon.[1012]

The daimon in this case would be Protogonos who Zeus later on swallows. Not only is Protogonos named daimon in the OR, too, but another verse from the *Rhapsodies* which describes what happens after the swallowing of Protogonos, refers to the [ἀ]λκήν of Protogonos being mixed in Zeus' belly: μεῖξε δ'ἑοῖς μελέεσσι θεοῦ δύναμίν τε καὶ ἀλκήν which is the same word used in the DP passage above.[1013] The verses from the DP note that Zeus received the daimon according to the 'prophesied rule', and the swallowing of Protogonos to which the OR verses refer to also takes place after Night's advice/oracle. Moreover, some of the remaining verses from OR59 (OF241F) are identical with verses quoted in the DP, in both cases describing the creation of the world by Zeus after the swallowing takes place:

> Πρωτογόνου βασιλέως αἰδοίου· τῶι δ' ἄρα πάντες
> ἀθάνατοι προσέφυν μάκαρες θεοὶ ἠδὲ θέαιναι
> καὶ ποταμοὶ καὶ κρῆναι ἐπήρατοι ἄλλα τε πάντα,
> ἄσσα τότ' ἦν γεγαῶτ', αὐτὸς δ' ἄρα μοῦνος ἔγεντο. (Col.XVI.3–6)
>
> Of the First-born king, the reverend one; and upon him all the immortals grew, blessed gods and goddesses and rivers and lovely springs and everything else that had then been born; and he himself became the sole one.
>
> καὶ ποταμοὶ καὶ πόντος ἀπείριτος ἄλλα τε πάντα
> πάντες τ' ἀθάνατοι μάκαρες θεοὶ ἠδὲ θέαιναι,
> ὅσσα τ' ἔην γεγαῶτα καὶ ὕστερον ὁπόσσ' ἔμελλεν,
> ἓν γένετο, Ζηνὸς δ' ἐνὶ γαστέρι σύρρα πεφύκει (OR59)

1011 Mētis/Protogonos as daimon: OR17 = OF140F. Zeus' words to daimon: OR54 = OF239F.
1012 Col.VIII.4–5.
1013 OR59 = OF241F.

...and rivers and the inaccessible deep, and everything else and all the immortal and blissful Gods and Goddesses and all that has already happened and all that will in the future became one, tangled inside the belly of Zeus and were brought forth again.

This not only shows that verses from the OR can be traced unchanged as early as the 5th century B.C. but also that it is indeed Protogonos who Zeus swallows in the DP, as was argued in Chapter 5. This latter point is moreover supported, as noted in Chapter 5, by the fact that the verse from the DP referring to the swallowing – "αἰδοῖον κατέπινεν, ὃς αἰθέρα ἔκθορε πρῶτος" – shows similarities with the one describing Phanes' birth in the *Rhapsodies*: ἐξέθορε πρώτιστος ἀνέδραμε τ' ἀρσενόθηλυς | Πρωτόγονος πολυτίμητος.[1014] It is becoming more and more evident that the points of contact between the DP and the OR in terms of narrative, entities, cosmology and text are abundant.

I have already argued that the Πρωτόγονος αἰδοῖος swallowed in the DP is the Protogonos whom Zeus swallows in the OR, and who is also identified with Metis.[1015] In the OR the following verse specifically refers to Metis being inside Zeus' belly:

καὶ Μῆτις, πρῶτος γενέτωρ καὶ Ἔρως πολυτερπής
πάντα γὰρ ἐν Ζηνὸς μεγάλωι τάδε σώματι κεῖται.

and also Metis, the first creator and much-delighting Eros, for all these lie inside Zeus' mighty body.[1016]

At an allegorical level, this good counsel, which is imperishable through time, is handed over from one ruler to the next and Kronos as signified by his epithets is the only one who did not use it wisely. The passing of Metis is perhaps symbolised through the passing of the sceptre, which Phanes/Metis first fabricated, from one ruler to the next.[1017] This is supported by the fact that the epithet ἀριδείκετε used for the daimon whom Zeus takes counsel from in the OR, is also used for the sceptre:[1018]

– ‿‿ – σκῆπτρον δ' ἀριδείκετον εἷο χέρεσσιν

1014 Col.XIII.4. OR10 (OF121F) = '...he sprang upwards first of all, the hermaphrodite and highly-honoured Protogonos'.
1015 Col.XIII.4. Col.XVI.3.
1016 OR61 = OF243F.
1017 OF98T(III) = Procl. *in Pl. Ti.* III.168,15: πρῶτος γὰρ ὁ Φάνης κατασκευάζει τὸ σκῆπτρον.
1018 OR54 = OF239F: 'ὄρθου δ' ἡμετέρην γενεήν, ἀριδείκετε δαῖμον': 'Guide our generation, most illustrious daimon.'

θῆκε θεᾶς Νυκτὸς, <ἵν' ἔχηι> βασιληΐδα τιμήν. (OR26)

He (Phanes) put the glorious sceptre in goddess Night's hands, giving her royal honour.

This suggestion would also explain the emphasis being put forth for the importance and supremacy of Nous/Mind by the Derveni author who explains its presence in each ruler through their names, as we saw.[1019] This is also evident in the use of the epithet μητίετα Ζεύς in a quoted verse in the DP in Col.XV which also includes the following quoted verse: "μῆτιν κα.[13]εν βασιληΐδα τιμ[ήν]".[1020] Even though lacunose, the similarities between this and the verse denoting the handing of the sceptre to Night by Phanes are evident and this time we also have the word *mētin*. The whole point of the Derveni author in this column is that Kronos and Zeus are essentially the same because they are both entities through which Nous/Metis is manifested in different ways. Considering the textual and conceptual evidence, then, it is possible that the sceptre in the OR signifies Protogonos/Phanes/Metis.

Moreover, the identification of counsel (*mētis*) through the figure of Protogonos with *aidoion* – and in turn with the sceptre, as was argued – that the Derveni author refers to might be explained through the episode of Ouranos' castration by Kronos in the *Rhapsodies*. The relevant verses refer to Ouranos' μήδεα falling in the sea:

μήδεα δ' ἐς πέλαγος πέσεν ὑψόθεν, ἀμφὶ δὲ τοῖσι
λευκὸς ἐπιπλώουσιν ἑλίσσετο πάντοθεν ἀφρός·(OR44)

(Ouranos') genitals fell into the ocean from high above and white foam wrapped them all around as they floated.

The word μήδεα is often found in Homer, Hesiod and also in Pindar and Aeschylus but it does not always mean genitals, it often means counsel.[1021] The fact that both meanings are found in archaic poetry means that this double meaning was established early on. The castration of Ouranos by Kronos and the identification of Ouranos' genitals with Protogonos/Metis suggests that it was the sceptre/Metis which Kronos took from Ouranos. The double meaning could not derive from

---

1019 See p.211 ff.
1020 Col.XV.6: "ἐκ τοῦ δὴ Κρόνος αὖτις, ἔπειτα δὲ μητίετα Ζεύς": "following him in turn was Kronos, and then Zeus the contriver." Bernabé-Piano: "μῆτιγ καὶ [μακάρων κατέχ]ωμ βασιληΐδα τιμ[ήν'."
1021 Hom. *Il.* 7.277; 15.467; 17.319–340; 24.77–92. Hes. *Theog.* 545ff; 371; 173ff. *Op.* 55. Pind. *Pyth.* 10.12. *Hom. Hymn* 4.456. *Hom. Hymn* 5.43ff. Aesch. *PV* 593–608.

Zeus' swallowing of Metis in Hesiod since in that case Metis is not likened to genitals. Considering that Protogonos is also called Metis and *aidoios* in the OR and DP, and if this entity was symbolised by the sceptre being passed from one ruler to the next in the OR, then this could be the origin of this double meaning, especially considering that Phanes/Protogonos is the primal generative force containing the seeds of creation, a clear parallel to the genitals, also indicated by his denomination as *aidoios*. Ouranos' genitals, thus, which fell into the sea would be Metis'/Protogonos'/sceptre. One could see how the word μήδεα could be a product of μῆτις and αἰδοίος put together, but there is no way to confirm this. This suggestion would mean that the above Orphic elements were either pre-Homeric or developed during the epic tradition. The Derveni author's reference to this equation of Ouranos' genitals with Protogonos-Metis-*aidoios* shows that this suggestion is possible since we can trace these ideas as early as the 5th century B.C. This would also mean that the DP was right to liken the sun to genitals and that the genitals are essentially Protogonos himself. Moreover, as we will see, we might have more reasons to believe that verses from the *Rhapsodies* originated in the epic rhapsodic tradition.

In many of the cases where the word μήδεα is mentioned in ancient authors it can be related to Orphic ideas. I will only refer to some examples from Pindar who was shown to have other points of contact with Orphic texts and ideas, as discussed in earlier chapters. A passage from his *Pythian Ode to Hippocleas of Thessaly* (498 B.C.) is of particular interest because it shows textual similarities with the *Rhapsodies*:

> Ἄπολλον, γλυκὺ δ' ἀνθρώπων τέλος ἀρχά
> τε δαίμονος ὀρνύντος αὔξεται·
> ὁ μέν που τεοῖς τε μήδεσι τοῦτ' ἔπραξεν,
> τὸ δὲ συγγενὲς ἐμβέβακεν ἴχνεσιν πατρός
>
> Apollo, grows sweet the end and the beginning for men when a daimon urges on. He achieved this through your counsels, and by inherited ability he has trod in the footsteps of his father...[1022]

Pindar here equates counsel with Apollo and says that Hippocleas' achievements are due to a συγγενὲς ability from his father who also was an Olympic victor. The same verb ὄρνυμι referring to the daimon is also used to describe Protogonos' birth in the OR: ὀρνυμένοιο Φάνητος (OR13 = OF122F), ὡρμήθη δ'ἀνὰ κύκλον

[1022] Pind. *Pyth.* 10.10–13. The fact that the victor was from Pelinna where gold tablets were found may or may not be relevant.

ἀθέσφατον (OR9 = OF118F). The phrase of following the footsteps of his father due to an innate ability is very similar to OR18 (OF173F) referring to a mighty daemon following Metis/Protogonos: οἷσιν ἐπεμβεβαὼς δαίμων μέγας αἰὲν ἐπ'ἴχνη. Pindar uses a similar expression in the *Nemean Ode to Alcimidas of Aegina*: ἴχνεσιν ἐν Πραξιδάμαντος ἑὸν πόδα νέμων | πατροπάτορος ὁμαιμίου.[1023] This ode also begins with the phrase: 'There is one race of men, one race of gods; and from a single mother we both draw our breath' which is strikingly similar to the Orphic belief of the divine soul's airy nature it being breath, culminated in a verse from the *Rhapsodies*: 'and as we draw in air, we collect the divine soul'.[1024] Pindar's *Olympian Ode to Theron of Acragas* was already argued to show several similarities with the eschatology of the gold tablets and it becomes more possible that he was familiar with Orphic ideas and texts. I would argue, thus, that it is possible that the Pindaric passage above either derives from Orphic poetry or both Pindar and 'Orpheus' derived from the same tradition. Considering, however, the use of the word μήδεα in Pindar's passage the first case seems more probable.

6.5.4 Zeus becomes the Fifth Ruler: OR45 – OR58

So far we have seen the kingship being passed on through the sceptre from one ruler to the next and it seems that the kingship was an important motif of the *Rhapsodies*. We have in total six different reigns which are in chronological order those of Phanes – Night – Ouranos – Kronos – Zeus – Dionysos. There is an allusion to the six kingships in Plato's *Philebus* where he quotes from an Orphic poem: '"And with the sixth generation", says Orpheus, "cease singing the order of the world"'.[1025] This suggests that the six rulers were an early part of the Orphic theogonical tradition. The element of successive kingship is also present in Hesiod but even though we might see rulers being overruled, this is not portrayed on the same scale as in the *Rhapsodies*, nor do we have any indication of a sceptre going from one ruler to the next one and, most importantly, the sceptre and kingship being given away *willingly*. In Hesiod we have the succession of Ouranos by Kronos and of Kronos by Zeus. The succession is always done violently: Kronos

---

1023 Pind. *Nem*. 6.15: 'as he plants his step in the tracks of his own true grandfather Praxidamas.' (Tr. Race).
1024 Pind. *Nem*. 6.1–2: ἕν ἀνδρῶν, ἕν θεῶν γένος· ἐκ μιᾶς δὲ πνέομεν ματρὸς ἀμφότεροι (Tr. Race). Careful examination of Pindar's Odes shows many parallels to Orphic ideas and texts and it is a matter worth further analysis. OR89 = OF422F: ἀέρα δ'ἕλκοντες ψυχὴν θείαν δρεπόμεσθα.
1025 Pl. *Phlb*. 66c: "ἕκτῃ δ' ἐν γενεᾷ", φησὶν Ὀρφεύς, "καταπαύσατε κόσμον ἀοιδῆς" (Tr. Lamb).

castrates Ouranos, and Zeus fights against Kronos and the rest of the Titans for ten years. This is very different from what we have in the *Rhapsodies*: Phanes, the first ruler creates the world for men and gods (OR19–24), he then willingly gives his sceptre to Night (OR26); Ouranos then peacefully becomes the third ruler who is then castrated by Kronos, a Titan (OR43); Zeus binds Kronos but only according to the prophecies (OR49–53); Zeus, finally, hands over sovereignty to Dionysos and announces to the gods that he is their new King (OR78–79); Dionysos eventually gets dismembered by the Titans (OR81–82).[1026] We notice, as already mentioned, that the violent acts are done only by the Titans while in all the other cases there is willingness and cooperation between the rulers. Some examples are the guidance of Zeus by Night, the fact that Phanes gives the sceptre and the power of prophecy to Night, and also that Zeus gives the sceptre to Dionysos, while when Zeus takes the kingship from Kronos he asks for guidance from the daimon representing counsel as it was argued.[1027] At the same time, the lawless and evil nature of the Titans is constantly emphasised in the OR (OR39–43/49/81) as a way of condemning their outrageous deeds.[1028]

The importance of kingship in the Orphic theogony is evident from the fact that the word king (βασιλεὺς) is found constantly throughout the OR and the DP, mostly as an epithet of Zeus. Examples from the DP are:

Col.VIII.2: "[ο]ἳ Διὸς ἐξεγένοντο [ὑπερμεν]έος βασιλῆος"	Col.VIII.2: "Who were born from Zeus, the mighty king."
Col.XIX.10: "Ζεὺς βασιλεύς, Ζεὺς δ' ἀρχὸς ἁπάντων ἀργικέραυνος"	Col.XIX.10: "Zeus the king, Zeus the ruler of all, he of the bright bolt."
Col.XVI.14: "[νῦν δ' ἐστὶ]ν βασιλεὺς πάντ[ων καί τ' ἔσσετ' ἔπ]ειτα"	Col.XVI.14: "And now he is king of all and will be afterwards."
Col.XV.7–8: 'ἐκ τοῦδε [ἀ]ρχή ἐστιν, ἐξ ὅσου βασιλεύει ἥδε ǀ ἀρχή'.	Col.XV.7–8: 'from that time is the beginning, from which this magistracy reigns.'[1029]

1026 OR19–24 = OF167F/152F/160F/158F/155F/156F/139F. OR26 = OF168F. OR43 = OF225F. OR49–53 = OF200F/208F/212F/ 214F/224F/223F/220F/239F. OR78–79 = OF299F/166F. OR81–82 = OF303F/311F/314F.
1027 OR54.
1028 OR39–43 = OF301F/232F/178F/186F/225F/181F/251F. OR49 = OF200F. OR81 = OF303F.
1029 All but last are quoted verses from the Orphic poem. Col.XVI.14 refers to Mind which is actually Zeus.

Examples from the DP not referring to Zeus are:

Col.XIV.6: "Οὐρανὸς Εὐφρονίδης, ὃς πρώτιστος βασίλευσεν"	Col.XIV.6: "Ouranos, son of Euphrone, who was the first to become king."
Col.XV.13: "μῆτιγ καὶ [μακάρων κατέχ]ωμ βασιληίδα τιμ[ήν]"	Col.XV.13: "Metis and having royal honour"
Col.XVI.3: "Πρωτογόνου βασιλέως αἰδοίου·..."	Col.XVI.3: "Of the First-born king, the reverend one..."
Col.XIV.8–9: ἀφ[αι]ρεθῆναι γὰρ	τὴν βασιλείαν αὐτόν.	Col.XIV.8–9: ...for the latter was deprived of the kingship.

Examples from the OR are: OR19: πρῶτος βασίλευσε περικλυτὸς Ἡρικεπαῖος, OR26: σκῆπτρον δ' ἀριδείκετον εἷο χέρεσσιν | θῆκε θεᾶς Νυκτὸς, <ἵν'ἔχηι> βασιληίδα τιμήν, OR33: ὃς πρῶτος βασίλευσε θεῶν μετὰ μητέρα Νύκτα, OR58: ἀθανάτων βασιλῆα θεῶν πέμπτον σε γενέσθαι, OR61: Ζεὺς βασιλεύς, Ζεὺς αὐτὸς ἁπάντων ἀρχιγένεθλος, OR74: ~ ἡ Δημήτηρ ἐγχειρίζουσα τῆι Κόρηι τὴν βασιλείαν φησίν ~, OR79: ~ ὁ γὰρ πατὴρ ἱδρύει τε αὐτὸν ἐν τῶι βασιλείωι θρόνωι καὶ ἐγχειρίζει τὸ σκῆπτρον ~, OR79: 'κλῦτε, θεοί· τόνδ' ὕμμιν ἐγὼ βασιλῆα τίθημι'.[1030] The particular epithet is never used by Homer for Zeus but it is found in Hesiod and most importantly in the two Orphic Hymns about Zeus: ἀστραπέα Δία, παγγενέτην, βασιλῆα μέγιστον and ὦ βασιλεῦ.[1031] The abundance of examples and the fact that this was not a common epithet of Zeus would suggest that this epithet signifying the importance of the element of kingship was distinctively Orphic.[1032] The fact that this word is so prominent in both the DP and the OR and in some cases found in similar verses, draws a narrative link between the Orphic theogony found in the DP and the OR, showing the preservation of traditional elements and supporting an early date for the contents of the OR.

6.5.4.1 Everything Becomes One and at the Same Time Separate

I have already referred to the important role of Night as a prophet and advisor of Zeus. She is the one that tells him how to bind Kronos and how to establish his kingship. It is on her answer to this latter question that I will now elaborate. Zeus

---

[1030] OR19 = OF167F. OR26 = OF168F. OR33 = OF174F. OR58 = OF219F. OR61 = OF243F. OR74 = OF284F. OR79 = OF299F. For translations see section 6.4.
[1031] To Zeus Astrapaios: 20.5 and To Zeus: 15.3 respectively. Sider, 2014.
[1032] It is found five times in Aristophanes (*Nub.* 1, *Nub.* 153, *Vesp.* 624, *Ran.* 1278, *Plut.* 1095), five times in Pindar (*Nem.* 7.82, *Nem.* 5.35, *Isthm.* 8.19, *Nem.* 10.16, *Ol.* 7.34) and two times in Hesiod (*Th.* 886, *Th.* 923).

asks 'How can everything become one to me and at the same time each separate?' to which Night replies:

> 'αἰθέρι πάντα πέριξ ἀφάτωι λάβε, τῶι δ' ἐνὶ μέσσωι
> οὐρανόν, ἐν δέ τε γαῖαν ἀπείριτον, ἐν δὲ θάλασσαν,
> ἐν δὲ τὰ τείρεα πάντα τά τ' οὐρανὸς ἐστεφάνωται...'

> 'Surround all things with ineffable aether, and in the middle of it place the heaven and amidst that place infinite earth and in that the sea, and in that all of the constellations with which the sky is crowned...'[1033]

Firstly, these verses are also found in the *Iliad*, but this matter will be discussed in a following paragraph. We notice that aether is presumably the primal substance of the universe since everything is encompassed in it. This is also evident by the fact that it was pre-existent at the beginning and it was the substance of the egg out of which the first creator Phanes came forth. Phanes himself is called Αἰθέρος υἱὸς (OR8) while in the episode describing the beginning of the cosmos and Phanes' birth, aether is mentioned five times (OR4, OR7, OR8, OR13, OR25).[1034] Moreover, at the beginning everything was undivided in the dark mist, under aether, and covered by Night (OR5–6 = OF106F/107F). It seems, then, that aether is the divine pre-existing substance which underlies everything while Phanes, the son of aether, could be identified with the generative intelligence and creative force of aether since he was the first creator. Aether, the first substance, then, is also the divine intelligence (*mētis*) as already discussed. Going back to Night's advice, if we were to visualise what she describes, it would look like this:

[1033] OR56 = OF237F.
[1034] OR4 = OF111F. OR7 = OF114F. OR8 = OF125F. OR13 = OF122F. OR25 = OF123F.

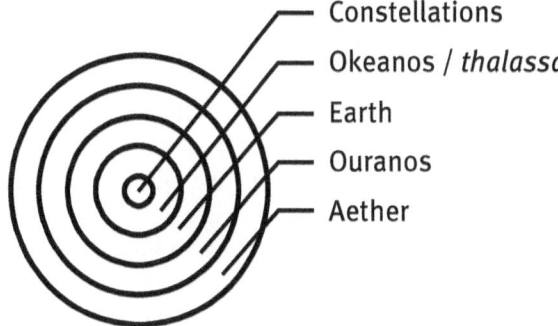

Fig. 1: The Cosmogony of Night's advice

When Zeus actually proceeds to the recreation of the world after swallowing Phanes he follows the same sequence:

> τοὔνεκα σὺν τῶι πάντα Διὸς πάλιν ἐντὸς ἐτύχθη,
> αἰθέρος εὐρείης ἠδ' οὐρανοῦ ἀγλαὸν ὕψος,
> πόντου τ' ἀτρυγέτου γαίης τ' ἐρικυδέος ἕδρη,
> ὠκεανός τε μέγας καὶ νείατα Τάρταρα γαίης

> Hence, everything was created anew inside Zeus, and along with the universe, the wide aether and also the bright heights of the sky, the infertile sea and the foundations of glorious Gaia, and the great ocean, and earthly Tartarus anew and rivers and the inaccessible deep.[1035]

Again, aether is the substance which encompasses everything while the other cosmic levels follow: Ouranos, Earth and Okeanos. We could identify these cosmic levels with the four elements. Aether, would be fiery air, and the rest air, earth and water. But if the stars which are placed in the middle also represent an element, this must be a fifth element, different from the rest. I will come back to this point shortly. It could be argued that this was the cosmology of the *Rhapsodies*, which was evident earlier in the narrative as well. Meaning that, apart from the early emphasis on aether and the idea that everything was undivided under aether, we also notice that, for example, Okeanos was singled out from the rest of the Titans as the only one who did not have a violent heart and abstained from overturning Ouranos' kingship. This might be due to his importance as representing one of the four elements.

1035 OR59 = OF241F.

At first glance the above schema would comply with Orphic ideas established so far. For example the airy nature of the soul which was breathed is located above the earth and it could be perceived as air mixed with aether. The βόρβορος which was identified many times in the previous chapters as the place of punishment in the afterlife through the image of lawless souls lying in the mud, could presumably be imagined as the subterranean area under the earth, and the mud which admittedly is a peculiar substance to be punished in, could be due to the mingling of earth with water.[1036] This representation suggests a spherical cosmos encompassed by aether with the stars being at the innermost, most difficult-to-reach location – as the gods' place of abode is described in the beginning of the OR. I have argued in the previous chapters that Orphics seemed to believe in an astral immortality with the stars and the Milky Way constituting the Isles of the Blessed; more particularly the Taurus and Charioteer constellations. It was suggested in Chapter 4 that the owners of the gold tablets performed an underground journey to Tartaros along with initiated and non-initiated souls to be judged, before proceeding to the special abode preserved for the purest of the pure and only after they had proven their status as initiates who had paid the penalty. In this case the stars in the above schema could represent the purest essence of aether, a different kind of fire. In the DP the author says that the moon is made from the whitest/brightest but cold substance and the stars are said to be of the same essence as Helios – who is identified with Protogonos/Phanes. This is evident from the author's observation that the stars are situated far away from each other out of necessity 'otherwise all those that have the same property as those from which the sun was composed would come together in a mass'.[1037] Finally, the above schema would also suggest that the path to the astral Isles of the Blessed was *watery* since the Ocean is located between the Earth and the Constellations. These suggestions will become clearer when we discuss the last section of the *Rhapsodies*.

Taking this schema further I would suggest that this central starry/aetherial element could be represented by a deity similar to Hestia – possibly bisexual Phanes – which the Stoics later considered to be the *pyr technikon* as portrayed by Crates of Mallus, for example. This is based on the fact that the Derveni author quotes a verse from an Orphic hymn where Hestia is equated to Gē Mētēr: 'Demeter, Rhea, Gē Mētēr, Hestia, Deio'.[1038] Secondly, we find references to the elements

---

1036 See p.133.
1037 Col.XXV.7–9: αἰωρεῖται δ' αὐτῶν ἔκαστα ἐν ἀνάγκηι, ὡς ἂν μὴ συνίηι | πρὸς ἄλληλα· εἰ γὰρ μή, συνέλθοι [ἂν] ἀλέα ὅσα τὴν αὐτὴν | δύναμιν ἔχει, ἐξ ὧν ὁ ἥλιος συνεστάθη.
1038 Col.XXII.12: "Δημήτηρ ['Ρ]έα Γῆ Μήτ.ηρ Ἑστία Δηιώι".

in Euripidean plays and other sources which might be relevant. In an unidentified play Euripides equates Gē Mētēr with Hestia just as the Orphic verse does and he says that it stands stable in the aether: '...and Gaia Meter, whom the wise amongst men call Hestia, as 'siting idly' in the aether'.[1039] According to Macrobius, one of the authors who quote this fragment, this means that Hestia is located in the centre of the cosmos.[1040] In the *Cratylus*, Plato interprets Hestia's name through the word ἐσσίαν, drawing a connection with the essence of reality, and in *Phaedrus* he says that while each god is assigned their sphere of duties, 'Hestia alone remains in the house of the gods'.[1041] Moreover, Euripides' representation of aether in other works agrees with its description in the *Rhapsodies*. In *Erechtheus*, the aether is associated with eschatology and immortality and it is clear that the immmortal's place of abode is in a different location from Hades: 'Therefore these girls' souls have not gone down to (Hades), but I have lodged their spirits in the aether'.[1042] In his *Phaethon* there are several references to aether in relation to Phaethon: 'Cypris most beautiful of goddesses, and to your newlywed boy, whom you keep hidden in the aether'.[1043] At this point I must emphasise that Protogonos/Phanes is also called Phaethon in the *Rhapsodies*, in the verse where he is referred to as the son of aether (OR8 = OF125F): Πρωτόγονος Φαέθων περιμήκεος Αἰθέρος υἱός. In Euripides' *Phaethon*, when Helios gives his chariot to Phaethon he advises him the following:

'ἔλα δὲ μήτε Λιβυκὸν <u>αἰθέρ'</u> εἰσβαλών
κρᾶσιν γὰρ <u>ὑγρὰν</u> οὐκ ἔχων ἁψῖδα σὴν
κάτω διήσει [... a short gap]
ἵει δ' ἐφ' ἑπτὰ Πλειάδων ἔχων δρόμον.'

1039 Eur. *TrGF* fr. 944: καὶ Γαῖα μῆτερ· Ἑστίαν δέ σ' οἱ σοφοὶ | βροτῶν καλοῦσιν ἡμένην ἐν αἰθέρι.
1040 Macrob. *Sat.* 1.23.8: *quod autem addit* μένει δὲ Ἑστία ἐν θεῶν οἴκῳ μόνη, *significat quia haec sola, quam terram esse accipimus, manet immobilis intra domum deorum, id est intra mundum, ut ait Euripides*: καὶ Γαῖα μῆτερ· Ἑστίαν δέ σ' οἱ σοφοὶ | βροτῶν καλοῦσιν ἡμένην ἐν αἰθέρι: 'The added thought that "Only Hestia [goddess of the hearth] stays behind in the gods' dwelling" means that only this god, whom we take to be the earth, remains unmoved within the gods' dwelling, that is, the cosmic order, as Euripides says: 'and mother Earth: the wise among mortals call you Hestia, sitting still in the ether.' (Tr. Kaster).
1041 Pl. *Cra.* 400d–401e. Pl. *Phdr.* 247a-b: μένει γὰρ Ἑστία ἐν θεῶν οἴκῳ μόνη.
1042 Eur. fr.370.71–72 Collard-Cropp: ψυχαὶ μὲν οὖν τῶνδ' οὐ βεβᾶσ' [Ἅιδ]ην πάρα, | εἰς δ' αἰθέρ' αὐτῶν πνεῦμ' ἐγὼ [κ]ατῴκισα· (Tr. Collard-Cropp).
1043 Eur. *TrGF* fr.781.19–21: Κύπρι θεῶν καλλίστα, | τῷ τε νεόζυγι σῷ | πώλῳ, τὸν ἐν αἰθέρι κρύπτεις (Tr. Collard-Cropp).

'Drive neither entering the heaven above Libya – for because it has no admixture of wet it will let your wheels fall [...] steer and hold a course for the seven Pleiads.'[1044]

From this passage it seems that aether is considered to be airy and its consistency changes depending on how it is mixed with the other elements. In relation to the Pleiades, we have discussed in Chapter 4 that they were part of the constellation of Taurus where I have located the Isles of the Blessed. When Phaethon fails to follow this course he is burned and falls down to earth.

The Pleiades are also mentioned in the following verses from the *Iliad* which are similar to the oracle of Night. In Homer's case the verses describe Achilles' shield made by Hephaestus:

πέντε δ' ἄρ' αὐτοῦ ἔσαν σάκεος πτύχες· αὐτὰρ ἐν αὐτῷ
ποίει δαίδαλα πολλὰ ἰδυίῃσι πραπίδεσσιν.
Ἐν μὲν γαῖαν ἔτευξ', ἐν δ' οὐρανόν, ἐν δὲ θάλασσαν,
ἠέλιόν τ' ἀκάμαντα σελήνην τε πλήθουσαν,
ἐν δὲ τὰ τείρεα πάντα, τά τ' οὐρανὸς ἐστεφάνωται,
Πληιάδας θ' Ὑάδας τε τό τε σθένος Ὠρίωνος
Ἄρκτον θ', ἣν καὶ Ἄμαξαν ἐπίκλησιν καλέουσιν,
ἥ τ' αὐτοῦ στρέφεται καί τ' Ὠρίωνα δοκεύει,
οἴη δ' ἄμμορός ἐστι λοετρῶν Ὠκεανοῖο.

Five were the layers of the shield itself; and on it he made many adornments with cunning skill. On it he fashioned the earth, on it the heavens, on it the sea, and the unwearied sun, and the moon at the full, and on it all the constellations with which heaven is crowned – the Pleiades and the Hyades and mighty Orion and the Bear, that men call also the Wain, that circles ever in its place, and watches Orion, and alone has no part in the baths of Ocean.[1045]

It is impossible to do justice here to this fine Homeric example of *ekphrasis*, but I must note a number of points of interest in this passage, which again entails cosmological elements, such as the position of the Arktos constellation which circles around itself. This could be, for example, a reference to the Polar Star belonging to the Arktos constellation and that it was considered to be the central point of the universe. As Edwards notes, the usual view on this passage is that the heavenly bodies are placed in the central position and there is an emphasis on movement and progression of time.[1046] Putting aside the striking fact of having almost identical verses between this passage and the OR, the location of the astral sphere

---

1044 Eur. *TrGF* fr.779.1–4 (Tr. Collard-Cropp).
1045 Hom. *Il.* 18.481–489 (Tr. Murray). See also *Il.*15.187–95. Arist. *Ph.* 4.212b–23.
1046 Edwards, 1991, p.206–207.

Analysis of the *Orphic Rhapsodies* — **327**

in the centre and in proximity to Okeanos is another similarity to the Orphic cosmology as described above. Orion is often perceived as a hunter and is located in between the Bull and Eriphos constellation which are the ones that have been related in Chapter 4 to the Isles of the Blessed and an aetherial/astral immortality. The shield includes several scenes of everyday life: of a lawsuit about a blood spilt crime for which the outcome is bound to remain forever unknown, of times of war and peace, of cultivation, cattle and sheep herding moving from water to earth, dancers performing cyclical dances, the Ocean surrounding the shield as it was imagined surrounding the earth. There are also some distinctive details which are uncharacteristic of Homer and reminiscent of the *Rhapsodies*: for example he considers the cattle that are taken to the riverside and back to the meadow to be owned by a king who watched in silence holding his sceptre [βασιλεὺς δ' ἐν τοῖσι σιωπῇ | σκῆπτρον ἔχων ἑστήκει ἐπ' ὄγμου γηθόσυνος κῆρ].[1047] Achilles' shield is also described in Euripides' *Electra* by the chorus:

> ἐν δὲ μέσῳ κατέλαμπε σάκει φαέθων
> κύκλος ἁλίοιο
> ἵπποις ἅμ πτεροέσσαις
> ἄστρων τ' αἰθέριοι χοροί,
> Πλειάδες, Ὑάδες, Ἕκτορος
> ὄμμασι τροπαῖοι

> In the center of the shield glowed the burning circle of the sun with his winged steeds, and the choruses of stars on high, Pleiades and Hyades, to turn Hector's eyes to flight.[1048]

Euripides describes Achilles' shield in a similar way to Homer but his reference to the aethereal dances of the stars is closer to the Orphic passage where everything is encompassed in aether, especially because aether is not mentioned by Homer. Could it be that Achilles' Shield was introduced in the *Iliad* by an *aoidos* who was familiar with Orphic poetry? Considering the early references to an elemental cosmology as the one found in the *Rhapsodies* it is possible that the Orphic verses were part of a common oral epic tradition.

As Martin notes, 'even in the context of live oral composition, it is possible for one performer to 'allude' to and even 'quote' other traditions known to him and recognised by the audience'.[1049] For this suggestion to be true it is necessary for Orphic texts, and in this case the *Rhapsodies*, to have been part of the epic

---

1047 Hom. *Il.* 18.556–557: 'and among them the king, staff in hand, was standing in silence at the swath, glad at heart.'
1048 Eur. *El.* 464–469 (Tr. Kovacs).
1049 Martin, 2001, p.25.

rhapsodic tradition and transmitted orally before being written down. Do we have any evidence for this? Firstly, the above representation of the world is not the only one found in Homer, meaning that there are multiple passages which have variations in their representation, as Havelock discusses.[1050] This supports but does not necessarily prove the hypothesis that this particular imagery might have been borrowed. Another case which might support a contact between Orphic oral poetry – and particularly the *Rhapsodies* – and Homer is the case of the sceptre as outlined earlier. As was said, the sceptre is not incuded in Hesiod, while it is greatly emphasised in the *Rhapsodies*. I suggested that the sceptre in the *Rhapsodies* might actually be Metis/Phanes representing the divine Nous/counsel and generative force; I also discussed its association with genitals and the word *aidoios* and *mēdea*, a point also discussed by the DP author. In the relatively few cases where a sceptre is mentioned in Homer, it is often in the hands of a mortal (king or hero) and associated with good counsel originating from god, while when Apollo holds it it is likened to the sun:

Il.7.277–278: μέσσῳ δ' ἀμφοτέρων σκῆπτρα σχέθον, εἶπέ τε μῦθον κῆρυξ Ἰδαῖος, πεπνυμένα μήδεα εἰδώς·

'Between the two they held their staffs, and the herald Idaeus, skilled in prudent counsel, spoke…'

Il.9.96–99: "Ἀτρεΐδη κύδιστε, ἄναξ ἀνδρῶν Ἀγάμεμνον,
ἐν σοὶ μὲν λήξω, σέο δ' ἄρξομαι, οὕνεκα πολλῶν
λαῶν ἐσσι ἄναξ καί τοι Ζεὺς ἐγγυάλιξε
σκῆπτρόν τ' ἠδὲ θέμιστας, ἵνα σφίσι βουλεύῃσθα…."

'Agamemnon, lord of men, with you will I begin and with you make an end, because you are king over many men, and Zeus has put into your hands the scepter and rights, so that you may take counsel for your people.'

Od.17.199: Εὔμαιος δ' ἄρα οἱ σκῆπτρον θυμαρὲς ἔδωκε.

'and Eumaeus gave him a staff to his liking'

Il.1.14–15: στέμματ' ἔχων ἐν χερσὶν ἑκηβόλου Ἀπόλλωνος
χρυσέῳ ἀνὰ σκήπτρῳ,

'…and in his hands he held the ribbons of Apollo, who strikes from afar, on a staff of gold'

Il.1.373–74: στέμματ' ἔχων ἐν χερσὶν ἑκηβόλου Ἀπόλλωνος

1050 Havelock, 1987.

χρυσέῳ ἀνὰ σκήπτρῳ

'holding in his hands on a staff of gold the ribbons of Apollo who strikes from afar'[1051]

There is no apparent explanation for the association of the sceptre with good counsel or the sun, as far as I am aware, and the fact that the element of the sceptre does not have a prominent role in the Homeric succession myth suggests that this was a borrowed element. The sceptre's association with good counsel or the sun, then, suggests that it was borrowed from an Orphic oral poem, elements of which have survived in the *Rhapsodies*. That the sceptre was a borrowed element might also be indicated in Book 2 of the *Iliad* where an ancestral and imperishable sceptre [*Il*.2.46: εἵλετο δὲ σκῆπτρον πατρώϊον ἄφθιτον] made by Hephaestus is handed down from a series of gods – starting from Zeus – and kings, to Agamemnon, as this is not mentioned elsewhere in the *Iliad*:

> ... ἀνὰ δὲ κρείων Ἀγαμέμνων
> ἔστη σκῆπτρον ἔχων, τὸ μὲν Ἥφαιστος κάμε τεύχων.
> Ἥφαιστος μὲν δῶκε Διὶ Κρονίωνι ἄνακτι,
> αὐτὰρ ἄρα Ζεὺς δῶκε διακτόρῳ ἀργεϊφόντῃ·
> Ἑρμείας δὲ ἄναξ δῶκεν Πέλοπι πληξίππῳ,
> αὐτὰρ ὁ αὖτε Πέλοψ δῶκ' Ἀτρέι, ποιμένι λαῶν·
> Ἀτρεὺς δὲ θνῄσκων ἔλιπεν πολύαρνι Θυέστῃ,
> αὐτὰρ ὁ αὖτε Θυέστ' Ἀγαμέμνονι λεῖπε φορῆναι,
> πολλῇσιν νήσοισι καὶ Ἄργεϊ παντὶ ἀνάσσειν.

Then among them lord Agamemnon stood up, holding in his hands the scepter which Hephaestus had toiled over making. Hephaestus gave it to lord Zeus, son of Cronos, and Zeus gave it to the messenger Argeïphontes; and Hermes, the lord, gave it to Pelops, driver of horses, and Pelops in turn gave it to Atreus, shepherd of men; and Atreus at his death left it to Thyestes, rich in flocks, and Thyestes again left it to Agamemnon to carry, to be lord of many isles and of all Argos.[1052]

[1051] The handing down of the sceptre from Zeus to Aristocratic families down to Agamemnon reflects perhaps the special priviledge of aristocracy which is absent from the Orphic perception of the divine soul/Nous pertaining all humans. See also 2.46 and 2.186 where the sceptre is called ἄφθιτον (imperishable); 9.295-299; 10.319-332. See also Combellack, 1948.

[1052] Hom. *Il*.2.100–108, Tr. Murray. Pausanias even mentions that this sceptre was worshipped by the Chaeroneans: IX.40.11–12: θεῶν δὲ μάλιστα Χαιρωνεῖς τιμῶσι τὸ σκῆπτρον ὃ ποιῆσαι Διί φησιν Ὅμηρος Ἥφαιστον, παρὰ δὲ Διὸς λαβόντα Ἑρμῆν δοῦναι Πέλοπι, Πέλοπα δὲ Ἀτρεῖ καταλιπεῖν, τὸν δὲ Ἀτρέα Θυέστῃ, παρὰ Θυέστου δὲ ἔχειν Ἀγαμέμνονα· τοῦτο οὖν τὸ σκῆπτρον σέβουσι, Δόρυ ὀνομάζοντες· καὶ εἶναι μέν τι θειότερον οὐχ ἥκιστα δηλοῖ τὸ ἐς τοὺς ἀνθρώπους ἐπιφανὲς ἐξ αὐτοῦ· φασὶ δ' ἐπὶ τοῖς ὅροις αὐτῶν καὶ Πανοπέων τῶν ἐν τῇ Φωκίδι εὑρεθῆναι, σὺν δὲ αὐτῷ καὶ χρυσὸν εὕρασθαι τοὺς Φωκεῖς, σφίσι δὲ ἀσμένοις ἀντὶ χρυσοῦ γενέσθαι τὸ σκῆπτρον:

This brings us to another important point about non-Homeric elements of oral tradition which contain non-Homeric mythological variants. Pavese refers to formulas such as Διὶ μητιόεντι, Διὸς πάρα μητιόεντος which have to do with the non-Homeric hymn of Metis as the first spouse of Zeus.[1053] Considering that in Hesiod Zeus swallows Metis, an act which contains one element of the Orphic myth in the *Rhapsodies* and the DP, and that in Homer the sceptre – which was identified with Metis/Phanes – is related to good counsel and the sun could suggest that this element and words including *metis* come from an Orphic tradition. In the *Rhapsodies* we find several times words such as: ἀφθιτόμιτης (OR4), κακομῆται (OR39), ἀγκυλομήτης (OR43) and the phrase μητίετα Ζεὺς is quoted by the Derveni author.[1054] Another example Pavese mentions is formulas such as φιλομμειδὴς Ἀφροδίτη deriving from the non-Homeric birth of Aphrodite from Ouranos' *medea* instead of Zeus's, as we see it happening in the *Rhapsodies* where the word μήδεα is specifically mentioned (OR44 = OF189F). Other non-Homeric examples are also the forms of Ζηνὸς, Ζηνὶ, Ζῆνα which are also found in the *Rhapsodies* (OR59, OR61, OR62, OR48).[1055] Pavese suggests that the rhapsodic epic tradition as a whole was oral and independent, and 'all the poems, Homeric and non-Homeric ones, depend on the rhapsodic epic tradition as a whole'.[1056]

An Orphic poem, thus, might have been part of the rhapsodic tradition.[1057] Martin has argued that 'Orphic poetry, whatever its private affiliations, formed part of the rhapsode's repertoire'.[1058] Similarly to Willamowitz and Böhme, who suggested that the whole of the Nekyia was an interpolation by an editor who was interested in Orphism, Martin suggests that the Nekyia was a result of a performance interaction where a rhapsode would appropriate contemporary and competing traditions, which would explain the Nekyia incongruities.[1059] He argues that the Orphic text which influenced the Nekyia is the *Descent to Hades*.

'Of the gods, the people of Chaeroneia honour most the sceptre which Homer says Hephaestus made for Zeus, Hermes received from Zeus and gave to Pelops, Pelops left to Atreus, Atreus to Thyestes, and Agamemnon had from Thyestes. This sceptre, then, they worship, calling it Spear. That there is something peculiarly divine about this sceptre is most clearly shown by the fame it brings to the Chaeroneans. They say that it was discovered on the border of their own country and of Panopeus in Phocis, that with it the Phocians discovered gold, and that they were glad themselves to get the sceptre instead of the gold.'

1053 Pavese, 1998, p.76.
1054 OR4 = OF111F. OR39 = OF301F. OR43 = OF181F. DP Col.XV.6/11
1055 OR59 = OF241F. OR61 = OF243F. OR62 = OF245V. OR48 = OF231F.
1056 Pavese, 1998, p.73.
1057 See also Nagy, 2011, p.50–51 and Obbink, 1997, p.41, fn.4.
1058 Martin, 2001, p.23.
1059 Martin, 2001, p.29.

Tsagarakis also argues that Homer's Nekyia combines two themes known to Homer, the *nekyomanteion* and the *katabasis*, the latter one including the *katabasis* related to Orpheus.[1060] In the following passage from the Nekyia the representation of the underworld topography has indeed many Orphic elements:

> ἔνθ' ἦ τοι Μίνωα ἴδον, Διὸς ἀγλαὸν υἱόν,
> χρύσεον σκῆπτρον ἔχοντα, θεμιστεύοντα νέκυσσιν,
> ἥμενον, οἱ δέ μιν ἀμφὶ δίκας εἴροντο ἄνακτα,
> ἥμενοι ἑσταότες τε κατ' εὐρυπυλὲς Ἄιδος δῶ.
> τὸν δὲ μέτ' Ὠρίωνα πελώριον εἰσενόησα
> θῆρας ὁμοῦ εἰλεῦντα κατ' ἀσφοδελὸν <u>λειμῶνα</u>,
> τοὺς αὐτὸς κατέπεφνεν ἐν οἰοπόλοισιν ὄρεσσι
> χερσὶν ἔχων ῥόπαλον παγχάλκεον, αἰὲν ἀαγές.

> There, you must know, I saw Minos, the glorious son of Zeus, golden scepter in hand, giving judgment to the dead from his seat, while they sat and stood about the king in the widegated house of Hades and asked him for judgment. And after him I became aware of huge Orion herding together over the field of asphodel the wild beasts he himself had slain on the lonely hills, and in his hands he held a club all of bronze, forever unbroken.[1061]

The description of the judge holding a sceptre and passing judgment on the dead in the house of Hades, and the subsequent description of the punishment of the lawless, is a very characteristic Orphic idea entailing the notion that our actions while alive affect our lot in the afterlife. The particular reference to Orion who in the previous Homeric passage has been acknowledged as a constellation in the sky could be evidence of an association of eschatological topography with the stars. Hesiod too refers to Orion as a constellation, in relation to the cultivation of grains, wine making and sailing, and notes that when Orion as a hunter chases away the Pleiades, storms and mighty winds happen in the sea and thus it is not a good time for sailing.[1062] Odysseus also used the Pleiades, Bootes, Arktos and Orion to sail (*Od.* 5.272–3). This reflects the very early use of these constellations, along with Sirius and Arcturus (Bear) also mentioned by Hesiod and Homer above, to navigate and measure the seasons of the year.[1063] The herding of cattle in general is often considered to refer to the stars being led by another celestial body – with perhaps the most evident representation, the cattle of the Sun in

---

1060 Tsagarakis, 2000, p.25–36/105–123.
1061 Hom. *Od.* 11.568–575 (Tr. Murray).
1062 Hes. *Op.* 597–626. See also OF341F: Olympiodorus and Damascius refer to the four rivers according to Orpheus: Puriflegethon (fire and east), Kokytos (earth and west), Acheron (air and meridian), Ōkeanos (water and arktos constellation). OF342F: Acherousia limne is called *aeria*.
1063 See also discussion in p.161–172.

Homer – and we saw in Chapter 4 that Dionysos is named as the leader of the chorus of the stars by Sophocles, and that Orphic initiates are called *boukoloi* (herdsmen).[1064] The word λειμῶνα is the word used to describe the groves of Persephone both in the *Rhapsodies*, as we will see, and the gold tablets. In this passage alone, then, there are many Orphic elements which support the argument that the Nekyia was influenced by an Orphic poem. Nagy also suggests that there was 'an Orphic phase in the evolution of the Homeric tradition' and argues that the element of Okeanos as a generative force, part of a cosmic fluidity was an Orphic element.[1065] It is also worth mentioning that in Homer, Odysseus and the suitors arrive to Hades through the Ocean as Circe instructs Odysseus to leave his ship on the shore of the Ocean before proceeding to the 'House of Hades':

> πὰρ δ' ἴσαν Ὠκεανοῦ τε ῥοὰς καὶ Λευκάδα πέτρην,
> ἠδὲ παρ' Ἡελίοιο πύλας καὶ δῆμον ὀνείρων
> ἤισαν· αἶψα δ' ἵκοντο κατ' ἀσφοδελὸν <u>λειμῶνα</u>,
> ἔνθα τε ναίουσι ψυχαί, εἴδωλα καμόντων.

> Past the streams of Oceanus they went, past the rock Leucas, past the gates of the Sun and the land of dreams, and quickly came to the meadow of asphodel, where the ghosts dwell, phantoms of men who have done with toils.

> τὴν δέ κέ τοι πνοιὴ Βορέαο φέρῃσιν.
> ἀλλ' ὁπότ' ἂν δὴ νηὶ δι' Ὠκεανοῖο περήσῃς,
> ἔνθ' ἀκτή τε λάχεια καὶ ἄλσεα Περσεφονείης,
> μακραί τ' αἴγειροι καὶ ἰτέαι ὠλεσίκαρποι,
> νῆα μὲν αὐτοῦ κέλσαι ἐπ' Ὠκεανῷ βαθυδίνῃ,
> αὐτὸς δ' εἰς Ἀίδεω ἰέναι δόμον εὐρώεντα.

> ...and the breath of the North Wind will bear her onward. But when in your ship you have now crossed the stream of Oceanus, where is a level shore and the groves of Persephone – tall poplars, and willows that shed their fruit – there beach your ship by the deep eddying Oceanus, but go yourself to the dank house of Hades.[1066]

At the same time, Hades is described as dark and murky ['beneath the murky darkness'] but also as having clouds ['shadowy clouds'], while Menelaos is told that his soul will not go to Hades but to the Elysian plain where the 'Ocean sends

---

1064 Hom. *Od.* 12.377ff. Soph. *Ant.* 1146–1154. For *boukolos* see p.268.
1065 Nagy, 2011, p.49–53. See also D'Alessio, 2004.
1066 Hom. *Od.* 24.11–14 (suitors). Hom. *Od.* 10.507–511 (Circe). Tr. Murray.

up blasts of Zephyros' to cool men; this comes in contrast to the previous description of Hades as also being proximate to Okeanos and the gates of the Sun.[1067] Such contradictions might demonstrate the existence of a tradition were the Netherworld was located at the celestial/astral sphere as indicated here by the 'gates of the Sun' and was proximate to Okeanos as was argued to be the case in the Orphic cosmogony in the previous paragraphs. Moreover, the dead are described in two contradicting ways: as shadowy and witless on the one hand, and as entities that maintain their bodily functions. It seems that Homer, as Tsagarakis argues, combined two prevailing eschatological views which 'underlie certain religious beliefs that belonged to the poet's cultural heritage and were an integral part of a unified and yet diverse poetic tradition'.[1068] Tzifopoulos argues that we may call these two views as the Homeric and the Orphic, noting however that each view has 'an array of differing and sometimes opposing views and approaches'.[1069] This combination of Homeric and Orphic eschatological beliefs might also take place in Polygnotos' (active in the second half of the 5th century B.C.) Nekyia painting at Delphi which depicts Orpheus and the Netherworld.[1070] Pausanias, who describes the painting in detail (X.25–31), says that Polygnotos was inspired by the work *Minyad* which according to him included punishments of known figures and as Manoledakis suggests, might have been particularly Orphic or dealing with Orpheus' *katabasis*.[1071] Depicting the Netherworld offered the best thematic opportunity to combine Homeric themes such as Odysseus standing next to the *bothros* recalling the *nekyomanteion* theme, and Orphic notions of personal accountability for the soul's fate in the afterlife through showing various punishments and placing Orpheus in a prominent place playing his lyre, presumably alluding to him describing in song what he saw during his *katabasis*. The fact that Homer's Nekyia seems to include many Orphic borrowed elements in relation to the afterlife suggests that the Orphic texts were the works which 'specialized' in such matters, filling in a gap left by other epic rhapsodic texts most of which fell short of answering the question of what happens to humans after death.

These suggestions might be considered controversial by some, but they are nonetheless based on the evidence discussed so far and supported by textual

---

1067 Hom. *Od*. 11.155: ὑπὸ ζόφον ἠερόεντα; 11.592: νέφεα σκιόεντα; 4.561–568.
1068 Tsagarakis, 2000, p.109.
1069 Tzifopoulos, 2010.
1070 Manoledakis, 2003, p.208–220.
1071 Manoledakis, 2003, p.186. Paus. X.28.2; IV.33.7; IX.5.9; X.31.3.

sources. Let us examine, then, if we have additional evidence to support the suggestion that an Orphic cosmology such as the one described in this section was linked to a soteriological eschatology (a matter to be discussed in the following section of this chapter). Firstly, I will discuss internal evidence from the *Rhapsodies*. The allegorical representation of the elements as described at the beginning of this section is evident in another verse from the *Rhapsodies*:

> ἓν δὲ δέμας βασίλειον. ἐν ὧι τάδε πάντα κυκλεῖται
> πῦρ καὶ ὕδωρ καὶ γαῖα καὶ αἰθήρ, νύξ τε καὶ ἦμαρ
> καὶ Μῆτις πρῶτος γενέτωρ
>
> One regal form, in whom everything is encircled, fire and water and Gaia and aether, night and day and also Metis, the first creator.[1072]

These verses come from a hymn to Zeus, parts of which are also quoted in the DP, suggesting their survival from early times. Several of these words are also found in gold tablet C, as discussed in Chapter 4.[1073] Some other verses from the *Rhapsodies* suggest that the soul underwent a constant transformation before returning to aether again: 'And water is death for the soul and for the water the same requital applies. From water comes into existence earth, and from earth water once again, and from that, soul, becoming aether in its entirety'.[1074] The soul goes back and forth between water and earth trapped in a circle until it becomes aether in its entirety (ἐκ τοῦ δὴ ψυχὴ ὅλον αἰθέρα). In both directions the path is watery. Another verse says 'as we draw in air we collect the divine soul' and 'men's soul is rooted in the aether' where it is clearly shown that air is distinguished from aether.[1075] The cosmological aspect of Orphic eschatology, thus, is straightforwardly mentioned in exegetical verses which agree with the above interpretation. If I am correct about aether being the divine substance which underlies everything, then the passing of the sceptre-Phanes from one ruler to the next might be a way to represent the participation of aether-Metis in every stage of the cosmology being mixed with the other elements – Okeanos might not be a ruler but he

---

1072 OR61 = OF243F.
1073 See p.171.
1074 OR90 = OF437F.
1075 OR89 = OF422F + OF436F. The distinction between *aer* and aether differs depending on the source but already in Homer aether seems to be the 'region' above the clouds: *Il*.15.20–21: σὺ δ' ἐν αἰθέρι καὶ νεφέλῃσιν | ἐκρέμω· 'And in the air among the clouds you hung...'.

is the one Titan who remains out of Tartaros between Ouranos' kingship and Kronos' kingship –.[1076] This idea also corresponds to the exegesis of the Derveni author who explains how Mind (Nous/Metis) participates in every ruler and equates the Mind and everything with air.[1077]

It might be possible to detect inklings of the above theory in other works such as Aeschylus' *Prometheus*. Seaford, in his analysis of this play, has argued that 'both Empedokles and the *Prometheia* draw on a certain subliterary current of ideas' and that this is irrespective of 'whether or not the dramatist and Empedokles knew each other's works'.[1078] Seaford does not draw a link to the *Rhapsodies* but includes the gold tablets in the texts that draw from this subliterary current of ideas and refers to the Olbian tablets as evidence that the style of Herakleitos originates in the mysteries, even though the similarities might be due to a 'shared tradition of mystic cosmology'.[1079] As he says, the strong presence of the four cosmological elements in the *Prometheia* cannot be explained through the Hesiodic versions but that the role of the elements in the play 'has a mystical rather than a purely philosophical origin' (p.10). The emphasis on the elements is evident from the first words of Prometheus:

ΠΡΟΜΗΘΕΥΣ
ὦ δῖος αἰθὴρ καὶ ταχύπτεροι πνοαί,
ποταμῶν τε πηγαί, ποντίων τε κυμάτων
ἀνήριθμον γέλασμα, παμμήτωρ τε γῆ,
καὶ τὸν πανόπτην κύκλον ἡλίου καλῶ·
ἴδεσθέ μ' οἷα πρὸς θεῶν πάσχω θεός.

PROMETHEUS
O bright Sky, and you swift-flying winds, and river-springs, and you countless twinkling waves of the sea, and Earth mother of all, *and all-seeing circle of the Sun*, behold what I, a god, am suffering at the hands of the gods! [1080]

Seaford wants to trace in various texts the mystic adaptation of the Hesiodic tradition where men are imagined as immortals who were punished in ancient times for lawless behaviour and which can eventually return to their prior immortality.[1081] However, even though the story of Prometheus stealing the fire and giving

---

1076 OR42 = OF186F.
1077 See p.211.
1078 Seaford, 1986, p.3.
1079 Seaford, 1986, p.4–8; 10–14; 21.
1080 Aesch. *PV* 88–92 (Tr. Sommerstein). The verse in * is translated by the author since it is not translated by Sommerstein for unknown reasons.
1081 Seaford, 1986, p.9.

it to humans is known and mentioned in Hesiod, he does not include the element of the final release, which is found in Orphic beliefs and Pre-Socratic philosophy through, for example, the return of the fallen daimon in Empedokles. The release of the Titans is also mentioned in Pindar in the passage referring to the repayment of a debt to Persephone which has been associated with the Orphic myth of Dionysos' dismemberment and the gold tablets. In any case, it is not clear based on the Hesiodic tradition alone, why humans would come to associate themselves with the Titans, who are linked to the punishment, neither why they would believe they were immortals, nor what the wrongdoing was exactly. The aetiology can be given only by Orphic mythology since for example we do not know what led to Empedokles' daimon's fall and in Homer, mere mortals certainly did not believe they used to be immortal. It is more probable, then, that the variations of Titanic punishment were derivations of Dionysos' dismemberment and as we will see in the last section, fire in Orphism was associated with mortality and incarnation. This rejects a possible relation to Herakleitos for example, who is also discussed by Seaford, since for him the primal element is fire. In contrast, for Orphics it is aether which is the first element, invoked by Prometheus in the above passage, from which fire is also entirely absent. The verse referring to the all-seeing sun is also reminiscent of Orphic theology/cosmogony as found in the DP and the *Rhapsodies* where the sun is said to be the guardian and ruler of all things.[1082]

Stafford refers to some indirect references to human creation in ancient Greek literature, the majority related to the Titan Prometheus, who is sometimes depicted in Etruscan/Italic and Roman art creating man and was also punished by Zeus for giving to men the gift of fire.[1083] Apollodorus also says that Prometheus 'moulded men out of water and earth'.[1084] Furthermore, Hesiod hints at a myth where mankind sprung forth from the Meliae (ash-tree Nymphs) who were born from the drops of blood falling on the earth from the castrated genitals of Ouranos by Kronos; they were in other words daughters of Earth and Heaven as the Titans were and as the initiates of the gold tablets proclaim.[1085] In the *Rhapsodies*, this version of the myth refers to the birth of the Titans and the fact that Meliae means ash-trees and that humans were born from the smoke of the ashes of the Titans in the Orphic myth, suggests that perhaps Hesiod is adapting external mythological elements of the oral tradition.[1086] Stafford identifies the absence of a 'strong

---

[1082] OR22 = OF158F. See also OR88 = OF340F. DP Col. XXV.10–12. Col.XIII.10–11. Col.XV.3–5.
[1083] Stafford, 2009, p.435–36.
[1084] Apollod. *Bibl.* I.7.1–2: Προμηθεὺς δὲ ἐξ ὕδατος καὶ γῆς ἀνθρώπους πλάσας,...
[1085] Stafford, 2009, p.431. Hes. *Op.* 106ff, 144–145. Hes. *Theog.* 560ff. See also Paus.X.4.4.
[1086] OR35 = OF188F.

early narrative tradition' for the creation of mankind.[1087] Moroever, the particular passage from Hesiod belongs to the episode where Prometheus' cunningness and the gift of fire are mentioned. However, the various indirect references to human creation can be understood as references to the Orphic cosmogony where men are created from the smoke of the ashes of the Titans. Seaford's suggestions are plausible, but perhaps a better explanation would be a religious eschatological cosmology as was identified in Orphism since it includes all the elements highlighted by Seaford, and we have found inklings of this cosmology in texts earlier than the Pre-Socratics such as Homer and Hesiod. Also, the fact that it is a Titan who is being punished and released through a cosmological transformation suggests that this is an idea closer to the Orphic mythological and cosmic eschatology rather than Pre-Socratic ones, or the fallen daimon of Empedokles. This, of course, does not reject the possibility that Seaford might be right and we have a combination of elements.

Obbink, developing these suggestions by Seaford, argues that the Derveni author 'might have seen his elucidation of cosmology as possible instruction for mystic initiates, in which an eschatological myth associated with the mysteries is combined with a dominant concern about relation between elements'.[1088] Obbink, though, seems to suggest that this was not a common practice and that the Derveni author's comments on the Orphic text is 'a singular and unique message fathomable only by a learned elite'.[1089] However, as I have suggested in Chapter 5 and after examining the *Rhapsodies*, the Derveni author's *exegesis* must not be an arbitrary one but a common exegesis of Orphic Theogony. It certainly corresponds to the cosmology of the *Rhapsodies*, as we already established, and so it does not seem probable that the Derveni author was a one-off phenomenon. To return to Seaford's earlier discussion, he notes that 'cosmology should not be regarded as an odd, alien kind of instruction for mystic initiates'.[1090] In fact, considering the discussion in this section and the suggestion that elements from the *Rhapsodies* were part of the rhapsodic oral tradition it is more probable that cosmological Pre-Socratic philosophies were either partly influenced by Orphic cosmological/theological poems or were influenced by the rhapsodic tradition as a whole which contained Orphic elements, as it reached them in the 6th century B.C. It could be that Ionia was an important centre of Orphic texts and mysteries, which would explain a possible influence on Pre-Socratic philosophers, based on

---

[1087] Stafford, 2009, p.444.
[1088] Obbink, 1997, p.40.
[1089] Obbink, 1997, p.52.
[1090] Seaford, 1986, p.20.

the following points: a) the Ionian colony Phanagoria which showed signs of worshipping Phanes through a triple identification with Apollo, Dionysos and Artemis; b) the Bone Tablets which contain a mixture of Orphic religious eschatological elements, and philosophical elements also found in Pre-Socratic philosophers such as Herakleitos, were found in Olbia which was a Milesian colony; and c) some Ionian traits of the oral tradition are maintained in the *Rhapsodies*.

6.5.5 A separate didactic *hieros logos* about the Soul and the Afterlife? – OR88 – OR97

Since I have already discussed the myth of Dionysos' dismemberment in Chapter 3, referring to all the available sources, including the *Rhapsodic* fragments and analysing its nature, it is not necessary to discuss it here again. I shall proceed, then, to the final section of the *Rhapsodies*. The fragments I have arranged from OR88 to OR97 are of a different nature to all the previous ones discussed so far. They do not refer to theogonical or mythological stories but they are exegetical, in the sense that they refer in a straightforward way to eschatological ideas about the afterlife and the nature of the soul. This suggests that this might have been a separate *hieros logos* concerning the nature of the soul and its fate in the afterlife. It shows, moreover, that the *Rhapsodies* were most probably not a continuous theogonical/cosmogonical narrative but that they also included exegesis and presumably hymns such as the one to Zeus in OR61–62 (OF243F/245V). Significantly, after juxtaposing this section with the text and eschatology of the gold tablets it will become evident that there are many points of contact in terms of topography and ideas. But let us first examine whether these exegetical verses agree with the Orphic eschatological cosmology I have outlined so far. The eschatology described in this section of the OR notes the aetherial divine nature of the soul, and distinguishes between a place where the blessed and just go post-mortem and a place where the unjust go. It refers to the notion of reincarnation, including that of animals, there is an elemental transformation of the soul and there is use of the terminology of escaping woes which I have identified as particularly Orphic religious terminology. Let us discuss these ideas in more detail.

The following verses note that those who will live a pure life while they are alive will enjoy a happy afterlife:

οἳ μέν κ' εὐαγέωσιν ὑπ' αὐγὰς ἠελίοιο,
αὖτις ἀποφθίμενοι μαλακώτερον οἶτον ἔχουσιν
ἐν καλῶι λειμῶνι βαθύρροον ἀμφ' Ἀχέροντα.

the ones who dwell purely under the rays of the sun, when they in turn perish, they have a more gentle fate in the beautiful meadow around deep-flowing Acheron.[1091]

The word εὐαγέωσιν is the same one which is used in the gold tablets by the deceased to denote that they are indeed pure and to be recognised as inititates who deserve to be sent to the *locus amoenus* of the Underworld. This can be seen in several gold tablets such as in A3 and A2 (4th B.C.): ὥς με{ι} πρόφ‹ρ›ω‹ν› πέμψη‹ι› ἕδρας ἐς εὐαγέ{ι}ων and in D4 (4th-3rd B.C.): εὐαγῆς ἱερὰ Διονύσου Βακχίου εἰμὶ Ἀρχέβου[λὴ] ἡ Ἀντιδώρου.[1092] The notion of purity is especially present in the gold tablets as can be seen from the frequent declaration by the deceased that he/she 'comes pure from the pure'.[1093] Could this acclamation essentially be the initiate's way to announce that he/she is now not 'mixed' with inferior mortal elements and he/she should thus reunite with his/her aetherial origin as described in the *Rhapsodies*? The cycle of rebirths is clearly defined in OR90 (OF437F) as a constant transformation through the elements while it ends when the soul is made of aether in its entirety [ψυχὴ ὅλων αἰθέρα ἀλλάσσουσα]. This elemental transformation of the soul has already been discussed but we should also mention that this cycle could be applied to the gold tablets. In the GT the souls of the initiated and unitiated alike perform an underground journey as is also the case in the *Rhapsodies*: 'But whenever a man leaves the sunlight, then Kyllenios Hermes leads the immortal souls down into the vast nether world'.[1094] In the case of the GT, the initiated souls are informed that in the Underworld they must avoid the first fountain they will come across and from which the uninitiated souls refresh themselves.[1095] The souls who drink water from this fountain presumably fail to escape the cycle of incarnations and are reborn again; some or all presumably after first receiving punishment in some other location such as for example the much referenced *borborō*/mire.[1096] This happens through the element of water and it must be of significance that in many tablets the initiates state in agony: 'I

1091 OR88 = OF340F.
1092 A3.7/A2.7: '...so that she (Persephone) may kindly send me to the seats of the pure'. D4.1–4: 'Pure and sacred to Dionysos Bacchios am I; Archeboule (daughter of) Antidoros.'
1093 A1.1: Ἔρχομαι ἐκ κοθαρῶ‹ν› κοθαρά, χθονί‹ων› βασίλεια. Same or slightly variant in: A3.1; A2.1; A5.
1094 OR91 = OF339F.
1095 B10.4 and B11.6: ἔνθα κατερχόμεναι ψυχαί νεκύων ψύχονται: 'there the descending souls of the dead refresh themselves.'
1096 See discussion in p.133, 179–183, 250–251 and fn.823.

am parched with thirst and dying...' [Δίψαι αὖος ἐγὼ καὶ ἀπόλλυμαι].[1097] This literally means that the soul is dying due to dryness (αὖος). If, however, the initiates of the GT wish to escape the cycle of rebirths they must ask for a drink from the fountain of Mnemosyne after which they will proceed to the Isles of the Blessed. The verses referring to the elemental transformation in the *Rhapsodies* note: 'From water comes into existence earth, and from earth water once again, and from that soul, becoming aether in its entirety'.[1098] In other words there are two watery paths which lead back to either afterlife punishment and mortality, or immortality. This might also be portrayed in OR88 (OF340F) where it is said that the pure ones will proceed to the beautiful meadow around deep-flowing Acheron, while the unjust will be led down under the surface of Kokytos; either route is through a river. Following the same logic, and if I am right, the acclamation of the gold tablets' initiates that they are 'The child of earth and starry heaven' culminates in a very simplified way the idea that humans are a mixture of non-divine (earth) and divine (aetherial stars) elements; the specification that they are the purest from the pure and their race is heavenly is the proof that they are now ready to return to their aetherial abode – the stars –, and their request for cold water is the means to get there, as long as they drink from the right one.[1099] The word ἀπόλλυμαι in the gold tablets, as mentioned in the previous paragraph, and the agony of dryness of the soul, thus, might mean that it is through heat that the soul materialises, since it might be a play on the word Apollo. This could also explain the phrase of being 'mastered by the lightning' which has a negative connotation in the GT.[1100] I have discussed in Chapter 4 the Myth of Er in the *Republic*, where I found similarities with the eschatology of the gold tablets. Perhaps it is relevant that Er describes the materialisation of the souls saying that they sleep in the Plain of Oblivion and then abruptly wake up from the 'sound of thunder and the quaking of the earth' and then materialise like shooting stars.[1101] The above are also reminiscent of the βίος-θάνατος-βίος of the Olbian tablets, in which case the zig-zag lines inscribed on them could represent lightning.[1102]

[1097] B1.8, B2.9, B3.1, B4.1, B5.1, B6.1, B7.1, B8.1, B9.1, B10.11, B11.13, B12.1.
[1098] OR90 = OF437F.
[1099] It might also be relevant that some of the names inscribed on the gold tablets have astrological connotations: e.g. B2: Ἀστέριος ὄνομα.
[1100] A1.4, A2.5, A3.5.
[1101] The etymological closeness of *astēr* with *astrapē* is also interesting.
[1102] See Graf and Johnston, Appendix, p.215 for drawings of the Olbian Bone Tablets.

At this point, I must refer back to Euripides' Phaethon as a case where a text could be interpreted in relation to Orphic texts and beliefs and in this case in relation to heat as a generative force and the use of the verb ἀπόλλυμι. In the following passage Euripides describes the burning of Phaethon's body:

<ΚΛΥΜΕΝΗ>:
πυροῦσσ' Ἐρινὺς ἐν †νεκροις θ.ρ.(.)νυαι†
ζώσης δ' ἀνίησ' ἀτμὸν ἐμφανῆ <φλογός>.
ἀπωλόμην·

'A Fury all of fire on the dead and sends up a visible exhalation of living (flame). I am destroyed!'[1103]

Phaethon was struck by Zeus' lightning because he was unable to keep the chariot of the sun at a safe distance from earth. The description of his body as smouldering is unique and reminiscent of the Titanic smoke out of which humans were created. The notion that the ἀτμὸς coming out of Phaethon's body is an exhalation of a living flame could be perceived as creating the same image of the materialisation of the soul from the Titan's smoke when they were striken by Zeus' thunderbolt. Perhaps related to this, is that Euripides does not follow Hesiod's version of Phaethon's parentage from Eos and Cephalus but makes him a son of Helios and Clymene instead who in Hesiod is the mother of Titan Prometheus who was punished by Zeus for giving to mortals the gift of fire. In the DP, too, it is when Kronos makes wrong use of Metis and strikes the *eonta* with heat uncontrollably, that Zeus takes from Kronos the daimon – argued to be Metis/Phanes – and after swallowing him (*aidoion*/Prōtogonon) recreates the world. In the *Rhapsodies* too, Phanes – also called Phaethon – is swallowed after Kronos' reign. The use of the verb ἀπόλλυμι, also found in the GT in reference to the soul's dryness, is reminiscent of Orphic ideas, as is the reference to a living exhalation, which is similar to the Orphic notion of soul being breath and the equation of this living exhalation to smoke. Is Euripides deliberately evoking Orphic ideas or is he just drawing from a pool of common traditional elements? We can never be sure or know a writer's motives but based on the vocabulary used, the Euripidean parentage from a Titaness mother and the fact that *Phaethon* has been suggested to include

---

[1103] Eur. *Phaethon* 214–215 Collard-Cropp (= *TrGF* fr.781).

other Orphic allusions make it plausible that Euripides is indeed referring to Orphic ideas here.[1104] In another passage from Euripides' *Phaethon* the same idea of two different post-mortem locations is expressed in the following verses which show textual similarities with the *Rhapsodies*: ἀν' αἰθέρ' ἢ γᾶς ὑπὸ κεῦθος ἄφαντον ἐξαμαυρωθῶ ['Should I vanish up into the aether, or down in an unseen hiding place in the earth?'].[1105] This is similar to OR91: ψυχὰς ἀθανάτας κατάγει Κυλλήνιος Ἑρμῆς | γαίης ἐς κευθμῶνα πελώριον.[1106] Not only, thus, is the Underworld defined through the same word in the *Phaethon*, but the alternative route the soul can take is upwards into the aether which is the belief expressed in the *Rhapsodies* (OR89) as we saw.[1107] Considering the cosmological similarities of the *Phaethon* to the OR discussed earlier it becomes more plausible that Euripides was familiar with Orphic eschatology. In his *Heracles* he also says that those mortals who were good, when they die they should 'run back to the light of the sun on the return leg of the course' [εἰς αὐγὰς πάλιν ἀλίου | δισσοὺς ἂν ἔβαν διαύλους].[1108] This 'return' leg of the course towards the light of the sun is the same as the last stage described above of the soul moving from water to aether while the vocabulary used is similar to the expression in the OR referring to those who dwell purely or unjustly 'under the rays of the sun': ὑπ'αὐγὰς ἠελίοιο.[1109] Admittedly Euripides is the tragedian whom I have been commenting on the most in relation to Orphic ideas and texts and perhaps Bremmer is right when he says that Euripides 'became increasingly interested in Orphism in the course of his career'.[1110]

1104 As Heath says: 'The criterion of acceptability <of an interpretation> depends on the nature of the interest which underlies a particular interpretative project: for some purposes, intentions are indispensable; for others, they are utterly irrelevant' (Heath, 2007, p.38).
1105 Eur. *TrGF* fr.781.63–64.
1106 OR91 = OF339F: 'Kyllenios Hermes leads the immortal souls down into the vast nether world.'
1107 OR89 = OF436F/422F/426F/425F.
1108 Eur. *Heracl.* 660–61 (Tr. Kovacs). The verses following this passage could also have an Orphic context, since the Chorus says that they still sing the praise of Mnemosyne and hymn Heracles' victory along Bromios the giver of wine and with the seven stringed lyre: μὴ ζώην μετ' ἀμουσίας, | αἰεὶ δ' ἐν στεφάνοισιν εἴην· | ἔτι τοι γέρων ἀοιδὸς | κελαδῶ Μναμοσύναν, | ἔτι τὰν Ἡρακλέους | καλλίνικον ἀείδω | παρά τε Βρόμιον οἰνοδόταν | παρά τε χέλυος ἑπτατόνου | μολπὰν καὶ Λίβυν αὐλόν: 'May I never live a Muse-less life! Ever may I go garlanded! Old singer that I am I still sing the praise of Mnemosyne, still hymn Heracles' glorious victory in company with Bacchus giver of wine, in company with the song of the seven-stringed tortoise shell and the Libyan pipe.' (Eur. *Heracl.* 676–684 Tr. Kovacs).
1109 OR88 = OF340F.
1110 Bremmer, 2014, p.68.

Going back to the description of the Netherworld in the *Rhapsodies*, we notice that the beautiful meadow is called λειμῶνι, which is the word used to describe the *locus amoenus* of the GT: λειμῶνάς θ'{ε} ἱερούς.[1111] Moreover, OR91 refers to the δόμον εἰς Ἀίδαο which is similar to the εὑρήσ{σ}εις ‹δ'› Ἀίδαο δόμων found in four of the lengthiest GT texts.[1112] OR91 includes further textual similarities to the gold tablets since the verse ὁππότε δ' ἄνθρωπος προλίπηι φάος ἠελίοιο, is found identical in the GT: ἀλλ' ὁπόταν ψυχὴ προλίπηι φάος ἀελίοιο, (A4.1). Moreover in both the OR and the GT we have the word λύσις which refers to the notion of deliverance from toil and wrongdoings.[1113] In addition, OR95 (OF350F) in its entirety is extremely similar to the vocabulary and ideas found in the GT. It is quoted by Damascius who notes that the god who gives deliverance is Dionysos. It says that people will offer sacrifices all year round and perform ὄργια in order to get deliverance (λύσιν) from the lawless deeds of their ancestors (προγόνων ἀθεμίστων). Referring to Dionysos it says: σὺ δὲ τοῖσιν ἔχων κράτος, οὕς κ'ἐθέλῃισθα, | <u>λύσεις ἔκ τε πόνων χαλεπῶν</u> καὶ ἀπείρονος οἴστρου.[1114] The 'deliverance from pain' expression is used very often in relation to escaping mortality in Orphic texts and as argued constitutes specific Orphic religious terminology. In the GT the toil and misery is also due to lawless actions since the initate announces that he/she has paid the penalty and we have phrases such as:

A2.4: πο‹ι›νὰν δ' ἀνταπέ{ι}τε{σε}ι‹σ›' ἔργων ἕνεκα οὔτι δικα‹ί›ων
B2.6: εἰρήσονται ὅ τι χρέος εἰσαφικάνεις·
D3.2: ἄποινος γὰρ ὁ μύστης

A2.4: Recompense I have paid on account of deeds not just.
B2.6: they will ask you for what <debt> have you come;
D.3.2: For the initiate is without penalty.[1115]

Moreover, in the GT also it is Dionysos who gives deliverance from the toil [D1.2/D2.2: εἰπεῖν Φερσεφόναι σ' ὅτι Β‹άκ›χιος αὐτός ἔλυσε] while the means seem also to be the same since we have a reference to the ὄργια of Demeter Chthonia (D5).[1116] Also, in the GT the misery and toil are cyclical as is evident from verses

---

1111 A4.6. D3.2.
1112 OR91 = OF339F. GT: B1.1. B2.1. B10.2. B11.4.
1113 OR95 = OF350F. GT: D1.2. D2.2.
1114 See section 6.4. for translation.
1115 B2.6: Translation in < > is by the author since the word χρέος does not mean need but 'debt', 'obligation' or that which one must pay.
1116 D1.2/D2.2: 'Say to Persephone that Bacchios himself freed you.'

such as: κύκλο‹υ› δ' ἐξέπταν βαρυπενθέος ἀργαλέοιο (A1.6).[1117] Not only do we have a very similar verse in the OR [OR94 = OF348F: Κύκλου τ'ἂν λήξαι καὶ ἀναπνεῦσαι κακότητος] but the cyclical element is prominent in the whole eschatological section. For example we have verses such as:

OR92 = OF338F: οὕνεκ' ἀμειβομένη ψυχὴ κατὰ κύκλα χρόνοιο
OR93 = OF438F: οὐδὲν ἔχει μίαν αἶσαν ἐπὶ φρεσίν, ἀλλὰ κυκλεῖται | πάντα πέριξ

OR92: because the soul of humans moves from one place to another with the circulation of time
OR93: none of them has one and the same destiny upon their existence, but all move around in a circle

The cyclical element is also present through the notion of rebirth and elemental transformation of the soul until its return back to aether which, as suggested, must be what the escape and deliverance from toil refers to. The important thing about these textual similarities is that they are present across all different groups of GT as classified in the recent edition by Edmonds, which constitutes another argument for their placement under one religious tradition, the Orphic one. Considering the eschatological similarities established earlier in this chapter in relation to astral immortality between the cosmological eschatology of the OR and the GT, the fact that we also have many textual similarities supports the suggestion that they were based on an Orphic *hieros logos* and it would not be surprising if many of the verses of this eschatological section of the *Rhapsodies* were part of the particular *hieros logos*. It does not seem probable that the compiler of the Orphic texts intercepted all these elements from the gold tablets since they were scattered in space and time and of a mystical nature from what we have seen. If this is true, then, it is another argument for assigning an eschatological philosophy with which the GT initiates had to be familiar, and reject – once more – the possibility that they were made by itinerant charlatan priests.

The distinction between the pure/just who will dwell in the Isles of the Blessed and the unjust who will be taken under the earth to Tartaros to be punished and/or reborn, as well as the notion of getting deliverance from lawless deeds presupposes the notion of justice and a specific way of life; a pure dwelling under the rays of the sun as emphasized in the *Rhapsodies* and the GT.[1118] This also suggests that the sun is all-seeing and nothing can escape his gaze, which is

---

[1117] A1.6: 'I flew out of the circle of wearying heavy grief.'
[1118] OR88 = OF340F: οἳ μέν κ' εὐαγέωσιν ὑπ' αὐγὰς ἠελίοιο: 'the ones who dwell purely under the rays of the sun'. GT: See fn.1092.

expressed earlier in the *Rhapsodies* when it is said that Phanes created him 'to be a guardian' and to 'rule over everything'.[1119] It is also emphasised in OR63 (OF233F) that, after Zeus recreated the world, he was followed by 'Justice the abundant punisher and protector of all'. We do not know in a detailed way what the Orphics had to do in order to act justly but the emphasis on purity and the phrase 'for many are the thyrsus-bearers, but few the Bacchoi' which is quoted by Plato and has been discussed extensively in a previous chapter, suggests that it was a lifelong effort of living a just life and not mere purifications of wrongdoings.[1120] In another passage from Plato's *Phaedrus* the *baccheuein* is related to the arousing of the soul through songs and poetry, which is identified as the third kind of mania, the one that comes from the Muses:

> τρίτη δὲ ἀπὸ Μουσῶν κατοκωχή τε καὶ μανία, λαβοῦσα ἀπαλὴν καὶ ἄβατον ψυχήν, ἐγείρουσα καὶ ἐκβακχεύουσα κατά τε ᾠδὰς καὶ κατὰ τὴν ἄλλην ποίησιν, μυρία τῶν παλαιῶν ἔργα κοσμοῦσα τοὺς ἐπιγιγνομένους παιδεύει·

> And a third kind of possession and madness comes from the Muses. This takes hold upon a gentle and pure soul, arouses it and excites it to Bacchic frenzy through songs and other poetry, and thus by adorning countless deeds of the ancients educates later generations.[1121]

baccheuein, thus, is associated with poetry and texts and stories of the past, which comes in accordance with what I have argued in relation to the importance of texts in Orphic beliefs and practices. The afterlife judgement is also perhaps suggested by OR91 (OF339F) which notes that when an animal or a bird dies their soul remains in the air until some other being snatches it through breathing in contrast to humans who are led down to the underworld by Hermes. This is presumably because birds and animals did not have to go through a judgement in the underworld as humans did and as was argued about the gold tablets.[1122] The importance of justice for Orphics is probably alluded to in Plato's *Laws* where he quotes Orpheus:

[1119] OR22 = OF158F.
[1120] See p.133 ff for text and discussion. OR96 = OF576F. See also Pind. *Nem.* 10.75–91: (78–79) παῦροι δ' ἐν πόνῳ πιστοὶ βροτῶν | καμάτου μεταλαμβάνειν: 'and few mortals remain faithful in time of toil to share the labor.' In this Ode Pindar refers to the Dioskouroi, Castor and Polydeuces in relation to matters of immortality and rebirth.
[1121] Pl. *Phdr.* 245a.
[1122] The guardians of the lake sometimes enquire with the chthonic king before allowing the initiate to proceed to the Isles of the Blessed. See B10 and B11 and as was mentioned we have the notions of paying a debt or being released from crimes.

ΑΘΗΝΑΙΟΣ: Ἄνδρες τοίνυν φῶμεν πρὸς αὐτούς, ὁ μὲν δὴ θεός, ὥσπερ καὶ ὁ παλαιὸς λόγος, ἀρχήν τε καὶ τελευτὴν καὶ μέσα τῶν ὄντων ἁπάντων ἔχων, εὐθείᾳ περαίνει κατὰ φύσιν περιπορευόμενος· τῷ δ' ἀεὶ ξυνέπεται Δίκη τῶν ἀπολειπομένων τοῦ θείου νόμου τιμωρός, ἧς ὁ μὲν εὐδαιμονήσειν μέλλων ἑχόμενος ξυνέπεται ταπεινὸς καὶ κεκοσμημένος, ὁ δέ τις ἐξαρθεὶς ὑπὸ μεγαλαυχίας ἢ χρήμασιν ἐπαιρόμενος ἢ τιμαῖς ἢ καὶ σώματος εὐμορφίᾳ, ἅμα νεότητι καὶ ἀνοίᾳ, φλέγεται τὴν ψυχὴν μεθ' ὕβρεως, ὡς οὔτ' ἄρχοντος οὔτε τινὸς ἡγεμόνος δεόμενος, ἀλλὰ καὶ ἄλλοις ἱκανὸς ὢν ἡγεῖσθαι, καταλείπεται ἔρημος θεοῦ, καταλειφθεὶς δὲ καὶ ἔτι ἄλλους τοιούτους προσλαβὼν σκιρτᾷ ταράττων πάνθ' ἅμα, καὶ πολλοῖς τισὶν ἔδοξεν εἶναί τις, μετὰ δὲ χρόνον οὐ πολὺν ὑποσχὼν τιμωρίαν οὐ μεμπτὴν τῇ δίκῃ ἑαυτόν τε καὶ οἶκον καὶ πόλιν ἄρδην ἀνάστατον ἐποίησε.

ATHENIAN: Let us, then, speak to them in this way: "O men, that God who, as the old *logos* tells, holds the beginning, the end, and the middle of all that exists completes his circuit according to nature in a straightforward way. With him Justice always follows, the avenger of those who fall short of the divine law; and she, again, is followed by whoever shall be truly happy, being humble and orderly, while the one who being carried away by arrogance or being proud about his money, or honours, or the beauty of his body, both because of insolence and folly, inflames his soul with hybris, thinking he does not need a ruler or guide, but that he is capable of leading others, he is abandoned by god, and being left behind he takes others with him too and disorderly troubles their mind. And to many he seems to be great, but after not so long, he receives the punishment, not unmerited and according to Justice, when he rouses up himself, his house and his city..."[1123]

I am quoting this passage at length because it can demonstrate how ideas found in the *Rhapsodies* can be traced unchanged in classical sources.[1124] Also, in the paragraphs following the above passage (4.716e–717a) Plato uses phrases such as: ἀκάθαρτος γὰρ τὴν ψυχὴν ὅ γε κακός, καθαρὸς δὲ ὁ ἐναντίος· and μάτην οὖν περὶ θεοὺς ὁ πολύς ἐστι πόνος τοῖς ἀνοσίοις, τοῖσι δὲ ὁσίοις ἐγκαιρότατος ἅπασι.[1125] These are reminiscent of the Orphic emphasis on purity and of the Orphic *ponos* terminology. We can be confident that the way of life Plato describes is the Orphic one since he associates it with a *logos* from which he paraphrases some verses which are the following Orphic verses found both in the *Rhapsodies* and the DP:

[1123] Pl. *Leg.* 4.715e–716b.
[1124] See also Ps-Demosthenes 25.11: καὶ τὴν ἀπαραίτητον καὶ σεμνὴν Δίκην, ἥν ὁ τὰς ἁγιωτάτας ἡμῖν τελετὰς καταδείξας Ὀρφεὺς παρὰ τὸν τοῦ Διὸς θρόνον φησὶ καθημένην πάντα τὰ τῶν ἀνθρώπων ἐφορᾶν, εἰς αὐτὸν ἕκαστον νομίσαντα βλέπειν οὕτω δεῖ ψηφίζεσθαι· 'Each juryman must reflect that he is being watched by hallowed and inexorable Justice, who, as Orpheus, that prophet of our most sacred mysteries, tells us, sits beside the throne of Zeus and oversees all the works of men' (Tr. Vince).
[1125] Pl. *Leg.* 4.716e: 'for the wicked is unpure in the soul and the good man is pure'. 717a: 'Therefore, all the great labour the impious spend on the gods is in vain, while for the pious it is profitable to them all.'

OR61 = OF243F:	OR61: Zeus was the first, Zeus the last
Ζεὺς πρῶτος γένετο, Ζεὺς ὕστατος ἀργικέραυνος· Ζεὺς κεφαλή, Ζεὺς μέσσα, Διὸς δ' ἐκ πάντα τέτυκται·	bright-thundering king, Zeus the head, Zeus the middle and from Zeus everything is created.
Col.XVII.12: "Ζεὺς κεφᾳ[λή, Ζεὺς μέσ]σᾳ, Διὸς δ' ἐκ [π]άντα τέτ[υκται"	Col.XVII.12: "Zeus is the head, Zeus the middle, and from Zeus is everything fashioned."
Col.XVIII.12–13: "Ζεὺς πρῶτος	[γέν]ετο"	Col.XVIII.12–13: "Zeus was born first"
Col.XIX.10: "Ζεὺς βασιλεύς, Ζεὺς δ' ἀρχὸς ἁπάντων ἀργικέραυνος	Col.XIX.10: "Zeus the king, Zeus the ruler of all, he of the bright bolt."

Significantly, Plato says that these words come from a παλαιὸς λόγος, supporting not only their being part of the *Rhapsodies* but also their early date. Most importantly, the reference to the text as a *logos* and its subsequent connection with a specific way of life evidences that Orphic texts were of an exegetical and aetiological nature, which in turn requires their studying and understanding. According to my reconstruction in OR61–62 (OF243F/245V) the praise of Zeus is indeed followed by a warning that not even the unjust men can escape from his gaze.[1126] Plato's linking of these verses to the notion of Justice being a helper of Zeus also supports the placement of OR63 (OF233F) which notes that Justice 'the abundant punisher and protector of all, follows' Zeus, right after this passage. The Orphic life according to Plato, then, seems to entail humbleness, simplicity, lawfulness and absence of greed and vanity. In this passage, too, we can see what was suggested earlier, that heat or fire is considered a harmful element for the soul (φλέγεται τὴν ψυχὴν μεθ'ὕβρεως) and must be related to mortality. As Bernabé claims, the idea of Zeus' justice having an important role in Orphism might be represented in several examples of Apulian pottery such as a ceramic fragment

---

1126 These verses from Homer's *Iliad* refer to an afterlife punishment for those who have sworn a false oath and are reminiscent of the OR and the DP since they mention that no one can escape the gaze of all-seeing and all-hearing Zeus and Helios: Hom. *Il.* 3.276–280: Ζεῦ πάτερ, Ἴδηθεν μεδέων, κύδιστε, μέγιστε | Ἠέλιός θ', ὃς πάντ' ἐφορᾷς καὶ πάντ' ἐπακούεις | καὶ ποταμοὶ καὶ γαῖα, καὶ οἳ ὑπένερθε καμόντας | ἀνθρώπους τίνυσθον, ὅτις κ' ἐπίορκον ὀμόσσῃ | ὑμεῖς μάρτυροι ἔστε, φυλάσσετε δ' ὅρκια πιστά: 'Father Zeus, who rule from Ida, most glorious, most great, and you Sun, who see all things and hear all things, and you rivers and you earth, and you who in the world below take vengeance on men who are done with life, whoever has sworn a false oath: be witnesses, and watch over the solemn oaths'. (Tr. Murray). The evocation of the rivers and the earth is further reminiscnent of the DP and the OR. See p.315. Considering the reference to afterlife punishments and the earlier discussion about the Nekyia, it is possible that these type of verses also derive from an Orphic tradition.

from Ruvo where we see Orpheus in the middle playing his lyre, Persephone and Hekate on the upper right part holding torches as if they are guiding in the underworld, Nike (Victory) half-opening a door and next to her Dike (Justice), both labelled.[1127] Finally, we have already discussed how being punished by the Erinyes for trespassing limits is emphasised by the Derveni author in relation to the sun and in Col.III.5 he says that Dike punishes those who were unjust, with the help of the Erinyes: 'For Dike punishes pernicious men through each of the Erinyes'.[1128] We can see, thus, that the notion of being just is directly related to securing escape from the cycle of rebirths and misery and the attainment of immortality.

Finally, the cycle of reincarnation is mentioned in OR92 (OF338F), where it is described how the soul moves between humans and animals through a circular passing of time. This is reminiscent of Empedokles' texts and we have textual similarities between the two. There are also many conceptual similarities between Empedoklean and Orphic eschatology and it is essential to mention that Empedokles himself attributes ideas identical with the ones we have discussed so far, and mentioned in the *Rhapsodies*, to 'an ancient decree of the gods, eternal, sealed by broad oaths' [θεῶν ψήφισμα παλαιόν, ἀίδιον, πλατέεσσι κατεσφρηγισμένον ὅρκοις·'].[1129] The fact that Empedokles identifies an external source for these ideas which are textually very close to verses from the *Rhapsodies* suggests that the cycle of reincarnation was not his idea. Also, the fact that this divine law was protected by oaths gives it a mystic nature, since it was bound by secrecy. It is, nonetheless, possible that there was a common tradition of mystic eschatology on which the Pre-Socratics drew. Riedweg, has suggested that Empedokles shows many similarities with the so-called *Orpheotelestae*.[1130] Betegh even compares him with the mythical figure of Orpheus himself, suggesting that he 'tries to elevate himself to Orpheus' religious and cultural standing by claiming the mythical poet's most important functions for himself'.[1131] He furthermore comments on the similarity of Empedokles' *Physika* with the text of the Derveni Papyrus noting that Empedokles also began the particular work with a demonological story which outlined his eschatology and framed his cosmological theory. OR97 (OF337F), which is also comparable to the DP since it could be perceived as a criticism or

---

[1127] Bernabé, 2009, p.98ff. Apulian, red figure fragment, 375–350 B.C. Ruvo di Puglia, Museo Nazionale Jatta, Inv.: ex Fenicia (1. Inv.). LIMC: Orpheus 83.
[1128] DP Col.III–IV.
[1129] Empedokles, DKB115.1–2.
[1130] Riedweg, 1995, p.39–40: 'Sieht man von der kontextbedingten negativen Färbung der platonischen Darstellung ab, so sind die zahlreichen phänomenologischen Übereinstimmungen mit Empedokles' Selbstvorstellung nicht zu verkennen.'
[1131] Betegh, 2004, p.371.

condemnation to the uninitiated similar to the one found in the DP, is very similar to a passage from a Stoic work by Cleanthes (4th-3rd B.C.):

> ὃν φεύγοντες ἐῶσιν ὅσοι θνητῶν κακοί εἰσι,
> δύσμοροι, οἵ τ'ἀγαθῶν μὲν ἀεὶ κτῆσιν ποθέοντες
> οὔτ' ἐσορῶσι θεοῦ κοινὸν νόμον, οὔτε κλύουσιν,
> ᾧ κεν πειθόμενοι σὺν νῷ βίον ἐσθλὸν ἔχοιεν.
> αὐτοὶ δ' αὖθ' ὁρμῶσιν ἄνοι κακὸν ἄλλος ἐπ' ἄλλο.

> This Word, however, evil mortals flee, poor wretches; though they are desirous of good things for their possession, they neither see nor listen to God's universal Law; and yet, if they obey it intelligently, they would have the good life. But they are senselessly driven to one evil after another.[1132]

It could be argued, thus, that these verses might actually be a later interpolation. However, they show some similarity to OR62 (OF245V) which seems to come from a hymn to Zeus which may indicate that at least the attitude of the verses towards mortals was part of the *Rhapsodies*. Also, the phrase ἀποστρέψαι κακότητος from OR97 which refers to the inability of mortals to stay away from evil, is similar to the phrase ἀναπνεῦσαι κακότητος from OR94 which refers to the aim of respiting from misery through escaping the cycle of rebirths.

6.6 Conclusion

In this Chapter I have analysed the text of the *Rhapsodies* and shown that it contained not only theogonical but also exegetical verses. It became evident that the reconstruction of the text enabled us to undertake a detailed analysis of the *Rhapsodies* which would not have been possible if we had to go through hundreds of fragments. The reconstructed text allowed us to identify patterns and draw a comparison with other Orphic sources and also to decipher the cosmological elements of the *Rhapsodies*. I agued that an elemental cosmology is expressed through allegorical verses and that this elemental cosmology corresponds to an elemental eschatology which was stated in a more straightforward way through exegetical verses at the last section of the *Rhapsodies*.

The elemental eschatology proclaims that aether is the primal substance which encompasses everything and its purest essence is the stars which constitute the Isles of the Blessed. The soul has an airy nature and is rooted in the aether, and corporeality's substance is earth. The soul has two watery paths after

---

[1132] Cleanthes, *Hymn to Zeus*, SVF I 537.18–22.

death: the one leads to the aether and immortality and the other leads back to the cycle of rebirths which could also include pre-rebirth punishments. It also seems that incarnation actualises through fire and there is a dual topography of the afterlife since the souls are led to the underworld post-mortem before taking one of the two watery paths. Several of these elements are also found in the GT and DP, indicating that there was a certain uniformity in Orphic texts and their interpretation. The last section of the *Rhapsodies* has so many textual and conceptual similarities with the GT, that it could contain verses form their *hieros logos*. The Orphic terminology of deliverance from pain which is used very often in relation to escaping mortality in Orphic texts, is also found in the *Rhapsodies* under the same premise. Based on the exegetical verses, it seems that the means to avoid the punishments in Hades and escape the cycle of rebirths is through leading a just life.

Also, textual and conceptual similarities between Homer and the *Rhapsodies* were identified and I argued that some distinctively Orphic elements might have been borrowed by a Homeric *aoidos*. Textual similarities to archaic sources such as Pindar and Hesiod and Pre-Socratic philosophers suggest that Orphic texts – elements of which have survived in the *Rhapsodies* – were likely to have been part of the same oral rhapsodic tradition. This suggestion is also supported by the fact that non-Homeric elements of oral tradition are found in the *Rhapsodies*, such as the importance of Metis and the birth of Aphrodite from Ouranos' genitals. It could be that Ionia was an important centre of Orphic texts and mysteries, which would explain a possible influence on pre-Socratic philosophers, based on the following points: a) the Ionian colony Phanagoria which showed signs of worshipping Phanes through a triple identification with Apollo, Dionysos and Artemis; b) the Olbian Bone Tablets, which contain a mixture of Orphic religious eschatological elements, and philosophical elements also found in Pre-Socratic philosophers such as Herakleitos, were found in Olbia which was a Milesian colony; and c) some Ionian traits of the oral tradition are maintained in the *Rhapsodies*.

7 Conclusion

One thing that has become evident through my book is that we can only define Orphism if we examine all the evidence together. The textual comparison between Orphic and non-Orphic sources allowed us to distinguish Orphic terminology and identify references to Orphism which might not have been discernible if the material had been examined in isolation. Through my analysis, three major patterns have emerged: the importance of texts and their correct understanding, the cosmological nature of the Orphic eschatology, and the curative and transformative nature of Orphic practices. Whether it was offering the means to escape the cycle of rebirths through acquiring knowledge and 'waking' the memory, or the atonement of wrongdoings, the Orphic texts and practices had the power to heal and restore.

Orphism can therefore be defined as a practical theology which spread throughout Greece and through time, influencing public rites, forming esoteric mysteries and becoming material for bricolage by religious practitioners. I distinguish three different strands:

(1) Public rites based on Orphic mythology: such would be some of the cases around Greece, examined in Chapter 2, where local cults were attached to the figure of Orpheus, or for example the Delphic rite performed by the Hyades to resurrect Dionysos, related to the Orphic myth of Dionysos' dismemberment and the subsequent collection and transfer of his parts to Delphi by Apollo.

(2) Esoteric initiation mysteries with specific eschatological beliefs of a cosmological nature based on Orphic texts, culminating in the perception of mortality as a punishment, and with the aim of returning to the initial divine state and substance.

(3) Religious practices performed by itinerant priests who made use of Orphic texts such as the Gurôb Papyrus, in combination with other religious elements.

The first category can be classed as Orphic because it was inspired by Orphic texts/mythology and ideas, but it belongs to the wider religious frame of ancient Greek religion, meaning that it was also inevitably intertwined with civic affairs and thus perhaps included non-Orphic elements such as sacrifices. Areas where such practices must have been prominent are Phlya, Laconia, Thessaly and Macedonia. The second category is the actualisation of Orphic beliefs into mysteries as they spread through time and space with a certain fluidity, but with some common and core beliefs between them: the most important was astral immortality, a cosmological eschatology and the importance of texts and knowledge; these were followed and performed by Orphic initiates and can be considered exclusively Orphic. The owners of the gold tablets and the recipients of the Derveni author's *exēgēsis* belong in this group. The third category can be classed as Orphic but it is not exclusively Orphic since it combines elements from other traditions. I have argued that there were two different attitudes toward Orphic rites and texts in ancient sources related to groups (2) and (3), meaning that the negative attitudes seem to address the wrong use of Orphic texts for personal gain and not the Orphic rites performed by Orphics nor the Orphic texts themselves.

Orpheus was most often mentioned as the poet, or *theologos*, and a plurality of works were attributed to him. These works are most often referred to as *logoi* or *hieroi logoi* indicating their explanatory justificatory nature in religious matters and their use in relation to mysteries. The clearest identification of people 'affiliated to Orpheus' is in relation to their understanding of Orphic texts, which confirms their complex nature and their enigmatic content as emphasised by the Derveni author. These people, moreover, are also associated in ancient sources with the performance of mysteries, which indicates that Orphic mysteries were based on Orphic *hieroi logoi*. The circulation of Orphic texts was most probably public and initially oral but the fact that ancient sources either straightforwardly refrain from referring to the interpretation of these *logoi*, or reveal only limited information, indicates that their interpretation was a secret revealed to the initiates during mysteries. This refrain of ancient sources referring to Orphic texts/mysteries and their meaning might also be due to their being highly revered, so sacred that they should not be uttered. It is also characteristic that later sources such as Plutarch are not as hesitant in revealing more details.

Orphic sacred stories are repeatedly linked to eschatological beliefs such as reincarnation, the afterlife and post-mortem rewards or punishments. The *Orphic Rhapsodies* include all these elements in combination with cosmogonical material intertwined with scientifical and astronomical observations, supporting that this was the nature of the Orphic *hieroi logoi*. A case where an *hieros logos* was behind the formation of mysteries would be the gold tablets. This is not to suggest that all the owners of the tablets were under a single religious administration. Perhaps the mystic initiation was not exactly the same for all the tablets' owners; but the knowledge they acquired and the justification for posthumous *kleos* and apotheosis remained the same. Initiations and Orphic mysteries had a common eschatology but a fluid practical manifestation in different areas. It is also possible that there were specific places of initiation or oracles of Dionysos – in Thrace and possibly other areas such as Lesbos – related to matters of post-mortem prophecy. Significantly, such oracles are associated with Orpheus in ancient sources. The text of the gold tablets was found to have many similarities in terms of eschatological theory and topography with the last section of the *Hieroi Logoi in 24 Rhapsodies* indicating that the latter could contain verses form their *hieros logos*. This would not have been immediately evident if these two sources had not been analysed together, which again demonstrates the importance of examining all the Orphic sources together, and indicates the rationale for following this methodology in this work. This co-ordinated examination would also have been impossible without a reconstruction of the text of the *Orphic Rhapsodies*.

The first Orphic texts are likely to have been rhapsodic theologies combining mythological elements with hymns and exegetical verses, as we see in the *Orphic Rhapsodies* and, thus, part of the rhapsodic oral tradition. It was argued that Orphic elements such as the association of the sceptre in the *Orphic Rhapsodies* with Metis/counsel/*medea* and the sun, which are also present in Homer were borrowed from the Orphic oral tradition and the Orphic identification of Phanes/Metis/*aidoios* with the sceptre being passed on from one ruler to the next representing Counsel/Nous. This is particularly supported by the fact that the myth of Metis and the myth of Aphrodite's birth from Ouranos' *mēdea* are non-Homeric myths and are both found in the *Orphic Rhapsodies*. Moreover, the Homeric Nekyia shows similarities to Orphic eschatology. Apart from these textual and conceptual similarities, it was also suggested that the elemental cosmology of the *Orphic Rhapsodies*, also found in Homer through the same verses, was borrowed by Homer. I have also identified textual and cosmological similarities between Orphic cosmology and the Pre-Socratic philosophers such as Herakleitos, Anaxagoras, and Empedokles, amongst others. The textual similarities between Orphic theological texts and Pre-Socratic philosophers corroborate the conclusion that they belong to the same current of ideas. Elements from the *Orphic Rhapsodies*, then, must have been part of the rhapsodic oral tradition, and it is probable that Pre-Socratic philosophers were either partly influenced by Orphic cosmological/theological poems or were influenced by the rhapsodic tradition as a whole which contained Orphic elements, as it reached them in the 6th century B.C.

It could be that Ionia was an important centre of Orphic texts and mysteries, which would explain a possible influence on Pre-Socratic philosophers, based on the following points: a) the Ionian colony Phanagoria showed signs of worshipping Phanes through a triple identification with Apollo, Dionysos and Artemis; b) the Bone Tablets which contain a mixture of Orphic religious eschatological elements and philosophical elements also found in Pre-Socratics such as Herakleitos, were found in Olbia, a Milesian colony; and c) some Ionian traits of the oral tradition are maintained in the *Orphic Rhapsodies*. This suggestion should not be considered controversial since Pre-Socratic philosophers were as much natural theologians as they were natural philosophers and there is no reason to deny the possible existence of a mystic cosmological eschatology. The Orphic cosmological eschatology, in particular, is also identifiable in many ancient authors such as Pindar, Plato, Euripides, Diodorus, Plutarch and others. Moreover, many ancient passages which might appear peculiar, exactly because they mingle mythological tradition with elemental cosmology, fall into place when explained with the Orphic cosmological and eschatological model.

The Orphic texts, then, were of a theological/cosmological character and described the nature of the gods through cosmological allegory. Juxtaposing the GT, DP and the OR has made it clear that the Orphic cosmological model was consistent throughout all of them. Aether is the purest essence which underlies everything, the primal substance of the cosmos out of which the astral sphere is made and where the Isles of the Blessed are situated and more specifically the constellations of the Bull (Taurus), Charioteer (Auriga) and the Pleiades. The soul is of an airy nature and enters the body through breath. As soon as the body dies and the soul exits the body, the soul descends in the underworld and the body returns to earth. A process of judgement takes place there where the Orphic initiate had to prove his/her status as initiate, his/her purity through leaving a just life and his/her repayment of an old debt. There were then two watery paths for the soul, signified allegorically through the two fountains of the GT and the two underworld rivers of the *Rhapsodies*. One watery path leads to immortality and returns to the aether in the stars, while the other leads back to punishment, incarnation and mortality. The lightning and fire was most probably a symbol of incarnation. This schema also explains the punishment of the wicked souls in the mire/mud in Tartaros, where they remain trapped, since mud is a mixture of earth and water. The Orphic topography of the afterlife, thus, is dual since Tartaros is subterranean and the Isles of the Blessed are celestial.

Perhaps the major difference of Orphism from Pre-Socratic cosmology is the promise for an individual immortality, the survival of the self, instead of anonymously becoming part of the universal soul. The Derveni author refers to innumerable souls, and many of the gold tablets have names inscribed on them. The Isles of the Blessed are located in the stars and the soul is aetherial but it seems that it still maintains some of its identity, which may be why Orpheus makes a world out of each star as Heraclides of Pontus says.[1133] This is also evident from the importance of Mnemosyne in the gold tablets so that the initiate will remember who he was and what he knows. A posthumous *kleos* and immortality, thus, stops being exclusive to the Homeric heroes of the distant past but becomes available to anyone who recollects the *alētheia* and recognises their divine ancestry. Based on the many references by ancient sources to the belief that the soul turned

---

1133 Heraclid. Pont. fr.75 Schütrumpf.

into aether and became a star post-mortem it is improbable that such ideas were 'marginal' or 'peripheral' to conventional religion but most likely personal, esoteric and 'supplementary'.

Another difference of Orphism from the rest of ancient Greek religion is the element of monotheism: even though we have many significant deities in Orphism (Zeus, Dionysos, Apollo, Persephone, Demeter/Ge Meter), these were constantly mingled and interchanged into one another and they represent different manifestations of the same divine entity. Dionysos and Apollo are two sides of the same coin, Zeus is everything, Aphrodite is the act of procreating, Phanes/Protogonos encompasses all the world within him and is also Dionysos and Apollo, Hestia is Demeter and Rhea became Demeter when she gave birth to Zeus, while the Derveni author quotes a verse from the Orphic Hymns which says that Demeter is Rhea and Rhea is Ge Meter and Hestia. Essentially, then, there is only one divine entity which encompasses all, and all these deities are simply different manifestations of the same entity.

The owners of the gold tablets considered it necessary for the achievement of afterlife bliss that they inscribe an Orphic *hieros logos* on gold, and they also emphatically stressed the importance of memory. This shows, not only the importance of *logos* (text) and memory, but also the existence of a collective belief shared by the owners of the tablets that they would be able to use this text, this information and this knowledge in the afterlife for a better lot. Such a belief could not exist without a specific eschatological and philosophical/theological framework, since it is closely linked with matters such as the 'substance' of the soul, its identity and abilities after death, with a specific underworld topography and afterlife expectations, and with the importance of specific gods in the soul's posthumous bliss. There is no doubt that the souls of the tablets' owners had to perform a journey into the underworld. From the moment of their death until they reached the guards of the fountain of Memory and addressed Persephone in order to convince her of their special status, they were as ordinary as any other uninitiated soul. In other words, the background knowledge was specific/practical on the one hand and analytical/ideological on the other.

The agonistic and heroic elements expressed in the gold tablets, especially through the use of the word *euchomai*, might indicate a shift from the heroic exclusivity of the Homeric epics to a more inclusive immortality. In this way, the tablets' owners legitimate their right to deification in a way that no one familiar with epic poetry could dispute. If my *genos* is divine, then I must be too, we can imagine the initiates realizing at some point of their initiation. Since both cases were based on divine lineage, an aetiological myth was essential in the case of Orphism. This was the Titanic anthropogony which has been shown to have been associated with Orphics from at least the early Hellenistic period, while the existence in humans of a Titanic and divine nature is mentioned in Plutarch and Plato, who also refers to the Orphic notion of the body being a tomb for the soul, indicating that Orphics considered incarnation an undesirable state. Other authors, such as Dio Chrysostom, also refer to incarnation in relation to humans being descended from the Titans. In the case of the myth of Titanic punishment by Zeus, the importance of examining various sources together was also evident, since the intertextual similarities between the Platonic passages, Damascius and Dio Chrysostom allow us to define as Orphic the idea of incarnation as a punishment and imprisonment of the soul, and relate it to the descent of mortals from the Titans. In particular, the use of the specific phrase for having respite from pain/troubles/misery, or lying in the *borborō*/mire, can be perceived as Orphic religious terminology and help us identify indirect references to Orphic ideas in sources as early as Herakleitos and Pindar.

Orphic initiations most probably included the re-enactment of myths such as the dismemberment of Dionysos by the Titans and the subsequent incarnation through the thunderbolt of Zeus as evidenced through the Orphic eschatological cosmology and non-Orphic sources. Also, in the case of the gold tablets, katabatic rites must have taken place as a re-enactment of death and 'rebirth' as a god, through the ascent and emergence to light where *legomena* and *dromena* would take place. This was evident from the echoes of such a mystery in the tablets themselves, through performative aspects in the text, such as dialogue, acclamations, formulaic phrases, repetition and instructions. Also, procession of light/torches must have been involved, representing Dionysos/Apollo. A katabatic mystery would not only serve as 'practice' for the actual afterlife journey but also symbolise the initiate's death and rebirth as a purified member of the holy *thiasos*. What distinguishes the tablets' owners and gives them an advantage is not a special status but knowledge. This knowledge is not confined to directions for an underworld journey, but also relates to matters of the soul. We can thus conclude that at some point during the Orphic initiation procedure the involvement of an expert who would give guidance in the understanding of Orphic literature through his teaching was essential. Also, texts such as the Derveni Papyrus were probably owned and used by the Orphic initiates, and the Orphic theogony was a key text that had to be understood and interpreted. Most importantly, and what again distinguished Orphism from the rest of the ancient Greek religion, is that deliverance from the cycle of rebirths, and the return to the divine state was done through living the *Orphikos bios* and *baccheuein* which constituted a constant effort to avoid bloodshed, live a just life and understand the cosmological eschatology of the Orphic texts.

My interpretation of the Orphic texts and sources and the above definition of Orphism differs from the scholarly understanding of the matter up to this date. During my journey I have identified various attitudes to Orphism in scholarship; there are those who categorise Orphism under ancient magic, those who approach anything Orphic with the presupposition of it being inferior and marginal to 'normal' ancient Greek religion – whatever that is –, those who choose to ignore the matter altogether due to its bafflingness, those who treat it as an external 'exotic' phenomenon, the list could go on and on. All these attitudes cannot be justified considering the vastness of Orphic material present in ancient Greek sources and I hope that the analysis I have pursued in this book has shown that Orphism was a much bigger and influential phenomenon. A phenomenon whose beginnings were rooted so deeply in archaic times that often our ancient sources are not entirely sure how to treat it. And this is one of the major reasons that studying Orphism often feels elusive and enigmatic. Orpheus being classified along Homer as one of the earliest poets, Plato quoting from an Orphic text which he refers to as ὁ παλαιὸς λόγος, the Derveni commentary on a text which was clearly well established and interpreted by the 5th century B.C., the early signs that Orphic religious activity and deities were already formed in the 7th–6th century B.C. in areas such as Olbia, Phanagoria and Chios, the close similarities of Orphic theologic texts to Pre-Socratic philosophies, the frequent treatment of Orphic beliefs and rites by ancient authors as highly revered and the reluctance of authors such as Herodotus to reveal any details, all point to the archaicness of Orphism. A phenomenon which continued to evolve and adapt in the following centuries, at the same time influencing the formation of Greek religious rites and eschatological beliefs and becoming material for bricolage. It is through observing the light coming in through the cracks of the door which keeps us, the modern versions of the profane, out of the locale where everything is explained, and through the aid of later authors who begun being more revealing about Orphic texts and beliefs that we were able to get an understanding of this major chapter of ancient Greek religion.

Appendix

Justification of the Reconstruction

The Beginning: OR0 – OR9

OR1 was placed at the beginning of the Theogony since it was suggested in Chapter 5 that this phrase might have been a typical beginning of Orphic *hieroi logoi*.[1134] Damascius informs us that the first entities of the OR are Chronos, Aether, Chaos and Phanes coming out of the egg (**OR0**). Ioannis Malalas (**OR2**) also says that the OR2 verses were at the beginning of Orpheus' poem which justifies their placement at the first episode. Proclus (**OR4**) and Simplicius (OR4) also identify Chronos and Aether as first principles. Based on this information, fragments referring to these entities were placed in the first episode of the *Rhapsodies*. The paraphrase referring to Chronos (**OR3**) was placed here based on the definitive Χρόνος οὗτος which follows in the next verse, suggesting a previous generic reference to Chronos. Simplicius (OF111F(VII)) also specifies that the verse οὐδέ τι πεῖραρ ὑπῆν, οὐ πυθμήν, οὐδέ τις ἕδρα refers to χάσμα πελώριον and thus was placed after the two verses quoted by Proclus referring to χάσμα πελώριον.

OR5 was placed at the beginning of the cosmogony because it states that everything was still undivided.

OR6 is quoted by Ioannis Malalas in a context referring to Chronos, Aether and Chaos while gloomy Night covered and overwhelmed everything: this suggests that the verse belongs in this episode. We already know from Damascius that Phanes who came out of the egg was one of the first entities and in **OR7** he also says that Chronos created the egg with Aether; it was therefore considered appropriate that these verses be placed in this episode. This is also supported by Lactantius (**OR8**) who says that Phanes was born from Aether, came out of infinity and nothing was born before him.

OR9 was considered to refer to Phanes' birth from the egg since, when quoting it, Proclus claims that the shape of the sphere is 'akin to the Demiurge' and 'ancestral (*progonikos*) to the cosmos having been made to appear first in the hidden order of the cosmos itself'.

1134 See p.254.

https://doi.org/10.1515/9783110678451-008

The Birth of Phanes from the Egg: OR10 – OR18

OR10 is reconstructed by Bernabé and even though there is doubt about the precise wording, the overall content is well attested in the sources on which the reconstruction is based. Damascius and Proclus [OF121F (I), (II), (IV), (V)] inform us that Phanes was born breaking through the egg.

Hermias (**OR11, OR12**) refers to the first principles of the Orphic Theogony which are in this order: Aether, Chaos, the Egg and Phanes which supports the placement of the episode of Phanes' birth from the Egg fabricated by Chronos with Aether at the beginning of the Theogony, and of these verses at the moment of Phanes' birth. OR12 has the same ending as OR11, which supports their being placed proximate to each other.

OR13 refers to the time of Phanes' birth as the present participle (ὀρνυμένοιο) of the verb ὄρνυμι suggests. The reference to 'Aether' and 'misty chasm' were previously mentioned and appear as information being recalled again.

OR14–OR15 are quoted by Proclus in the same context as a description of Phanes whom he identifies as the first god, distinguishing him from the previous 'abstract' entities. His description could only take place after he broke through the egg into the light, which is why these verses were placed here.

Proclus quotes **OR16**, specifying that it refers to Phanes who contains intellectual life, which is why it was considered to be part of his description and placed proximate to **OR17** which notes that Phanes carried the seed of the gods. It was therefore placed at the beginning, before the other gods appear, since they are still inside Phanes/Metis as a seed.

Proclus quotes **OR18** specifying that it refers to Metis and Eros which are epithets of Phanes, as we saw. It was placed here bearing in mind that the pronoun οἷσιν could refer to the gods μάκαρες.

The First Creation of the World by Phanes: OR19 – OR24

Syrianus (**OR19**) confirms that Phanes rules before Night and Ouranos and this is why these verses were placed here in reference to his kingship.[1135] Lactantius (**OR20**) explains why Phanes was the first creator and this is why these verses were considered as part of his creative process. They were placed first because Lactantius says that the immortals' home was heaven, which would presumably

---

1135 These verses could also refer to the episode of Zeus' swallowing but Syrianus does not give any helpful information.

come prior to other celestial bodies and mortal beings. **OR21** was placed after OR20 since it refers to the home of the mortals and is thematically similar to OR20 describing the home of the immortals.

OR22 seems to further specify the function of the Sun which must have already been mentioned and this is why it was placed after OR21 which describes the location of the Sun and its distance from the earth. **OR23** refers to the creation of a different world (ἄλλην γαῖαν) which suggests that the creation of the earth has already been mentioned; thus OR23 was placed after OR21 which refers to the mortal's home, which can be none other than the earth. Aristocritus (**OR24**) notes that these verses, which refer to the creation of the cosmos by Phanes, were a part of the 4th rhapsody of Musaeus (as discussed in the introduction of Chapter 6).

The Second and Third Ruler: Night and Ouranos: OR25 – OR34

OR25 was placed here because it refers to the Night, and so it bridges the previous episode with the episode where Night takes the kingship from Phanes. The phrase τοὶ δ' ἄλλοι ἅπαντες suggests that the world and its beings have already been created by Phanes; so these verses should be placed after Phanes' creation.

Proclus **(OR26)** refers to the succession of rulers and says that Phanes passes the sceptre to Night willingly. He also mentions that Night gives the sovereignty of the universe willingly to Ouranos, but Cronus 'who has been allotted the fourth regal order' takes the sceptre from Ouranos and gives it to Zeus in a violent way. Proclus says that the last ruler was Dionysos and in another fragment that Dionysos succeeds Zeus: the total number of rulers, thus, is six [OF98T(III)]. In the same passage Proclus notes that Phanes fabricated the sceptre (πρῶτος γὰρ ὁ Φάνης κατασκευάζει τὸ σκῆπτρον = 'For first of all Phanes fabricated the sceptre'). The verses **(OR26, OR27)** referring to Night taking the kingship from Phanes were therefore placed right after Phanes' kingship and creation.

Hermias **(OR28)** notes that this verse refers to Night; it was placed here in the light of another Orphic fragment cited by Hermias (OF113F), where he notes that Phanes sits in Night's innermost sanctuary where she prophesies. This suggests that she acquired her prophetic powers during Phanes' reign. We know that she already had prophetic powers when she gives an oracle to Zeus later on. **OR29** was placed here considering the fragment in Hermias mentioned above which refers to Night's innermost shrine as Phanes' place of abode. The verse also signifies the end of the creative procedure by Phanes which will be continued by Night after she copulates with Phanes (OR30).

OR30 links to the previous verses through the word ἑῆς...παιδός since the verse refers to a child of Phanes and we know from Proclus that this child was Night. They also link to the following ones (OR31) that begin with Ἡ δὲ πάλιν since the word Ἡ refers to Night as is noted by Hermias in OR31. Since at this point of the Theogony the subject is Night, it is now that any of her off-spring should be mentioned.

OR33 was placed here because the second reign of Ouranos must have been stated in the theogony, and this is the only available quotation where it is mentioned. Proclus [(**OR32**= OF113 (Kern)] notes that this verse by Orpheus refers to Ouranos and it was placed here as a definition of his nature during his reign.

OR34 refers to the offspring of Gaia and Ouranos who was the third and current ruler and this is why it was placed here. Several fragments also attest that the first marriage in the Theogony was between Gaia and Ouranos (OF175F). **OR35** was placed here because it gives another name for the offspring of Gaia and Ouranos. It comes from *Etymologicum Magnum* and we are also informed that these verses are from the 8th rhapsody of the *hieros logos* [οὕτως Ὀρφεὺς ἐν τῷ ὀγδόῳ τοῦ ἱεροῦ λόγου].[1136] **OF36** was placed here since Proclus informs us that the second dyad was Okeanos and Tethys. In the same passage he notes that there was not a marriage between Phanes and Night who were only 'intelligibly united to each other'. That is why, as he notes, the first marriage was that of Gaia and Ouranos and the second that of Okeanos and Tethys.

Ouranos' Castration by Cronos: OR37 – OR44

OR37 and **OR38** were paired together because both refer to Night's capacity as a nurse. They were placed here since they single out Kronos from all the Titans who were mentioned in the previous verses. **OR39** was combined with **OR40** and **OR41** because they all refer to the Titans' evil nature and how it led them to conspire against their father and to their punishment from Ouranos.[1137] **OR40** is quoted by Proclus in reference to the Titanomachy between the Olympians and the Titans. The reference to the Titans' lawless heart ὑπέρβιον ἦτορ ἔχοντες corresponds to ἀμείλικτον ἦτορ ἔχοντες of **OR41** forming perhaps a cyclic composition.

After the negative description of the Titan's nature in OR40 which will lead them to attack their father, there was presumably a punishment: this is where

---

1136 *Etym. Magn.* 231.21.
1137 In OR41 I have accepted Bernabé's supplement.

OR41 comes. Proclus specifies in **OR41** that it is Ouranos who punished the Titans for their lawless nature. Also, **OR41, OR42** and **OR34** (referring to the Titans' birth) are quoted by Proclus in the same context: this might indicate that there was proximity between them in the OR or that they belong to the same episode of the Titans' birth. Proclus quotes **OR42** saying that Okeanos did not follow the other Titans at their attack against Ouranos, and at the same time married Tethys, an episode for which we do not seem to have any verses surviving. In **OR43** the Cronian epithet ἀγκυλομήτης is taken from OF181F) and it was a usual epithet of his. The paraphrase by Proclus referring to the castration episode was inserted to link Ouranos' castration mentioned further on with the entity that did it. The verse from OF251F is quoted by Proclus as an oracle from Night. It foreshadows Zeus' birth and Cronos' castration forming a thematic group with the previous verses, while it is consistent with the characterisation of Night as a prophet. Finally, Proclus **(OR44)** specifies that it is Ouranos' genitals that these verses refer to.

Zeus becomes the Fifth Ruler: OR45 – OR58

As already mentioned the succession of rulers is known from other sources and so we know that Kronos succeeded Ouranos. **OR45** was placed here since after Ouranos' castration there must have been some verses announcing Kronos' reign as happens with every ruler. **OR46** is placed here because it relates to Zeus' birth from Rhea and Kronos as Proclus notes. Proclus quotes **OR46** and **OR47** in the same context, which is why **OR47** was placed here since he also notes that Demeter was the first to distribute these types of nourishment among the gods, which suggests that this took place early in the Theogony. What is more the honey (ἀγλαὰ ἔργα μελισσάων ἐριβόμβων) needs to be in existence when Zeus uses it to drunken Kronos in this episode; the fact that the same phrase is used in **OR53** (ἔργοισιν μεθύοντα μελισσάων ἐριβόμβων) perhaps constitutes a cyclic composition, echoing **OR47**, which supports the placement of these verses here.

OR48 refers to the race of men under Kronian Zeus as also asserted by Proclus, and they should be placed here at the time when Kronos was still a ruler and before his succession by Zeus with the help of Rhea. **OR49**, is a paraphrase from Damascius who refers to the Orphic Kronos, and it bridges the gap between the birth of Zeus and Rhea's trick to save Zeus from Kronos quoted in **OR50** and **OR51**. In **OR50** we are informed about the plot of Rhea to save Zeus in a scholium on Lycophron who claims that this episode is mentioned in Hesiod's *Theogony* who took it from Orpheus.[1138] Hermias **(OR50)** notes that Ide and Adrasteia protected Zeus who was hidden in Night's cave where he was also nurtured by Amaltheia.

Proclus quotes **OR51** in relation to Kronos and Rhea and this episode and this is why it was placed here. **OR52** quoted by Clement refers to Kronos; it should be placed here since it relates to the plan of deceiving Kronos and the action taken by Zeus as foreshadowed by Night's oracle in **OR53**. Porphyry **(OR53)** notes that Kronos was asleep when Zeus bound him and that these verses were Night's oracle to Zeus. Proclus **(OR54)** refers to the binding of Kronos by Zeus and says that Zeus said this to Kronos 'after the bonds' (Procl. *in Pl. Ti.* I.207.1). Proclus, also quotes this verse elsewhere and says that Zeus called his father *daemon* (Procl. *in Pl. Cra.* 391a, 27.21) and this is why this verse was placed here since it belongs to this episode. However, it is possible that the word daimon refers to Phanes/Metis and not Kronos. It seems at this point that Zeus is seeking guidance for his reign.

Proclus **(OR55)** records that Zeus addresses his questions to Night *before* the creation of all things. So we know that this is where these verses should be placed: immediately after Zeus acquires the power and right before the creative procedure. Next, Proclus goes on to quote Night's answer. Her answer is quoted by Proclus in **OR56** (OF237F) at greater length and this is the quotation used here. Proclus **(OR57)** says that 'Zeus establishes the golden chain on the advice of Night' and this is why these verses were considered part of Night's oracle to Zeus. Syrianus **(OR58)** refers to the successive rulers according to the theologist Orpheus, and to the sceptre. He records that this verse was a part of Night's oracles about Zeus and this is why it was placed here where Night is addressing Zeus giving him her advice on how to establish his reign.

Zeus swallows Phanes and creates the world anew: OR59 – OR63

OR59 is a combination of Procl. in Pl. *Tim* 29a, I.324.14–I.325.3 and I.313.10–16. These verses were placed here because they fulfil Night's advice for everything to become one unto Zeus, through the swallowing of Phanes and the world created by him. Proclus **(OR60)** quotes these verses right after **OR59**. It is necessary for them to be placed here in order to denote that Zeus held everything inside him but brought them out to light again, thus creating the universe anew. The reference to 'these' could be to all the things described above, reinforcing the placement of these verses here. Also, we find the same lines in OF243F **(OR61)** as part

---

1138 λιγυηχές suggested by Wilamowitz.

of a long Orphic quotation by Porphyry which gives credibility to their being part of the Theogony.

In Kern's edition, OF168 (**OR61**) is one of the most important ones including an abundance of quotations of Orpheus' praise to Zeus for being the One and only Creator from whom everything comes. We have quotations from Proclus going back to Porphyry and even Plutarch of the same and almost identical verses, which gives strong credibility to a substantially unchanged survival of these particular verses. The placing of OR61 here is reinforced by Porphyry quoting them after saying that Zeus created all things after containing the world in himself, which has just happened in the previous verses. Also, Proclus (Procl. *in Pl. Tim.* 28c, I.313.17) quotes these verses, saying that Zeus achieved this after acting according to Night's oracles which suggests that they should be placed after Night's oracle in OR56–OR58.

OR62 combines quotations from Aristocritus and Proclus. Aristocritus' quotation [OF245V] continues the quotation of OF243F from Porphyry, meaning that the verses 'ἓν κράτος, εἷς δαίμον...σώματι κεῖται' are included in the Aristocritus quotation while he continues the quotation differently than Porphyry. The Porphyry quotation has therefore been included up to the point that is also found in Aristocritus and then continued with the rest of Aristocritus' quotation. The verse ὅσσα τ' ἔην γεγαῶτα... ἔμελλεν is taken from Proclus' quotation, which includes part of the Aristocritus' quotation. These verses correspond to the narrative and complete the image of almighty Zeus watching and reigning over his creation by describing everything that dwells under his eyes and how nothing can escape his attention. In **OR63** Proclus says that Justice follows Zeus 'now reigning over, and beginning to arrange and adorn the universe' which suggests that this verse should be placed at the time that Zeus reigned and created the universe.

The Era of Zeus and the generation of the Gods: OR64 – OR77

Proclus (**OR64**) discusses how Orpheus celebrated the demiurgic cause of Phanes and Zeus and how 'all the – creative – causes participate in each other and are in each other' since he calls Zeus Metis, Dionysos, Phanes and Erikepaios. It seemed appropriate then to place it here, after the swallowing of Phanes by Zeus where they become one, and before the creative process begins. At this point of the theogony, I have placed all the fragments referring to the birth of specific gods from Zeus. However, even though the episode of the gods' generation by Zeus should be placed here, the order of the gods' generation could be different since we do not have enough contextual evidence to be confident about the order.

I suggest that Athena was one of the first entities born based on the context in Proclus (**OR65**) who says that she was one of the first 'intellectual entities subsisting in the Demiurgus' (Creator = Zeus) (Procl. *In Ti.* 24d, I.166). Proclus also records that Zeus gave birth to Athena from his head. **OR66** is quoted in the same context as the previous ones where Proclus explains Athena's various names and role in aiding Zeus in the creative process. OF264F is quoted after Proclus says: 'Hence the theologist Orpheus says, that the father produced her: <quotation>' and so we know that this verse must have belonged to the episode of Athena's birth. **OR67** was placed here on the grounds that it has the same meaning as the previous one, of Athena being the helper of Zeus. **OR68** refers to Athena as the leader of the Kouretes and the most appropriate place for it is here where her birth and characteristics are described. **OR69** specifies why the Kouretes belong in the order of Athena; it complements and derives from the previous one (OR68) and this is why it was placed here.

Hermias **(OR70)** records that Orpheus says in his Theology that the Cyclops were called τεκτονόχειρας because they were one of the first principles and causes of forms. They also taught Hephaestus and Athena about the variety of the forms. This verse was placed here, therefore, because the Cyclops belonged to the first principles but the reference to Athena and Hephaestus implies that their birth has already been described and in terms of narrative it would not make sense to refer to deities who have not been born yet. Proclus **(OR71)** refers to the Cyclopes as being the instructors of Athena and Hephaestus and identifies weaving as a special skill of Athena and its allegorical meaning of weaving the order in cosmos. He then quotes these verses which seem to belong to the same episode and this was the reason for placing them here.

Proclus **(OR72)** notes that these verses refer to the second birth of Aphrodite from Zeus. The episode of Aphrodite's birth was placed here in order to leave Demeter's birth at the end of the female goddesses' birth because this way there is a better transition to the episode of the abduction of Demeter's daughter, Kore.

Aphrodite's birth was placed before Artemis', on the grounds that she appears to have a significant role in Orphism since not only is this the second birth of Aphrodite but she is also mentioned in the DP as a generative force. Both quotations (OF257F, OF317F) of **OR73** refer to Artemis and have the same narrative and theme of Artemis' virginity and this is why they were placed together. Proclus (OR73) notes that Artemis, Kore and Hecate are closely related in a context where he explains the gods' names.

OR74 (OF284F) where Persephone is coupled with Apollo was placed first because the rest of the verses refer to Persephone's ravishment by Hades which should take place at the end, since after it took place Persephone became Hades' wife in the Underworld. Proclus' paraphrase informs us that these words were addressed by Demeter to Persephone when she handed over to her the kingdom. These verses are puzzling since in no other source is it attested that Kore took the kingship from Demeter, who in fact did not have the kingship either. Proclus' discussion is also not very helpful. It is possible that Demeter is referring to the kingship of nature/life, and considering Apollo's role in Orphism as described in this book, this might have been an episode where Apollo as the god of life (also associated with the element of fire), was contrasted with the following abduction of Persephone and the dominion of death/Hades. I have placed these verses here since the rest of the verses available about Persephone refer to her ravishment by Hades which should take place at the end, since after it took place Persephone became Hades' wife in the Underworld. The previous verses (**OR73**) might also essentially refer to Kore, since Artemis, Hecate and Kore are equated by Proclus.

Apart from Tzetzes (**OR75**) we have many references to Kore weaving an unfinished web when being abducted in Porphyry (OF286F: *De Antro Nym.* 14, p.66.13), Proclus (OF286F: Procl. *in Pl. Ti.* 41b-c, III.223.3 and I.134.26; OF290F: Procl. *in Pl. R.* II.62.9), and Damascius (*De Princ.* 339). **OR75** was placed here because it provides a narrative complement to the following verses which also refer to the unfinished web (ἱστόν) and create the episode of Persephone's kidnapping. Proclus' paraphrase (**OR76**) was placed here as a better transition to the part of the theogony where Persephone becomes Hades' wife, through the episode of her ravishment by him. The quoted verse in **OR77** is ἐννέα... ἀνθεσιουργοὺς (OF293F), while Proclus' paraphrase (OF292F) makes the narrative clearer by explaining that Persephone bore with Hades the Eumenides. In this fragment too, Proclus equates Artemis and Athena to Persephone.

Dionysos takes the Kingship and is then Dismembered by the Titans: OR78 – OR87

Proclus (**OR78**) informs us that Zeus established Dionysos as the king of the gods. Through Proclus' context and this verse we know that Zeus gave the kingship to Dionysos when he was still an infant, so this episode should take place soon after Dionysos' birth for which, however, we do not have any verses. According to Proclus, Zeus announces to all the gods that Dionysos is now their king, which creates the image of all the gods being gathered together with Zeus giving them a speech announcing Dionysos' kingship. **OR79** (OF299F: κλῦτε...τίθημι) is the announcement of Dionysos' kingship by Zeus when he transfers to him the sceptre as Proclus' paraphrase notes, and so it was placed here. The quoted verse from

OF166F is a poetic fragment of Musaeus and was inserted after Proclus' paraphrase because in the same context he says that according to Orpheus these were the dimensions of Zeus' sceptre (OF166F: Procl. *in Pl. Cra.* 396b, 53.26), which are the same dimensions in Musaeus' fragment.

Proclus (**OR80**) refers to the gods' help in perfecting the fabrication of the world, something in which Dionysos has a special role. It is logical that Zeus gave the kingship to Dionysos in order to fulfil this role and this point of the *Rhapsodies* would be the appropriate time for him to make his contribution.

Since **OR81** comes from Nonnus' *Dionysiaca* it is not suggested that it was an actual part of the theogony, but that the story which it narrates was. Even though Nonnus is not quoting from Orpheus, he might have had in mind the narrative of the OR and based on the first line –'But he did not hold the throne of Zeus for long…'– we can suggest that it is at this point of the Theogony that Dionysos' dismemberment takes place. The verse from OF303F was placed here because Proclus records that Dionysos was often called 'Wine', and the person who would feel jealous of him would have to be Hera. Under OF210 in Kern there are many passages referring to the Zagreus myth going back to Diodorus (1st B.C., V.75.4) and Plutarch (1st A.D.).

OR82: Proclus quotes these verses in the same context noting that according to the theologian, the Titans divided Dionysos into seven parts but that the heart was preserved by Athena. Several passages in OF210 (Kern) mention that Dionysos' heart was preserved by Athena [See also OF314F–OF316F]. Olympiodorus' paraphrase **(OR83)** records that it was Apollo who gathered Dionysos' pieces after his dismemberment. In OF322F(IV) we are informed by Proclus that he acted according to Zeus' wishes. Proclus (**OR84**) attests that Dionysos was often called by the theologians Οἶνος (Wine) and then quotes three verses from Orpheus as an example. This particular verse was placed here because it fits with Zeus' order to Apollo to bring him the scattered parts of Dionysos which is known to us from other fragments. For a lengthy discussion of this myth and OR82–OR86 see Chapter 3.

Proclus' paraphrase (**OR85**) (OF329F) was placed here because he records that Ipta received Dionysos 'when he was brought forth from Zeus' and proceeded into her from his thigh', while we also find the word κραδιαῖος which means 'from the heart' or 'of the heart'. The quoted verse (OF296F) is quoted in the same passage and this is why it was placed here. **OR86** is a paraphrase by Olympiodorus: for a discussion about the creation of the human race from the Titans' smoke after being struck by Zeus' thunderbolt see Chapter 3. **OR87** includes verses which belong to Hesiod's *Theogony*, but Proclus quotes them after saying that the other Titans were punished after Dionysos' dismemberment, which is not a part of the

Hesiodic Theogony. We can therefore accept that the reference to Atlas was a part of the *Rhapsodies*.

A separate didactic *hieros logos* about the Soul and the Afterlife?: OR88 – OR97

The remaining fragments used for the reconstruction of the OR all refer to the 'condition' of the human race, the soul and the cycle of reincarnation, thus constituting a thematic group which should be placed at the end and after the creation of cosmos and the gods since humans are the 'least perfect' beings of the world.

OR88 gives an introduction to the double topography of the netherworld and the connection of the soul's fate to living a just life. It was placed at the beginning of this section since it seems to give new information about where the soul goes after death. It also relates to the previous section's ending which refers to the creation of the mortal race from the Titans (OR86). **OR89–OR90** forms a thematic group referring to the nature of the soul and the reincarnation process. I have placed the fragments referring to the soul (OF436F, OF422F, OF426F, OF425F and OF437F) first because it is more probable that the general information about the soul was given first, followed by the more specific information about what exactly happens to it after we die. The mentioning of facts such as 'the immortal souls are brought down by Kyllenian Hermes' **(OR91)** presupposes that the information about the soul's immortality has already been given.

OR89, OR90 and **OR91** were grouped together because they refer to the cycle of rebirth and reincarnation. **OR89** was placed first because the other two fragments mention more specific information on the cycle of rebirth. **OR91** links the previous information about the soul, to the following information about the cycle of rebirth, through referring to what happens to the soul after humans and animals decease. There is also a connection with the previous verses from OR89, through the idea of soul dwelling in the air, making it thus more probable that they belonged to the same thematic episode of the theogony and should be placed proximate to each other.

OR92 was placed after the general description of the soul in relation to the cycle of reincarnations as well as the reasons that lead to it – namely unjust deeds (OR88) – because it describes reincarnation in a more specific way. Moreover, when Proclus quotes these verses, he notes that Orpheus says these things after the retribution of the Titans and the creation of the human race from them. This supports the placement of this exegetical section after the myth of Dionysos' dismemberment (OR81–86). **OR93** specifies that everyone must take part in the cycle of rebirth and links the earlier general information about reincarnation (OR92) to the way through which someone can escape the endless cycle of rebirths (OR94,OR95). **OR95** is placed here because it refers to a deliverance from 'grievous toil and endless agony', something that connects to the previous idea of getting free from the cycle of rebirths and the previous verse (**OR94**) that refers to a 'respite from the misery'.

Olympiodorus' context (**OR96**) refers to the dyadic nature of humans in relation to the Titans and Dionysos. The passage has an eschatological context referring to the afterlife and its punishments and to how the 'real Bacchoi' have a happy afterlife, while he refers to Dionysos as the guardian and ruler of death. These ideas can be found in the previous verses of OR95 and this is why this verse was placed here.

OR97 is relevant to the Orphic ideas of living a life as far from evil as possible and it was considered that they would be part of a didactic exegesis such as this section. Also, the verse οὔτ'ἀπόθεν μάλ'ἀποτρέψαι κακότητος has a parallel to the previous verse from OR94 κύκλου τ'ἂν λῆξαι καὶ ἀναπνεῦσαι κακότητος.

Bibiliography

Adam, J. (ed.) (1963). *The Republic of Plato: Edited with Critical Notes, Commentary and Appendices*, Vol. II. Cambridge: Cambridge University Press.
Alderink, L.J. (1981). *Creation and Salvation in ancient Orphism*. California: American Philological Association.
Alonge, M. (2005). 'The Palaikastro Hymn and the modern myth of the Cretan Zeus'. Version 1.0. December. *Princeton/Stanford Working Papers in Classics*.
Astour, M.C. (1985). 'Ancient Greek Civilization in Southern Italy', in: *Journal of Aesthetic Education* 19 (1), Special Issue: Paestum and Classical Culture, Past and Present, 23–37.
Athanassakis, A.N. (1977). *The Orphic Hymns: Text, translation and notes*. Missoula, Montana: Scholars Press.
Avagianou, A.A. (2002). 'Physiology and Mysticism at Pherai. The Funerary Epigram for Lykophron', in: *Kernos* 15, 75–89.
Baltussen, H. (2007). 'Playing the Pythagorean: Ion's *Triagmos*', in: Jennings, V. and Katsaros, A. (eds.). *The world of Ion of Chios*. Leiden: Brill, 295–318.
Beaumont, L. et al. (1999). 'New Work at Kato Phana, Chios: The Kato Phana Archaeological Project Preliminary Report for 1997 and 1998', in: *The Annual of the British School at Athens*, Vol. 94, 265–287.
Bernabé, A. (2014). 'On the Rites Described and Commented Upon in the Derveni Papyrus, Columns I–VI', in: Papadopoulou, I. and Muellner, L. (eds.) *Poetry as Initiation: The Center for Hellenic Studies Symposium on the Derveni Papyrus*. Hellenic Studies Series 63. Washington, DC./Cambridge, MA: Harvard University Press, 19–53.
Bernabé, A. (2013). 'The Commentary of the Derveni Papyrus: The Last of Pre-Socratic Cosmogonies', in: *Littera Antiqua* 7, 4–31.
Bernabé, A. (2010). 'The Derveni Papyrus: Problems of Edition, Problems of Interpretation', in: Gagos, T. (ed.). *Proceedings of the Twenty-Fifth International Congress of Papyrology, Ann Arbor 2007* American Studies in Papyrology, 79–86.
Bernabé, A. (2009). 'Imago Inferorum Orphica', in: Casadio, G. and Johnston, P.A. (eds.) *Mystic cults in magna graecia*. Austin: University of Texas Press, 95–130.
Bernabé, A. (2007). 'The Derveni Theogony: Many Questions and Some Answers', in: *Harvard Studies in Classical Philology* 103, 99–133.
Bernabé, A. (2006). Myths of the Underworld Journey: Plato, Aristophanes, and the 'Orphic' Gold Tablets, by R.G. Edmonds III. Reviewed in: *Aestimatio* 3, 1–13.
Bernabé, A. (ed.) (2005a). *Orphicorum et Orphicis similium testimonia et fragmenta*. Poetae Epici Graeci. Pars II. Fasc. 2. Bibliotheca Teubneriana. München/Leipzig: K.G. Saur.
Bernabé, A. (2005b). '¿Qué se puede hacer con un pájaro? ὀρνίθειον en el papiro de Derveni', in: Alvar Ezquerra, A. and González Castro, J.F. (eds.). *Actas del XI Congreso Español de Estudios Clásicos*. Madrid: Sociedad Española de Estudios Clásicos, 287–297.
Bernabé, A. (ed.) (2004a). *Orphicorum et Orphicis similium testimonia et fragmenta*. Poetae Epici Graeci. Pars II. Fasc. 1. Bibliotheca Teubneriana. München/Leipzig: K.G. Saur.
Bernabé, A. (2004b). *Textos órficos y filosofía presocrática: materiales para una comparación*. Madrid: Editorial Trotta.
Bernabé, A. (2003). 'Autour du mythe orphique sur Dionysos et les Titans. Quelque notes critiques', in: Accorinti D. and Chuvin P. (eds.) *Des Géants à Dionysos. Mélanges de mythologie et de poésie grecques offerts à Francis Vian*. Alessandria: Edizioni dell'Orso, 25–39.

Bernabé A. and Jiménez San Cristóbal, A.I. (2011). 'Are the 'Orphic' gold leaves Orphic?', in: Edmonds III, R.G. (ed.) *The 'Orphic' Gold Tablets and Greek Religion. Further along the Path*. Cambridge: Cambridge University Press, 68–102.

Bernabé, A. and Jiménez San Cristóbal, A.I. (2008). *Instructions for the Netherworld: The Orphic Gold Tablets*. Boston: Brill.

Bernabé, A. and Piano, V. (2016). 'Derveni Papyrus, cols. VII–XXVI', *IMouseion Project*. Center for Hellenic Studies. [Accessed 10 January 2013] http://dp.chs.harvard.edu/index.php?col=7&ed=Bac

Bernabé, A., Casadesús, F. and Santamaría, M.A. (eds.) (2010). *Orfeo y l'Orfismo: nuevas perspectivas*. Alicante: Biblioteca Virtual Miguel de Cervantes.

Betegh, G. (2011). 'The «Great Tablet» from Thurii (OF 492)', in: Herrero de Jáuregui, M. *et al.* (eds.). *Tracing Orpheus. Studies of Orphic Fragments*. Berlin: De Gruyter, 219–25.

Betegh, G. (2007). 'The Derveni Papyrus and Early Stoicism', in: *Rhizai* IV.1, 133–152.

Betegh, G. (2004). *The Derveni Papyrus: Cosmology, Theology and Interpretation*. Cambridge: Cambridge University Press.

Betz, H. (2011). "A child of Earth am I and of starry Heaven': Concerning the anthropology of the Orphic gold tablets', in: Edmonds III, R.G. (ed.). *The 'Orphic' Gold Tablets and Greek Religion. Further along the Path*. Cambridge: Cambridge University Press, 102–109.

Betz, H. (1992). *The Greek Magical Papyri in translation: Including the Demotic Spells*, (2nd ed). Chicago: The University of Chicago Press.

Bond, G.W. (ed.) (1963). *Euripides' Hypsipyle*. Oxford: Oxford University Press.

Bossi, B. (2011). 'Herakleitos B 32 Revisited in the Light of the Derveni Papyrus', in: *Anales del Seminario de Historia de la Filosofía*, 28, 9–22.

Boutsikas, E. and Ruggles, C. (2011). 'Temples, Stars, and Ritual Landscapes: The Potential for Archaeoastronomy in Ancient Greece'. *American Journal of Archaeology* 115(1), 60–66.

Bowden, H. (2015). 'Nameless Gods: Mystery Cults, Myths, Ritual and Greek Polis Religion', in: *Kodai, Journal of Ancient History* 16, 31–42.

Bowden, H. (2013). 'Seeking Certainty and Claiming Authority: The Consultation of Greek Oracles from the Classical to the Roman Imperial Periods', in: Rosenberger, V. (ed.) *Divination in the Ancient World: Religious Options and the Individual. Potsdamer Altertumswissenschaftlichen Beiträge* 46. Stuttgart: Franz Steiner Verlag, 41–60.

Bowden, H. (2008). 'Before Superstition and After: Theophrastus and Plutarch on Deisidaimonia', in: *Past and Present* 199 (3), 56–71.

Braun, R.E. (ed.) (1992). *Rhesos*. Oxford: Oxford University Press.

Bremmer, J.N. (2015). 'Preface: The Materiality of Magic', in: Boschung D. and Bremmer, J.N. (ed.). *The Materiality of Magic*. Paderborn: Wilhelm Fink, 7–20.

Bremmer, J.N. (2014). *Initiation into the Mysteries of the Ancient World*. Göttingen: Hubert & Co. GmbH & Co. KG.

Bremmer, J.N. (2013). 'Divinities in the Orphic Gold Leaves: Euklês, Eubouleus, Brimo, Kybele, Kore and Persephone', in: *Zeitschrift für Papyrologie und Epigraphik* 187, 35–48.

Bremmer, J.N. (2011). 'The Place of Performance of Orphic Poetry (OF1)', in: Herrero de Jáuregui, M. *et al.* (eds.). *Tracing Orpheus. Studies of Orphic Fragments*. Berlin: De Gruyter, 1–6.

Bremmer, J.N. (2010). 'From holy books to holy bible: an itinerary from ancient Greece to modern Islam via second temple Judaism and early Christianity', in: Popović, M. (ed.). *Authoritative Scriptures in Ancient Judaism*. Netherlands: Brill, 327–360.

Brisson, L. (2009). 'Zeus did not Commit Incest with his Mother. An Interpretation of Column XXVI of the Derveni Papyrus', tr. Chase M, in: *Zeitschrift für Papyrologie und Epigraphik*, 168, 27–39.

Brisson, L. (2003). 'Sky, Sex and Sun. The Meanings of αἰδοῖος/αἰδοῖον in the Derveni Papyrus', in: *Zeitschrift für Papyrologie und Epigraphik*, 144, 19–29.

Brown, A.S. (1998). 'From the Golden Age to the Isles of the Blest', in: *Mnemosyne*, Fourth Series, 51 (4), 385–410.

Burkert, W. (1997). 'Star Wars or One Stable World? A Problem of Presocratic Cosmogony (PDerv. Col. XXV)', in: Laks, A. and Most, G.W. (eds.). *Studies on the Derveni papyrus*. Oxford: Clarendon Press, 167–174.

Burkert, W. (1985). *Greek religion*, tr. Raffan, J. Cambridge, Mass.: Harvard University Press.

Burkert, W. (1972). *Lore and Science in Ancient Pythagoreanism*. Harvard: Harvard University Press.

Calame, C. (2011). 'Funerary gold lamellae and Orphic papyrus commentaries: Same use, different purpose', in: Edmonds III, R.G. (ed.). *The 'Orphic' Gold Tablets and Greek Religion. Further along the Path*. Cambridge: Cambridge University Press, 203–219.

Calvo-Martínez, J.L. (2011). 'Col. VI of the Derveni Papyrus and the Ritual Presence of Poultry', in: Herrero de Jáuregui, M. *et al.* (eds.). *Tracing Orpheus: Studies of Orphic Fragments in honour of Alberto Bernabé*. Berlin: De Gruyter, 371–375.

Campbell, D.A. (ed. and tr.). (1988). Anacreon. *Greek Lyric, Volume II: Anacreon, Anacreontea, Choral Lyric from Olympus to Alcman*. Cambridge, MA: Harvard University Press.

Carpenter, T.H. (2000). 'Images and Beliefs: Thoughts on the Derveni Krater', in: Tsetskhladze, G.R. *et al.* (eds.), *Periplous: papers on classical art and archaeology presented to Sir John Boardman*. London: Thames & Hudson, 51–59.

Carpenter, T.H. and Faraone, C.A. (eds.). (1993). *Masks of Dionysus*. Ithaca: Cornell University Press.

Carrington, P. (1977). 'The Heroic Age of Phrygia in Ancient Literature and Art', in: *Anatolian Studies* 27, 117–126.

Casadesús, F. (2010). 'Similitudes entre el Papiro de Derveni y los primeros filósofos estoicos', in: Bernabé, A., Casadesús, F., Santamaría (eds.). *Orfeo y el orfismo. Nuevas perspectivas*. Alicante: Biblioteca Virtual Miguel de Cervantes, 192–239.

Casadesús, F. (1995). 'Heráclito y el orfismo', in: *Enrahonar: quaderns de filosofia* 23, 103–116.

Caskey, M.E. (1986). *Keos II, The temple at Ayia Irini. Part I: The statues*. New York: Town House Press.

Catling, H.W. (1989). 'Archaeology in Greece 1988–89', in: *Archaeological Reports* 35 (1988–1989), 3–116.

Chadwick, J. (1967). *The decipherment of Linear B*. Cambridge: Cambridge University Press.

Clinton, K. (2007). 'The Mysteries of Demeter and Kore', in: Ogden, D. (ed.). *A Companion to Greek Religion*. Oxford: Blackwell, 342–356.

Clinton, K. (2003). 'Stages of Initiation in the Eleusinian and Samothracian Mysteries', in: Cosmopoulos, M.B. (ed.). *Greek Mysteries: The Archaeology and Ritual of Ancient Greek Secret Cults*. London: Routledge, 50–78.

Combellack, F.M. (1948). 'Speakers and Scepters in Homer', in: *The Classical Journal*, 43 (4), 209–217.

Comparetti, D. and Smith, C. (1882). 'The Petelia Gold Tablet', in: *The Journal of Hellenic Studies* 3, 111–118.

Connelly, J.B. (2007). *Portrait of a Priestess: Women and Ritual in Ancient Greece*. Princeton, NJ: Princeton University Press.
Cooper, F.A. (1996). *The Temple of Apollo Bassitas: The architecture*. Princeton, NJ: ASCSA.
Cooper, F.A. (1978). *The Temple of Apollo at Bassai: a preliminary study. Outstanding dissertations in the fine arts*. New York: Garland Publishing.
Cosmopoulos, M.B. (2015). *Bronze Age Eleusis and the Origins of the Eleusinian Mysteries*. Cambridge: Cambridge University Press.
Coxe, C.A. et al. (eds.). (1885). *Ante-Nicene Fathers. Volume 2: Fathers of the Second Century: Hermes, Tatian, Athenagoras, Theophilus, and Clement of Alexandria (Entire)*. Revised and chronologically arranged with brief prefaces and occasional notes by A. Cleveland Coxe. New York: Christian Literature Publishing Co.
D'Alessio, G.B. (2004). 'Textual Fluctuations and Cosmic Streams: Ocean and Acheloios', in: *The Journal of Hellenic Studies*, 124, 16–37.
Damyanov, M. (2015). 'The Greek Colonists', in: Valeva, J. et al. (eds.). *A Companion to Ancient Thrace*. West Sussex: Wiley, Blackwell, 295–307.
Depew, M. (1997), 'Reading Greek Prayers', in: *Classical Antiquity* 16 (2), 229–258.
Despoini, A. (1996). *Ελληνική Τέχνη. Αρχαία χρυσά κοσμήματα*. Athens.
Diels, H. (ed.). (1897). *Parmenides Lehrgedicht: griechisch und deutsch*. Berlin: G. Reimer.
Diggle, J. (2004). *Theophrastus' Characters edited with introduction, translation and commentary*. Cambridge: Cambridge University Press.
Diggle, J. (1994). *Euripidea: collected essays*. Oxford: Oxford University Press.
Dillon, J.M. and Finamore, J.F. (2002). *Iamblichus, De Anima: Text, Translation, and Commentary*. Society of Biblical Literature.
Dixon, D.W. (2014). 'Reconsidering Euripides' *Bellerophon*'. *Classical Quarterly* 64 (2), 493–506.
Dodds, E.R. (1973). *The Ancient Concept of Progress and Other Essays on Greek Literature and Belief*. Oxford: Oxford University Press.
Dodds, E.R. (ed.) (1960). *Euripides' Bacchae: edited with introduction and commentary* (2nd ed.). Oxford: Clarendon Press.
Dodds, E.R. (1951). *The Greeks and the irrational*. Berkeley: University of California Press.
Dover, K.J. (1986). 'Ion of Chios: his place in the history of Greek literature', in: Boardman, J. and Vaphopoulou-Richardson, C.E. (eds.). *Chios: A Conference at the Homereion in Chios 1984*. Oxford: Oxford University Press, 27–37.
Edmonds III, R.G. (2015). 'When I walked the dark road of Hades: Orphic katabasis and the katabasis of Orpheus', in: *Les Études classiques* 83, 261–279.
Edmonds III, R.G. (2013). *Redefining Ancient Orphism: a study in Greek Religion*. Cambridge: Cambridge University Press.
Edmonds III, R.G. (ed.). (2011a). *The 'Orphic' Gold Tablets and Greek Religion. Further along the Path*. Cambridge: Cambridge University Press.
Edmonds, R.G. III. (2011b). 'Sacred scripture or oracles for the dead? The semiotic situation of the "Orphic" gold tablets', in: Edmonds, R.G. III (ed.) *The 'Orphic' Gold Tablets and Greek Religion: Further along the path*. Cambridge: Cambridge University Press, 257–270.
Edmonds III, R.G. (2009). 'Who are you? Mythic Narrative and Identity in the 'Orphic' Gold Tablets', in: Casadio, G. and Johnston, P.A. (eds.) *Mystic cults in magna graecia*. Austin: University of Texas Press, 73–94.

Edmonds III, R.G. (2008a). *Recycling Laertes' Shroud: More on Orphism and Original Sin*. Center for Hellenic Studies, Harvard University. [Online]. [Accessed 10 May 2016]. Available at: http://nrs.harvard.edu/urn-3:hlnc.essay:EdmondsR.Recycling_Laertes_Shroud.2008.

Edmonds III, R.G. (2008b). 'Extra-ordinary People: *Mystai* and *Magoi*, Magicians and Orphics in the Derveni Papyrus', in: *Classical Philology*, 103, 16–39.

Edmonds, III, R.G. (2004). *Myths of the Underworld Journey: Plato, Aristophanes and the 'Orphic' Gold Tablets*. Cambridge: Cambridge University Press.

Edmonds III, R.G. (1999). 'Tearing Apart the Zagreus Myth: A Few Disparaging Remarks on Orphism and Original Sin', in: *Classical Antiquity*, 18 (1), 35–73.

Edwards, M.J. (2000). 'In Defense of Euthyphro', in: *The American Journal of Philology*, 121 (2), 213–224.

Edwards, M.W. (1991). *The Iliad: A Commentary, Volume V: books 17–20*. Cambridge: Cambridge University Press.

Faraone, C.A. (2011). 'Rushing into milk: New perspectives on the gold tablets', in: Edmonds III, R.G. (ed.). *The 'Orphic' Gold Tablets and Greek Religion. Further along the Path*. Cambridge: Cambridge University Press, 310–331.

Faraone, C.A. (1991). 'The Agonistic Context of Early Greek Binding Spells', in: Faraone, C.A. and Obbink, D. (eds.). *Magika Hiera: Ancient Greek Magic and Religion*. Oxford University Press: Oxford, 3–32.

Ferrari, F. (2014). 'Democritus, Heraclitus, and the Dead Souls: Reconstructing Columns I–VI of the Derveni Papyrus', in: Papadopoulou, I. and Leonard, M. (eds.). *Poetry as Initiation: The Center for Hellenic Studies Symposium on the Derveni Papyrus*. Hellenic Studies Series 63. Washington, DC: Center for Hellenic Studies, 53–66.

Ferrari, F. (2012). 'Derveni Papyrus: Ferrari edition'. *CHS: The iMouseion Project*. [Online]. [Accessed 10 January 2013]. Available at: http://dp.chs.harvard.edu/index.php?col=1&ed=Ftacb

Ferrari, F. (2011a). 'Frustoli erranti. Per una ricostruzione di P.Derveni coll. I–III', in: *Papiri Filosofiki: Miscellanea di Studi, VI*. Florence: L.S. Olschki, 39–54.

Ferrari, F. (2011b). 'Rites without frontiers: Magi and Mystae in the Derveni Papyrus', in: *Zeitschrift für Papyrologie und Epigraphik*, 179, 71–83.

Ferrari, F. (2011c). 'Eraclito e i Persiani nel Papiro di Derveni (col. IV 10–14)', in: Herrero de Jauregui M. *et al.* (eds.). *Tracing Orpheus: Studies of Orphic Fragments: in Honour of Alberto Bernabé*. Berlin: De Gruyter, 363–68.

Ferrari, F. (2011d). 'Oral Bricolage And Ritual Context In The Golden Tablets', in: Lardinois, A.P.M.H. *et al.* (eds.). *Sacred Words: Orality Literacy and Religion*. Orality and Literacy in the Ancient World, Vol.8. Leiden: Brill, 205–216.

Ferrari, F. (2010). 'Democrito a Derveni? PDERV col. 4.1–6', in: *La Parola del passato: Rivista di Studi Antichi, Fascicolo CCCLXXI*. Napoli: Gaetano Macchiaroli Editore, 137–149.

Ferrari, F. and Prauscello, L. (2007). 'Demeter Chthonia and the Mountain Mother in a new Gold Tablet from Magoula Mati', in: *Zeitschrift für Papyrologie und Epigraphik*, 162, 193–202.

Ferella, C. (2018). 'Ζεὺς μοῦνος and Parmenides' *What-is*', in: Santamaría Álvarez, M.A. (eds.). *The Derveni Papyrus: Unearthing Ancient Mysteries*. Leiden, The Netherlands: Brill, 65–74.

Filonik, J. (2013). 'Athenian Impiety Trials: a reappraisal', in: *Dike*, 16, 11–96.

Finkelberg, A. (1986). 'On the Unity of Orphic and Milesian Thought', in: *The Harvard Theological Review*, 79(4), 321–335.

Flower, M.A. (2008). *The Seer in Ancient Greece*. California: University of California Press.

Fontenrose, J. (1978). *The Delphic Oracle: Its Responses and Operations with a Catalogue of Responses.* Berkley, CA: University of California Press.
Ford, A. (1988). 'The Classical Definition of ΡΑΨΩΙΔΙΑ', in: *Classical Philology*, 83 (4), 300–307.
Forrest, W.G. (1963). 'The Inscriptions of South-East Chios, I', in: *The Annual of the British School at Athens*, 58, 53–67.
Fowler, R.T. (2013). *Early Greek Mythography, Vol.2 Commentary.* Oxford: Oxford University Press.
Fowler, R.L. (2000). *Early Greek Mythography, Vol.1 Text and Introduction.* Oxford: Oxford University Press.
Gager, J.G. (2006). 'Curse Tablets and Binding Spells in the Greco-Roman World', in: Wygant, A. (ed.). *The Meanings of Magic from the Bible to Buffalo Bill.* New York: Berghahn Books, 69–87.
Gager, J.G. (ed.) (1992). *Curse Tablets and Bindnig Spells from the Ancient World.* Oxford: Oxford University Press.
Gagné, R. (2013). *Ancestral fault in ancient Greece.* New York: Cambridge University Press.
Gagné, R. (2007). 'Winds and Ancestors: The "Physika" of Orpheus', in: *Harvard Studies in Classical Philology* 103, 1–23.
Gallop, D.A. (1972). 'Hippias: Fragments and Testimonies', in: Rosamond Kent, S. (ed.) *The older sophists: a complete translation by several hands of the fragments in Die Fragmente der Vorsokratiker edited by Diels-Kranz [...] : with a new edition of Antiphon and of Euthydemus.* Columbia SC: University of South Carolina Press, 94–105.
Gantz, T. (1993). *Early Greek Myth: A Guide to Literary and Artistic Sources.* Baltimore/London: The Johns Hopkins University Press.
Gottschalk, H. (1998). *Heraclides of Pontus.* Oxford: Sandpiper.
Graf, F. (2011). 'Text and Ritual: The corpus Eschatologicum of the Orphics', in: Edmonds III, R.G. (ed.). *The 'Orphic' Gold Tablets and Greek Religion. Further along the Path.* Cambridge: Cambridge University Press, 53–67.
Graf, F. (2003). 'Initiation: A concept with a troubled history', in: Dodd, D.B. and Faraone, C.A. (eds.). *Initiation in Ancient Greek Rituals and Narratives. New Critical Perspectives.* London: Routledge, 3–24.
Graf, F. (1993). 'Dionysian and Orphic eschatology: New texts and old questions', in: Carpenter, T.H. and Faraone, C.A. (eds.). *Masks of Dionysus.* Ithaca: Cornell University Press, 239–258.
Graf, F. (1991). 'Prayer in magic and religious ritual', in: Faraone, C.A. and Obbink, D. (eds.) *Magika hiera: Ancient Greek Magic and Religion.* Oxford: Oxford University Press, 188–97.
Graf, F. and Johnston, S.I. (2013). *Ritual Texts for the Afterlife: Orpheus and the Bacchic Gold Tablets.* Second edition. London/New York: Routledge.
Granger, H. (2013). 'Early Natural Theology: The purification of the Divine Nature', in: Sider, D. and Obbink D. (eds.), *Doctrine and Doxography: Studies on Herakleitos and Pythagoras.* Berlin/Boston: Walter de Gruyter, 163–200.
Gregory, A.D. (2016). 'Magic, Curses and Healing', in: Irby, G.L. (ed.). *A Companion to Science, Technology, and Medicine in Ancient Greece and Rome.* Vol.1 Blackwell Companions to the Ancient World. USA: John Wiley & Sons, 418–433.
Grenfell, B.P. and Hunt, A.S. 1907. *The Hibeh Papyri. Part 1.* Oxford: Horace Hart.
Gruppe, O. (1890). *Die rhapsodische Theogonie und ihre Bedeutung innerhalb der orphischen Litteratur.* Leipzig: B.G. Teubner.
Guthrie, W.K.C. (1962). *A History of Greek Philosophy.* Cambridge: Cambridge University Press.

Guthrie, W.K.C. (1952). *Orpheus and Greek Religion: A study of the Orphic movement*. London: Methuen.
Guthrie, W.K.C. (1950). *The Greeks and their Gods*. London: Methuen and Co. Ltd.
Halliwell, S. (2007). 'The Life-and-Death Journey of the Soul: Interpreting the Myth of Er', in: Ferrari, G.R.F. (ed.). *The Cambridge Companion to Plato's Republic*. New York: Cambridge University Press, 445–473.
Harrison, J.E. (1903). *Prolegomena to the Study of Greek Religion*. Cambridge: Cambridge University Press.
Hasluck, F.W. (1910). *Cyzicus: Being Some Account of the History and Antiquities of that City, and of the District Adjacent to it, with the towns of Apollonia ad Rhyndacum, Miletupolis, Hadrianutherae, Priapus, Zeleia, etc.* Cambridge: Cambridge University Press.
Havelock, E.A. (1987). 'The Cosmic Myths of Homer and Hesiod', in: *Oral Tradition*, 2/1, 31–53.
Heath, M. (2007). *Political Comedy in Aristophanes*. Revised edition. [Online] [Accessed 12 December 2014] Available at: http://eprints.whiterose.ac.uk/3588/1/Political_Comedy_
Henderson, J. (ed.) (1959). *Plutarch. Moralia*, Volume VII: *On Love of Wealth. On Compliancy. On Envy and Hate. On Praising Oneself Inoffensively. On the Delays of the Divine Vengeance. On Fate. On the Sign of Socrates. On Exile. Consolation to His Wife*. Translated by De Lacy, P.H. and Einarson, B. Loeb Classical Library 405. Cambridge, MA: Harvard University Press.
Henrichs, A. (2011). 'Dionysos Dismembered and Restored to Life', in: Herrero de Jáuregui M. *et al*. (eds.). *Tracing Orpheus: Studies of Orphic Fragments in Honour of Alberto Bernabé*. Boston: De Gruyter, 61–68.
Henrichs, A. (2003). '"Hieroi Logoi" and "Hierai Bibloi": The (Un)Written Margins of the Sacred in Ancient Greece', in: *Harvard Studies in Classical Philology* 101, 207–266.
Herrero de Jáuregui, M. (2011). 'Dialogues of immortality from the Iliad to the gold leaves', in: Edmonds III, R.G. (ed.) *The 'Orphic' Gold Tablets and Greek Religion. Further along the Path*. Cambridge: Cambridge University Press, 271–291.
Herrero de Jáuregui, M. (2010). *Orphism and Christianity in Late Antiquity*. Volume 7 of Sozomena. Berlin: Walter de Gruyter.
Herrero de Jáuregui M. *et al*. (eds.). (2011). *Tracing Orpheus: Studies of Orphic Fragments in Honour of Alberto Bernabé*. Boston: De Gruyter.
Herrmann, P. *et al*. (eds.) (2006). *Inschriften von Milet, Teil 2. Inschriften n. 1020–1580*. Berlin/New York: Walter de Gruyter.
Hiller von Gärtringen, F. (1903). '444. Chronicum Parium', in: *Inscriptiones Graecae. Vol. XII.5, Inscriptiones Cycladum praeter Tenum*, Berlin, 100–111.
Himmelmann, N. (2000). 'Quotations of Images of Gods and Heroes on Attic Grave Reliefs of the Late Classical Period', in: Tsetskhladze, G.R. *et al*. (eds.). *Periplous: Papers on Classical Art and Archaeology Presented to Sir John Boardman*. London: Thames & Hudson, 136–144.
Hordern, J. (2000). 'Notes on the Orphic Papyrus from Gurôb (P. Gurôb 1; Pack^2 2464)', in: *Zeitschrift für Papyrologie und Epigraphik* 129, 131–140.
Horky, P.S. (2006). 'The imprint of the soul: Psychomatic affection in Plato, Gorgias and the 'Orphic' Gold Tablets', in: *Mouseion, Series III* 6, 383–398.
Huxley, G. (1965). 'Ion of Chios', in: *Greek, Roman and Byzantine Studies*, 6(1), 29–46.
Iliev, J. (2013). 'Oracles of Dionysos in Ancient Thrace', in: *Haemus Journal* 2, 61–70.
Instone, S. (2009). *Greek personal religion: a reader*. Oxford: Aris & Phillips Ltd.
Jakob, D.J. (2010). '*Milk* in the Gold Tablets from Pelinna', in: *Trends in Classics* 2(1), 64–76.

Janko, R. (2016). 'Parmenides in the Derveni Papyrus: New Images for a New Edition', in: *Zeitschrift Für Papyrologie Und Epigraphik* 200, 3–23.
Janko, R. (2010). 'Orphic Cosmogony, Hermeneutic Necessity and the Unity of the Derveni Papyrus', in: Bernabé, A., Casadesús, F. and Santamaría, M.A. (eds.). *Orfeo y el Oprhismo: Nuevas Perspectivas*, Alicante: Biblioteca Virtual Miguel de Cervantes, 178–191.
Janko, R. (2002). 'The Derveni Papyrus: An Interim Text', in: *Zeitschrift Für Papyrologie Und Epigraphik*, 141, 1–62.
Janko, R. (1984). 'Forgetfulness in the golden tablets of memory', in: *Classical Quarterly*, 34, 89–100.
Jiménez San Cristóbal, A.I. (2018). 'Rites and Officiants in Col.xx of the Derveni Papyrus', in: Santamaría Álvarez, M.A. (eds.). *The Derveni Papyrus: Unearthing Ancient Mysteries*. Leiden, The Netherlands: Brill, 129–142.
Jiménez San Cristóbal, A.I. (2015). 'Thiasoi in the underworld', in: *'EX PLURIBUS UNUM', EDIZIONI QUASAR STUDI IN ONORE DI GIULIA SFAMENI GASPARRO a cura di Concetta Giuffré Scibona e Attilio Mastrocinque con la collaborazione di Anna Multari estratto.* Roma: Edizioni Quasar di Severino Tognon srl., 109–120.
Jiménez San Cristóbal, A.I. (2011). 'Do not drink the water of Forgetfulness (OF 474–477)', in: Herrero de Jáuregui, M. et al. (eds.). *Tracing Orpheus. Studies of Orphic Fragments in Honour of Alberto Bernabé*. Berlin/Boston: De Gruyter, 163–170.
Jiménez San Cristóbal, A.I. (2009). 'The meaning of βάκχος and βακχεύειν in Orphic texts', in: Johnston P.A. and Johnston S.I. (eds.), *Mystic Cults of Magna Graecia*. Austin: University of Texas Press, 46–60.
Jones, H.L. (1924). *The Geography of Strabo*. Cambridge, MA: Harvard University Press.
Jones, W.H.S. (tr.) (1935). Pausanias. *Description of Greece, Volume IV: Books 8.22–10 (Arcadia, Boeotia, Phocis and Ozolian Locri)*. Loeb Classical Library 297. Cambridge, MA: Harvard University Press.
Jourdan, F. (2003). *Le papyrus de Derveni*. Paris: Les Belles Letres.
Kapsomenos, S.G. (1964). 'Ο ορφικός πάπυρος της Θεσσαλονίκης', in: *Αρχ. Δελ.* 19, 17–25.
Kearns, E. (1989). 'The Mysteries of Demeter'. (Review of G. Sfameni Gasparro, *Misteri e culti mistici di Demetra*. 1986), in: *Classical Review*, 39, 61–62.
Kennedy, E.C. and Davis, A.R. (1998). *Euripides: Scenes from Rhesus and Helen*. GB: Bristol: Bristol Classical Press.
Kerényi, C. (1996). *Dionysos: Archetypal Image of Indestructible Life*, tr. Manheim, R. Princeton: Princeton University Press.
Kern, O. (1935). Review of W.K.C. Guthrie, *Orpheus and Greek Religion. A study of the Orphic Movement*, in: *Gnomon*, 11(9), 473–78.
Kern, O. (1922). *Orphicorum Fragmenta*. Berolini: Apud Weidmannos.
Kotwick, M.E. (ed.). (2017). *Der Papyrus von Derveni. Griechisch-deutsch*. Berlin/Boston: De Gruyter.
Kotwick, M.E. (2014). 'Reconstructing ancient constructions of the Orphic Theogony: Aristotle, Syrianus and Michael of Ephesus on Orpheus' succession of the first gods', in: *The Classical Quarterly*, 64 (3), 75–90.
Kraay, C. and Hirmer, M. (1966). *Greek Coins*. New York: Thames & Hudson Ltd.
Kuznetsov, V.D. (2016). *Phanagoria*. Moscow.
Lada-Richards, I. (1999). *Initiating Dionysos: Ritual and Theatre in Aristophanes' Frogs*. Oxford: Clarendon Press.

Laks, A. (1997). 'Between Religion and Philosophy: The Function of Allegory in the 'Derveni Papyrus', in: *Phronesis,* 42 (2), 121–142.
Laks, A. and Most, G.W. (ed/tr.). (2016a). *Early Greek Philosophy, Volume VI: Later Ionian and Athenian Thinkers. Part 1.* Loeb Classical Library 529. Cambridge, MA: Harvard University Press.
Laks, A. and Most, G.W. (ed/tr.). (2016b). *Early Greek Philosophy, Volume III: Early Ionian Thinkers, Part 2.* Loeb Classical Library 526. Cambridge, MA: Harvard University Press.
Laks, A. and Most, G.W. (ed.). (1997). *Studies on the Derveni papyrus.* Oxford: Clarendon Press.
Larson, J.L. (2007). *Ancient Greek cults: a guide.* New York: Routledge.
Lattimore, R. (1958). 'Introduction to Rhesus, by Euripides', in: Grene, D. and Lattimore, R. (eds.) *Euripides IV.* Chicago: University of Chicago Press, 1–49.
Levaniouk, O. (2007). 'The Toys of Dionysos', in: *Harvard Studies in Classical Philology,* 103, 165–202.
Lévi-Strauss, C. (1955). 'The Structural Study of Myth', in: *The Journal of American Folklore,* 68 (270), 428–444.
Liapis, V. (2012). *A Commentary on the Rhesus attributed to Euripides.* Oxford: Oxford University Press.
Liapis, V. (2009). '*Rhesus* revisited: the case for a fourth-century Macedonian context', in: *Journal of Hellenic Studies,* 129, 71–88.
Lifshitz, B. (1966). 'Le Culte d'Apollon Delphinios a Olbia', in: *Hermes,* 94 (2), 236–238.
Linforth, I.M. (1941). *The Arts of Orpheus.* Los Angeles: University of California Press.
Lissarrague, F. (2000). 'A Sun-Struck Satyr in Malibu', in: Tsetskhladze, G.R. *et al.* (eds.). *Periplous: Papers on Classical Art and Archaeology Presented to Sir John Boardman.* London: Thames & Hudson, 191–197.
Lloyd-Jones, H. (ed. and tr.) (1996). *Sophocles. Fragments.* London: Harvard University Press.
Lopez-Ruiz, C. (2010). *When the Gods were born: Greek cosmogonies and the Near East.* Harvard: Harvard University Press.
MacGillivray, A. and Sackett, H. (2000). 'The Palaikastro Kouros: The Cretan God as a Young Man', in: MacGillivray, A., Driessen, J.M., and Sackett, H. (eds.). *The Palaikastro Kouros: A Minoan Chryselephantine Statuette and its Aegean Bronze Age Context.* London: British School at Athens Studies 6, 165–169.
Manoledakis, M. (2003). «Νέκυια». Ερμηνευτική Προσέγγιση της Σύνθεσης του Πολύγνωτου στη «Λέσχη των Κνιδίων» στους Δελφούς. Θεσσαλονίκη: Εκδόσεις Κορνήλια Σφακιανάκη.
Martin, G. (2009). *Divine Talk: Religious Argumentation in Demosthenes.* Oxford: Oxford University Press.
Martin, R.P. (2001). 'Rhapsodizing Orpheus', in: *Kernos,* 14, 23–33.
Mayhew, R. (1999). 'Behavior Unbecoming a Woman: Aristotle's Poetics 15 and Euripides' Melanippe the Wise', in: *Ancient Philosophy,* 19 (1), 89–104.
McCabe, Donald F. (1986). *Chios Inscriptions. Texts and List.* The Princeton Project on the Inscriptions of Anatolia. Princeton: The Institute for Advanced Study. Packard Humanities Institute CD #6, 1991. [Online]. [Accessed 21 July 2019] Available at: https://epigraphy.packhum.org/book/488?location=455
Mead, G.R.S. (1965). *Orpheus.* New York: Barnes and Noble.
Megino Rodríguez, C. (2018). 'Daimons in the Derveni Papyrus and in Early Stoicism', in: Santamaría Álvarez, M.A. (eds.). *The Derveni Papyrus: Unearthing Ancient Mysteries.* Leiden, The Netherlands: Brill, 30–44.

Morand, A.F. (2010). 'Etymologies of Divine Names in Orphic texts', in: Bernabé, A. Casadesús, F. and Santamaría, M.A. (eds.). *Orfeo y el Oprhismo: Nuevas Perspectivas*. Alicante: Biblioteca Virtual Miguel de Cervantes, 157–175.

Most, G.W. (ed. and tr.) (2007). Hesiod. *Theogony. Works and Days. Testimonia*. Loeb Classical Library 57. Cambridge, MA: Harvard University Press.

Most, G.W. (1997). 'The Fire Next Time: Cosmology, Allegoresis, and Salvation in the Derveni Papyrus', in: *The Journal of Hellenic Studies*, 117, 117–135.

Muellner, L.C. (1976). *The meaning of Homeric εύχομαι through its formulas*. Innsbruck: Innsbrucker Beitrage Zur Sprachwissenschaft.

Murray, A.T. (1939). *Demosthenes with an English translation*. Cambridge: MA, Harvard University Press.

Murray, G. (ed.) (1913). *The Rhesus of Euripides*. Oxford: Oxford University Press.

Mylonas, G.E. (1961). *Eleusis and the Eleusinian Mysteries*. Princeton, N.J.: Princeton University Press.

Nagy, G. (2011). 'Comments on OF22', in: Herrero de Jáuregui M. *et al.* (eds.). *Tracing Orpheus: Studies of Orphic Fragments in honour of Alberto Bernabé*. Berlin: De Gruyter, 49–53.

Nauck, A. (1889). *Tragicorum Graecorum Fragmenta*. Leipzig: Lipsiae. (Reprinted with Supplementum continens nova fragmenta Euripidea etc., ed. B. Snell, Hildesheim, 1964).

Nilsson, M.P. (1935). 'Early orphism and kindred religious movements', in: *Harvard Theological Review*, 28 (3), 181–230.

Obbink, D. (2011). 'Poetry and Performance in the Orphic gold leaves', in: Edmonds III, R.G. (ed.) *The 'Orphic' Gold Tablets and Greek Religion. Further along the Path*. Cambridge: Cambridge University Press, 291–309.

Obbink, D. (1997). 'Cosmology as Initiation vs. the Critique of Orphic Mysteries', in: Laks, A. and Most, G.W. (eds.), *Studies on the Derveni papyrus*. Oxford: Clarendon Press, 39–54.

Obbink, D. (ed.) (1996). Philodemus. *Philodemus on piety: critical text with commentary*. Oxford: Clarendon Press.

Olson, S.D. (ed. and tr.) (2006). *Athenaeus II: The Learned Banqueters. Books III.106e–V*. Cambridge, MA: Harvard University Press.

Papadopoulou, I. and Muellner, L. (eds.) (2014). *Poetry as Initiation: The Center for Hellenic Studies Symposium on the Derveni Papyrus*. Hellenic Studies Series 63. Washington, DC./Cambridge: Harvard University Press.

Parke, H.W. and Wormell, D.E.W. (1956). *The Delphic Oracle* (Vol. 1). New Jersey: Blackwell.

Parker, R. (2007). *Polytheism and Society at Athens*. Oxford: Oxford University Press.

Parker, R. (1991). 'The 'Hymn to Demeter' and the 'Homeric Hymns', in: *Greece & Rome*, 38 (1), 1–17.

Pavese, C.O. (1998). 'The Rhapsodic Epic Poems as Oral and Independent Poems', in: *Harvard Studies in Classical Philology*, 98, 63–90.

Payne, H.G.G. (1934). 'Archaeology in Greece, 1933–34', in: *The Journal of Hellenic Studies*, 54, Part 2, 185–200.

Pelling, C.B.R. (2011). 'Putting the –viv– into convivial: the Table-Talk and the lives', in: Klotz, F. and Oikonomopoulou, K. (eds.). *The Philosopher's Banquet: Plutarch's Table Talk in the Intellectual Culture of the Roman Empire*. Oxford: Oxford University Press, 207–231.

Piano, V. (2018). 'Some Textual Issues on Column III (ed. Piano)', in: Santamaría Álvarez, M. (eds.). *The Derveni Papyrus: Unearthing Ancient Mysteries*. Leiden, The Netherlands: Brill, 19–29.

Piano, V. (2016). *Il papiro di Derveni tra religione e filosofia*. Studi e testi per il Corpus dei papiri filosofici greci e latini (STCPF), 18. Firenze: Leo S. Olschki.
Pinchard, A. (2012). 'The salvific function of memory in archaic poetry, in the Orphic Gold Tablets and in Plato: what continuity, what break?'. Paper presented at the International Society for Neoplatonic Studies Tenth Annual Conference, June 2012, Cagliari, Sardinia. [Online]. [Accessed 10 January 2017]. Available at: https://www.academia.edu/1621447/The_Salvific_Function_of_Memory_in_the_Archaic_Poetry_in_the_Orphic_Gold_Tablets_and_in_Plato_What_Continuity_What_Break
Powell, J.U. (1925). *Collectanea Alexandrina: Reliquiae minores Poetarum Graecorum Aetatis Ptolemaicae 323–146 A.C. Epicorum, Elegiacorum, Lyricorum, Ethicorum*. Oxford: Clarendon Press.
Propp, V. (1968). *Morphology of the Folktale*, tr. by Scott, L. Austin: University of Texas Press.
Pugliese-Caratelli, G. (2001). *Le lamine d'oro orfiche. Istruzioni per il viaggio oltremondano degli iniziati greci*, Biblioteca Adelphi 419. Milan: Adelphi.
Pugliese-Caratelli, G. (1993). *Le lamine d'oro 'orfiche'. Edizione e comment*. Milan.
Purves, A.C. (2010). *Space and Time in Ancient Greek Narrative*. New York: Cambridge University Press.
Race, W.H. (ed. and tr.) (1997). *Pindar. Nemean Odes. Isthmian Odes. Fragments*. Cambridge: Harvard University Press.
Ranzato, S. (2018). 'The Sage Speaks in Riddles: Notes on Col.VII of the Derveni Papyrus', in: Santamaría Álvarez, M. (eds.). *The Derveni Papyrus: Unearthing Ancient Mysteries*. Leiden, The Netherlands: Brill, 100–107.
Rhodes, P.J. (2009). 'State and Religion in Athenian Inscriptions', in: *Greece and Rome* 56, 1–13.
Riedweg, C. (2011). 'Initiation – death – underworld: Narrative and ritual in the gold leaves', in: Edmonds III, R.G. (ed.) *The 'Orphic' Gold Tablets and Greek Religion. Further along the Path*. Cambridge: Cambridge University Press, 219–257.
Riedweg, C. (1995). 'Orphisches bei Empedokles', in: *Antike und Abendland* 41, 34–59.
Ritchie, W. (1964). *The Authenticity of the Rhesus of Euripides*. Cambridge: Cambridge University Press.
Rohde, E. (1894). *Psyche: Seelencult und Unsterblichkeitsglaube der Griechen*. Freiburg (Breisgau): Mohr.
Roochnik, D. (2004). *Retrieving the Ancients. An Introduction to Greek Philosophy*. Oxford: Blackwell.
Rotstein, Andrea. (2016). *Literary History in the Parian Marble*. Hellenic Studies Series 68. Washington, DC: Center for Hellenic Studies.
Rubel, A. and Vickers, M. (2014). *Fear and Loathing in Ancient Athens: Religion and Politics During the Peloponnesian War*. London: Routledge.
Rusjaeva, A.S. (2003). 'The Main Development of the Western Temenos of Olbia in the Pontos', in: Bilde, P.G. et al. (ed): *The Cauldron of Ariantas. Studies presented to A.N. Ščeglov on the Occasion of his 70th Birthday*. Aarhus: Aarhus University Press, 93–117.
Rutter, N.K. (1973). 'Diodorus and the Foundation of Thurii', in: *Historia: Zeitschrift für Alte Geschichte*, 22 (2), 155–176.
Santamaría Álvarez, M. (eds.). (2018). *The Derveni Papyrus: Unearthing Ancient Mysteries*. Leiden, The Netherlands: Brill.
Schaps, D.M. (2011). *Handbook for Classical Research*. New York: Routledge.
Schibli, H.S. (1989). *Pherekydes of Syros*. Oxford: Clarendon.
Schoene, P. (ed.) (1866–1875). Eusebi. *Chronicorum*. Vol. 1. Berolini: Weidmannos.

Schütrumpf, E. *et al.* (eds.) (2008). *Heraclides of Pontus: Texts and Translation*, Vol.XIV. N.J: Transaction Publishers.
Schwartz, E. (1887). *Scholia in Euripidem, Vol.II*. Berolini: G. Reimer.
Seaford, R. (2006). *Dionysos. Gods and heroes of the ancient world*. London: Routledge Ltd.
Seaford, R. (2005). 'Mystic Light in Aeschylus' *Bassarai*', in: *The Classical Quarterly, New Series*, 55 (2), 602–606.
Seaford, R. (2004). 'An unedited text and the beginnings of 'philosophy': the Derveni papyrus', Review: in: *Classical antiquity. The Derveni Papyrus: Cosmology, Theology and Interpretation by Gabor Betegh*. Cambridge: Cambridge University Press. *Critical Quarterly*, 48 (2), 453.
Seaford, R. (1986). 'Immortality, Salvation, and the Elements', in: *Harvard Studies in Classical Philology*, 90, 1–26.
Segal, C. (1990). 'Dionysus and the gold tablets from Pelinna', in: *Greek, Roman and Byzantine Studies*, 31 (4), 411–419.
Sider, D. (2014). 'The Orphic poem of the Derveni Papyrus', in: Papadopoulou, I. and Muellner, L. (eds.). *Poetry as Initiation: The Center for Hellenic Studies Symposium on the Derveni Papyrus*. Hellenic Studies Series 63. Washington, DC/Cambridge, MA: Harvard University Press, 225–254.
Sider, D. (1997). 'Herakleitos in the Derveni Papyrus', in: Laks, A. and Most, G.W. (eds.). *Studies on the Derveni papyrus*. Oxford: Clarendon Press, 129–148.
Smyly, J.G. (1921). *Greek Papyri from Gurôb*. Dublin.
Sommerstein, A.H. (ed. and tr.) (2009). *Aeschylus. Fragments*. Cambridge: Harvard University Press.
Sourvinou-Inwood, C. (2003). 'Aspects of the Eleusinian Cult', in: Cosmopoulos, M.C. (ed.). *Greek Mysteries: The Archaeology and Ritual of Ancient Greek Secret Cults*. London: Routledge, 25–49.
Sourvinou-Inwood, C. (1996). *"Reading" Greek Death: To the End of the Classical Period*. Oxford: Clarendon Press.
Sourvinou-Inwood, C. (1990). 'What is polis religion?', in: Murray, O. and Price, S. (eds.). *The Greek City from Homer to Alexander*. Oxford: Oxford University Press, 295–322.
Stafford, E.J. (2009). 'Visualizing Creation in Ancient Greece', in: *Religion and the Arts* 13, 419–447.
Stafford, E.J. (2007). 'Personification in Greek Religious Thought and Practice', in: Ogden, D. (ed.). *A Companion to Greek Religion*. Oxford: Blackwell Publishing Ltd, 71–85.
Strauss Clay, J. (2003). *Hesiod's Cosmos*. Cambridge: Cambridge University Press.
Swain, S. (2002). *Dio Chrysostom: Politics, Letters, and Philosophy*. Oxford: Oxford University Press.
Torjussen, S. (2014). 'Milk as symbol of immortality in the 'Orphic' Gold Tablets from Thurii and Pelinna', in: *Nordlit [S.l.]*, 33, 35–46.
Torjussen, S. (2005). 'Phanes and Dionysos in the Derveni Theogony', in: *Symbolae Osloenses*, 80 (1), 7–22.
Tortorelli Ghidini, M. (2006). *Figli della Terra e del Cielo stellato. Testi orfici con traduzione e commento*. Napoli: M. D'Auria.
Tsagarakis, O. (2000). *Studies in the Odyssey 11*. Hermes Einzelschriften 82. Stuttgart: F. Steiner.

Tsantsanoglou, K. (1997). 'The first columns of the Derveni papyrus and their religious significance', in: Laks, A. and Most, G.W. (eds.). *Studies on the Derveni papyrus*. Oxford: Clarendon Press, 93–128.

Tzifopoulos, Y. (2014). 'The Derveni Papyrus and the Bacchic-Orphic Epistomia', in: Papadopoulou, I. and Leonard, M. (eds.). *Poetry as Initiation: The Center for Hellenic Studies Symposium on the Derveni Papyrus*. Hellenic Studies Series 63. Washington, DC: Center for Hellenic Studies, 135–164.

Tzifopoulos, Y. (2011). 'Center, periphery, or peripheral center: A Cretan connection for the gold lamellae of Crete', in: Edmonds III, R.G. (ed.) *The 'Orphic' Gold Tablets and Greek Religion. Further along the Path*. Cambridge: Cambridge University Press, 165–201.

Tzifopoulos, Y. (2010). *Paradise Earned: The Bacchic-Orphic Gold Lamellae of Crete*. Hellenic Studies Series 23. Washington, DC: Center for Hellenic Studies.

Van Hook, L.R. (tr.) (1945). *Isocrates. Evagoras. Helen. Busiris. Plataicus. Concerning the Team of Horses. Trapeziticus. Against Callimachus. Aegineticus. Against Lochites. Against Euthynus. Letters*. Loeb Classical Library 373. Cambridge, MA: Harvard University Press.

Versnel, H.S. (2015). 'Prayer and Curse', in: Eidinow, E. and Kindt, J. (ed.). *The Oxford Handbook of Ancient Greek Religion Oxford Handbooks in Classics and Ancient History*. Oxford: Oxford University Press, 447–461.

Von Arnim, H.F.A. (1964). *Stoicorum veterum fragmenta Vol.1: Chrysippus, the Stoic; Cleanthes, the Stoic*. Stutgardiae In aedibus: B.G. Tuebneri.

West, M.L. (ed. and tr.) (2003). *Greek Epic Fragments from the seventh to the fifth centuries*. Cambridge MA: Harvard University Press.

West, M.L. (1997). 'Hocus-Pocus in East and West. Theogony, Ritual, and the Tradition of Esoteric Commentary', in: Laks, A. and Most, G.W. (eds.). *Studies on the Derveni papyrus*. Oxford: Clarendon Press, 81–92.

West, M.L. (1983). *The Orphic Poems*. New York: Oxford University Press.

Westerink, L.G. (1977). *The Greek Commentaries on Plato's Phaedo, Vol.2 Damascius*. Amsterdam, Oxford: North-Holland Publishing Company.

Westerink, L.G., Combès, J. (1986-1991). *Damascius, Traité des Premiers Principes*, 3 vol., texte établi, traduit et annoté. Paris: Les Belles Lettres.

White Muscarella, O. (2013). *Archaeology, Artifacts and Antiquities of the Ancient Near East: Sites, Cultures, and Proveniences*. Leiden: Brill.

Winiarczyk, M. (2016). *Diagoras of Melos: A contribution to the History of Ancient Atheism*. Volume 350 of Beiträge zur Altertumskunde. Berlin/Boston: Walter de Gruyter.

Wixon, D.W. (2014). 'Reconsidering Euripides' Bellerophon', in: *Classical Quarterly*, 64 (2), 493–506.

Wygant, A. (2006). *The Meanings of Magic: From the Bible to Buffalo*. Vol.11 of Polygons: cultural diversities and intersections. New York/Oxford: Berghahn Books.

Yunis, H. (2005). *Demosthenes, Speeches 18 and 19*. Austin: University of Texas Press.

Zuntz, G. (1971). *Persephone: Three essays on religion and thought in Magna Graecia*. Oxford: Clarendon Press.

Index for the *Orphic Rhapsodies*

OR 0. OF96T: Damascius, De Princ. 123.
OR 1. OF1F: DP Col.VII.9. Plut. *Quaest. conv.* 2.3.2, 636d-636e. Reconstructed verse by Bernabé from multiple sourses (see OF1F).
OR 2. OF102F: Ioan. Mal. *Chrono.* IV 88–92.
OR 3. OF109F: Procl. *in Pl. Cra.* 396b, p.59.14.
OR 4. OF111F: Procl. *in Pl. R.* II.138.8 and Simplic. *in Arist. Ph.* IV, 1 p.208b29.
OR 5. OF106F: Procl. *in Pl. Prm.* 139b, 1175.7.
OR 6. OF107F: Ion. Mal. *Chrono.* 4.74.
OR 7. OF114F: Dam. *De Princ.* 55.
OR 8. OF125F: Lactant. *Div. Inst.* 1.5.4-6.
OR 9. OF118F: Procl. *in Pl. Ti.* 33b, II.70.3.
OR 10. OF121F: See discussion in p.283 and p.359.
OR 11. OF132F: Hermias *in Pl. Phdr.* 246e, p.138.11.
OR 12. OF136F: Hermias *in Pl. Phdr.* 246e, p.138.11.
OR 13. OF122F: Procl. *in Pl. R.* II.138.18.
OR 14. OF130F: Procl. *in Pl. Ti.*30c, I.427.20.
OR 15. OF134F: Procl. *in Pl. Ti.* 30c, I.429.26.
OR 16. OF144F: Procl. *in Pl. Ti.* 33c, II.85.23.
OR 17. OF140F: Procl. *in Pl. Cra.* 391d, 32.29.
OR 18. OF173F: Procl. *in Pl. I Alcibiades*, 103a, 66.
OR 19. OF167F: Syrianus *in Arist. Metaph.* N 4, p.1091b4.
OR 20. OF152F: Lactant. *Div. Inst.* I.5.4-6.
OR 21. OF160F: Procl. *in Pl. Ti.* 40e, III.172.20.
OR 22. OF158F: Procl. *in Pl. Ti.* 41c, III.227.3.
OR 23. OF155F, OF155F(I), OF156F.
OR 24. OF138F: Aristocritus Manich. *Theoso.* 61, p.116.15.
OR 25. OF123F: Hermias *in Pl. Phdr.* 247c, p.148.25.
OR 26. OF168F: Procl. *in Pl. Cra.* 396b, 54.21.
OR 27. OF170F: ps-Alexander (Michael of Ephesus?) *in Arist. Metaph.* N4, p.1091b4[1139].
OR 28. OF113F: Hermias *in Pl. Phdr.* 247c, p.147.20.
OR 29. OF163F: Procl. *in Pl. Ti.* 41c, III.227.31.
OR 30. OF148F: Procl. *in Pl. Ti.* 31a, I.450.22.
OR 31. OF149F: Hermias *in Pl. Phdr.* 247d, p.154.23 a.
OR 32. OF113 (Kern):   Dam. *De Princ.* 257.

1139 It is now generally agreed that this commentary is not by Alexander of Aphrodisias, and it has been argued that it is by Michael of Ephesus (12th century A.D.). Kotwick maintains that the latter's reading of the Aristotelean passage was heavily influenced by Syrianus' commentary on it, and that he attempted to combine all the entities mentioned by Aristotle and promote his argumentation through using and adjusting the verses that Syrianus quoted from the OR (Kotwick, 2014, p.75ff; p.84–90).

OR 33. OF174F: ps-Alexander (Michael of Ephesus?) *in Arist. Metaph.* N4, 1091b4[1140].
OR 34. OF179F: Procl. *in Pl. Ti.* 40e, III.184.1.
OR 35. OF188F: Etym. Magn. 231.21 s. Γίγας.
OR 36. OF183F: Procl. *in Pl. Ti.* 40e, III.176.10.
OR 37. OF182F: Dam. *De Princ.* 67.
OR 38. OF112F: Procl. *in Pl. Cra.* 404b, p.92.9.
OR 39. OF301F: Procl. *in Pl. Ti.* 24e, I.175.9.
OR 40. OF232F: Procl. *in Pl. Ti.* 25b, I.187.4.
OR 41. OF178F: Procl. *in Pl. Ti.* 40e, III.185.20.
OR 42. OF186F: Procl. *in Pl. Ti.* 40e, III.185.28.
OR 43. OF225F: Procl. *in Pl. Cra.* 396b, 55.11 and OF181F: Dam. *De Princ.* 67 and OF251F: Procl. *in Pl. Ti.* 30a, I.396.29.
OR 44. OF189F: Procl. *in Pl. Cra.* 406c, 110.15.
OR 45. OF363F: Lactant. *Div. Inst.* 1.13.11 .
OR 46. OF206F: Procl. *in Pl. Cra.* 403e, 90.28.
OR 47. OF221F: Procl. *in Pl. Cra.* 404b, 92.14.
OR 48. OF231F: Procl. *Theol. Pl.* V10, p.264.20:
OR 49. OF200F: Dam. *in Pl. Parm.* 267.
OR 50. OF208F: Hermias *in Pl. Phdr.* 248c, p.161.15 and OF212F: Procl. *Theol. Pl.* IV 17, p.206.4 and OF214F: Schol. Lycoph. 399, p.149.11.
OR 51. OF224F: Procl. *in Pl. R.* I.138.23.
OR 52. OF223F: Clem. Al. *Strom.* VI 2.26.2.
OR 53. OF220F: Porph. *De Antr. Nymph.* 16, p.67.21.
OR 54. OF239F: Procl. *in Pl. Cra.* 391a, 27.21. See also Procl. *in Pl. Ti.* I.207.1.
OR 55. OF237F: Procl. *in Pl. Ti.* I.206.26.
OR 56. OF237F: Procl. *in Pl. Ti.* 28c, I.314.31.
OR 57. OF237F: Procl. *in Pl. Ti.* 31c, II.24.23.
OR 58. OF219F: Syrian. *in Arist. Metaph.* N p.1091b4.
OR 59. OF241F: These eight verses are a combination of Procl. *in Pl. Ti.* 29a, I.324.14–I.325.3 and I.313.10-16.
OR 60. OF243F(XXXI): Procl. *in Pl. Ti.* 29a, I.325.9.
OR 61. OF243F: Porph. *In Euseb. Praep. evang.* III 8-9, p.100a-105d; Aristoc. Manich. *Theoso.* 50, p.109.23 and Procl. *in Pl. Ti.* 28c, I.313.17. For various other sources see also OF168 (Kern) and OF243F.
OR 62. OF245V: Aristoc. Manich. *Theoso.* 50, p.109.23 and Procl. *in Pl. Prm.* IV 959, 21.
OR 63. OF233F: Procl. *Theol. Pl.* VI 8, 363.15
OR 64. OF141F: Procl. *in Pl. Ti.* 29a-b, I.336.6.
OR 65. OF263F: Procl. *in Pl. Ti.* 24d, I.166.21.
OR 66. OF266F and OF264F: Procl. *in Pl. Ti.* 24d, I.170.3 and 24d, I.169.1.
OR 67. OF265F: Procl. *in Pl. R.* I.102.11.
OR 68. OF267F: Procl. *in Pl. Cra.* 406d, 112.14.
OR 69. OF268F: Procl. *in Pl. R.* I.138.12.
OR 70. OF269F: Procl. *in Pl. Ti.* 29a, I.327.23 and Hermias *in Pl. Phaedr.* 247c, 149.9.

[1140] See previous footnote.

OR 71. OF271F: Procl. *in Pl. Cra.* 389b, 21.13.
OR 72. OF260F: Procl. *in Pl. Cra.* 406c, 110.23.
OR 73. OF317F and OF257F: Procl. *in Pl. Cra.* 404b, 106.10 and 406b, 106.25.
OR 74. OF284F: Procl. *in Pl. Cra.* 404e, 96.13.
OR 75. OF288F: Tzetz. Exeges. in Iliad. 26.18: Apart from Tzetzes we have many references to Kore weaving an unfinished web in Porph. (OF286F: *De Antr. Nymph.* 14, p.66.13), Procl. (OF286F: *In Ti.* 41b-c, III.223.3 and I.134.26), and Dam. (*De Princ.* 339).
OR 76. OF288F: Procl. *in Pl. Ti.* 41b-c, III.223.7.
OR 77. OF292F: Procl. *in Pl. Cra.* 404d, 95.10 and OF293F: Procl. *in Pl. Cra.* 406b, 106.5.
OR 78. OF299F: Procl. *in Pl. Ti.* 42d, III.310.30.
OR 79. OF299F: Procl. *in Pl. Cra.* 396b, 55.5 and Olympiod. *In Pl. Phd.* 85.9 and OF166F: Mus. fr.103 = Alcidam. *Ulix.* 25 and Procl. *in Pl. Cra.* 396b, 52.26.
OR 80. OF300F: Procl. *in Pl. Ti.* 42e, III.316.3.
OR 81. OF308V: Nonnus, *Dion.* VI 169 and OF303F: Procl. in Pl. Cra. 406c, 108.13.
OR 82. OF311F and OF314F: Procl. *in Pl. Ti.* 35a, II.145.18-II.146.9.
OR 83. OF322F: Olympiod. *In Pl. Phd.* 111.14 and Olympiod. *In Pl. Phd.* 67c, p.43.14 and Procl. *in Pl. Ti.* 35b, II.198.2.
OR 84. OF321F: Procl. *in Pl. Cra.* 406c, 108.13.
OR 85. OF296F: Procl. *in Pl. Ti.* 30b, I.408.7 and OF329F: Procl. *in Pl. Ti.* 30b, I.407.22.
OR 86. OF320F: Olympiod. *In Pl. Phd.* 61c, p.2.21.
OR 87. OF319F: Procl. *in Pl. Ti.* 24e, I.173.1.
OR 88. OF340F: Procl. *in Pl. R.* II.340.11.
OR 89. OF436F, OF422F, OF426F, OF425F: Vet. Val. *Anthol.* IX 1, p.330.23.
OR 90. OF437F: Clem. Al. *Strom.* VI.2.17.1.
OR 91. OF339F: Procl. *in Pl. R.* II.339.17.
OR 92. OF338F: Procl. *in Pl. R.* II.338.10 .
OR 93. OF438F: Clem. Al. *Strom.* V.8.45.
OR 94. OF348F: Procl. *in Pl. Ti.* 42c, III.297.3 .
OR 95. OF350F: Dam. *In Phd.* I 87.11.
OR 96. OF576F: Olympiodor. *In Pl. Phd.* 69c, p.48.20.
OR 97. OF337F: Ioan. Mal. *Chrono.* IV 91.75.

General Index

Abaris 48
abduction 110–11
abode 137, 143, 168, 310, 314, 324–25
–aetherial, 340
–blessed 143
–special 324
acclamations 60, 156, 178, 261, 268, 339–40
–cultic 145
Achaea 113
Acheloos 209
Acheron 188–89, 331, 339–40
Acherousia limne 331
Achilles 140–41
–Achilles' Shield 326–27
Acragas 257, 319
Adeimantus 21–23, 73, 135
Admetus 146
Aegina 51–52, 319
Aeneas 140
Aeolians 65
aer/air 55, 67, 79–80, 159–61, 187, 211–17, 220, 225–33, 248, 258, 301–3, 319, 323–24, 334–35
Aeschines 35–39, 149
Aeschylus 55, 182, 185, 317
–Bassarai 184
–Prometheus 335
Aesop 57
aether 15, 80, 137–38, 158, 161, 168–71, 186–88, 196–98, 213–16, 242–44, 248, 286–305, 322–27, 334–44
–astral 203
aetherial 138, 338
afterlife 20–25, 41–43, 73, 100, 125, 131–34, 170–72, 181–89, 196–98, 234–39, 251, 258, 324, 331–48
–blissful 31–32, 49, 70, 111, 131, 158, 168
–happy 25, 28, 95, 135, 142, 157, 178–79, 181, 190, 338
–journey 183, 193, 203–4, 239
–punishments 41, 182, 340, 347
–topography 197, 203
Agamemnon 328–30

Agathon 255
Aiakos 208
aidoion 210–11, 241–55, 272, 316–18, 328, 341
Aigialos 51
Aigina 51–52
Aion 300
Aischylos, Sisyphos 88
Alcamenes 51
Alcimidas 319
Alcman 163, 373
Alexander 53–54, 56–57
Alexandria 57–58, 77, 148, 274, 277, 284
Alexis 71
Alkmaionis 88
Amalkeides 78
Amaltheia 166
Amelios 237
Amphipolis 208
Anaxagoras 221, 225, 227, 232, 273
Anaximander 225, 232–33
Anaximenes 220, 225, 229–30
Antaugês 186
anthropogony 4, 101, 107, 112, 128, 136, 274, 336–37
aphrodisiazein 213, 229, 309
Aphrodite 31, 48, 188, 199, 213, 309, 330
–birth 330, 350
–Ourania 209, 213, 228–29, 308–9
Apollo 55, 91, 104, 119–21, 165, 184–86, 196, 202, 218, 237, 261, 299–318, 338
–Delphinios 199
–Iatros 199
–Patroios 217
–Phanaeus 306–8
Apollodorus 91, 281–82, 336
Apollonides 81
Apollonius Rhodius 59, 69
–Argonautika 69, 282
Apulian pottery 118, 347–48
Aratus 165–67, 169–70
Arcturus 331
Argeïphontes 329
Argives 118

Ariadne 205
Arideus 196
Aristander 56
Aristodemus 255
Aristophanes 38, 43, 72, 80, 182–83, 202, 251, 255, 302–3
–Birds 80, 301–2
–Frogs 38, 165, 182, 188
–Peace 159
Aristotle 14–16, 55, 79, 216–17
Arkteia 178
Arktos 331
Artemis 31–32, 165, 294, 309–10, 338, 350
–Orthia 163
Asia Minor 44, 59, 68, 83, 309
asphodel 331–32
Asteropaeus 140
astral immortality 143, 162, 196–97, 203–4, 215, 248, 257–58, 324, 344, 351
astronomy 75, 143, 161, 187, 200, 202, 214–15, 310–11
Athena 87, 269
Athenagoras 39–40, 72, 280
Athenodorus 275
Athens 24, 28–29, 33, 37, 51, 69, 117, 132–33, 188
Atlas 296, 368
atonement 21, 23, 41, 99, 182, 270–72
Atreus 329–30
Atthidographers 78
Atthis 79
Attica 45, 52
Augē 174

Babylon 65
Bacchae 54, 61–62, 64, 305
baccheuein 132, 134, 136, 255, 345
Bacchic 17, 30, 40, 60, 76, 180, 183, 201
–cult 66
–frenzy 62, 64, 105, 109, 345
–Hymn 164
–initiates 53, 251
–inscription 202
–mysteries 30, 120, 134, 183
–orgies 45
–rites 17, 30–31, 68, 103–4

Bacchic-Orphic 123, 145
bacchoi 90, 122, 129, 132, 134–35, 149–50, 154–55, 183, 215, 237, 298, 345
Bassarai 56, 184
Baubo 73
Bellerophon 138
Bendideian 60
Berlin Papyrus 82
Bessi 63
bibloi 20, 34–35, 39
birth 69, 80, 88, 90–91, 163, 213, 243
body 10–11, 15, 32, 43, 67, 82–83, 97, 100, 150, 180–81, 199, 217, 231
Boeotia 65
Bone Tablets 199, 201–2, 249, 338
Bootes 331
borborō 339
boukolos 268, 332
Briareus 79
bricolage 25, 33, 37, 177, 269–70, 273
Brimo 126, 155, 265–67, 269
Bromios 61–62, 218, 342
Brontinos 77, 79
Bryges 67
Brygians 68
bull 118, 126, 154, 156–58, 162–64, 166, 173, 184, 187, 189, 201, 213, 268, 309
–constellation 164, 166–68, 201, 203, 327
bull-roarer 86, 93, 266–67

Calabria 113, 118, 128, 131, 191
Callimachus 50–51, 81, 91
Calliope 200
cannibalism 98–99
Castor 307, 345
castration 72, 242, 317
Caucon 46
Celaenus 46
Celeus 45
Cephalus 341
Cercops 77–78, 275
Ceres 45
Chaeremon 279
chaos 299, 301, 305
Charon 146
Chios 306, 308

chronos (Time) 80, 174, 243, 259, 286, 299–300, 302
Chrysippus 220
chthonic, Zeus 224
Chthonic, Zeus 170
Cicero 78
Cleanthes 185–86, 219, 277, 349
Clement of Alexandria 72, 77, 92, 148–49, 247, 251, 256–57, 267–68, 277
Clitodemus 78–79
Clymene 341
Conflagration 219
Conon 66
constellations 164–66, 168, 200, 203, 213, 292, 322, 324, 326, 331
–Arktos 326
–Auriga 164, 166, 187
–Charioteer 166–68, 187, 203, 324
–Cygnus 200
–Eriphoi 168, 201, 327
–Gemini 307
–Lyra 55, 200
–Orion 163, 326–27, 331
–Pleiades 163–65, 200, 326–27, 331
–Taurus 163–66, 187–88, 200–201, 324, 326
Corybantes 60
cosmogonical 16, 33, 79–80, 113, 215, 219, 224, 240, 276–78, 311
cosmology 215, 218–19, 221–22, 254, 299, 323, 334, 337, 342
–cosmological eschatology 197, 204, 337, 344
–mystic 335
Cotytian 60
Crates 324
creation 19, 80, 101, 106–7, 139, 186–87, 209–19, 244, 255, 261, 301–18, 336–37
–creator 79–80, 107, 176, 209, 243, 257, 301–5, 316, 322, 334
Crete 62, 92, 119–20, 123, 126, 131
Cybele 60
Cyclopes 294
Cyzicus 68–69

dadouchos 47–48, 183, 185, 239, 269
daimons 79, 221, 238–39, 243–44, 305, 314–16, 318, 320, 341
–fallen 336–37
Damagetus 56
Damascius 74, 100–101, 105–9, 274, 276, 280, 343
Damascius and Dio Chrysostom 101
darkness 179, 183, 188
Deceit 311
Deception 290
Deio 223, 324
deisidaimōn 26–28
Delos 170
Delphi 91, 94, 120, 165, 196, 333
–omphalos 303
–rites 120
Demeter 47–48, 50–52, 73, 126, 152–53, 223, 271, 291, 295, 305, 309, 324
–Chthonia 49, 59, 83, 155, 203, 343
–Eleusinia 70
–grief 111, 152
–hymn to 46–47
–Lykomidae 46–47
–search 72, 135
Democritus 221, 246
Demon 78–79
Demosthenes 35–38, 149
Derveni Krater 205
Diagoras of Melos 39–40
Dikē 226, 238–39, 245–46, 293, 348
Dio Chrysostom 57–58, 100–101
Diodorus Siculus 43–44, 62–63, 92, 164, 171–72, 222–24, 306
Diogenes of Apollonia 220, 225, 228–29, 231, 273
Dionysiac context 93
Dionysiac elements 95
Dionysios, Dionysiac nature 95
Dionysos 58–59, 136, 141–42, 148–49, 163–66, 170–71, 184–86, 205, 208, 218–19
–Apollo 120–21, 185, 202, 237, 303, 308
–Attes 149
–Baccheios 126, 154, 202
–Bacchos 13, 45, 56, 60, 89, 92, 142, 148, 201, 203, 215, 266

–birth 69, 88, 90–91, 148, 171
–bull 118
–bull-eating 118
–deliverance 343
–Delphi 120
–Dionysiac nature 95–106, 108–9
–dismemberment 54–55, 82, 85–88, 91–99, 106, 109, 141, 186–87, 219, 267, 273–74, 306, 336
–Eleleus 218
–Iacchos 165, 188
–kingship 320
–Lyseus 106
–Macedonian cult 54
–oracle 63–66, 236–38
–Phallen 66
–Phanagoria 309
–Phanes 176, 223, 306
–prophet 64, 237
–rites 19, 53, 60, 90, 92, 148, 267, 304
–tomb 94, 120
–toys 86, 92–93, 267, 270, 273
–Zagreus 85–109, 113–48, 176–77, 185–87, 219, 267–68, 271
Dioskouroi 199, 307–9
Doliones 69
dromena 152–53, 156, 181, 189, 204, 260

Earth Mother 67, 79, 136–39, 155, 158, 161–63, 223, 301, 305, 323–26, 335–36, 340
Edonian 53–55
egg 17–20, 34, 75, 80, 243, 254–55, 286–87, 301–5, 307, 309
Egypt 57, 67, 264
–rites 17–18
Eleusis 14, 39–40, 45, 47, 62–63, 70, 90, 111–12, 134–35, 179–80, 182–83
–Iacchos 165
–Mysteries 14, 24, 42–45, 47–48, 72–73, 89–90, 152–53, 157, 180–82, 268, 271
Eleutherna 119–20
Elis 113, 118, 163
Empedokles 46, 98, 277, 335–37, 348
Empedotimus 161
Ennodia 118
Eos 341

Ephesus 309–10
Epicharmus 71
Epigenes 77–78
Epimenides 120, 303
epiphany 162, 173–74, 183
Epipurgidia 51
Eratosthenes 55–56
Erebus 301
Erikepaios 267, 287–89, 292, 311
Erinyes 79, 105, 226, 238, 246–47, 252
eriphos 166
Eros 47, 69, 287, 293, 301–2, 305, 309, 316
Erotylos 173
Eubouleus 147, 170–71, 186–87, 266, 271
Eudemus 74
Euklēs 121, 147, 170–71
Eumenides 239, 295
Eumolpus 23–24, 68, 73, 82, 164
Euphorion 91–92
–Mopsopia 91
Euripides 12, 31–32, 50, 54, 61–63, 72, 132, 137–38, 185, 299, 305, 327, 341–42
–Alcestis 63–64, 146
–Andromeda 308
–Bacchae 184, 237
–Cretans 88, 119
–Electra 327
–Erechtheus 325
–Helen 138, 169
–Herakles 50, 71, 145, 182, 342
–Hippolytus 29, 33, 136
–Hypsipyle 305
–Iphigeneia 105
–Melanippe the Wise 138
–Phaethon 325, 341–42
–Phoenissae 218
–Rhesus 12–14, 16, 38, 43, 64, 183
–Suppliants 137

Firmus 17–19
frenzy 62, 104–5, 109, 184
–philosophic 255

Gaia 107, 210, 311, 323, 325, 334. See also Earth mother

gala 158, 164, 171
Glaucothea 36–37
Great Goddesses 47–48

Hades 22–23, 41–42, 76–78, 88, 110, 128–35, 145–46, 160, 172, 178, 234–38, 251, 325, 331–33
–god 42, 49–50, 56, 88, 110, 170, 187, 208, 215, 250–51, 295, 331
Haemus 63–64
Harmonia 209, 213, 228, 308–9
Harpokration 78, 81
Heaven god 79, 134, 136, 138–39, 336
Hekate 51–52, 294, 310, 348
Helios 52, 55, 175–76, 184, 202, 211, 270, 299, 302–3, 324–25, 341
Hellanikos 74
Hephaestos 296, 326, 329–30
Hera 103, 281, 295, 309
Heraclides Ponticus 15–16, 63, 75, 143, 160–61
Herakleitos 201, 209, 219, 221, 225, 245–52, 259–61, 273, 335–36
Herakles 39, 50, 69, 146, 306
Hermaios 168
Hermes 168, 170, 188, 199, 208, 297, 329–30, 339, 342, 345
Hermias 305
Hermione 49–51
Herodikos 77
Herodotus 16–18, 20, 34–35, 40, 49, 63, 67, 81, 180, 202
Hesiod 10, 25, 42, 70–71, 88, 101, 247, 276–81, 299–300, 311, 317–41
Hesperides 92
Hestia 210, 223, 309, 324–25
Hibeh Papyri 163
Hieronymos 74, 280–81
Hippias 70, 376
Hippolytos 29–32, 132–33
Hippolytus (author) 46
Hipta 54, 87
Homer 25, 46, 70–71, 74, 88, 139–43, 247, 276, 279–80, 299, 317, 321, 326–37
–Iliad 140–41, 322, 326, 329
–Nekyia 330–33

Homeric Hymns 52, 137, 152–53, 307
Hyades 165–66, 326–27

Iacchos 73, 165, 218
Iamblichus 77–78, 216
immortality 150, 166–70, 192–93, 198, 239, 251, 307, 325–27, 335, 340, 345, 348, 350
incarnation 58, 83, 97–101, 112, 130, 144, 201, 268, 336, 339, 350
Ino 259
Ionia 308–9, 337
Ionian 65, 207
Ion of Chios 71, 76–77, 81, 160
Irikepaios 266–67. See also Erikepaios
Isles of the Blessed 125, 129–32, 143–44, 154, 166–68, 172, 195, 200–204, 258–59, 271, 324–27, 340, 344–45, 349
Isocrates 71
Italy 118, 123–28
itinerant priests 20–43, 48, 69, 83, 240, 260, 263, 269–71, 273

Justice 42–43, 226, 245, 250, 293, 345–48. See also Dikē

Kabeiroi 60, 148, 308
–mysteries 39–40, 48
Kairos 174
Kalliope 13, 57–58
katabasis 50, 146–51, 172, 177–84, 196–97, 331–33
Kato Phana 306, 308
Kikones 62–63
Kithairon 61
kleos 140–43, 192–93, 198
Klodones 53
Klymenos 49–50
knuckle-bones 86, 93, 266–67
Kokytos 189, 297, 340
Kore 48–49, 51, 110, 142, 148, 153, 205, 271, 295
–Protogone 48
–rape 24
–Soteira 49, 68–70, 83
Korybantic 76, 148

Kouretes 119–20, 265, 294
Kronos 209–14, 221–24, 227, 235, 249, 258, 289–91, 311–21, 335–36, 341
Kybele 59, 62, 157, 171, 269, 306, 372

Lacedaemonia 48
Lachesis 194
Lactantius 278
Lasos 49–50
laws 101, 105
legomena 34, 40, 44–46, 134, 142, 153, 183, 189, 260
Leibethra 56, 58, 64
Lemnos 50
Leotychidas 28
Lesbian, oracle 65
Lesbos 64–66, 116–18, 236
Lethe 130, 150–51, 168, 192–96, 201
Leto 165, 286, 294
Leucippus 246
lightning 106–8, 142, 147–48, 196, 201, 268, 294, 340–41
Linus 45, 71
locus amoenus 140, 339, 343. See also Isles of the Blessed
Lucian 66, 200, 236, 262, 279
Lykomidae 46–48, 269
Lykophron 91, 161–62
lyre 56–57, 65–66, 76, 119, 199–200, 333, 348

Macedonia 52–58, 67–68, 113, 116, 123–24, 126, 169–70, 208
Macrobius 161, 187, 217–18
–Saturnalia 185, 217
Maenads 54, 69, 118, 200, 205, 251, 259
magoi 234, 239–41, 251
mania 237, 255, 345. See also frenzy
mantis 64, 185, 237, 253
meadow 165, 168, 179, 183–84, 188–89, 191, 193, 197, 204, 296, 327, 332, 339–40, 343
Megalopolis 68
Meliae 336
memory 110, 125–30, 139, 150, 191–98
–fountain of 140, 172, 203
Menander Rhetor 277

Metapontum 79
Methapos 48
Methymna 66
Metis 187, 224, 228, 243–44, 287, 293, 314–19, 328, 330, 334, 341, 350
Metrodorus of Lampascus 220
Midas 68
Miletus 51, 68, 168, 199, 338, 350
milk (see also gala) 110, 126, 147, 154, 156, 156–66, 172–75, 178, 189, 203
Milky Way 158, 160–61, 164, 166, 168, 171, 188, 195–96, 259, 324
Mimallones 53
Minoan 59, 163
Minos 331
mire 133, 180, 182, 251. See also borborō
mirror 86, 93, 97, 201, 266–67, 296
Mnemosyne 110, 122, 126, 130, 189, 191–97, 201, 289
–fountain 132, 143, 150, 340
–See also memory
Moira 194–95, 217, 231, 250
moon 163–64, 195, 215, 233, 243, 248, 256, 263, 288, 310, 324, 326
Mountain Mother 59, 89–90, 155, 203
Mount Haemus 53
Mount Olympus 56
Mount Pangaion 13, 53–58
Mount Parnassos 87
mud 22–23, 73, 250–51, 324
Musaeus 11, 21–25, 28, 31, 45–50, 70–73, 77, 81–82, 160, 256, 269
Mycenaean 114

nature 102–3
Nemesis 311
Neoplatonists 262, 274–78
netherworld 49–52, 73, 115, 121–39, 145–72, 177–97, 258, 295, 331–50
–topography 129, 189, 193, 195–96, 204, 338
Night 80, 170, 209, 211, 214, 280–81, 299, 301–3, 311–26
Nike 348
Nikias of Elea 77
Nino 36–37
Nonnus 284

Nous 227–28, 272, 317, 335

Odrysians 65
Odysseus 331–33
Oeagrus 13, 58, 200, 256
offerings 29, 109, 116, 199, 238, 252
Oinopoion 306
Oinos 87, 295
oistros 105–9
Okeanos 209, 228, 258–59, 281, 289–92, 301, 317, 323–27, 332–34
Olbia 199–202, 308, 338
–Bone Tablets 8, 198–202, 250, 335, 340, 350
Olympias 53–54
Olympiodorus 95–97, 100–101, 108, 112, 134, 183, 274
Olympus 13, 58, 64, 158, 168, 186, 294, 300
omphalos 119–21, 303
Onomakritos 46, 49–50, 77, 81–82, 92, 269
oracle 149–51, 236–37, 261, 299
orgia 17, 45, 53, 60, 82, 92, 154–55, 172, 178, 180, 200, 203, 256
Orpheotelestae 25–26, 28–29, 38, 83, 198, 240–41, 348
Orphikos Bios 29, 31, 43, 58, 62, 109, 182, 239, 267, 271–72, 304
Orthi Petra 119
Osiris 17, 164
Ouranos 86, 107, 137, 209–12, 241–43, 281, 289–90, 311–13, 317–21, 323, 330, 336
Ovid 54–55, 66, 68, 218

Palaikastro Hymn 162–63
Pamphos 46
Pan 69, 309
Parian Marble 24, 58, 72–73, 82
Parmenides 158, 225–26, 229–30, 273, 277–78
passwords 127, 148–49, 155, 176, 189–90, 203, 266–68
Pausanias 43–52, 55–56, 64–66, 70, 74, 82, 120, 150, 180, 183, 255, 269, 329, 333

Peitho 209, 213, 228–29, 308–9
Pelops 329–30
penalty 10–11, 41–43, 83, 99, 109–11, 136, 154–55, 181, 184, 188, 324, 343
Pentheus 184–85, 255–56
Pergamum 275
Persephone 49–52, 92, 109–11, 122, 126–28, 132–42, 146–48, 154, 170–72, 189–90, 195, 208, 267–71
–Artemis 310
–debt 13, 64, 336
–Dionysos' mother 69, 85, 119, 148, 165
–search 73, 153, 180
Persia 56, 65
–magoi 240–41
Persinos the Milesian 77
Persuasion 309
Phaedra 29
Phaethon 286, 325–26, 341–42
Phanagoria 308–10, 357, 378
Phanes 18–19, 174–76, 184–87, 213, 223, 245, 267, 274, 280, 287–88, 302–22, 341–45
–birth 18, 175, 213, 287, 301–2, 305
–Phanagoria 308–10
–swallowing 241–45, 292, 312, 323
–See also Protogonos
Phanocles 65
Phanodemus 78
phantoms 153, 332
Pherekydes of Syros 300
Philip II 53, 205
Philochorus 63, 78–79, 120
Philodemos 90–95
Philolaus 220
Philostratus 64
Phlya 45–48, 69–70, 83, 184, 253, 269
Phocis 65, 330
Phoebe 289
Phoenicia 201
Phorkys 281, 289
Phōs 174
Phrygia 36, 58–68
Physika 77–79
Pindar 58, 109–11, 136–37, 163, 184, 257–61, 299–300, 317–19, 336
Pisistratids 82

Plato 9–21, 43, 66, 74, 97–112, 142, 168, 181–83, 193–98, 216, 267–73, 279–81, 345–47
–Apology 71
–Cratylus 9–16, 98, 100–102, 163, 181, 221–22, 247, 262, 325
–Ion 71
–Laws 28–29, 41–43, 47, 101–5, 345–47
–Meno 109–11, 136–37, 261
–Phaedo 100, 133, 182–83
–Phaedrus 182, 255, 325, 345
–Philebus 102, 319
–Protagoras 10–15
–Republic 21–32, 56, 73, 134–37, 160, 193, 198, 340
–Symposium 197, 255
–Timaeus 103, 141–43, 167–68, 234, 237, 280–81
Plotinos 237
Plotinus (author) 97
Plutarch 18–20, 28, 34–35, 53–56, 66–67, 98–101, 108–9, 120, 179–88, 196–97, 216–20, 249, 254, 304
Pluto 126, 146
Pollux 307
Polycaon 46
Polygnotos 333
post-mortem rewards 22–26, 33, 73, 83, 133, 160, 184, 195–96, 239, 258
prayer 25, 66, 135, 140, 152, 246, 266–67, 269
Pre-Socratic 78, 201, 204, 209, 220–21, 225–33, 245–47, 252, 263, 273, 299, 337–38, 348, 350
–philosophy 224–25, 247, 263, 273, 299, 336
priests/priestesses 28–29, 36–38, 42, 63, 110–11, 119–20, 137, 154, 190–91, 196, 253, 261, 269, 291
Proclus 96–103, 141–42, 148, 274, 315
Prodicus of Samos 77
profane 125, 134, 255–56, 262, 286
Prometheus 163, 335–37
prophecy 65, 83, 151, 209, 224, 235–37, 251, 311–14, 320
prophet 25–26, 38, 63–64, 135, 194, 221–22, 234–38, 253–58

Protogonos 171, 174–75, 185, 218, 241–45, 255, 266, 286–87, 302–6, 314–18, 324–25
–birth 80, 163, 213, 243, 302, 318
–creator 80, 150
Protoklea 78
Protokreon 78
punishment 10–12, 22–26, 41–43, 83, 98–101, 106–12, 134, 181–84, 196, 235, 239, 258, 268, 331–50
purification 21, 33, 43, 76, 132, 149, 177, 240, 250–51, 253, 270–71, 345
Puriflegethon 331
purity 26, 31–33, 90, 123, 127, 130–39, 152, 186, 195, 221, 270, 339, 345–46
Pylos 59
pyr technikon 324
Pythagoreanism 15–20, 33–34, 41, 76–83, 121–22, 129, 180, 304
–Pythagoras 77–78
–Pythagoreans 15–19, 30, 33, 77–83, 180
Pythia 66

ram 126, 154–73, 189–90, 213, 266–67
rebirth 56, 99, 103, 110–11, 162, 170, 179, 195–96, 200–201, 271, 295, 339, 344
–cycle of 143, 167, 196, 201, 271–72, 339–40, 348–50
reincarnation (see also incarnation) 41, 67, 83, 95–103, 122, 137, 142–43, 167, 201, 258, 338–48
Rhadamanthys 208
rhapsode 279, 330
Rhea 59–62, 91, 210, 223, 265–66, 269, 305, 309, 324
riddles 19, 186, 235–36, 247, 261, 299, 313
Ruvo 348

Sabaoth 175
Sabazian mysteries 36, 60, 148, 157, 268–69
sacrifice 21–29, 41, 66, 106, 116–17, 173, 240, 267–71, 273, 343, 351
Samothrace 53, 62–63, 119
scepter 174–75, 288–89, 295, 311, 316–20, 327–31, 334

secrecy 14–20, 33–40, 44–46, 63, 71, 100–106, 114, 127, 183, 190, 254, 263–64, 269, 298
seers 27, 39–40, 185, 236
Selene 21, 288, 310
Semele 259
serpent/snake 53–54, 69, 87, 148–49, 171, 201, 268, 296–97
Sethians 45
Sibylline Oracles 278
Sicily 113, 128, 191
Sikyon 120
Silenus 68
Simonides 10, 48
sing 18, 47, 186, 286, 304
–song 22, 43, 47, 55–57, 74, 146, 191, 236, 333, 345
Sirius 163–64, 331
Sithone 13, 58
sky 158–61, 163–65, 167, 175, 184–85, 194–96, 214, 292, 296, 300–301, 322–23, 331
Skyles 202
sleep 53, 291, 311, 340
smoke 30, 69, 88, 94–95, 101, 296, 336–37, 341
Socrates 10–11, 16, 22–23, 56, 95, 100, 110–11, 133–34, 163, 167, 193–96, 221–25, 255, 261–62
soothsayer 10–11, 236, 253
Sophocles 118, 165, 202, 300, 332
Sossius Senecio 19, 304
soul 9–16, 41–43, 57–62, 95–101, 109–12, 125–45, 159–61, 164–72, 179–82, 192–200, 222, 237–39, 296–97, 338–50
–airy 14–16, 55, 79–84, 137–38, 143, 150, 159–61, 187–200, 213–22, 231, 263, 324–26, 334, 349
–body 10–15, 32, 42–43, 67, 82–83, 97–100, 150, 180–81, 199, 217, 222, 231
–divine 67, 80, 139, 198, 248, 257–58, 297, 319, 334
–transmigration 58, 96–99, 248, 267
–water 248–51
Sparta 51, 68, 70, 163
stag 309–10

stars 15–16, 143, 158–68, 175, 184–88, 195–201, 213–14, 233, 248, 259, 307, 323–32, 340
–child of starry Heaven 110, 126–39, 155, 162, 192, 203, 261, 340
Stesichorus 257
Stesimbrotus of Thasos 220
Stoicism 219–25, 324, 349
Strabo 14, 60
Suda 34, 51, 74, 76–79, 81, 200, 274–75
sun 55, 79, 171, 175–76, 184–90, 198, 202, 211–33, 241–52, 257, 286–88, 296–97, 299, 309–48
swallowing 211, 229, 242, 244, 254, 315–18, 341. *See also* Phanes, swallowing
swan 56, 194–200
symbols 93, 125, 127, 149, 176, 189–90, 267, 269
symposium 54, 117, 160, 188, 197, 295
Syrianus 79

Tartarus 82, 108, 168, 188–89, 290–97, 301, 303, 323–24, 335, 344
Tatian 82, 120
Teiresias 237
temple 48–51, 70, 165, 306–10
Teos 308
Tethys 74, 247, 281, 289
Thales 225, 229
Thamyras 47
Theagenes of Rhegium 220
Themistocles 48
Theognetos the Thessalian 76, 78, 275
theogony 18, 71, 80, 174–75, 209–11, 241, 274–81, 285, 300–305, 310–14
theology 45, 96, 218–20, 236, 247, 252–53, 256–57, 262–63, 274, 277
Theonoe 138, 169
Theophrastus 26–36
Theron of Acragas 257, 319
Theseus 29–32, 132, 136
Thesmophoria 18, 148, 271
Thessaly 113, 118, 123–24, 128, 146, 156–57, 161
thiasos 36, 54, 149, 151, 154–55, 178, 182–83, 202–3

Thrace 13, 36, 53–68, 118–19, 146, 236–37
thunder 53, 67, 69, 88, 94–98, 142, 147, 195–96, 250, 259, 294–96, 340–41
Thyestes 329–30
Thyiades 165
thyrsus 133–35, 182, 267, 298, 309, 345
Timarchus 150
Timockles the Syracusan 77
Titans 42, 67–69, 82, 91–112, 121–23, 134–37, 141, 267–71, 290–91, 295–96, 303, 314, 320, 335–37
tombs 9, 11, 54, 56, 58–59, 64, 83, 117, 125, 181, 205, 208
Torchbearer 46–47, 183
Triptolemus 45, 271
Tritopatores 78–79
Trophonios 150–51
Trygaeus 159–60

Varro 200
vegetarianism 29–31, 58, 132, 136, 267, 271
Vergina 208
Virgil, 66, 200

water 67, 103, 130, 138–39, 150, 168, 186, 192–95, 219, 248, 323–24, 334–36, 339–40, 342
winds 14, 78–80, 186, 216–19
wine 22, 103–5, 157, 160, 173–74, 178
wreath 117, 157, 173, 307

Xenokrates 100–101

Zagourē 175–76
Zephyros 333
Zopyros of Heraklea 77
Zoroaster 67

Index of Primary Sources

Aeschylus
fr. 5 TrGF — 88 n.267
fr.23a TrGF — 55–56
fr.228 TrGF — 88 n.267
fr.341 Nauck — 185 n.603
Choephoroe
845 — 159 n.515
Edonians
fr.57.8–11 TrGF — 268 n.880
Prometheus Vinctus
88–92 — 335
593–608 — 317 n.1021

Alcman
fr.2 Campbell — 307 n.975
fr.34 Campbell — 308 n.976
PMG 1.60–63 — 163

Alexis
fr. 135 — 71

Anaxagoras
fr. 467 KRS — 232 n.751
fr. 468 KRS — 232 n.752
fr. 476 KRS — 227
fr. 477 KRS — 227
fr. 488 KRS — 232 n.752
fr. 489 KRS — 232 n.752
fr. 490 KRS — 232 n.752
fr. 492 KRS — 227

Anaximander
fr. 121 KRS — 233

Anaximenes
fr. 139 KRS — 229 n.741

Apollonius Rhodius
Argonautica
I.1134–39 — 60
I.989–1012 — 69

Apollodorus
Bibliotheca
1.1.1–1.2.1.4 — 281 n.923
1.3.2 — 146 n.468
1.7.1–2 — 336 n.1084
2.5.12 — 146 n.468

Aratus
Phaenomena
1–6 — 169
156–164 — 166 n.545
167–178 — 166–167
264–268 — 166 n.544

Aristophanes
Birds
145–152 — 251 n.823
268–276 — 251 n.823
693–704 — 301–302
695 — 80
746 — 59 n.168
1072 — 39 n.109
Clouds
1 — 321 n.1032
153 — 321 n.1032
603 — 120 n.365
Frogs
145–150 — 182
154–159 — 183 n.594
316 — 39 n.109
342–344 — 165 n.542
1031–1036 — 276 n.903
1032 — 38, 182
1278 — 321 n.1032
Peace
825–841 — 159–160
Plutus
288 — 68 n.193
1095 — 321 n.1032
Thesmophoriazusae
986–91 — 202 n.656
Wasps
624 — 321 n.1032

Aristotle
De anima
405b28–31   216
410b28–411a3   216 n.698
410b29–411a3   14, 231 n.746
Metaphysica
983b19–23   229 n.741
984a6–7   229 n.741
1091b   217 n.700
Meteorologica
1.8 (345a 11)   158 n.513
Poetica
1447b.21–23   279 n.911
Physika
4.212b–23   326 n.1045

Arrian
Anabasis
1.11.2   56 n.159

Athenaeus
Deipnosophistae
IV.164b–c   71 n.209

Athenagoras
Legatio pro Christianis
4.1   39
18.3   72
18–20   280 n.919

Cicero
De Natura Deorum
1.107   78
2.141   225 n.728

Cleanthes
SVF
fr. I 495   220 n.709
fr. I 537.18–22   349
fr. I.538   185
fr. I.546   186 n.605

Clement of Alexandria
Stromata
1.21.107.4   24 n.54
1.21.131.3   77
1.21.134   236 n.766

6.2.17   247–248
15.2   71 n.206
Protrepticus
2.12   152 n.489
2.14   148, 268 n.876
2.15   92, 148 n.473,
                         267 n.875
2.16   148 n.474
2.17   72–73, 268 n.881
2.18   268
6.61   277
7.63   256, 277 n.907

Clitodemus
DFHG p.363 F19   79

Damascius
In Phaedo
I 84.22   100
I 85.5–86.7   106–107
I 86–87.9   108
I 86–87.8   107
I 87.11   106
I 87.7   106 n.321
De Principiis
123–124 (III 160, 17–162,
19 Westerink)   74 n.225, 277
                         n.904/905, 280
                         n.919, 303 n.948

Damagetus
Anthologia Palatina 7.9 56 n.162

Democritus
fr. D74 Laks–Most   246 n.808

Demon
DFHG p.378 F2   79

Demosthenes
18.259   35, 149 n.475
19.281   36
39.2   36 n.91
47.68   70 n.202

Index of Primary Sources —— 401

[Demosthenes]
Against Aristogeiton I
25.11   38, 346 n.1124

Derveni Papyrus
Col.I   238
Col.II   238
Col.III   238–39, 348
Col.IV   238, 226, 240
                                n.784, 245–46,
                                311 n.988
Col.V   222, 233–234,
                                235, 238
Col.VI   207, 238, 239,
                                240
Col.VII   18–19, 133, 207,
                                235, 236 n.764,
                                247 n.812, 254,
                                261 n.855, 262
                                n.860, 263
Col.VIII   243, 314, 315,
                                320
Col.IX   232 n.750, 263,
                                310 n.987
Col.X   214, 261 n.855,
                                310 n.987, 313
Col.XI   313–314
Col.XII   300
Col.XIII   176, 232 n.750,
                                241–245 n.796,
                                311 n.988, 316,
                                336 n.1082
Col.XIV   211–12, 227, 312
                                n.997, 321
Col.XV   212, 214, 224,
                                228, 311 n.988,
                                317, 320, 321,
                                330 n.1054, 336
                                n.1082
Col.XVI   170, 210, 212–13,
                                227–30, 242,
                                244, 257, 315,
                                316, 320, 321
Col.XVII   79, 209, 212, 215,
                                230–31, 257, 303
                                n.952, 347
Col.XVIII   217, 228, 231,
                                257, 303 n.952,
                                347
Col.XIX   209, 228–229,
                                230 n.743, 231,
                                250 n.821, 303
                                n.952, 320, 347
Col.XX   210 n.679, 240,
                                260, 264
Col.XXI   213, 227–28,
                                232, 308 n.981,
                                310 n.987
Col.XXII   72, 210, 223, 252
                                n.828, 324
                                n.1038
Col.XXIII   228, 258–259,
                                263
Col.XXV   197 n.642, 214–
                                15, 226, 232
                                n.750, 233, 243
                                n.797, 324
                                n.1037, 336
                                n.1082
Col.XXVI   263

Dio Chrysostom
Orations
30.10   100
32.64–65   57
32.69   58 n.164

Diodorus Siculus
I.11   176
I.11.3   164, 223, 302
                                n.947
I.12.4   223
I.23.6   277 n.907
I.96.4–6   172 n.556
IV.25.1–4   146 n.468, 277
                                n.907
V.64.4   43 n.119
V.70.1   223–224
V.72.2   223–224
V.75.4   92
V.77.3   62–63, 119 n.359
XIII.6   39 n.109

Diogenes of Apollonia
fr. 602 KRS	231
fr. 603 KRS	231

Diogenes Laertius
Prooem. 3	3

Epimenides
DK3 A1–5	303 n.950
DK3 B5	303
DK3 B11	120

Empedokles
DKB115.1–2	348

Euphorion
fr. 14	91–92
fr. 40	59 n.169

Euripides
fr. 477 Nauck	185 n.603
fr. 944 *TrGF*	325
Alcestis	
357–363	146
864–869	147 n.471
962–72	63
965–969	146 n.470
Andromeda	
fr.124 *TrGF*	308 n.977
Antiope	
fr. 203 Collard–Cropp	268 n.880
Bacchae	
32–33	105, 180 n.585
50–63	61
73–87	61–62
120–134	305 n.959
298–301	237
471–475	255 n.840
725	165 n.542
918–924	185 n.602
Bellerophon	
fr.307a	138
fr.308.3	138 n.440
Cretans	
fr.472 Nauck	89, 59 n.168, 119
Electra	
464–469	327
Erechtheus	
fr.370.71–72 Collard–Cropp	325
Hecuba	
70	305 n.959
Helen	
865–867	169
1015–1017	138
1301	59 n.168, 305 n.959
1364	305 n.959
Heraclidae	
900	300 n.939
Heracles	
607–615	50
613	50
660–661	342
676–684	342 n.1108
Hippolytus	
948–949	132 n.418
949–961	30
953–955	132 n.419
1416–19	31–32
1456–1458	133 n.420
Hypsipyle	
fr.759a Collard–Cropp	54
fr.57 Bond	305
Ion	
550	120 n.365
715	120 n.365
Melanippe the Wise	
fr.484	138–139
fr.487	138
Phaethon	
fr.779.1–4 *TrGF*	325–326
fr.781 *TrGF*	341
fr.781.19–21 *TrGF*	325
fr.781.63–64 *TrGF*	342
Rhesus	
346	13 n.26
943–44	13
962–73	12
942–944	183 n.597
Suppliants	
531–536	137–138

Eusebius
Chronicon II 46 Schone	24 n.54

Index of Primary Sources

Gold Tablets

A1   115, 116 n.346, 117, 121 n.373, 121 n.374, 122, 126, 140 n.444, 142, 147, 149, 154, 156, 157, 170, 178, 190, 195, 196, 250, 266, 268, 307 n.971, 339, 340. 344

A2   115, 116 n.346, 121 n.373, 121 n.374, 140 n.444, 141, 154, 170, 189, 190, 195, 250, 266, 307 n.971, 339, 340, 343

A3   115, 116 n.346, 121 n.373, 121 n.374, 140 n.444, 141, 142, 154, 170, 189, 190, 195, 250, 266, 307 n.971, 339, 340

A4   115, 116 n.346, 117, 121 n.374, 126, 127, 154, 156, 157, 170, 187, 188, 190, 343

A5   115, 117, 121 n.373, 126 n.400, 149, 156, 170, 190, 192, 266, 307 n.971, 339 n.1093

B1   114, 115, 121 n.374, 122 n.380, 126, 127, 128, 129, 130, 144, 155, 196 n.638, 340 n.1097, 343 n.1112

B2   114 n.340, 115, 122 n.378, 126 n.398–400, 128, 130, 144, 162, 191, 192, 340 n.1097/1099, 343

B3   115, 126 n.399, 144, 156, 340 n.1097

B4   115, 126 n.399, 144, 340 n.1097

B5   115, 126 n.399, 144, 340 n.1097

B6   114, 115, 126 n.399, 340 n.1097

B7   115, 122 n.378, 126 n.399, 144, 340 n.1097

B8   115, 122 n.378, 126 n.399, 144, 340 n.1097

B9   114 n.340, 115, 126 n.399, 144, 340 n.1097

B10   114 n.340, 115, 122 n.380, 126 n.398–400, 128, 129, 130, 136, 143 n.456, 144, 149, 151, 154 n.499, 155, 178 n.579, 191, 340 n.1097, 343 n.1112, 345 n.1122

B11   114 n.340, 115, 126 n.398–400, 128, 129, 130, 154, 155, 190, 191, 340 n.1097, 343 n.1112

B12   115, 126 n.399, 155, 340 n.1097

C1   115, 116 n.346, 117, 121 n.374, 155, 171

D1	90 n.271, 114, 115, 126, 127, 131, 136, 154, 155, 156, 157, 160, 171 n.554, 178 n.579, 190, 266, 343	F8	113 n.337, 116
		F9	113 n.337, 116
		F10	116 n.346, 117 n.349
		F11	116
		F12	116
D2	90 n.271, 114, 115, 117, 126, 131, 136, 154, 155, 156, 157, 160, 190, 266, 343	F13	113 n.337
		Greek Magical Papyri	
		PGM XIII.29–37	172–173
		PGM XIII.129–147	173 n.561
D3	116, 127, 136, 154 n.499/501, 155, 156, 188, 266, 267, 343	*PGM* XIII.164–167	174
		PGM XIII.186–190	174
		PGM XIII.443–452	175
		PGM XIII.646–651	173
D4	90 n.271, 114 n.340, 116 n.346, 126 n.401, 154 n.499, 189, 266, 339	*PGM* XIII.890–892	173 n.561
		PGM XIII.898–901	174 n.562
		PGM XIII.935	173
		PGM XIII.940–950	173
		PGM XIII.1052–1054	174 n.563
D5	90 n.271, 114 n.340, 116, 154 n.499, 155, 266, 307 n.971, 343	**Gurôb Papyrus**	See p.264–272
		22	306 n.962
		27–30	93 n.282
E1	116		
E2	116, 122 n.378, 125, 156	**Harpocration Lexixon**	
		s.v. Ἴων	81
E3	116, 126 n.401, 154 n.499	s.v. Τριτοπάτορες	78
E4	114 n.342, 116, 117 n.349, 126 n.401	**Hecataeus**	
		FGrHist 1 F 219	69 n.199
E5	114 n.340, 116 n.346, 156	**Heraclided Ponticus**	
		fr.50 Schütrumpf	161 n.521
F1	116, 117 n.349	fr.75 Schütrumpf	15, 143 n.454, 354
F2	114 n.342, 116, 154 n.499		
F3	114 n.340, 116, 117	**Heraclitus Paradox.**	
		21	146 n.468
F4	114 n.342, 116, 154 n.499	**Herakleitos**	
F5	114 n.342, 116, 117 n.349	B15 DK	88 n.267
		D1 Laks–Most	259–260
F6	114 n.342, 116, 117 n.349	D4 Laks–Most	259–260
		D15 Laks–Most	250
F7	114 n.340/342, 116	D16 Laks–Most	170 n.551, 250
		D18 Laks–Most	251

Index of Primary Sources — **405**

D48 Laks–Most	249	148–150	79 n.241
D51 Laks–Most	248, 249 n.816	173	317 n.1021
D54 Laks–Most	248, 249 n.816	211–226	311 n.989/990
D60 Laks–Most	246 n.809	371	317 n.1021
D63 Laks–Most	249	463–91	59 n.168
D65 Laks–Most	246 n.809	545	317 n.1021
D67 Laks–Most	248	560	336 n.1085
D76 Laks–Most	246 n.809	744	311 n.989
D80 Laks–Most	251	745–760	311 n.989
D82 Laks–Most	250 n.820	886	321 n.1032
D84 Laks–Most	249 n.817	923	321 n.1032
D85 Laks–Most	249	*Work and Days*	
D86 Laks–Most	249 n.817	1–10	299 n.934
D87 Laks–Most	249 n.817	55	317 n1021
D89 Laks–Most	246 n.807	106	336 n.1085
D90 Laks–Most	249	144–145	336 n.1084
D100 Laks–Most	247–248	560	312 n.998
D101 Laks–Most	248, 251	597–626	331 n.1062
D103 Laks–Most	248 n.815	618	166 n.544
D119 Laks–Most	252		
D120 Laks–Most	251 n.826	**Hesychius**	
		ω 108–109	258 n.845
Hermesianax			
Leontion		**Hippias**	
fr.7.1–14	146 n.468	DK 6B	71 n.206
Hermias		**Hippolytus**	
In Phaedrus		*Refutatio Omnium Haeresium*	
247c, 149.9	102 n.312	V.15	45
Herodotus		**Homer**	
2.61	17	*Iliad*	
2.81	16, 34	1.14–15	328
2.81.2	180	1.373–374	328
2.171.1–2	18 n.40	2.46	329
5.67.1	279 n.911	2.82	140 n.445
7.6.2	82	2.100–108	329
7.6.3	49–50	2.186	329 n.1051
7.73.1	68 n.190	2.846–847	63 n.176
7.110–111	63 n.176	3.276–280	347 n.1126
		4.405	140 n.445
Hesiod		5.172–73	140 n.445
Theogony		5.246–248	140 n.445
1–35	299 n.934	6.121–236	140
94–95	299 n.935	6.200	141 n.450
110	300 n.943	6.211	140 n.445
124–126	311 n.989	7.277	317 n.1021

7.277–278	328	**Homeric Hymns**	
9.96–99	328	*Demetra*	
9.161	140 n.445	2.20–75	52 n.142
9.295–299	329 n.1051	2.438–440	52 n.143
10.319–332	329 n.1051	*Hermes*	
13.54	140 n.445	4.456	317 n.1021
14.113	140 n.445	*Aphrodite*	
14.279	82	5.43	317 n.1021
15.20–21	334 n.1075	*Gaia Mother of All*	
15.187–95	326 n.1045	30.17	137
15.467	317 n.1021	*Dioskouroi*	
17.70–74	63 n.176	33.16–17	307–308
17.319–340	317 n.1021		
18.119	142 n.452	**Hyginus**	
18.481–489	326	*Astronomica*	
18.497–501	140–141	2.7	56 n.156
18.556–557	327		
20.177–352	140	**Iamblichus**	
20.209	140 n.445	*De anima*	
20.241	140	1.8	217
21.149–160	140	*De vita Pythagorica liber*	
21.182–189	140	28.145–146	77 n.232
21.186–187	140 n.445	28.151	77 n.233
24.77–92	317 n.1021	*Protrepticus*	
Odyssey		77.27	181 n.589
1.1–12	299 n.934		
1.180	140 n.445	**Isaeus**	
1.187	140 n.445	*Speeches*	
4.561–568	333 n.1067	8.39	70 n.202
5.272–3	331		
9.39–61	63 n.176	**Isocrates**	
9.263	140 n.445	*Busiris*	
9.519	140 n.445	11.8	146 n.468
10.507–511	332	11.38	72
11.155	333 n.1067	*Discourses*	
11.568–575	331	10.64	257 n.842
11.592	333 n.1067		
12.377	332 n.1064	**Kallimachos**	
14.199	140 n.445	fr43.117 Pfeiffer	88 n.267
14.204	140 n.445		
15.426	140 n.445	**Leukippus**	
16.63	140 n.445	fr. 569 KRS	246 n.808
17.199	328		
17.373	140 n.445	**Lucian**	
21.335	140 n.445	*Astrology*	
24.11–14	332	10	200, 236, 262
24.269	140 n.445		

Lycorphron
Alexandra
209–210   118 n.357
564   307 n.975

Lysias
Against Andocides
6.17   39 n.109
6.10   70 n.203

Macrobius
Saturnalia
1.17.42   217–218
1.17.46   218
1.17.52–56   218 n.701
1.18.12–14   185–186
1.18.17–18   187 n.607
1.23.8   325 n.1040

Marmor Parium
saec. III a.C.n. (*IG* 12 (5), 444,14 24 n.56
saec. III a.C.n. (IG 12 (5), 444,15) 24 n.55

Menander Rhetor
1.333   278 n.908

Orphic Fragmenta and Testimonia   See p.75–76 and 85–88
OF1F   284, 304, 386
OF20F– OF27V   280
OF34V   85
OF36F   361
OF59F   91
OF69T– OF89F   280
OF91T   34
OF96T   386
OF98T   175, 316, 360
OF102F   302, 386
OF106F   299, 386
OF106F   322
OF107F   305, 322, 386
OF109F   386
OF111F   301, 314, 322, 330, 358, 386
OF112F   281, 387
OF113F   360, 386
OF114F   244, 302, 322, 386
OF118F   244, 302, 319, 386
OF121F   175, 244, 283, 302, 309, 316, 359, 386
OF122F   244, 318, 322, 386
OF123F   243, 302, 305, 322, 386
OF125F   244, 322, 325, 386
OF130F   244, 309, 386
OF132F   244, 386
OF134F   244, 267, 305, 309, 386
OF136F   244, 302, 386
OF138F   243, 386
OF139F   267
OF140F   243–44, 267, 300, 305, 307, 314–15, 386
OF141F   387
OF144F   244, 386
OF148F   386
OF149F   300, 386
OF152F   243, 386
OF155F   281, 386
OF155F–OF157F 243
OF156F   386
OF158F   176, 243, 336, 345, 386
OF160F   243, 386
OF163F   314, 386
OF166F   85, 320, 367, 387
OF167F   243, 312, 321, 386
OF168F   320–21, 386
OF170F   386
OF173F   319, 386
OF174F   312, 321, 387
OF175F   361
OF178F   387
OF179F   387
OF181F   314, 330, 362, 387

OF182F	387	OF284F	321, 365, 387
OF183F	387	OF286F	366, 387
OF186F	335, 387	OF288F	387
OF188F	336, 387	OF290F	366
OF189F	330, 387	OF292F	366, 387
OF200F	320, 387	OF293F	366, 387
OF206F	305, 387	OF296F	85, 87, 367, 387
OF208F	387	OF299F	85, 88, 320, 321, 366, 387
OF209F	86, 87		
OF211F	86	OF300F	85, 387
OF212F	86, 387	OF301F	314, 330, 387
OF214F	387	OF303F	320, 367, 387
OF219F	312–313, 321, 387	OF304F	86
		OF306F	86
OF220F	313, 387	OF308V	86, 284, 387
OF221F	387	OF309F	86
OF223F	387	OF310F	86
OF224F	387	OF311F	86, 387
OF225F	320, 387	OF313F	86, 87, 88
OF231F	330, 387	OF314F	86, 87, 367, 387
OF232F	387	OF315F	87
OF233F	345, 347, 387	OF316F	87, 367
OF237F	311, 322, 363, 387	OF317F	310, 365, 387
		OF318F	87, 88
OF237F	312–13	OF319F	387
OF239F	315–16, 387	OF320F	88, 387
OF241F	244, 315, 323, 330, 387	OF321F	87, 387
		OF322F	87, 367, 387
OF243F	244, 314, 316, 321, 330, 334, 338, 347, 363–64, 387	OF326F	88
		OF327F	87
		OF328F	87
		OF329F	87, 88, 367, 387
OF245V	244, 330, 338, 347, 349, 364, 387	OF331F	85
		OF337F	348, 387
		OF338F	88, 96, 344, 348, 387
OF251F	313, 362, 387		
OF257F	310, 365, 387	OF339F	339, 342–43, 345, 387
OF260F	387		
OF263F	387	OF340F	189, 336, 339–40, 342, 344, 387
OF264F	365, 387		
OF265F	387	OF341F	331
OF266F	387	OF342F	331
OF267F	387	OF348F	102, 142, 344, 387
OF268F	387		
OF269F	102, 387	OF350F	106, 343, 387
OF271F	102, 387	OF363F	312, 387
OF283F	85, 86	OF383T	82

OF403T–OF405F	76	OF768T–OF776F	75
OF406T–OF407F	76	OF777F	75
OF408T	76	OF778F	75
OF409T–OF412F	76	OF779F	75
OF413F–OF416F	76	OF780T–OF781V	75
OF417F–OF420T	76	OF782T	75
OF422F	80, 231, 319, 334, 368, 387	OF792T–OF794F	76
		OF800T–OF803F	76
OF425F	231, 368, 387	OF805F	75
OF426F	161, 231, 368, 387	OF806T–OF810F	75
		OF811T	75, 304
OF430F	181	OF835T	76
OF433F	41, 43	OF836T	75
OF436F	80, 161, 231, 334, 368, 387	OF837T	76
		OF838T	76
OF437F	334, 339–40, 368, 387	OF839T	76
		OF840T	76
OF438F	344, 387	OF841T	76, 81
OF506T	76	OF842T	76
OF510T–OF535F	43	OF874T	58
OF513T	58, 72	OF890T	13, 58
OF524T	67	OF891T	13, 58
OF526T	60	OF902T	58
OF528T	60	OF904T	58
OF557T	39	OF923T–OF937T	13, 58
OF576F	134, 183, 345, 387	OF980T	146
		OF985T	146
OF578F	86, 266	OF1036T	56
OF602T–OF605T	76	OF1096T	24, 72
OF606T	76	OF2 Kern	305
OF607T	76	OF63 Kern	282
OF608T	76	OF86 Kern	305
OF609T	76	OF113 Kern	361, 386
OF610T–OF611T	76	OF168 Kern	364, 387
OF612T	76	OF210 Kern	367
OF613T	76		
OF614T–OF624V	76	**Olympiodorus**	
OF692T–OF694T	76	*In Phaedo*	
OF695T–OF705F	76	61c, p.2.21	95–96
OF706F	76	69c, 48.20	134, 183 n.595
OF707T–OF717	76		
OF713T	145 n.467	**Orphic Hymns**	
OF714T	145 n.467	OH 11.23	105 n.319
OF715T	145 n.467	OH 27.11–12	59 n.169
OF716T	145 n.467	OH 32.6	105 n.319
OF726T–OF752F	75	OH 37.1–6	107–108
OF753T–OF767F	75	OH 70.9	105 n.319

OH 71.11	105 n.319	OR26	175, 311, 317, 320–21, 360
OH 76.9–10	192 n.626	OR27	175, 360
		OR28	311, 360
Orphic Rhapsodies		OR29	314, 360
(According to my reconstruction)		OR30	360, 361
OR0	358	OR31	300, 361
OR1	175, 284, 299, 304, 358	OR32	361
OR2	302, 358	OR33	312, 321, 361
OR3	358	OR34	311, 360–62
OR4	301, 314, 322, 330, 358	OR35	336, 361
		OR37	361
OR5	299, 322, 358	OR38	311, 361
OR6	80, 358	OR39	314, 320, 330, 361
OR7	19, 244, 302, 322, 358	OR40	361
OR7–OR17	244	OR41	361–62
OR8	213, 322, 325, 358	OR42	335, 362
		OR43	313–14, 320, 330, 362
OR8–OR24	150		
OR9	175, 299, 302, 319, 358	OR44	317, 330, 361–62
		OR45	312, 319, 362
OR10	163, 213, 243–44, 283, 301–2, 309, 316, 359	OR46	305, 362
		OR47	362
		OR48	330, 362
OR11	359	OR49	320, 362
OR12	359	OR50	362–63
OR13	244, 318, 322, 359	OR51	362
		OR52	363
OR14	309, 359	OR53	362–63
OR15	267, 305, 309, 359	OR54	315–16, 320, 363
		OR55	311, 363
OR17	243–44, 300, 305, 307, 314–15, 359	OR56	312–13, 322, 363–64
		OR57	363
OR18	319, 359	OR58	319, 321, 362–64
OR19	312, 320–21, 359	OR59	170, 244, 315, 323, 330, 363
OR19–OR24	176, 243		
OR20	359–60	OR60	363
OR21	360	OR61	314, 316, 321, 330, 334, 338, 347, 363–64
OR22	176, 336, 345, 360		
		OR62	330, 349, 364
OR23	360	OR63	345, 347, 363, 364
OR24	301, 359–60		
OR25	243, 302, 305, 311, 322, 360	OR64	364
		OR65	365

OR66	365	11.50	66 n.185
OR67	365	11.67–70	54–55
OR68	365	11.85–102	68 n.193
OR69	365		
OR70	365	**P. Berol.**	
OR71	365	13426, saec. II, 1469ss	56 n.161
OR72	365		
OR73	310, 365–66	**Parmenides**	
OR74	321, 365	fr. 295 KRS	230 n.742
OR75	366	fr. 296 KRS	230 n.742
OR76	366	fr. 307 KRS	226
OR77	364, 366	*On Nature*	
OR78	320, 366	D11	158
OR78–OR87	85	D12	158
OR79	321, 366		
OR80	215, 367	**Parmenion**	
OR81	284, 320, 367–68	*Anthologia Palatina* 16.217	58 n.165
OR82	367	**Pausanias**	
OR83	367	I.22.7	46
OR84	367	I.31.4	48 n.130
OR85	367	II.13.7	120 n.370
OR86	96, 367–68	II.30.2	51
OR87	366–67	II.35.4–11	49 n.132
OR88	189, 336, 338–40, 342, 344, 368	II.35.10	50
		III.19.13–20	257 n.842
OR89	80, 161, 231, 319, 334, 342, 368	III.20.5	70 n.204
		IV.1.5	46
OR90	334, 339–40, 368	IV.1.7–8	48
		IV.33.7	333 n.1071
OR91	339, 342–43, 345, 368	VIII.31.1–8	68 n.195
		VIII.37.5	82, 180
OR92	96, 100, 344, 348, 368–69	IX.5.9	333 n.1071
		IX.27.2	46, 184 n.598
OR93	344, 368	IX.30.4	44 n.120
OR94	344, 349, 369	IX.30.5	56
OR95	105, 343, 369	IX.30.6	146 n.468
OR96	183, 345, 369	IX.30.9	56, 64
OR97	338, 348–49, 368–69	IX.30.12	46
		IX.39.3	150 n.482
		IX.39.8	150 n.483
Ovid		IX.40.11–12	329 n.1052
Metamorphosis		X.4.4	336 n.1085
4.9–17	218 n.702	X.19.3	66
10.77	64 n.179	X.25–31	333
11.1–84	54	X.28.2	333 n.1071
11.41–43	55	X.31.3	333 n.1071

Phanocles
fr. 1.10–17 Powell　　65

Phanodemus
DFHG p.367 F4　　78

Pherekydes of Syros
fr. 14 Schibli = 7B1DK　　300 n.940

Philochorus
DFHG p.384 F2　　79
FGrHist 22　　120

Philodemus
On Piety
N 247 III(*HV²* II44)1–13　　90–91
N 1088 XI 14–21 (*HV²* II 9)　　91 n.273

Philostratus
Heroicus
5.3　　118 n.358
28.8–11　　65
Imagines
6.16–21　　277 n.907

Pindar
fr.128c Race　　13 n.26
fr.133 Race　　109, 136
fr.153 Race　　163 n.537
Nemean Odes
5.35　　321 n.1032
6.1–2　　319 n.1024
6.15　　319
7.82　　321 n.1032
10.16　　321 n.1032
10.49–51　　307 n.975
10.75–91　　345 n.1120
Olympian Odes
2.17　　299 n.937
2.21–30　　259 n.847
2.55–68　　184 n.600
2.55–56　　258 n.844
2.68–73　　258
2.83–85　　257
7.34　　321 n.1032
10.50–55　　299 n.937

Pythian Odes
10.10–13　　318
10.12　　317 n.1021
11.61–64　　307 n.975

Plato
Apology
41a　　71, 276 n.903
Cratylus
396a–397a　　221 n.716
396b　　221
396d　　221–222, 262 n.861
397c–d　　163 n.538
399d–e　　222
400b　　181
400c　　9, 222, 310 n.985
400d–401e　　325 n.1041
402a–c　　247
402b　　74
404c　　222 n.721
Epinomis
981d　　164 n.538
Epistles
3.319e　　257 n.842
7.335a　　43 n.117
Ion
536b　　71
Laws
2.653d　　104
2.658b　　279 n.911
2.669 d　　74
2.672b　　103–104
2.672d　　104
3.701b　　94 n.289
3.701b–c　　101–102
4.715e–716b　　346
4.716e　　346
6.782c–d　　29, 267 n.874
6.759c–e　　70 n.202
6.775a　　70 n.202
8.829d–e　　47 n.125
9.854a–b　　105
9.869b　　42 n.115
9.870d–e　　41
9.872e　　42
10.899a–899c　　167 n.547

Index of Primary Sources — 413

Meno
81a–b   110 n.335, 261
81a–d   110 n.334, 137 n.433
81b–c   109, 136 n.431
Phaedo
63c   100 n.307
69c–d   133, 182, 251 n.823
Phaedrus
243b   257 n.842
245a   345
247a–b   325 n.1041
Philebus
66c   74, 319
Protagoras
316d   10, 15, 236 n.766
Respublica
1.363d   251 n.823
2.358a   23
2.362c   21–22
2.363c–d   73
2.363c–e   22, 160 n.519/520
2.364b–e   25
2.364e–365a 21, 270, 271
2.366a–b   135
2.379a   277 n.907
3.395b   102 n.311
7.533d   251 n.823
10.600d–e   279 n.914
10.613   56 n.160
10.614a–621d 193 n.631
10.616b–c   194
10.618a   194 n.634
10.619e   194 n.635
10.620a   56 n.161
10.621a–b   194 n.636
10.621b   195 n.637
10.621c–d   195
Statesman
268e7   102 n.312
Symposium
179d   146 n.468. 197 n.643
218b   255

Timaeus
40e   281 n.920
41d–e   167
42b   167
42b–c   143
42c–d   103
71e–72b   234–235

Plotinus
Enneades
IV.3.12.1–13 97

Plutarch
fr.177 Sandbach   181
fr.178 Sandbach   179–180
Alexander
2   53–54
14.5   56
53   257 n.842
Apopthegmata
224e   28
De communibus notitiis adversus Stoicos
1065b   219
De defectu oraculorum
10.414f–415a 66–67
10.415b–c   67
415f–416a   219 n.707
De E apud Delphos
388c   120 n.366
388f–389a   120 n.368, 186, 219
389a   120 n.368, 219 n.705, 261 n.856
De esu carnium
1.2 994a   108–109
1.7, 996b–c 98–99
De genio Socratis
21(590a)   150 n.481, 237 n.768

De Iside et Osiride
364e–f   118 n.357
De sera numinis vindicta
563e   196 n.640
563f   197
566a–c   196 n.639

De Stoicorum repugnantiis
1052f   220 n.710
Themistocles
1.3   48
Quaestiones convivales
2.3.1, 635e   19, 304
2.3.2, 636d–636e   18, 254, 304 n.955
2.3.2, 636e   19, 304 n.956
7.714c   170 n.551

[Plutarch]
De fluviis
3.4   56 n.161

Proclus
In Cratylus
389b, 21.13   102 n.312
400d1–5, 77.25–78.4   98
In Respublica
II.338.10   96
II.340.11   188–189
In Timaeus
29a, I.327.23   102 n.312
41c, III.227.31   176 n.569
42c, III.297.3   102, 141–142
Theologia Platonica
1.6   2 n.2

Ps–Moschus
3.115–125   146 n.468

Scholia
Apollonius Rhodius
Argonautica
III.467   52 n.142
Euripides
Alcestis
968 Schwartz,
Vol.2 p.239   63, 236 n.765, 237
Euripides
Hecuba 1267,
Schwartz, Vol.1, p.89   64

Servius
In Virgil Aeneid
VI.645   200 n.650

Sophocles
fr.959 Lloyd–Jones   118 n.357
Antigone
1126   120 n.365
1131–1136   202 n.656
1146–1154   165, 332 n.1064
Electra
179   300 n.939
Oedipus Tyrannus
391–392   279 n.911
Trachiniae
218–220   202 n.656
Tyro
fr.668 Lloyd–Jones   118 n.357

Stobaeus
Eclogae
4.52.49   179–180
20.2.47, IV 461–2   65

Strabo
10.3.9   14 n.29
10.3.15–16   60
12.4.4   69 n.199

Suda
s.v. Ὀρφεὺς, ο' 654–660 74, 200 n.652
s.v. Πορθμήϊον, π' 2072 51

Syrianus
On Aristotle Metaphysics
165,33–166,6 Kroll   79

Tatianus
Oratio ad Graecos
8   120 n.365
41.3   82 n.259

Tertullian
Ad nationes
II.7   152 n.489

Thales
fr. 85 KRS 229 n.741

Theophrastus
Characters
16.2 27
16.6 70 n.202
16.11 27

Timotheus
Persae
fr.791, 221–224 58 n.165

Vettius Valens
Anthology
IX 1, p.330.23 161 n.525

Virgil
Georgics
IV 523 66 n.185

Xenophon
fr.20 Heinze 100 n.306

www.ingramcontent.com/pod-product-compliance
Lightning Source LLC
Chambersburg PA
CBHW031411230426
43668CB00007B/269